DATE DUE

OC 1 2 '98			
AP 24 00			
DE 18 00			
JE 9 04			

DEMCO 38-296

Criminal Justice

Contemporary Literature in Theory and Practice

Series Editors
Marilyn McShane
Frank P. Williams III
California State University – San Bernardino

GARLAND PUBLISHING, INC.
New York & London
1997

Contents of the Series

The American Court System

Edited with introductions by
Marilyn McShane
Frank P. Williams III
California State University – San Bernardino

GARLAND PUBLISHING, INC.
New York & London
1997

Library of Congress Cataloging-in-Publication Data

The American court system / edited with introductions by Marilyn
McShane, Frank P. Williams III.
     p. cm. — (Criminal justice ; v. 5)
    Includes bibliographical references.
    ISBN 0-8153-2512-6 (alk. paper)
    1. Criminal justice, Administration of—United States. 2. Law
enforcement—United States. 3. Criminal courts—United States.
I. McShane, Marilyn D., 1956– . II. Williams, Franklin P.
III. Series: Criminal justice (New York, N.Y.) ; 5.
KF9223.A955 1997
345.73'05—dc21   96-39145
                                      CIP

Printed on acid-free, 250-year-life paper
Manufactured in the United States of America

Contents

Series Introduction

At the turn of the century the criminal justice system will be confronting many of the same demons, although the drugs of choice, the technology of crime fighting, and the tools and techniques of management have evolved. Despite the enhancements of twenty-first century technologies, funding, crowding, and public concerns about effectiveness continue to be discussed in "crisis" terminology, and criminal justice scholars remain somewhat cynical about the ability to reform the criminal justice system. This pessimistic attitude may be fueled, at least in part, by the drama of real-life crime that plays itself out in courtrooms, newspapers, and talk shows across America every day. The combination of emotional political maneuvering and campaigning on punitive rhetoric assures us of a steady stream of legislation designed to reflect a zero tolerance for crime.

Testing the constitutional limits of our times, we have devised even more ways of imposing severe punishments, seizing assets, reinstituting corporal punishment, and penalizing the parents of delinquents. We have also created new offenses, such as recruiting someone into a gang, transmitting "indecent" images on the Internet, and knowingly passing along a disease. Despite these politically popular solutions to crime, problems of enforcement, equity, and affordability remain. The public's preoccupation with "what works?" and quick fixes to crime problems have never been reconciled with the more realistic ideas of "what can we live with?" and long-range preventive solutions.

Ironically, despite public perceptions that crime has been getting worse, statistics seem to indicate that the rates for virtually all offenses are either no worse than they were in 1980 or are now lower. Drug-related arrests and the rates for most forms of adult crime (in particular, most violent crimes) have actually decreased. Against this general backdrop, the rate of violent juvenile crime appears to be the sole increasing trend, leading to a situation in which risks of victimization by violent crime have also increased for juveniles. The contrary public perception of a massive and growing crime problem has created a situation in which the number of cases of juveniles transferred to adult court has increased, as has the proportion of inmates facing life sentences, life in prison without parole, and death sentences. On the other hand the risk of incarceration also appears to have increased for minorities, directing attention to questions of racial and economic disparity in the quality of protection and justice available in this country today.

While all this has been happening over the past two decades, academia has rather quietly developed an entire discipline dedicated to the study of crime and the criminal justice system. Though crime policy is still dominated largely by political interests swayed by public opinion, crime scholars have begun to have an impact on how crime is viewed and what can be done about it. While this impact is not yet a major one, it continues to gain weight and shows promise of some day achieving the influence that economists have come to wield in the realm of public policy-making.

Simultaneously with this growing scholarship comes an irony: academic journals, the major repository of scholarly wisdom, are being discontinued by libraries. Access, although ostensibly available in an electronic form, is decreasing. In many academic libraries, only a few select, "major" journals are being retained. Clearly, there is so much being done that the few "top" journals cannot adequately represent current developments (even if these journals were not focused in particular directions). Thus, the knowledge of the field is being centralized and, at the same time, more difficult to obtain. The multitude of criminal justice and criminology degree programs now face an interesting dilemma: how do students and faculty access current information? Or put differently, how does the field distribute its hard-gained knowledge to both assure quality of education and pursue efforts to offset the often ill-informed myths of public opinion?

Electronic access would appear to be one possible answer to the problem, especially with libraries facing yet another squeeze, that of space. On-line and media-based (CD-ROM) services promise quick availability of periodical literature, but remain futuristic. The costs associated with downloading articles can approximate the cost of the journal subscriptions themselves and many libraries cannot afford to participate in on-line periodical services. In addition, there is the inconvenience of translating the electronic images into the user's still-preferred paper-based format. Moreover, the paper-based serendipitous value of "browsing" decreases as only specific articles appear on-line, without surrounding materials.

An alternative solution is to review the range of journals and collect the "best" of their articles for reprinting. This is the approach this criminal justice periodical series has taken. By combining both depth and scope in a series of reprints, the series can offer an attractive, cost-effective answer to the problem of creating access to scholarship. Moreover, such a compact format yields the added advantage that individuals searching for a specific topic are more likely to experience the serendipity of running across related articles. Each of the six volumes presents a comprehensive picture of the state of the art in criminal justice today and each contains articles focused on one of the major areas of criminal justice and criminology: Police, Drugs, Criminological Theory, Corrections, Courts, and Victimology. Each volume contains approximately twenty articles.

The Article Selection Process

The articles appearing in the series represent the choices of the editors and a board of experts in each area. These choices were based on four criteria: (1) that the articles were from the time period of 1991–1995, (2) that they represent excellent scholarship, (3) that collectively they constitute a fair representation of the knowledge of the period, and (4) that where there were multiple choices for representing a knowledge area, the articles appeared in journals that are less likely to be in today's academic library holdings. We believe the selection criteria and the board of experts were successful in compiling truly representative content in each topical area. In addition, the authors of the selected articles constitute a list of recognizable experts whose work is commonly cited.

Finally, there is one other advantage offered by the volumes in this series: the articles are reprinted as they originally appeared. Scholars using anthologized materials are commonly faced with having to cite secondary source pages because they do not have access to the original pagination and format. This is a difficulty because mistakes in reprinting have been known to alter the original context, thus making the use of secondary sources risky (and synonymous with sloppy scholarship). In order to overcome this problem, the series editors and the publisher made the joint decision to photoreproduce each article's original image, complete with pagination and format. Thus, each article retains its own unique typesetting and character. Citations may be made to pages in confidence that the reproduced version is identical in all respects with the original. In short, the journal article is being made available exactly as if the issue had been on a library shelf.

We believe this series will be of great utility to students, scholars, and others with interests in the literature of criminal justice and criminology. Moreover, the series saves the user time that would have otherwise been spent in locating quality articles during a typical literature search. Whether in an academic or personal library, the only alternative to this collection is having the journals themselves.

Volume Introduction

Depending on whom one talks to, today's criminal courts are either the savior or the demon of our social order. While everyone seems to have an answer about what needs to be done, the solutions are neither simple, nor within our current allocation of resources. Media hype and political posturing emotionally dilute the reality of what motivates crime and what constitutes effective punishment. The essays and research in this anthology give the reader a realistic view of complex problems affecting our juvenile and adult courts and, consequently, the rest of the criminal justice system. Topics include sentencing disparity, sentencing reform, and wrongful convictions. Some traditionally controversial issues are covered, such as the insanity defense and the death penalty as well as the more recent "three-strikes-and-you're-out" movement and mandatory minimums.

Judicial Philosophy

While observers of recent criminal philosophy would view an unquestionable orientation toward punitiveness, there are still debates over what the proper goals of sentencing should be. Ernest van den Haag and Andrew von Hirsch and Lisa Maher engage in one such debate. Van den Haag proffers that the compensatory aspects of the philosophy of *lex talionis* are more realistic in tort law, than in contemporary criminal law. While the primitive practice may suggest minimum punishments, it is perhaps less appropriate for considering maximums which should be guided by social harm rather than the damage to any individual victim. In the quest for a rational sentencing policy, von Hirsch and Maher argue that the inability to accurately predict the success of rehabilitation makes it unsuitable as a justification for sentences. They also critique the notion of advocating rehabilitation from the perspectives of humaneness and fairness.

Court Decisions

The search and seizure issue has been a controversial one, particularly during the "war on drugs." Reviewing Supreme Court decisions during the Burger and Rehnquist tenures, Joseph Davey concludes that present interpretations of the Fourth Amendment have created a situation where there are virtually no restrictions on police search and seizure. He believes that the drug war was instrumental in justifying the expansion of government authority. Viewing this lack of restriction as problematic, Davey issues warnings about the threat posed to a free society by a largely unfettered police.

On the matter of judicial activism in correctional settings, Rudolph Alexander reviews the "hands off" doctrine. He notes that claims of a reemergence of the "hands off" doctrine during the 1970s and early 1980s are questionable because the U.S. Supreme Court had not produced a significant decision articulating the issue. A 1987 decision, however, produced a "reasonableness" test that deferred to prison officials. Under this decision, institutional order is declared to be superior to inmates rights, thus any conflict between the two should be resolved in favor of maintaining order. Alexander refers to this approach as a new "semi-hands-off" doctrine.

Legal Reform

Among other events, reform of criminal law has been a favored tactic in the past decade's war against crime. One reasonable query about these reforms is the simple and straightforward question, "have they had any effect?" Ronet Bachman and Raymond Paternoster attempt to answer this question in an analysis of cases filed under state and federal rape laws. Using pre- and post-reform periods, they conclude that neither criminal justice system practice nor victim behavior has been affected significantly. Bachman and Paternoster do find two small effects: post-reform offenders were more likely to be imprisoned and offenders who were acquaintances are more likely to be treated like strangers.

Another type of legal reform derived from attacks on the insanity defense. Seeking more control and less "lenient" treatment of criminal defendants, one-quarter of the states have adopted a "guilty-but-mentally-ill" (GBMI) verdict. Lisa Callahan, Margaret McGreevy, Carmen Cirincione, and Henry J. Steadman analyze before and after data, concluding that GBMI increased the likelihood of an insanity verdict and resulted in harsher sentences than defendants who plead guilty but not mentally ill. They believe that GBMI verdicts will ultimately reduce the number of insanity pleas.

Three-strikes legislation is perhaps the *pièce de resistance* of judicial reform. Politicians have embraced such bills as the ultimate way to prove they are tough on crime. Many in the criminal justice system, however, have roundly criticized three-strikes legislation, citing the many undesirable effects. In an essay originally appearing in *Federal Probation*, Peter Benekos and Alida Merlo point out the political benefits and problems of three-strikes through an examination of legislation in three states. They conclude that such approaches will do much more damage than good.

Barry Feld examines another major reform movement of the past few decades: that of transforming juvenile courts into criminal courts. He concludes that reforms have resulted in a juvenile court that punishes in the name of treatment, with inadequate procedural safeguards. Feld provides three policy remedies ranging from a return to the previous structure and goals to the elimination of juvenile courts.

Sentencing

In the view of the public, sentencing is the prime ingredient in the criminal justice stew. When crime appears to increase, the public blames "lenient" sentencing and demands tougher and harsher laws to insure sentencing is punitive. What they refer to, of course, is imprisonment, not other forms of sanctions—virtually all of which are perceived as lenient. Over the course of the past two decades our sentencing practices have gotten progressively more punitive and vengeful. Micheal Tonry's essay provides a review and analysis of sentencing reforms of the past twenty years. His overview generates food for thought, particularly concerning what has, or has not, worked and what the effects of many of the reforms have been.

One of the nagging questions concerning policy-making is whether conservative or liberal ideologies really affect actual sentencing behavior. Throughout the past fifteen years, such effects have been assumed. David Bowers and Jerold Waltman look at the issue by comparing felony sentences of more conservative states to more liberal states. They found that, except for homicide, violent crime offenders were sentenced more harshly in conservative states. On the other hand, property crime sentences had no such relationship. In short, it seems that conservative ideologies mostly affect violent offenders.

Another sentencing issue is that of how to handle white-collar offenders and corporations. In answer to these concerns, the U.S. Sentencing Commission enacted sentencing guidelines for organizations. William Laufer looks at these guidelines in light of relevant provisions in the U.S. Code. He argues that, because of Congress' failure to reform the U.S. Code over the past twenty years, the value of the organizational sentencing guidelines is questionable. Laufer ends with an assessment of proposals to determine intent under existing codes.

Another essay examines the effect of mandatory minimum sentences on the work of the U.S. Sentencing Commission. Henry Wallace argues that congressionally created mandatory minimum sentences are antithetical to the construction of sentencing guidelines and are impractical. Because of prosecutorial pressures, most cases are decided by plea bargaining, even if unofficially. If mandatory minimum sentences are not eliminated, the integrity and viability of the Sentencing Commission are questioned.

Discrimination and Prejudice in Judicial Process

The topics of discrimination and inequity have long been staples for social science researchers. Indeed, there are criminological theories that literally assume the system is discriminatory. With the recent harsher sentencing policies, questions have again arisen about the effect of offender characteristics on judicial decision-making. In their article, John Kramer and Darrell Steffensmeier examine the effect of racial differences on sentencing decisions. Analyzing data from Pennsylvania sentences, they found only a small racial discrimination effect on decisions to incarcerate (in favor of whites) and none on length of incarceration. Offense severity and prior record were the primary sentencing variables.

Bennett Gershman also focuses on the issue of prejudice, although more broadly. Arguing that recent criminal justice reforms have made the system more complex and burdened the courts, he notes that efficiency and not justice has become the common denominator. A system in crisis, however, should be even more concerned with justice, particularly the possible conviction of innocent defendants. Gershman contends that increasing racial prejudice and lawyer incompetence results in more frequent wrongful convictions of minorities.

Gender disparity is the subject of Deborah Denno's essay. She analyzes data from the Biosocial Study and matches the results with existing research evidence. Women appear to engage in crime more as the result of biological factors, whereas environmental factors are more predictive of male criminality. Using these results to focus on gender-based defenses to crime, Denno proposes that females may be more successful in employing a neurological abnormality defense. However, in examining the gamut of gender-based defenses, Denno questions their use and concludes that it would be unwise to consider these defenses in sentencing because of the danger of negative stereotyping.

Death Penalty

While the public has come to overwhelmingly support capital punishment (at least simplistically), several appellate issues have surfaced recently. Kenneth Haas' article deals with the recent trends in Supreme Court decisions on the death penalty. He argues that, after 1978, the Court has partially justified the constitutionality of death penalty statutes on the legitimacy of retribution. While retribution has been philosophically separate from vengeance, Haas finds evidence in more recent decisions that vengeance has now been added as an acceptable justification.

In an article focusing on capital murder statutes, James Acker and Charles Lanier examine the primary components of these statutes. They conclude that the statutes alone do not sufficiently narrow the range of defendants who are eligible for capital punishment. The addition of relevant aggravating factors at the penalty phase of the trial becomes critical to determining who is considered for the death penalty.

* * * * * *

We would like to thank the board members of this volume who assisted us in the selection of articles. Because only a limited number of pieces could be selected for this volume, an expanded bibliography is included to provide additional materials. Articles marked with an asterisk (*) are included in this anthology.

Acker, James (1992). Affirmed: Using social science research evidence in appellate court decision-making. *Criminal Justice Research Bulletin* 7(3): 1–6.

Acker, James and Charles Lanier (1994). In fairness and mercy: Statutory mitigating factors in capital punishment laws. *Criminal Law Bulletin* 30(4): 299–345.

*Acker, James and Charles Lanier (1993). The dimensions of capital murder. *Criminal Law Bulletin* 29(5): 379–417.

Acker, James and Charles Lanier (1993). Aggravating circumstances and capital punishment: Rhetoric or real reforms? *Criminal Law Bulletin* 29(6): 467–501.

Ainsworth, Janet (1991). Re-imagining childhood and reconstructing the legal order: The case for abolishing the juvenile court. *North Carolina Law Review* 69: 1083–1133.

Alexander, Rudolph, Jr. (1992). Cruel and unusual punishment: A slowly metamorphosing concept. *Criminal Justice Police Review* 6(2): 123–35.

*Alexander, Rudolph, Jr. (1994). Hands-off, hands-on, hands-semi-off: A discussion of the current legal test used by the United States Supreme Court to decide inmates' rights. *Journal of Crime and Justice* 17(1): 103–28.

Allen, Francis (1996). *The habits of legality: Criminal justice and the rule of law.* New York: Oxford University Press.

*Bachman, Ronet and Raymond Paternoster (1993). A contemporary look at the effects of rape law reform: How far have we really come? *Journal of Criminal Law and Criminology* 84(3): 554–74.

Bales, William and Linda Dees (1992). Mandatory minimum sentencing in Florida: Past trends and future implications. *Crime and Delinquency* 38(3): 309–29.

*Benekos, Peter and Alida Merlo (1995). Three strikes and you're out: The political sentencing game. *Federal Probation* 59(1): 3–9.

Blankenship, Michael, Jerry Sparger, and W. Richard Janikowski (1992). Accountability v. independence: Myths of judicial selection. *Criminal Justice Policy Review* 6(1): 69–79.

Bloom, Robert (1993). Judicial integrity: A call for its re-emergence in the adjudication of criminal cases. *Journal of Criminal Law and Criminology* 84(3): 462–501.

*Bowers, David and Jerold Waltman (1993). Do more conservative states impose harsher felony sentences? An exploratory analysis of 32 states. *Criminal Justice Review* 18(1): 61–70.

Bowman, Cynthia (1992). The arrest experiments: A feminist critique. *The Journal of Criminal Law and Criminology* 83: 201–8.

Bradley, Craig (1993). The courts' "two model" approach to the Fourth Amendment: Carpe diem! *Journal of Criminal Law and Criminology* 84(3): 429–61.

Bumby, Kurt (1993). Reviewing the guilty but mentally ill alternative: A case for the blind "pleading" the blind. *Journal of Psychiatry and Law* 21(2): 191–220.

*Callahan, Lisa, Margaret McGreevy, Carmen Cirincione, and Henry Steadman (1992). Measuring the effects of the guilty but mentally ill (GBMI) verdict: Georgia's 1982 GBMI reform. *Law and Human Behavior* 16(4): 447–62.

Clarkson, Chris and Rod Morgan, eds. (1995). *The politics of sentencing reform.* Oxford: Clarendon Press.

Cohen, Mark (1992). Environmental crime and punishment: Legal/economic theory and empirical evidence on enforcement of federal environmental statutes. *Journal of Criminal Law and Criminology* 82(4): 1054–1108.

*Davey, Joseph (1994). The death of the Fourth Amendment under the Rehnquist court: Where is the original intent when we need it. *Journal of Crime and Justice* 17(1): 129–48.

*Denno, Deborah (1994). Gender, crime and the criminal law defenses. *The Journal of Criminal Law and Criminology* 85: 80–180.

DiMento, Joseph (1993). Criminal enforcement of environmental law. *The Annals of the American Academy of Political and Social Science* 525 (Jan): 134–46.

Fabelo, Tony (1994). Sentencing reform in Texas: Can criminal justice research inform public policy. *Crime and Delinquency* 40(2): 282–94.

*Feld, Barry (1993). Juvenile (in)justice and the criminal court alternative. *Crime and Delinquency* 39(4): 403–24.

Feld, Barry (1991). Justice by geography: Urban, suburban and rural variations in juvenile justice administration. *Journal of Criminal Law and Criminology* 82: 156–210.

Feld, Barry (1991). The transformation of the juvenile court. *Minnesota Law Review* 75: 691–725.

Frase, Richard (1994). Purposes of punishment under the Minnesota Sentencing Guidelines. *Criminal Justice Ethics* 13(1): 11–20.

*Gershman, Bennett (1993). Themes of injustice: Wrongful convictions, racial prejudice, and lawyer incompetence. *Criminal Law Bulletin* 29(6): 502–15.

Goldman, Sheldon and Matthew Saronson (1994). Clinton's nontraditional judges: Creating a more representative bench. *Judicature* 78(2): 68–73.

Grubin, Don and Robert Prentky (1993). Sexual psychopathy laws. *Criminal Behaviour and Mental Health* 3(4): 381–92.

*Haas, Kenneth (1994). The triumph of vengeance over retribution: The U.S. Supreme Court and the death penalty. *Crime, Law and Social Change* 21(2): 127–54.

Heaney, Gerald (1991). The reality of guidelines sentencing: No end to disparity, *American Criminal Law Review* 28(2): 161–232.

Horney, Julie and Cassia Spohn (1991). Rape law reform and instrumental change in six urban jurisdictions. *Law and Society Review* 25(1): 117–54.

Jacobs, James (1993). Should hate be a crime? *The Public Interest* (Fall): 3–14.

Kadish, Sanford (1994). Forward: The criminal law and the luck of the draw. *The Journal of Criminal Law and Criminology* 84(4): 679–702.

Karle, Theresa and Thomas Sager (1991). Are the federal sentencing guidelines meeting congressional goals? An empirical and case law analysis. *Emory Law Journal* 40(2): 393–444.

Kendall, Kathy (1991). The politics of premenstrual syndrome: Implications for feminist justice. *Journal of Human Justice* 2(2): 77–98.

*Kramer, John and Darrell Steffensmeier (1993). Race and imprisonment decisions. *Sociological Quarterly* 34(2): 357–76.

*Laufer, William (1992). Culpability and the sentencing of corporations. *Nebraska Law Review* 71(4): 1049–94.

Lofquist, William (1993). Legislating organizational probation: State capacity, business power, and corporate crime control. *Law and Society Review* 27(4): 741–83.

McGarrell, Edmund and Thomas Castellano (1991). An integrative conflict model of the criminal law formation process. *Journal of Research in Crime and*

Delinquency 28: 174–96.

Miller, Robert (1994). The criminalization of the mentally-ill: Does dangerousness take precedence over need for treatment? *Criminal Behaviour and Mental Health* 3(4): 241–50.

Moenssens, Andre (1993). Novel scientific evidence in criminal cases: Some words of caution. *The Journal of Criminal Law and Criminology* 84(1): 1–21.

Morse, Stephen (1995). The new syndrome excuse syndrome. *Criminal Justice Ethics* 14(1): 3–15.

Nelson, James (1994). A dollar a day: Sentencing misdemenants in New York state. *Journal of Research in Crime and Delinquency* 31(2): 183–201.

Odubekun, Lola (1992). A structural approach to differential gender sentencing. *Criminal Justice Abstracts* 24(2): 343–60.

Russell, Katheryn (1994). A critical view from the inside: An application of critical legal studies to criminal law. *The Journal of Criminal Law and Criminology* 85: 222–40.

Schoenfeld, C.G. (1993). Crime, punishment and the criminal law: A psychoanalytic summary and analysis. *Journal of Psychiatry and the Law* 21(3): 337–61.

Spohn, Cassia and Jerry Cederblom (1991). Race and disparities in sentencing: A test of the liberation hypothesis. *Justice Quarterly* 8(3): 305–27.

Stahl, Marc (1992). Asset forfeiture, burdens of proof and the war on drugs. *Journal of Criminal Law and Criminology* 83: 274–337.

*Tonry, Michael (1995). Twenty years of sentencing reform: Steps forward, steps backward. *Judicature* 78(4): 169–72.

Tonry, Michael (1993). The failure of the U.S. Sentencing Commission's Guidelines. *Crime and Delinquency* 39(2):131–49.

Tonry, Michael (1994). Racial disproportion in U.S. prisons. *British Journal of Criminology* 34: 97–115.

Towberman, Donna (1994). Racial bias in the criminal justice system: Shifting focus from outcome to underlying causes. *Juvenile and Family Court Journal* 45(1): 15–25.

*Van den Haag, Ernest (1992). The *lex talionis* before and after criminal law. *Criminal Justice Ethics* 11(1): 2, 62.

Von Hirsch, Andrew (1994). Sentencing Guidelines and penal aims in Minnesota. *Criminal Justice Ethics* 13(1): 39–49.

Von Hirsch, Andrew (1995). The future of the proportionate sentence. Chapter 9, of *Punishment and Social Control,* edited by Thomas Blomberg and Stanley Cohen. New York: Aldine de Gruyter.

Von Hirsch, Andrew and Judith Greene (1993). When should reformers support creation of sentencing guidelines? *Wake Forest Law Review* 28(2): 329–43.

*Von Hirsch, Andrew and Lisa Maher (1992). Should penal rehabilitationism be revived? *Criminal Justice Ethics* 11(1): 25–30.

*Wallace, Henry Scott (1993). Mandatory minimums and the betrayal of sentencing reform: A legislative Dr. Jekyll and Mr. Hyde. *Federal Probation* 57(3): 9–19.

The Dimensions of Capital Murder

By James R. Acker* and C. S. Lanier**

This is the third in a series of articles analyzing U.S. death penalty statutes. The previous article in this series presented a review of the evolution of capital murder statutes in this country, as well as a general description of contemporary murder statutes in death penalty jurisdictions. The present article resumes with a more detailed examination of modern capital murder statutes. Four aspects of those statutes are addressed in this article: mens rea requirements, felony murder provisions, the breadth or scope of offense and offender characteristics that help define capital murder, and categories of offenders who are excluded from death penalty eligibility. Subsequent articles will discuss aggravating sentencing circumstances, mitigating circumstances, and the formulas employed to balance these circumstances in imposing sentence.

When a man is hung, there is an end of our relations with him. His execution is a way of saying, ''You are not fit for this world, take your chance elsewhere.''

—Sir James Fitzjames Stephen[1]

If the criminal law cannot make persuasive distinctions between life and death cases of murder, a modern death penalty has no use.

—Franklin Zimring and Gordon Hawkins[2]

A previous article in this series presented a review of the evolution of capital murder statutes in this country, as well as a general description of contemporary murder statutes in death penalty jurisdictions.[3] This description explained the significance of whether the class of offenders eligible for capital punishment is circumscribed by statutes that incorporate specific aggravating circumstances as elements of the crime of murder, or whether

---

* Assistant Professor, School of Criminal Justice, University at Albany, State University of New York, Albany, N.Y.

** Assistant Editor, *Sourcebook of Criminal Justice Statistics*, Hindelang Criminal Justice Research Center, and doctoral student, School of Criminal Justice, University at Albany, State University of New York, Albany, N.Y.

[1] Stephen, ''Capital Punishments,'' 69 Fraser's Mag. 753, 763 (1864), *quoted in* Furman v. Georgia, 408 U.S. 238, 290 (1972) (Brennan, J., concurring).

[2] F. Zimring & G. Hawkins, *Capital Punishment and the American Agenda* 77 (1986).

[3] Acker & Lanier, ''Capital Murder from Benefit of Clergy to Bifurcated Trials: Narrowing the Class of Offenders Punishable by Death,'' 29 Crim. L. Bull. 291 (1993).

1

instead murder is defined broadly and the class of death-eligible offenders is narrowed at the penalty phase of capital trials through proof of aggravating sentencing factors. A conviction for capital murder, standing alone, does not expose the offender to the risk of capital punishment in most jurisdictions. Rather, the prosecution ordinarily must prove one or more statutory aggravating factors at a sentencing hearing before a murderer crosses the threshold of death penalty eligibility.[4]

The present article resumes with a more detailed examination of modern capital murder statutes. Although jurisdictions use different terminology, "capital murder" is considered here to be the crime that, if proven at the guilt phase of the trial, permits the prosecution to advance a case to a sentencing hearing for purposes of seeking the death penalty.[5] Four aspects of capital murder statutes are addressed in this article: mens rea requirements, felony murder provisions, the breadth or scope of offense and offender characteristics that help define capital murder, and categories of offenders who are excluded from death penalty eligibility.[6]

Mens Rea

Judgments about culpability in the criminal law normally depend on both the offender's mens rea, or state of mind, and

---

[4] Only in Utah and Washington does proof of capital murder, without more, render an offender eligible for capital punishment. See Utah Code Ann. § 76-3-207 (Supp. 1992); Wash. Rev. Code Ann. § 10.95.030(2) (1990). The laws in California and Ohio require that the prosecution allege and prove a special circumstance or an aggravating circumstance (respectively) prior to the penalty trial before a murderer is eligible for capital punishment. See Cal. Penal Code § 190.2(a) (West Supp. 1993); Ohio Rev. Code Ann. § 2929.04(A) (Anderson 1993). In Oregon, Texas, and Virginia, the sentencer must answer affirmatively to one or more special questions at a capital sentencing hearing before the offender is eligible to receive a death sentence. See Or. Rev. Stat. § 163.150(1)(b) (1991); Tex. Crim. Proc. Code Ann. arts. 37.071(2)(b), 37.071(2)(c), 37.071(2)(e) (Vernon Supp. 1993); Va. Code Ann. §§ 19.2-264.2(1), 19.2-264.2(2) (1990). In the remaining thirty death penalty jurisdictions, a convicted murderer is not eligible for capital punishment unless the prosecution proves at least one statutory aggravating circumstance at the penalty phase of the trial.

[5] Many jurisdictions call this crime by a name other than capital murder, such as first-degree murder, aggravated murder, or simply murder.

[6] Although different death penalty provisions exist under federal law, we limit our consideration to the only one that includes detailed sentencing procedures that typify the modern statutes enacted after the Court's decision in Furman v. Georgia, 408 U.S. 238 (1972). This law, which became effective in 1988, provides for a federal death penalty in certain cases of drug-related killings. 21 U.S.C. § 848(e) (Supp. 1993). See Acker & Lanier, *supra* note 3, at 300 n. 36; Jordan, "Death for

the harm caused by the offender.[7] The primary harm in all criminal homicides is the same: the death of a human being.[8] Since this is a constant, the severity of the law's response ordinarily varies according to whether the offender killed "purposely" (or intentionally),[9] "knowingly,"[10] "recklessly,"[11] "negligently,"[12] or with another type of mens rea.[13] Felony murder, which is considered in the next section, is unique because capital punishment may be imposed irrespective of the offender's mens rea for the homicide.

Culpability correlates highly, although not perfectly, with the purposeful quality of harm-causing conduct. The criminal law

Drug Related Killings: Revival of the Federal Death Penalty," 67 Chi.-Kent. L. Rev. 79 (1991).

[7] J. Hall, *General Principles of the Criminal Law* 93 (2d ed. 1960). See also Tison v. Arizona, 481 U.S. 137, 156 (1987).

[8] Traditionally, all human life has been treated as equally valuable for purposes of the criminal law. For example, no discrimination is made between the life of a newborn child and an octogenarian, between a Fortune 500 company president and a homeless person. See Booth v. Maryland, 482 U.S. 496, 506 n.8 (1987) ("We are troubled by the implication that defendants whose victims were assets to their community are more deserving of punishment than those whose victims are perceived to be less worthy. Of course, our system of justice does not tolerate such distinctions."). But see Payne v. Tennessee, 111 S. Ct. 2597 (1991) (overruling *Booth* in part, and holding that some forms of victim impact evidence are admissible at capital sentencing hearings). See generally Berger, "*Payne* and Suffering—A Personal Reflection and a Victim-Centered Critique," 20 Fla. St. U. L. Rev. 21 (1992).

[9] See Model Penal Code § 2.02(2)(a)(i) (Proposed Official Draft 1962) ("A person acts purposely . . . when . . . it is his conscious object to engage in conduct of that nature or to cause such a result.").

[10] Model Penal Code § 2.02(2)(b)(ii) (Proposed Official Draft 1962) ("A person acts knowingly . . . when . . . he is aware that it is practically certain that his conduct will cause such a result.").

[11] Model Penal Code § 2.02(2)(c) (Proposed Official Draft 1962) ("A person acts recklessly with respect to a material element of an offense when he consciously disregards a substantial and unjustifiable risk that the material element exists or will result from his conduct. The risk must be of such nature and degree that, considering the nature and purpose of the actor's conduct and the circumstances known to him, its disregard involves a gross deviation from the standard of care that a law-abiding person would observe in the actor's situation.").

[12] Model Penal Code § 2.02(2)(d) (Proposed Official Draft 1962) ("A person acts negligently with respect to a material element of an offense when he should be aware of a substantial and unjustifiable risk that the material element exists or will result from his conduct. The risk must be of such a nature and degree that the actor's failure to perceive it, considering the nature and purpose of his conduct and the circumstances known to him, involves a gross deviation from the standard of care that a reasonable person would observe in the actor's situation.").

[13] Other specific forms of mens rea, such as that the killing was "willful, premeditated and deliberate," may be required by murder statutes. See *infra* notes 17–27 and accompanying text.

generally punishes intentional killings more harshly than unintentional ones,[14] and further recognizes distinctions between various kinds of purposeful homicides. For example, an intentional killing committed in the heat of passion, in response to provocation,[15] or in a pique of anger[16] may evoke significantly different legal consequences than a purposeful killing committed after premeditation[17] and calm deliberation.[18] The cold and calculated nature of the latter brand of homicide may indicate depravity above and beyond what is associated with an intentional, "hotblooded" killing. For this reason, the first formal distinction between first-degree (capital) murder and second-degree (noncapital) murder depended largely on whether the homicide was "willful, deliberate and premeditated."[19]

---

[14] The two most notable exceptions to this statement involve felony murder and "depraved heart" murder or reckless killings that manifest extreme indifference to the value of life. See *infra* notes 42–49, 62–67 and accompanying text.

[15] Under common law, an intentional killing committed in the heat of passion after reasonable provocation was considered voluntary manslaughter rather than murder. See W. LaFave & A. Scott, *Criminal Law* 653–665 (2d ed. 1986). Analogously, the Model Penal Code recognizes that a killing "which otherwise would be murder"—for example, a purposeful criminal homicide—is manslaughter if "committed under the influence of extreme mental or emotional disturbance for which there is reasonable explanation or excuse." Model Penal Code § 210.3(1)(b) (Proposed Official Draft 1962).

[16] Where recognized, second-degree murder generally involves an intentional killing committed "in hot blood" or on impulse. It is punished less severely than first-degree murder because it lacks the "cold blooded" quality of that more serious grade of murder. See Austin v. United States, 382 F.2d 129, 137 (D.C. Cir. 1967).

[17] In simplest terms, " 'premeditation' . . . requires that the [offender] did in fact reflect, at least for a short period of time before his act of killing." LaFave & Scott, *supra* note 15, at 643. " 'Premeditation means "thought of beforehand" for some length of time, however short.' " R. Perkins & R. Boyce, *Criminal Law* 131 (3d ed. 1982), *quoting* State v. Chavis, 231 N.C. 307, 311, 56 S.E.2d 678, 681 (1949).

[18] The "deliberation" requirement for first-degree murder has defied precise definition, but "perhaps the best that can be said of 'deliberation' is that it requires a cool mind that is capable of reflection." LaFave & Scott, *supra* note 15, at 643 (footnote omitted). " 'Deliberation means that the act is done in a cool state of blood.' " Perkins & Boyce, *supra* note 17, at 131, *quoting* State v. Bowser, 214 N.C. 249, 253, 199 S.E. 31, 34 (1938). In application, the meanings of "deliberation" and "premeditation" become far more obscure than their definitions would suggest. See LaFave & Scott, at 643–646; Perkins & Boyce, at 131–133; Acker & Lanier, *supra* note 3, at 295 & n.16.

[19] Pa. Laws 1794, c. 257, §§ 1, 2. See Keedy, "History of the Pennsylvania Statute Creating Degrees of Murder," 97 U. Pa. L. Rev. 759 (1949); Acker & Lanier, *supra* note 3, at — & ns. 13–14. This early Pennsylvania statute also made certain types of felony murder first-degree murder, as it did with killings committed by poison or by lying in wait.

Statutory Mens Rea Requirements

In five states—Maryland,[20] Missouri,[21] Pennsylvania,[22] Virginia,[23] and Washington[24]—a homicide is a capital murder if and only if the offender killed intentionally, and with premeditation and/or deliberation. Maryland, Pennsylvania, and Virginia all require that a killing be "willful, deliberate and premeditated" in order to constitute capital murder.[25] In Missouri, one who "knowingly causes the death of another person after deliberation"[26] commits capital murder, while in Washington the offender must cause the death of another "with premeditated intent."[27] Felony murder in its traditional form, which does not require an intentional homicide, does not exist as a category of capital murder in any of these states.[28]

Under federal law[29] and in seven states—Alabama,[30] Louisi-

---

[20] Md. Ann. Code art. 27, § 407 (1992) ("[M]urder . . . perpetrated by means of poison, or lying in wait, or by any kind of willful, deliberate and premeditated killing.").

[21] Mo. Ann. Stat. § 565.020(1) (Vernon Supp. 1992) ("knowingly causes the death of another person after deliberation on the matter").

[22] Pa. Stat. Ann. tit. 18, § 2502(a) (Purdon 1983) ("A criminal homicide . . . committed by an intentional killing."); *id.* at § 2502(d) (" 'Intentional killing' [is defined as] [k]illing by means of poison, or by lying in wait, or by any other kind of willful, deliberate and premeditated killing.").

[23] Va. Code Ann. §§ 18.2-31(1)–18.2-31(9) (Supp. 1992) (all forms of capital murder require a "willful, deliberate, and premeditated killing").

[24] Wash. Rev. Code Ann. §§ 10.95.020 (1988), 9A.32.030(1)(a) (Supp. 1993) ("With the premeditated intent to cause the death of another person, [the offender] causes the death of such person or of a third person."); *id.* at § 9A.32.020(1) (1988) ("the premeditation required in order to support a conviction of the crime of murder in the first degree must involve more than a moment in point of time").

[25] *Supra* notes 20, 22, 23.

[26] *Supra* note 21.

[27] *Supra* note 24.

[28] For a discussion of felony murder, see *infra* notes 62–104 and accompanying text.

[29] 21 U.S.C. §§ 848(e)(1)(A), 848(e)(1)(B) (Supp. 1993) ("intentionally kills or counsels, commands, induces, procures, or causes the intentional killing of an individual and such killing results"). See *supra* note 6. See also *infra* note 32.

[30] Ala. Code §§ 13A-5-40(b) (Supp. 1992), 13A-6-2(a)(1) (1982) ("With intent to cause the death of another peson, he causes the death of that person or of another person.").

383

ana,[31] New Hampshire,[32] New Jersey,[33] Ohio,[34] Texas,[35] and Utah[36]—there cannot be capital murder unless the offender intentionally (purposely) or knowingly caused death or serious bodily injury.[37] Additionally, only intentional killings are capital crimes

[31] La. Rev. Stat. Ann. §§ 14:30(A)(1)–14:30(A)(6) (West 1986 & West Supp. 1993) (killing "[w]hen the offender has specific intent to kill or to inflict great bodily harm"); La. Rev. Stat. Ann. § 14:30(A)(7) (West Supp. 1993) (offender kills with "specific intent to kill" during designated "ritualistic acts").

[32] N.H. Rev. Stat. Ann. § 630:1(I) (Supp. 1991) ("knowingly causes the death"). The New Hampshire statute, which appears to be modeled in some respects after the federal death penalty procedures codified at 21 U.S.C. §§ 848(m), 848(n) (Supp. 1993), suffers from an inconsistency similar to the federal statute. As a prerequisite to imposing the death penalty, the jury at the sentencing phase must find that the defendant either purposely killed, purposely inflicted serious bodily injury resulting in death, or engaged in conduct that created a grave risk of death and in fact resulted in death. N.H. Rev. Stat. Ann. § 630:VII(a) (Supp. 1991). Compare 21 U.S.C. § 848(n)(1) (Supp. 1993). However, in order to convict for capital murder, the jury already must have found under the New Hampshire law that the defendant "knowingly" caused death, and under the federal law the jury must have found that the defendant killed "intentionally." See Jordan, *supra* note 6, at 104.

[33] N.J. Stat. Ann. §§ 2C:11(3)(c), 2C:11(3)(a)(1), 2C:11(3)(a)(2) (West Supp. 1992) ("The actor purposely causes death or serious bodily injury resulting in death; or [t]he actor knowingly causes death or serious bodily injury resulting in death."). Voters in New Jersey recently approved an amendment to the state constitution's cruel and unusual punishments clause that provides:

> It shall not be cruel and unusual punishment to impose the death penalty on a person convicted of purposely or knowingly causing death or purposely or knowingly causing serious bodily injury resulting in death who committed the homicidal act by his own conduct or who as an accomplice procured the commission of the offense by payment or promise of payment of anything of pecuniary value.

N.J. Const. art. I, para. 12 (Supp. 1993). This amendment nullified state supreme court rulings that capital punishment could not be imposed consistently with the state constitution unless the offender specifically intended to kill the homicide victim. See, e.g., State v. Gerald, 113 N.J. 40, 549 A.2d 792 (1988).

[34] Ohio Rev. Code Ann. § 2903.01(B) (Anderson 1993) (For felony related killings, offender must "purposely cause the death of another." However, for other killings to constitute aggravated murder, the offender must "purposely, and with prior calculation and design, cause the death of another." Ohio Rev. Code Ann. § 2903.01(A) (Anderson 1993).). See also Ohio Rev. Code Ann. § 2903.01(D) (Anderson 1993).

[35] Tex. Penal Code Ann. §§ 19.03(a), 19.02(a)(1) (Vernon 1989) ("intentionally or knowingly causes the death of an individual").

[36] Utah Code Ann. § 76-5-202(1) (Supp. 1992) ("intentionally or knowingly causes the death of another").

[37] Among the jurisdictions just discussed, in addition to the intent to kill, only Louisiana and New Jersey include the intent to inflict great bodily harm or serious bodily injury as mens rea for capital murder. See *supra* notes 31, 33. Conceptually, intent to kill and intent to do serious bodily injury are distinct, with the latter state of mind perhaps being closer to extreme recklessness or "depraved heart" murder when death results. As a practical matter, of course, it may be difficult to distinguish

384

in Oregon in all but exceptional circumstances.[38] The mens rea requirements for capital murder in these jurisdictions, as in the states that require premeditation and/or deliberation, preclude unintentional felony murders from being considered capital crimes.

In the other twenty-three death penalty states, or in roughly three out of five of the nation's capital punishment jurisdictions, offenders can be convicted of capital murder *even though they have no intent to kill or to inflict serious bodily injury*. This owes largely to the fact that felony murder or a closely related form of unintentional killing can be a capital offense in these jurisdictions.[39] However, outside of the felony murder context, in eleven of these states, capital murder must be committed intentionally or knowingly, coupled with premeditation and/or deliberation.[40]

---

between intent to kill and intent to inflict serious injury. *See* LaFave & Scott, *supra* note 15, at 616–617.

[38] Eleven general types of "murder," as defined by Or. Rev. Stat. § 163.115 (1991), are considered "aggravated murder" or capital murder, under Or. Rev. Stat. § 163.095 (1991). By joint operation of these statutes, aggravated murder must be committed "intentionally," Or. Rev. Stat. §§ 163.115(1)(a), 163.095(2)(d) (1991) (felony-related homicides must be committed "personally and intentionally" by the defendant). One narrow exception is recognized. This exception concerns a criminal homicide involving the death of either a child under age 14 or a dependent person when the homicide is caused "[b]y abuse when a person, recklessly under circumstances manifesting extreme indifference to the value of human life [kills such a victim] . . ., and the person has previously engaged in a pattern or practice of assault or torture of the victim or another child under 14 years of age or a dependent person." Or. Rev. Stat. § 163.115(1)(c) (1991). To be capital murder, this type of killing must be aggravated by one of the considerations enumerated in the capital murder statute. Or. Rev. Stat. § 163.095 (1991).

[39] See *infra*, notes 70–78 and accompanying text.

[40] Ariz. Rev. Stat. Ann. § 13-1105(A) (1989) ("Intending or knowing that his conduct will cause death, such person causes the death of another with premeditation."); Ark. Stat. Ann. §§ 5-10-101(3)–5-10-101(6) (Supp. 1991) (requiring "premeditated and deliberate purpose" of causing death; Ark. Stat. Ann. §§ 5-10-101(7), 5-10-101(8) (Supp. 1991) (killing pursuant to agreement); Cal. Penal Code § 189 (West Supp. 1993) ("willful, deliberate, and premeditated killing"); Fla. Stat. Ann. § 782.04(1)(a)(1) (West Supp. 1993) (killing with "a premeditated design" to effect death). (However, two forms of drug-related capital murder in Florida permit conviction either for intentional killings, or for killings where the offender manifested reckless disregard of human life by drug trafficking.) Fla. Stat. Ann. §§ 893.135(1)(b)(2), 893.135(1)(c)(2) (West Supp. 1993); Neb. Rev. Stat. § 28-303(1) (1989) (kills "purposely and with deliberate and premeditated malice") (Nebraska law also defines killing by poison or by procuring the execution of an innocent person through perjury to be capital murder. Neb. Rev. Stat. § 28-303(3) (1989)); Nev. Rev. Stat. Ann. § 200.030(1)(a) (Michie 1992) ("willful, deliberate and premeditated killing") (A killing to avoid or prevent a lawful arrest, or to escape from legal custody also is capital murder in Nevada. Nev. Rev. Stat. Ann. § 200.030(1)(c) (Michie 1992)); N.C. Gen. Stat. § 14-17 (Supp. 1992) ("willful, deliberate, and premeditated killing"); Okla. Stat. Ann. tit. 21, § 701.7(A) (West

In three other states, capital murders other than felony murder must be committed knowingly or with the intent to cause death or serious bodily injury.[41] Only nine states allow that capital murder has been committed even though the offender kills neither intentionally nor during the course of an enumerated felony.

The most common basis for this type of capital murder involves conscious risk-taking activity by an offender who, although harboring no intent to kill, manifests through his behavior a "don't give a damn" attitude about the consequences, which predictably could include the loss of human life. This general form of criminal homicide, known as depraved heart murder at common law,[42] was recognized as capital murder in the Model Penal Code (MPC) for killings "committed recklessly under circumstances manifesting extreme indifference to the value of human life."[43] The inclusion of such murders as capital crimes "reflects the judgment that there is a kind of reckless homicide that cannot fairly be distinguished in grading terms from homicides committed purposely or knowingly."[44] Capital murder provisions of this basic form are in effect in Colorado,[45]

Supp. 1992) (killing with "malice aforethought," which is "deliberate intention" to kill) (Oklahoma also recognizes aggravated child abuse resulting in death as capital murder. Okla. Stat. Ann. tit. 21, § 701.7(C) (West Supp. 1992)); S.D. Codified Laws Ann. § 22-16-4 (1988) (killing with a "premeditated design to effect . . . death"); Tenn. Code Ann. § 39-13-202(a) (1991) (an "intentional, premeditated and deliberate killing"); see Tenn. Code Ann. §§ 39-13-201(b)(1), 39-13-201(b)(2) (1991) (defining "deliberate" and "premeditated"). (Tennessee also defines aggravated child abuse resulting in death as capital murder. Tenn. Code Ann. § 39-13-202(4)(1991)); Wyo. Stat. § 6-2-101(a) (Supp. 1992) (where offender kills "purposely and with premeditated malice").

[41] Conn. Gen. Stat. Ann. § 53a-54a (West Supp. 1993) (where offender acts "with intent to cause the death of another person"); Conn. Gen. Stat. Ann. § 53a-54b (West Supp. 1993); Ind. Code Ann. § 35-42-1-1(1) (Burns Supp. 1992) (where offender "knowingly or intentionally kills another"); Mont. Code Ann. § 45-5-102(1)(a) (1987) (where offender "purposely or knowingly causes the death of another").

[42] Model Penal Code and Commentaries § 210.2, pp. 15, 22 (Official Draft & Revised Comments 1980); LaFave & Scott, *supra* note 15, at 617–621.

[43] Model Penal Code § 210.2(1)(b) (Proposed Official Draft 1962).

[44] Model Penal Code and Commentaries § 210.2, p. 21 (Official Draft & Revised Comments 1980). See also G. Fletcher, *Rethinking Criminal Law* 254 (1978) ("Wanton killings are generally regarded as among the most wicked, and the feature that makes a killing wanton is precisely the absence of detached reflection before the deed . . . . Killing without a motive can usually be just as wicked as killing after detached reflection about one's goals.").

[45] Colo. Rev. Stat. § 18-3-102(1)(d) (1986) ("Under circumstances evidencing an attitude of universal malice manifesting extreme indifference to the value of human life generally, he knowingly engages in conduct which creates a grave risk

Illinois,[46] Kentucky,[47] Mississippi,[48] and New Mexico.[49] Under Delaware law, simple recklessness (rather than the aggravated recklessness contemplated under the MPC and the states accepting this formulation) suffices as the mens rea for capital murder when the victim is "a law-enforcement officer, corrections employee or fireman [killed] . . . in the lawful performance of his duties."[50]

Statutes in three states—Georgia,[51] Idaho,[52] and South Carolina[53]—define murder as the killing of another person "with

---

of death to a person, . . . other than himself, and thereby causes the death of another."). For intentional capital murder, Colorado law requires that the offender killed "[a]fter deliberation, and with the intent to cause" death. Colo. Rev. Stat. § 18-3-102(1)(a) (1986).

[46] Ill. Ann. Stat. ch. 720, § 5/9-1(a)(2) (Smith-Hurd Supp. 1993) (killing where the offender "knows that such acts create a strong probability of death or great bodily harm to that individual or another"). Intentional capital murder is committed if the offender "either intends to kill or do great bodily harm . . . or knows that such acts will cause death." Ill. Ann. Stat. ch. 720, § 5/9-1(a)(1) (Smith-Hurd Supp. 1993).

[47] Ky. Rev. Stat. Ann. § 507.020(1)(b) (Michie/Bobbs-Merrill 1990) ("Including, but not limited to, the operation of a motor vehicle under circumstances manifesting extreme indifference to human life, he wantonly engages in conduct which creates a grave risk of death to another person and thereby causes the death of another person."). Intentional capital murder is defined simply: "With intent to cause the death of another person, he causes the death of such person or of a third person." Ky. Rev. Stat. Ann. § 507.020(1)(a) (Michie/Bobbs-Merrill 1990).

[48] Miss. Code Ann. § 97-3-19(1)(b) (Supp. 1992) (A killing "done in the commission of an act eminently dangerous to others and evincing a depraved heart, regardless of human life, although without any premeditated design to effect the death of any particular individual."). Intentional capital murder must be "done with deliberate design" to kill. Miss. Code Ann. § 97-3-19(1)(a) (Supp. 1992). See Miss. Code Ann. § 97-3-19(2) (Supp. 1992).

[49] N.M. Stat. Ann. § 30-2-1(A)(3) (1984) (Killing "by any act greatly dangerous to the lives of others, including a depraved mind regardless of human life."). Intentional capital murder is "any kind of willful, deliberate and premeditated killing." N.M. Stat. Ann. § 30-2-1(A)(1) (1984).

[50] Del. Code Ann. tit. 11, § 636(a)(4) (1987). Intentional capital murder is committed when the offender "intentionally causes the death of another person." Del. Code Ann. tit. 11, § 636(a)(1) (1987).

[51] Ga. Code Ann. § 16-5-1(a) (1992). "Malice" is defined as follows: "Express malice is that deliberate intention unlawfully to take the life of another human being which is manifested by external circumstances capable of proof. Malice shall be implied when no considerable provocation appears and where all the circumstances of the killing show an abandoned and malignant heart." Ga. Code Ann. § 16-5-1(d) (1992).

[52] Idaho Code § 18-4001 (1987) (defining murder as an unlawful killing "with malice aforethought or the intentional application of torture" resulting in death). Capital murder involves the commission of specific types of murder, as defined under Idaho Code §§ 18-4003(a)–18-4003(f) (Supp. 1992).

[53] S.C. Code Ann. § 16-3-10 (Law Co-op. 1985) (" *Murder* is the killing of

387

9

malice aforethought,'' and make all or a subclass of such killings capital crimes. Because of the inherent ambiguity in the term ''malice aforethought,'' the specific contours of capital murder in these states are fashioned primarily through judicial decisions.[54] While legislatures are presumed to act with knowledge of judicial decisions, and terms like ''premeditation'' and ''deliberation'' also require judicial definition,[55] there is little reason to commend language as vague as ''malice aforethought'' as an essential provision of capital murder statutes. Legislative policy concerning the mens rea requirements for capital murder certainly is capable of more precise expression.

Suggested Mens Rea Threshold

Considerable variation exists in legislative judgments about the minimum mens rea requirements for capital murder. These differences, in part, may reflect a lack of consensus as to the comparative culpability of offenders who kill with ''premeditation and deliberation,'' or ''intentionally,'' or ''recklessly, manifesting extreme indifference to the value of human life,'' or who simply kill ''recklessly'' or ''with malice aforethought.'' They also may indicate different conceptions about the minimum threshold of culpability that should characterize the crime of capital murder.[56] Judgments of this nature obviously do not reduce to simple exercises of logic that start from shared premises

---

any person with malice aforethought, either express or implied.'') (emphasis in original).

[54] See generally LaFave & Scott, *supra* note 15, at 605 (''[I]t is preferable not to rely upon that misleading expression ['malice aforethought'] for an understanding of murder, but rather to consider the various types of murder . . . which the common law came to recognize and which exist today in most jurisdictions: (1) intent-to-kill murder; (2) intent-to-do-serious-bodily-injury murder; (3) depraved-heart murder; and (4) felony murder.'').

[55] See *supra* notes 17, 18.

[56] The Supreme Court has not established a minimum threshold of culpability for capital punishment except to rule out the rape of an adult as a capital crime, Coker v. Georgia, 433 U.S. 584 (1977); to prohibit the execution of fifteen-year-old murderers, Thompson v. Oklahoma, 487 U.S. 815 (1988), see *infra* notes 167–168 and accompanying text; and in the context of vicarious liability for felony murder. Tison v. Arizona, 481 U.S. 137 (1987), see *infra* notes 65–68 and accompanying text. Otherwise, the Court has ruled that the death penalty is to be reserved for aggravated forms of murder, Godfrey v. Georgia, 446 U.S. 420, 433 (1980) and Zant v. Stephens, 462 U.S. 862, 877–878 (1983), but has not elaborated on how ''aggravated'' a criminal homicide must be to render an offender eligible for the death penalty.

and evolve according to agreed-on principles of penology or jurisprudence.

Murder is an inherently condemnable act, and in all cases deserves serious punishment. Because the death penalty is qualitatively different from other punishments,[57] though, it seems persuasive that such a uniquely severe sanction should be reserved for murderers who evidence a similarly unique quality of culpability. It seems intuitive that a murder committed intentionally, after thought and reflection, reflects a greater depravity than a spontaneous, intentional murder that is not distinguished by premeditation and deliberation.[58] Furthermore, it is persuasive that

> a determination that the defendant acted with intent is qualitatively different from a determination that the defendant acted with reckless indifference to human life. The difference lies in the nature of the choice each actor has made. The reckless actor has not *chosen* to bring about the killing in the way the intentional actor has. The person who chooses to act recklessly and is indifferent to the consequences often deserves serious punishment. But because that person has not chosen to kill, his or her moral and criminal culpability is of a different degree than that of one who . . . intended to kill.[59]

If the conclusions from these twin lines of argument are accepted, then there is considerable merit in the legislative judgments reflected in the murder statutes of Maryland, Missouri, Pennsylvania, Virginia, and Washington.[60] Reckless killings and intentional killings, without more, lack the exceptional moral depravity to qualify as capital murder. The death penalty should be available only for uniquely culpable offenders: intentional murderers who have premeditated and deliberated in advance of their killings.[61]

---

[57] Woodson v. North Carolina, 428 U.S. 280, 305 (1976) (plurality opinion). See Acker & Lanier, *supra* note 3, at 302 & n.43.

[58] See *supra* notes 15–19 and accompanying text. However, some killings that transpire after considerable brooding and reflection may relate back to an incident that would have been adequate provocation to reduce an intentional killing from murder to manslaughter, had the offender killed when originally provoked. See State v. Gounagias, 88 Wash. 304, 153 P. 9 (1915). See generally C. Black, *Capital Punishment: The Inevitability of Caprice and Mistake* 48–49 (1974).

[59] Tison v. Arizona, 481 U.S. 137, 170–171 (1987) (Brennan, J., dissenting) (emphasis in original). Obviously, some will disagree with this proposition. See *supra* notes 42–44 and accompanying text.

[60] See *supra* notes 20–24 and accompanying text.

[61] The capital murder statutes in Maryland, Pennsylvania, and Virginia require

389

Felony Murder

The United States not only is one of the few countries in the western hemisphere that retains capital punishment,[62] but it "remains virtually the only western country still recognizing a rule which makes it possible 'that the most serious sanctions known to law might be imposed for accidental homicide.'"[63] That rule is the felony murder rule. Under the law of felony murder, even an unintentional killing, committed by a felon during the course of a serious crime, such as rape, robbery, and burglary, may result in a conviction for murder and a commensurately serious punishment. Moreover, under vicarious liability principles, even a felon who does not personally claim another's life is guilty of murder when an accomplice commits a homicide in furtherance of the underlying felony. Obviously, making felony murder a capital offense is inconsistent with policies that restrict capital murders to intentional, premeditated, and deliberate killings.[64]

In *Tison v. Arizona*[65] the Supreme Court ruled (5-4) that the Constitution does not forbid capital punishment for felony murder, even for a participant in the felony who did not personally kill nor intend that anyone be killed during the crime.[66] "[M]ajor

---

premeditation and deliberation, while Missouri requires only deliberation, and Washington requires only premeditation. See *supra* notes 20-24.

[62] *See* Acker & Lanier, "Doing the Devil's Work: Toward Model Death Penalty Legislation," 29 Crim. L. Bull. 219, 228 & n.26 (1993).

[63] Roth & Sundby, "The Felony-Murder Rule: A Doctrine at Constitutional Crossroads," 70 Cornell L. Rev. 446, 447-448 (1985), *quoting* Jeffries & Stephan, "Defenses, Presumptions, and Burden of Proof in the Criminal Law," 88 Yale L.J. 1325, 1383 (1979).

[64] For a collection of the epithets that have been used to characterize the felony murder rule—e.g., a "living fossil," an "astonishing" and "monstrous" doctrine, an "anachroni[sm]," and a rule that "erodes the relation between criminal liability and moral culpability"— see Finkel, "Capital Felony-Murder, Objective Indicia, and Community Sentiment," 32 Ariz. L. Rev. 819, 819-821 (1990) (citations omitted). See also Roth & Sundby, *supra* note 63, at 446 (criticisms of the felony murder rule include that it is "an unsupportable 'legal fiction,' 'an unsightly wart on the skin of the criminal law,' and . . . an 'anachronistic remnant' that has 'no logical or practical basis for existence in modern law.' ") (citations omitted).

[65] 481 U.S. 137 (1987).

[66] Five years prior to the decision in *Tison*, the Court had ruled that "the Eighth Amendment [forbids] imposition of the death penalty on one . . . who aids and abets a felony in the course of which a murder is committed by others but who does not himself kill, attempt to kill, or intend that a killing take place or that lethal force will be employed." Enmund v. Florida, 458 U.S. 782, 797 (1982). The decision in *Tison*, which purported to distinguish *Enmund*, substantially eroded the rule

390

participation'' in the underlying felony, coupled with the mens rea of ''reckless indifference to human life,''[67] establish the requisite culpability for death penalty eligibility under the majority opinion in *Tison*. The Court's opinion relied heavily on a survey of state death penalty legislation in reaching the conclusion that the death penalty is not a disproportionate punishment for felony murder committed under these circumstances.[68] A review of the legislation, which is based on the statutes themselves rather than judicial decisions that interpret and sometimes limit the scope of the statutes, reveals additional details about felony murder as a capital crime.

Legislative Recognition of Capital Felony Murder

Fourteen of thirty-seven death penalty jurisdictions preclude capital punishment for unintentional felony murder by requiring that a killing be committed intentionally or knowingly to qualify as capital murder.[69] In eighteen of the remaining death penalty states, felony murder simpliciter, which requires no specific mens rea and applies to killings committed during a variety of dangerous felonies, is made a capital crime.[70] North Carolina's

---

propounded in *Enmund*. See Rosen, ''Felony Murder and the Eighth Amendment Jurisprudence of Death,'' 31 B.C. L. Rev. 1103, 1150 (1990).

[67] Tison v. Arizona, 481 U.S. 137, 158 (1987). The Court explained that the twin requirements of major participation in the underlying felony and reckless indifference to human life ''often overlap.'' *Id*. at 158 n.12. The Court declined ''to precisely delineate the particular types of conduct and states of mind warranting imposition of the death penalty.'' *Id*. at 158.

[68] *Id*. at 152–154. The dissent in *Tison* took issue with the majority opinion's characterization of the death penalty statutes. *Id*. at 174–175 (Brennan, J., dissenting). In Enmund v. Florida, 458 U.S. 782 (1982), there was similar disagreement and confusion about the precise scope of state death penalty laws in the context of felony murder and vicarious liability. Compare *id*. at 789–793 (majority opinion of White, J.) and *id*. at 819–823 (dissenting opinion of O'Connor, J.).

[69] See *supra* notes 20–38 (included here are Louisiana and New Jersey, which also have intent-to-inflict-serious-bodily-injury capital murder, and Oregon, which has an exceptional form of nonintentional capital murder based on aggravated abuse of a child or dependent person).

[70] See Ariz. Rev. Stat. Ann. §§ 13-1105(A)(2), 13-1105(B) (1989); Ark. Stat. Ann. §§ 5-10-101(a)(1), 5-10-101(a)(2) (Supp. 1991); Cal. Penal Code §§ 189 (West Supp. 1993), 190.2(17) (West 1988) (special circumstances); Colo. Rev. Stat. § 18-3-102(1)(b) (Supp. 1992); Fla. Stat. Ann. § 782.04(1)(a)(2) (West Supp. 1993); Ga. Code Ann. § 16-5-1(c) (1992); Idaho Code § 18-4003(d) (Supp. 1992); Ill. Ann. Stat. ch 720, § 5/9-1a(3) (Smith-Hurd Supp. 1993); Ind. Code Ann. §§ 35-42-1-1(2), 35-42-1-1(3) (Burns Supp. 1992); Miss. Code Ann. § 97-3-19(2)(e) (Supp. 1992); Mont. Code Ann. § 45-5-102(1)(b) (1987); Neb. Rev. Stat. § 28-303(2) (1989); Nev. Rev. Stat. Ann. § 200.030(1)(b) (Michie 1992); N.M. Stat. Ann. § 30-2-1(A)(2) (1984); N.C. Gen. Stat. § 14-17 (Supp. 1992); Okla.

391

felony murder provision is illustrative: "A murder . . . committed in the perpetration or attempted perpetration of any arson, rape or a sex offense, robbery, kidnapping, burglary, or other felony committed or attempted with the use of a deadly weapon shall be deemed to be murder in the first degree."[71]

The felony murder statutes in other jurisdictions deviate from the more typical model. Under Connecticut law, capital felony murder includes only homicides associated with the commission of three specific offenses: kidnapping; the illegal sale of cocaine, heroin, or methadone; or first-degree sexual assault.[72] Tennessee punishes felony murders as capital crimes only if the offender killed recklessly,[73] whereas Delaware law makes both reckless and criminally negligent homicides capital murder if committed in the course of designated felonies.[74] In South Carolina, capital murder is simply "the killing of any person with malice aforethought, either express or implied";[75] felony murder is included as a matter of judicial construction.[76] Kentucky does not recognize felony murder. However, under related legislation in that state, an offender who "wantonly engages in conduct which creates a grave risk of death to another person and thereby causes death"[77] is guilty of capital murder. This category is broad enough to

---

Stat. Ann. tit. 21, § 701.7(B) (West Supp. 1993); S.D. Codified Laws Ann. § 22-16-4 (1988); Wyo. Stat. § 6-2-101(a) (Supp. 1992).

[71] N.C. Gen. Stat. § 14-17 (Supp. 1992).

[72] Conn. Gen. Stat.Ann. §§ 53a-54b(5)–53a-54b(7) (West Supp. 1993). The Connecticut statutes are structured so that capital felonies (Conn. Gen. Stat. Ann. § 53a-54b (West Supp. 1993)) require proof of murder, which is defined at Conn. Gen. Stat. Ann. § 53a-54a (West Supp. 1993) (intent to kill) and at Conn. Gen. Stat. Ann. § 53a-54c (West Supp. 1993) (felony murder). It appears that felony murder can serve as the basis for a capital felony. See State v. Usry, 205 Conn. 298, 533 A.2d 212, 219–220 (1987) (life sentence imposed).

[73] Tenn. Code Ann. § 39-13-202(a)(2) (1991).

[74] Del. Code Ann. tit. 11, § 636(a)(2) (1987) ("In the course of and in furtherance of the commission or attempted commission of a felony or immediate flight therefrom, he recklessly causes the death of another person."); Del. Code Ann. tit. 11, § 636(a)(6) (Supp. 1992) ("He with criminal negligence, causes the death of another person in the course of and in furtherance of the commission or attempted commission of rape, unlawful sexual intercourse in the first or second degree, kidnapping, arson in the first degree, robbery in the first degree, burglary in the first degree, or immediate flight therefrom.").

[75] S.C. Code Ann. § 16-3-10 (Law Co-op. 1985).

[76] See, e.g., State v. Copeland, 278 S.C. 572, 300 S.E.2d 63 (1982), cert. denied, 460 U.S. 1103 (1983).

[77] Ky. Rev. Stat. Ann. § 507.020(1)(b) (Michie/Bobbs-Merrill 1990).

include unintentional homicides committed in the course of dangerous felonies.[78]

Specifics of Legislation

The crimes that serve most commonly as predicate felonies for capital felony murder are kidnapping; robbery; burglary; arson; and rape, sodomy, and other sexual assaults. Virtually all capital felony murder statutes include these offenses. This is consistent with the philosophy that the offender's intentional commission of an inherently dangerous felony justifies punishing a related homicide as murder, without further regard for the offender's mens rea for the killing.[79]

Many states similarly define as capital murder killings that occur during felonious activities, such as the delivery of controlled substances,[80] the use of a bomb or destructive device,[81] child abuse,[82] and hijacking.[83] In Georgia and New Mexico, there are no statutory limits on the types of felonies on which capital felony murder can be predicated.[84] Capital murder statutes in Illinois and Montana require only that a homicide be committed

---

[78] For example, felony murder is not recognized under the MPC. However, the MPC does recognize as murder a criminal homicide "committed recklessly under circumstances manifesting extreme indifference to the value of human life." Model Penal Code § 210.2(1)(b) (Proposed Official Draft 1962).

Such recklessness and indifference are presumed if the actor is engaged or is an accomplice in the commission of, or an attempt to commit, or flight after committing or attempting to commit robbery, rape or deviate sexual intercourse by force or threat of force, arson, burglary, kidnapping or felonious escape.

Model Penal Code § 210.2(1)(b) (Proposed Official Draft 1962).

[79] LaFave & Scott, *supra* note 15, at 623–625.

[80] See, e.g., Colo. Rev. Stat. § 18-3-102(1)(e) (Supp. 1992); Fla. Stat. Ann. §§ 893.135(1)(b)(2)(b), 893.135(1)(c)(2)(b) (West Supp. 1993); Ind. Code Ann. § 35-42-1-1(3) (Burns Supp. 1992); Okla. Stat. Ann. tit. 21, § 701.7(D) (West Supp. 1993).

[81] See, e.g., Miss. Code Ann. § 97-3-19(2)(c) (Supp. 1992); Neb. Rev. Stat. §§ 28-1223(4), 28-1224(1), 28-1224(4) (1989); S.D. Codified Laws Ann. § 22-16-4 (1988).

[82] See, e.g., Miss. Code Ann. § 97-3-19(2)(f) (Supp. 1992); Okla. Stat. Ann. tit. 21, § 701.7(C) (West Supp. 1993); Or. Rev. Stat. §§ 163.115(c), 163.095 (1991). See *supra* note 38. See *infra* note 154 and accompanying text.

[83] See, e.g., Ark. Stat. Ann. § 5-10-101(1) (Supp. 1991); Neb. Rev. Stat. § 28-303(2) (1989).

[84] Ga. Code Ann. § 16-5-1(c) (1992) ("in the commission of a felony"); N.M. Stat. Ann. § 30-2-1(A)(2) (1984) ("in the commission of or attempt to commit any felony").

during a "forcible" felony.[85] Killings committed during crimes like escape,[86] train wrecking,[87] product tampering,[88] mayhem,[89] and even theft[90] are treated as capital murder in scattered jurisdictions.[91]

Statutes differ in describing the connection between "felony" and "homicide" that must exist to transform a felony-related killing into capital murder. The most general provisions stipulate only that the homicide must be committed "in the perpetration or attempted perpetration of" the qualifying felonies, or some closely related variation of that standard.[92] More specific statutes typically require that a killing be committed "in the course of

---

[85] Ill. Ann. Stat. ch. 720, § 5/9-1(a)(3) (Smith-Hurd Supp. 1993) ("a forcible felony other than second-degree murder"); Mont.Code Ann. § 45-5-102(b) (1987) (enumerating several specific felonies, in addition to "any other forcible felony").

[86] See, e.g., Ariz. Rev. Stat. Ann. § 13-1105(A)(2) (1989); Ark. Stat. Ann. § 5-10-101(a)(1) (Supp. 1991); Colo. Rev. Stat. § 18-3-102(1)(b) (Supp. 1992); Fla. Stat. Ann. § 782.04(1)(a)(2)(g) (West Supp. 1993); Mont. Code Ann. § 45-5-102(1)(b) (1987); Okla. Stat. Ann. tit. 21, § 701.7(B) (West Supp. 1993); Wyo. Stat. § 6-2-101(a) (Supp. 1992).

[87] Cal. Penal Code § 189 (West Supp. 1993).

[88] Ind. Code Ann. § 35-42-1-1(2) (Burns Supp. 1992).

[89] Cal. Penal Code § 189 (West Supp. 1993); Idaho Code § 18-4003(d) (Supp. 1992). See also Mont. Code Ann. § 45-5-102(1)(b) (1987) (including felony assault and aggravated assault); Tenn. Code Ann. § 39-13-202(a)(2) (1991) (including first-degree murder). The previous felonies are unusual predicates for felony murder because of the merger doctrine, which normally requires that the felony on which a felony murder conviction is based be independent of the homicidal assault. See LaFave & Scott, *supra* note 15, at 637–639; Fletcher, *supra* note 44, at 294.

[90] Tenn. Code Ann. § 39-13-202(a)(2) (1991) (By this same provision, the killing committed in the perpetration of a theft, as with other felonies, must be committed recklessly.).

[91] Oregon, which requires that killings in the course of felonies be committed intentionally in order to qualify as capital murder, Or. Rev. Stat. § 163.095(2)(d) (1991), includes compelling prostitution as a predicate felony for felony murder. Or. Rev. Stat. § 163.115(1)(b)(I) (1991).

[92] Statutes of this basic variety include Cal. Penal Code §§ 189 (West Supp. 1993) 190.2(17) (West Supp. 1993) (special circumstance, also including homicides committed during immediate flight); Fla. Stat.Ann. § 782.04(1)(a)(2) (West Supp. 1993); Idaho Code § 18-4003(d) (Supp. 1992); Ill. Ann. Stat. ch. 720, § 5/9-1(a)(3) (Smith-Hurd Supp. 1993); Ind. Code Ann. § 35-42-1-1(2) (Burns Supp. 1992); Miss. Code Ann. § 97-3-19(2)(e) (Supp. 1992); Neb. Rev. Stat. § 28-303(2) (1989); Nev. Rev. Stat. Ann. § 200.030(1)(b) (Michie 1992); N.M. Stat. Ann. § 30-2-1(A)(2) (1984); N.C. Gen. Stat. § 14-17 (Supp. 1992); S.D. Codified Laws Ann. § 22-16-4 (1988); Wyo. Stat. § 6-2-101(a) (Supp. 1992). In addition, statutes in two states specify that the killing must occur "in the commission of" the felony, thus omitting the common clause "or attempted commission" of the felony. Ga. Code Ann. § 16-5-1(c) (1992); Okla. Stat. Ann. tit. 21, § 701.7(B) (West Supp. 1993).

394

and in furtherance of'' the felony, thus demanding that a causal connection and not merely a coincidental link be established between the felony and the homicide. Many of these statutes specifically include killings committed ''in immediate flight'' from the felony as a punishable offense.[93] The Colorado capital murder statute exemplifies this latter type of legislation:

> Acting either alone or with one or more persons, he commits or attempts to commit [enumerated felonies] . . . and, in the course of or in furtherance of the crime that he is committing or attempting to commit, or of immediate flight therefrom, the death of any person, other than one of the participants, is caused by anyone.[94]

This statute raises additional issues relevant to the scope of felony murder provisions that arise in other death penalty jurisdictions. Colorado is one of three states that, by statute, does not hold an offender guilty of felony murder if another participant in the crime is the homicide victim.[95] Nor does the Colorado statute by its terms limit murder liability to a killing committed by a felon; its coverage extends to deaths ''caused by anyone.''[96]

Many statutes are vague about whether capital felony murder can be committed if one of the felons does not personally kill a homicide victim.[97] Statutes in seven states expressly provide that a felon will be guilty of murder if an accomplice or co-participant

---

[93] See Ariz. Rev. Stat. Ann. § 13-1105(A)(2) (1989); Ark. Stat. Ann. § 5-10-101(a)(1) (Supp. 1991); Colo. Rev. Stat. § 18-3-102(1)(b) (Supp. 1992); Conn. Gen. Stat. Ann. § 53a-54c (West Supp. 1993) (''flight,'' rather than ''immediate flight''); Mont. Code Ann. § 45-5-102(1)(b) (1987) (''in the course of the forcible felony or flight thereafter''). Several jurisdictions that make intentional killing in the course of felonies, or immediate flight thereafter, a form of capital murder have similar limitations. One rather unique provision of this type appears in New Hampshire's statute, which includes knowingly causing death ''before, after, while engaged in the commission of, or while attempting to commit'' the named felonies. N.H. Rev. Stat. Ann. §§ 630:1(I)(b), 630:1(I)(e), 630:1(I)(f) (Supp. 1991).

[94] Colo. Rev. Stat. § 18-3-102(1)(b) (Supp. 1992).

[95] See also Conn. Gen. Stat. Ann. § 53a-54c (West Supp. 1993); Or. Rev. Stat. §§ 163.115(1)(b), 163.095(2)(d) (1991) (Oregon requires that felony-related homicides be committed intentionally to qualify as capital murder.).

[96] See supra text accompanying note 94.

[97] See, e.g., Cal. Penal Code §§ 189 (West Supp. 1993), 190.2(d) (West 1988); Idaho Code § 18-4003(d) (Supp. 1992); Nev. Rev. Stat. Ann. § 200.030(1)(b) (Michie 1992); N.C. Gen. Stat. § 14-17 (Supp. 1992). Correctly categorizing the statutes relevant to this point caused the Court considerable confusion in Tison v. Arizona, 481 U.S. 137 (1987) and in Enmund v. Florida, 458 U.S. 782 (1982). See supra note 68. See also Rosen, supra note 66, at 1125–1127.

in the felony causes the death of the victim.[98] The felony murder provisions in Colorado (a death is caused "by anyone")[99] and Arizona (the felon "or another person" causes a death)[100] appear to invite liability even if a third party, such as a police officer or a resisting victim, commits the homicide. With varying degrees of clarity, legislation in fifteen jurisdictions implies or states that only the actual killer is guilty of murder in felony-related homicides.[101]

Inadequate Justification

Under felony murder statutes, there is great risk that offenders will be convicted and condemned to die, even though they have not manifested that unique culpability that should be a prerequisite to the imposition of capital punishment. Where it is recognized, capital felony murder at a minimum should encompass only killings committed in the course of and in furtherance of[102] a select few, inherently dangerous felonies.[103] Further, only the actual killer should be liable for murder unless a cofelon who did not kill intended that a homicide be committed.[104] Even with

---

[98] These statutes are not confined to jurisdictions that permit capital murder to be based on nonintentional felony murder. These statutes include: Ala. Code § 13A-5-40(c) (Supp. 1992); Ark. Stat. Ann. § 5-10-101(a)(1) (Supp. 1991); Conn. Gen. Stat. Ann. § 53a-54c (West Supp. 1993); Fla. Stat. Ann. § 782.04(1)(a)(2) (West Supp. 1993) (capital murder if killing by person engaged in felony), Fla. Stat. Ann. § 782.04(1)(a)(3) (West Supp. 1993) (second-degree murder if killing by person other than one engaged in felony); Miss. Code Ann. § 97-3-19(2)(e) (Supp. 1992); Mont. Code Ann. § 45-5-102(1)(b) (1987); S.D. Codified Laws Ann. § 22-16-4 (1988).

[99] See *supra* text accompanying note 94.

[100] Ariz. Rev. Stat. Ann. § 13-1105(A)(2) (1989).

[101] The statutes listed here include jurisdictions in addition to those that permit capital felony murder for nonintentional killings. Different interpretations that may have been made of these statutes by judicial decision are not included. The statutes include: Del. Code Ann. tit. 11, §§ 636(a)(2) (1987), 636(a)(6) (Supp. 1992); Ga. Code Ann. § 16-5-1(c) (1992); Ill. Ann. Stat. ch. 720, § 5/9-1(a)(3) (Smith-Hurd Supp. 1993); Ind. Code Ann. §§ 35-42-1-1(2), 35-42-1-1(3) (Burns Supp. 1992); La. Rev. Stat. Ann. § 14:30(A)(1) (West Supp. 1993); Neb. Rev. Stat. § 28-303(2) (1989); N.H. Rev. Stat. Ann. § 630:1(I) (Supp. 1991); Ohio Rev. Code Ann. § 2903.01(B) (Anderson 1993); Okla. Stat. Ann. tit. 21, § 701.7(B) (West Supp. 1993); Or. Rev. Stat. § 163.095(2)(d) (1991); Tex. Penal Code Ann. § 19.03(a)(2) (Vernon 1989); Utah Code Ann. § 76-5-202(1) (Supp. 1992); Wash. Rev. Code Ann. §§ 10.95.020, 10.95.020(9) (1990); Wyo. Stat. § 6-2-101(a) (Supp. 1992); 21 U.S.C. §§ 848(e)(1)(A), 848(e)(1)(B) (Supp. 1993).

[102] See *supra* notes 92, 93 and accompanying text.

[103] See *supra* notes 79–91 and accompanying text.

[104] See *supra* notes 96–101 and accompanying text.

such limitations, though, the major problem with the felony murder doctrine is not rectified because unintended killings can still be treated as capital crimes. In short, there is no persuasive justification for classifying felony murder simpliciter as a capital offense.

The Scope of Capital Murder Provisions

An earlier article in this series presented an argument for detailed capital murder legislation, in preference to statutes that define capital murder generally and then limit death penalty eligibility by requiring that one of several aggravating factors be proven during the sentencing phase of capital trials.[105] Statutes vary widely in how specifically they define capital murder and in whether they narrow the class of death-eligible offenses primarily through proof of the elements of murder or through proof of sentencing factors after guilt has been established. For example, Missouri and South Carolina each define capital murder generally, and then enumerate sixteen and ten aggravating circumstances, respectively, to be considered at sentencing.[106] In contrast, Utah has seventeen specific forms of capital murder, and no additional circumstances need to be considered or proven at the sentencing trial to make the offender eligible for capital punishment.[107] Similarly, Virginia law itemizes nine types of capital murder, and the sentencing trial focuses on either of two statutory issues.[108] Some states define several different forms of capital murder, and also specify numerous aggravating factors that may be considered during the penalty trial.[109]

The factors that aggravate a murder for death penalty purposes—either by incorporation in the definition of capital murder, or by inclusion among the sentencing circumstances that help

---

[105] Acker & Lanier, *supra* note 3.

[106] Mo. Ann. Stat. § 565.020(1) (Vernon Supp. 1992); S.C. Code Ann. §§ 16-3-10 (Law Co-op. 1985), 16-3-20(C)(a)(1)–20(C)(a)(10) (Law Co-op. Supp. 1992).

[107] Utah Code Ann. §§ 76-5-202(1)(a)–76-5-202(1)(q), 76-3-207 (Supp. 1992).

[108] Va. Code Ann. §§ 18.2-31(1)–18.2-31(9) (Supp. 1992), 19.2-264.2 (1990).

[109] For example, Alabama law defines fourteen different types of capital murder, and also incorporates eight aggravating sentencing circumstances. Ala. Code §§ 13A-5-40(a)(1)–13A-5-40(a)(14), 13A-5-49(1)–13A-5-49(8) (Supp. 1992). Mississippi law has seven forms of capital murder, and also includes eight aggravating sentencing circumstances. Miss. Code Ann. §§ 97-3-19(2)(a)–97-3-19(2)(f), 99-19-101(5)(a)–99-19-101(5)(h) (Supp. 1992).

determine death penalty eligibility—can be classified according to four different dimensions of the crime: offender characteristics, the manner in which the crime was committed, the motive for the crime, and characteristics of the victim. Considerations that aggravate a criminal homicide do so regardless of whether they are called elements of capital murder or sentencing circumstances, and it is artificial to treat crime elements and sentencing factors as if they were conceptually distinct. While aggravating factors are the focus of the next article in this series, what follows here is a brief summary of the aggravating factors that have been identified as elements of capital murder in different statutes.[110] This section also discusses a noteworthy form of capital murder that is recognized by statute in four states, procuring the execution of an innocent person through perjury.

Offender Characteristics

An otherwise unaggravated form of murder is transformed into capital murder in four states if the offender has a prior murder conviction or, in Oregon, a prior conviction for manslaughter.[111] In Utah, prior record has greater significance, as any past conviction for "a felony involving the use or threat of violence to a person" can convert an unaggravated killing to a capital crime.[112] An offender who commits murder during service of a sentence of life imprisonment or while sentenced to death commits a capital crime in six states.[113] A killing committed by

---

[110] Excluded from this review is legislation that defines capital murder only by reference to mens rea and felony murder provisions, and that does not itemize the aggravating circumstances that distinguish capital murder from less serious criminal homicide. Included for present purposes are the statutes from California and Ohio, which define murder generally, but which require the proof of additional circumstances prior to the penalty phase of a trial before a death sentence may be sought. See Acker & Lanier, *supra* note 3, at 301–302 & ns. 38–42.

[111] Ala. Code & 13A-5-40(a)(13) (Supp. 1992) (convicted of another murder within twenty years preceding the crime); Cal. Penal Code § 190.2(a)(2) (West Supp. 1993) (special circumstance) (prior conviction for first-degree or second-degree murder); Conn. Gen. Stat. Ann. § 53a-54b(3) (West Supp. 1993) (prior conviction for intentional murder or murder committed during the course of a felony); Idaho Code § 18-4003(c) (Supp. 1992) (offender under sentence, including probation or parole, for first-degree or second-degree murder); Or. Rev. Stat. § 163.095(1)(c) (1991) (prior conviction for murder or manslaughter).

[112] Utah Code Ann. § 76-5-202(1)(h) (Supp. 1992).

[113] Ala. Code § 13A-5-40(a)(6) (Supp. 1992); Ark. Stat. Ann. § 5-10-101(a)(6) (Supp. 1991); Conn. Gen. Stat. Ann. § 53a-54b(4) (West Supp. 1993); Miss. Code Ann. § 97-3-19(2)(b) (Supp. 1992); N.H. Rev. Stat. § 630:1(I)(d) (Supp. 1991); Utah Code Ann. § 76-5-202(1)(p) (Supp. 1992). See generally Sumner v. Shuman, 483 U.S. 66 (1987) (discussing why murder committed by prisoners serving sentence

anyone who is incarcerated, or by one who is attempting to escape from a place of lawful confinement, is a form of capital murder in six additional states.[114]

Manner in Which the Crime Was Committed

Causing a death during a contemporaneous felony, including drug offenses, is by far the most common way that a homicide is committed that distinguishes a killing as capital murder.[115] Using a destructive device, bomb, or explosive to cause death also is capital murder in several jurisdictions.[116] Utah more generally recognizes that a killing is capital murder if the offender ''knowingly created a great risk of death to a person other than the victim and the actor.''[117]

Eight states make killing more than one victim during the same criminal episode or course of conduct a form of capital murder.[118] In Delaware, the rather unlikely crime of causing

---

of life imprisonment without parole can properly be considered aggravated murder, but rejecting mandatory capital punishment for this category of murder).

[114] Idaho Code §§ 18-4003(e), 18-4003(f) (Supp. 1992); Or. Rev. Stat. §§ 163.095(2)(b), 163.095(2)(f) (1991); Tex. Penal Code Ann. § 19.03(a)(4) (Vernon 1989); Utah Code Ann. § 76-5-202(1)(a) (Supp. 1992); Va. Code Ann. § 18.2-31(3) (Supp. 1992); Wash. Rev. Code Ann. §§ 10.95.020(2), 10.95.020(3) (1990).

[115] See generally *supra* notes 79–91 and accompanying text.

[116] Ala. Code § 13A-5-40(a)(9) (Supp. 1992); Cal. Penal Code §§ 190.2(a)(4), 190.2(a)(6) (West Supp. 1993); Del. Code Ann. tit. 11, § 636(A)(5) (1987); Fla. Stat. Ann. §§ 782.04(2)(i), 790.161(4) (West Supp. 1993); Miss. Code Ann. § 97-3-19(2)(c) (Supp. 1992); Neb. Rev. Stat. § 28-1223(4) (1989); Or. Rev. Stat. § 163.095(2)(c) (1991); Tenn. Code Ann. § 39-13-202(a)(3) (1991); Utah Code Ann. § 76-5-202(1)(1) (Supp. 1992).

[117] Utah Code Ann. § 76-5-202(1)(c) (Supp. 1992). (This provision presumes the commission of a related intentional or purposeful killing. Utah Code Ann. § 76-5-202(1) (Supp. 1992)).

[118] Ala. Code § 13A-5-40(a)(10) (Supp. 1992) (at least two people murdered during the same act, scheme, or course of conduct); Cal. Penal Code § 190.2(a)(3) (West Supp. 1993) (special circumstance) (in the instant proceeding, the offender was convicted of more than one first-degree or second-degree murder); Conn. Gen. Stat. Ann. § 53a-54b(8) (West Supp. 1993) (at least two victims murdered at the same time or during the course of a single transaction); Or. Rev. Stat. § 163.095(1)(d) (1991) (the murder of more than one person during the same criminal episode); Tex. Penal Code Ann. § 19.03(a)(6) (Vernon 1989) (the murder of more than one person during the same criminal transaction or during different transactions but the same scheme or course of conduct); Utah Code Ann. § 76-5-202(1)(b) (Supp. 1992) (at least two people killed in one act, scheme, or course of conduct); Va. Code Ann. § 18.2-31(7) (more than one person killed during the same act or transaction) (Supp. 1992); Wash. Rev. Code Ann. § 10.95.020(8) (1990) (more than one victim killed during a common scheme or plan or during one act). See also La. Rev. Stat. Ann. § 14:30(A)(3) (West 1986) (''when the offender has a specific intent to kill or to inflict great bodily harm upon more than one person'').

399

"another person to commit suicide by force or duress" is a capital offense.[119] Many other jurisdictions define homicides as capital murder when they reflect extraordinary calculation and premeditation, such as causing death by poison or after lying in wait.[120]

Because of its imprecise definition, the most troublesome form of capital murder involves killings committed by torture, or in an "especially heinous, atrocious, cruel, or exceptionally depraved manner."[121] Torture killing is capital murder in Idaho,[122] Nevada,[123] Oregon,[124] and in California, which requires "proof of the infliction of extreme physical pain no matter how long its duration" to support the allegation of torture.[125] California and Utah recognize the "especially heinous, atrocious, cruel, or depraved" variety of capital murder. The statutes in each state provide further definition of these operative terms.[126] Provisions

---

[119] Del. Code Ann. tit. 11, § 636(a)(3) (1987).

[120] This type of capital murder was recognized as first-degree murder in the 1794 Pennsylvania statute that originally discriminated between first-degree (i.e., capital) and second-degree murder. See Acker & Lanier, *supra* note 3, at 295 n.14 and accompanying text. See also *supra* note 19 and accompanying text. Statutes of this kind presently are in effect, as follows: Cal. Penal Code §§ 190.2(a)(15), 190.2(a)(19) (West Supp. 1993) (special circumstances); Idaho Code § 18-4003(a) (Supp. 1992); Md. Ann. Code art. 27, § 407 (1992); Neb. Rev. Stat. § 28-303(3) (1989); Nev. Rev. Stat. Ann. § 200.030(1)(a) (Michie 1992); Tenn. Code Ann. §§ 39-13-202(a)(1), 39-13-201(b)(2) (1991); Utah Code Ann. § 76-5-202(1)(n) (Supp. 1992).

[121] Utah Code Ann. § 76-5-202(1)(q) (Supp. 1992). See *infra* note 126 for the entirety of this provision.

[122] Idaho Code § 18-4003(a) (Supp. 1992) ("[a] murder which is perpetrated by . . . torture, when torture is inflicted with the intent to cause suffering, to execute vengeance, to extort something from the victim, or to satisfy some sadistic inclination").

[123] Nev. Rev. Stat. Ann. § 200.030(1)(a) (Michie 1992).

[124] Or. Rev. Stat. § 163.095(1)(e) (1991) ("The homicide occurred in the course of or as a result of intentional maiming or torture of the victim.").

[125] Cal. Penal Code § 190.2(a)(18) (West Supp. 1993) (special circumstance) ("The murder was intentional and involved the infliction of torture. For the purpose of this section torture requires proof of the infliction of extreme pain no matter how long its duration.").

[126] Cal. Penal Code § 190.2(a)(14) (West Supp. 1993) (special circumstance) ("The murder was especially heinous, atrocious, or cruel, manifesting exceptional depravity. As utilized in this section, the phrase especially heinous, atrocious or cruel manifesting exceptional depravity means a conscienceless, or pitiless crime which is unnecessarily torturous to the victim."); Utah Code Ann. § 76-5-202(1)(q) (Supp. 1992) ("The homicide was committed in an especially heinous, atrocious, cruel, or exceptionally depraved manner, any of which must be demonstrated by physical torture, serious physical abuse, or serious bodily injury of the victim before death.").

of this nature appear more commonly as aggravating sentencing circumstances, where they are equally troublesome.[127]

Motive

Numerous states consider killings committed for hire, for pecuniary gain, or pursuant to agreement to be especially reprehensible, and define such homicides as capital murder.[128] Killing for the purpose of avoiding a lawful arrest, or to escape from lawful custody, are other relatively common types of capital murder.[129] Murders motivated by the desire to conceal the commission of a crime or the identity of the perpetrator,[130] or to prevent or retaliate against a person for testifying in a legal proceeding are capital crimes in five jurisdictions.[131] Killing "for the purpose of . . . disrupting or hindering any lawful governmental function or enforcement of laws" is made a capital murder in Utah.[132] In California, a murder is a capital crime if

---

[127] These factors are considered in greater detail in a future article in this series. See Arave v. Creech, 113 S. Ct. 1534 (1993) (upholding similar aggravating circumstance under Idaho law); Walton v. Arizona, 497 U.S. 639 (1990) (upholding, as applied, Arizona aggravating circumstance of this nature); Maynard v. Cartwright, 486 U.S. 356 (1988) (invalidating Oklahoma aggravating circumstance of this nature, as applied); Godfrey v. Georgia, 446 U.S. 420 (1980) (invalidating Georgia aggravating circumstance of this type, as applied). See generally Rosen, "The 'Especially Heinous' Aggravating Circumstance in Capital Cases—The Standardless Standard," 64 N.C.L. Rev. 941 (1986).

[128] Ala. Code § 13A-5-40(a)(7) (Supp. 1992); Ark. Stat. Ann. §§ 5-10-101(A)(7), 5-10-101(A)(8) (Supp. 1991); Cal. Penal Code § 190.2(a)(1) (West Supp. 1993) (special circumstance); Conn. Gen. Stat. Ann. § 53a-54b(2) (West Supp. 1993); La. Rev. Stat. Ann. § 14:30(A)(4) (West 1986); Miss. Code Ann. § 97-3-19(2)(d) (Supp. 1992); N.H. Rev. Stat. § 630:1(I)(c) (Supp. 1991); Or. Rev. Stat. §§ 163.095(1)(a), 163.095(1)(b) (1991); Tex. Penal Code Ann. § 19.03(a)(3) (Vernon 1989); Utah Code Ann. § 76-5-202(1)(f), 76-5-202(1)(g) (Supp. 1992); Va. Code Ann. § 18-2-31(2) (Supp. 1992); Wash. Rev. Code Ann. §§ 10.95.020(4), 10.95.020(5) (1990).

[129] Cal. Penal Code § 190.2(a)(5) (West Supp. 1993) (special circumstance); Del. Code Ann. tit. 11, § 636(a)(7) (1987); Idaho Code § 18-4003(f) (Supp. 1992); Nev. Rev. Stat. Ann. § 200.030(1)(c) (Michie 1992); Utah Code Ann. § 76-5-202(1)(e) (Supp. 1992).

[130] Or. Rev. Stat. § 163.095(2)(e) (1991); Wash. Rev. Code Ann. § 10.95.020(7) (1990).

[131] Ala. Code § 13A-5-40(a)(14) (Supp. 1992); Cal. Penal Code § 190.2(a)(10) (West Supp. 1993) (special circumstance); Or. Rev. Stat. § 163.095(2)(a)(E) (1991); Utah Code Ann. §§ 76-5-202(1)(i)(i)–76-5-202(1)(i)(iii) (Supp. 1992); Wash. Rev. Code Ann. § 10.95.020(6) (1990).

[132] Utah Code Ann. § 76-5-202(1)(i)(iv) (Supp. 1992).

401

the "victim was intentionally killed because of his or her race, color, religion, nationality, or country of origin."[133]

Victim Characteristics

Fifteen jurisdictions make killing a law-enforcement officer a form of capital murder. Such laws recognize that a unique social harm has been inflicted when a police officer or other law-enforcement official is murdered. As one dissenting justice expressed it, "Because these people are literally the foot soldiers of ordered liberty, the State has an especial interest in their protection."[134] However, there are many differences in the statutes that define murdering a law-enforcement officer as a capital crime, and these differences significantly alter the scope of this offense in the various jurisdictions in which it is recognized.

One important difference between statutes involves the offender's mens rea as relevant to the victim's status as a law-enforcement officer. The statutes are clear in Mississippi and Texas that the offender must have known that his victim was a peace officer in order for the homicide to be a capital murder.[135] In contrast, in four jurisdictions, it is sufficient that the offender knew or reasonably should have known that the murder victim was a law-enforcement officer.[136] The remaining statutes either

---

[133] Cal. Penal Code § 190.2(a)(16) (West Supp. 1993) (special circumstance). See generally Wisconsin v. Mitchell, 113 S. Ct.—(1993) (in which the Supreme Court ruled that a criminal sentence may be enhanced when an offender is motivated to commit a crime based on the race, religion, sexual orientation, color, disability, or national origin or ancestry of his victim); Dawson v. Delaware, 112 S. Ct. 1093 (1992) (offender's membership in white supremacist group inadmissible at capital sentencing hearing when such group membership is not connected to the commission of capital crime).

[134] Roberts v. Louisiana, 431 U.S. 633, 646–647 (1977) (Rehnquist, J., dissenting). The Court in *Roberts* invalidated a Louisiana statute that provided for mandatory capital punishment for the murder of a police officer. However, the per curiam majority opinion did recognize that "the fact that the murder victim was a peace officer performing his regular duties may be regarded as an aggravating circumstance. There is a special interest in affording protection to these public servants who regularly must risk their lives in order to guard the safety of other persons and property." *Id.* at 636 (footnote omitted).

[135] Miss. Code Ann. § 97-3-19(2)(a) (Supp. 1992); Tex. Penal Code Ann. § 19.03(a)(1) (Vernon 1989) (Offender must know that murder victim is a peace officer or fireman. When a prisoner murders an employee of a penal institution, there is no corresponding requirement that the offender knew the victim's status as an employee, although that status likely would be apparent.) Tex. Penal Code Ann. at § 19.03(a)(5) (Vernon 1989).

[136] Cal. Penal Code §§ 190.2(a)(7)–190.2(a)(9) (West Supp. 1993) (special circumstances); Idaho Code § 18-4003(b) (Supp. 1992); Utah Code Ann. § 76-5-202(l)(k) (Supp. 1992); Wash. Rev. Code Ann. § 10.95.020(1) (1990) (The

402

are ambiguous or silent in this regard.[137] Such statutes present the possibility that killing an undercover or plain clothes peace officer, or killing an officer who the offender could not reasonably have known had a law-enforcement status, could be capital murder.[138]

All statutes require that the killing somehow be related to the victim's performance of his duties as a law-enforcement officer, if the murder is to be regarded as a capital crime. Nevertheless, there are significant differences in the way in which this limitation is expressed. Some statutes require that the officer be engaged in duties at the time of the killing,[139] while others simply state that the killing ''relate to'' the victim's official duties.[140] Still others

Washington statute also makes it a capital offense to murder a probation or parole officer. The statute does not specify that the offender must have known or reasonably should have known about his victim's official status, but it does require that the ''murder was related to the exercise of official duties performed or to be performed by the victim.'' Wash. Rev. Code Ann. § 10.95.020(6)(b) (1990).).

[137] Ala. Code § 13A-5-40(a)(5) (Supp. 1992) (see *infra* note 138); Ark. Stat. Ann. § 5-10-101(a)(3) (Supp. 1991); Conn. Gen. Stat. Ann. § 53a-54b(1) (West Supp. 1993); Del. Code Ann. tit. 11, § 636(a)(4) (1987); La. Rev. Stat. Ann. § 14:30(A)(2) (West 1986); N.H. Rev. Stat. § 630:1(I)(a) (Supp. 1991); Or. Rev. Stat. § 163.095(2)(a) (1991); Va. Code Ann. § 18.2-31(6) (Supp. 1992); 21 U.S.C. § 848(e)(1)(B) (Supp. 1993). Once again, only the statutes themselves and not the judicial interpretations of the statutes are considered here.

[138] The Alabama statute was amended in 1987 to make the murder of a law-enforcement officer a capital homicide ''regardless of whether the defendant knew or should have known the victim was an officer or guard on duty.'' Ala. Code § 13A-5-40(a)(5) (Supp. 1992). This amendment was entitled ''The Undercover Officers Protection Act of 1987.'' *Id.*, Code Commissioner's Note. See generally Baker, '' 'Protecting the Foot Soldiers of an Ordered Society': An Analysis of State Statutory Aggravating Circumstances of Murdering a Police Officer in the Performance of His or Her Duty,'' 58 U. Mo. K. C. L. Rev. 675 (1990); Case Note, ''Knowledge is Not Required to Satisfy the Aggravating Circumstance of Killing a Police Officer: *State v. Compton*,'' 17 N.M. L. Rev. 433 (1987); United States v. Feola, 420 U.S. 671 (1975) (holding that crime of assaulting federal officers under 18 U.S.C. § 111 (Supp. 1993) does not require proof that offender knew victim was a federal officer at time of assault or conspiracy to commit assault).

[139] The statute that exemplifies this most clearly is Washington's, which requires that the law-enforcement officer victim ''was performing his or her official duties at the time of the act resulting in death.'' Wash. Rev. Code Ann. § 10.95.020(1) (1990). Other statutes that require that the officer be on duty when killed include: Ark. Stat. Ann. § 5-10-101(a)(3) (Supp. 1991); Cal. Penal Code § 190.2(a)(9) (West Supp. 1993) (special circumstance) (killing of firefighter; for other law-enforcement officers, a killing in retaliation for the performance of duties is capital murder, see *infra* note 141 and accompanying text); Conn. Gen. Stat. Ann. § 53a-54b(1) (West Supp. 1993); Del. Code Ann. tit. 11, § 636(a)(4) (1987); Idaho Code § 18-4003(b) (Supp. 1992); La. Rev. Stat. Ann. § 14:30(A)(2) (West 1986); N.H. Rev. Stat. § 630:1(I)(a) (Supp. 1991); Tex. Penal Code Ann. §§ 19.03(a)(1), 19.03(a)(5) (Vernon 1989); Va. Code Ann. § 18.2-31(6) (Supp. 1992).

[140] Or. Rev. Stat. § 163.095(2)(a) (1991); Utah Code Ann. § 76-5-202(1)(k)

403

specifically include killings that retaliate for the past performance of official duties.[141] Statutes in four states specify that the peace officer must have been engaged in or has been discharging lawful duties,[142] while other statutes more ambiguously require that the slain officer was in the performance of "official" duties[143] or was killed "in the line of duty."[144] Some laws state only that the officer must have been "on duty," without further limitation.[145]

The range of victims encompassed under these statutes is similarly diverse. All statutes include police officers. Many also cover firefighters and correctional officers, and some specifically apply to the killing of probation and parole officers.[146] Other statutory provisions make the murder of judicial officials, including judges, prosecuting attorneys, and occasionally jurors and defense lawyers, a capital crime.[147] In some jurisdictions, killing elected officials, candidates for public office, or other holders of

---

(Supp. 1992); Wash. Rev. Code Ann. § 10.95.020(6) (1990) (relating to the murder of, inter alia, probation and parole officers, and members of the indeterminate sentence review board (board of prison terms and paroles)).

[141] Ala. Code § 13A-5-40(a)(5) (Supp. 1992); Cal. Penal Code §§ 190.2(a)(7), 190.2(a)(8) (West Supp. 1993) (special circumstances); Miss. Code Ann. § 97-3-19(2)(a) (Supp. 1992); 21 U.S.C. § 848(e)(1)(B) (Supp. 1993).

[142] Del. Code Ann. tit. 11, § 636(a)(4) (1987); Idaho Code § 18-4003(b) (Supp. 1992); La. Rev. Stat. Ann. § 14:30(A)(2) (West 1986); Tex. Penal Code Ann. § 19.03(a)(1) (Vernon 1989).

[143] Miss. Code Ann. § 97-3-19(2)(a) (Supp. 1992) (official capacity); Or. Rev. Stat. § 163.095(2)(a) (1991); Va. Code Ann. § 18.2-31(6) (Supp. 1992); Wash. Rev. Code Ann. §§ 10.95.020(1), 10.95.020(2) (1990); 21 U.S.C. § 848(e)(1)(B) (Supp. 1993).

[144] N.H. Rev. Stat. § 630:1(I)(a) (Supp. 1991). See also Conn. Gen. Stat. Ann. § 53a-54b(1) (West Supp. 1993) ("within the scope of his duties").

[145] Ala. Code § 13A-5-40(a)(5) (Supp. 1992); Cal. Penal Code §§ 190.2(a)(7)-190.2(a)(9) (West Supp. 1993) (special circumstances); Utah Code Ann. § 76-5-202(1)(k) (Supp. 1992).

[146] See, e.g., Ark. Stat. Ann.§ 5-10-101(a)(3) (Supp. 1991) (firefighter, correctional officer, probation or parole officer); Cal. Penal Code § 190.2(a)(9) (West Supp. 1993) (special circumstance) (firefighter); La. Rev. Stat. Ann. §§ 14:30(A)(2) (West 1986), 14:30(B) (West Supp. 1993) (corrections officer, parole officer); N.H. Rev. Stat. §§ 630:1(I)(a), 630:1(II) (Supp. 1991) (corrections officers, probation and parole officers); Utah Code Ann. § 76-5-202(1)(k) (Supp. 1992) (firefighter, corrections officer, probation or parole officer), Wash. Rev. Code Ann. § 10.95.020(6)(a) (1990) (probation or parole officer, member of indeterminate sentence review board (board of prison terms and parole)).

[147] See, e.g., Idaho Code § 18-4003(b) (Supp. 1992) (judicial officer or prosecuting attorney); Miss. Code Ann. § 97-3-19(2)(a) (Supp. 1992) (judge, prosecutor, other court officials); Utah Code Ann. § 76-5-202(1)(k) (Supp. 1992) (prosecutor, judge, other court officials, juror); Wash. Rev. Code Ann. § 10.95.020(6)(a) (1990) (judge, juror, prosecutor, defense attorney).

404

public office is capital murder.[148] In Arkansas, killing military personnel acting in the line of duty is a capital offense,[149] and in Washington killing a news reporter "to obstruct or hinder the investigative, research or reporting activities" of the reporter is made a form of capital murder.[150]

A number of jurisdictions make killing a child under specific circumstances a capital homicide. In Louisiana, intentionally killing a child under age 12 qualifies as capital murder.[151] The willful, deliberate, and premeditated killing of a child under age 12 is a capital crime in Virginia, when the murder is committed during an abduction for the purpose of extorting money or defiling the child.[152] Statutes in five states make killing a child through aggravated or prolonged child abuse a form of capital murder. These statutes typically do not require that the child have been killed intentionally.[153] Several other jurisdictions include child sex abuse or aggravated child abuse among the predicate felonies that will support a conviction for capital felony

---

[148] See, e.g., Ala. Code § 13A-5-40(a)(11) (Supp. 1992); Ark. Stat. Ann. § 5-10-101(a)(5) (Supp. 1991); Cal. Penal Code § 190.2(a)(13) (West Supp. 1993) (special circumstance); Miss. Code Ann. § 97-13-19(2)(g) (Supp. 1992); Ohio Rev. Code Ann. § 2929.04(A)(1) (Anderson 1993) (specified aggravating circumstance); Utah Code Ann. § 76-5-202(1)(j) (Supp. 1992).

[149] Ark. Stat. Ann. § 5-10-101(a)(3) (Supp. 1991).

[150] Wash. Rev. Code Ann. § 10.95.020(10) (1990).

[151] La. Rev. Stat. Ann. § 14:30(A)(5) (West 1986).

[152] Va. Code Ann. § 18.2-31(8) (Supp. 1992).

[153] See Miss. Code Ann. § 97-3-19(2)(f) (Supp. 1992) ("[w]hen done with or without any design to effect death, by any person engaged in the commission of the crime of felonious abuse and/or battery of a child . . . or in any attempt to commit such felony"); Nev. Rev. Stat. Ann. § 200.030(1)(a) (Michie 1992) ("[p]erpetrated by means of . . . child abuse"); Okla. Stat. Ann. tit. 21, § 701.7(C) (West Supp. 1993) ("when the death of a child results from the willful or malicious injuring, torturing, maiming or using of unreasonable force by said person or who shall willfully cause, procure or permit any of said acts to be done upon the child."); Or. Rev. Stat. § 163.115(1)(C) (1991) (One form of noncapital murder, which becomes capital murder if aggravated by any of the factors set forth in Or. Rev. Stat. § 163.095 (1991), is causing death by abuse of a child or dependent person. See *supra* note 38.); Tenn. Code Ann. § 39-13-202(a)(4) (1991) ("A killing of a child less than thirteen (13) years of age, if the child's death results from a protracted pattern or multiple incidents of bodily injury committed by the defendant against such child and the death is caused either by the last injury or the cumulative effect of such injuries.") But see State v. Hale, 840 S.W.2d 307 (Tenn. 1992) (declaring application of the previous statutory provision unconstitutional under the state constitution, as disproportionate to the crime, because it dispenses with a requirement for mens rea). See generally "Number of Capital Domestic Homicide Cases on Increase," 30 Cap. Rep. 1, 7 (Mar./Apr. 1993).

405

murder.[154] Causing the death of a child under age 18 by the unlawful sale of drugs to the victim on school grounds is one type of capital murder in Colorado.[155] In one form or another, thirteen jurisdictions consider killing a child to be sufficiently heinous to qualify as capital murder.[156]

Perjury Resulting in Execution of the Innocent

An unusual and particularly noteworthy type of homicide is defined as capital murder in California, Colorado, Idaho, and Nebraska. Colorado's statutory provision is representative:

> (1) A person commits the crime of murder in the first degree if . . .
> (c) By perjury or subordination of perjury he procures the conviction and execution of any innocent person.[157]

The statutes in these four states officially recognize the risk that inevitably stalks the death penalty whenever and wherever it is administered, that innocent men and women will be executed. Two academic authorities have uncovered evidence suggesting that at least twenty-three innocent people have been executed in this country during the twentieth century.[158] Some disagree with the precise number of erroneous executions identified by these researchers,[159] while others forthrightly accept erroneous executions as a "cost of doing business."[160] However, no one seriously

---

[154] See, e.g., Ariz. Rev. Stat. Ann. § 13-1105(A)(2) (1989); Cal. Penal Code §§ 189, 190.2(a)(17)(v) (West Supp. 1993); Colo. Rev. Stat. § 18-3-102(1)(b) (Supp. 1992); Fla. Stat. Ann. § 782.04(1)(a)(2)(h) (West Supp. 1993); Ind. Code Ann. § 35-42-1-1(2) (Burns Supp. 1992); Miss. Code Ann. § 97-3-19(2)(e) (Supp. 1992); Nev. Rev. Stat. Ann. § 200.030(1)(b) (Michie 1992); Utah Code Ann. § 76-5-202(1)(d) (Supp. 1992) (Utah, in common with some other states, requires that a felony-related homicide be intentional to constitute capital murder. See *supra* notes 20–38 and accompanying text).

[155] Colo. Rev. Stat. § 18-3-102(1)(e) (Supp. 1992).

[156] These states are Arizona, California, Colorado, Florida, Indiana, Louisiana, Mississippi, Nevada, Oklahoma, Oregon, Tennessee, Utah, and Virginia. See *supra* notes 151–155 and accompanying text.

[157] Colo. Rev. Stat. § 18-3-102(1)(c) (1986). See also Cal. Penal Code § 128 (West 1988); Idaho Code § 18-5411 (1987); Neb. Rev. Stat. § 28-303(3) (1989).

[158] Bedau & Radelet, "Miscarriages of Justice in Potentially Capital Cases," 40 Stan. L. Rev. 21 (1987). See also M. Radelet, H.Bedau & C. Putnam, *In Spite of Innocence: Erroneous Convictions in Capital Cases* (1992).

[159] Markmam & Cassell, "Protecting the Innocent: A Response to the Bedau-Radelet Study," 41 Stan. L. Rev. 121 (1988). But see Bedau & Radelet, "The Myth of Infallibility: A Reply to Markmam and Cassell," 41 Stan. L. Rev. 161 (1988).

[160] See, e.g., van den Haag, "Why Capital Punishment?," 54 Alb. L. Rev. 501, 512–513 (1990). But see Radelet & Bedau, "Fallibility and Finality: Type II Errors

can dispute that innocent people have been executed in the past,[161] and that it is impossible to guard absolutely against such miscarriages of justice in the future. The startling number of revelations of erroneous convictions in capital cases in recent years (perhaps most widely publicized by the *The Thin Blue Line*, a documentary focusing on Randall Dale Adams's conviction and sentence of death in Texas) refutes the facile assumption that modern death penalty procedures serve as a fail safe against executing the innocent.[162]

Erroneous convictions, sentences, and executions in capital cases have been produced by many factors, including perjury, prosecutorial misconduct, and honest human error,[163] the very factors that are impossible to eliminate with even the most sophisticated legal procedures. Moreover, the Supreme Court has made it clear that, except under highly unusual circumstances, state prisoners cannot raise claims of actual innocence when seeking federal court review of their capital convictions and sentences.[164] Numerous procedural pitfalls routinely await death-

---

and Capital Punishment," in *Challenging Capital Punishment: Legal and Social Science Approaches* 91, 104–108 (K. Haas & J. Inciardi, eds. 1988).

[161] Even van den Haag concedes that "[t]he existence of the death penalty implies the possibility, and, in the long run, the statistical likelihood, that innocent people will be executed. Courts are not infallible. Therefore, miscarriages of justice will occur." Van den Haag, *supra* note 160, at 512. The discovery in England that Timothy John Evans almost certainly was an innocent man when executed precipitated the abolition of capital punishment in that country in 1965. Bedau & Radelet, *supra* note 158, at 22–23; D. Hook & L. Kahn, *Death in the Balance: The Debate Over Capital Punishment* 112–113 (1989).

[162] There have been many erroneously condemned individuals who have nearly been executed in the post-*Furman* era of capital punishment, in which modern procedures have been used. See, e.g., Tabak & Lane, "The Execution of Injustice: A Cost and Lack-of-Benefit Analysis of the Death Penalty," 23 Loy. L.A. L. Rev. 59, 99–114 (1989); Carmody, "The *Brady* Rule: Is It Working?," 15 National L.J. 1 (May 17, 1993). See generally Rosenbaum, "Inevitable Error: Wrongful New York State Homicide Convictions, 1965–1968," 18 N.Y.U. Rev. L. & Soc. Change 807 (1990–1991) (describing wrongful homicide convictions in New York, which does not have capital punishment, between 1965 and 1988).

[163] See Bedau & Radelet, *supra* note 158; Tabak & Lane, *supra* note 162; Carmody, *supra* note 162.

[164] Herrera v. Collins, 113 S. Ct. 853 (1993). The Court suggested that:

We may assume, for the sake of argument in deciding this case, that in a capital case a truly persuasive demonstration of "actual innocence" made after trial would render the execution of a defendant unconstitutional, and warrant federal habeas relief if there were no state avenue open to process such a claim. But because of the very disruptive effect that entertaining claims of actual innocence would have on the need for finality in capital cases, and the enormous burden that having to retry cases based on often stale evidence would place on the States, the sentenced prisoners who petition for federal habeas corpus review of their cases.[165] It is no small irony that the murder statutes in California, Colorado, Idaho, and Nebraska threaten capital punishment as a sanction for a crime that is possible only because these jurisdictions' capital punishment systems are fallible and have malfunctioned in a related case. These statutes explicitly acknowledge and accept the risk that innocent people will be executed under a regime that allows capital punishment. This same risk exists in the other thirty-three death penalty jurisdictions in this country as the execution of innocent people is a danger against which no statutes offer adequate protection.

Exclusions From Death Penalty Eligibility

There may be good reason to rule out the death penalty as a criminal sanction, even when an offender's conduct fits within the statutory definition of capital murder. Although constrained by law, capital punishment decisions are uniquely moral judgments. Under some circumstances there may be no constitutional constraints on the power of prosecutors to seek, or judges or juries to impose, a capital sentence, yet lawmakers may choose to safeguard the moral quality of death penalty decisions by exempting categories of offenders or offenses from this ultimate sanction. At least three classes of cases merit consideration for statutory exclusion from death penalty eligibility.

Youthful Offenders

In *Stanford v. Kentucky*,[166] the Supreme Court ruled that the Eighth Amendment does not prohibit capital punishment for sixteen- and seventeen-year-old murderers. One year prior to *Stanford*, four members of the Court agreed in *Thompson v.*

---

threshold showing for such an assumed right would necessarily be extraordinarily high.

Id. at 869.

[165] For recent, comprehensive reviews of the Court's limitations on federal habeas corpus, see Hoffmann, "Starting from Scratch: Rethinking Federal Habeas Review of Death Penalty Cases," 20 Fla. St. U. L. Rev. 133 (1992); Tabak & Lane, "Judicial Activism and Legislative 'Reform' of Federal Habeas Corpus: A Critical Analysis of Recent Developments and Current Proposals," 55 Alb. L. Rev. 1 (1991); Liebman, "More than 'Slightly Retro:' The Rehnquist Court's Rout of Habeas Corpus Jurisdiction in *Teague v. Lane*," 18 N.Y.U. Rev. L. & Soc. Change 537 (1990–1991).

[166] 492 U.S. 361 (1989) (plurality decision).

408

Oklahoma[167] that to execute an offender who was only fifteen years old when he committed his crime would be cruel and unusual punishment. Justice O'Connor concurred in the judgment in *Thompson*, but noted that Oklahoma's statutes "specifie[d] no minimum age at which the commission of a capital crime can lead to the offender's execution."[168] She reserved judgment about whether a fifteen-year-old offender could be executed consistently with the Constitution if a "legislative body . . . rendered a considered judgment approving the imposition of capital punishment on juveniles who were below the age of 16 at the time of the offense."[169]

Now, as when *Stanford* and *Thompson* were decided, the statutes in eighteen states define no minimum age for death penalty eligibility.[170] No jurisdiction that establishes a minimum death-eligibility age by statute authorizes capital punishment for offenders younger than age 16. Statutes in four states define 16 years of age at the time of the offense as the threshold for death penalty eligibility;[171] two states opt for age 17;[172] and in twelve states and under federal law an offender must be age 18 or older to risk capital punishment for a crime.[173]

---

[167] 487 U.S. 815 (1988). *Thompson* was decided by an eight-member Court; Kennedy, J., did not participate in the decision.

[168] Thompson v. Oklahoma, 487 U.S. 815, 857–858 (1988) (O'Connor, J., concurring) (footnote omitted).

[169] *Id.* at 852.

[170] Stanford v. Kenucky, 492 U.S. 361, 385 (1989) (Brennan, J., dissenting); Thompson v. Oklahoma, 487 U.S. 815, 827 n. 26 (1988) (plurality opinion) (listing states, including Vermont, which no longer has a death penalty). The states that do not specifically set a minimum age by statute for death penalty eligibility are Alabama, Arizona, Arkansas, Delaware, Florida, Idaho, Louisiana, Mississippi, Missouri, Montana, Oklahoma, Pennsylvania, South Carolina, South Dakota, Utah, Virginia, Washington, and Wyoming.

[171] Ind. Code Ann. § 35-50-2-3(b) (Burns Supp. 1992); Mo. Ann. Stat. § 565.020(2) (Vernon Supp. 1992); Nev. Rev. Stat. Ann. § 176.025 (Michie 1992); Wyo. Stat. § 6-2-101(b) (Supp. 1992).

[172] N.C. Gen. Stat. § 14-17 (Supp. 1992) (exempting offenders under 17 years of age from death penalty eligibility, with the exception that "any person under the age of 17 who commits murder in the first degree while serving a prison sentence imposed for a prior murder or while on escape from a prison sentence imposed for a prior murder" may be punished by death); Tex. Penal Code Ann. § 8.07 (Vernon Supp. 1993).

[173] Cal. Penal Code § 190.5 (West Supp. 1993); Colo. Rev. Stat. § 16-11-103(1)(a) (Supp. 1992); Conn. Gen. Stat. Ann. § 53a-46a(g)(1) (West 1985) (including age of less than 18 as a mitigating factor, proof of which exempts the offender from death penalty eligibility); Ill. Ann. Stat. ch. 720, § 5/9-1(b) (Smith-Hurd Supp. 1993); Md. Ann. Code art. 27, § 412(f)(1) (Supp. 1992); Neb. Rev.

409

Although age is measured in standard terms of years, there is no objective measure of culpability for a crime, nor is there an agreed on standard of sufficient culpability for purposes of imposing capital punishment. It is evident, historically, logically, and experientially, that young people are treated differently than adults because they lack the experience, maturity, and judgment to be accepted as fully responsible citizens.[174] It is equally obvious that the progression from adolescence to adulthood is a varied experience for different individuals. This transition is incremental and continuous, rather than an abrupt one that magically culminates on an eighteenth or twenty-first birthday.[175]

Statutes defining age 18, age 17, or age 16 as the minimum age for death penalty eligibility almost inevitably will make mistaken classifications. For some youths, who are immature or irresponsible notwithstanding their chronological age, the statutory line for death eligibility will certainly have been fixed too low. Conversely, some adolescents will be ''older than their years,'' and may fortuitously escape death penalty eligibility when minimum ages are set by statute. This latter group of youths may be functioning at the same maturation level as young

---

Stat. § 28-105.01 (1989); N.H. Rev. Stat. Ann. § 630:5(XVII) (Supp. 1991) (Prohibiting death penalty ''for an offense committed by a minor.'' This provision would appear to be in conflict with N.H. Rev. Stat. Ann. § 630:1(V) (1986), which provides that, ''In no event shall any person under the age of 17 years be culpable of a capital murder.'' We assume that the former provision takes precedence, thus prohibiting capital punishment in New Hampshire for offenders younger than 18 years of age.); N.J. Stat. Ann. § 2C:11-3(g) (West Supp. 1992); N.M. Stat. Ann. § 31-18-14(A) (1990); Ohio Rev. Code Ann. § 2929.02(A) (Anderson 1993); Or. Rev. Stat. § 161.620 (1991); Tenn. Code Ann. §§ 37-1-134(a)(1)(A), 37-1-134(a)(1)(B) (1991); 21 U.S.C. § 848(1) (Supp. 1993).

[174] For a comprehensive review, see V. Streib, *The Death Penalty for Juveniles* (1987). An excellent summary of the psychological and developmental factors relevant to youth and capital punishment is presented in the Brief for the American Society for Adolescent Psychiatry and the American Orthopsychiatric Association as Amici Curiae, in Thompson v. Oklahoma, 487 U.S. 815 (1988) (No. 86-6169). As of April 20, 1993, approximately 34 of the 2,729 individuals on death row were under 18 years of age when they committed the offense for which they were sentenced to die. NAACP Legal Defense and Educational Fund, Inc., *Death Row, U.S.A.* 1, 40 (Spring 1993).

[175] Developmental studies suggest that age 21, rather than age 18, may be a more valid age at which to assume psychological and emotional maturity. See Brief for the American Society for Adolescent Psychiatry and the American Orthopsychiatric Association as Amici Curiae, in High v. Zant, 487 U.S. 1233 (1988) (No. 87-5666); and Wilkins v. Missouri, 492 U.S. 361 (No. 87-6026) (consolidated in Stanford v. Kentucky, 492 U.S. 361 (1989) (No. 87-5765)). See Stanford v. Kentucky, 492 U.S. at 396 (Brennan, J., dissenting).

410

adults, perhaps as a result of their relatively rich life experiences or their accelerated intellectual and emotional development.

If erroneous classifications regarding death eligibility are inevitable, they will assume one of two forms in this context. First, statutory thresholds may be set too high, as when eighteen is the statutory minimum age for death penalty eligibility, and some "deserving" sixteen- and seventeen-year-old murderers avoid capital punishment and instead are sentenced to a term of imprisonment for their crimes. On the other hand, the age for exclusion from death penalty eligibility may be fixed too low, as when sixteen is the minimum age established by statute, and a sixteen- or seventeen-year-old murderer who is not "fully culpable," in the same way that adults are, is sentenced to death because of the shocking magnitude of his crime. The latter type of error, setting the minimum age for death penalty eligibility too low, and potentially subjecting immature offenders to capital punishment, is by far the more serious.[176]

As the laws in thirteen death penalty jurisdictions presently attest, a state does no significant disservice to the penological objectives of capital punishment if it excludes sixteen- and seventeen-year-olds from the reach of its capital murder statutes.[177] As a group, children of this age are more impressionable than adults, more compulsive, more susceptible to peer pressure, and are less fully appreciative of the final consequences of their actions. They also are more malleable and amenable to change.[178] If laws are to err, they should err on the side of protecting this class of children, rather than exposing individual sixteen- and seventeen-year-olds to execution for crimes that well may not have been committed but for their youth. Statutes that limit capital punishment eligibility to offenders age 18 and older will

---

[176] Acker, "Dual and Unusual: Competing Views of Death Penalty Adjudication," 26 Crim. L. Bull. 123, 150–152 (1990).

[177] Thompson v. Oklahoma, 487 U.S. 815, 838 (1988) (plurality opinion) ("[W]e are not persuaded that the imposition of the death penalty for offenses committed by persons under 16 years of age has made, or can be expected to make, any measurable contribution to the goals that capital punishment is intended to achieve."); Stanford v. Kentucky, 492 U.S. at 361, 405 (Brennan, J., dissenting) ("[I]mposition of the death penalty on persons for offenses committed under the age of 18 makes no measurable contribution to the goals of either retribution or deterrence.").

[178] The amicus curiae briefs filed by the American Society for Adolescent Psychiatry and the American Orthopsychiatric Association in *Thompson v. Oklahoma* and *Stanford v. Kentucky* provide an excellent summary in documentation of these points. See *supra* notes 174, 175.

411

prevent the execution of some youthful offenders whose lives can be salvaged, and who may not be fully responsible for their crimes. Such laws will sacrifice little in return.

Mentally Retarded Offenders

In 1989, the Supreme Court ruled that the Eighth Amendment does not prohibit the execution of murderers who are moderately or mildly mentally retarded.[179] These classifications include the vast majority of mentally retarded individuals, and correspond to IQ assessments that dip to fifty and below.[180] When the Supreme Court issued its ruling in *Penry v. Lynaugh*,[181] only the federal death penalty statute and the law in one state, Georgia, excluded the mentally retarded from death penalty eligibility.[182] In the relatively brief time since *Penry* was decided, Kentucky, Maryland, New Mexico, Tennessee, and Washington all have acted to prohibit the capital punishment of these mentally retarded individuals convicted of murder.[183]

These more recently enacted statutes are unlike the Georgia and federal laws in that each provides a specific definition of "mentally retarded." The definition given in New Mexico's statute is typical: "As used in this section, 'mentally retarded' means significantly subaverage general intellectual functioning existing concurrently with deficits in adaptive behavior. An

---

[179] Penry v. Lynaugh, 492 U.S. 302 (1989). The petitioner, Johnny Paul Penry, was described as "having an IQ between fifty and sixty-three, which indicates mild to moderate retardation." *Id.* at 307–308 (footnote omitted). Mentally retarded individuals have deficits in adaptive behavior, coupled with subaverage intellectual functioning. Different ranges of IQ scores are used to classify the level of mental retardation as mild (IQ between seventy and fifty to fifty-five), moderate (IQ between fifty to fifty-five and thirty-five to forty, severe (IQ between thirty-five to forty and twenty to twenty-five), and profound (IQ lower than twenty to twenty-five). *Id.* at 308 n. 1, citing American Association on Mental Deficiency (now Retardation) *Classification in Mental Retardation*, 11–13 (H. Grossman ed. 1983). The *Penry* Court suggested that the Eighth Amendment would prohibit the execution of profoundly and severely mentally retarded offenders. Penry v. Lynaugh, 492 U.S., at 333.

[180] Approximately 89 percent of mentally retarded individuals are classified as mildly retarded. Penry v. Lynaugh, 492 U.S. at 302, 308 n. 1.

[181] 492 U.S. 302 (1989).

[182] *Id.* at 334. See Ga. Code Ann. § 17-7-131(j) (Supp. 1992); 21 U.S.C. § 848(1) (Supp. 1993).

[183] Ky. Rev. Stat. Ann. § 532.140(1) (Michie/Bobbs-Merrill 1990); Md. Ann. Code art. 27, § 412(f)(1) (Supp. 1992); N.M. Stat. Ann. § 31-20A-2.1(B) (Supp. 1992); Tenn. Code Ann. § 39-13-203(b) (1991); Wash. Rev. Code Ann. § 10.95.030(2) (Westlaw, effective July 25, 1993).

412

intelligence quotient of seventy or below on a reliably administered intelligence quotient test shall be presumptive evidence of mental retardation.''[184]

The Kentucky, New Mexico, Tennessee, and Washington statutes all specify that the trial judge, rather than the jury, must make the finding of mental retardation.[185] Under Georgia law, the jury, or the judge in a case tried before the court, considers returning a verdict of guilty but mentally retarded.[186] Statutes in the other jurisdictions are silent about whether the judge or jury determines mental retardation. In New Mexico, Tennessee, and Washington the defendant has the burden of producing evidence and also the burden of persuasion, by a preponderance of the evidence, on the issue of mental retardation.[187] Kentucky law places the burden of producing evidence of mental retardation on the defendant but, like the statutes in the other jurisdictions, does not assign the burden of persuasion.[188]

The arguments to be made in favor of excluding mentally retarded offenders from death penalty eligibility are similar to those offered for excluding sixteen- and seventeen-year-old murderers.[189] Although mental retardation is not as readily verifiable as an offender's age, mental retardation usually is manifested early in life, and is a chronic condition rather than one that has a sudden onset or that changes over time.[190] This condition thus is

---

[184] N.M. Stat. Ann. § 31-20A-2.1(A) (Supp. 1992). See also Ky. Rev. Stat. Ann. § 532.130(2) (Michie/Bobbs-Merrill 1990); Md. Ann. Code art. 27, § 412(e)(3) (Supp. 1992); Tenn. Code Ann. § 39-13-203(a) (1991); Wash. Rev. Code Ann. § 10.950.030(2)(a)–10.950.030(2)(e) (Westlaw effective July 25, 1993).

[185] Ky. Rev. Stat. Ann. § 532.135(2) (Michie/Bobbs-Merrill 1990); N.M. Stat. Ann. § 31-20A-2.1) (C) (Supp. 1992); Tenn. Code Ann. § 39-13-203(c) (1991); Wash. Rev. Code Ann. § 10.95.030(2) (Westlaw effective July 25, 1993).

[186] Ga. Code Ann. § 17-7-131(j) (Supp. 1992).

[187] N.M. Stat. Ann. § 31-20A-2.1(C) (Supp. 1992); Tenn. Code Ann. § 39-13-203(c) (1991); Wash. Rev. Code Ann. § 10.95.030(2) (Westlaw effective July 25, 1993).

[188] Ky. Rev. Stat. Ann. § 532.135(1) (Michie/Bobbs-Merrill 1990).

[189] See Blume & Bruck, "Sentencing the Mentally Retarded to Death: An Eighth Amendment Analysis," 41 Ark. L. Rev. 725 (1988); Penry v. Lynaugh, 492 U.S. 302, 343–349 (1989) (Brennan, J., dissenting). An excellent summary of the arguments against capital punishment for mentally retarded offenders, from a developmental perspective, may be found in the Brief for American Association on Mental Retardation et al. as Amici Curiae, in Penry v. Lynaugh, 492 U.S. 302 (1989) (No. 87-6177).

[190] Ellis & Luckasson, "Mentally Retarded Criminal Defendants," 53 Geo. Wash. L. Rev. 414, 422–423 (1985) (but noting, for purposes of the criminal law, that the age of onset of mental retardation should not matter). The Maryland law

413

hard to fabricate, even though there may be borderline cases in which it is difficult to distinguish between mentally retarded offenders and offenders of low intelligence who are not mentally retarded. As with youthful offenders, the prospects of erroneously executing a mentally retarded individual who is not "fully culpable" for a murder, and who may be incarcerated for life as punishment for his crime, should be considered far more weighty than any benefits associated with a statutory scheme that authorizes capital punishment for mentally retarded offenders.

Lingering Doubt

Death penalty statutes in four states expressly acknowledge the risk that innocent people may be convicted of capital murder and erroneously executed.[191] This risk, present in all death penalty jurisdictions, is one that even the most ardent supporters of capital punishment wish to guard against. Still, it cannot be eliminated in any legal system that uses the death penalty. When the drafters of the MPC finalized their proposals on the death penalty,[192] they included a provision designed to help minimize the chance that people who actually were innocent of crimes for which they were convicted would be executed. Although the death penalty proposals of the MPC have significantly influenced modern death penalty statutes, the particular provision that would help guard against the risk of executing innocent people mysteriously has been ignored. This provision prohibits the imposition of a death sentence in cases where, "although the evidence suffices to sustain the verdict, it does not foreclose all doubt respecting the defendant's guilt."[193]

The Supreme Court has indicated that a defendant has no constitutional right to have lingering or "residual" doubts about

---

exempting mentally retarded offenders from death penalty eligibility requires that mental retardation be manifested by age 22, while Tennessee and Washington statutes set 18 as the age by which mental retardation must be exhibited. Md. Ann. Code art. 27, § 412(e)(3) (Supp. 1992); Tenn. Code Ann. § 39-13-203(a)(3) (1991); Wash. Rev. Code Ann. §§ 10.95.030(2)(a), 10.95.030(e) (Westlaw effective July 25, 1993).

[191] See *supra* notes 157–165 and accompanying text.

[192] The American Law Institute took no position on whether capital punishment should be abolished or retained, although the Advisory Committee and Reporters who drafted the MPC overwhelmingly favored abolition. Acker & Lanier, *supra* note 62, at 228 n. 25; Zimring & Hawkins, *supra* note 2, at 82.

[193] Model Penal Code § 210.6(1)(f) (Official Draft and Revised Comments 1980).

guilt considered as a mitigating factor for capital sentencing purposes.[194] However, the justices also have credited the view that "jurors who decide both guilt and penalty are likely to form residual doubts or 'whimsical' doubts . . . about the evidence so as to bend them to decide against the death penalty. Such residual doubt has been recognized as an extremely effective argument for defendants in capital cases."[195]

"Proof beyond a reasonable doubt" is an abstract concept that may be difficult to explain to lay jurors,[196] especially in a way that can be applied meaningfully to a concrete set of facts. There are different ways that an accused may be "not guilty" of capital murder, ranging from total noninvolvement in the alleged crime to having a legal justification or excuse for the killing. The defendant also may have committed a criminal homicide, such as manslaughter or second-degree murder, but not capital murder.[197] Accordingly, there are many different reasons why residual doubts may exist about whether an accused offender is guilty of a capital crime. Researchers have corroborated the proposition that lingering doubt about a defendant's guilt can affect whether a sentencing jury decides to impose capital punishment.[198]

---

[194] Franklin v. Lynaugh, 487 U.S. 164, 172–174 (1988) (plurality opinion).

[195] Lockhart v. McCree, 476 U.S. 162, 181 (1986), *quoting* Grigsby v. Mabry, 758 F.2d 226, 247–248 (8th Cir. 1985) (en banc) (Gibson, J., dissenting) (citations omitted).

[196] See generally Cage v. Louisiana, 111 S. Ct. 328 (1990) (per curiam). The Court in *Cage* vacated the petitioner's capital murder conviction because of the trial court's defective instruction to the jury about the meaning of proof beyond a reasonable doubt.

The charge did at one point instruct that to convict, guilt must be found beyond a reasonable doubt; but it then equated a reasonable doubt with a "grave uncertainty" and an "actual substantial doubt," and stated that what was required was a "moral certainty" that the defendant was guilty. It is plain to us that the words "substantial" and "grave," as they are commonly understood, suggest a higher degree of doubt than is required for acquittal under the reasonable doubt standard. When these statements are then considered with the reference to "moral certainty," rather than evidentiary certainty, it becomes clear that a reasonable juror could have interpreted the instruction to allow a finding of guilt based on a degree of proof below that required by the Due Process Clause.

(footnote omitted). *Id.* at 329–330.

[197] C. Black, *supra* note 58, at 45–55.

[198] *See* Geimer & Amsterdam, "'Why Jurors Vote Life or Death: Operative Factors in Ten Florida Death Penalty Cases," 15 Am. J. Crim. L. 1, 28–34 (1988); Barnett, "Some Distribution Patterns for the Georgia Death Sentence," 18 U.C. Davis L. Rev. 1327, 1338–1345 (1985).

The MPC's exclusion of capital punishment in cases in which the evidence "does not foreclose all doubt" about guilt is directed at the trial court rather than the jury.[199] Because the jury and not the trial judge normally determines guilt, it seems logical to present this same issue to the capital jury—after a guilty verdict has been returned, but before a death sentence may be considered. Resolution of this issue could be the first order of business for penalty deliberations in jurisdictions where juries make capital sentencing decisions. Where judges impose the sentence in capital trials, the guilt phase jury could be asked to address this question following the return of the guilty verdict. Absent unanimous agreement that the evidence in fact did "foreclose all doubt" about the offender's guilt, the defendant would not be eligible for capital punishment. The judge's subsequent affirmation that the evidence did foreclose all doubt about guilt, as proposed under the MPC, would serve as an additional safeguard for the reliability of the jury's verdict.

Preventing the execution of an innocent person cannot be accomplished through legislation. Proof that appears utterly conclusive may be based on evidence that is perjured, incomplete, colored by passion, or simply erroneous. Yet, to do less than is possible through statute to diminish the risk of an erroneous execution should not be condoned. This proposition should be noncontroversial. It should be implemented through legislative provisions that forbid capital punishment when the trial jury and judge are not convinced that the evidence is sufficient to "foreclose all doubt respecting the defendant's guilt."

Conclusion

This article has considered four different aspects of capital murder statutes: mens rea requirements, felony murder provisions, the relative breadth or scope of the elements of capital murder, and classes of offenders who should be excluded categorically from death penalty eligibility under capital murder statutes. The definition of "capital murder" has important procedural ramifications,[200] and also is important because it helps to narrow the class of offenders who may be considered for capital punish-

---

[199] Model Penal Code § 210.6(1)(f) (Official Draft and Revised Comments 1980).

[200] Acker & Lanier, *supra* note 3.

ment. In most jurisdictions, though, this narrowing process is not complete until additional aggravating factors have been proven at the penalty phase of the capital trial. A comprehensive review of the offender and offense circumstances that ultimately define death penalty eligibility can be completed only by considering the elements of capital murder in combination with the sentencing factors made relevant at the penalty trial. The next article in this series continues the analysis of statutory aggravating factors and related sentencing circumstances.

HANDS-OFF, HANDS-ON, HANDS-SEMI-OFF: A DISCUSSION OF THE CURRENT LEGAL TEST USED BY THE UNITED STATES SUPREME COURT TO DECIDE INMATES' RIGHTS

Rudolph Alexander, Jr.
The Ohio State University

ABSTRACT

Beginning in the 1970s, a few criminal justice professionals alerted the justice community that the U.S. Supreme Court was returning to a "hands-off" doctrine, and thereby was reversing advances made in prisoners' rights. These warnings were generally made following a decision which was adverse to prisoners. The Court had not articulated a full legal test by which one could ultimately conclude that a hands-off doctrine had reemerged. However, the Court announced such a test in 1987 that is called the reasonableness test. Although the reasonableness test connotes prudence and fairness, it is extremely deferential to state prison officials and provides a constitutional vehicle for regressing prisoners' rights. This paper retraces the hands-off doctrine, discusses the reasonableness test, analyzes several cases where the test has been applied, and concludes that a semi-hands-off doctrine has unfolded.

INTRODUCTION

During the past two decades, criminal justice professionals have stated that the United States Supreme Court has been moving penology more and more toward a return to a "hands-off" doctrine or a reluctance to interfere in prison administrators' decisions (Crouch & Marquart, 1989; Huff, 1980; Nagel, 1985). For instance, Huff (1980) wrote that the Court had returned to a hands-off doctrine in a North Carolina case in which the Court sided with prison officials who, on the grounds of needing to maintain prison order, had blocked inmates from unionizing. Bronstein (1985) and Nagel (1985) analyzed the prison-related decisions announced by the Burger Court and concluded that the Court had returned to a hands-off doctrine. Haas and Albert (1989) opined that the Court had returned to a modified hands-off doctrine. Even Justices on the Supreme Court stated that the Court was returning this country to a hands-off doctrine (*Hudson v Palmer*, 1984).

For the most part, these concerned writers were reacting to specific decisions which were adverse to inmates. The U.S. Supreme Court had not used a clearly enunciated legal test that one could conclude was the vehicle by which a hands-off doctrine had returned. In 1987 the U.S. Supreme Court pronounced just such a test— named the reasonableness test— that all courts were to use in adjudicating inmates' rights. Although the name of the test connotes prudence and fairness, it is highly deferential to prison officials and has the potential for a significant erosion in prisoners' rights. The purpose of this paper is to discuss the development of the hands-off doctrine and analyze the reasonableness test and its effect upon inmates and prison administrators.

DEVELOPMENT OF THE HANDS-OFF DOCTRINE

19th Century

The hands-off doctrine emanated from a Virginia case involving Woody Ruffin. About 1870, Ruffin was convicted of a felony and sentenced to a Virginia prison. Soon after his confinement, he was contracted out by the State of Virginia to work on the Chesapeake and Ohio railroad. During one work day, Ruffin attempted to escape and killed the guard hired by the railroad to supervise him. Ruffin was convicted of murder and sentenced to hang. His appeal to the Court of Appeals of Virginia maintained that he should have been tried in the County of Bath where the offense had occurred, instead of the City of Richmond. However, the court summarily rejected Ruffin's contention and made the following observation about the status of prisoners:

> The bill of rights is a declaration of general principles to govern a society of freemen, and not of convicted felons and men civilly dead. Such men have some rights it is true, such as the law in its benignity acccords [sic] to them, but not the rights of freemen.

42

They are the slaves of the State undergoing punishment for heinous crimes committed against the laws of the land. While in this state of penal servitude, *they must be subject to the regulations of the institution of which they are inmates*, [emphasis added] and the laws of the State to whom their service is due in expiation of their crimes (*Ruffin v The Commonwealth*, 1871, p. 796).

With this decision, the court declared that inmates were the slaves of the state and did not enjoy any rights guaranteed by the United States Constitution. Moreover, the court suggested that prison administrators must have a free hand in regulating their prisons in order to extract inmates' expiation for their wrongs. Thus, the courts should maintain a hands-off approach and allow prison administrators to do their jobs.

As *Ruffin* noted, individuals who were civilly dead also did not enjoy the protection of the Bill of Rights, and the hands-off doctrine evolved indirectly from this status, according to another view. Once individuals were convicted of a felony, civil death ensued. Prisoners could be sued but had no standing to sue. Civil death effectively deprived imprisoned felons of access to the courts in civil matters (Del Russo, 1980).

20th Century

Molanphy (1984) wrote that the refusal of courts to interfere in the prison environment evolved from their perceived lack of expertise in prison management. Giving a broader perspective than Molanphy, Justice Lewis Powell stated that the hands-off doctrine emerged from the realization by federal courts that the problems in prison could not be effectively addressed by judicial decree. Rather, the problems could only be addressed by the executive and legislative branches because those two branches controlled the resources. As a result, courts had a very limited role to play (*Procunier v Martinez*, 1974). Whether considering prisoners to be civilly dead, slaves of the state, or difficult to help, courts have appeared to give tacit approval to the Virginia court's decision because legal decisions favorable to inmates have been notably absent from prison case law.

The major consequence of the hands-off doctrine has been that inmates were left virtually to the mercy of prison administrators, as suggested they should be by the *Ruffin* case. During this period, the hands-off doctrine has engendered considerable abuse of inmates, involving gross medical neglect, physical brutality, economic exploitation, and poor living conditions (Bronstein, 1980; Crouch & Marquart, 1989; Del Russo, 1980). Nagel, a New Jersey prison administrator in the 1950s and 1960s, regrettably recalled transferring troublesome inmates in the middle of the night to the mental hospital and the maximum security prison, censoring reading materials and mail thought to be critical, denying visitors, banning the writing of poetry, prohibiting the wearing of watches and wedding rings, and ordering segregation of inmates for unspecified reasons and time. At the same time, Nagel was credited with running a model prison. But he later acknowledged that he grossly violated inmates' rights (Nagel, 1985). Inmates, for the most part, had no legal recourse to address these abuses and could only count upon the irregular advocacy of prison reform groups.

Courts' Recognition of Prisoners' Rights

The commonly stated belief is that the hands-off doctrine was not abandoned until the 1960s, during the tenure of Chief Justice Earl Warren and the civil rights movement (Mays & Olszta, 1989; Singer, 1980). However, the foundation for the erosion of the hands-off doctrine had been laid years earlier in cases not directly involving prisoners. This was accomplished by the U.S. Supreme Court's informing the States that questions involving the violation of the United States Constitution were federal questions. For instance, in 1892, the United States Supreme Court considered the convictions of several Texas federal officials who had been convicted of conspiring with a mob to deprive several federal detainees of their right to be protected while in federal custody. Attorneys for the defendants argued that any punishment for failing to protect a prisoner awaiting trial is an issue for a state court. (The detainees had killed a sheriff following a shootout initiated by a deputy; however, the detainees were being held in federal custody. The detainees were acquitted at trial.) However, the Court rejected this argument and noted that a prisoner in federal custody enjoys the right to be free from unlawful violence while awaiting trial and a conspiracy to deprive a prisoner of this right is punishable by federal law (*Logan v United States*, 1892).

Although *Logan* involved the deprivation of rights of prisoners who were awaiting trial in federal custody and had not been convicted, the Court ruled also in a case involving a state prisoner in 1941 that some questions are strictly within the province of the federal court. In this case, the warden of a Michigan state prison enacted a policy forbidding inmates to submit any legal papers to the courts unless the papers had first been submitted to a state legal counsel who was charged with the responsibility of ensuring that the papers were properly drawn and contained accurate allegations. The Court thanked the warden for his regulation but stressed that decisions regarding the correctness of legal claims to federal courts were for the courts to determine (*Ex parte Hull*, 1941).

A few years later a federal Court of Appeals made an important decision with respect to inmates' rights. In this case, Lyman Coffin was confined to the U.S. Public Health Service Hospital and filed an application for a writ of habeas corpus. Although the case was rejected at the District Court level, the Court of Appeals observed that Coffin's

> conviction and incarceration deprive him only of such liberties as the law has ordained he shall suffer for his transgressions [and] a prisoner retain all the rights of an ordinary citizen except those expressly or by necessary implication, taken from him by law (*Coffin v Reichard*, 1944, p. 445).

The latter phrase was a key pronouncement by declaring for the first time that prisoners retain some rights, and similar declarations were made during the civil rights era in the 1960s and early 1970s. One justice reminded the states that no iron curtain exists between prisons and the Constitution (*Wolff v McDonnell*, 1974).

Two other cases were decided in the 1970s in which the U.S. Supreme Court struggled with the proper standard to use in deciding prisoners' rights. In *Procunier v Martinez* (1974) the Court avoided viewing the case as involving prisoners' rights and chose to decide it on different grounds. At issue was a policy enacted by the California Department of Corrections involving mail censorship and a ban against law students and paraprofessionals conducting interviews for attorneys. The Court ruled that the latter ban infringed upon inmates' access to the courts and thus was unconstitutional. With respect to mail censorship, the Court decided it from the perspective of the right of free individuals to communicate by letter with prisoners. On this basis, the Court held mail censorship to be unconstitutional (*Procunier v Martinez*, 1974).

But in *Pell v Procunier* (1974), the Court upheld a policy of the California Department of Corrections prohibiting face-to-face interviews between reporters and inmates. The Court discussed the need to balance restriction of free speech against the state's legitimate interest in confining offenders as a mean of deterrence, protecting society by incapacitating offenders and exposing them to rehabilitative efforts, and maintaining internal security. It noted that alternative means of communicating were still open to inmates as they could communicate with reporters by mail or through other visitors.

In deciding this case, the Court discussed the legal test it used; however, the test consisted primarily of weighing prisons' security concerns against inmates' assertions of unconstitutional infringement. This type of test is often referred to as a balancing test. In 1987, the Court significantly transformed and expanded the balancing test.

THE NEW STANDARD FOR DECIDING ISSUES OF INMATES' RIGHTS

Background of the Case

In 1984, Mr. Len Safley and Miss P.J. Watson were inmates at the Renz Correctional Institution, a coed Missouri penal institution. According to prison rules, inmates who become romantically involved would require one of them being transferred to another institution. As a result, Safley was transferred and began trying to communicate with Watson. Safley's letters to Watson were returned and their attempt to get married was denied. Thereupon, Safley and Watson filed a lawsuit for monetary damages and injunctive relief in the Western Division of the U. S. District Court. They contended that three specific policies violated their rights— the prohibition against marrying, the receiving of inmate mail, and the visiting by former inmates unless they have been freed for six months.

The judge, making 45 finding of facts involving inconsistencies in the marriage and mailing regulations, ruled the prison policies to be violative of the constitutional rights of Safley and Watson. The judge further ruled that the visitation ban did not amount to a constitutional violation but some flexibility was wise. The judge denied monetary damages to Safley and Watson (*Safley v Turner*, 1984). Dissatisfied with the U.S. District Court's ruling, Safley appealed to the Eighth Circuit Court of Appeals. A three-judge panel unanimously affirmed the lower court. Although the U.S. District Court relied upon previous case decisions to make it decision, the Court of Appeals was more explicitly in the legal test applicable for deciding the marriage and mail issue. Specifically, the Court of Appeals relied upon a strict scrutiny test, which is the highest standard employed by the courts (*Safley v Turner*, 1985). It is the same test that is employed when free persons have alleged that a governmental action has violated their fundamental rights. The State, under a strict scrutiny test, must show a compelling interest and a policy narrowly tailored to serve that interest.

The U.S. Supreme Court's Development of the Reasonableness Test

However, on further appeal by the state of Missouri to the U.S. Supreme Court, the majority found strict scrutiny to be incompatible with legal issues arising within a prison environment. Before articulating the proper standard, the majority began its legal framework by expressing two key principles. First, the Court noted that federal courts must protect the valid constitutional claims of inmates and that "prison walls do not form a barrier separating prison inmates from the protections of the Constitution" (*Turner v Safley*, 1987 p. 2259). It declared, for instance, that inmates have the right to petition the government for redress of grievances, to be free from racial discrimination, and to due process protections.

Second, the Court stated that courts lack the expertise to administer prisons, and many necessary reforms are not conducive to remediation by judicial decrees. It observed that

> running a prison is an inordinately difficult undertaking that requires expertise, planning, and the commitment of resources, all of which are peculiarly within the province of the legislative and executive branches of government (p. 2259).

More importantly, the Court stated that

> prison administration is, moreover, a task that has been committed to the responsibility of those branches, and separation of powers concerns counsels a policy of judicial restraint. Where a state penal system is involved, federal courts have . . . additional reason to accord deference to the appropriate prison authorities (p. 2259).

Given these guiding principles, the Court announced its reasonableness test, whose scope was to encompass *fundamental* as well as *nonfundatmental* rights. The test consisted of four criteria that courts should weight in determining whether prisoners' rights had been violated. Two of the four criteria evolved from four cases that it had ruled on in the 1970s and 1980s, and the other two criteria appeared to emanate just from the conservative Justices' philosophical beliefs.

As stated previously, in 1974 the Court held in *Pell v Procunier* that inmates do not have a constitutional right to face-to-face interviews with the news media. The Court observed from this decision that

> judgments regarding prison security are peculiarly within the province and professional expertise of corrections officials and, in the absence of substantial evidence in the record to indicate that the officials have exaggerated their response to these considerations, courts should ordinarily defer to their expert judgment in such matters (*Turner v Safley*, 1987, p. 2260).

In *Jones v North Carolina Prisoners' Union* (1977) the Court rejected inmates' challenge to a ban on prison unions and bulk mailing of union literature. The state's response to the union was that unionized inmates would present a challenge to prison order and unions should be banned. The Supreme Court accepted this argument, stating that "the ban on inmate solicitation and group meetings . . . was rationally related to the reasonable, indeed to the central, objectives of prison administration." From *Bell v Wolfish* (1979) the Court upheld a ban on books entering a federal institution unless they were mailed directly from the publisher. In this case the Court stated that the prison administrators' expertise regarding security should prevail. Finally, in *Block v Rutherford* (1984) the Court, also on security concerns, upheld a ban on contact visits.

From these four cases, the Court constructed the reasonableness test and created a watershed in prisoners' rights. It specifically declared that "when a prison regulation impinges on inmates' constitutional rights, the regulation is valid if it is reasonably related to legitimate penological interest" (*Turner v Safley*, 1987, p. 2261). Whether a regulation is legitimate is measured by one or more parts of a four-part test. The Court must determine:

(1) whether there is a "valid, rational connection between the prison regulation and the legitimate governmental interest put forward to justify it";

(2) "whether there are alternative means of exercising the right that remain open to prison inmates";

(3) "the impact accommodation of the asserted constitutional right will have on guards and other inmates, and on the allocation of prison resources generally"; and

(4) "The absence of ready alternatives is evidence of the reasonableness of a prison regulation."

The Court gave the rationale for its first two criteria and specifically cited *Pell, Jones, Bell,* and *Block* as justification for these parts of the reasonableness test. However, the Court did not indicate where it derived the last two criteria and no previously decided cases were cited for their inclusion. The absence of such citations and discussions suggests that the last two criteria came from the conservative justices' philosophical beliefs.

Using this reasonableness test, the Court held in *Turner* that the Missouri prison's ban on inmate-to-inmate mail was reasonable and thereby constitutional because it was related to the legitimate goal of prison security. Inmates could communicate plans to assault other inmates through inmate-to-inmate mail or plan escapes. On the other hand, the ban on inmates' marrying could not be justified under the reasonableness test as it was not related to security. Moreover, the Court stated that allowing inmates to marry might be rehabilitative.

CASE EXAMPLES OF THE APPLICATION OF THE REASONABLENESS TEST

Decisions Favorable to Prison Systems

Armed with the reasonableness test, the Supreme Court and lower courts have applied it in deciding several cases since *Turner*. In *O'Lone v. Estate of Shabazz* (1987) the Court considered Muslim inmates' claim that they had been denied the right to participate in an important Muslim religious event on Friday afternoons in violation of their rights under the

First Amendment. The inmates were incarcerated at a minimum security state prison in New Jersey that required them to work outside their living quarters and not to return to their living quarters until the work day had ended. The District Court ruled in favor of the prison, but the Court of Appeals remanded the case back to the District Court, ruling that prison policies could be justified only by convincing evidence from the prison administrator that these policies were necessary based on security. On appeal to the United States Supreme Court, the majority reversed the Court of Appeals, holding that placing the burden on prison administrators to justify their decision disrespected the deference owed to the state. Moreover, using the reasonableness test, the Court concluded that the policies were justified (*O'Lone v Estate of Shabazz*, 1987).

Particularly, the Court agreed with prison administrators that requiring the inmates to work outside conformed with rehabilitation because inmates would be exposed to the work ethic. The Court also accepted testimony from the warden that security would be compromised by allowing inmates to congregate. Congregation, according to the warden, creates an "affinity group" with a leadership structure that invariably challenges the administrator's authority. Additionally, security would be compromised by not regulating traffic through the main gate, a stated high-risk area. Further, the Court accepted that adjusting the work schedule for weekend work would require additional supervision and diminish scarce resources. For all of these reasons and inmates' opportunity to participate in other religious activities, the Court ruled that the prison policies did not infringe on Muslim inmates' rights to practice their religion (*O'Lone v Estate of Shabazz*, 1987).

In *Thornburgh v Abbott* (1989) federal inmates filed suit against a Federal Bureau of Prisons regulation banning publications from publishers to inmates if these materials are found by the warden to be detrimental to the security, good order, or discipline of a prison, or promote criminal activities. The warden may not, however, reject materials because their content is religious, philosophical, political, social, sexual, unpopular, or repugnant. Besides this policy, the warden adopted an all or none regulation, whereas all contents of a magazine had to be acceptable. The inmates stated in their suit that 46 publications had been banned unconstitutionally. Further, the inmates objected to the all or none regulation, contending that if one part of a magazine is objectionable, the other parts should be allowed into the institution. The District Court, however, found the regulation constitutional under *Turner*, but the Court of Appeals remanded the case to the District Court for further consideration under a different standard. The U.S. Supreme Court agreed to hear the Federal Bureau of Prisons' appeal and upheld the District Court's determination.

Writing for the majority, Justice Blackmun found that the broad discretion provided to the warden was rationally related to security considerations. Although no conclusive evidence was presented at the trial in the District Court that the rejected materials had caused a security problem, the Supreme Court, nonetheless, sided with the Bureau of Prisons. In fact, the testimony given was that most of the rejected materials were provided to inmates in other prisons without causing any security problems. Nevertheless, Justice Blackmun stated that

> we agree that it is rational for the Bureau to exclude materials that, although not necessarily likely to lead to violence, are determined by the warden to create an intolerable risk of disorder under the conditions of a particular prison at a particular time (*Thornburgh v Abbott*, 1989, p. 1883).

Under this rationale, the Court agreed that the all or none regulation was reasonable based on the administrator's testimony that tearing out objectionable portions of reading materials was likely to provoke confrontations between staff and inmates.

In another application of the reasonableness test, the U.S. Supreme Court sanctioned the use of involuntary medication of mentally ill inmates. Walter Harper, a mentally ill inmate in the State of Washington, was returned to prison following a revocation of his parole for assaulting two nurses in a state mental institution where he had been civilly committed. After returning to prison and being transferred to a mental health unit, Harper refused to continue taking his medication. The state, having instituted a forced medication policy, initiated a committee hearing (consisting of a psychiatrist, a psychologist, and an associate warden) to determine whether Harper should be involuntarily medicated. A decision to medicate involuntarily needed to be made by at least two persons on the committee with the psychiatrist being in the majority. An adverse decision could be appealed to the warden. Harper filed suit to prevent the state from medicating him involuntarily, arguing that a judge, deciding what Harper would do if Harper were competent, should decide whether involuntary medication was justified. The trial court rejected the issues raised in Harper's suit, but the Washington Supreme Court held for Harper, agreeing that a judicial hearing is required before an individual can be involuntarily medicated. The State of Washington appealed to the U.S. Supreme Court and the Court held for the state and rejected that a judicial hearing was required.

The majority of the Court held that

> given the requirements of the prison environment, the Due Process Clause permits the State to treat a prison inmate who has a serious mental illness with antipsychotic drugs against his will, if the inmate is dangerous to himself or others and the treatment is in the inmate's medical interest (*Washington v Harper*, 1990, pp. 1039-1040).

The Court further wrote

> there are few cases in which the State's interest in combating the danger posed by a person to both himself and others is greater than in a prison environment, which, by definition, is a made up of persons with a demonstrated proclivity for antisocial, criminal, and often violent, conduct . . . Prison administrators have not only an interest in ensuring the safety of prison staffs and administrative personnel, but the duty to take reasonable measures for the prisoners' own safety. These concerns have added weight when a penal institution . . . is restricted to inmates with mental illnesses. Where an inmate's mental disability is the root cause of the threat he poses to the inmate population, the State's interest in decreasing the danger to others necessarily encompasses an interest in providing him with medical treatment for this illness (*Washington v Harper*, 1990, pp. 1038-1039).

In another case, involving a mentally ill prisoner named Perry who was on death row in Louisiana and who had become incompetent to be executed as a result of refusing to take anti-psychotics, the State of Louisiana obtained a court order to medicate him involuntarily. The State of Louisiana's theory was that its state interest in carrying out justice outweighed the prisoner's interest in refusing medications. The United States Supreme Court vacated the court order and remanded the case back to Louisiana for reconsideration based on the reasonableness test (*Perry v Louisiana*, 1990).

Seemingly, the State of Louisiana went about the medication issue incorrectly. From previous Court's rulings using the reasonableness test, the State of Louisiana could easily have medicated the inmate involuntarily. It would have needed testimony from prison administrators that Perry's psychosis was threatening to security and order on death row. Because Perry was on death row for murder, the Court would easily have accepted that he was dangerously violent and his mental illness exacerbated his danger. Thus, it would have been reasonable for the state to have medicated him involuntarily to reduce his dangerousness and to provide security to employees on death row as well as to other prisoners for whom the state was responsible for caring until their sentences were carried out. Once medicated involuntarily to increase the level of security for everyone, and concomitantly made sane, the state would have been free to execute him.

Harper and *Perry* involved the application of the reasonableness test to the prison environment. However, the U. S. Supreme Court has indicated that it is applicable to a mentally ill jailed defendant who has not been convicted as long as the State has provided the structure and processes in *Harper* (*Riggins v Nevada*, 1992). Thus, *Riggins* represents an extension of the reasonableness test from the prison environment where inmates possess fewer rights to the jail environment where some defendants have more rights by virtue of not being convicted felons.

Moreover, the reasonableness test has been applied to mentally ill parolees. A Wisconsin parolee brought legal action against Wisconsin parole authorities for compelling him to take psychotropic drugs. The parties agreed that the reasonableness test was used in *Harper* and *Riggins* and these environments, while different in some respects, were penal in nature. The State argued that it had a greater right to compel the parolee to take psychotropic drugs because it does not have the prison environment to help control dangerous behavior. Further, the State argued that the parolee was still in the custody of the Department of Corrections. After considering the arguments, the Court of Appeals determined that the reasonableness test was applicable to a parolee but decided that Wisconsin had not implemented the structure and processes announced in *Harper*, which are the establishing of need and appropriateness of forced medication by a hearing panel (*Felce v Fiedler*, 1992).

In a somewhat related case, a state court held that a prisoner named Kallinger who was trying to starve himself to death could be forced fed based on the reasonableness test (United States Law Week, October 2, 1990). Before the reasonableness test was handed down, one state court had ruled that a competent prisoner may starve himself to death based on a right to privacy (*Zant v Prevatte*, 1982). However, in the Pennsylvania case, a psychiatrist testified that if the court allowed Kallinger to starve to death, his death would have an adverse effect upon the mental health staff whose moral obligation is to help people. Also, the psychiatrist stated that Kallinger's death would have an adverse effect on the prison environment in that prisoners would lose faith in the mental health unit. Because the reasonableness test requires courts to consider the impact upon the prison environment of accommodating prisoners' rights, the Pennsylvania court authorized prison officials to force feed Kallinger (United States Law Week, October 2, 1990).

Lower federal courts have applied or remanded cases to the District Court in light of the reasonableness test. One case involved a male Michigan inmate who objected to female correctional officers viewing him showering and using the toilet. He filed a grievance and alleged that the officers, in retaliation, intensified their surveillance of him. As a result, he filed a lawsuit. A federal District Court summarily dismissed the suit, but the Court of Appeals remanded the case back to the District Court with instructions to use the reasonableness test. Although the Court of Appeals hinted that the inmate might lose with the application of the reasonableness test, it stated that his case had merit and should not have been summarily dismissed. The Court of Appeals observed that a Court of Appeals in a different circuit had recently upheld damages for a female inmate who had been forced to take off her underwear in the presence of male guards. Although inmates do not have a right to privacy, they retain a limited right with respect to a person of the opposite sex viewing genitals unnecessarily. The Court of Appeals noted also that the Michigan Department of Corrections had been sued for sex discrimination by female correctional officers. Because equal treatment of correctional officers is a valid penological goal, the Michigan inmate was likely to lose his case with the application of the reasonableness test (*Kent v Johnson*, 1987).

Another Court of Appeals upheld a District Court ruling in favor of a federal prison that barred Native American inmates from wearing religious headgear in the dining area. According to the warden, other inmates were complaining about the cleanliness of the headgear and threatened to resolve the situation themselves if he did not. Perceiving these statements to be a threat to order and security, the warden banned the headgear. The Native American inmates said that instead of banning all headgear, the correctional officers should inspect headgears for cleanliness. However, the warden indicated that this might lead to confrontations and thus a total ban was reasonable. The Court of

Appeals, using the reasonableness test, agreed with the warden and concurred with the District Court (*Standing Deer v Carlson*, 1987).

Additionally, the reasonableness test has been used to determine whether a Missouri prison could prohibit prisoners from opening a saving account at a nearby local bank. In response to the inmate's lawsuit, the Director of the Department of Corrections provided an affidavit to the court which stated that a prohibition against banking was needed to deter escapes. Inmates with access to funds, according to the Director, were more likely to escape. Also, the Director stated that prohibiting access to funds prevented weak inmates from being robbed and prevented inmates from gambling. The Director stated that inmates could earn interest on their money by buying U. S. Saving Bonds, and their purchase was allowed. Based on the Director's explanations and the reasonableness test, the U. S. District Court and the Eighth Circuit Court of Appeals upheld the prison's prohibition against prisoners opening saving accounts (*Foster v Hughes*, 1992).

Decisions Unfavorable to Prison Systems

Although courts have upheld prison regulations in several cases based on the reasonableness test, they also have rejected some states' justifications for some of their policies. In an Arkansas case, a prisoner converted to the Muslim faith and legally changed his name. However, the Department of Corrections refused to recognize the prisoner's new name and cited security as a reason for maintaining the prisoner's old name. The Court of Appeals refused to accept the Arkansas officials' justification and ordered them to use the prisoner's new name (*Lockhart v Salaam*, 1990).

Another case involving a religious issue concerned Rastafarian inmates who fought an attempt by New York officials to cut their hair. New York officials stated that the inmates needed to get haircuts so that prison officials could take their pictures without hair, and nearly balded prisoners' pictures were needed in case of future escapes. New York officials contended that after the pictures were taken, the inmates could grow their hair back. Thus, the need to cut the inmates' hair was reasonable and met the reasonableness test. The inmates contended that the cutting of their hair would violate their religion. The Court of Appeals held that the cutting of the hair was unnecessary and the inmates could be asked to hold their hair back which would accomplish the objective of getting a picture with little hair being shown (*Coughlin v Benjamin*, 1990).

In another New York case involving an AIDS prisoner, prison officials argued that the reasonableness test allowed them to segregate inmates with viruses and have their records indicate their affliction. The officials argued that these practices were needed to protect the prison staff and were security related. However, the court rejected New York prison officials' argument (United States Law Week, December 3, 1991).

IMPLICATIONS OF THE REASONABLENESS TEST

Several problems exist with the reasonableness test. First, it confers too much deference to correctional administrators. As the minority justices in *O'Lone* pointed out, administrators in other social institutions are not afforded the deference that is conferred to prison administrators. Justice Marshall conceded that the realities of running prisons are complex and difficult, and prison administrators have special expertise. By comparison, the realities of running a school or city are equally complex and difficult, and these administrators also possess special expertise. However, in cases involving the First Amendment the Court does not defer to these professionals because their behavior appears rational on the surface. Justice Marshall stated that with respect to the First Amendment, the courts cannot blindly defer to the judgment of prison administrators, or any administrator, because of the nature of their jobs. In prisons, the administrator's job is to maintain order, and an administrator can be dismissed for disorder in his or her institution. Thus, a natural tendency is to err on the side of too little freedom, which may violate the Constitution (*Jones v North Carolina Prisoners' Union*, 1976).

A more telling example consistent with Justice Marshall's reasoning involves police officers. Everyone would acknowledge that police officers, and their supervisors, have a difficult job in maintaining order and protecting society. In all likelihood, the rate of police officers who are killed and injured probably exceeds that of correctional officers. For instance, from 1980 to 1990 the average number of law enforcement officers assaulted each year by weapons was 61,438 and the average number killed during this same period was 79 (Bureau of Justice Statistics, 1992). Comparatively, in 10 states and the Federal Bureau of Prisons, 21 persons were killed in correctional institutions from 1984 to 1989 (Bureau of Justice Statistics, 1992). With respect to assaults,

California had 774 assaults upon prison staff, New York had 717, Texas had 155, 28 states had less than 100, and many states had no assaults (Bureau of Justice Statistics, 1992).

Despite these statistics, the Court repeatedly stresses how dangerous prisons are as justification for conferring considerable deference to prison officials. At the same time, few statements have come from the Court about the dangers in free society as justifications for restricting free individuals' rights. Like prison administrators, police officers possess special expertise. But the Supreme Court likely would not allow police officers to confiscate from citizens reading materials, such as the *Onion Field* which depicted the murder of a Los Angeles police officer in the early 1960s, the *Badge of the Assassin* which depicted the murder of two New Jersey police officers, or *Foster and Laurie* which depicted the murder of two New York police officers. Despite the seriousness of the injuries police officers suffer each year, the Supreme Court is not likely to uphold confiscation of these books because the officers believe that these books might likely promote, or pose a risk of, violence against them. Thus, when Justice Marshall asked why a different standard exists for prisons that does not exist in free society, he questioned the lower standard afforded prisoners.

Justice Brennan answered that

> prisoners are persons whom most of us would rather not think about . . . They exist in a shadow world that only dimly enters our awareness . . . When prisons emerge from the shadows to press a constitutional claim, they invoke no alien set of principles drawn from a distant culture. Rather, they speak the language of the charter upon which all of us rely to hold official power accountable. They ask us to acknowledge that power exercised in the shadows must be restrained at least as diligently as power that acts in the sunlight (*O'Lone v Estate of Shabazz*, 1987, pp. 354-355).

Justice Brennan, disagreeing with the majority and particularly Chief Justice Rehnquist, wrote that

> The Constitution was not adopted as a mean of enhancing the efficiency with which government officials conduct their affairs, nor as a blueprint for ensuring sufficient reliance on administrative expertise (*O'Lone v Estate of Shabazz*, 1987, p. 356).

In both of these cases, *Jones* and *O'Lone*, the majority justices relied on statements that were unsupported by the evidence. In the *Jones* case, the warden offered no evidence to support his conclusion that a prison union would lead to disruption or disorder, and in the *O'Lone* case no evidence was offered to support the warden's conclusion that security was compromised. In fact, the record in the *O'Lone* case indicated that special working arrangements had been made to accommodate Jewish inmates' religious activities on Saturday and Christian inmates' on Sunday.

Moreover, in the case of *Thornburgh v. Abbott* (1989), one can readily understand why deference to prison administrators with respect to reading materials under the guise of security is ill-formed. The Federal Bureau of Prison's policy is that reading materials can be banned that constitute a threat to order and security, but they cannot be banned because they are critical, political, sexual, repugnant, or unpopular. Yet all the banned materials were critical of, or unpopular with, prison administrators and staff. One banned publication contained an article regarding an inmate who died because of an asthma attack that the guards allegedly did not respond to quickly enough. The article was entitled "Murder by Neglect." The real question is: Did the prison administrators want this publication banned from the institution because they were afraid of potential disorder or because they did not want the inmates to have knowledge of medical deficiencies that might be the basis for a lawsuit against them?

The reasonableness test allowed the Court to accept uncritically the warden's statement about security concerns, although the same publication was received in another prison without incident. The Court has provided further protection for prison administrators by ruling that even if no evidence of potential security problems is offered by the warden, the courts should still defer to the warden's judgment. The majority wrote

> it is rational for the Bureau to exclude materials that although not necessarily likely to lead to violence, are determined by the warden to create an intolerable risk of disorder under the conditions of a particular prison at a particular time (*Thornburgh v Abbott*, 1989, p. 1883).

As a consequence, there is really no way to determine whether a warden has banned a publication because the content, for instance, is political. Once he or she says that the publication is a risk to order or likely to pose a risk, a finding that the decision is contrary to the policy is nil because the court would defer to the warden's expertise.

Although one cannot be sure about the truthfulness of a prison administrator's testimony regarding the dynamics of a prison at a given time, the Missouri Director's affidavit regarding the saving account issue is highly suspect to professionals knowledgeable of prisons. According to the Director, prohibiting prisoners from having access to money would deter prisoners' escapes, robberies, and gambling. First, prisoners' plans to escape are totally unrelated to whether the prisoners have money in the bank. If they are successful in their escape plans, they will get money from friends, relatives, or steal some. It is doubtful that an inmate will say that he does not plan to escape because he or she does not have any money in the bank or does not have access to money on the outside. Second, cigarettes are currency in prisons and prisoners gamble with cigarettes and take them from weaker prisoners. While opening a saving account at a bank may not be a constitutional right, the Director's testimony reveals the questionableness of some testimony regarding prison conditions.

Another major problem with the reasonableness test is that it provides legal sanctions for the use of psychotropic drugs for social control purposes. In the case of *Washington v. Harper* (1989), the Court sanctioned involuntary medication of Harper because his mental illness threatened the security of the institution. The majority ignored that Harper's medication was increased on one occasion because the prison was short of staff. Alexander (1991) argued that Harper's medication increase for this purpose is very inappropriate. Alexander (1991) further argued that the Washington policy specified that inmates with a serious mental disorder could be involuntarily medicated, and this would encompass almost the entire prison population. Because prisons contain a very high percentage of inmates who have been diagnosed with an anti-social personality disorder and because medication is sometimes given to persons with this disorder (Kaplan & Sadock, 1988), most inmates could be involuntarily medicated under the guise that they constitute a threat to prison security.

Support for Alexander's contention is provided by a Pennsylvania court decision which allowed the involuntary medical care of a state prisoner who "suffers from a serious mental illness, diagnosed as a borderline personality disorder" (United State Law Week, October 2, 1990, p. 2193). According to the *Diagnostic Statistical Manual of Mental Disorders Third Edition Revised*, the essential features of a borderline personality disorder are a pervasive pattern of instability of self-image, interpersonal relationships, and mood, beginning in early adulthood and present in variety of contexts (American Psychiatric Association, 1987). This disorder, as well as antisocial personality disorder, characterizes most prisoners and makes them candidates for involuntary medication. The reasonableness test facilitates and justifies involuntary medication of these prisoners.

The reasonableness test also dismantles one of the key principles in remedying constitutional deficiencies in prisons. That is, the courts have consistently rejected arguments from the executive branch that they do not have money to remedy deficiencies in their state prisons. A District Court judge in Arkansas wrote that the duty of administrators to eliminate constitutional deficiencies is not determinable by the actions of the executive or legislative branch. Thus, the judge said that if Arkansas wants to operate a prison system, it must do so within the Constitution (*Holt v Sarver*, 1970).

The reasonableness test challenges this principle because it mandates the courts to consider the cost of accommodating inmates' rights. Justice Kennedy, in writing *Washington v. Harper*, specifically referred to the cost of providing mentally ill inmates with a judicial hearing, noting that funds for providing such hearings could better be used to operating the mental health unit. Costs were again referred to in the O'Lone case as the Court was sympathetic to the warden's testimony that it would cost more to provide weekend work assignments for Muslim inmates. Before the reasonableness test, courts had repeatedly rejected states' claims that providing constitutional remedies would cost too much because they knew that the states could always rely on this argument, and it was mostly a sham argument (*Battle v Anderson*, 1979; *Hamm v Dekalb County*, 1985; *Ohlinger v Watson*, 1980; *Wyatt v Aderholt*, 1974; *Wright v Rushen*, 1981). Historically, prisons have been underfunded and the states have been mandated to provide only a minimum level of constitutional remedies.

The inclusion of cost as a factor in deciding the reasonableness of prison policies threatens other rights that inmates enjoy. For example, inmates now have the right to a law library. If prison administrators want to rid their prisons of these law libraries, they could manipulate their budgets to create a shortage of funding. Then, they could decry the expense of maintaining law libraries and how the money could be better used to increase the number of correctional officers and thereby increase security. Prison administrators could announce that they are abolishing law libraries because of the cost of maintaining them. Inmates, then, would probably sue, and the issue would be decided based on the reasonableness test. Because deference is to be given to prison administrators with respect to testimony about budgetary problems and security needs, abolishment of the law libraries might be upheld.

Another threat involves legal mail. Before the announcement of the reasonableness test, numerous courts had ruled that legal mail to prisoners may not be read and could only be opened in the presence of the prisoners to scan for contrabands (*Parrish v Johnson*, 1986). *Parrish* was decided in the Sixth Circuit Court of Appeals. However, after the reasonableness test was announced in Turner and mandated to the lower courts, the view of the Sixth Circuit Court of Appeals appeared to have changed. In a recent case, the court stated

> it may seem perfectly reasonable to this court that prison officials have authority to read certain inmate's mail, where for example, there is probable cause to believe this inmate is conspiring with persons outside the prison to traffic in contraband or to arrange a breakout (*Reneer v Sewell*, 1992, p. 260).

Reneer does not give prison officials the right to read a prisoner's legal mail, but it does give them the right to read legal mail if they have probable cause to believe that an escape is being planned. If a correctional administrator does not need to produce concrete evidence of a threat to security in the institution, he or she, under the reasonableness test, may also be afforded deference regarding whether probable cause exists.

A final threat concerns inmates' right to mental health treatment. In *Ohlinger v. Watson* (1980), an Appeals Court disagreed with the State of Oregon's plan to treat some convicted sex offenders, who had been given indeterminate life sentences under a mental health act, with the same type of treatment afforded to the general inmate population. The Appeals Court ruled that inmates convicted under this sex offender statute had a constitutional right to treatment that would give them a realistic opportunity to be cured or to improve their mental condition. Moreover, the Appeals Court stated that the State of Oregon's failure to provide individualized treatment could not "be justified by lack of funds, staff or facilities" (p. 775). Clearly, if this case were relitigated today using the reasonableness test, the State of Oregon would prevail. The Court would now say that the prison administrators have the expertise and know better than the courts what type of treatment is appropriate. In other words, the court should defer to the prison authorities if they state that the treatment afforded to the general population is adequate. Further, the reasonableness test would be extremely sensitive to arguments from the State of Oregon regarding a lack of funds, staff, or facilities, and this argument would be given considerable weight.

CONCLUSION

As stated early in this article, several commentators in the 1970s and early 1980s have stated that the Court had returned to a hands-off doctrine regarding prisoners' rights. Each commentary followed an adverse ruling by the Court against prisoners. None could articulate a standard or legal framework that the courts were following in restricting prisoners' rights because the U. S. Supreme Court had not clearly articulated a standard by which all courts were to follow until the reasonableness test was announced in 1987. This article has attempted to explain this test, its uses in several cases, and its implications. Despite the connotation involving its name, the reasonableness test is not reasonable and represents a watershed in prisoners' rights.

The most problematic aspect of this decision is its deference to correctional officials. As Nagel described his tenure as warden of a prison in the 1950s, he grossly violated prisoners' rights while purported to be running a model institution. Accepting at face value from a prison administrator that he or she needs to restrict prisoners' rights because such rights might create "an intolerable risk of disorder under conditions of a particular prison at a particular time" (*Thornburgh v Abbott*, 1989, p. 1883) takes institutional corrections almost back to a hands-off period.

An almost equally problematic aspect of the reasonableness test is its impact on mentally disordered prisoners. It allows and justifies not only the involuntary medication of schizophrenic inmates, but also inmates diagnosed with borderline and antisocial personality disorders. A prisoner with an antisocial personality disorder or a borderline personality disorder is a typical prisoner and does not need medication. The reasonableness test sanctions the involuntary medication of any mentally disordered prisoner who poses a danger to institutional order. Previous litigation has documented the abuse and overuse of psychotropic medication in correctional institutions, and court orders have been issued halting the practice (Alexander, 1991). The reasonableness test facilitates the retrieving of such practices, and sanctions their use as long as the Harper requirements are followed.

A complete hands-off doctrine has not developed and prisoners retain some rights. They may legally change their names, keep their hair for religious purposes, and resist the stigmatization of having AIDS. Although these rights are important, other major rights may be denied, such as freedom from involuntary medication and freedom to read sensitive or thought-provoking literature. When these rights conflict with institutional order, the reasonableness test assures that the courts defer to institutions. In this respect, a semi-hands-off doctrine has been developed.

REFERENCES

Alexander, R. Jr. (1991) "The United States Supreme Court and an Inmate's Right to Refuse Mental Health Treatment." *Criminal Justice Policy Review* 5:225-240.

American Psychiatric Association (1987) *Diagnostic Statistical Manual of Mental Disorders*. 3rd Ed. Washington, DC: author.

Battle v Anderson, 594 F.2d 786 (10th Cir. 1079).

Block v Rutherford, 468 U.S. 576 (1984).

Bronstein, A.J. (1980) "Prisoners' Rights: A History." In G.P. Alpert (ed.), *Legal Rights of Prisoners*. Beverly Hills, CA: Sage.

____ (1985) "Prisoners and Their Endangered Rights." *The Prison Journal* 65:3-17.

Bureau of Justice Statistics (1992) *Sourcebook of Criminal Justice Statistics-1991*. Washington, DC: author.

Coffin v Reichard, 143 F.2d 443 (6th Cir. 1944).

Coughlin v Benjamin, 905 F.2d 571 (2nd Cir. 1990).

Crouch, B.M. and J.W. Marquart (1989) *An Appeal to Justice: Litigated Reform of Texas Prisons*. Austin, TX: University of Texas Press.

Del Russo, A.L. (1980) "Prisoners' Right of Access to the Courts: A Comparative Analysis of Human Rights." In G.P. Alpert (ed.), *Legal Rights of Prisoners*. Beverly Hills, CA: Sage.

Ex Parte Hull 312 U.S. 546 (1941).

Felce v Fiedler, 974 F.2d 1484 (7th Cir. 1992).

Foster v Hughes, 979 F.2d 130 (8th Cir. 1992).

Haas, K.C. and G.P. Albert (1989) "American Prisoners and the Right of Access to the Courts: A Vanishing Concept of Protection." In L. Goodstein & D.L. MacKenzie (eds.), *In the American Prison: Issues in Research and Policy.* New York: Plenum Press.

Hamm v Dekalb County, 774 F.2d 1567 (11th Cir. 1985).

Holt v Sarver, 309 F. Supp 385 (ED Ark 1970).

Hudson v Palmer, 104 S.Ct. 3202 (1984).

Huff, C.R. (1980) The Discovery of Prisoners' Rights: A Sociological Analysis." In G.P. Alpert (ed.), *Legal Rights of Prisoners.* Beverly Hills, CA: Sage.

Kaplan, H.I. and B.J. Sadock (1988) *Synopsis of Psychiatry: Behavioral Sciences and Clinical Psychiatry.* 5th Ed. Baltimore, MD: Williams & Wilkins.

Kent v Johnson, 821 F.2d 1220 (6th Cir. 1987).

Lockhart v Salaam, 905 F.2d 1168 (8th Cir. 1990).

Mays, G.L. and M. Olszta (1989) "Prison Litigation: From the 1960s to the 1990s." *Criminal Justice Policy Review* 3:279-298.

Molanphy, H.C. (1984) "The U.S. Courts and Prison Reform: Ruiz v. Estelle." *The Prison Journal* 64:68-75.

Nagel, W.G. (1985) "Hands Off, Hands On, Hands Off: An Editorial." *The Prison Journal* 65:i-iii.

O'Lone v Estate of Shabazz, 482 U.S. 342 (1987).

Ohlinger v Watson, 652 F.2d 775 (9th Cir. 1980).

Parrish v Johnson, 800 F.2d 600 (6th Cir. 1986).

Pell v Procunier, 417 U.S. 817 (1974).

Perry v Louisiana, 110 S. Ct. 1317 (1990).

Procunier v Martinez, 94 S. Ct. 1800 (1974).

Reneer v Sewell, 975 F.2d 258 (6th Cir. 1992).

Riggins v Nevada, 112 S. Ct. 1810 (1992).

Ruffin v Commonwealth, 62 Va. Reports 790 (1871).

Safley v Turner, 586 F. Supp. 589 (W.D. Missouri 1984).

Safley v Turner, 777 F. Supp 1307 (8th Cir. 1985).

Singer, R. (1980) "The Wolfish Case: Has the Bell Tolled for Prisoner Litigation in the Federal Courts?" In G.P. Alpert (ed.), *Legal Rights of Prisoners*. Beverly Hills, CA: Sage.

Standing Deer v Carlson, 831 F.2d 1525 (9th Cir. 1987).

Thornburgh v Abbott, 109 S.Ct 1874 (1989)

Turner v Safley 107 S.Ct 2254 (1987)

United States Law Week, October 2, 1990.

United States Law Week, December 3, 1991.

Washington v Harper, 110 S.Ct 1028 (1990).

Wolff v McDonnell, 418 U.S. 555 (1974).

Wright v Rushen, 642 F.2d 1129 (9th Cir. 1981).

Wyatt v Aderholt, 503 F.2d 1305 (5th Cir. 1974).

Zant v Prevatte, 286 S.E.2d 715 (1982).

0091-4169/93/8403-0554
THE JOURNAL OF CRIMINAL LAW & CRIMINOLOGY
Copyright © 1993 by Northwestern University, School of Law

Vol. 84, No. 3
Printed in U.S.A.

A CONTEMPORARY LOOK AT THE EFFECTS OF RAPE LAW REFORM: HOW FAR HAVE WE REALLY COME?*

RONET BACHMAN, PH.D**
& RAYMOND PATERNOSTER, PH.D.***

I. INTRODUCTION

The reform of state and federal rape statutes has been the product of a fragile alliance among feminist groups, victim's rights groups, and organizations promoting more general "law and order" themes.[1] As can be expected from such a diverse coalition, the intended goals of rape law reform have not always been clear, and different reform groups have had somewhat different agendas. For example, feminist groups were largely motivated by ideological issues. These organizations focused on societal perceptions about rape and rape victims.[2] Such perceptions included: (a) the belief that rape was not a serious and violent offense; (b) the notion that acquaintance rapes or rapes perpetrated by intimates[3] were less serious than and different from "real rapes"—those that fit a cultural

---

* An earlier version of this Article was presented at the 1992 meeting of the American Society of Criminology in New Orleans, Louisiana. Points of view and opinions expressed herein are those of the authors and do not necessarily represent the official position or policies of the United States Department of Justice. The authors would like to thank Patsy Klaus for providing a supportive environment in which to work on this project, Pat Langan for supplying data from the National Prisoner Statistics reporting program, and Lawrence Greenfeld for assistance with the prison survey data.

** Bureau of Justice Statistics, United States Department of Justice; Ph.D. University of New Hampshire, 1989.

*** Institute of Criminal Justice and Criminology, University of Maryland; Ph.D. Florida State University, 1978.

[1] See generally JEANNE C. MARSH ET AL., RAPE AND THE LIMITS OF LAW REFORM (1982); Ronald J. Berger et al., The Social and Political Context of Rape Law Reform: An Aggregate Analysis, 72 SOC. SCI. Q. 221 (1991); Leigh Bienen, Rape III—National Developments in Rape Reform Legislation, 6 WOMEN'S RTS. L. REP. 170 (1980); Vicki M. Rose, Rape as a Social Problem: A By-product of the Feminist Movement, 25 SOC. PROBS. 75 (1977).

[2] See Rose, supra note 1, at 76.

[3] "Intimates," as used in this Article, refers to either husbands, common-law spouses or boyfriends.

stereotype involving a stranger jumping out from a place of hiding and violently raping a physically resisting woman; and (c) the various "rape myths" which suggested, among other things, that rape victims were somehow partially to blame for their own victimization.[4] For feminist groups, then, a very important intended consequence of rape law reform was largely symbolic and ideological—to educate the public about the seriousness of all forms of sexual assault, to reduce the stigma experienced by victims of rape, and to neutralize rape myth stereotypes.[5]

Different concerns motivated victim's rights and "law and order" groups. Their intentions were somewhat more pragmatic and instrumental. The problem with extant rape statutes for these groups was that, too frequently, rape offenders were not arrested for their crime because many victims were reluctant to report the offense. These groups also believed that many offenders arrested for rape were not convicted or were convicted of a less serious offense because frequently the victim rather than the offender was put on trial.[6] For instance, the defense would use the victim's own sexual history to question her lack of consent. Further, they perceived that many offenders who were convicted of rape or sexual assault did not receive prison sentences because the sexual assaulter was known to the victim, and that therefore the public did not view the victimization by an acquaintance or intimate as real rape.[7] In addition to changing the public's conceptualization of the crime of rape and of the victims of sexual assault, rape law reformers also intended to modify existing criminal justice practices.

Although differing in emphasis, the impact of the symbolic and instrumental effects of rape law reform were intended to be complementary. Changes in public conceptions about what rape "really is" and who rape "really victimizes" were expected to lead to more reports of rape. Simultaneously, jurors were expected to become more sensitive to both the victimization and stigmatization of rape victims. Consequently, rape reports, arrests, convictions and rates of imprisonment (especially for "non-stereotypical" acquaintance rapes) were all expected to increase.[8]

---

[4] *See* Rose, *supra* note 1, at 78.

[5] *Id.* at 78-79; *see generally* Mary Ann Largen, *Rape-law reform: An Analysis, in* RAPE AND SEXUAL ASSAULT II 271 (A.W. Burgess ed., 1988).

[6] *See* Julie Horney & Cassia Spohn, *Rape Law Reform and Instrumental Change in Six Urban Jurisdictions,* 25 LAW & SOC'Y REV. 117, 119-21 (1991). *See generally* MARSH ET AL., *supra* note 1; Berger et al., *supra* note 1; Bienen, *supra* note 1.

[7] *See* SUSAN ESTRICH, REAL RAPE 8-26 (1987).

[8] For a detailed discussion of rape law reform, see generally CASSIA SPOHN & JULIE HORNEY, RAPE LAW REFORM: A GRASS ROOTS REVOLUTION AND ITS IMPACT (1992).

Significant questions still exist, however, regarding the extent to which the reporting and handling of rape cases has actually changed within the legal system subsequent to rape law reforms. That is, questions remain as to whether rape law reforms have actually produced the more instrumental public policy reforms that their proponents envisioned. At least four important public policy questions exist. First, are victims of sexual assault more likely to report their victimization now than they were in the past? Second, has there been an increase in the number of rape arrests and convictions from pre- to post-reform years? Third, are those convicted of rape more likely to do some prison time? Finally, are non-stereotypical rapes being handled as seriously as those rapes which more closely approximate a stereotypical sexual assault by a stranger?

Surprisingly, there has been little research to address these important public policy issues, and the results of the few studies which have been undertaken remain somewhat equivocal. Many of these studies find weak and inconsistent support for the assumption that rape law reform has had a significant impact on the criminal justice system's processing of rape cases. In Michigan, for example, where the first and most comprehensive reforms were implemented, researchers have found increases in the number of arrests and convictions for rape, but no change in the number of rapes reported to the police.[9] Statistics from other jurisdictions have shown even less of an impact for rape law reform. In fact, except for a few jurisdictions that experienced extremely zealous reforms, research has demonstrated that in the vast majority of jurisdictions, legal reforms have *not* been followed by significant increases in either the reporting of rape cases or the arrest and conviction probabilities for rape.[10]

---

[9] Marsh et al. performed an interrupted time-series analysis for data before and after rape law reforms were implemented in Michigan. These investigators found increases in the number of arrests and convictions for rape, but found no change in the number of rapes that were reported to the police. MARSH ET AL., *supra* note 1. Susan Caringella-MacDonald compared pre- and post-reform attrition (the extent to which cases were dropped) and conviction rates from two jurisdictions in Michigan (Kalamazoo county and Detroit). She found decreases in rates of attrition and increases in rates of conviction for both Michigan jurisdictions after reforms had been implemented. Susan Caringella-MacDonald, *Sexual Assault Prosecution: An Examination of Model Rape Legislation in Michigan*, 4 WOMEN & POL. 65 (1984).

[10] Polk examined data for the entire state of California from 1975 to 1982. Although he found an increase in the probability that those convicted of rape would be sentenced to a state institution, his data revealed that police clearance rates for rape and the rate of court filings for rape remained relatively unchanged during this time period. *See* Kenneth Polk, *Rape Reform and Criminal Justice Processing*, 31 CRIME & DELINQ. 191 (1985). Horney and Spohn studied the impact of rape law reforms in six jurisdictions: Detroit, Chicago, Philadelphia, Atlanta, Houston, and Washington, D.C. Only two jurisdictions displayed significant increases in rape adjudication outcomes. Detroit data showed in-

Horney and Spohn conducted the most recent and perhaps most extensive study to date to address these issues.[11] After evaluating the impact of rape law reforms on reports of rape and on the processing of rape cases in six urban jurisdictions, these authors pessimistically concluded that, "[o]ur primary finding was the overall lack of impact of rape law reforms. . . . [w]e have shown that the ability of rape reform legislation to produce instrumental change is limited."[12] While this study and others have provided important information regarding the effects of rape law reform in particular jurisdictions, they all have several limitations. Perhaps the foremost limitation is the fact that, except for Horney and Spohn, who investigated six jurisdictions, all the others have relied on single states or jurisdictions. The available knowledge base, therefore, is very restricted and precludes any general conclusion about the effects of rape law reform. In addition, all of the studies have confined their inquiries to data from the late 1970s or early 1980s, thereby leaving a large gap in our understanding about what has occurred with rape reporting and processing during the last decade. Finally, all of the above studies have examined changes in rape reporting and adjudication in isolation, not in comparison to other violent crimes.[13] Necessarily, one must examine rape in relation to other crimes of violence in order to control for extraneous factors, such as an increase in the general efficiency or punitiveness of the criminal justice system. These and other extraneous factors may be affecting the reporting and processing of *all* crimes, not simply the crime of rape. Only if the reporting and adjudication of rape increases relative to other violent crimes can any researcher attribute this trend to the influence of rape law reforms.

For these reasons, it is clear that, in order to advance our understanding of the effects of rape law reforms, it is necessary to conduct a *national* accounting of the *recent* trends in rape reporting and adjudication *relative* to other crimes of violence. Horney and Spohn adopted this very position after their recent review of the rape reform literature. "These empirical studies provide some evidence of

---

creases in reports and indictments of rape, and Houston data revealed slight increases in reporting and sentence lengths for rapes. *See* Horney & Spohn, *supra* note 6, at 117. In another study, Loh found no significant changes in conviction rates for rape in King County, Washington (Seattle). *See* Wallace D. Loh, *The Impact of Common Law and Reform Rape Statutes on Prosecution: An Empirical Study*, 55 WASH. L. REV. 543 (1981). *See also* Largen, *supra* note 5.

[11] Horney & Spohn, *supra* note 6.

[12] *Id.* at 149-50.

[13] *See supra* notes 9-13 and accompanying text for a brief overview of previous rape reform studies.

the impact of rape law reforms in four jurisdictions but leave many unanswered questions about the *nationwide* effect of the reforms."[14]

This Article both contributes to and extends the previous literature on the effectiveness of rape law reforms in this country. Using a number of national data sources, we investigate the degree to which there has been a change in three aspects of the rape adjudication process relative to two other crimes of violence—robbery and aggravated assault. We will address three questions regarding rape: (a) to what extent has reporting rape to the police changed from the 1970s to the present; (b) to what extent has the probability of going to prison for rape (conditioned on arrest) changed from the 1970s to the present; and (c) to what extent does the victim/offender relationship composition of rape victimizations reflect the composition of offenders going to prison for rape, and to what extent has this composition changed from the 1970s to the present? Specifically, has there been an increase in the number of "date" or "acquaintance" rape offenders who have been imprisoned?

II. RAPE LAW REFORM

Perhaps the most illuminating characterization of rape laws in this country was provided by Sir Matthew Hale, Lord Chief Justice of the King's Bench: " 'rape is an accusation easy to be made, hard to be proved, and harder to be defended by the party accused though ever so innocent.' "[15] This concern with protecting men from false accusations of rape went beyond the "not guilty until proven innocent" standard, and led to arguments for nearly unlimited admissibility of evidence regarding the accused's character.[16] This, combined with cultural conceptions of rape and early rape laws, placed serious impediments on the adjudication of rape cases.[17] Such offender-bias affected the entire adjudication sequence of rape cases, from the victim's reporting of the attack to the state's prosecution of the event.

Pressure from various organizations in the early seventies led to a growing societal awareness that rape laws in this country were an-

---

[14] Horney & Spohn, *supra* note 6, at 122 (emphasis added).

[15] MATTHEW HALE, THE HISTORY OF THE PLEAS OF THE CROWN 634-35 (1847), *quoted in* Andrew Z. Soshnick, Comment, *The Rape Shield Paradox: Complainant Protection Amidst Oscillating Trends of State Judicial Interpretation*, 78 J. CRIM. L. & CRIMINOLOGY 644, 650 (1987).

[16] *See* I.A. JOHN HENRY WIGMORE, EVIDENCE 62 (Tiller's rev. ed. 1983).

[17] *See* Andrew Z. Soshnick, Comment, *The Rape Shield Paradox: Complainant Protection Amidst Oscillating Trends of State Judicial Interpretation*, 78 J. CRIM. L. & CRIMINOLOGY 644, 649 (1987).

tiquated at best.[18] This awareness, in turn, provided the impetus for the enactment of some form of rape law reform in all fifty states.[19] Michigan was the first state to modify its rape statute when it enacted a comprehensive criminal sexual assault law in 1974.[20] Several other states soon followed by reforming their own rape statutes. The reform of state rape statutes also had a "spill over" effect on procedural law, as evidenced by Congress' 1978 enactment of Rule 412 of the Federal Rules of Evidence.[21] This rule excluded from evidence all reputation and opinion testimony concerning a rape complainant's prior sexual conduct, but still allowed for the limited admissibility of evidence of a complainant's specific prior sexual acts.[22]

Although the nature of rape law reforms varied across jurisdictions in comprehensiveness and specific detail,[23] Horney and Spohn identified four common reform themes:

(1) Many states replaced the single crime of rape with a series of offenses graded by seriousness and with commensurate penalties . . . . Traditional rape laws did not include attacks on male victims, acts other than sexual intercourse, sexual assaults with an object, or sexual assaults by a spouse [or an intimate]. The new crimes typically are gender neutral and include a range of sexual assaults.

(2) A number of jurisdictions changed the consent standard by modifying or eliminating the requirement that the victim resist her attacker. Under traditional rape statutes, the victim, to demonstrate her lack of consent, was required to 'resist to the utmost' or, at the very least, exhibit, 'such earnest resistance as might reasonably be expected under the circumstances. Reformers challenged these standards, arguing not only that resistance could lead to serious injury but also that the law should focus on the behavior of the offender rather than on that of the victim.

(3) The third type of statutory reform was elimination of the corroboration requirement—the rule prohibiting conviction for forcible rape on the uncorroborated testimony of the victim. Critics cited the diffi-

---

[18] *Id.* at 651.

[19] *See id.* at 644 nn.1-3; Vivian Berger, *Man's Trial, Woman's Tribulation: Rape Cases in the Courtroom*, 77 COLUM. L. REV. 1, 22-39 (1977); Abraham P. Ordover, *Admissibility Patterns of Similar Sexual Conduct: The Unlamented Death of Character for Chastity*, 62 CORNELL L. REV. 90 95-102 (1977).

[20] *See* Act of August 12, 1974, Pub. L. No. 266, 1974 Mich. Pub. Acts 1025 (codified as amended at MICH. COMP. LAWS ANN. §§ 750.520a-.5201 (West Supp. 1987)).

[21] The Privacy Protection for Rape Victims Act of 1978, Pub. L. No. 95-540, 92 Stat. 2046, was signed into law on October 28, 1978, and as FED. R. EVID. 412 applies to all trials conducted after November 29, 1978.

[22] FED. R. EVID. 412.

[23] *See generally* Berger et al., *supra* note 1; Jack E. Call et al., *An Analysis of State Rape Shield Laws*, 72 SOC. SCI. Q. 774 (1991); Harriet R. Galvin, *Shielding Rape Victims in the State and Federal Courts: A Proposal for the Second Decade*, 70 MINN. L. REV. 763 (1986); Horney & Spohn, *supra* note 6.

culty in obtaining evidence concerning an act that typically takes place in a private place without witnesses. They also objected to rape being singled out as the only crime with such a requirement.

(4) Most states enacted rape shield laws that placed restrictions on the introduction of evidence of the victim's prior sexual conduct. Under common law, evidence of the victim's sexual history was admissible to prove she had consented to intercourse and to impeach her credibility . . . . Critics argued that the rule was archaic in light of changes in attitudes toward sexual relations and women's role in society . . . . [S]tate legislatures enacted rape shield laws designed to limit the admissibility of evidence of the victim's past sexual conduct.[24]

Advocates of the new statutes expected a number of positive outcomes from the reforms. First, they expected the treatment of rape victims to improve and, in turn, increase the reporting of rape. Second, they expected an increase in the arrest, conviction and imprisonment rates of all types of rape, including date and marital rape. As noted earlier, however, there is a paucity of research attempting to measure the success of these reforms, but the literature which does exist remains somewhat equivocal.[25]

The primary objective of this Article is to provide a national accounting of the extent to which rape reforms have succeeded in producing three expected outcomes. First, if such procedural reforms as rape shield laws have reduced the reluctance of victims of rape to report their victimizations to the police, then we should see an increase in the number of these victimizations reported to police during the past decade. Second, if statutes aimed at eliminating the resistance and corroboration requirements have indeed increased the probability that rapists will be convicted and sent to prison, then the probability of going to prison for rape should have increased relative to other violent crimes over the past twenty years. Third, if new criminal codes which replaced the single crime of rape with a series of offenses have indeed increased the probability that rape offenders who victimize intimates or acquaintances will be convicted and go to prison, then we should see an increased incarceration rate for these types of rapists as compared to the late seventies and early eighties.

III. METHODS

To address the research questions posed above, this study relies on several data sources: the National Crime Victimization Survey ("NCVS"),[26] the Uniform Crime Reports ("UCR"),[27] the

---

[24] Horney & Spohn, *supra* note 6, at 118-19 (citations omitted).

[25] *See supra* notes 9-13 and accompanying text.

[26] BUREAU OF JUSTICE STATISTICS, NATIONAL CRIME VICTIMIZATION SURVEY (1991).

National Prisoner Statistics program ("NPS"),[28] and the National Corrections Reporting Program ("NCRP").[29] While we are primarily interested in the extent to which there has been a change in rape reporting and rape case adjudication, it is important to control for other factors which may also affect trends in these outcomes, such as the increased efficiency or punitiveness of the criminal justice system over time. To control for these factors, rape data will be compared to both robbery and assault data in all analyses. If rape law reforms have increased the effectiveness of the criminal justice system's handling of rape cases and of rape victims' willingness to report to the police, then we should expect to see increases in these measures for rape, over and above those increases observed for robbery and assault.

IV. DEPENDENT VARIABLES

A. POLICE REPORTS

This study focused on two indicators to examine trends in the reporting of rape, robbery and assault incidents to the police: the NCVS tally of victims who reported their victimization to the police, and the UCR tally of the same group. Both of these reporting trends are traced from 1973-1990.[30]

The Bureau of Justice Statistics ("BJS") sponsored and the U.S. Census Bureau conducted both the NCVS and prison inmate surveys. For a more detailed discussion of the methodologies employed in the NCVS, see BUREAU OF JUSTICE STATISTICS, CRIMINAL VICTIMIZATION IN THE UNITED STATES (1973-91).

[27] FEDERAL BUREAU OF INVESTIGATION, UNIFORM CRIME REPORTS (1991). The Uniform Crime Reporting program is sponsored by the Federal Bureau of Investigation ("FBI"). For a detailed description of this data, see FEDERAL BUREAU OF INVESTIGATION, CRIME IN THE UNITED STATES (1990). For a critical evaluation of the UCR data, see LARRY BARON & MURRAY A. STRAUS, FOUR THEORIES OF RAPE IN AMERICAN SOCIETY 26-32 (1989).

[28] BUREAU OF JUSTICE STATISTICS, NATIONAL CRIME REPORTS (1991). The collection of admissions data for the NPS is also sponsored by BJS. For a more detailed discussion of this program, see PATRICK A. LANGAN, U.S. DEP'T OF JUSTICE, NCJ-125618, RACE OF PRISONERS ADMITTED TO STATE AND FEDERAL INSTITUTIONS, 1926-86 (1991).

[29] BUREAU OF JUSTICE STATISTICS, NATIONAL CORRECTIONS REPORTING PROGRAM (1991). Data tapes and technical documentation for each of the data sets utilized in this Article can be obtained from the National Archive of Criminal Justice Data at the University of Michigan, Ann Arbor.

[30] It is important to note that the definitions of rape used by the UCR and the NCVS are not the same. The UCR defines rape as "carnal knowledge of a female against her will." UNIFORM CRIME REPORTS, *supra* note 27, at 23. The NCVS, for the time period studied here, relied on a respondent's self-classification of an incident as rape. That is, in response to a series of questions related to being attacked, threatened, or harmed, those women who voluntarily reported that they had been raped comprise the NCVS

75

B.   PROBABILITY OF GOING TO PRISON

To estimate the probability of going to prison for rape, robbery and assault, this study divided the number of individuals admitted to prison for each of the three crimes by the number of individuals arrested for that same crime during a given year. In making this probability estimate we utilized two sources of data: admission series data from the NPS and arrest data from the UCR. As part of the NPS data, the admission series obtains information on each individual admitted to prison during a given year. Because of budgetary concerns, however, the federal government sporadically collected this data during the 1970s. Consequently, for that decade we can only estimate the probability of going to prison for the years 1970, 1974, 1978 and 1979. Thereafter, however, we have continuous trend data from 1981 to 1989.

C.   VICTIM/OFFENDER RELATIONSHIP FOR THOSE COMMITTING
     OFFENSES AND THOSE IMPRISONED

In order to investigate the extent to which the relationship between the victim and offender for the crimes of rape, robbery and assault reflects the victim/offender relationship for those offenders in prison for these same crimes, and to determine whether there has been increased correspondence between these two measures during the past decade, we have utilized two sources of data: the NCVS for the time periods of 1979-1986 and 1987-1990, and a survey of inmates in state correctional facilities conducted in 1986 and in 1991

---

sample. RONET BACHMAN, U.S. DEP'T OF JUSTICE, NCJ-145325, VIOLENCE AGAINST WOMEN 1 (1994).

The accuracy of both data sources have been criticized for the extent to which they estimate incident rates of rape in this country. *See* Mary P. Koss, *The Underdetection of Rape: Methodological Choices Influence Incidence Estimates*, 48 J. SOC. ISSUES 61 (1992). This Article, however, *does not* purport in any way to estimate incidence rates of rape victimization in the United States. Because the objective of this study was to discern national trends in rape reporting behavior and in the adjudication process of rape cases by the criminal justice system, it was important to utilize *consistent* sources of data that were available at the national level. We believe these data are reasonably consistent over time.

It should also be noted that the NCVS procedures for measuring rape have changed as a result of a 10-year redesign project. The survey now asks direct questions about sexual assault, including rapes involving family members or other intimates. For example, NCVS interviewers now ask the following screening question: "Incidents involving forced or unwanted sexual acts are often difficult to talk about. Have you been forced or coerced to engage in unwanted sexual activity by (a) someone you didn't know before, (b) a casual acquaintance, or (c) someone you know well?" This, along with other questions that specifically address sexual assault victimization, were implemented into 100% of the NCVS sample in July of 1993. Estimates of rape and sexual assault from these new questions will be available in the fall of 1994.

as part of the NCRP. In both sources, analysis was restricted first to female victims and victimizations; second, to those incidents which involved single offenders and single victims; and third, to those victimizations involving adults over 18 years of age.[31]

D. TIME PERIODS

Constructing a perfect interrupted time-series model to evaluate the national impact of rape law reforms was virtually impossible for several reasons. Most important, perhaps, is the fact that even though most state level statutes were enacted during the late seventies,[32] the majority of these statutes have undergone numerous revisions based on appellate court decisions in virtually every state. In fact, these revisions and amendments to original reform statutes continue in states across the country today.

Some have noted that this proliferation of litigation has been necessary because most statutes were hastily enacted by state legislatures in response to constituent pressures.[33] As a result of their hasty construction, many statutes were ambiguous and vague, if not incomprehensible. As Galvin explains, "[u]nder pressure from powerful interest groups to proceed with haste and to embrace a symbol of sexual autonomy and equality with one quick stroke of the legislative pen, drafters of rape-shield legislation failed to approach the task of evidentiary reform functionally."[34] Perhaps the most noteworthy example of these reformulations occurred in 1989 when Steven Lord was acquitted of rape and kidnapping charges in Brow-

---

[31] Analyses were restricted in these ways to obtain the purest sample possible. While many sexual assault statutes today are written in gender-neutral terms, the vast majority of victims still remain female. Throughout this Article, the male gender will be used to refer to the perpetrator and the female gender will be used to refer to a victim of rape. The sample was restricted to adult victims as well because crimes of rape involving juveniles are also much different in circumstance, for example incest, compared to rapes involving adults.

In addition, because there may have been differential proportions of strangers and acquaintances in prison due to the fact that victims differentially report these types of victimizations to the police, analyses were replicated using *only* those victims from the NCVS who reported their victimization to the police. As there were no significant differences between analyses in which only reported cases were used and the total sample, results presented in this Article are those obtained for the total sample. The fact that the victim/offender relationship does not have a significant effect on reporting behavior of rape victims is supported by recent research as well. *See* Ronet Bachman, *Predicting the Reporting of Rape Victimization: Have Rape Reforms Made a Difference?*, 20 CRIM. JUST. & BEHAV. 254 (1993).

[32] For a detailed account of these early state reform statutes, see HUBERT S. FEILD & LEIGH B. BIENEN, JURORS AND RAPE: A STUDY OF PSYCHOLOGY AND LAW (1980).

[33] Soshnick, *supra* note 17, at 646.

[34] Galvin, *supra* note 23, at 776.

ard County, Florida. During Mr. Lord's trial, the jury was repeatedly shown the clothes worn by the alleged victim: a lacy white miniskirt with no underwear and a green tanktop. Newspapers nationwide published accounts of this trial, including the following statement made by the jury foreman: " '[w]e all felt she asked for it, the way she was dressed.' "[35] After this trial, Florida revised its existing rape shield statute to preclude the presentation of evidence at trial which suggests that an alleged victim's manner of dress incited a sexual assault.[36]

Because most state rape reform statutes have undergone so many reformulations since their implementation, it would be virtually impossible to establish a single time point by which to distinguish between pre- and post-reform periods. Therefore, we refer to pre- and post-reform periods in the sections that follow very loosely.

---

[35] Elinor J. Brecher, *The Whole Story*, MIAMI HERALD, Nov. 26, 1989, at 10.

[36] *See* FLA. STAT. ANN. § 794.022 (West 1993). A glance through virtually every state's penal and evidentiary codes will reveal numerous changes to original rape and sexual assault statutes. It is not our purpose to delineate them all here; a few examples will suffice.

Pennsylvania did not address the proper interpretation of its rape shield statute until 1983 in Commonwealth v. Majorana, 470 A.2d 80 (Pa. 1983). In that case, the defense counsel sought to introduce evidence that the alleged victim had engaged in consensual intercourse with a codefendant two hours prior to the alleged incident. The Commonwealth of Pennsylvania objected on the ground that the evidence was inadmissible under Pennsylvania's rape shield statute. *Id.* at 82. After a lower court sustained the Commonwealth's objection, the Supreme Court reversed the trial court's decision that "evidence which directly contradicts the act or occurrence at issue is not barred by [the rape shield] statute." *Id.* at 83, *cited in* Soshnick, *supra* note 17, at 681. More recently, in Commonwealth v. Johnson, 566 A.2d 1197 (Pa. Super. Ct.), *appeal granted*, 581 A.2d 569 (Pa. 1990), the appellate court ruled that a trial court should conduct an in camera hearing to determine whether the probative value of exculpatory evidence of prior sexual conduct involving the victim outweighs the prejudicial effect. *Id.* at 1202.

Other states, such as California, have made recent changes in their rape reform statutes through legislation. For example, the following changes were made to the California Penal Code § 1127d in 1990:

(a) In any criminal prosecution for the crime of rape, or for violation of Section 261.5, or for an attempt to commit, or assault with intent to commit, any such crime, the jury shall not be instructed that it may be inferred that a person who has previously consented to sexual intercourse with persons other than the defendant *or with the defendant* would be therefore more likely to consent to sexual intercourse again. *However, if evidence was received that the victim consented to and did engage in sexual intercourse with the defendant on one or more occasions prior to that charged against the defendant in this case, the jury shall be instructed that this evidence may be considered only as it relates to the question of whether the victim consented to the act of intercourse charged against the defendant in the case, or whether the defendant had a good faith reasonable belief that the victim consented to the act of sexual intercourse. The jury shall be instructed that it shall not consider this evidence for any other purpose.*

(b) A jury shall not be instructed that the prior sexual conduct in and of itself of the complaining witness may be considered in determining the credibility of the witness . . . .

CAL. PENAL CODE § 1127d (West 1988) (emphasis indicates amendments).

Keep in mind that we are simply assuming that, over the time period analyzed, there should be increases in the reporting, convicting and incarcerating of rape offenders, particularly those who rape someone known to them.

It should also be noted that, because the data we utilized were taken from several different nationally representative samples, we were not able to make pre- and post-periods completely consistent across all sources. With these data limitations in mind, however, we believe the important information to be gained from the analyses reported in this Article is a contemporary picture of the criminal justice system as it relates both to rape victims and to the adjudication of rape offenders since the years of reform.

V. RESULTS

A. POLICE REPORTS

This Section will examine the extent to which rape law reforms such as rape shield laws and modifications in the consent standard have, in fact, increased the probability that victims of rape will report their victimization to the police. To investigate this question, we will first examine the NCVS' violent crime victimization data for the years 1973 to 1990. Figure 1 displays the proportion of rape, robbery and assault victims who reported their victimization to the police. As this figure demonstrates, the proportion of victims who reported to the police is far more variable for rape than for both robbery and assault. One reason for this may be the relatively small sample size of rapes in the NCVS. With such small numbers, minor variations in reporting will produce seemingly large effects. To reduce the influence of extreme annual fluctuations, we smoothed the proportion of police reports by rape victims using a moving average span of three.[37] Both the original data proportions of rape victimizations reported to the police and the computed smoothed proportions are presented in Figure 2.

From both Figures 1 and 2, it appears that the proportion of rape victims who reported their victimization to the police has increased slightly since 1980. Looking at the original data points,

---

[37] Smoothing is a technique often done to time series data in order to detect visual patterns in data from original data points which change in a rapid and sporadic fashion. We adopted a moving average span of three. After basing both axes at their true values, a moving average span of three involves replacing each year value with the average of the previous year, the current year and the next year. For example, the smoothed data point for the year 1981 would be ascertained by computing the average of the proportion of police reports for the years 1980, 1981 and 1982. For a detailed explanation of smoothing techniques, see LAWRENCE C. HAMILTON, MODERN DATA ANALYSIS (1990).

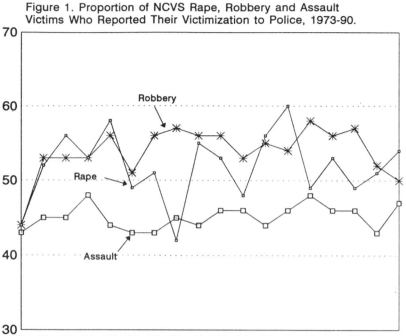

Figure 1. Proportion of NCVS Rape, Robbery and Assault Victims Who Reported Their Victimization to Police, 1973-90.

Note: Assaults include both Aggravated and Simple

there was a 28% increase in rape victims who reported to the police from 1980 to 1990. When these data are smoothed, however, the increase in victim reporting is only 10%. In spite of this small increase, it is greater than the increases for assault (4%) and robbery (a 12% decrease). On the basis of NCVS data, then, it appears that rape reform legislation may have slightly increased the willingness of rape victims to report their victimization to the police. UCR data corroborates this small increase of 10% in rape victim reporting.

Figure 3 displays UCR data on the rates of rape, robbery, and assaults reported to police departments for the years 1973-1990. The UCR data reveals a 13% increase in rape reporting from 1980 to 1990. Rates of reported robbery increased by only 6% over the same time period, while assault reports increased 46%. Thus, the NCVS and UCR data together paint a comparable picture concerning the impact of rape reform legislation on rape reporting. Both data sources show that rape victims were slightly more likely to report their victimizations after statutory reforms were in place.

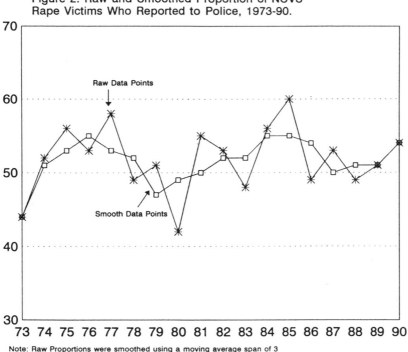

Figure 2. Raw and Smoothed Proportion of NCVS
Rape Victims Who Reported to Police, 1973-90.

Note: Raw Proportions were smoothed using a moving average span of 3

B.   PROBABILITY OF GOING TO PRISON FOR CRIMES OF VIOLENCE

This section of the Article will examine the extent to which
there has been an increase over time in an arrestee's probability of
going to prison for rape, robbery or assault. If rape law reforms
have achieved their intended goal, we should observe an increase
over time in the probability that arrested rape offenders will serve
time in prison relative to either robbery or assault offenders.

Recall that the probabilities used here were computed at the
national level by dividing the number of individuals admitted to
prison for rape, robbery and assault (NPS) by the number of individuals arrested for that same crime during a given year (UCR). The
estimated probabilities of going to prison for rape, robbery and assault are presented in Figure 4.

It appears from Figure 4 that the probability of going to prison
for rape has increased over the 1970 to 1989 period. In fact, with
only a few exceptions, there has been a monotonically increasing
probability of imprisonment for arrested rapists since 1981. It also
appears that the greater probability of imprisonment for arrested

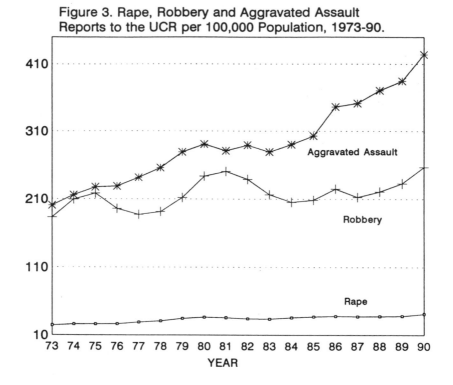

Figure 3. Rape, Robbery and Aggravated Assault Reports to the UCR per 100,000 Population, 1973-90.

rapists over time is not due to the growing general punitiveness of the criminal justice system, since the likelihood of imprisonment for arrested rapists has increased at a faster rate than that for either robbery or assault. In fact, since 1981 the probability that an arrested rapist will go to prison has increased by over 200% compared with a 9% increase for robbery and a 25% increase for assault.

C.   VICTIM/OFFENDER COMPOSITION OF CRIMINAL ACTIVITY VERSUS COMPOSITION OF PRISON POPULATION

Earlier we alluded to the symbolic impact of rape law reform. One dimension of this was the expectation that persons would begin to consider "non-traditional" or non-stereotypical forms of sexual assault as real rape.[38] One type of "non-traditional" sexual assault is an assault occurring between acquaintances. If the educational purpose of rape law reform has been successful, rapists who victimized acquaintances should be as likely to be imprisoned as those who victimized strangers (the stereotypical rape). The final issue to

---

[38] *See* ESTRICH, *supra* note 7, at 826.

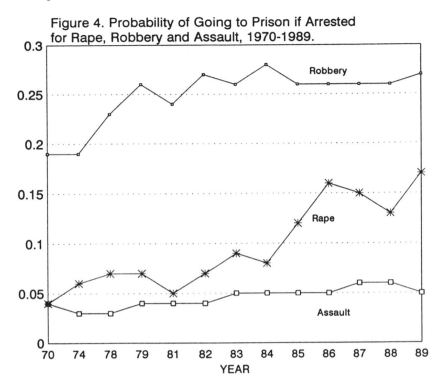

Figure 4. Probability of Going to Prison if Arrested for Rape, Robbery and Assault, 1970-1989.

be examined here is the extent to which rape law reforms have increased the probability that those who rape acquaintances will be sent to prison relative to those who rape strangers.

Our inquiry focuses on the correspondence between crime victims' descriptions of their relationships with their respective attackers (NCVS) and imprisoned violent crime offenders' descriptions of their relationships with their respective victims (NCRP). We make a few assumptions. First, because acquaintance rapes have historically been treated by the legal system as less serious than those involving strangers, we first assume that rape events (victimization incidents) will involve a larger proportion of acquaintance relationships than sanction events (incarcerations). Thus, we would expect to see a higher proportion of acquaintance rapes in the victimization data than the incarceration data. Second, we assume that if rape reforms have had their intended effect, this difference in proportions involving acquaintances between victimization events and sanction events will decrease over time. As a result of rape law reform, then, a larger proportion of acquaintance rapists will be incarcerated in the latter years of the time period than in earlier years.

In testing this latter hypothesis, two additional issues should be kept in mind. First, while the victimization data includes annual reports of victimization over the years 1979-1986 and 1987-1990, the NCRP compiled incarceration data at only two points in time, 1986 and again in 1991. We will, therefore, consider the first time period (1979-1986) as the "pre-reform" period and the second time period (1987-1992) as the "post-reform" period. Second, because of these data limitations, we are conducting a very conservative test for the impact of rape law reform. Many states began to revise their rape statutes to some degree during what we are calling the pre-reform period. If the effect of these reforms was relatively instantaneous, our comparison over the two time periods may minimize the observed impact of rape reform legislation on this outcome variable.

Table 1 compares the proportion of rape, robbery and assault victimizations who were strangers, acquaintances or relatives/intimates as reported by crime victims to the same proportions for the crimes committed by incarcerated offenders.

TABLE 1. PERCENTAGE OF STRANGER, ACQUAINTANCE AND RELATIVE OFFENDERS BASED ON VICTIM'S REPORTS TO THE NCVS COMPARED WITH THE PERCENTAGE OF STRANGER, ACQUAINTANCE AND RELATIVE OFFENDERS IN PRISON ACCORDING TO NATIONAL PRISONER STATISTICS

Crime	NCVS Proportion*			NPS Proportion		
	Years: 1979-1986 - "Pre-Reform" Period			Year: 1986 - "Pre-Reform" Period		
	Stranger	Acquaintance	Relative	Stranger	Acquaintance	Relative
Rape	45%	41%	14%	56%	29%	15%
Robbery	70	18	12	85	14	1
Assault	38	46	16	45	36	19
	Years: 1987-1990 - "Post-Reform" Period			Year: 1991 - "Post-Reform" Period		
	Stranger	Acquaintance	Relative	Stranger	Acquaintance	Relative
Rape	36%	48%	16%	43%	40%	17%
Robbery	83	13	4	86	12	1
Assault	52	36	12	48	32	20

* Proportions for the NCVS are based on all single-offender victimizations.

Table 1 indicates that in the pre-reform period (1979-1986) the proportion of rape crimes that involved a victim who was acquainted with her offender was higher (41%) than the proportion found for those offenders who were incarcerated (29%). Given their proportion in offense data, then, we find an underrepresentation of rapists who victimized acquaintances in the incarceration data. There is a corresponding overrepresentation of rapes involving stranger victims in the incarceration data (56%) relative to their proportion in the victimization data (45%). It is probable that juries during this period did not view acquaintance rapes to be as serious as rape by strangers, and were therefore less likely to send an acquaintance to prison. This is precisely the understanding of sexual assault that rape law reform attempted to modify. A similar and comparable "acquaintance discount" seems to be at work for assault. Acquaintance victims are more likely to be found in the victimization data (46%) than the incarceration data (36%).

The fact that rapists who victimize acquaintances are less likely to be incarcerated than those who victimize strangers may not be due to the fact that the former are perceived to be less serious than the latter. Rather, it may be that objectively *they are* less serious. Rapes committed against acquaintances may be less brutal and violent and less likely to involve another felony (such as kidnapping) than those committed against strangers. These factors may explain the underrepresentation of acquaintance rapists in the incarceration data. If, however, the underrepresentation of acquaintance rapists declines subsequent to rape reform legislation, we may speculate that such crimes are, more likely than in the past, being viewed by juries as "real rape"—in other words, viewed as comparable in seriousness to those rapes involving strangers.

The second panel of Table 1 shows the representation of acquaintance rapists in victimization and incarceration data during the post-reform period. In comparison to pre-reform years (1979-1986), the correspondence between victimization data and incarceration data with regard to acquaintance rapes is slightly closer in the post-reform period (12% as opposed to 8%). In the latter years, 48% of rape victims identified their offender as an acquaintance, as did 40% of those incarcerated. Another indication that rape law reform may have had an impact on how acquaintance rapes were being handled by the legal system can be seen in the increase in acquaintance rapists in prison from pre- to post-reform years. In 1986, 29% of those incarcerated for rape victimized an acquaintance. In 1991, this had grown to 40%. There was, then, an 11% increase in the number of acquaintance rapists who were in prison while the number of acquaintance rape victimizations increased by only 7% (41% versus 48%) over this same period. Correspondingly, the proportion of incarcerated offenders who victimized acquaintances in robberies and assaults declined by 2% and 4%

85

respectively, while the proportion victimized by acquaintances for these same two offenses declined by 5% (robbery) and 10% (assault). At the end of the reform period, then, there is some evidence to indicate that those who raped acquaintances were treated more comparably to those who victimized strangers. Although consistent, we must note that the observed changes are not very substantial.

There is yet another way to examine whether acquaintance rapists are being incarcerated with the same consistency as stranger rapists. Using a demographer's technique which Blumstein introduced to criminological research in 1982 and which Langan reinforced in 1985,[39] we explored the extent to which the criminal justice system differentially handles cases of stranger and acquaintance rape by calculating the proportion of acquaintance rapists expected to be in prison based on the probability of a stranger rapist being in prison. Table 2 describes these expected proportions and the supporting mathematical calculations.

For both pre- and post-reform periods, the observed proportion of incarcerated offenders who had raped an acquaintance was significantly lower (.01 level, two-tailed) than the proportion expected. In what we have termed the pre-reform period (1979-1986), the expected proportion of imprisoned acquaintance rapists was 49%, but the proportion of those incarcerated who actually did victimize an acquaintance was only 29%. This difference of 20% between expected and observed proportions is much greater for rape than for both robbery (7%) and assault (14%).

More importantly, however, is whether the difference between the expected and observed proportion of acquaintance offenders in prison narrowed at the end of the reform period. The bottom half of Table 2 demonstrates that the discrepancy for robbery and assault offenses has improved and, in fact, has almost disappeared. In other words, for these two offenses, the observed proportion of acquaintance offenders in prison nearly matches the expected proportion. In contrast, there is still a large discrepancy between expected and observed proportions for the offenses of rape. Of those incarcerated for rape in 1991, 58% should have involved acquaintance rapes, but only 40% of them actually did. This 18% difference is only slightly lower than the 20% difference observed during the pre-reform period. In spite of legal reforms, then, a strong "acquaintance discount" continues to exist for those who rape.

---

[39] Alfred Blumstein, *On the Racial Disproportionality of United States Prison Populations*, 73 J. CRIM. L. & CRIMINOLOGY 1259 (1982); Patrick A. Langan, *Racism on Trial: New Evidence to Explain the Racial Composition of Prisons in the United States*, 76 J. CRIM. L. & CRIMINOLOGY 666 (1985).

**TABLE 2. EXPECTED VERSUS OBSERVED PROPORTION OF
ACQUAINTANCE OFFENDERS IN THE NATION'S STATE PRISONS
BASED ON THE PROBABILITY OF GOING TO PRISON IF THE
OFFENDER IS A STRANGER**

	(a)	(b)	(c=b/a)	(d)	(e=c × d)	(f)
Years: 1979-1986 - "Pre-Reform" Period						Observed
		% of	Probability of		Expected %	% of
	% of	Stranger	a Stranger	% of	of Acquaint.	Acquaint.
Type of	Stranger	Offenders	Going to	Acquaint.	Offenders	Offenders
Crime	Offender	in Prison	Prison	Offenders	in Prison	in Prison
Rape	45%	56%	1.2	41%	49%	29%
Robbery	70	85	1.2	18	21	14
Assault	38	45	1.1	46	50	36
Years: 1987-1991 - "Post-Reform" Period						
	(a)	(b)	(c=b/a)	(d)	(e=c × d)	(f)
		% of	Probability of		Expected %	Observed
	% of	Stranger	a Stranger	% of	of Acquaint.	% of
Type of	Stranger	Offenders	Going to	Acquaint.	Offenders	Acquaint.
Crime	Offender	in Prison	Prison	Offenders	in Prison	Offenders in Prison
Rape	36%	43%	1.2	48%	58%	40%
Robbery	83	86	1.0	13	13	12
Assault	52	48	.92	36	33	32

VI.   DISCUSSION

Proponents of rape law reform intended that revisions of state rape statutes would produce a number of specific outcomes.[40] Our empirical examination of the extent to which these expected outcomes have been achieved reveals mixed results. The most obvious impression from these data is that statutory rape law reform has not had a very substantial effect on either victim behavior or actual practices in the criminal justice system. We found no large increase over time in the proportion of victims who reported being raped, and a very small change in the likelihood that individuals who raped an acquaintance would be imprisoned. In this regard, our generally null findings are consistent with other research concerning the impact of rape law reform.[41]

We would like to emphasize, however, that we observed some

---

[40] *See supra* notes 2-7 and accompanying text.
[41] *See supra* notes 9-13 and accompanying text.

partial success. Although not dramatic, both victim-based (NCVS) and law enforcement (UCR) data suggest that from the 1970s to 1990 there was a slight (approximately 10%) increase in the proportion of women who reported being the victim of a rape. One symbolic effect that rape law reform may have had, then, is a reduction in rape victims' perceptions that the legal process would stigmatize them, which in turn made them more likely to report their victimization. We also found that, subsequent to rape law reforms, rape offenders were more likely to be sent to prison. This increased probability of incarceration in recent years was not due to the general punitiveness of the criminal justice system, because we did not observe comparable increases for robbery or assault. Finally, we also found a small increase in the likelihood that the legal system would sanction acquaintance rapes and stranger rapes similarly. While there continues to be a large "acquaintance discount," treatment of rapes committed against an acquaintance in the post-reform period more closely approximate the treatment of stranger-perpetrated cases of rape.

There is, then, a silver lining to the general clouds revealed by our empirical analyses. In spite of this partial success, however, proponents of rape law reform must be disappointed with the results of our study and those of others before us. Although attitudes about rape and rape victimization may have become more enlightened over the past two decades, there is little evidence to suggest that these attitudes have been translated into significant performance changes in the criminal justice system. Our generally null findings, however, may in part be due to methodological imperfections. For example, our examination of national data over a long period of time may somewhat confound "pre-reform" and "post-reform" periods. In addition, this national analysis may also mask any impact reforms may have had at state-specific levels. The consistency of our findings with previous research, however, would suggest that although statutory revisions of rape laws have had some effect, significant progress still awaits us.

Three Strikes and You're Out!: The Political Sentencing Game

By Peter J. Benekos and Alida V. Merlo*

THE "WAR on crime" has added another weapon to the arsenal of getting tough on crime: "three strikes and you're out." From the ogans of "just say no" to "if you can't do the time, n't do the crime," it is ironic that the latest meta- or for crime policy parallels the baseball players' rike of 1994. The recent initiatives to mandate life ntences for three-time convicted felons are re- onses to the public's fear of crime and frustration ith the criminal justice system and indicate the ntinuation of politicized crime policy.

In the 30 states that have introduced "three-strikes" gislation and in the 10 that have passed tougher ntencing for repeat offenders (*Criminal Justice ewsletter*, 1994c, p. 1), politicians have demonstrated iick-fix responses to the complex and difficult issues crime, violence, and public anxiety over the disorder id decline in America. The United States Congress so finally overcame differences to legislate a new t-tough crime bill that not only includes a provision life imprisonment for a third felony conviction but so authorizes the death penalty "for dozens of exist- g or newly created federal crimes" (Idelson, 1994, p. 38).

Notwithstanding the critics of these sentencing poli- es (Currie, 1994; Gangi, 1994; Gladwell, 1994; Kra- er, 1994; Lewis, 1994; Raspberry, 1993) politicians ive rushed to embrace the "get *even* tougher" sen- ncing proposals because they have learned that "po- ically, it still works" (Schneider, 1993, p. 24). "Crime ed to be the Republicans' issue, just as the economy as the Democrats'. No more" (Schneider, 1993, p. 24). his commentary on how the "misbegotten" three- rikes piece of legislation became part of the crime ll, Lewis writes that "the answer is simple: politics. emocrats wanted to take the crime issue away from epublicans. Republicans responded by sounding ugher'" . . . and "President Clinton wanted some- ing—anything—labeled 'crime bill'" (Lewis, 1994, p. 13).

This article reviews the ideological and political ntext of these sentencing reforms, examines get- ugh legislation in three states and on the Federal vel, and considers the consequences of increasing

sentencing severity. The review suggests that baseball sentencing will further distort the distribution of pun- ishments and will contribute to an escalation of politi- cal posturing on crime policies.

Politicalization of Crime

In a sense, this is what baseball sentencing is about: using the fear factor as a political issue; relying on what Broder calls "bumper sticker simplicity" to for- mulate crime policy (1994b, p. 6), and taking a tough stance on sentencing criminals as symbolic of doing something about crime. The politicizing of crime as a national issue can be traced to the 1964 Presidential election when Barry Goldwater promoted the theme of "law and order" and challenged Lyndon Johnson's "war on poverty" as a soft-headed response to crime and disorder (Cronin, Cronin, & Milakovich, 1981).

Thirty years ago the voters chose "social reform, civil rights, and increased education and employment op- portunities" over a "get-tough response to crime that included expanding police powers and legislating tougher laws" (Merlo & Benekos, 1992a, p. x). Today's election results reflect a reversal of policy and the expansion of the Federal role in crime control (*Con- gressional Digest*, 1994).

Even though Johnson won the 1964 election, the "nationalization" of the crime issue was established and the Federal Government began "a new era of involvement in crime control" (*Congressional Digest*, 1994, p. 162): "the law and order issue just wouldn't go away" (Cronin et al., 1981, p. 22) and it became em- bedded in the public's mind and on the national agenda (Merlo and Benekos, 1992a, p. x).

In his 1965 address to Congress, President Johnson "called for the establishment of a blue ribbon panel to probe 'fully and deeply into the problems of crime in our Nation'" (*Congressional Digest*, 1994, p. 162). This led to the Law Enforcement Assistance Act of 1965, the Omnibus Crime Control and Safe Streets Act of 1968, and more recently to the Comprehensive Crime Con- trol Act of 1984, the Anti-Drug Abuse Act of 1986, the Anti-Drug Abuse Act of 1988, the Crime Control Act of 1990, and finally, the Violent Crime Control and Law Enforcement Act of 1994 (*Congressional Digest*, 1994, pp. 163, 192), which was signed by President Clinton on September 13, 1994. Since 1965 to 1992, the Fed- eral spending for the "administration of justice" has "risen from $535 million to an estimated $11.7 billion" (*Congressional Digest*, 1994, p. 162).

*Dr. Benekos is professor, Administration of Justice, Mer- hurst College. Dr. Merlo is professor, Department of Crimi- l Justice, Westfield State College. This article is based on paper presented at the annual meeting of the American ciety of Criminology, November 1994 in Miami, Florida.

From Horton to Davis and McFadden

The lessons of crime and politics were learned again in the Presidential election of 1988 when the then Vice President George Bush invoked the get-tough issue when he challenged Massachusetts Governor Michael Dukakis on his state's correctional policies that allowed a convicted murderer serving a life sentence to participate in the furlough program (Merlo & Benekos, 1992a, p. x).

Willie Horton became the poster child of Republicans and reminded Democrats (as well as doubting Republicans) that appearing to be soft on crime (and criminals) was politically incorrect. The Willie Horton incident "effectively crystalized a complex problem by presenting it as a dramatic case history of one individual" (The Sentencing Project, 1989, p. 3). Ironically, even without the Willie Horton incident, the 1980's were a period of conservative crime policy in which get-tough sentencing reforms were implemented throughout the country (Merlo & Benekos, 1992b). As part of these get-tough, get-fair, just deserts, determinate sentencing reforms, penalties were increased, mandatory sentences were legislated, and prisons became overcrowded (Shover & Einstadter, 1988, p. 51).

Similar to the Willie Horton situation, in 1993 another tragic case also became a "condensation symbol" for the public's perception that crime was increasing, that violent criminals were getting away with murder, that sentences were too lenient, and that offenders were getting out of prison after serving only small portions of their sentences. The California case which outraged the public was the October 1, 1993, abduction and murder of 12-year-old Polly Klaas by a parolee who had been released after serving 8 years of a 16-year sentence for a 1984 kidnapping (New York Times, 1993, p. A22).

Richard Allen Davis, who was arrested November 30, 1993, had convictions for two kidnappings, assault, and robbery and had spent "a good part of his adult life in jail" (New York Times, 1993, p. A22). At the time of his arrest, he was in violation of a pass from the halfway house that he was released to and therefore was also charged as a parole violator.

This type of crime fuels public fear and outrage and becomes fodder for politicians who respond by calling for tougher sentences to curb the perceived increases in crime and violence. Coincidently to Davis' arrest, the FBI released its semiannual tabulation of crime which "showed that the rate of crime as a whole declined 5 percent in the first six months of 1993 from the same period the year before and that the rate of violent crime dropped 3 percent" (Lewis, 1993, p. B6).

These data, however, are not comforting to a public which sees the Klaas incident as evidence of the horrific and violent crimes which grip the Nation in fear.

"The public doesn't rely on statistics to generate the perception of the level of crime. People's perceptior are based on what they see and hear going on arour them" (Michael Rand of the Justice Department, cite in Lewis, 1993, p. B6). In reviewing 1994 state politic campaigns, Kurtz observed that "although other tr ditional hot-button issues—welfare, taxes, immigr tion, personal ethics—also are prominent, crin remains the 30-second weapon of choice, and tl charge most often is that an incumbent is responsib for turning dangerous inmates loose" (1994, p. 12).

Recent "Baseball Sentencing" Legislation

In order to provide a clearer picture of the legislatic that is designed to impose mandatory life sentenc (without possibility of parole or early release), v examined the recently enacted Violent Crime Contr and Law Enforcement Act of 1994 and similar statut in the states of Washington, California, and Georgi The Violent Crime Control and Law Enforcement A of 1994, signed by President Clinton on September 1 1994, authorizes mandatory life imprisonment for pe sons convicted on two previous separate occasions two serious violent felonies or one or more seriot violent felonies and one or more serious drug offense According to the new Federal code, a "serious viole felony" includes offenses ranging from murder ar aggravated sexual abuse to arson, aircraft piracy, ca jacking, and extortion (U.S. Government Printing C fice, 1994, pp. 194-195).

In the State of Washington, the "Persistent Offend Accountability Law" was approved by the voters November 1993 by a 3 to 1 victory and became effecti in December 1993 (Corrections Digest, 1994a). Und the revised statute, an offender who is categorized : a "persistent offender" must be sentenced to life ir prisonment without any hope of parole if he or she h: been convicted of a "most serious offense" and has tv prior separate convictions for crimes that meet tl "most serious offense" definition (Washington Lau 1994, p. 1). Included in the definition of "most seriot offense" are crimes ranging from "manslaughter in tl second degree" to "promoting prostitution in the first degree" or any felony defined under any law as a Cla: A felony or criminal solicitation of or criminal conspi acy to commit a Class A felony (Washington Lau 1994, p. 13).

In March 1994, Governor Pete Wilson signed Ca fornia Assembly Bill 971 into law. Its most publiciz provision is the requirement that judges impose ". an indeterminate sentence of a minimum of 25 yea to life, or triple the normal sentence, whichever greater, on offenders convicted of certain serious violent felonies if they have two previous convictior for any felony" (Tucker, 1994, p. 7). The offenses i cluded in the category of serious or violent felony range from murder and rape to burglary, any felony using a firearm, and selling or giving drugs such as heroin, cocaine, and PCP to a minor (California Penal Code, s1192.7).

In Georgia the voters approved "The Sentence Reform Act of 1994" which authorizes life imprisonment without possibility of parole, pardon, early release, leave, or any other measure designed to reduce the sentence for any person convicted of a second "serious violent felony." Under Georgia law, a serious violent felony is defined as "...murder or felony murder, armed robbery, kidnapping, rape, aggravated child molestation, aggravated sodomy and aggravated sexual battery" (Georgia Statutes, 17-10-6.1).

Despite the fact that this law became effective January 1, 1995, any felony committed before that date in Georgia or in another jurisdiction, which meets the Georgia definition of a "serious violent felony," would count as one of the "strikes." The Federal code and the Washington and California laws contain similar language. The offender's criminal record in the state where the most recent conviction occurs as well as his or her record in other states or on the Federal level determine the number of "strikes." In short, an offender may already have the requisite number of convictions even as the mandatory sentencing provisions first become effective.

When the Federal criminal code and the three strikes laws are compared, it appears that the Georgia law is the most restrictive. Unlike the others, it contains a "two strikes" versus a "three strikes" provision. However, upon closer inspection, Georgia's law is the only one of the four reviewed here that requires mandatory life imprisonment for crimes that can be strictly identified as violent. By contrast, the Federal law and the Washington and California laws include a variety of nonviolent crimes such as burglary, prostitution, and drug trafficking that can result in a mandatory life sentence in prison. In California, for example, a criminal twice convicted of the property crime of burglary may be sentenced to life in prison for a third burglary conviction.

In order to clarify the intent of the legislation—that these offenders serve lengthy prison sentences—some states such as Washington stipulate that the Governor is "urged to refrain from pardoning or granting clemency" to offenders sentenced until the offender has reached the age of 60 (*Final Legislative Report*, 1994, p. 1). In order to discourage the Governor's use of pardons as a way to minimize the effects of the legislation, Washington law mandates that the Governor provide reports twice each year on the status of these "persistent offenders" he or she has released during his or her term of office and that the reports continue to be made for as long as the offender lives or at least 10 years after his or her release from prison (*Final Legislative Report*, 1994, p. 1).

Effects of Baseball Legislation

Thermodynamic Effects of Baseball Punishment

While the get-tough rhetoric continues to capture the public's support, the consequences of increased sentencing penalties are having an unintended but not unanticipated impact on the criminal justice system. In California where the mandatory statute "makes no distinction between 'violent' and 'serious' felonies . . . a superior court judge, Lawrence Antolini, declared the three-strikes law unconstitutional" because it "metes out 'cruel and unusual' jail terms" for nonviolent criminals and "robs justices of the power to evaluate the nuances of individual cases" (Peyser, 1994, p. 53). In an article about the tough California sentencing law, a *New York Times* report indicated that "judges in many California jurisdictions have been indicating their reluctance to follow the new law . . . by changing some felony charges to misdemeanors" (1994c, p. A9). In addition, Supreme Court Justice Anthony Kennedy has also criticized the "increasing use of mandatory minimum sentences, saying the practice was unwise and often unfair" (*New York Times*, 1994a, p. A14).

And, as some judges find fault with the harsher sentencing laws, prosecutors are also raising doubts about the ability of the courts to handle the number of cases which fall under the baseball sentencing provisions. In California, where the District Attorneys' Association opposed the three-strikes law, Los Angeles County District Attorney Gil Garcetti voiced concerns that the broad nature of California's sentencing law would expand the number of felons subject to life in prison (*Criminal Justice Newsletter*, 1994a, p. 6). In an interview with National Public Radio, Garcetti stated that Los Angeles County alone would need 40 more prosecutors to handle the increase in the number of cases (National Public Radio, 1994).

What Garcetti was referring to is the potential increase in the number of accused offenders who refuse to plea-bargain and would rather take their chances on a trial (Peyser, 1994, p. 53). For example, a convicted murderer in California, Henry Diaz, originally entered guilty pleas to three counts of child molestation. When he learned that "one of the incidents occurred after the 'three-strikes' law went into effect on March 7 (1994), making (him) eligible for sentencing under the new law," he withdrew his guilty plea and requested a trial (*New York Times*, 1994d, p. A19). Responses such as this give the California Judicial Council reason to "estimate that the new law will require an additional $250 million per year to try more felony cases" (*Criminal Justice Newsletter*, 1994a, p. 7).

These types of judicial responses illustrate a hydraulic, thermodynamic effect where getting tough may in fact result in being softer. For example, "the law allows prosecutors to move to dismiss criminals' prior convictions 'in the furtherance of justice'—namely, if they believe the law mandates an elephantine sentence for a puny offense" (Peyser, 1994, p. 53). Another avenue to circumvent the law is a "wiggle" factor where district attorneys can "classify certain crimes that straddle the felony-misdemeanor line as misdemeanors" (Peyser, 1994, p. 53).

In addition, some district attorneys have reported "instances in which crime victims had told prosecutors they would not testify if a conviction meant the defendant would fall under the requirements of the new law" (*New York Times*, 1994c, p. A9). As Griset observed in her study of determinate sentence reforms, legislators fail to "recognize the inevitability of the exercise of discretion at all points in the criminal justice system" and as a result develop policies which are incongruent and inconsistent with the reality of the criminal justice system (1991, p. 181). The above examples illustrate her conclusions and also suggest an inverse relationship between the severity of sanctions and the likelihood that those sanctions will be applied (Black, 1976).

Police officers are also experiencing the effects of these baseball "swings" at offenders: "suspects who are more prone to use violence when cornered" (Egan, 1994, p. A11). In one case in Seattle, a suspect threatened to shoot police after he was cornered. "After the suspect was taken into custody, the police were told by his acquaintances that he thought he was facing a three-strikes charge. Rather than face life in prison, he decided to confront officers" (Egan, 1994, p. A11).

Prisons and Prisoners: Economic and Social Impact

With crime uppermost in voters' minds, the new Federal crime bill was frequently featured in the 1994 election campaigns. Incumbent members of Congress informed their constituents of the immediate effects of the legislation on their home state. For example, New Jersey has been promised $77 million for new prisons and 3,800 police officers. Pennsylvania is slated for $110 million for prisons and 4,200 new police officers (*The Vindicator*, 1994, p. A5). These tangible results of the crime bill are intended to provide voters with a sense of security and satisfaction. However, the public has not yet focused on the long-term costs of these new initiatives.

There is little doubt that an immediate effect of the legislation will be to increase the already enormous prison population in the United States. According to

The Sentencing Project research, there are currently 1.3 million Americans incarcerated (Mauer, 1994a, p. 1). The incarceration rate is 519 per 100,000, making the United States' rate second only to Russia's (Mauer, 1994a, p. 1). In the United States, the incarceration rate of African-Americans (1,947 per 100,000) as compared to the incarceration rate of whites (306 per 100,000) is even more striking; Mauer's analysis illustrates that there are currently more African-American males in prisons and jails in the United States than enrolled in institutions of higher education (Mauer, 1994a, pp. 1-2). In terms of future projections, the National Council on Crime and Delinquency (NCCD) contends that if the remainder of the states follow in the footsteps of the Federal Government and of those states such as Washington and California, the inmate population in American prisons will rise to a minimum of 2.26 million within the next 10 years (*Corrections Digest*, 1994b, p. 1).

An increase of over a million inmates will mandate an increase in the level of funding necessary to accommodate such a large population. According to NCCD estimates, the Federal Government and the states will need an additional $351 billion during the next 10 years (*Corrections Digest*, 1994b, p. 1). In California, the effects of the three strikes provision are estimated to increase the costs of operating the state prisons by $75 million for fiscal year 1994-1995 (Tucker, 1994, p. 7). The requisite prison construction that will be necessary to fulfill the legislative provisions is estimated to cost California residents $21 billion (Mauer, 1994a, p. 22). The Federal grants that the states are hoping to receive from the Federal Government will fall far short of these costs.

In addition, there are also the costs associated with providing health care and security for inmates over the age of 50. Based upon demographic data obtained from the California Department of Corrections, NCCD projects that the number of inmates who are 50 years of age or older will increase by 15,300 from 1994 to 1999. Although these older inmates comprised only 4 percent of California's prison population in 1994, it is estimated that they will represent 12 percent of the prison population in 2005 (NCCD, 1994, p. 3). State officials in California expect that the full impact of this legislation will be realized in the year 2020 at which time over 125,000 inmates or 20 percent of the prison population will be 50 years of age or older (NCCD, 1994, p. 3).

The New Jersey Department of Corrections has estimated that a new baseball sentencing bill would have a substantial financial impact on prison costs. In a financial impact statement, the Office of Legislative Services reported that "for every inmate who is not paroled as a result of this bill, an additional $80,000 in construction costs and $1 million in operating costs would be incurred over the lifetime of that inmate...that accounting breaks down to $25,000 per year per inmate for operating costs or an additional $3.75 million each year for 30 years, or $1.7 billion" (Gray, 1994, p. B9). In other words, Todd Clear estimates it would cost " $1 million to lock up a 30-year criminal for life" (Clear cited in Levinson, 1994, p. B2).

In his review of the costs of crime and punishment, Thomas not only finds that "the fastest growing segment of state budgets in fiscal 1994 is corrections" but he considers that as more funds are put into public safety and crime control, there are fewer funds for other public and social programs (Thomas, 1994, p. 31). For example, Geiger reports that "seventy percent of all the prison space in use today was built since 1985. Only 11 percent of our nation's classrooms were built during the 1980s" (1994, p. 22).

In an assessment of the consequences of baseball sentencing laws on prison costs, The Sentencing Project cautioned that "the most significant impact of these proposals, though, will begin to take place 10-20 years after their implementation, since the prisoners affected by these proposals would generally be locked up for at least that period of time under current practices" (1994, p. 2).

Confronted with the fact that an older inmate population will have a higher incidence of circulatory, respiratory, dietary, and ambulatory difficulties than younger inmates, prison officials need to anticipate and plan for geriatric services and programs now. Another realization is that these inmates pose the least risk in terms of criminal behavior. As a group, they are not a threat to society since crime is primarily an activity of young males. As a result, while the United States will be spending millions of dollars on the incarceration of these older prisoners, this is unlikely to reduce the incidence of crime.

Mauer (1994a) contends that these sentencing policies will have several lasting effects. First, the money spent to build new prisons will represent a commitment to maintain them for at least 50 years. Once the public has invested the requisite capital for construction, the courts will continue to fill the beds. Second, the funds that will be allocated to the increased costs of corrections will not be able to be used for other crime prevention measures. There will be little money available to improve the effectiveness of other components of the system such as juvenile justice, and diversion or early intervention programs will receive only limited funding and support. Third, the incarceration rate of African-American males will continue to increase. As a result, there is little reason to believe that the status of young African-American males will improve when their representation in American prisons and jails

exceeds their representation in college classrooms. Fourth, there will be little opportunity to fully examine and discuss crime in the political arena because prevailing policies will be so dependent upon a limited range of sentencing initiatives (Mauer, 1994a, p. 23). Once the "quick fix" mentality to crime has been adopted, it is less likely to expect a divergence from the "punitive-reactive" response to crime.

Assessing the Effectiveness of Baseball Sentences

While some legislatures and policy wonks would disagree, "there is no reason to believe that continuing to increase the severity of penalties will have any significant impact on crime" (The Sentencing Project, 1994, p. 2). In their critique of incarceration trends, Irwin and Austin observed that political rhetoric has distorted rational sentencing policies and resulted in large increases in the number of prisoners, many of whom are nonviolent, without any corresponding reductions in crime (1994).

In a study of California's get-tough-on-crime strategy, "which quadrupled the prison population between 1980 and 1992," Joan Petersilia concluded "that the much higher imprisonment rates in California had no appreciable effect on violent crime and only slight effects on property crime" (Petersilia, cited in Broder, 1994a, p. 4). Despite such findings that these measures may be ineffective in reducing crime, and notwithstanding the spiraling costs of baseball sentencing, the punishment model continues to prevail.

In her review of retributive justice and determinate sentencing reforms, Griset (1991, p. 186) concludes that :

> the determinate ideal arose as a reaction, a backlash against the perceived evil of the reigning paradigm. While the theoretical underpinnings of determinacy attracted a large following, in practice the determinate ideal has not lived up to the dreams or the promises of its creators.

With a similar argument, Robert Gangi, executive director of the Correctional Association of New York, writes that "three strikes and you're out represents extension of a policy that has proven a failure" (1994, p. A14).

With a strong momentum toward tougher sentences and the success of get-tough political posturing on crime issues, it is unlikely that baseball metaphors will fall into disuse. For example, a proposal in Oregon would offer voters a "grand slam" package for crime. This package would require prisoners to work or study, prohibit sentence reductions without a two-thirds legislative vote, make sentencing alternatives to prison more difficult, and impose mandatory minimum sentences for all violent offenders older than 15 (Rohter, 1994, p. A12).

Conclusion

In this review of the recently enacted Federal crime bill and the Washington, California, and Georgia statutes, and in the assessment of the anticipated consequences of recent sentencing statutes, baseball punishment is characterized as the latest episode in the search for the "quick fix" to a complicated and disturbing social problem. These attempts to prevent crime, however, are misguided and will prove to be far more costly and ineffective than their proponents and the public could have anticipated. In the rush to enact "three strikes legislation," elected officials and the electorate appear to have given little thought to the long-term effects of these provisions.

In terms of additional systemic costs, these laws will have a considerable effect on an already over-burdened court system. The process of justice relies extensively on an offender entering into a plea agreement. Once these laws become enacted, there will be little incentive for an offender to plead guilty to any charges which could result in longer periods of incarceration. If offenders know that pleading guilty will constitute a first or second strike let alone a third, there is a greater likelihood that they will demand a trial. As a result, such legislation will necessitate additional funding for more prosecutors, judges, and court administrative and support staff.

One of the distressing aspects of these sentencing proposals is that they seem to have far-reaching effects on other offender populations. Included in the newly enacted Federal code is a provision to try as adults those juveniles who are 13 years of age and charged with certain violent crimes. It will be possible for the first strike to have been committed at age 13. This tendency to treat juvenile offenders more harshly is but one manifestation of a trend in juvenile justice mandating waiver into the adult court and sentencing younger juveniles to prison. Efforts to confront the crime problem would be more effective if society addressed the tough issues of gun availability, family violence, and drug prevention (Mauer, 1994c).

The "three strikes" legislation has also raised public expectations far beyond the likelihood of success. A *Wall Street Journal*/NBC News poll found that 75 percent of Americans interviewed believed that enacting such legislation would make a "major difference" in the crime rate (*Criminal Justice Newsletter*, 1994d, p. 1). Apparently, elected officials and the media have succeeded in pandering to the American penchant for oversimplifying the causes of crime.

Despite legislative sentencing changes, the *crime* problem has not been addressed. Absent a commit-

ment to do more than get tough on criminals, the "three strikes" legislation is just one more costly slogan which will have no appreciable benefit for society. Research and commentary on the consequences of baseball punishment suggest that prison populations will continue to grow, corrections expenditures will consume larger percentages of government budgets, and sentence severity will have "no discernible effect on the crime rate" (Currie, 1994, p. 120). As the rhetoric pushes punitive policies to the margin, baseball metaphors and politicalization of sentencing will continue to divert attention from addressing the antecedents and correlates of crime. It is not surprising that the emotionalizing of policy results in "feel-good bromides, like 'three-strikes'...that create the illusion of problem solving" (Kramer, 1994, p. 29).

REFERENCES

Allen, Harry (1994) Personal Communication. (September 17).

Balz, Dan (1994) "Pete Wilson: Practicing the Politics of Survival." *The Washington Post National Weekly Edition.* (August 29-September 4): 14.

Black, Donald (1976) *The Behavior of Law.* New York, NY: Academic Press.

Booth, William (1994) "Florida Turns Up the Heat on Crime." *The Washington Post National Weekly Edition.* (February 21-27): 37.

Broder, David (1994a) "Population Explosion." *The Washington Post National Weekly Edition.* (April 25-May 1): 4.

_____ (1994b) "When Tough Isn't Smart." *The Criminologist.* (July/August) 19:4; 6.

California Legislative Service (1994) Chapter 12 (A.B. No. 971) (West) 1994 Portion of 1993-94 Regular Session "An Act to Amend Section 667 of the Penal Code."

California Penal Code Section 1192.7

Congressional Digest (1994) "The Federal Role in Crime Control." Washington, DC (June-July).

Corrections Digest (1994a) "Experts Doubt '3 Strikes You're Out' Laws Will Effectively Curb Crime." (February 9): 7-9.

_____ (1994b) "Senate Crime Bill Will More Than Double American Prison Population by Year 2005." (March 9): 1-4.

Crime Control Digest (1994) "'Three-Time Loser' Bill to Be Introduced in House." (January 24): 5-6.

Criminal Justice Newsletter (1994a) "California Passes a Tough Three-Strikes-You're-Out Law." (April 4): 6-7.

_____ (1994b) "Texas Comptroller Warns of 'Prison-Industrial Complex.'" (May 2): 2-3.

_____ (1994c) "State Legislators Moving Toward Tougher Sentencing." (June 15): 1-2.

_____ (1994d) "State Chief Justices Oppose Senate Crime Bill Provisions." (February 15): 1-3.

Cronin, Thomas, Tania Cronin, and Michael Milakovich (1981) *U.S. v. Crime in the Streets.* Bloomington, IN: Indiana University Press.

Currie, Elliot (1994) "What's Wrong with the Crime Bill." *The Nation.* (January 31) 258:4; 118-121.

Egan, Timothy (1994) "A 3-Strike Penal Law Shows It's Not as Simple as It Seems." *New York Times.* (February 15): A1; A11.

Final Legislative Report (1994) Fifty-Third Washington State Legislature. 1994 Regular Session and First Special Session.

Gangi, Robert (1994) "Where Three-Strikes Plan Takes Us in 20 Years." *New York Times.* (February 7): A14.

Geiger, Keith (1994) "Upgrading School Buildings." *The Washington Post National Weekly Edition.* (September 26-October 2): 22.

rgia Statutes 17-10-6.1 Code of Georgia, Title 17. Criminal Procedure, Chapter 10 Sentence and Punishment, Article 1. Procedure for Sentencing and Imposition of Punishment.

dwell, Malcolm (1994) "The Crime Bill May Not Be the Cure." The Washington Post National Weekly Edition. (June 6-12): 33.

son, Bucky (1994) "Anti-Crime Packages Don't Work." Erie Times News. (October 9): A1; A12.

y, Jerry (1994) "New Jersey Senate Approves Bill to Jail 3-Time Criminals for Life." New York Times. (May 13): A1; B9.

et, Pamala (1991) Determinate Sentencing: The Promise and the Reality of Retributive Justice. Albany, NY: State University of New York Press.

son, Holly (1994) "Crime Bill's Final Version." Congressional Quarterly. (July 30) 52: 30; 2138.

n, John and James Austin (1994) It's About Time: America's Imprisonment Binge. Belmont, CA: Wadsworth Publishing Co.

ner, Michael (1994) "Tough. But Smart?" Time. (February 7): 29.

tz, Howard (1994) "The Campaign Weapon of Choice." The Washington Post National Weekly Edition. (September 19-25): 2.

nson, Arlene (1994) "Three Strikes and You're Out." Erie Morning News. (January 25): B2.

is, Anthony (1994) "Crime and Politics." New York Times. (September 16): A13.

is, Neil (1993) "Crime Rates Decline; Outrage Hasn't." New York Times. (December 3): B6.

er, Marc (1994a) "Americans Behind Bars: The International Use of Incarceration, 1992-1993." The Sentencing Project. Washington DC.

_ (1994b) "An Assessment of Sentencing Issues and the Death Penalty in the 1990s." The Sentencing Project. Washington DC.

_ (1994c) "Testimony of Marc Mauer before the House Judiciary Committee, Subcommittee on Crime and Criminal Justice on Three Strikes and You're Out.'" (March 1): 1-13.

lo, Alida and Peter Benekos (1992a) "Introduction: The Politics of Corrections" in Peter Benekos and Alida Merlo (eds.) Corrections: Dilemmas and Directions. Cincinnati, OH: Anderson Publishing Co.

_ (1992b) "Adapting Conservative Correctional Policies to the Economic Realities of the 1990s." Criminal Justice Policy Review. (March) 6:1; 1-16.

onal Council on Crime and Delinquency (1994) "The Aging of California's Prison Population: An Assessment of Three Strikes Legislation." 1-6.

onal Public Radio (1994) Broadcast on "All Things Considered" (September 30).

, Albert (1994a) "With Candidates in Dead Heat, Ridge Uses Casey in Ad." Erie Morning News. (October 6): A14.

_____ (1994b) "Singel Faces Up to His Worst Nightmare." Erie Times News. (October 9): B3.

New York Times (1993) "Hunt for Kidnapped Girl, 12, Is Narrowed to Small Woods." (December 3): A22.

_____ (1994a) "Mandatory Sentencing is Criticized by Justice." (March 10): A14.

_____ (1994b) "Georgia Voters to Consider '2-Strikes' Law." (March 16): A10.

_____ (1994c) "California Judge Refuses to Apply a Tough New Sentencing Law." (September 20): A9.

_____ (1994d) "Killer Withdraws Plea in a '3 Strikes' Case." (September 28): A19.

Peyser, Marc (1994) "Strike Three and You're Not Out." Newsweek. (August 29): 53.

Raspberry, William (1993) "Digging In Deeper." The Washington Post National Weekly Edition. (November 1-7): 29.

Reno, Janet (1994) "Memorandum from the Attorney General: The Violent Crime Control and Law Enforcement Act of 1994." (September 15): 1-5.

Rohter, Larry (1994) "States Embracing Tougher Measures for Fighting Crime." New York Times. (May 10): A1; A12.

Schneider, William (1993) "Crime and Politics: Incumbents Got Mugged by Fear in Our Streets." The Washington Post National Weekly Edition. (November 15-21): 24.

Shover, Neal and Werner Einstadter (1988) Analyzing American Corrections. Belmont, CA: Wadsworth Publishing Co.

The Sentencing Project (1989) "The Lessons of Willie Horton." Washington, DC.

_____ (1994) "Why '3 Strikes and You're Out' Won't Reduce Crime." Washington, DC.

The Vindicator (1994) "Law Will Star in Fall Campaigns." (August 28): A5.

Thomas, Pierre (1994) "Getting to the Bottom Line on Crime." The Washington Post National Weekly Edition. (July 18-24): 31.

Tucker, Beverly (1994) "Can California Afford 3 Strikes?" California Teachers Association Action (May): 7; 17.

U.S. Government Printing Office (1994) "The Violent Crime Control and Law Enforcement Act of 1994." Conference Report. Washington, DC.

Walker, Samuel (1994) Sense and Nonsense About Crime and Drugs: A Policy Guide, Third Edition. Belmont, CA: Wadsworth Publishing Co.

Washington Laws (1994) 1994 Pamphlet Edition Session Laws Fifty-Third Legislature 1994 Regular Session. Chapter 1 "Persistent Offenders-Life Sentence on Third Conviction." (Statute Law Committee) Olympia, WA.

Criminal Justice Review
Volume 18, Number 1, Spring 1993

Research Note:
DO MORE CONSERVATIVE STATES IMPOSE HARSHER FELONY SENTENCES? AN EXPLORATORY ANALYSIS OF 32 STATES

David A. Bowers and Jerold L. Waltman

Felony sentencing is a state public policy outcome lying at the end of a long chain of decisions by legislatures, bureaucracies, and courts. Using data from the 1986 National Judicial Reporting Program study of 32 states, the authors discovered that felony sentences for rape, assault, and robbery were linked to the Erikson, McIver, and Wright index of state conservatism (1987), whereas those for homicide and property crimes were not correlated with ideology. The addition of resource variables such as tax capacity and prison capacity was found not to alter these findings. These results make sense, given the intense public antipathy to crimes against persons; the exception for murder may derive from the fact that a uniform abhorrence of murderers subdues the effect of liberal and conservative ideologies. Therefore, the preferences of the public seem to weigh heavily in the sentencing of violent offenders (other than murderers) but have much less if any effect on the fate of other criminals.

Criminal sentencing is probably the most extensively studied of governmental activities. Analysts have probed the effects of any number of variables—various attributes of the defendant (Myers and Talarico, 1987, offer a good overview of this extensive literature), characteristics of the judge (Myers, 1988, and works cited therein), the legal culture of the jurisdiction (Levin, 1977), and the organizational work routines of the criminal courts (Eisenstein & Jacob, 1977; Nardulli, Fleming, & Eisenstein, 1984). Occasionally, some people have reached beyond the courthouse and examined ecological variables of political units, such as racial composition, income levels, and degree of urbanization (Myers & Talarico, 1987). The purpose of the present article is not to critique any of these approaches to explaining sentencing behavior—for there is nothing flawed in the rationale or in the data collection efforts that this type of research has spawned—but rather to complement them through taking a somewhat different perspective. We take the view that sentencing can profitably be analyzed as a state public policy, a policy outcome lying at the end of a long chain of decisions by legislatures, bureaucracies, and courts. The literature on comparative state policy, therefore, is a useful intellectual departure point for examining the sentences meted out to lawbreakers.

PUBLIC OPINION AND COMPARATIVE STATE POLICY

For many years the major debate among those who studied state policy was whether socioeconomic variables or political variables (such as the degree of party competition) were the more important determinants of policy outcomes. Following in the steps of the early efforts of Dawson and Robinson (1963) and Dye (1966), an entire subfield developed that was devoted to redefining the independent and dependent variables and constructing ever more elegant tests (Wright, Erikson, & McIver, 1987). The avalanche of articles and papers often degenerated into what Uslaner called a contest over "whether scholar X's measure of a given variable is really that much better than scholar Y's" (Uslaner, 1978, p. 140). In general, the research results pointed to a greater role for socioeconomic factors, a finding that was clearly disturbing to political scientists.

Somewhat curiously, most of these studies ignored the possible role that public preferences might play in determining public policy. Students of more authoritarian polities might be excused for looking elsewhere for explanatory factors, but the relative openness of the American states surely suggests that if public opinion is relevant anywhere it is relevant here. In fact, students of the comparative politics of democratic nations have long attributed a good deal of strength to public preferences (see King, 1973). Certainly the magnitude of differences in political culture is greater across nations, and it is therefore easier to study public opinion and to separate it from other effects, but the American states are far from uniform in their political cultures, as any traveler can testify (see Pierce & Hagstrom, 1983). Plausibly, these differences in attitudes should show up in public policy. In fact, most of us, if queried about the difference in education policy between, say, Iowa and Alabama, would immediately adduce a cultural and attitudinal explanation.

Some studies began to examine public attitudes after Elazar (1972) offered his famous classification of subcultures. Lowery (1987), for example, combined these categories with party control of the legislature and governorship to develop one independent variable that might explain variations in state tax policy. Nice (1983) used the percentages of votes cast for George McGovern in 1972 to develop a scale for liberalism, which he then tried to correlate with several policies. Erikson (1978) conducted an analysis of state policies in the 1930s and correlated them to public opinion polls taken then, when Gallup samples were much larger. Plotnick and Winters (1985) have recently devised an intriguing index consisting of contributions to the United Way and federal income tax deductions for charitable contributions; supposedly the index measures sympathy for redistributive policies.

By far the most comprehensive and sophisticated study of public opinion and public policy, however, has been conducted by Wright, Erikson, and McIver (1987), who combined all CBS News/*New York Times* polls from

1976 to 1982, many of which had questions asking for ideological self-identification. These aggregations produced usable measures for every state except Nevada. It was then possible to construct a "conservatism" score for 48 states (or, by reversing the coefficients, a "liberalism" score), including an estimate for Nevada.[1] The scores were next weighted to reflect voting turnout. The authors believed that this "measure of state ideology in the late 1970s and early 1980s is, conceivably, a reasonable reflection of state ideology throughout, say, most of the post-World War II era" (Wright, Erikson, & McIver, 1987, p. 998). For their substantive analysis, they constructed measures of policy liberalism for eight policy areas (including criminal justice), each of which showed significant correlations with public opinion. When controls were introduced for spurious correlations, the correlations held. In short, the authors concluded that, "across an impressive range of policies, public opinion counts, and not just a little" (Wright, Erikson, & McIver, 1987, p. 999). Seemingly, therefore, there are solid grounds for believing that sentences should be affected by public opinion.

Several disparate studies of sentencing, in fact, lend some credence to that belief. For example, Cox (1984) found that the top and bottom 10 states in terms of prison population per 100,000 persons and as a percentage of the total in custody correlated well with Elazar's political subcultures and with little else. Cook (1977) argued that federal district courts, in their sentencing of draft offenders during the Vietnam war, were sensitive to public opinion and its shifts.[2] Levin (1977) found significant differences in the sentencing practices of judges in Pittsburgh and Minneapolis and attributed at least part of it to differences in political beliefs. Myers and Talarico (1987) uncovered differences in jurisdictions having different racial compositions and in urban and rural sentencing patterns in Georgia, but they argued that public values may be as important in explaining this phenomenon as demographics, particularly because there was no simple urban/rural correlation in either case. More tenuously, Gruhl, Welch, and Spohn (1981) found that both black and women judges were more evenhanded in sentencing offenders in "Metro City" than white males, a finding that accorded with Gottschall's earlier discovery (1983) of significant differences between black and white federal judges' handling of appeals cases involving criminal defendants and prisoners' rights.[3] To some degree, Welch, Gruhl, and Spohn argued, this evenhandedness flows from a desire on the judges' part to "represent" their respective communities. If so, it seems equally likely that trial court judges consider themselves analogously regarding their local communities.

---

[1]The CBS News/*New York Times* poll omitted Alaska and Hawaii.

[2]However, see the critique of some of her measures in Kritzer (1979a) and the more general discussion in Kritzer (1979b).

[3]However, see Walker and Barrow (1985) for evidence that the appointments made little difference. Like Gottschall, though, Walker and Barrow focused on an area other than sentencing.

METHODOLOGY

For many years, the study of comparative sentencing has been hampered by a serious lack of data and by the lack of comparability in the data that were available. Few states collect sentencing data systematically, and this deficiency has meant that researchers have had to search through the original records of trial courts. This daunting task has inevitably limited most research efforts to a handful of jurisdictions at most. Furthermore, because different states define felonies in different ways it is difficult for investigators to make meaningful comparisons across states. For example, the dollar amounts for grand larceny vary considerably from one state to the next.

Fortunately, the National Institute of Justice has now published a solid body of data derived from 1986 felony sentencing in 96 counties representing 32 states.[4] The Institute has taken considerable time and effort to carefully compare state statutes and arrive at standard definitions of the felonies used in the data base. According to the BJS, "state felony statutes in force in 1986 were identified in each state's annotated code. At the same time, the wording of individual felony statutes was closely examined to determine the appropriate NJRP offense classification code for each statute" (Inter-University Consortium for Political and Social Research, 1991, p. 65).[5]

From these data, an adjusted mean sentence was constructed for each crime for each state.[6] This adjusted mean, which became the dependent

---

[4] The data for this paper were gathered by the United States Department of Justice, Bureau of Justice Statistics, National Judicial Reporting Program (NJRP) and were provided to the researchers through the Inter-University Consortium for Political and Social Research (ICPSR Study Number 9073), 1991. For more complete information on the data set, see Bureau of Justice Statistics (1990). Neither the collector of the original data nor the consortium bear any responsibility for the analyses or interpretations presented here. The data, which were aggregated to both the county and state levels, are based on a sample of 55,966 convicted felons sentenced in state courts in 1986. The NJRP used a two-stage stratified cluster sampling design. Weighting was not relevant to our research design. The National Judicial Reporting Program used each state's 1986 annotated code to classify each felony in one of eight categories.

One major concern with this type of research is sample selection bias, which results from the manner in which the sample is selected and means that the regression coefficients may not accurately estimate the true causal effects. Instead, the results may be confounded by the way in which individuals are selected to reach the sentencing stage in the judicial process. For example, some counties may have prosecuting attorneys who are very lax and allow everyone but the most serious offenders to be released without being sentenced. These counties might appear to have the most harsh sentences, because only the most serious offenders are being sentenced. However, it is our belief that in the case of these felonies, particularly the most serious felonies, all defendants will be sentenced, not merely released. For crimes such as larceny, of course, the risk of sample selection bias is greater. For these less serious crimes there is simply a greater chance of the exercise of discretion throughout the whole judicial process, starting with the arresting officer.

Sample selection bias is not as serious a problem here as it often is, because the sentences have been broken down by seriousness. When this is done, according to Myers and Talarico (1986), "for two reasons the hazard rate is almost a surrogate for, and consequently controls for the effect of, offense seriousness. First, it is strongly determined by offense seriousness. Second, in preliminary equations including both variables, the regression estimates for two variables were correlated at -.95" (p. 378, note 8). Thus, if offense seriousness and the hazard rate are the same, running separate regressions on the various types of offenses should deal with the problem.

[5] For more complete information, consult Logan, Stellwagen, and Langan (1987).

[6] The mean sentence used here is the maximum prison sentence, coded in months, for the most serious felony offense. This measure does not include offenders who did not receive prison terms, and the study did

variable, was calculated as the mean sentence weighted according to the number of cases from the various counties. Therefore, a county with many criminals sentenced had a greater impact on the mean than one with only a few. The independent variable is the conservatism score assigned to each state by the Wright-Erikson-McIver article. The data are presented in Table 1. The hypothesis is that the higher a state scores on the conservatism scale the longer that state's sentences should be.

Table 1

Mean Sentences and State Conservatism Scores

State	Homicide	Rape	Assault	Robbery	Burglary	Larceny	Drug	Conservatism
Arizona	181	111	78	106	60	43	71	.20
California	214	a	55	49	38	26	35	.05
Colorado	276	243	98	126	91	75	75	.08
Connecticut	240	68	47	65	94	30	46	.05
Florida	208	164	62	77	44	33	53	.16
Georgia	262	143	60	110	47	36	39	.15
Hawaii	340	179	97	160	108	62	166	—
Illinois	222	100	60	82	55	27	55	.10
Indiana	344	175	100	109	60	20	a	.17
Kansas	257	205	128	227	113	50	138	.14
Kentucky	265	170	91	116	54	40	64	.13
Louisiana	271	229	96	148	54	33	67	.21
Maryland	276	169	85	89	60	35	44	.07
Massachusetts	—	131	85	119	—	73	86	.01
Michigan	181	214	50	126	140	65	a	.09
Minnesota	169	85	41	50	36	21	22	.13
Missouri	408	155	93	189	66	49	98	.14
Nevada	557	416	84	109	78	50	65	.20
New Jersey	252	109	70	148	60	a	56	.02
New York	313	148	102	104	69	42	155	.04
North Carolina	—	120	50	115	47	36	33	.22
Ohio	362	243	135	236	122	22	36	.10
Oklahoma	393	638	123	204	61	45	59	.28
Oregon	406	179	100	113	81	56	78	.10
Pennsylvania	295	140	89	91	86	49	78	.10
South Carolina	a	a	45	a	52	17	15	.26
Tennessee	252	148	59	182	69	50	48	.18
Texas	325	198	82	159	94	64	107	.22
Utah	a	638	298	483	55	84	a	.33
Virginia	290	182	95	218	130	a	153	.20
Washington	171	71	44	52	31	23	23	.09
Wisconsin	197	87	35	85	48	32	33	.11

Note. Mean sentence is given in months for the most serious felony sentence.
"a" indicates five cases or fewer, which were omitted from the analysis.
— indicates that data were not available from BJS study.

not have any method to determine actual time served.

To make it possible to have an interval scale, life sentences and death sentences had to be assigned a value in months. We believed that 420 months was an appropriate approximation for life sentences with the possibility of parole, and 480 months when there was no possibility for parole. In the case of death sentences, 720 months was believed to be a useful approximation.

One question immediately arises concerning the unit of analysis, in that county-level sentencing data are being correlated with state-level opinion data. This is admittedly a potentially serious problem, but two factors weaken its impact.

One is that sentencing is not solely in the hands of a local-level decision maker. First, the minimums and maximums, along with a variety of guidelines, are set by the state legislatures. In some states, for example, the legislature sets "presumptive guidelines," such as those in Minnesota, which provide that all violent offenders should be incarcerated for some period. Second, a variety of pressures conspire to press for uniformity across a state. Formal networks, such as judicial conferences, and informal contacts among judges and prosecutors are very important. Moreover, the court system itself is a creature of the state government, and its hierarchical structure brings its disparate parts into at least a rudimentary system. Inevitably, too, when study groups or commissions on sentencing are set up, they are state-level bodies. Third, judicial selection patterns often allow state-level factors to enter. This is most clear in the case of gubernatorial appointment, but merit systems are also subject to this feature. The governor's appointments to the commissions usually have statewide connections, and often so do the others. Even when judicial elections are employed, the districts are often larger than an individual county. Furthermore, research has shown that even in states with judicial elections about half the judges come to office through gubernatorial appointment (Stumpf, 1988, p. 173).

The other factor that mitigates the levels-of-analysis problem is that, in those states that have only one county represented, that county is usually the state's largest and thus would contribute disproportionately to the state-level variable, public preferences.[7]

To buttress this claim, within the data set the variation between states is greater than the variation within states. Table 2 presents the F statistics and significances for the analysis of variance (ANOVA) for all states that have more than three counties in the data set. Note that for all but one category of crime considered in this article the likelihood that the variation occurred by chance is less than 1 in 100. This fact strongly suggests that states internally exhibit a significant degree of uniformity in sentencing. In sum, it seems that sentences, although handed down formally by local courts, in actuality reflect state as much as local policies.

---

[7]This fact means that the present analysis is skewed toward urban areas, and some scholars have argued that there are differences between urban and rural sentencing practices. For examples see Austin (1981), Hagan (1977), and Myers and Talarico (1986).

Table 2

ANOVA of Mean Sentence by County and State

Crime	*F* statistic	Significance
Homicide	5.7	.01
Rape	15.8	.00
Assault	1.5	.22
Robbery	10.5	.00
Burglary	8.4	.00
Larceny	17.9	.00
Drug offenses	14.7	.00
Other	6.9	.00

DISCUSSION

Table 3 shows the standardized beta weights, the significance levels, and R-squares for the regression. As it turns out, only three crimes—assault, rape, and robbery—are significantly correlated with public preferences. For the others—homicide, larceny, burglary, and drug offenses—there is no discernible influence for public opinion. In gross terms, the public opinion hypothesis does very badly.

Table 3

Regression of Conservatism, Prison Capacity, and Tax Capacity With Sentences

Crime	Conservatism	Prison capacity	Tax capacity	R^2
Homicide	-.01	——	——	.00
	.04	.11	.55**	.31
Rape	.50**	——	——	.25
	.54**	.12	.00	.26
Assault	.45**	——	——	.21
	.46*	.09	-.02	.19
Robbery	.50**	——	——	.25
	.55**	.14	-.11	.26
Burglary	-.05	——	——	.00
	.08	.49**	-.04	.22
Larceny	.15	——	——	.02
	.21	.19	.10	.07
Drug offenses	-.11	——	——	.01
	-.11	.01	.19	.05

Note. These equations give the estimated standardized beta coefficients with adjusted mean sentence. Prison capacity is percentage of capacity in 1987 based on Bureau of Justice Statistics data cited in Skogan (1990, p. 395). Tax capacity is relative tax capacity for 1982 based on Advisory Commission on Intergovernmental Relations data cited in Aronson and Hilley (1986, p. 41).
* $p \leq .05$ ** $p \leq .01$

Perhaps, therefore, sentencing is not related to how the public feels. The criminal justice professionals may set their own agenda, or possibly they take their cues exclusively from an elite political culture that is detached from mass political culture. Or, perhaps, the assumption about state-level attitudes is incorrect, and local opinion would do a better job of predicting sentences.

However, a close examination of the regression coefficients reveals that the hypothesis may not be completely nullified. First, let us remove homicide. This is such a heinous crime that it could be argued that almost everyone, whatever their political orientation, is in favor of harsh sentences for murderers. Therefore it may not be a good measure of the sensitivity of sentencing policy to public opinion. The remaining crimes divide neatly into crimes against people and offenses against property or transactional crimes. The public opinion hypothesis seems to predict the sentences given in the former group rather well. In fact, for these three crimes, more than 21 percent of the variance in the dependent variable, mean maximum sentence, is explained by one variable, a state's conservatism.

These results are plausible insofar as the public reacts to crimes against people more strongly than to crimes involving property, and these intense feelings are communicated to those in power. It is primarily violent crimes that lead to lurid articles in the newspapers and that breed the greatest public outrage. When most people speak of fear of crime, they usually have these three violent crimes in mind: the random rape, the brutal assault on an innocent stranger, the robbery of a wallet at gunpoint. Therefore, although citizens in conservative states may favor lengthy sentences for those who commit property crimes, they do not feel as intensely about the matter, and this opens the door to other variables.

RESOURCE CAPACITY

One alternative, or at least mitigating, variable that needs to be examined is resource capacity. The amount of prison space a state has, or conceivably the amount it can afford to build, could affect the sentences that judges impose. Thus, in a very conservative but poor state sentences might be lighter than in an equally conservative but wealthy state because the former has less space to house the convicted.[8]

To introduce a control for this variable, a multiple regression analysis was conducted using the state conservatism scores, prison capacity, and tax capacity as independent variables. This analysis is also presented in Table 3. For the three violent non-homicidal crimes, public opinion proved to be dramatically more important than either of the other variables. It seems,

---

[8]The literature is rather thin on the direct effect of resource constraints on sentencing. However, Finn (1984) does address this issue. According to his survey, "nearly half the judges (15) reported that the capacity of prison facilities in their states has been a factor in the sentencing decision of felony court judges" (p. 322).

therefore, that resource capacity has only a minimal effect on sentences for these crimes.[9]

CONCLUSION

Because sentencing criminals lies at the core of government's activities, it offers important clues into the ways in which political structures operate. From the analyses presented here, it would appear that the preferences of the public at large weigh heavily in the sentencing of violent offenders (other than murderers) but have much less, if any, effect on the fate of other criminals. Precisely how the public's attitudes filter into the decision-making process and why they have so little effect on nonviolent offenders offer important avenues for further research.

REFERENCES

Aronson, R. J., & Hilley, J. L. (1986). *Financing state and local government.* Washington, DC: Brookings Institute.

Austin, T. L. (1981). The influence of court location on type of criminal sentence: The rural-urban factor. *Journal of Criminal Justice, 9,* 305-316.

Bureau of Justice Statistics, United States Department of Justice. (1990). *Special report: Felony case processing in state courts, 1986.* Washington, DC: United States Department of Justice.

Cook, B. B. (1977). Public opinion and federal judicial policy. *American Journal of Political Science, 21,* 567-600.

Cox, G. (1984). Values, culture, and prison policy. *Prison Journal, 64,* 5-15.

Dawson, R. E., & Robinson, J. A. (1963). Inter-party competition, economic variables, and welfare policies in the American states. *Journal of Politics, 25,* 265-289.

Dye, T. R. (1966). *Politics, economics, and the public.* Chicago, IL: Rand McNally.

Eisenstein, J., & Jacob, H. (1977). *Felony justice: An organizational analysis of criminal courts.* Boston, MA: Little, Brown.

Elazar, D. (1972). *American federalism: A view from the states* (2nd ed.). New York, NY: Crowell.

Erikson, R. (1978). The relationship between public opinion and state policy: A new look based on some forgotten data. *American Journal of Political Science, 20,* 25-38.

Finn, P. (1984). Judicial responses to prison crowding. *Judicature, 67,* 319-325.

Gottschall, J. (1983). Carter's judicial appointments: The influence of affirmative action and merit selection on voting on the U.S. Court of Appeals. *Judicature, 67,* 165-173.

Gruhl, J., Welch, S., & Spohn, C. (1981). Women as policy makers: The case of trial judges. *American Journal of Political Science, 25,* 308-322.

Hagan, J. (1977). Criminal justice in rural and urban communities: A study of the bureaucratization of justice. *Social Forces, 55,* 597-612.

Inter-University Consortium for Political and Social Research. (1991). *Codebook for study number 9073.* Ann Arbor, MI: Author.

King, A. (1973). Ideas, institutions and the policies of governments: A comparative analysis. *British Journal of Political Science, 3,* 291-313 and 409-423.

Kritzer, H. (1979a). Federal judges and their political environments: The influence of public opinion. *American Journal of Political Science, 23,* 194-205.

Kritzer, H. (1979b). Political culture, trial courts and criminal cases. In P. Nardulli (Ed.), *The study of criminal courts: Political perspectives* (pp. 131-169). Cambridge, MA: Ballinger.

Levin, M. (1977). *Urban politics and the criminal courts.* Chicago, IL: University of Chicago Press.

---

[9]The effects of tax capacity on homicide and of prison capacity on burglary are intriguing and in need of investigation.

Logan, W., Stellwagen, L. A., & Langan, P. A. (1987). *Felony laws of the 50 states and the District of Columbia*. Washington, DC: U.S. Department of Justice, Bureau of Justice Statistics.

Lowery, D. (1987). The distribution of tax burdens in the American states. *Western Political Quarterly, 40*, 137-158.

Myers, M. (1988). Social background and the sentencing behavior of judges. *Criminology, 26*, 649-675.

Myers, M., & Talarico, S. (1986). Urban justice, rural injustice? Urbanization and its effect on sentencing. *Criminology, 24*, 367-391.

Myers, M., & Talarico, S. (1987). *The social context of criminal sentencing*. New York, NY: Springer-Verlag.

Nardulli, P., Fleming, R., & Eisenstein, J. (1984). Unraveling the complexities of decision making in face-to-face groups: A contextual analysis of plea-bargained sentences. *American Political Science Review, 78*, 912-928.

Nice, D. (1983). Representation in the states: Policymaking and ideology. *Social Science Quarterly, 64*, 404-411.

Pierce, N., & Hagstrom, J. (1983). *The book of America: Inside the 50 states today*. New York, NY: Norton.

Plotnick, R., & Winters, R. (1985). A politico-economic theory of income redistribution. *American Political Science Review, 79*, 458-473.

Skogan, W. (1990). Crime and punishment. In V. Gray, H. Jacob, & R. B. Albritton (Eds.), *Politics in the American states*. Glenview, IL: Little, Brown.

Stumpf, H. (1988). *American judicial politics*. San Diego, CA: Harcourt, Brace, Jovanovich.

Uslaner, E. (1978). Comparative state policy formation, interparty competition and malapportionment: A new look at V. O. Key's hypothesis. *Journal of Politics, 40*, 409-432.

Walker, T., & Barrow, D. (1985). The diversification of the federal bench: Policy and process ramifications. *Journal of Politics, 47*, 596-616.

Welch, S., Gruhl, J., & Spohn, C. (1988). Do black judges make a difference? *American Journal of Political Science, 32*, 126-136.

Wright, G., Erikson, R., & McIver, J. (1987). Public opinion and policy liberalism in the American states. *American Journal of Political Science, 31*, 980-1001.

Law and Human Behavior, Vol. 16, No. 4, 1992

Measuring the Effects of the Guilty but Mentally Ill (GBMI) Verdict

Georgia's 1982 GBMI Reform*

Lisa A. Callahan,† Margaret A. McGreevy,‡
Carmen Cirincione,‡ and Henry J. Steadman‡

We studied effects of guilty but mentally ill (GBMI) legislation on use of the insanity defense in Georgia using data on all defendants entering an insanity plea before (1976–1981) and after (1982–1985) the introduction of the GBMI verdict. In contrast to earlier studies, our results indicated that GBMI did decrease the likelihood of an insanity verdict and affected the composition of those found not guilty by reason of insanity. Defendants pleading insanity and found GBMI were typically white males with a serious mental disorder, charged with murder or robbery in which an unrelated female victim was involved. The data also indicated that defendants who pleaded insanity and were found GBMI received harsher sentences than their guilty counterparts. We conclude that the GBMI verdict will make the insanity plea a less appealing option for mentally ill defendants.

In the face of public concerns for longer and more secure detention of defendants acquitted by reason of insanity, one of the more popular revisions of insanity defense procedures in the United States during the past 15 years has been the guilty but mentally ill (GBMI) verdict. The GBMI verdict was first adopted in Michigan (1975) in the aftermath of the Michigan Supreme Court ruling in *People v. McQuillan* (1974). That ruling struck down the state's automatic commitment law and ultimately resulted in the release of approximately 150 insanity acquittees who did not currently meet civil commitment standards (Smith & Hall, 1982).

---

* Requests for reprints should be sent to Margaret McGreevy, Policy Research Associates, 262 Delaware Ave., Delmar, NY 12054.
† Russell Sage College.
‡ Policy Research Associates.

0147-7307/92/0800-0447$06.50/0 © 1992 Plenum Publishing Corporation

Several other states, including Indiana, Illinois, and New Mexico, adopted the GBMI verdict during the late 1970s and early 1980s as tensions surrounding the use of the insanity defense heightened. Following John Hinckley's attempted assassination of President Reagan and his subsequent plea of insanity, the Attorney General recommended the adoption of a GBMI verdict in federal courts (Smith & Hall, 1982). In 1982, after Hinckley's not guilty by reason of insanity (NGRI) acquittal, public dissatisfaction with the insanity defense intensified, fostering pervasive calls for reform (Appelbaum, 1982; Hans, 1986). Thirty-four states subsequently made changes in their insanity defense laws, 8 of which enacted GBMI verdicts bringing to 12 the number of states that have passed GBMI legislation (Callahan, Steadman, McGreevy, & Robbins, 1991).

Since Michigan's first enactment of the GBMI option, there has been much debate in the legal community about the GBMI verdict (Fentiman, 1985; Keilitz, 1987; McGraw, Farthing-Capowich, & Keilitz, 1985; Slobogin, 1985). Advocates of GBMI reform believe that this law will protect the public by reducing the number of insanity acquittals and providing lengthy confinement in prisons for those found GBMI. Keilitz states that "legislators hoped that the GBMI verdict would offer juries an attractive alternative to the verdict of not guilty by reason of insanity and thereby curb the use of the insanity plea and verdict and prevent the early release of dangerous individuals" (Keilitz, 1987). On the other hand, many scholars and professionals believe that the GBMI verdict is conceptually flawed and procedurally problematic (McGraw et al., 1985). They argue that the verdict is misleading in that the phrase *but mentally ill* connotes a diminished capacity that is not part of the verdict, and that a more correct phrase would be *guilty and mentally ill* (Petrella et al., 1985; Smith & Hall, 1985). Others have argued that the definitions of mental illness and insanity overlap, making distinctions between them difficult and discretionary (Slobogin, 1985). Another concern is that juries will use it as a compromise verdict and find defendants guilty but mentally ill who actually fit the "legal" definition of insane, in order to ensure their incapacitation.

In general, the courts' reaction to the GBMI verdict has been overwhelmingly supportive. To date, the GBMI verdict has withstood challenges on the grounds of equal protection, due process, cruel and unusual punishment, ex post facto law, and right to treatment (Fentiman, 1985; McGraw et al., 1985). The courts have held that the verdict satisfies legislative intent. Courts have also rejected the contention that it is unfair to excuse those found insane while holding the mentally ill responsible and ruled that the GBMI verdict actually clarified the legal meaning of insanity (*People v. Sorna,* 1979). Further, courts have held that the verdict does not stigmatize the defendant, as, for example, in *Kirkland v. State* (Georgia, 1983), where the court held that the additional finding of mental illness in the GBMI proceedings actually diminished the guilty verdict and offered treatment. In terms of right to treatment issues, the Illinois Appelate Court ruled that there is no constitutional right to treatment for those found GBMI. Similarly, courts in Michigan and Indiana have held that the proper way to address the right to treatment claims is through legal petition to the department of correctional services to provide the mandated services (Fentiman, 1985; McGraw et al., 1985).

The empirical data that exist on the impact of GBMI reforms generally indicate that the reforms have had marginal or no impact (Keilitz, 1987; McGraw et al., 1985; Smith & Hall, 1982). The majority of GBMI research has come from Michigan. To a lesser degree, the experiences of Illinois, Pennsylvania, and Georgia have also been examined. The issue most frequently addressed by prior research is whether GBMI legislation decreased the number of insanity acquittals. In both Michigan and Illinois, the research demonstrated that the GBMI option did not reduce the number of NGRI findings (Blunt & Stock, 1985; Criss & Racine, 1980; Klofas & Weisheit, 1986). The overall conclusion was that while the intent of the Michigan legislation was to reduce insanity acquittals, the number and rate of NGRI findings actually increased following the GBMI enactment (Smith & Hall, 1982). The Illinois data are less extensive than Michigan's, yet the conclusion is similar: NGRI acquittals were not reduced by Illinois's adoption of the GBMI statute. In Georgia, the number of acquittals actually decreased after GBMI, although not immediately (Keilitz, 1987). Although MacKay and Kopelman (1988) determined that NGRI acquittals decreased somewhat following the adoption of the GBMI verdict in Pennsylvania, they hesitate to conclude that the law affected the reduction as there were other changes in insanity defense laws.

In an effort to determine whether those found GBMI were more likely to be drawn from the NGRI or guilty group, Keilitz (1987) analyzed data on GBMI, NGRI, and guilty defendants in Michigan, Illinois, and Georgia. He concluded that the typical GBMI resembled the NGRI on some variables and guilty defendants on others and stressed that more useful results would come from a study of changes in the population pleading insanity and those acquitted NGRI both before and after enactment of GBMI legislation. He also compared the sentences received by a small cohort of GBMI with those of guilty defendants and tentatively concluded that the average GBMI received a longer sentence than the average guilty defendant.

Though prior studies on the GBMI verdict have consistently found that the GBMI verdict has had little impact on use of the insanity defense, as Keilitz (1987) noted, their analyses have examined only the basic differences in the number and composition of insanity acquittals and GBMIs to assess the impacts of GBMI statues. For a clearer picture of what actually happens under GBMI, it is important also to examine the characteristics of all persons pleading insanity before and after the GBMI verdict and how they compare with those found GBMI. Without data on all defendants pleading insanity, and without controls for key factors such as offense and sociodemographic variables, conclusions drawn about the impact of GBMI legislation from NGRI acquittals alone may be misleading. The purpose of the research reported here is to evaluate the impact of Georgia's 1982 GBMI reform on the use of the insanity defense with a range of data not available in prior research. Our sample includes all persons entering an insanity plea in 12 Georgia counties before and after the GBMI alternative was enacted. We also examine data on sentence and the confinement history for those found GBMI in relation to those found guilty and NGRI.

Georgia enacted the GBMI alternative to the insanity defense in 1982 (Ga. Code A. 17-7-131). The GBMI reform was implemented in Georgia shortly after the release of an insanity acquittee who subsequently murdered three people. As in Michigan, the adoption of the GBMI alternative in Georgia closely followed a U.S. District Court's ruling (*Benham v. Edwards*, 1980) in which Georgia's automatic commitment procedure for insanity acquittees was overturned (Hauser, 1981). Georgia's GBMI verdict applies only in felony cases, provides that persons found GBMI be sentenced as if found guilty, allows the GBMI verdict for both NGRI and GBMI pleas, and calls for treatment within available resources. Defendants pleading GBMI waive their right to a trial, must receive a psychiatric exam, and are sentenced after the judge reviews the psychiatric report.

Findings from the more comprehensive data we gathered in Georgia do not fully support the conclusions of prior work: that GBMI statutes have negligible impact on findings of insanity and that defendants found GBMI are drawn primarily from the group that would have been found guilty. Rather, we found that the GBMI statute in Georgia did have an impact on the insanity defense, particularly in the acquittal rate of insanity pleas, that certain types of cases that formerly may have been found NGRI were being found GBMI, and that those found GBMI receive more severe punishment than their guilty counterparts.

METHOD

We collected data in 12 Georgia counties on all persons who were indicted for a felony and pled NGRI from 1976 through 1985 ($N = 2,553$). We obtained 6½ years of data prior to the 1982 GBMI law and 3½ years of post-GBMI data. The counties selected were those that had the most NGRI acquittals prior to the reform. Together they produced 60% of all the state's insanity acquittals. The counties studied ranged in population from approximately 35,000 to 600,000 and varied from rural to highly urbanized.[1] In each county, court dockets were searched to identify all persons raising the insanity defense from 1976 through 1985. In addition, we identified all persons who pled and/or were found GBMI after June 1982, when the new law went into effect. Once all insanity and GBMI pleas were identified, information was obtained from court case files, the Department of Mental Health and Hospitals, and the Department of Corrections. The cases of those persons who were still institutionalized when we completed the initial data collection were followed to determine whether they had been released in the subsequent 3 years. The data obtained include sociodemographics, current criminal charges, victim information, psychiatric diagnosis, and information on sentencing and length of confinement.

The major focus of our analyses was on (1) whether the enactment of a GBMI statute affected the volume and rate of NGRI pleas and acquittals, (2) whether it affected the characteristics of those raising the plea and those acquitted NGRI, (3) how those found GBMI compare to those acquitted NGRI or found guilty, and

---

[1] The counties are Bibb, Chatham, Cherokee, Clarke, Cobb, Dekalb, Dougherty, Floyd, Fulton, Newton, Richmond, and Thomas.

(4) how the confinement careers of NGRIs and GBMIs compare to those found guilty.

RESULTS

Volume of Insanity Pleas and Acquittals

The number of insanity pleas and acquittals in the 12 Georgia counties studied are shown by year in Figure 1. The volume of insanity pleas rose steeply during 1976–1977 and then leveled off to just over 250 per year from 1978 to 1982. The number of insanity pleas increased to over 300 per year in 1983 and 1984 and then returned to its prior level in 1985. The noted increase in insanity pleas did not occur immediately following the July, 1982, changes in the law. In fact, we found that the number of insanity pleas did not show an increase until the last half of 1983 and lasted just one year, after which the number began to diminish again. The delay makes it somewhat difficult to attribute the increase in insanity pleas directly to the GBMI legislation. Other factors, such as the change in the automatic commitment of insanity acquittees and new release procedures that preceded the GBMI legislation, may also have had an impact on the use of the insanity defense in Georgia.

Insanity acquittals, shown in the lower portion of Figure 1, increased steadily from 1976 to 1979 when they peaked at 65. The volume of acquittals decreased in 1980–1982 and then remained relatively stable at 30–35 acquittals per year through 1985. Despite a relatively large increase in the number of insanity pleas in 1983 and 1984, the number of insanity acquittals actually decreased slightly.

Interrupted time series analyses of the plea rate (number of insanity pleas per

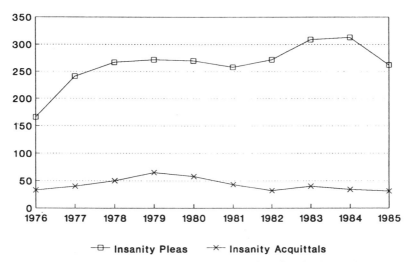

Fig. 1. Number of insanity pleas and acquittals in Georgia 1976–1985.

111

100 felony indictments) and the acquittal rate (number of acquittals divided by the number of insanity pleas) were conducted to determine whether there were any significant changes due to the introduction of the GBMI verdict. Time series designs have been widely used to assess the impact of policy interventions (Campbell & Stanley, 1963; Fox, 1984; Lewis-Beck, 1986; Simonton, 1977). An advantage of the time series design (as opposed to a before–after design) is that it explicitly accounts for trends prior to the intervention. The assessment of the intervention is equal to testing for changes in level (intercept) and/or trend (slope) associated with the introduction of the intervention.

In this study, an F test was used to evaluate the combined changes in the slope (trend) and intercept (level) associated with the introduction of the GBMI reform. This analysis was performed for both the plea rate and the acquittal rate. As can be seen in Table 1, changes in the rate of insanity pleas around the introduction of the GBMI verdict were not statistically significant, although the changes in the acquittal rate were significant. The level of the acquittal rate dropped from .221 (22.1% of insanity pleas were successful) before the GBMI law was passed to .124 (12.4%) after the law.

A further analysis, in which crime was separated into violent offenses (murder, physical assault, and other violent offenses) and nonviolent offenses, revealed striking results. Figure 2 depicts the acquittal rate for violent and nonviolent crimes during the study years. Prior to the reform, the acquittal rate for insanity pleas for violent crimes was substantially higher than that for nonviolent crimes, especially in the 3 years preceding the GBMI law. With the reform came a significant drop in the acquittal rate for violent crimes (29.5% in 1981 to 15.5% in 1982), bringing it down to the level for nonviolent offenses.

These results suggest that the GBMI reform was associated with a change in the success rate of insanity pleas, particularly for violent crimes. These types of crimes, the highly publicized murders and other violent crimes, were what had prompted the call for the GBMI verdict. The fact that the acquittal rate for violent

Table 1. Results of Multiple Regression Equation Assessing Change in Plea and Acquittal Rates Due to 1982 GBMI Legislation

	Pre-GBMI		Post-GBMI		Change	
Rate	Slope	Level	Slope	Level	Slope	Level
Plea rate	− .0004	.016	.0007	.017	.0011	.001
					$F = .266$	
					$p < .77$	
Acquittal rate	.0061	.221	− .0005	.124	− .0066	− .097
					$F = 6.70$	
					$p < .03$	
Violent	.0271	.349	.0154	.123	− .0117	− .226
					$F = 8.33$	
					$p < .02$	
Nonviolent	− .0077	.140	− .0119	.127	− .0042	− .013
					$F = .18$	
					$p < .84$	

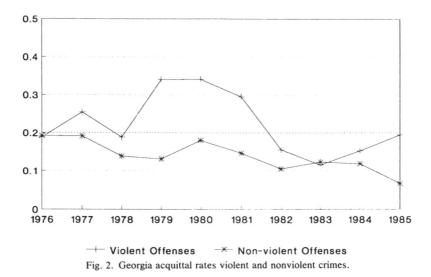

Fig. 2. Georgia acquittal rates violent and nonviolent crimes.

offenses increased in 1984 and 1985 makes any long-term trend unclear. The noted decline in successful use of the insanity defense for violent crimes may simply have been temporary.

Outcome of Insanity Pleas

Figure 3 presents data on the distribution of verdicts for persons pleading NGRI before and after the GBMI law became effective (July, 1982). The percent-

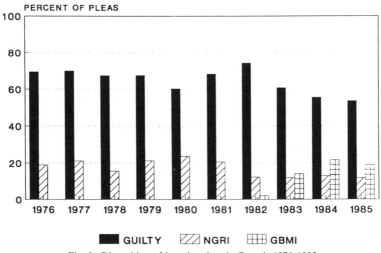

Fig. 3. Disposition of insanity pleas in Georgia 1976–1985.

113

age of pleas resulting in an "other" verdict (not shown), which includes not guilty, withdrawn, dismissed, or pending, remained relatively constant before and after the GBMI verdict, whereas the percentage resulting in a guilty or NGRI verdict both declined following the legislation. Consistent with the data presented above on the acquittal rate, prior to the GBMI reform defendants pleading insanity had about a 20% chance of being successful, whereas after the reform their chances of being successful were 12%. Similarly, the percentage of those pleading insanity who were found guilty dropped from approximately 70% to 55% after the introduction of GBMI. These data suggest that the GBMI group was drawn from both the NGRI and guilty groups.

Characteristics Associated with Outcomes of Insanity Pleas

Prior research suggests that a number of factors are associated with successful insanity pleas. Consistently, the most important factor has been a forensic evaluation recommendation of nonresponsibility and/or a psychiatric diagnosis of schizophrenia (Steadman, Keitner, Braff, & Arvanites, 1983). Other important factors include sociodemographic characteristics as well as variables related to the specific crime and criminal justice processing (Hawkins & Pasewark, 1983; Jeffrey, Pasewark, & Beiber, 1988; Klofas & Weisheit, 1986; Steadman, 1985; Stokeman & Heiber, 1984). Persons who successfully plead NGRI, compared with those who fail with the insanity defense, tend to be older, better educated, black, single, unskilled, and unemployed. Earlier work shows that NGRI acquittals are more likely to occur in violent crimes, and the plea is more successful in crimes where the victim and offender are related. Further, the presence of a jury decreases the chances of an acquittal (Finkel, 1989).

Little is known about what factors are associated with a GBMI verdict. Keilitz (1987) and Klofas and Weisheit (1986) suggest that GBMIs are white males who have committed a violent crime. The range of psychiatric diagnoses associated with a GBMI verdict is broader than that for an NGRI acquittal, but GBMI defendants also tend to have a diagnosed mental disorder.

Data on the characteristics of persons pleading insanity who were ultimately found guilty, NGRI, and GBMI in Georgia before and after the reform are presented in Table 2. We found that the characteristics of those pleading insanity and the subset found guilty showed a number of significant changes from the period preceding the GBMI law to the period following its passage. Generally, the changes observed in the plea group were mirrored in the subset found guilty. For example, the average age of insanity pleas increased from 28 to 30 years pre- to postreform. A similar increase, from 27 to 29 years, was observed in the guilty group. The fact that the majority of those pleading insanity were found guilty (58%–68%) explains much of the observed correlation between the two groups. Other changes seen in the plea and guilty groups after the GBMI verdict were an increase in the percentage of women and minorities, a decrease in the percentage diagnosed with schizophrenia, and an increase in the percentage diagnosed with personality disorder.

Table 2. Composition of Insanity Pleas, and Defendants Found Guilty, NGRI, and GBMI Before and After the Enactment of GBMI Legislation[a]

Characteristics	Insanity pleas		Guilty		Acquittals		GBMI
	Pre (N = 1461)	Post (N = 1114)	Pre (N = 978)	Post (N = 656)	Pre (N = 289)	Post (N = 131)	Post (N = 180)
Age							
X Age	28.1	***30.0	27.0	***29.3	31.2	30.5	30.6
Gender							
Percent Female	8.5	**11.5	7.0	**11.3	13.1	18.3	7.8
Ethnicity							
Percent Minority	61.6	*65.7	59.7	*65.8	65.8	74.8	63.2
Diagnosis							
Percent Schizophrenic	44.3	*38.5	34.1	***23.5	68.7	69.2	53.0
Percent Other maj. MI	11.4	13.1	11.8	12.1	9.9	12.8	16.8
Percent Person. dis.	6.3	11.0	7.6	12.9	3.3	5.1	8.7
Percent Other MI	15.9	14.4	15.0	16.2	16.8	12.0	9.4
Percent No MI	22.0	23.1	31.5	35.4	1.2	0.9	12.1
Crime							
Percent Murder	11.0	10.2	11.2	*9.9	12.5	6.2	18.9
Percent Phys. assault/ other violent	25.0	26.2	23.0	23.2	36.3	41.1	27.8
Percent Robbery	11.8	9.1	13.7	9.3	7.7	4.7	16.1
Percent Property/other minor	52.2	54.5	52.0	57.6	43.5	48.0	37.2
Victimization[b]							
Percent Female victim	41.0	***47.2	45.3	46.0	33.3	33.3	59.3
Percent Not related victim	26.2	36.5	31.1	35.8	16.7	23.8	50.4
Adjudication							
Percent Judge	20.3	***16.3	4.9	2.8	73.3	**86.7	15.1
Percent Jury	16.7	12.2	13.5	12.5	20.0	6.3	9.6
Percent Plea	63.0	71.5	81.6	84.7	6.7	7.0	75.3

[a] Information on defendants found GBMI is only postreform.
[b] Data on victim are only for those crimes with victims.
* $p < .05$.
** $p < .01$.
*** $p < .001$.

It is important to note that pre–post changes occurred among insanity acquittals that were of similar or greater magnitude but did not show statistical significance due to the relatively small N of the pre and post cohorts. For example, the increase in the percentage of female and nonwhite insanity acquittees after the GBMI verdict was of a larger magnitude than the increases in either the plea or guilty groups yet they were only marginally significant ($p < .10$) compared to the other groups. Similar changes occurred in diagnosis.

The only significant change seen in the crime categories occurred in the guilty cohort. There was a decline in the proportion of insanity pleas found guilty of murder and robbery and an increase in property crimes after the GBMI verdict was enacted. As above, the changes observed in the target offenses for insanity acquittals pre- and post-GBMI did not reach statistical significance but were of greater magnitude than changes observed in the guilty group. Insanity acquittees were about half as likely to be acquitted of murder or robbery charges after the introduction of GBMI as prior to the reform.

There were also major pre–post changes in the variables related to victim-

115

ization. These data reported are only for crimes in which there were victims, that is, murder, physical assault, other violent crimes, and robbery.[2] Significantly larger percentages of defendants charged with crimes in which there were female and/or unrelated victims pled insanity after the GBMI verdict was introduced than before. There was little change in the percentage of persons found guilty or acquitted NGRI who were charged with these types of crimes. The noted increase in the plea group was largely reflected in those found GBMI.

There were significant differences in the method of adjudication for the plea group as a whole as well as for those acquitted NGRI before and after the GBMI law. A significantly larger percentage of the plea group was adjudicated by a plea following the GBMI legislation as compared with earlier years. Among the NGRIs, there was a decrease in jury trials and a concommitant increase in those acquitted by bench trials. A comparison across the three groups in the postreform period revealed significant differences in the method of adjudication. The large majority of guilty and GBMI verdicts came from a plea or plea bargain, whereas the vast majority of insanity acquittals resulted from a bench trial.

A multinomial logit regression was run on the post-GBMI data to determine which variables were associated with the respective verdict groups: GBMI, NGRI, and guilty. Table 3 presents the coefficient and the odds ratio for the major independent variables shown in Table 2. The cohort of guilty defendants was used as the reference group to predict those found NGRI and GBMI. The results presented are based on the sample of post-GBMI cases in which data were available for all the independent variables except those related to victimization. We excluded a large number of guilty defendants for whom we did not have information on diagnosis.[3]

The odds ratio provides an estimate of the "odds" of someone with the independent characteristic (male) falling into the predicted group compared to the reference (guilty) group. A 1.0 indicates an equal likelihood of the variable for both groups. For example, we found that males were one third (.34) as likely to be found NGRI as guilty, a statistically significant result. In contrast, males were almost as likely (.90) to be found GBMI as guilty. Minorities were somewhat less likely (.89) to be found NGRI than guilty and significantly less likely (.61) to be found GBMI than guilty as compared to whites.

The findings present a predictable pattern for diagnosis. As expected, defendants who were diagnosed as schizophrenic as compared to other mental illness (the diagnostic category to which all other categories were compared) were significantly more likely to be found either NGRI (3.69) or GBMI (4.94) than guilty. Those diagnosed as "not mentally ill" were less likely to be found GBMI (.50) and significantly less likely to be found NGRI (.03) than guilty.

Violent offenses are clearly associated with being found NGRI or GBMI.

---

[2] These data are reported because they offer new insights into the make-up of the GBMI population; however, it is important to note that information was missing in a considerably high percentage (25%) of cases.

[3] We performed a similar analysis in which cases with missing information were placed in the excluded or omitted category. The results were quite consistent with those presented.

Table 3. Results of Multinomial Regression Predicting NGRI and GBMI Verdicts with Guilty Verdict as Reference Group

Factors	Prediction of NGRI		Prediction of GBMI	
	B	Odds ratio	B	Odds ratio
Sociodemographic				
Male	** − 1.087	.34	− 0.101	.90
Minority	− 0.116	.89	* − 0.493	.61
Diagnosis				
Schizophrenia	***1.305	3.69	***1.597	4.94
Other psychosis	0.401	1.49	0.844	2.33
Personality disorder	− 0.684	.50	0.123	1.13
Not mentally ill	*** − 3.504	.03	− 0.692	.50
Target Offense				
Murder	− 0.327	.72	***1.230	3.42
Physical assault	**0.872	2.39	*0.613	1.84
Other violent	0.939	2.55	0.114	1.12
Robbery	− 0.814	.44	0.343	1.41
Victimization				
Female victim	− 0.095	.91	0.280	1.32
Unrelated victim	− 0.232	.79	*0.434	1.54
Trial by jury	** − 1.473	.23	** − 0.902	.41

Note. This analysis includes 609 cases in which data were available for all the independent variables except those related to victimization. Cases with missing data on the victim's gender ($N = 81$) and relationship ($N = 168$) to defendant was included in the omitted category for this analyses.
  * $p < .05$.
 ** $p < .01$.
*** $p < .001$.

Someone who committed a murder and pled NGRI was significantly more likely to be found GBMI (3.42) than guilty. Similarly, those who committed physical assault and pled NGRI were significantly more likely to be found NGRI (2.39) or GBMI (1.84) than guilty. Further, GBMIs were more than twice as likely (2.38) to offend against unrelated victims. A jury trial was significantly less likely to result in either an NGRI (.23) or GBMI (.41) verdict than a guilty verdict.

Differences between insanity acquittals and those pleading insanity who were found GBMI can also be assessed with these results. For instance, someone charged with murder and pleading insanity was five times (3.42 divided by .72) more likely to be found GBMI than acquitted by reason of insanity. Similarly, a defendant charged with robbery and pleading insanity was three times as likely to be found GBMI as NGRI. Other major distinctions between those acquitted NGRI and those found GBMI appear in gender, diagnosis, and victim. A male pleading insanity was two and one half times more likely than a female to be found GBMI than NGRI. Someone diagnosed with a personality disorder was twice as likely to be found GBMI than NGRI, and someone committing an offense against an unrelated victim was nearly four times as likely to be GBMI as NGRI.

Our data support earlier observations that the prototypical GBMI is a white male with a serious mental disorder, who commits murder, particularly if his victim is an unrelated female. After the introduction of the GBMI verdict, the

117

prototypical NGRI is a female, diagnosed with schizophrenia, and charged with physical assault or a minor felony. The defendant pleading insanity who is most likely to be found guilty in Georgia is a nonwhite male with a personality disorder or no mental illness who commits robbery, a property crime, or a minor felony.

Sentencing and Lengths of Confinement

The Georgia GBMI law states that defendants who plead NGRI but are found GBMI shall be sentenced in the same manner as defendants found guilty (Ga. Code A. 17-7-131). Four approaches were used to determine whether those defendants pleading insanity who were found GBMI were punished equitably. First, we compared the proportion of each group sentenced to prison, jail, or the hospital. Nearly all NGRIs (98.4%) were hospitalized following acquittal. For the GBMI verdict group, 80% went to prison, 1.7% to jail, and 16.7% were given probation. Only 3 people went to a psychiatric hospital. Defendants pleading insanity and found guilty were confined least often, with 62.8% going to prison, 7.5% to jail, and the remaining 29.3% being placed on probation or released outright. A comparison of the GBMI with the guilty indicated that a greater proportion of the GBMI were imprisoned for all crime types except robbery. The differences were statistically significant ($p < .05$) for physical assaults and minor crimes.

Next, we compared the sentences received by GBMI and guilty defendants; NGRIs do not receive a sentence so they are not included in these analyses. We found that GBMI defendants (14%) were significantly ($p < .01$) more likely than guilty defendants (5.5%) to receive a life sentence. For murder, 70.6% of GBMIs as compared to 49.2% of guilty defendants received life sentences. For those defendants not receiving a life sentence, we disaggregated the data by crime and examined the differences in the average sentence. Sentences for GBMIs were typically longer than for those found guilty, and the differences were significantly larger for murder and minor crimes. For murder, the typical sentence for a GBMI was 5 years longer than for a guilty defendant.

Length of confinement was assessed using a Cox proportional hazards model to evaluate the chances of release of all three verdict groups (NGRI, GBMI, and guilty). The model was used to predict the "hazard" of release, which is the probability of being released at a specific point in time given that one has not been previously released (Allison, 1984; Blassfeld, 1989; Schmidt, 1988). This approach is particularly well suited for data such as ours where many of the defendants are still confined. These data are referred to as "censored." Data on their length of confinement can be used in the analyses up until the point that they become censored.[4] The data in Table 4 require some explanation. For the crimes presented, each is compared to minor crimes. In other words, the chance of release for murder is 14% of the probability of release for minor crimes, whereas the chances for the release for the other three crimes are about half that of minor

---

[4] We recorded lengths of confinement as the date of admission after verdict to the date of release. If a defendant was not released by November, 1989, that date was used as the time of "censoring."

Table 4. Prediction of Release into
Community (Cox Proportional
Hazards Results)

	B[a]	Hazard multiplier[b]
Crime		
Murder	*** − 1.968	.14
Physical assault	*** − .679	.51
Other violent	*** − .652	.52
Robbery	*** − .800	.45
Verdict		
NGRI	.279	1.32
GBMI	− .282	.75

[a] These numbers represent the relative height of the hazard for the different crimes and verdict groups as compared to the omitted categories. Positive values represent a higher probability while negative values represent the opposite.
[b] These figures are calculated by exponentiating the coefficients in the model.
* $p < .05$.
** $p < .01$.
*** $p < .001$.

crimes. These results indicate that, as expected, the probability of release is lower for more serious crimes.

The fourth comparison is of length of confinement among the three verdict groups with guilty serving as the comparison. NGRIs are 1.32 times more likely than the guilty to be released, while GBMI defendants were .75 times as likely to be released as the guilty. Given their increased likelihood of receiving life sentences and longer sentences, it was not surprising that they were the least likely to be returned to the community.

What these four analytic strategies demonstrate is that no matter how one defines *punishment,* whether it be likelihood of imprisonment, likelihood of life sentence, length of sentence, or time served, GBMI defendants fared the least well of the three verdict groups. GBMIs were more likely than guilty defendants to go to prison, to receive life sentences, and to receive longer sentences for the same crimes. And they were the least likely of the three groups to return to the community.

DISCUSSION

Contrary to the findings from earlier work, our data suggest that the GBMI verdict was associated with changes in the use of the insanity defense in Georgia. Although the introduction of the GBMI alternative did not affect the rate of insanity pleas, other changes did occur. There was a decrease in both the number and rate of insanity acquittals, especially those associated with the most violent offenses; the proportion of insanity pleas found guilty and NGRI both decreased; and there were significant changes in the characteristics of those pleading insanity following the introduction of the GBMI verdict. After 1982, the population raising the insanity plea was older and comprised of more women, nonwhites, and individuals diagnosed with personality disorders. Similar changes were seen in the subset that were found guilty. Although the changes observed in the characteristics of those acquitted NGRI did not reach statistical significance, they were of comparable magnitude to changes in the plea and guilty groups and indicated that more women, more minorities, and fewer persons charged with murder or robbery were acquitted NGRI after the introduction of the GBMI verdict.

There was other evidence to suggest that some GBMIs were drawn from the NGRI group. The distribution of verdicts for insanity pleas showed a decline in the proportion found guilty and NGRI after the GBMI verdict was introduced, suggesting that those found GBMI were pulled from both groups. This, in conjunction with the significant decline in the acquittal rate, especially among those acquitted of violent crimes, suggests that the GBMI verdict did impact on the insanity defense. Further, those found GBMI differed significantly from the other two groups in their characteristics, crimes, and path through the system. The results of the logit analysis indicated that GBMI drew some of the seriously mentally ill males charged with murder or robbery from both the NGRI and guilty groups. GBMIs were also more likely to have offended against an unrelated victim than either of the other two groups.

Like Keilitz (1987), we found that defendants pleading insanity who were found GBMI were more likely to be confined, received longer sentences, and were imprisoned for longer periods of time than those pleading insanity and found guilty of similar offenses. The GBMI verdict seems to provide a means of assuring long terms of confinement for mentally ill offenders who have committed violent offenses. Our data clearly contradict the notion, put forth by the court in the *Kirkland* case, that GBMI has a diminishing effect on a guilty verdict.

Nor does the GBMI verdict appear to be a compromise verdict that results in both confinement and treatment. There is little reason to believe that the GBMI verdict does anything other than simply acknowledge the presence of a mental disorder. Data from other states indicate that the treatment available to GBMIs is no different from that available to other prisoners with mental health needs (Keilitz, 1987; Smith & Hall, 1982). The Georgia statute specifically states that treatment will be given to GBMIs only within available resources. And it is well known that prisons do not have the mental health resources to provide anything but the most cursory services for those requiring mental health services (Fentiman, 1985). Our data suggest that the GBMI verdict is creating a new category of prisoner with mental health needs, relatively serious needs that may be going virtually untreated. To date, courts in Michigan and Indiana asked to rule on right to treatment issues regarding GBMIs have determined that it is not an issue of constitutional rights but rather that legal petitions or class action suits may be used to make the Department of Correctional Services provide the mandated services (Fentiman, 1985; McGraw et al., 1985). This has yet to occur.

The addition of a GBMI verdict will undoubtedly make the insanity plea a less appealing option for mentally ill defendants. In all states in which GBMI has been enacted, defendants are required to either plead insanity or indicate their intent to raise mental illness as a factor in their defense. Given the harsh reality of what can happen when mentally ill defendants are not successful in their bids for insanity acquittals but are instead found GBMI, we would predict that, over time, defense attorneys for mentally ill defendants will be less willing to enter an insanity plea for their clients. GBMI has, without question, changed the odds on an insanity plea in Georgia.

REFERENCES

Allison, P. D. (1984). *Event history analysis: Regression for longitudinal event data.* Beverly Hills, CA: Sage.

Appelbaum, P. (1982). The insanity defense: New calls for reform. *Hospital and Community Psychiatry, 33,* 13–14.

Benham v. Edwards, 501 F. Supp. 1050, 1076 (N.D. Ga. 1980).

Blossfeld, H., Hamerle, A., & Mayer, K. U. (1989). *Event history analysis: Statistical theory and application in the social sciences.* Hillsdale, NJ: Erlbaum.

Blunt, L. W., & Stock, H. V. (1985). Guilty but mentally ill: An alternative verdict. *Behavioral Sciences and the Law, 3,* 49–67.

Callahan, L. A., Steadman, H. J., McGreevy, M. A., & Robbins, P. C. (1991). The volume and composition of insanity defense pleas: An eight state study. *Bulletin of the American Academy of Psychiatry and Law, 19,* 331–338.

Campbell, D. T., & Stanley, J. C. (1963). *Experimental and quasi-experimental designs for research.* Boston, MA: Houghton Mifflin.

Criss, M. L., & Racine, D. R. (1980). Impact of change in legal standard for those adjudicated not guilty by reason of insanity. *Bulletin of American Academy of Psychiatry and Law, 8,* 261–271.

Faulstich, M. E. (1985). Effects upon social perceptions of the insanity plea. *Psychological Reports, 55,* 183–187.

Fentiman, L. C. (1985). Guilty but mentally ill: The real verdict is guilty. *Boston College Law Review, 26,* 603–653.

Finkel, J. J. (1990). Defacto departures from insanity instructions. *Law and Human Behavior, 14,* 105–122.

Fox, J. (1984). Detecting changes of level and slope in repeated measures data. *Sociological Methods and Research, 12,* 263–277.

Georgia Code Annotated § 17-7-131.

Hans, V. P. (1986). An analysis of public attitudes toward the insanity defense. *Criminology, 24,* 393–413.

Hans, V. P., & Slater, D. (1984). Plain crazy: Lay definitions of legal insanity. *International Journal of Law and Psychiatry, 7,* 105–114.

Hauser, S. (1981). Commitment and release of persons found not guilty by reason of insanity: A Georgia perspective. *Georgia Law Review, 15,* 1065–1103.

Hawkins, M. R., & Pasewark, R. A. (1983). Characteristics of persons utilizing the insanity plea. *Psychological Reports, 53,* 191–195.

Janofsky, J. S., Vandeville, M. B., & Rappeport, J. R. (1989). Defendants pleading insanity: An analysis of outcome. *Bulletin of the American Academy of Psychiatry and Law, 17,* 203–210.

Jeffrey, R. W., Pasewark, R. A., & Bieber, S. (1988). Insanity plea: Predicting not guilty by reason of insanity adjudications. *Bulletin of the American Academy of Psychiatry and Law, 16,* 35–39.

Keilitz, I. (1987). Researching and reforming the insanity defense. *Rutgers Law Review, 39,* 289–322.

Kirkland v. State, 166 Ga. App. 578 (1983).

Klofas, J., & Weisheit, R. (1986). Pleading guilty but mentally ill: Adversarial justice and mental health. *International Journal of Law and Psychiatry, 9,* 491–501.

Lewis-Beck, M. S. (1986). *Interrupted time series in new tools for social scientists.* W. D. Berry & M. S. Lewis-Beck (Eds.), Beverly Hills, CA: Sage Publications, 209–240.

Mackay, R. D., & Kopelman J. (1988). The operation of the "guilty but mentally ill" verdict in Pennsylvania. *Journal of Psychiatry and Law,* 247–268.

McGraw, B., Farthing-Capowich, D., & Keilitz, I. (1985). The guilty but mentally ill plea and verdict: Current State of the knowledge. *Villanova Law Review, 30,* 117–191.

Michigan Compiled Laws Annotated 768.36 (1982).

Moran, R. (1985). The origin of insanity as a special verdict: The trial for treason of James Hadfield (1800). *Law and Society Review, 19,* 601–633.

Pasewark, R. A., & Seidenzahl, D. (1979). Opinions concerning the insanity plea and criminality among mental patients. *Bulletin of the American Academy of Psychiatry and Law, 7,* 199–202.

Pasewark, R. A., & McGinley, H. (1985). Insanity plea: National survey of frequency and success. *Journal of Psychiatry and Law, 13,* 101–108.

People v. DeWitt, 463 N.E. 2d 742 (211 App. 1984).

People v. McQuillan, 393 Mich. 511, 221 N.W. 2d 569 (1974).

People v. Sorna, 88 Mich. App. 351, 362, 276 N.W. 2d 892 (1979).

Petrella, R. C., Benedek, E. P., Bank, S. C., & Packer, I. K. (1985). Examining the application of the guilty and mentally ill verdict in Michigan. *Hospital and Community Psychiatry, 36,* 254–260.

Schmidt, P., & Whitte, A. D. (1988). *Predicting recidivism using survival models.* New York: Springer-Verlag.

Simonton, D. K. (1977). Cross-sectional time-series experiments: Some suggested statistical analyses. *Psychological Bulletin, 84,* 489–502.

Slobogin, C. (1985). The guilty but mentally ill verdict: An idea whose time should not have come. *George Washington Law Review, 53,* 494–527.

Smith, G. A., & Hall, J. A. (1982). Evaluating Michigan's guilty but mentally ill verdict: An empirical study. *Journal of Law Reform, 16,* 75–112.

Steadman, J. J. (1985). Empirical research on the insanity defense. *Annals, 477,* 58–71.

Steadman, H. J., & Cocozza, J. J. (1978) Public perceptions of the criminally insane. *Hospital and Community Psychiatry, 29,* 457–459.

Steadman, H. J., Keitner, L., Braff, J., & Arvanites, T. (1983). Factors associated with a successful insanity plea. *American Journal of Psychiatry, 140,* 401–405.

Stokman, C. L. J., & Heiber, P. G. (1984). The insanity defense reform act in New York State, 1980–1983. *International Journal of Law and Psychiatry, 7,* 367–384.

THE DEATH OF THE FOURTH AMENDMENT UNDER THE REHNQUIST COURT: WHERE IS ORIGINAL INTENT WHEN WE NEED IT?

Joseph D. Davey
Hartnell College

ABSTRACT

The U.S. Supreme Court has significantly modified the meaning of the Fourth Amendment over the past two decades. Numerous police practices that very often have developed as part of the "war-on-drugs" have been ruled to be acceptable. The framers of the Fourth Amendment required a showing of "probable cause" before a search or seizure could be undertaken by police. While it is true that some exceptions to the requirement of "probable cause" had been allowed by the Supreme Court prior to Burger's appointment as Chief Justice, these exceptions were very carefully limited and supported by specific public policy rationales. The Court under Burger and Rehnquist have added so many exceptions to the requirement of probable cause that there are few restrictions on police searches and seizures under the present interpretation of the Fourth Amendment. This paper will argue that the "war-on-drugs" is far more likely to destroy the Fourth Amendment than it is to destroy the drug problem and Congress or State Legislatures should rectify this situation by re-instating those reasonable restrictions on searches and seizures which the present U.S. Supreme Court believes are not required by the Fourth Amendment.

INTRODUCTION

The purpose of the Fourth Amendment is to protect the right of the individual to "privacy", i.e., one's right to be free from unauthorized intrusion by government. The Amendment says that such an intrusion is unauthorized unless the government agent has "probable cause" to believe he or she will find evidence of a crime in the search. Without probable cause there is no authority to search or seize persons, houses, papers and effects. However, this standard of "probable cause" appears to be seriously endangered by decisions of the U.S. Supreme Court under the leadership of Chief Justices Burger and Rehnquist.

Richard Nixon promised in his campaign to appoint "strict constructionists" to the Supreme Court. There never was widespread consensus on exactly what the term "strict constructionist" meant and, in fact, some have argued that liberal justices like Hugo Black and William O. Douglas were "strict constructionists." However, it would appear that Nixon's use of the term meant "conservative," "law and order" justices who would narrowly interpret the meaning of the Bill of Rights when it came to the rights of criminal suspects.

In other words, terms in the Constitution such as "privacy" or "equal protection" or "due process" are broad enough to allow for a wide variety of interpretations. For example, in the 1986 case of *Bowers v Hardwick* (1986) the Court was asked whether or not it was a denial of "due process" for the state of Georgia to criminalize sodomy. Four justices said that it was. Five said that it was not. The term "due process" itself retains what has been called a "convenient vagueness" and liberal and conservative justices will probably never agree on it's exact meaning.

This lack of a precise definition, of course, also applies to the Fourth Amendment. The majority in the Fourth Amendment cases of the recent past that have modified or changed the interpretation of the Amendment given it by the Warren Court, has raised the argument that the Constitution should be narrowly construed. They have advanced the position that many of the complaints about the law that are brought to them in the form of constitutional cases, should be taken to a legislature instead. In other words, the majority in *Bowers v Hardwick* is not saying that they would vote to criminalize sodomy if they were members of the Georgia legislature. These justices are simply saying that they know of nothing in the Constitution that prohibits the Georgia legislature from doing so.

Likewise, when finding no constitutional infirmity with the various police procedures, the majority are not saying that they would authorize such practices if they were State legislators; only that they do not interpret the meaning of the Fourth amendment to prohibit such practices. However, they frequently state that they are simply interpreting the original intent of the Framers of the Fourth Amendment when, as we shall see, they seem to be doing just the opposite.

ORIGINAL INTENT

Ronald Reagan's rejected nominee for the Supreme Court, Judge Robert Bork, made the argument, both in his ill-fated confirmation hearings and in his book, *The Tempting of America*, that the Court should concern itself solely with the "original understanding" of the framers of the constitution.   Bork argued that the Supreme Court is constantly tempted to read into the Constitution a justification for results that the Justices like (Kaus, 1989).

The very heart of Robert Bork's argument, indeed the essence of all the arguments against "judicial activism", is summed up by Bork in *The Tempting of America* in these words: "Once the Court begins to employ its own notions of reasonableness . . . it cannot avoid legislating the Justices own personal views" (Bork, 1989). But if Bork and his supporters are serious about original intent, then certainly the probable cause standard of the Fourth Amendment is not something that they would lightly abandon.

The present Court, however, in what amounts to a radical departure from past precedent, is abandoning the probable cause requirement and deciding case after case on the basis of the "reasonableness" of the search, i.e., balancing the extent of the intrusion into the suspect's privacy with the need of government to protect society against some real or imagined evil.

However, the framers of the Fourth Amendment understood that searches and seizures would be based upon "probable cause." Robert Bork was probably not thinking of the present Court when he complained about how harmful it can be for appellate courts to abandon the "original understanding" concept and apply a standard of "reasonableness" to each case, but that does appear to be exactly what they are doing in Fourth Amendment cases, especially during the past decade.

The process of tolerating exceptions to the probable cause requirement began under the Warren Court, in *Terry v Ohio*. But the door Terry opened was very limited.   Police could detain an individual, the Court argued, when there was less than "probable cause" to arrest him. For the protection of the officer, the Court stated that the officer could pat down the individual and remove anything that felt like it could be a weapon. Government clearly had an interest in investigating an individual engaged in "unusual behavior" which may suggest a particular type of criminal activity but which does not   establish probable cause for arrest.   The progeny of *Terry* carefully spelled out the limitations upon these "stop and frisk" situations. If the Court was going to tolerate exceptions to the probable cause requirement, they would carefully scrutinize and restrict how far the police could go in these situations.

Suddenly, in the last decade, that original opening has become enormous. Case after case has relied on the *Terry* exception to justify searches and seizures that lack warrant or probable cause. Year after year, the Court has approved searches that were not only not based on probable cause, but sometimes not based on any suspicion at all. In each of these cases, the Supreme court ruled that the search was "reasonable" when they balanced the needs of government and the invasion of the individual's privacy. The "probable cause" standard of the framers of the Fourth Amendment was apparently abandoned in each of these cases because no one could argue that probable cause existed in any of these cases. And yet, ironically, there are many members of this Court who would claim to pay the utmost respect to "the original understanding" of the framers.

BACKGROUND OF THE FOURTH AMENDMENT'S DEATH

The Bill of Rights was ratified by the States in 1791. During the following century there were very few Fourth Amendment cases because even when evidence had been illegally seized by police, the courts would still allow the evidence to be used against the defendant. Of course, in the rural,agrarian society of 19th century America constitutional rights in dealing with police were of little significance. Organized police forces did not begin replacing bounty hunters until around mid-century and their role in society was very different than the role they would play in the 20th century. Accordingly, judicial review of police behavior is rare in the 19th century.

In *Weeks v United States* (1914) the U.S. Supreme Court accepted the argument that if the evidence seized in violation of the Fourth Amendment was allowed to be used to convict the defendant, the Court would be encouraging police to violate constitutional rights and acquiescing in situations in which the Fourth Amendment offered a "right without a remedy." In other words, unless the evidence were excluded, the Fourth Amendment would have no teeth. But this new "exclusionary rule" applied to federal officials only.

State and local police officers were not subject to the exclusionary rule until 1961. In *Mapp v Ohio* (1961) the Court ruled that the due process clause of the Fourteenth Amendment required that the exclusionary rule be applied to State police officers. Prior to the *Mapp* case, the exact restrictions on government officials demanded by the Fourth Amendment were not very important. Federal officers made relatively few arrests. The vast majority of searches were conducted by state police officers. Therefore, there was little more than academic interest in the limits of police authority to search and seize.

The *Mapp* case took that issue off the back burner. Henceforth, every arrest, search and seizure in the nation would be subject to the restrictions of the Fourth Amendment. And the extent of those restrictions would be dramatically changed by the Rehnquist Court.

WARRANTLESS SEARCHES: FROM WARREN TO REHNQUIST

The Court has long acknowledged that there are situations where it would be unreasonable to insist that the police secure a search warrant before conducting a search. However, the Court has always indicated that the preferred method of conducting a search is after a magistrate has determined that probable cause exists and then issued a warrant. The situation wherein a police officer makes the decision that probable cause exists and conducts a search without a warrant was treated by the Warren Court as an exception to the warrant rule that must be carefully limited. Under the Burger and Rehnquist Court, the list of allowable exceptions has grown rapidly.

Searches Incident to Arrest: Chimel to Robinson to Chadwick

A search incident to arrest was examined by the Warren Court in the case of *Chimel v California* (1968). Chimel was arrested for burglary by two police officers who were waiting for him when he arrived home. They had an arrest warrant. They did not have a search warrant. Nonetheless, after placing him in custody, and searching his person and the area immediately surrounding him, the officers went down the hallway and searched his bedroom. They found some of the coins that had been taken during the burglary in Chimel's night table.

The Court had previously ruled that police are justified in conducting a warrantless "search incident to arrest" whenever they are facing "exigent circumstances." The dangers involved in taking an individual into custody justify a warrantless search of an area in which the individual may have concealed either a weapon with which to facilitate his escape, or easily destructible evidence of the crime for which he is being arrested. However, to extend this search beyond that "lunge area" was to needlessly expand the exception to the warrant requirement. In other words, there is no reason why the police in the *Chimel* case, having ended the exigency by arresting and removing Chimel from the premises, could not then secure a warrant and search the entire apartment. This they failed to do. And for that reason the Court reversed Chimel's conviction.

Five years later the limitation laid down in *Chimel* seemed to evaporate in *U.S. v Robinson* (1973). Richard Nixon had delivered on his campaign promise with four appointees to the Court who were, in Nixon's term, "strict constructionists." In *U.S. v Robinson* the suspect was arrested for driving a car with an expired license. The police conducted a search of the suspect at the scene and after removing a pack of cigarettes from his pocket they opened and examined the package and found drugs. The officers indicated at the suppression hearing that they were not looking for weapons in the cigarette pack and that there was no other evidence to be found for this type of crime.

In other words, there were no "exigent circumstances" to justify a warrantless arrest and these officers were on what used to be called a "fishing expedition." Nonetheless, Justice Rehnquist, writing for the majority, ruled that if the arrest is lawful, "a search incident to the arrest requires no additional justification" (*U.S. v Robinson*, 1973). That is, the exigent circumstances required in *Chimel* were no longer necessary. In dissent, Marshall, Douglas and Brennan wrote: "The majority's approach represents a clear and marked departure from our long tradition" of Fourth Amendment adjudication. This may have been the first such departure, but there would certainly be more.

However, if the *Chimel* principle seemed to disappear in the Robinson case, it was not completely gone. Four years later it re-appeared in the *Chadwick* case. In the case of *Chadwick v U.S.* (1977), federal agents had probable cause to believe that Chadwick had two hundred pounds of marijuana in a footlocker in the trunk of his car. He was arrested and the footlocker seized and removed to a Federal Office Building in Boston. The footlocker was searched without a warrant. The Court agreed to hear Chadwick's appeal.

Rehnquist again argued that exigent circumstances were not necessary to justify a warrantless search incident to arrest, even where the arrest had occurred over an hour before the search. But in *Chadwick*, Rehnquist was writing in dissent. The majority concluded that the search was a violation of the Fourth Amendment. The Court appeared to be upholding a simple, bright-line rule: if there is no exigency, there must be a warrant. "When no exigency is shown to support the need for an immediate search," wrote the Court in reversing the conviction, "the Warrant Clause places the line at the point where the property to be searched comes under the exclusive dominion of police authority" (*Chadwick v U.S.*, 1977).

The decision in Chadwick encouraged the supporters of the Warren Court. One such observor hailed the decision in *Chadwick* as he beginning of "a significantly less police-oriented Court" (Schwartz, 1987). But the noted constitutional authority, Yale Kamisar, was a lot less sanguine about what he called the "third Burger Court" which he traced to the summer of 1981 and the appointment of Sandra Day O'Connor. It was this Court that abandoned the principle enunciated in *Chimel* and *Chadwick*, while maintaining that no precedent was being over-turned.

Car Searches:
Ross to Class to Bertine to Sitz

In 1982 the Court heard the case of *U.S. v Ross*. Ross was arrested by police who had probable cause to believe that Ross was selling drugs out of his car. After the arrest, police conducted a warrantless search of the car. In the trunk they found a leather pouch and a brown paper bag. They searched the contents and found drugs and cash. Ross's defense argued that *Chadwick* required the exclusion of the evidence since the police should have obtained a warrant after the bags had been seized and the exigency had passed. The Court disagreed. It ruled that the police had the right to search the trunk without a warrant because they had probable cause to search the whole car. They claimed that their decision was not inconsistent with *Chadwick*, even though the facts of the two cases seemed indistinguishable.

In dissent, Marshall and Brennan argued that the majority "never explains why these concerns permit the warrantless search of a container, which can easily be seized and immobilized while police are obtaining a warrant" (*Ross v U.S.*, 1982). More ominously, the dissenters argued that "the majority today not only repeals all realistic limits on warrantless automobile searches, it repeals the Fourth Amendment warrant requirement itself."

Automobiles have always presented problems for the Court's Fourth Amendment jurisprudence. The mobility of moving-vehicles intensify the exigent circumstances associated with the need to search and the Court has been more lenient with warrantless searches of automobiles. But even if warrants are not always required to search a car, probable cause is. To paraphrase William Pitt the Elder, "a man's car may not be his castle, but before the forces of the king can enter that humble vehicle, they must have some reason to believe they are going to find some kind of evidence of some kind of crime." Or at least that is what the law use to be.

In *New York v Class* (1986) the Court heard a case in which the police had entered the vehicle of an individual who had been stopped for a traffic offense. There was no reason to believe Class had been involved in any offense other than the traffic offense. The police wanted to know the Vehicle Identification Number (V.I.N.) which is located on the front dash. They stated that a newspaper was on top of the V.I.N. which blocked a view of it from outside they vehicle. The officer entered the vehicle to remove the newspaper. While in the vehicle, the officer spotted a gun and an arrest was made. The Court acknowledged that in this case there was neither a warrant nor probable cause to justify the entering of the vehicle. Nonetheless, the majority ruled that the police had the right to enter the vehicle in order to read the V.I.N., even though the driver could have been asked to remove the object that blocked its view from outside the car.

A year later the Court expanded the authority of police to search vehicles in *Colorado v Bertine* (1987). Here, Bertine was arrested for driving while intoxicated. The police took control of his car and then searched it and its contents. A closed back pack was found in the back seat. Unlike *Chadwick* or *Ross* there was no reason to expect to find any contraband inside the back pack; unlike *Class*, there was no reason to check the vehicle identification number. Nonetheless, the officer searched the back pack and found drugs.

The Colorado Supreme Court reversed the conviction based on the reasoning in *Chadwick*. But Justice Rehnquist writing for the majority of the U.S. Supreme Court concluded that this search was not a violation of Bertine's Fourth Amendment rights since this was an "inventory search" and no warrant or probable cause was necessary. There was no explanation as to why an inventory search could not have been completed by seizing and storing the back pack rather than examining it's contents. Would an attorney's brief case located in the same position as the back pack be seized and stored? Or would it and the client files it contained be scrutinized by police for evidence of crime?

Ross, *Class* and *Bertine* all involved searches of vehicles that had been legally stopped. In each case, reasonable suspicion existed to justify the stop. What if the police lack any evidence of any criminal activity when they order a vehicle to pull over? In 1990 the Court heard the case of Michigan v Sitz (1990). In that case, the police had set up "checklanes" and simply stopped everyone on the highway. They questioned each driver to determine if he or she were sober. Sitz was one such driver who was stopped and arrested. He appealed his conviction saying that the practice of stopping every car violated the Fourth Amendment. Chief Justice Rehnquist wrote the majority opinion upholding this procedure as "reasonable."

THE WAR ON DRUGS

The problem of widespread drug abuse is generally viewed from two very distinct perspectives. One side sees it as a spiritual problem wherein alienated souls seek oblivion from the pain of the human experience. This side sees the solution lying in the hands of ministers, priests, rabbis, psychologists and other counselors. The other side sees the solution in ever greater police authority. The present Court seems clearly lined up with the latter perspective. Their decisions appear to establish a clear cut belief: if law enforcement is granted greater and greater legal powers in dealing with the public, at some point the drug problem will go away.

Yale Kamisar argued that:

"Because the Court had become convinced that more law enforcement tools were needed to combat drug traffic during the 1982-83 term, the government gained complete or partial victory in all nine search-and-seizure cases decided that term (all involving drugs)" (Schwartz, 1987).

But in the years following those nine decisions, drugs have been instrumental in Fourth Amendment cases involving far more extravagant invasions of privacy than any of those cases.

For example, the Court considered a drug search in the case of *T.L.O. v New Jersey* (1985). A high school student had been caught smoking a cigarette in the ladies room of her school. The school administrator searched her pocket book, found a small quantity of marijuana and turned it over to police to be used in a criminal prosecution of the student. No evidence existed that would suggest the student was carrying drugs in her pocket book. The administrator was on a "fishing expedition." The New Jersey court excluded the marijuana, finding that the search violated the Fourth Amendment. The Supreme Court reversed the decision. The majority held that the probable cause standard of the Fourth Amendment did not apply to teachers or school administrators. The Court found that the necessities of the "war on drugs" demanded that government authority be expanded once again.

In 1993, the "war on drugs" appears to be spiraling out of control. For instance, there are more inmates in Federal prisons today for drug crimes than were in Federal prison for all crimes when Ronald Reagan took office. Moreover, there does not seem to be any end in sight. The Justice Department estimates that by 1995 more than two-thirds of all convicts in Federal prisons will be inside for drugs offenses (Baum,1992).

Even with the tripling of the incarceration rate in the U.S. over the past twenty years, we are still only able to lock up about 1.25 million people. The most responsible estimates are that there are 50 to 60 million people who still use an illegal drug at least once a year. There are about 18 to 35 million regular marijuana users in the US, five to ten million cocaine users and five million heroin users (Trebach & Engelsmen, 1985). Therefore, even an exponential increase in incarceration of drug offenders would only affect a small percentage of all users.

And even the war on the supply of drugs seems to have failed. For instance, a study by Manhattan District Attorney Robert Morgenthau found that between 1984 and 1988, New York State tripled the number of drug dealers sent to prison— from 1,376 to 4,089. Yet during this same period, cocaine became even cheaper and easier to buy (Morganthau, 1988). The war on drugs would appear to have a far greater impact on the right of individuals to be left alone by government agents then it has on the availability of drugs.

A Drug User's Home is Not His Castle:
Oliver, Ciraolo, Riley and Greenwood

One method of attacking the problem of drugs is to prevent the cultivation of marijuana. This rationale has provided law enforcement with an excuse for some of the most invasive tactics ever used by American police. In *Oliver v U.S.* (1984), police officers without search warrants or probable cause, or consent of the owner, went onto the defendant's secluded, wooded property, hiked past the "no trespassing" signs that Oliver had posted and discovered marijuana plants growing in a remote area. The Court ruled that the police were justified in their procedure because an individual may not expect privacy for activities conducted out-of-doors in open fields, unless the area is part of the "curtilage," i.e., the area immediately surrounding the home. Marshall, Brennan and Stevens dissented.

This area immediately surrounding the home was reconsidered two years later in *California v Ciraolo* (1986). Here the marijuana was not being grown in a secluded area; it was being grown in Ciraolo's backyard and he clearly did expect privacy in this area. He had surrounded the area with two fences, one six feet high and the other ten feet. Was this area within the curtilage of Ciraolo's home? Was Ciraolo entitled to expect privacy in such an area from police in the absence of either a warrant or probable cause to believe he was engaging in criminal activities?

The police had received an anonymous tip that Ciraolo was growing marijuana. The courts have repeatedly held that an anonymous tip alone cannot establish probable cause since there is no way to evaluate the credibility of the informant. Should the rule be otherwise, any angry neighbor could target anyone they chose and expose them to a police search. Thus, in the *Ciraolo* case, the police had no probable cause and no warrant authorizing a search of his backyard. So they rented a plane.

The police flew over Ciraolo's backyard and observed the plants growing in his "curtilage." Ciraolo's attorney argued that the Oliver case gave the defendant an expectation of privacy in his "curtilage." Chief Justice Burger answered for the majority by saying that since the plane was more than a thousand feet in the air over Ciraolo's backyard, he could have no reasonable expectation of privacy from observers in the plane. Therefore, the search was reasonable and Ciraolo's conviction was affirmed.

The Oliver majority opinion had been written by Justice Powell who went along with the majority's argument that Oliver could reasonably expect privacy only within the "curtilage." In *Ciraolo*, Powell angrily dissented and argued that given the state of the art in space satellites, the majority decision allowing over flight observation was no different than allowing police to use listening devices to pick up conversations within the home.

Two years after *Ciraolo*, the Court heard the case of *Florida v Riley* (1989). Police had once again observed marijuana growing within the defendant's curtilage, but here the overflight question had two differences: first, a helicopter was used instead of a fixed wing plane; and, second, the height of the plane was 400 feet instead of 1000. The Court ruled that it made no difference. The search was good since there was no legitimate expectation of freedom from aerial observation, regardless of the altitude of the observers, the nature of the aircraft, or the lack of probable cause. Justice Powell's earlier observations about police surveillance from space may not be as far fetched as they had seemed.

Meanwhile, back on the ground, police in California were conducting warrantless searches of garbage. In the 1988 case of *California v Greenwood* (1988), the Court considered the extent to which an individual can reasonably expect his trash to be free from government inspection. Every week for around two months, Laguna Beach police, without a warrant or probable cause, seized and examined the trash that Greenwood left for the disposal company in opaque, sealed bags on the curb outside his home. Ultimately, they found evidence of criminal drug activity on Greenwood's part. Greenwood's conviction was reversed by the California Supreme Court because California law recognizes a right to expect privacy in trash.

However, the U.S. Supreme Court reversed the California court and ruled that since the trash was placed outside the curtilage and abandoned, there could be no expectation to privacy in it and no need to get a warrant to search it. This case left several unanswered questions. Would the trash outside an attorney's office containing a client's files be viewed in the same light as Greenwood's plastic bags? Although this would appear to be a legitimate implication of their decision, the majority did not address the question. In his dissent, Justice Brennan stated:

> The American society with which I am familiar chooses to 'dwell
> in reasonable security and freedom from surveillance' (*Johnson
> v U.S.*, 1948) and is more dedicated to individual liberty and

more sensitive to intrusions on the sanctity of the home than the Court is willing to acknowledge" (*California v Greenwood*, 1988).

The majority in *Greenwood* may not have disagreed with Brennan's distaste for "surveillance." They would simply suggest that the Constitution does not prohibit such practices and it is the legislature that should decide the issue. The same argument would be made concerning the use of the "drug courier profile."

Airport Searches: "Drug Courier Profiles": Mendenhall to Sokolow

The detention of an individual by police is subject to different regulations in a free society than in a police state. When probable cause does not exist for an arrest, the legal rights of the individual who is detained by the police is a good indicator of how free that society remains. May the police detain anyone they like? If the police lack probable cause or even rational suspicion about an individual's behavior and they ask that individual to stop and answer questions, does the individual have the right to simply walk away? Substantial changes in this area occurred during the last decade.

When Sylvia Mendenhall stepped off a plane in Detroit airport in 1980, she was approached by two agents of the Drug Enforcement Agency. The agents knew very little about Mendenhall other than the fact that she fit the D.E.A.'s "drug courier profile." After a brief conversation, they all went to a D.E.A. office, a female agent was brought in and Sylvia was stripped and searched. Drugs were found in her undergarments. When she appealed her conviction to the Supreme Court, a sharply divided Court ruled that the procedures were acceptable under the Fourth Amendment.

In the landmark case of *Terry v Ohio* (1968), the Warren Court had laid down the rules for police detention based on less than probable cause. Police may constitutionally "stop and frisk" an individual if there is "reasonable suspicion" that he or she is involved in a crime. This standard of "reasonable suspicion" requires less evidence to establish than does "probable cause" and only a detention is justified by the presence of reasonable suspicion; in order to search someone who has been detained, the police need probable cause.

However, the reasoning of the Court in the Mendenhall case seemed to blur the bright line rule laid down in *Terry*. Four justices concluded that the newly created "drug courier profile" did not establish even reasonable suspicion and therefore Mendenhall's detention was unlawful, and clearly her search was unlawful. They would exclude the evidence and reverse her conviction.

The other five agreed that the stop and search was acceptable but they were divided about how this procedure could be justified. Three said that the stop and search had been pursuant to Mendenhall's freely given consent which they apparently felt was implied by the fact that she did not forcibly resist the agents. The remaining two justices held that the stop was justified by the "drug courier profile." This final argument was probably the most disturbing position from the perspective of civil libertarians. How could a vaguely worded "profile" justify a strip search in a free society?

Nonetheless, by 1989, with Reagan's three appointees added to the Court, this view of "drug courier profiles" would become a majority opinion. In *U.S. v Sokolow* (1989), the suspect had fit the "drug courier profile" because he had left Miami for a brief trip, paid in cash for his ticket, and brought only carry on luggage; in addition, the suspect was dressed in a black jumpsuit, wore gold jewelry and had his phone number listed in another persons name. The Court ruled that these circumstances established the right to detain Sokolow. When a drug sniffing dog indicated that his bags contained drugs, he was arrested.

The validity of the assumptions upon which the "drug courier profile" is based are, to say the least, open to question. Justice Marshall has pointed out in *Sokolow* that these profiles have been used in various cases to include the fact that the suspect was the first off the plane, or the last off the plane, or in the middle of the crowd that was getting off the plane; in some cases they have included the fact that the suspect purchased a one way ticket, and in other cases, a round trip ticket; that the suspect took a non-stop flight, or that the suspect changed planes; that the suspect had a shoulder bag or the suspect had a new suitcase; that the suspect was travelling alone or that the suspect was traveling with a companion; that the suspect acted too nervously or that he acted too calmly; in other words, it may be that anyone could fit this most flexible profile.

D.E.A. does not reveal its records on the stopping of people under the drug courier profile so we have no way of knowing how accurately the profile identifies drug couriers. Does the profile prove to be an accurate indicator in ninety percent of all detentions? Or is it closer to five percent? D.E.A. will not say. But we do know that these profiles have now been put into use in train stations, on interstate buses and on highways.

Drug Testing: Von Raab

When the U.S. Treasury Department required 3,600 employees to urinate in jars and turn the samples over to labs for drug testing, it was likely that the expectation of the Treasury Department administrators was that a substantial number of employees would test positive. If not, why go through such a humiliating and debasing exercise? Actually, the tests revealed that only five of the 3,600 tested employees had traces of drugs in their urine.

There was no probable cause to believe that any of these people would test positive. There was no "reasonable suspicion" to believe they had used drugs. But in order to keep their jobs in the U.S. Customs Office, they had to submit to the drug test. Their union took the case to the Rehnquist Court in 1989 arguing that the regulation reversed the presumption of innocence.

In a five-four decision the Court concluded that the Fourth Amendment was not violated by this urine testing. Justice Kennedy argued simply that "it is necessary to balance the individual's privacy expectations against the Government's interests . . ." (*National Treasury Employees v Von Rabb*, 1989). The absence of warrants was unimportant; the absence of some level of individualized suspicion was unimportant. Only the 'Government's interest' was significant.

Justices Scalia and Stevens joined Marshall and Brennan in dissenting. Scalia wrote a scathing dissent which excoriated the majority for sacrificing constitutional freedoms as a result of the public hysteria about drug use. He stated: ". . . neither the frequency of use nor the connection to harm is demonstrated or even likely. In my view, the Custom Service rules are a kind of immolation of privacy and human dignity in symbolic opposition to drug use" (*National Treasury Employees v Von Rabb*, 1989). Justice Scalia, no one's idea of a civil libertarian, seemed to have finally gotten a glimpse of what other justices had been warning the Court about since *U.S. v Robinson* (1973).

THE DEATH OF THE FOURTH AMENDMENT

Perhaps the most serious threat to the future of the Fourth Amendment, however, comes from the idea of "the good faith exception." This idea— which was incorporated in the recently vetoed federal crime bill— began in the case of *U.S. v Leon* (1984). In that case the police were given a warrant that was not based on probable cause. They executed the warrant and the trial court accepted the evidence found. An appellate court reversed the conviction, finding that the warrant was no good. The Supreme Court granted certiorari.

The Court reasoned that the exclusionary rule had little impact on the behavior of police who violate Fourth Amendment rights of an individual while acting in good faith ignorance of the situation. Therefore, they concluded, there was no point in applying the exclusionary rule to these situations. They re-instated the conviction. In dissent, Justice Brennan stated: "Since [1974], in case after case, I have witnessed the Court's gradual but determined strangulation of the [exclusionary] rule. It now appears that the Court's victory over the Fourth Amendment is complete . . ." (*U.S. v Leon*, 1984). Brennan concludes his lengthy dissent by saying: "Today, for the first time, this Court holds that although the Constitution has been violated, no court should do anything about it . . ." (*U.S. v Leon*, 1984).

When the logic of the Court in the *Leon* case is examined, there is nothing in the reasoning of the majority that in anyway precludes the extension of the "good faith exception" to other types of searches and seizures. What are American police likely to do in the absence of an exclusionary rule?

Between 1948 and 1961, American police were told by the Court that they had to respect the Fourth Amendment rights of the individual but that the evidence they seized in violation of those rights did not have to be excluded from trial. There is widespread agreement that during this time period there was little, if any, respect shown for the Fourth Amendment by local police (Lowenthal, 1980). That, of course, was in the relatively placid fifties. But what will law enforcement be like in a society that lives with a level of fear of crime that borders on hysteria? In a society that considers itself inundated with drug dealers, illegal immigrants and urban "underclass" undesireables? How much self-restraint will police exercise if there is no longer the restraining influence of an exclusionary rule?

CONCLUSION

In the sixties, the Bureau of Narcotics and Dangerous Drugs estimated that of all the drugs that are sent by drug dealers toward American streets, law enforcement probably does not seize more than about five percent. Today, the estimate is that about the same percentage of drugs is still being seized. This raises two important questions: first, how much harm would it do if that other five percent also made it to the street? And, secondly, is it really worth surrendering the right to privacy that the Framers thought so critical to a free society in order to continue a stalemated war on drugs?

Efforts at seizing supplies of drugs after production hold very little promise. The most intense efforts of law enforcement have been directed at the cocaine market. Still in 1990 alone, of the nearly 900 metric tons of cocaine produced worldwide, only a little over 300 tons were seized by the combined efforts of all military and law enforcement efforts throughout the U.S. and throughout the entire hemisphere region (Lane, 1992).

Furthermore, to put these figures in perspective, according to the National Narcotics Intelligence Consumers Committee, the total amount of cocaine consumed in the U.S. in the mid-eighties was around 70 tons annually (Reuter & Crawford, 1988). It would appear that the supply is far greater than the demand will ever be. In short, these figures strongly suggest that an attack on the supply of drugs is a waste of time. The Rand Corporation reached a similar conclusion. A careful study of interdiction efforts conducted by the Rand Corporation determined that "even massively stepped-up drug interdiction efforts are not likely to greatly affect the availability of cocaine and heroin in the United States" (Reuter & Crawford, 1988).

In the United States of today, people routinely discuss the last urine test for drugs which they were forced to take by their employer and they seem to forget that twenty years ago the only people being compelled to submit to such tests were people like S.A.C. bomber pilots and prison parolees. Police checkpoints routinely pull over every car on the road to test the driver's level of sobriety.

At airports, dogs sniff at everyone's luggage and at bus and train stations police agents detain and question strangers who seem to fit some vague "profile" which apparently changes constantly. In schools, students are forced to submit to searches based on the whim of school administrators and anything that is found can be used against the student in a criminal trial. Backyard gardens are examined by government agents in helicopters with neither warrants nor probable cause, and police laboratories analyze the garbage of anyone they wish.

The coercive extinction of substance abuse may well prove to be a cure that is worse than the illness. The social damage from drug use may one day be seen as a minor problem when compared to the social cost of the expansion of government authority to search for drugs. Congress and State legislatures should be encouraged to revise the penal codes in order to reinstate those restrictions on police procedures which should exist in a free society.

Perhaps the time has come to consider the warning of Justice Marshall in his dissent in Von Raab: "History teaches that grave threats to liberty often come in times of urgency when constitutional rights seem too extravagant to endure" (*National Treasury Employees v Von Rabb*, 1989). Thurgood Marshall understood the "original intent" of the Framers of the Fourth Amendment.

REFERENCES

Baum, D. (1992) "Drug War on Your Rights." *The Nation* 254(25):886.

Bork, R. (1989) *The Tempting of America: The Political Seduction of the Law.* New York: Free Press.

Bowers v Hardwick, 478 U.S. 1039 (1986)

California v Ciraolo, 476 U.S. 207 (1986)

California v Greenwood, 486 U.S. 35 (1988)

Chadwick v U.S., 433 U.S. 1 (1977)

Chimel v. California, 395 U.S. 792 (1968)

Colorado v Bertine, 479 U.S. 367 (1987)

Florida v Riley, 488 U.S. 445 (1989)

Kaus, M. (1989) "Bork Chop." *New Republic* 3:18-20.

Lane, C. (1992) "The Newest War." *Newsweek* January 6:18-23.

Loewenthal, M. (1980) "Evaluating the Exclusionary Rule in Search and Seizure." *University of Missouri-Kansas City Law Review* 49:24-32.

Mapp v Ohio, 367 U.S. 643 (1961)

Michigan Dept of State Police v Sitz, 496 U.S. 444 (1990)

Morgenthau, R. (1988) "We Are Losing the War on Drugs." *The New York Times* Feb. 16:A21.

National Treasury Employee v Von Raab, 489 U.S. 656 (1989)

New York v Class, 475 U.S. 106 (1986) p.144

Oliver v U.S., 466 U.S. 170 (1984)

Reuter, P., G. Crawford and J. Cace (1988) *Sealing the Borders: The Effects of Increased Military Participation in Drug Interdiction.* Santa Barbara, CA: The Rand Corporation.

Schwartz, H. (1987) *The Burger Years: Rights and Wrongs in the Supreme Court, 1969-1986.* New York: Viking.

Terry v Ohio, 392 U.S. 1 (1968)

T.L.O. v New Jersey, 469 U.S. 325 (1985)

Trebach, A. and E. Engelsman (1989) "Why Not Decriminalize?" *NPQ* Summer:40-45.

U.S. v Leon, 468 U.S. 897 (1984)

U.S. v Mendenhall, 446 U.S. 544 (1980)

U.S. v Robinson, 414 U.S. 218 (1973)

U.S. v Ross, 456 U.S. 798, (1982)

U.S. v Sokolow, 490 U.S. 1 (1989)

Weeks v United States, 232 U.S. 383 (1914)

0091-4169/94/8501-0080
THE JOURNAL OF CRIMINAL LAW & CRIMINOLOGY
Copyright © 1994 by Northwestern University, School of Law

Vol. 85, No. 1
Printed in U.S.A.

GENDER, CRIME, AND THE CRIMINAL LAW DEFENSES

DEBORAH W. DENNO*

I. INTRODUCTION

Gender is among the strongest predictors of crime,[1] particularly violent crime.[2] Arrest, self report, and victimization data consistently

* Associate Professor, Fordham University School of Law. B.A., University of Virginia, 1974; M.A., University of Toronto, 1975; Ph.D., 1982, J.D., 1989, University of Pennsylvania. I presented an earlier version of this Article at the Third Annual Feminist Symposium at Northwestern University School of Law, where I benefitted from questions and discussions. I am most grateful to the following individuals for their comments on this Article: Cynthia Bowman, James Fleming, Bruce Green, John Monahan, and Stephen Schulhofer. These individuals are not responsible for my mistakes or misjudgments. I give special thanks to Kevin Downey for his ideas and artistry in the creation from data of Figures 1-4 and Table 1, and to Erica Ginsburg for drawing Figures 5 and 6. Further appreciation is extended to Steven Aurand for his help with statistical analyses, to Robert Renzulli and Kira Watson for their exceptional research assistance, and to Kathleen Smith-Ruggiero for her care and diligence in typing tables. Fordham University School of Law provided generous research support, for which I am thankful. The results of the Biosocial Study presented in this Article were also supported in part by Grant # 85-IJ-CX-0034, awarded by the National Institute of Justice. Points of view are those of the author and do not necessarily represent the views of the United States Department of Justice.

[1] See JAMES W. MESSERSCHMIDT, MASCULINITIES AND CRIME: CRITIQUE AND RECONCEPTUALIZATION OF THEORY 1 (1993); JAMES Q. WILSON & RICHARD J. HERRNSTEIN, CRIME AND HUMAN NATURE 104-05 (1985); David F. Greenberg, *The Gendering of Crime in Marxist Theory*, in CRIME AND CAPITALISM: READINGS IN MARXIST CRIMINOLOGY 405, 405 (David F. Greenberg ed., 1993); Kenneth E. Moyer, *Sex Differences in Aggression*, in SEX DIFFERENCES IN BEHAVIOR 335, 335 (Richard C. Friedman et al. eds., 1974); Darrell Steffensmeier & Emilie Allan, *Gender, Age, and Crime*, in CRIMINOLOGY: A CONTEMPORARY HANDBOOK 67, 67 (Joseph F. Sheley ed., 1991); June Andrew, *Delinquency: Correlating Variables*, 10 J. CLIN. CHILD PSYCH. 136, 136-40 (1981). Recent analyses of historical data show, however, that such gender differences have not always existed. *See* Greenberg, supra; Helen Boritch, *Gender and Criminal Court Outcomes: An Historical Analysis*, 30 CRIMINOLOGY 293 (1992); Malcolm M. Feeley & Deborah L. Little, *The Vanishing Female: The Decline of Women in the Criminal Process, 1687-1912*, 25 L. & SOC'Y REV. 719 (1991).

[2] *See infra* notes 21 to 24 and accompanying text; *see also* MARTIN DALY & MARGO WILSON, HOMICIDE 156-86 (1988); DONNA MARTIN HAMPARIAN ET AL., THE VIOLENT FEW: A STUDY OF DANGEROUS JUVENILE OFFENDERS 51-87 (1978); Candace Kruttschnitt, *Gender and Interpersonal Violence*, in 3. UNDERSTANDING AND PREVENTING VIOLENCE: SOCIAL INFLUENCES 295, 295-378 (Albert J. Reiss, Jr. & Jeffrey A. Roth eds., 1994); Moyer, *supra* note 1, at 335; Deborah R. Baskin & Ira Sommers, *Females' Initiation into Violent Street Crime*, 10 JUST. Q. 559, 559-60 (1993); Ira Sommers & Deborah R. Baskin, *The Situational Context of Violent Female Offending* 30 J. RES. CRIME & DELINQ. 136, 140, 150-55 (1993); Steffensmeier & Allan,

show that men and boys commit significantly more crime, both serious and not, than women and girls.[3] This pattern persists despite data indicating that crimes committed by females may be rising.[4] Evidence also suggests that males are generally more aggressive than females,[5] even before the preschool years.[6] Yet most theories and explanations

---

supra note 1, at 67-70.

[3] *See* FREDA ADLER ET AL., CRIMINOLOGY 43-45 (1991); 1 UNDERSTANDING AND PREVENTING VIOLENCE 5 (Albert J. Reiss, Jr. & Jeffrey A. Roth eds., 1993); RITA JAMES SIMON, WOMEN AND CRIME 33-47 (1975); Kruttschnitt, *supra* note 2, at 298-314; Henry J. Steadman et al., *Designing a New Generation of Risk Assessment Research, in* VIOLENCE AND MENTAL DISORDER: DEVELOPMENTS IN RISK ASSESSMENT 297, 309 (John Monahan & Henry J. Steadman eds., 1994); Lynn Kratzer & Sheila Hodgins, *Adult Outcomes of Childhood Conduct Problems: A Cohort Study* (1994) (manuscript submitted for publication); *see also* John Monahan et al., *Ethical and Legal Duties in Conducting Research on Violence: Lessons From the MacArthur Risk Assessment Study,* 8 VIOLENCE AND VICTIMS 387, 388 (1993) (identifying gender as one of the risk markers for violence in planning the MacArthur Risk Assessment Study). Official statistics, however, show a greater gender disparity than self report studies. Whereas official statistics report male/female juvenile offense ratios as ranging between 3:1 and 7:1, self report studies show male/female offense ratios as ranging between 1.2:1 and 2.5:1. *See* Ronda L. Romanowski, Female Juvenile Offenders: Prevalence, Patterns and Etiology (1991) (unpublished manuscript, Northwestern University Medical Graduate School). Therefore, the nature and extent of female delinquency appears to more closely resemble that of male delinquency than official statistics demonstrate. *See* Rachelle J. Canter, *Family Correlates of Male and Female Delinquency,* 20 CRIMINOLOGY 146, 146-67 (1982). Kruttschnitt emphasizes that this male-female crime convergence is particularly apparent for less serious offenses. *See* Kruttschnitt, *supra* note 2.

[4] *See* FREDA ADLER, SISTERS IN CRIME: THE RISE OF THE NEW FEMALE CRIMINAL 5-30, 85-169 (1975); SIMON, *supra* note 3, at 19-67; Susan K. Datesman & Frank R. Scarpitti, *The Extent and Nature of Female Crime, in* WOMEN, CRIME, & JUSTICE 1, 8-64 (Susan K. Datesman & Frank R. Scarpitti eds., 1980); Roy L. Austin, *Recent Trends in Official Male and Female Crime Rates: The Convergence Controversy,* 21 J. CRIM. JUST. 447 (1993); Deborah Baskin et al., *The Political Economy of Female Violent Street Crime,* 20 FORDHAM URB. L.J. 401, 402-03 (1993). *But see* Kruttschnitt, *supra* note 2, at 314-17 (concluding that gender patterns are stable, rather than changing, over time); Darrell J. Steffensmeier, *Sex Differences in Patterns of Adult Crime, 1965-77: A Review and Assessment,* 58 SOCIAL FORCES 1080 (1980) (questioning whether female crime is rising); Darrell J. Steffensmeier, *National Trends in Female Arrests, 1960-1990: Assessment and Recommendations for Research,* 9 J. QUANTITATIVE CRIM. 411 (1993) (contending that the profile of female offenders has not changed over time relative to males and any changes that have been demonstrated have been in terms of rises in property crimes only, particularly minor thefts and fraud).

[5] *See* KATHERINE BLICK HOYENGA & KERMIT T. HOYENGA, GENDER-RELATED DIFFERENCES: ORIGINS AND OUTCOMES 337-56 (1993); GERDA SIANN, ACCOUNTING FOR AGGRESSION: PERSPECTIVES ON AGGRESSION AND VIOLENCE 33-37 (1985); Alice H. Eagly & Valerie J. Steffen, *Gender and Aggressive Behavior: A Meta-Analytic Review of the Social Psychological Literature,* 100 PSYCH. BULLETIN 309 (1986).

[6] *See* Eleanor Maccoby & Carol Jacklin, *Sex Differences in Aggression: A Rejoinder & Reprise,* 51 CHILD DEV. 964, 964-80 (1980). *But see* WILSON & HERRNSTEIN, *supra* note 1, at 117-19 (noting that each of the reasons for Maccoby's and Jacklin's conclusion can "with varying plausibility, be challenged"); Kruttschnitt, *supra* note 2, at 330 (contending that, irrespective of "a child's inborn or early acquired disposition, parental behaviors appear to have a strong mediating effect"); Todd Tieger, *On the Biological Basis of Sex Differences in Aggression,* 51 CHILD DEV. 943, 945-51 (1980) (contending, among other things, that the role of hormonal influences on aggressive human behavior is unclear and that cross cul-

of crime are gender blind. They either bypass the gender issue entirely or focus solely on why females fail to resemble males in their behavior.[7] These theories also ignore the possibility that explanations for the gender disparity in crime may help account for the underlying correlates of crime in general.[8]

This Article attempts to explain some of this gender disparity by analyzing the results of the "Biosocial Study," one of this country's largest longitudinal[9] studies of biological, psychological, and sociological predictors of crime.[10] The Biosocial Study followed nearly 1000 Philadelphia residents from birth through early adulthood and examined numerous variables. The individuals came from families who participated in the Philadelphia Collaborative Perinatal Project at Pennsylvania Hospital between 1959 and 1966. Pennsylvania Hospital was one of twelve medical centers the National Institute of Neurological Diseases and Stroke included in an unprecedented, nationwide study of biological and environmental influences upon the pregnancies of 60,000 women, as well as the physical, neurological, and psychological development of their children.[11]

---

tural studies of children reveal strong social and environmental influences on children's early behavior).

[7] *See* Meda Chesney-Lind, *Women and Crime: The Female Offender*, 12 Signs 78, 78-96 (1986); Douglas A. Smith & Raymond Paternoster, *The Gender Gap in Theories of Deviance: Issues and Evidence*, 24 J. Res. Crime & Delinq. 140, 140-72 (1987); *see also* Stephen J. Schulhofer, *The Gender Question in Criminal Law*, 7 Soc. Phil. & Pol'y 105, 105 (1990) ("[C]riminal law, constructed and expounded almost exclusively by males, can fairly be characterized (descriptively) as 'sexist' or at least 'gendered' (that is, male-oriented) in its core assumptions."); Robin West, *Jurisprudence and Gender*, 55 U. Chi. L. Rev. 1, 2 (1988) (contending that "all of our modern legal theory . . . is essentially and irretrievably masculine").

[8] *See* Judith Allen, *Men, Crime, and Criminology: Recasting the Questions*, 17 Int'l J. Soc. L. 19, 19-39 (1989) (noting that any explanation for the gender disparity in crime "might be posed as a litmus test for the viability of the discipline" of criminology).

[9] A longitudinal study analyzes the same group of individuals over a period of time. *See* John M. Neale & Robert M. Liebert, Science and Behavior: An Introduction to Methods of Research 109 (3d ed. 1986); Julian L. Simon & Paul Burstein, Basic Research Methods in Social Science 90 (3d ed. 1985). For a general discussion of the use of social science research methods in legal contexts, see John Monahan & Laurens Walker, Social Science in Law: Cases and Materials 31-81 (3d ed. 1994).

[10] The Biosocial Study is described in detail in two sources: Deborah W. Denno, Biology and Violence: From Birth to Adulthood (1990) [hereinafter Denno, Biology and Violence]; Deborah W. Denno, Comment, *Human Biology and Criminal Responsibility: Free Will or Free Ride?*, 137 U. Pa. L. Rev. 615 (1988).

[11] *See* Kenneth Niswander & Myron Gordon, The Women and Their Pregnancies (1972). Examination of the study children from the time of their birth through age seven continued until 1974, completing a total project cost exceeding 100 million dollars. *See* Joseph A. McFalls, Jr., *Social Science and the Collaborative Perinatal Project: An Opportunity for Research*, 4 Public Data Use 37, 37-47 (1976). Numerous publications have resulted from examining these data. *See, e.g.,* Sarah Broman et al., Preschool IQ: Prenatal and Early Developmental Correlates (1975); Janet B. Hardy et al., The First Year of Life (1979);

The Biosocial Study and its data are unique in this country. Few researchers have conducted longitudinal studies of crime and behavioral disorders,[12] and no one has been able to intensively analyze a large sample of individuals both before and after the start of their criminal careers. Moreover, many studies examine only males or do not focus on gender differences when they include both males and females.[13]

As this Article discusses, the results of the Biosocial Study confirmed past research which had demonstrated gender differences in the prevalence of crime. Males engaged in more crime and violence than females, and they were more likely to repeat their crimes. However, the Biosocial Study also corresponded with some research and theory which had indicated gender differences in the prediction of crime. With some exceptions, biological factors were found to be more predictive of crime among females, whereas environmental factors were found to be more predictive of crime among males.[14] Also, more factors overall were correlated with crime among females than males. This Article considers the consequences of these results with respect to whether there should be a gender-based standard for punishment or defenses.

This Article uses loose definitions of the terms "biological" and "environmental" or "sociological," because of their close association with related terms, and with one another. Generally, "biological" factors are "nonsocial, nonbehavioral measures of . . . constitution and functioning,"[15] such as neurological abnormalities. "Environmental" factors include measures without a biological base, such as family income. Factors comprising "behaviorally-defined characteristics," like cognitive or intellectual ability and achievement, may have a partial biological base,[16] which a certain environment could perpetuate or alter. The term "sex" refers to the chromosomal constitution of an individual; the term "gender" refers to the sociological, psychological, and cultural constructions of male and female differences.[17] Lastly,

---

PAUL L. NICHOLS & TA-CHUAN CHEN, MINIMAL BRAIN DYSFUNCTION: A PROSPECTIVE STUDY (1981).

[12] *See infra* notes 123 to 131 and accompanying text.

[13] Although prior research on the Biosocial Study examined gender differences, *see* DENNO, BIOLOGY AND VIOLENCE, *supra* note 10, it emphasized possible variations in cognition, such as laterality and verbal and spatial IQ, as well as crime predictors that males and females shared. It did not focus on gender in the theoretical and legal context discussed in this Article.

[14] *See infra* Section III.

[15] Sarnoff A. Mednick et al., *Biology and Violence, in* CRIMINAL VIOLENCE 21, 22 (Marvin E. Wolfgang & Neil Alan Weiner eds., 1982).

[16] *See id.*

[17] *See* Kruttschnitt, *supra* note 2, at 295-96. As Kruttschnitt notes, a reference to "sex

the term "defenses" includes three types: (1) "complete" defenses, such as insanity, which may result in total acquittal; (2) "partial" defenses, such as provocation; and (3) mitigating factors, such as mental impairment. These latter two defenses may reduce either the charge (*e.g.*, from murder to manslaughter) or the sentence (*e.g.*, from life imprisonment to twenty years).

Section II analyzes the literature and research on gender differences in crime. Section III describes the Biosocial Study and its results, noting the gender differences in the prevalence and prediction of crime and the inability of any one factor to be a strong predictor of crime. Relying on the Biosocial Study's results, this Article proposes a new gender-based defense which incorporates the finding of gender variations among predictors of crime. This "gender-variant" defense recognizes that crime among females may be more strongly linked to certain biological factors, such as neurological abnormalities, whereas crime among males may be more strongly linked to certain environmental factors, such as lead poisoning. Such results suggest that gender is a factor in determining whether any particular condition renders individuals less culpable for their behavior.

Section IV considers whether gender differences warrant disparate types of punishment or treatment within the criminal justice system by analyzing the gender-variant defense within a continuum of four gender-based defenses. This continuum ranges from biologically-based defenses to socially or culturally constructed ones: (1) gender-specific (*e.g.*, post partum depression); (2) gender-dominant (*e.g.*, high testosterone); (3) gender-variant (*e.g.*, neurological factors or lead poisoning); and (4) gender-cultural (*e.g.*, battered woman syndrome). Commentators have rarely examined or compared these defenses in the aggregate since they typically focus on just one. Yet, looking at these defenses together, and more broadly, provides a perspective on how the criminal justice system views gender and gender-stereotyping. These defenses have not been widely-used, but they are rapidly gaining popularity. This Article questions whether they

---

differences" in any explanation of crime rates would suggest that the differences are biologically-based; a reference to "gender differences," however, would recognize social, psychological, and cultural influences. *See id.* at 296-97. Deborah Rhode properly discusses the difficulty with this "sex-gender" distinction, noting for example the interaction and interdependence between biological and social factors. *See* Deborah L. Rhode, *Theoretical Perspectives on Sexual Difference*, *in* THEORETICAL PERSPECTIVES ON SEXUAL DIFFERENCE 1, 2 (Deborah L. Rhode ed., 1990). She also critiques "a historical tradition that ascribed overriding importance to biological explanations for differences in the sexes' social roles and status." *Id.* at 3. This Article relies on this sex-gender distinction, however, for the very purpose that Rhode critiques it, *i.e.*, to illustrate how cultural stereotyping can inappropriately amplify biological differences between the genders through the use of certain criminal law defenses. Similarly, this Article recognizes that the distinction is artificial.

should be accepted.

Next, this section discusses and critiques the tendency for the criminal law to view the more biologically-based defenses as manifestations of gender stereotypes and to explain the more culturally-constructed defenses in terms of supposed biological or psychological gender differences. Even though defendants use stereotypes to make their defenses more persuasive to a jury, they are frequently irrelevant and have no basis in fact. Thus, courts should render them inadmissible. Moreover, gender-stereotyping stifles the criminal justice system's "greater" goal of gender neutrality.[18] For example, a gender-stereotyped defense may appear to win an acquittal, but other factors, such as severity of the crime, are actually far more influential on case outcomes. Further, gender-stereotyping can result in personal stigmatization, or harm men or women as a group.[19] If poorly used, it can ease conviction.[20] For these reasons, this section concludes that the potential harm of gender-stereotyping outweighs any perceived benefit.

Section V concludes that gender differences in prevalence and prediction should not be considered in sentencing. Sentencing decisions based upon generalizations about immutable individual characteristics such as gender offend society's notions of justice. This constitutes the worst form of stereotyping.

In sum, gender differences in prevalence or prediction or gender-stereotyping should not justify either mitigations in punishment or the underlying rationales for criminal law defenses, unless the de-

---

[18] *But see* Myrna S. Raeder, *Gender and Sentencing: Single Moms, Battered Women, and Other Sex-Based Anomalies in the Gender-Free World of the Federal Sentencing Guidelines*, 20 PEPP. L. REV. 905, 909 (1993) (contending, with respect to the Federal Sentencing Guidelines, that "the lofty goal of gender neutrality has backfired, wreaking havoc in the lives of female offenders and their children who are forgotten by the Sentencing Guidelines structure"); *see also infra* notes 397 to 408 and accompanying text.

[19] *See* ALAN M. DERSHOWITZ, THE ABUSE EXCUSE AND OTHER COP-OUTS, SOB STORIES, AND EVASIONS OF RESPONSIBILITY (1994); Anne M. Coughlin, *Excusing Women*, 82 CAL. L. REV. 3 (1994); *infra* notes 343 to 353 and accompanying text. Alan Dershowitz includes gender-stereotyped defenses among those he considers to be "abuse excuses," *i.e.*, legal strategies "by which criminal defendants claim a history of abuse as an excuse for violent retaliation." DERSHOWITZ, *supra*, at 3. He claims that such excuses can: (1) stigmatize all abuse victims even though only a very few have ever engaged in violent crime or have used their particular abuse to justify their conduct, *see id.* at 6, 29; (2) impair the credibility of sound defenses that are used appropriately, *see id.* at 29; (3) "confirm the sexist stereotype of the woman out of control"; *see* id. at 30; and hinder civil liberties by promoting vigilante justice. *See id.* at 28.

[20] Gender-stereotyping can ease conviction in a particular case if the jury finds it to be repugnant, *see infra* notes 267 to 268 and accompanying text, or future cases as a kind of "backlash." For example, Charles P. Ewing, a psychologist and a law professor, claims that one jury deadlocked in a substantial battered woman syndrome case as a "backlash" created by the media coverage of the Eric and Lyle Menendez and Lorena Bobbitt cases. *See* Stephanie B. Goldberg, *Fault Lines*, 80 A.B.A. J. 40, 42 (June 1994).

fenses are appropriately factually-based. It is beyond the scope of this Article to discuss the evidentiary issues involved in such a fact-based determination. At the same time, this Article's account of the Biosocial Study and its critique of gender-based defenses illustrate ways to make one. Lastly, this Article questions whether differential treatment is warranted for distinguishing among biological factors other than gender, given the results of the Biosocial Study and the dubious rationale that the criminal law offers for some biological defenses, but not others.

II. THE NATURE AND PREVALENCE OF GENDER DIFFERENCES IN CRIME

Males comprised eighty-eight percent of those persons arrested for violent crime in 1992[21] and approximately ninety-five percent of new court commitments for violent offenses in 1991.[22] Most conventional theories of crime do not sufficiently explain the overwhelming domination of males in violent crime.[23] Yet, because crime and violence are associated with maleness, society deems women who engage in crime to be "doubly deviant"—defying both the law and their gender role.[24] As the following sections show, this perspective toward female criminals has remained constant.

A. A HISTORICAL VIEW OF FEMALE CRIME

Historically, commentators have explained women's lesser involvement in crime as an "underachievement"[25] attributable to their biology or sexuality.[26] Moreover, they have often confused sex with

---

[21] FEDERAL BUREAU OF INVESTIGATION, UNIFORM CRIME REPORTS FOR THE UNITED STATES Table 42 at 234 (1992).

[22] BUREAU OF JUSTICE STATISTICS, NATIONAL CORRECTIONS REPORTING PROGRAM, 1991 Table 1-8 at 15, Table 5-4 at 57 (1992) (In 1991, males comprised 95% of new court commitments to state prison and 93.1% of new court commitments to federal prison).

[23] *See* MESSERSCHMIDT, *supra* note 1, at 2-4. For a review of the literature on the etiology of female crime, see CAROL SMART, WOMEN, CRIME, AND CRIMINOLOGY: A FEMINIST CRITIQUE, 27-76 (1976); Dorie Klein, *The Etiology of Female Crime: A Review of the Literature, in* WOMEN, CRIME, AND JUSTICE 70, 70-105 (Susan K. Datesman & Frank R. Scarpitti eds., 1980); Kathleen Daly & Meda Chesney-Lind, *Feminism and Criminology,* 5 JUST. Q. 497, 514-27 (1988).

[24] *See* Baskin, et al., *supra* note 4, at 402; Coughlin, *supra note* 19, at 3; Patricia Erickson & Glenn F. Murray, *Sex Differences in Cocaine Use and Experiences: A Double Standard Revived?,* 15 AM. J. DRUG ALCOHOL ABUSE 135, 136 (1989). This position for female offenders was recognized by Cesare Lombroso at the turn of the century. "[T]he born female criminal is, so to speak, doubly exceptional, as a woman and as a criminal. For criminals are an exception among civilised people, and women are an exception among criminals . . . . " CESARE LOMBROSO & WILLIAM FERRERO, THE FEMALE OFFENDER 151 (1895).

[25] Beverly R. Fletcher & Dreama G. Moon, *Introduction, in* WOMEN PRISONERS: A FORGOTTEN POPULATION 5, 12 (Beverly R. Fletcher et al. eds., 1993).

[26] As Carol Smart notes, classical studies of female criminality are based upon a biologi-

gender, characterizing crime among females as masculine or malelike, a perspective that remains in current research on female crime.[27]

Cesare Lombroso, an Italian physician, was the first to explain female crime in this manner.[28] Near the turn of the twentieth century, Lombroso espoused his belief that criminals possess an innate and "atavistic" predisposition toward crime.[29] Lombroso and William Ferrero attributed women's lower crime rate to their "piety, maternity, want of passion, sexual coldness, weakness, and undeveloped intelligence."[30] Women criminals, however, were deficient in such typical feminine characteristics. Instead, they exhibited "strong passions and intensely erotic tendencies," as well as high intelligence and physical strength.[31] Still, society believed that women criminals were capable only of a lower level of criminality because, as women, they lacked the "combination of intellectual functions" required of more demanding (*i.e.*, masculine) crimes, such as highway robbery, murder, and assault.[32]

Early socialist criminologists, emphasizing the importance of economic conditions on crime, criticized Lombroso's theories.[33] However, Willem Bonger, a prominent socialist criminologist, shared Lombroso's views[34]—despite his emphasis on economic conditions. According to Bonger, women commit fewer crimes because they have less "strength and courage" than men.[35] Likewise, women are not involved in "sexual crimes" both because they are physically unable to

---

cal determinist view that emphasizes a "non-cognitive, physiological" explanation for crimes committed by women. *See* SMART, *supra* note 23, at 27.

[27] *See id.* at 33.

[28] For a thorough profile of Lombroso's life and work, see Marvin E. Wolfgang, *Cesare Lombroso, 1835-1909, in* PIONEERS IN CRIMINOLOGY 232 (Hermann Mannheim ed., 1955; 2d ed. 1973).

[29] *See* CESARE LOMBROSO, CRIMINAL MAN 135 (1911). According to Lombroso, "[a]tavism, the reversion to a former state, is the first feeble indication of the reaction opposed by nature to the perturbing causes which seek to alter her delicate mechanism." *Id.*

[30] LOMBROSO & FERRERO, *supra* note 24, at 151.

[31] *Id.* Lombroso describes female offenders as more masculine. "Her maternal sense is weak because psychologically and anthropologically she belongs more to the male than to the female sex." *Id.* at 153.

[32] *See* CESARE LOMBROSO, CRIME: ITS CAUSES AND REMEDIES 185 (1911) ("To conceive an assassination, to make ready for it, to put it into execution demands, in a great number of cases at least, not only physical force, but a certain energy and a certain combination of intellectual functions. In this sort of development women almost always fall short of men.").

[33] *See* MESSERSCHMIDT, *supra* note 1, at 6; *see also* Wolfgang, *supra* note 28, at 257-71, for a more modern critique of Lombroso's theories and research.

[34] *See* MESSERSCHMIDT, *supra* note 1, at 6.

[35] WILLEM BONGER, CRIMINALITY AND ECONOMIC CONDITIONS 60 (1916).

commit them,[36] and because "the role of women in sexual life (and thus in the criminal sexual life) is rather passive than active."[37] Thus, Bonger emphasized both the impact of women's biology and their social conditions and positions in capitalist societies, as the reasons for their lower crime rate.[38] In 1923, W.I. Thomas continued this sexual nature-nurture theme depicting female criminality as primarily the result of sexual "demoralization," evidenced by casual sexual relations and poor socialization.[39] Indeed, a 1926 treatise on cocaine addiction viewed female cocaine users as particularly sexually "insatiable" under the drug's influence. The authors believed that such sexuality was the "stimulus" for later addiction and prostitution.[40]

Postwar views of female crime further emphasized sexuality and biological and sociological influences. For example, scholars compare Otto Pollak's book, *The Criminality of Women,*[41] to the works of Lombroso, Ferrero, and Thomas, because it takes a similar approach to the study of female crime.[42] Unlike Lombroso and Ferrero, Pollak did not rely entirely on a biological analysis, yet he did recognize the significance of biological and physiological foundations to female crime in the context of social and cultural influences.

According to Pollak, females are inherently manipulative and deceitful, characteristics derived from a number of their physiological and social attributes.[43] These include their passive roles during sexual intercourse and their ability to feign arousal, as well as social norms requiring women to hide menstruation and sexual information from children.[44] Such deceit allows females to conceal their crimes which,

---

[36] *See id.*

[37] *Id.*

[38] *See id.* at 59-64.

[39] *See* WILLIAM I. THOMAS, THE UNADJUSTED GIRL 98-150 (1923). Correspondingly, in the late nineteenth and early twentieth centuries, middle-class women could be acquitted for shop-lifting by attributing their behavior to kleptomania, then considered to be a "mental disorder" caused by "womb disease mania." It was believed that the disease lead to "larceny and eroticism with hysteria." ELAINE S. ABELSON, WHEN LADIES GO A-THIEVING: MIDDLE-CLASS SHOPLIFTERS IN THE VICTORIAN DEPARTMENT STORE 173-76 (1989).

[40] *See* ORIANA JOSSEAU KALANT, MAIER'S COCAINE ADDICTION 82 (1987) (translating DER KOKAINISMUS (1926)).

[41] OTTO POLLAK, THE CRIMINALITY OF WOMEN (1950).

[42] *See* SMART, *supra* note 23, at 46.

[43] *See* POLLAK, *supra* note 41, at 8-10.

[44] *See id.* at 10. As Pollak explained, a man "must achieve an erection in order to perform the sex act and will not be able to hide his failure." *Id.* For women, however,

> lack of orgasm does not prevent her ability to participate in the sex act. It cannot be denied that this basic physiological difference may well have a great influence on the degree of confidence which the two sexes have in the possible success of concealment and thus on their character pattern in this respect.

Id.

if detected, would be similar in frequency to males'.[45] Pollak particularly emphasized the significance of women's "generative" phases—menstruation, pregnancy, and menopause—as illustrations of the biological or psychological imbalances leading to crime.[46] Like Bonger, however, Pollak also attributed women's criminality to gender inequality in society.[47]

Pollak's theory, as well as other earlier theories of female crime, has been criticized.[48] Moreover, researchers have begun to rely more heavily on sociological explanations of women's lower criminality. They focus in particular on the propensity for society to more strongly persuade girls than boys to avoid delinquent behavior[49] and risk taking.[50] Essentially, society expects girls to follow biologically and culturally based "gender norms."[51] Although some researchers maintain that crime among females has increased as a consequence of growing gender equality,[52] others discount this explanation, focusing instead on the greater formalization of social control.[53] Social control theorists contend that the increase in arrests of female offenders is due to changes in law enforcement and reporting practices that create more consistent standards for decision making when an arrest is made. These changes reduce the effects of gender on the probability of arrest and the amount of "hidden" female crime.[54]

---

[45] *See id.* at 5-6.

[46] *See id.* at 157. "[T]hese generative phases are frequently accompanied by psychological disturbances which may upset the need and satisfaction balance of the individual or weaken her internal inhibitions, and thus become causative factors in female crime." *Id.*

[47] *See id.* at 2-3.

[48] *See* FRANCES HEIDENSOHN, WOMEN AND CRIME 120-21 (1985); SMART, *supra* note 23, at 46-53 (1976).

[49] *See* Greenberg, *supra* note 1, at 407-09; Ruth Morris, *Attitudes Toward Delinquency by Delinquents, Non-Delinquents, and Their Friends,* 5 BRITISH J. CRIMINOLOGY 249, 265 (1965); Raeder, *supra* note 18, at 909.

[50] *See* JOHN HAGAN, STRUCTURAL CRIMINOLOGY 158 (1989); John Hagan & Fiona Kay, *Gender and Delinquency in White-Collar Families: A Power-Control Perspective,* 36 CRIME & DELINQ. 391, 391-407 (1990).

[51] *See* Darrell Steffensmeier & Emilie Anderson Allan, *Sex Differences in Urban Arrest Patterns, 1934-1979,* 23 SOCIAL PROBLEMS 37, 37-50 (1981).

[52] *See supra* note 4 and accompanying text.

[53] For a discussion of this debate, see Steffensmeier (1993), *supra* note 4, at 411-41; Darrell Steffensmeier et al., *Development and Female Crime: A Cross-National Test of Alternative Explanations,* 68 SOCIAL FORCES 262, 262-83 (1989); Darrell Steffensmeier et al., *World War II and Its Effect on the Sex Differential in Arrests: An Empirical Test of the Sex-Role Equality and Crime Proposition,* 21 SOCIOLOGICAL Q. 403, 403-06 (1980); Darrell Steffensmeier & Cathy Streifel, *Time-Series Analysis of the Female Percentage of Arrests for Property Crimes, 1960-1985: A Test of Alternative Explanations,* 9 JUST. Q. 77, 77-103 (1992); Darrell Steffensmeier & Cathy Streifel, *Age, Gender, and Crime Across Three Historic Periods: 1935, 1960 and 1985,* 69 SOCIAL FORCES, 869, 870-71 (1991).

[54] *See* Steffensmeier & Streifel (1992), *supra* note 53, at 77-103.

B.   A MODERN VIEW OF FEMALE CRIME

The social-biological approach persists in more recent research on female crime which has focused on a variety of factors: parental deprivation and an inability to adjust to "feminine roles;"[55] psychiatric and familial disorders and impaired physical health;[56] sexual corruption;[57] conduct disorders;[58] and premenstrual and menstrual syndromes.[59] Commentators have criticized the methodology of these studies,[60] and their results remain inconclusive.

For example, most research has focused on females who commit minor offenses such as prostitution or drug use, and therefore may not vary significantly from nonoffenders. Research results are stronger when a study compares either nonoffenders or minor offenders to violent or habitual female offenders.

Researchers have linked violence among females to a host of factors: homosexuality, alcohol abuse, and psychiatric disturbances;[61] neurological abnormalities and problems with impulse control;[62] severe maternal loss, parental punishment, and neurological disorders among relatives;[63] and poor medical histories (indicated by injuries and perinatal and neurological abnormalities).[64] Although some research reports lower intelligence and achievement levels among female delinquents,[65] additional research indicates that other factors are more important contributors to female crime.[66]

Familial and environmental factors are more consistently significant. For example, considerable evidence shows that a broken home

---

[55] *See* MABEL RUTH FERNALD ET AL., A STUDY OF WOMEN DELINQUENTS IN NEW YORK STATE 525-26 (1986); CLYDE B. VEDDER & DORA B. SOMERVILLE, THE DELINQUENT GIRL 49-50, 153-54 (1970).

[56] *See* JOHN COWIE ET AL., DELINQUENCY IN GIRLS 169-79 (1968).

[57] *See* Erickson & Murray, *supra* note 24, at 137.

[58] *See* Kratzer & Hodgins, *supra* note 3.

[59] *See infra* notes 269 to 303.

[60] *See, e.g.*, SMART, *supra* note 23, at 54-76 (1976); Denno, *supra* note 10, at 619-45; Deborah W. Denno, Sex Differences in Cognition and Crime: Early Developmental, Biological, and Sociological Correlates 35-73 (1982) (unpublished Ph.D. dissertation, University of Pennsylvania); Erickson & Murray, *supra* note 24, at 137.

[61] *See* David A. Ward et al., *Crimes of Violence by Women, in* WOMEN, CRIME, AND JUSTICE 171, 171-91 (Susan K. Datesman & Frank R. Scarpitti eds., 1980).

[62] *See* Carlos E. Climent et al., *Epidemiological Studies of Female Prisoners. IV. Homosexual Behavior*, 164 J. NERV. & MENTAL DISEASE 25, 25-29 (1977).

[63] *See* Carlos E. Climent et al., *Epidemiological Studies of Women Prisoners. I. Medical and Psychiatric Variables Related to Violent Behavior*, 130 AM. J. PSYCH. 985, 985-90 (1973).

[64] *See* Shelley S. Shanok & Dorothy O. Lewis, *Medical Histories of Female Delinquents: Clinical and Epidemiological Findings*, 38 ARCHIVES OF GEN. PSYCH. 211, 211-13 (1981).

[65] *See* WILSON & HERRNSTEIN, *supra* note 1, at 116.

[66] *See* Climent et al., *supra* note 63, at 985-90; David R. Offord & Mary F. Poushinsky, *School Performance, IQ and Female Delinquency*, 27 INT'L J. SOCIAL PSYCH. 53, 53-62 (1982).

is one of the strongest predictors of delinquency among females.[67] Yet, the research is mixed with respect to whether a broken home or other negative family experiences have a greater impact on males or on females.[68] Some researchers contend that the consequences of family disorganization are more detrimental for females in light of the greater importance of the family for their supervision and attachment to conventional norms.[69] Others believe that the effects of family life show either no gender differences[70] or that stressful life events are more strongly associated with behavioral problems among males than among females.[71] One recent study concluded that the relationship was more complex, noting that the greater vulnerability of males or females may depend on the particular risk factor being analyzed (*e.g.*, marital stability and change).[72] For example, researchers found a significant association between delinquency among females and negative family events such as marital discord, recent marital disruption, and living in a single-parent home. They did not find any associations between those events and delinquency among males. Instead, males were more likely to appear depressed and anxious in the face of their parents' marital dissolution.[73]

Similar to research on the correlates of male delinquency, results with females may vary according to different samples and methodological techniques.[74] In general, however, research results show the following with respect to gender differences in the prediction of crime: (1) With some exceptions,[75] the factors found to be influential

---

[67] *See* COWIE ET AL., *supra* note 56, at 164-65; Susan K. Datesman & Frank R. Scarpitti, *Female Delinquency and Broken Homes: A Reassessment, in* WOMEN, CRIME, AND JUSTICE 129, 129 (Susan K. Datesman & Frank R. Scarpitti eds., 1980). This finding may be influenced by the racial composition of the sample. For example, one analysis of female violence showed no evidence of lower intelligence scores or a higher incidence of broken homes among offenders, while controlling for race. *See* Ward et al., *supra* note 61, at 171-91. However, in one study, loss of a father before age 10 was found to be highly correlated with depression among violent female offenders. *See* Carlos E. Climent et al., *Parental Loss, Depression and Violence. III. Epidemiological Studies of Female Prisoners,* 55 ACTA PSYCHIATRICA SCANDINAVICA 261, 261-68 (1977).

[68] *See* Maude Dornfeld & Candace Kruttschnitt, *Do the Stereotypes Fit? Mapping Gender Specific Outcomes and Risk Factors,* 30 CRIMINOLOGY 397, 397 (1992).

[69] *See* Datesman & Scarpitti, *supra* note 67, at 129; Steffensmeier & Allan, *supra* note 1, at 73-74.

[70] *See* Canter, *supra* note 3, at 149-67; Dornfeld & Kruttschnitt, *supra* note 68, at 397.

[71] *See* Dornfeld & Kruttschnitt, *supra* note 68, at 397.

[72] *See id.*

[73] *See id.* at 409-12. Because the sample in this study was young (the great majority of subjects were under age 16), the authors rightly emphasize that the results of their study could change if the subjects were older. *See id.* at 407, 413.

[74] *See generally* DENNO, BIOLOGY AND VIOLENCE, *supra* note 10.

[75] For example, there is some evidence that some minor physical anomalies may be associated with hyperactive behavior among boys but not with hypoactive behavior among

in crime among males are also influential in crime among females;[76] and (2) because society places stricter cultural constraints on female behavior,[77] females who become delinquent or violent appear to deviate more significantly from the norm—biologically, psychologically, or sociologically—than their male counterparts.[78] Thus, females who decide to engage in crime "must traverse a greater moral and psychological distance than males."[79]

C.   GENDER AND PREVALENCE

Gender differences in the prediction of crime may substantially

---

girls. The bases for these differences could be attributed to biological factors (*e.g.*, different hormonal or central nervous system structures) or socialization processes that accentuate behavioral problems among boys but inhibit them among girls. *See* Mary F. Waldrop et al., *Minor Physical Anomalies and Inhibited Behavior in Elementary School Girls*, 17 J. CHILD PSYCHOLOGY & PSYCHIATRY & ALLIED DISCIPLINES 113, 113-22 (1976).

[76] *See* WILSON & HERRNSTEIN, *supra* note 1, at 115-16; Steffensmeier & Allan, *supra* note 1, at 71; Romanowski, *supra* note 3, at 204. The research of Sheldon and Eleanor Glueck on both males and females has had comparable results. *Compare generally* SHELDON GLUECK & ELEANOR T. GLUECK, FIVE HUNDRED DELINQUENT WOMEN (1934) *with* SHELDON GLUECK & ELEANOR T. GLUECK, FIVE HUNDRED CRIMINAL CAREERS (1930). According to Steffensmeier and Allan, *supra* note 1,

> [g]roups or societies that have high male rates of crime also have high female rates, whereas groups or societies that have low male rates also have low female rates. Over time, when the male rate rises, declines, or holds steady across a specific historic period, the female rate behaves in a similar fashion. This suggests that the rates of both sexes are influenced by similar social and legal forces, independent of any condition unique to women.

Id. at 71.

[77] Steffensmeier & Allan, *supra* note 1, at 71.

> [I]t is probable that the lower involvement of girls in delinquency continues to be primarily related to existing socialization patterns, in particular the greater restrictions placed on the freedom of movement of most girls at the age when their male peers are "discovering" delinquency. . . . The realization of a lack of access to illegitimate opportunity structures for adolescent girls and women is of course a most perceptive insight into an understanding of female criminality.

SMART, *supra* note 23, at 68.

[78] *See* COWIE ET AL., *supra* note 56, at 166; C. Robert Cloninger et al., *Implications of Sex Differences in the Prevalences of Antisocial Personality, Alcoholism, and Criminality for Familial Transmission*, 35 ARCH. GEN. PSYCH. 941, 941-51 (1978); C. Robert Cloninger et al., *The Multifactorial Model of Disease Transmission: II. Sex Differences in the Familial Transmission of Sociopathy (antisocial personality)*, 127 BRITISH J. PSYCH. 11, 11-22 (1975).

[79] Steffensmeier & Allan, *supra* note 1, at 71; *see also* WILSON & HERRNSTEIN, *supra* note 1, at 117 ("If aggression or its antisocial expression is stronger in the average male than the average female, then females would be less likely to pass over the threshold into criminal behavior and, when they did, they would be more atypical, or deviant, among women than male offenders are among men."). Lombroso drew a similar, albeit more strongly put, conclusion:

> As a double exception [to her gender and to criminality], the criminal woman is consequently a monster. Her normal sister is kept in the paths of virtue by many causes, such as maternity, piety, weakness, and when these counter influences fail, and a woman commits a crime, we may conclude that her wickedness must have been enormous before it could triumph over so many obstacles.

LOMBROSO & FERRERO, *supra* note 24, at 152.

affect differences in prevalence. Gender becomes particularly important when assessing the "criminal careers"[80] of individual offenders, because predictive influences may vary depending on an individual's age and physiological development. An analysis of a criminal career focuses on two key elements: (1) *participation*—the difference between those who do or do not commit a crime; and (2) *frequency*—the number of crimes an active offender commits.[81] Certain factors, such as the offender's age at the initiation of a criminal career, the escalation and desistance of the offender's criminal behavior, and the policy approaches for restraining criminal careers, are influential in determining the onset and continuation of criminal careers. The most pertinent policies include the "three- strikes-and-you're-out" legislation that Congress has included in the new federal Crime Bill,[82] and which is currently implemented in a number of states.[83]

---

[80] A criminal career is the depiction of the number and types of crimes committed by an individual over a period of time. *See* 1 CRIMINAL CAREERS AND "CAREER CRIMINALS" 12 (Albert Blumstein et al. eds., 1986).

[81] *See* Kruttschnitt, *supra* note 2, at 318-19.

[82] The federal statute imposing penalties for manufacture or distribution of controlled substances already contains a provision that if a "person commits a violation . . . of this title after two or more prior convictions for a felony drug offense have become final, such person shall be sentenced to a mandatory term of life imprisonment without release . . . " 21 U.S.C.A. § 841(b)(1)(A) (West Supp. 1994). In addition, the recently enacted federal Crime Bill contains a provision that "a person who is convicted in a court of the United States of a serious violent felony shall be sentenced to life imprisonment if: (A) the person has been convicted (and those convictions have become final) on separate prior occasions in a court of the United States or of a State of: (i) 2 or more serious violent felonies; or (ii) one or more serious violent felonies and one or more serious drug offenses. . . . " H.R. REP. No. 711, 103d Cong., 2d Sess., title VIII, § 70001, 1994 WL 454841 (1994). Furthermore, the portion of the Crime Bill allocating federal funding to states in need of prison space attempts to induce states to enact similar legislation. It requires that, in order to be eligible for funding, states "shall demonstrate that the State: (1) has in effect laws which require that persons convicted of violent crimes serve not less than 85 percent of the sentence imposed; or (2) since 1993: (A) has increased the percentage of convicted violent offenders sentenced to prison; (B) has increased the average prison time which will be served in prison by convicted violent offenders sentenced to prison; (C) has increased the percentage of sentences which will be served in prison by violent offenders sentenced to prison; and (D) has in effect at the time of application laws requiring that a person who is convicted of a violent crime shall serve not less than 85 percent of the sentence imposed if: (i) the person has been convicted on 1 or more prior occasions in a court of the United States or of a State of a violent crime or a serious drug offense; and (ii) each violent crime or serious drug offense was committed after the defendant's conviction of the preceding violent crime or serious drug offense." *Id.* at tit. II, § 20102.

[83] For example, Washington places third-time felons and fourth-time fraudulent misdemeanors in prison for life. WASH. REV. CODE ANN. § 9.92.090 (West 1994). California sets forth a number of specific violent crimes for which three-time felons receive twenty year sentences and four-time felons receive life without parole. CAL. PENAL CODE § 667.7 (West 1994). Florida sentences those with two prior felony convictions to life, 30 years, or 10 years, depending on the degree of the current felony. FLA. STAT. ANN. § 775.084 (West 1994). Texas sentences third-time felons to "life, or for any term of not more than 99 years

The limited research that has compared violent male and female career criminals has found substantial differences: (1) although violent offenses comprise only a small percentage of all the offenses committed by offenders in any population, females participate in substantially less violent crime than males during the course of their criminal careers;[84] (2) the careers of violent females both begin and peak earlier than those of males;[85] (3) females are far less likely than males to repeat their violent offenses; and (4) females are far more likely to desist from further violence.[86]

Other researchers have shown, however, that although females are far less apt to participate in serious criminal activity than males, once they do participate, they commit crime at a comparable rate.[87] These researchers suggest that the large differences reported for males and females in aggregate crime statistics may be due to the differences found in rates of participation, not in frequency of offending.[88] This is a viable suggestion, but the limited amount of research comparing gender differences in crime rates prevents certainty. The next section of this Article demonstrates that comparisons between male and female offenders in the Biosocial Study did not support this proposal; males had both higher rates of participation in crime, as well as greater frequency in offending.[89]

---

or less than 25 years." TEX. PENAL CODE ANN. § 12.42 (West 1994). Alabama adopted a scheme which sentences second-, third-, and fourth-time felons more harshly based on the class of the offense, with the result being life without parole or similarly long sentences. ALA. CODE § 13A-5-9 (1977). Arkansas has a similar 'class of the offense' scheme that results in sentences ranging from three years to life without parole. ARK. CODE ANN. § 5-4-501 (Michie 1987). Kentucky sentences second-time felons "for the next highest degree than the offense for which convicted" and third-time felons from ten years to life, without parole. KY. REV. STAT. ANN. § 532.080 (Michie/Bobbs-Merrill 1971). Minnesota sentences third-time sex criminals to life. MINN. STAT. ANN. § 609.346 (West 1994). Indiana allows third-time felons to be given sentences three times longer than the presumptive sentence for the crime, and third-time violent felons to be given life sentences without parole. IND. CODE ANN. § 35-50-2-8 (Burns 1994). Illinois sentences certain third-time felons to "natural life imprisonment." 730 ILCS 5/5-5-3 (Michie 1993). Colorado sentences third-time felons to "three times the maximum of the presumptive range" and fourth-time felons to four times that, or "at least forty calendar years". COLO. REV. STAT. ANN. § 16-13-101 (West 1994). Maryland sentences third-time felons to 25 years and fourth-time felons to life without possibility of parole. MD. CODE ANN. 1957, Art. 27, § 643b.

[84] See Neil Alan Weiner, *Violent Criminal Careers and Violent Career Criminals, in* VIOLENT CRIME, VIOLENT CRIMINALS 35, 49, 56, 121 (Neil Alan Weiner & Marvin E. Wolfgang eds., 1989); 1 CRIMINAL CAREERS AND "CAREER CRIMINALS," *supra* note 80, at 40.

[85] See Weiner, *supra* note 84, at 102.

[86] See *id.* at 108-09.

[87] See 1 CRIMINAL CAREERS AND "CAREER CRIMINALS," *supra* note 80, at 67.

[88] See *id.* Kruttschnitt notes that the differences in results among research studies may be due to the different kinds of data sets that the researchers used. *See* Kruttschnitt, *supra* note 2, at 319-20.

[89] See *infra* notes 133 to 153 and accompanying text.

Gender differences in the prevalence and seriousness of crime hold within all ethnic groups, but in different magnitudes. For example, there are fewer gender differences in the prevalence of crime among black offenders relative to white offenders. Further, the discrepancy in crime rates between black females and white females is considerably greater than the discrepancy between black males and white males.[90] In some studies, however, black females have demonstrated a higher incidence of violence than white males,[91] a disparity some have attributed to a differential exposure to poverty.[92] In general, there has been relatively little crime research on blacks, a limitation that has been roundly criticized.[93]

The following sections of this Article examine possible gender differences in crime within a sample of black males and females, relying on an unusually rich data base of biological, psychological, and sociological variables. These sections focus on two issues: (1) differences in prevalence, with a particular emphasis on criminal careers, and (2) differences in prediction and how it may be interrelated with prevalence. Prevalence is important in determining the nature and extent of gender differences in crime and violence and in examining whether such differences justify gender-based standards of punishment or sentencing. Prediction is important in assessing what factors may have contributed to criminal acts over various developmental stages and, more particularly, why there may be some gender differences in the types of predictors. This approach also enables some investigation of the suggestion that biological factors can better explain crime among females, whereas social or environmental factors can better explain crime among males.[94] Whether such differences should justify differences in punishment, or gender-based defenses, is addressed in the last part of this Article.

---

[90] *See* Susan K. Datesman & Frank R. Scarpitti, *The Extent and Nature of Female Crime, in* WOMEN, CRIME, AND JUSTICE 3, 3-64 (Susan K. Datesman & Frank R. Scarpitti eds., 1980); Kruttschnitt, *supra* note 2, at 311-12; Lee H. Bowker, *The Incidence of Female Crime and Delinquency—A Comparison of Official and Self-Report Statistics,* 1 INT'L J. WOMEN'S STUDIES 178, 178-92 (1978).

[91] *See* Kruttschnitt, *supra* note 2, at 311-12; Baskin et al., *supra* note 4; Bowker, *supra* note 90, at 178-92; Roland Chilton & Susan K. Datesman, *Gender, Race, and Crime: An Analysis of Urban Arrest Trends, 1960-1980,* 1 GENDER & SOC'Y 152, 152-71 (1987); Gary D. Hill & Elizabeth M. Crawford, *Women, Race, and Crime,* 28 CRIMINOLOGY 601, 601-23 (1990); John H. Laub & M. Joan McDermott, *An Analysis of Serious Crime by Young Black Women,* 23 CRIMINOLOGY 81, 81-98 (1985).

[92] *See* Baskin et al., *supra* note 4.

[93] *See infra* note 96 and accompanying text.

[94] *See* SMART, *supra* note 23, at 56.

III. The Biosocial Study of Crime

The 987 subjects who participated in the Biosocial Study were born at Philadelphia's Pennsylvania Hospital between 1959 and 1962. The subjects and their families were originally part of the Collaborative Perinatal Project, one of the largest medical projects ever conducted in the United States.[95] Each one of the subjects was black because there were too few white subjects to study, and because, at the time, commentators had complained that little research had been devoted to studying crime among black youths.[96] The sample was se-

---

[95] In 1957, the National Institute of Neurological Diseases and Stroke launched the Collaborative Perinatal Project, a nationwide study of biological and environmental influences on pregnancy, and infant and childhood mortality, as well as physical, neurological, and psychological development in children. Nearly 60,000 pregnant women participated in the study between 1959 and 1966 in 15 different medical centers. One of these medical centers was located in Philadelphia. Examination of the children from the time of their birth through age seven continued until 1974. *See* Niswander & Gordon, *supra* note 11, at 3-7.

The Philadelphia Perinatal Project comprised the nearly 10,000 pregnant patients who delivered their children at Pennsylvania Hospital between 1959 and 1965; the children were later tested at Children's Hospital of the University of Pennsylvania. *See id.* at 11. All pregnant women who attended Pennsylvania Hospital during this time were included in the Philadelphia Perinatal Project if they wanted to be, except for those women who were unregistered emergency deliveries or who were planning to deliver elsewhere. The total sample in the Philadelphia Perinatal Project reflects, in part, the characteristics of families who would be interested in receiving inexpensive maternity care provided by a public clinic. The sample was comprised predominantly (87%) of black families whose socioeconomic levels were slightly lower than those of the United States population at the time. *See id.* at 10, 475, 498. In 1978, the National Institute of Justice awarded a grant to the Sellin Center for Studies in Criminology and Criminal Law at the University of Pennsylvania to examine the Philadelphia Perinatal Project children. As part of the grant, public school and police record data were collected on all 10,000 youths. For eight years thereafter, detailed data were organized and analyzed on a subsample consisting of the nearly 1000 individuals who constituted the subjects for the Biosocial Study. These 1000 subjects were selected from the first four years (1959-62) or from "cohorts" of 2958 black mothers who participated in the Philadelphia Perinatal Project. A "cohort" is "[a]ny group that passes through a set of experiences or institutions at the same time." Neale & Liebert, *supra* note 9, at 309.

[96] The Biosocial Study's research on black youths was initiated in 1980 at a time when black commentators were criticizing the Office of Juvenile Justice and Delinquency Prevention ("Office") for spending most (80%) of its monies researching white youths. *See* William Raspberry, *Youth Crime Funds Go to the Whites*, Phila. Inquirer, Apr. 1, 1980, at 9A. Essentially, commentators accused the Office of using crime statistics on black youths in order to acquire money, which the Office would then spend on research or rehabilitation programs for white youths. One result was that a growing number of white youths were being removed from the criminal justice system through deinstitutionalization and diversion programs, while a growing number of black youths were populating the prisons. Some commentators claimed that the premise underlying such differential treatment was that serious black offenders could not be similarly treated through counselling or diversion. *See id.* Because of these claims, many federal programs providing research funding on crime today urge grant applicants "to assess carefully the feasibility of including the broadest possible representation of minority groups" in their samples. Dept. of Health and

lected according to certain criteria to ensure that all subjects attended Philadelphia public schools and remained in the city, and thus the same urban environment, from the time of their birth to age twenty-two.[97] To test different theories of crime, the Biosocial Study used, in addition to urban environment, three primary data sources: (1) the Collaborative Perinatal Project's data set of early biological and environmental factors; (2) public school records; and (3) official police records for juveniles and adults.

The amount of data available for early biological and environmental factors was extraordinarily comprehensive. Upon registration for the Perinatal Project, each mother underwent a battery of interviews and physical examinations that provided data for each pregnancy, including the mother's reproductive history, recent and past medical history, and labor and delivery events. Data recorded for each child included information on neurological examinations conducted at birth, throughout the hospital stay, at four months, and at ages one and seven. Additionally, the children had their speech, language, and hearing examined at ages three and eight. Researchers collected socioeconomic and family data during the mother's registration and the child's seven-year examination.[98]

Philadelphia public school records also contained a variety of

---

Human Services, Public Health Service, Nat'l Insts. of Health, Nat'l Inst. on Alcohol Abuse and Alcoholism, *Program Announcement: Research on Relationships Between Alcohol and Violence* (June 1993). The racial and socioeconomic characteristics of the Biosocial Study's sample (black and lower-class) limits the extent to which the results of the Study can be generalized to other groups that may comprise individuals of a different race and socioeconomic status, such as middle-class whites. However, the demographic homogeneity of the Biosocial Study's sample provides built-in "controls" for those racial and socioeconomic factors that have been strongly linked to crime and its determinants. *See generally* Marvin E. Wolfgang et al., Delinquency in a Birth Cohort (1972). Therefore, it can be assumed that the results of the Biosocial Study are not attributed to racial and socioeconomic variations among individuals.

97 These subjects were selected according to the following criteria: (1) attended a Philadelphia public school, (2) stayed in Philadelphia from ages 10 through 17, (3) received selected intelligence tests within six months of age seven and achievement tests at ages 13 and 14, and (4) did not have a sibling in the sample to prevent the possible biases that could result in examining family members. Comparisons between the final sample of 987 subjects and the excluded sample of 2158 black subjects showed no significant differences in key variables: total family income, per capita family income, the number of prenatal examinations attended by the mother, the mother's age, and the distribution of males and females. In general, the final sample appeared to be representative of the sample from which it was drawn. *See* Denno, Biology and Violence, *supra* note 10, at 30.

98 Data were collected immediately after an event occurred. Highly structured forms and manuals were used to ensure comprehensiveness and comparability among the coders who recorded the data. All coders were either medical doctors or psychologists trained to record data systematically. For descriptions of the numerous procedures used to ensure reliability in the Project's coding, see Niswander & Gordon, *supra* note 11, at 17-19, 500-24.

161

data about each subject. The Biosocial Study relied predominately on two types: (1) academic achievement during ages thirteen and fourteen[99] and (2) evidence of learning or disciplinary problems.[100]

In addition, the Biosocial Study collected official police records for all subjects from ages seven to twenty-two. The Study used three different measures of juvenile and adult crime: (1) number of offenses; (2) categorization of juvenile offenders according to levels of the most serious offense recorded (violence, property, and nonindex);[101] and (3) seriousness of offenses.[102]

---

[99] The California Achievement Test measured academic achievement in grades seven and eight, which were attended during ages 13 and 14. Social scientists have described the California Achievement Test as an excellent data source for measuring both verbal and mathematical achievement. *See* DENNO, BIOLOGY AND VIOLENCE, *supra* note 10, at 171-73. Researchers have found a high correlation between that test and the other tests measuring achievement that were administered in the Perinatal Project at age seven. *Id.* at 169. Moreover, the standardization sample for the California Achievement Test allowed for "proportionate representation in the national norms of minority group students in the total school population." *Id.* at 171 (citation omitted). However, social scientists have found evidence of test bias in a number of other psychological tests administered in the Perinatal Project based upon a wide range of possible racial, socioeconomic, and cultural influences. *Id.* at 173. Because the individuals in the Biosocial Study were racially and socioeconomically homogenous, many of the factors most influential in creating test bias did not exist in the Study's analyses.

[100] Learning and disciplinary problems during school were measured, respectively, by the presence of any record of the child's involvement in special school programs for those classified as being mentally retarded or as having disciplinary problems. Children with disciplinary problems were diagnosed as having normal intelligence but some record of asocial behavior in school, including a history of starting fires, physical aggression toward teachers, maladjustment to school, and conduct disturbance. The Philadelphia School Board stated that any school's recommendation of a child to a special school program was made independently of any knowledge of that child's official delinquency status. *See id.* at 32, 62-63.

[101] *See id.* at 32. Violent offenders were those individuals who had a record of at least one violent offense at any time during their juvenile criminal career. Violent offenses consisted of murder, assault with intent to kill, aggravated assault, simple assault, rape, robbery with injury, and any other offense that involved injury to the victim. Property offenders had a record of at least one property-related offense, but no history of violent offenses. Property-related offenses included vandalism, burglary, robbery without injury, and auto theft. Nonindex offenders had a record of at least one nonindex offense, but no history of violent or property-related offenses. Nonindex offenses comprised truancy, disorderly conduct, running away, fraud, and possession of alcohol, marihuana, or hard drugs. *See id.* at 39.

[102] The method of ranking and scoring offense seriousness was based on a widely accepted and validated system of assigning numerical weights to different components of an offense that was derived from a national survey of crime severity. *See generally* MARVIN E. WOLFGANG ET AL., THE NATIONAL SURVEY OF CRIME SEVERITY (1985). The different components of an offense included the seriousness of personal injury to the victim, the amount of property theft or damage, the extent to which the victim was intimidated (*e.g.*, through a threat of gross bodily harm), the number of premises that the offender entered, and the number of vehicles stolen. *Id.* at 129-36.

A.   BIOLOGICAL AND SOCIOLOGICAL THEORIES OF CRIME

A multidisciplinary approach to crime is crucial for understanding both why crime occurs and the conditions for any possible gender differences. This approach also requires some sense of the Biosocial Study sample's surroundings.

1.   *Urban, Socioeconomic, and Environmental Factors*

When the Biosocial Study's subjects were young children, most blacks with low incomes were concentrated in Philadelphia's inner city areas, which were socially and culturally isolated.[103] It is difficult to measure whether any improvement occured during the Study's twenty-two year period.[104] In Philadelphia and other large cities, other types of problems had increased substantially since the 1960s, such as homelessness,[105] drug abuse,[106] and the social isolation of the ghetto.[107] These factors have been found to be significant contributors to crime generally,[108] and to the likelihood of criminal behavior among females in particular.[109]

---

[103] *See* CONRAD WEILER, PHILADELPHIA: NEIGHBORHOOD, AUTHORITY, AND THE URBAN CRISIS 181-82 (1974); John F. Bauman et al., *Public Housing, Isolation, and the Urban Underclass*, 17 J. URB. HIST. 264, 265, 273-86 (1991).

[104] *See* ROGER LANE, WILLIAM DORSEY'S PHILADELPHIA AND OURS ON THE PAST AND FUTURE OF THE BLACK CITY IN AMERICA 374-409 (1991); William J. Wilson, *The Ghetto Underclass and the Social Transformation of the Inner City, in* THE BLACK SCHOLAR at 10-11 (May/June 1988); *see generally* WILLIAM J. STULL & JANICE FANNING MADDEN, POST-INDUSTRIAL PHILADELPHIA: STRUCTURAL CHANGES IN THE METROPOLITAN ECONOMY (1990).

[105] *See* Elaine R. Fox & Lisa Roth, *Homeless Children: Philadelphia as a Case Study*, 506 ANNALS AM. ACAD. POL. & SOC. SCI. 141 (1989).

[106] *See, e.g.*, Michael deCourcy Hinds, *Pennsylvania City Hopes It's Bouncing Back From the Bottom*, N.Y. TIMES, Jan. 5, 1992, at A14; Tom Morganthau, *Children of the Underclass*, NEWSWEEK, Sept. 11, 1989, at 16.

[107] *See* Wilson, *supra* note 104, at 14-16.

[108] Evidence that crime is associated with community and urban factors was first investigated on a large scale by Clifford Shah and Henry McKay in Chicago and other metropolitan areas. *See* CLIFFORD R. SHAW & HENRY D. MCKAY, JUVENILE DELINQUENCY IN URBAN AREAS (1972). A substantial amount of research since that time has confirmed their conclusion that high rates of crime are concentrated in areas where residents are deprived socioeconomically. *See* Reiss & Roth, *supra* note 3, at 131-39; E. Britt Patterson, *Poverty, Income Inequality, and Community Crime Rates*, 29 CRIMINOLOGY 755, 755-64 (1991) (reviewing recent research on poverty and crime). Other researchers contend, however, that social instability, and not socioeconomic deprivation, accounts for the association between community characteristics and crime. *See* Patterson, *supra*, at 762-63 (noting that although a considerable amount of research demonstrates a link between poverty and crime, other research has uncovered additional factors indicating a link between crime and factors associated with social instability, including: residential mobility, family disorganization, and population density); *see also* Richard Block, *Community, Environment, and Violent Crime*, 17 CRIMINOLOGY 46 (1979) (emphasizing factors other than poverty).

[109] *See, e.g.*, Baskin & Sommers, *supra* note 2, at 577 (showing that initiation into violent street crime for the women offenders in their study was "influenced strongly by the neighborhood environment").

Aside from "controlling," or accounting for the effects of urban environment, the Biosocial Study examined other kinds of socioeconomic and environmental data, as well as indicators of family instability or disorganization. These data included: parents' occupation, education, and employment history; family income and size; religion; welfare status; child's residence in a foster home; and number of persons supported in the household. Many of these factors were interrelated.[110]

2. *Biological and Psychological Factors*

Biological and psychological theories of crime emphasize the physiological and psychological capacities for individuals to adjust to their environments and to learn appropriate behavior. Individuals who show central nervous system disorders, delayed maturation, or low intelligence test scores, for example, may be more vulnerable to negative or stressful environments.[111] These relationships exist regardless of the racial or socioeconomic characteristics of those individuals, although low income minorities are more likely to be raised in stressful environments.[112]

In the Biosocial Study, indicators of developmental or psychological theories were grouped very generally into six types: (1) early central nervous system development (*e.g.*, prenatal, perinatal, and pregnancy complications and the Apgar score, which is an accepted and validated scale of health and development immediately following birth);[113] (2) intelligence and cerebral dominance or laterality (*e.g.*, measures of verbal and spatial ability, as well as indicators of cerebral dominance or laterality, such as the child's hand, eye, and foot preference, which are indicative of learning disabilities);[114] (3) physical

---

[110] For a description of how these variables were measured and interrelated, see DENNO, BIOLOGY AND VIOLENCE, *supra* note 10, at 19-24.

[111] *See id.* at 24-28.

[112] *See id.* at 19.

[113] The term "prenatal" refers to the period between conception and birth. The term "perinatal" refers to the period near the time of birth. Considerable research points to associations among prenatal and perinatal complications and central nervous system dysfunction. Generally, early brain damage, primarily due to hypoxia (a severe lack of oxygen), may be related to later neuropsychiatric disturbances such as impaired intelligence or achievement, attention-deficit disorder (minimal brain dysfunction), pathological cerebral dominance, and reading failure. Directly or indirectly through these disturbances, pregnancy complication may also lead to general physical or behavioral disorders and delinquency. *See id.*

[114] Evidence of anatomic and functional differences in the lateralization of the two (left and right) hemispheres of the brain provides one explanation for intellectual variation in the general population. "Lateralization" refers to the "localization of a psychological function in a single hemisphere." Bonnie Burstein et al., *Sex Differences in Cognitive Functioning: Evidence, Determinants, Implications*, 23 HUMAN DEVELOPMENT 289, 204 (1980). Individuals

growth and development (*e.g.*, measures of height and weight);[115] (4) neurological status (*e.g.*, "soft neurological signs" or lack of coordination); (5) attention deficit disorder and hyperactivity (*e.g.*, evidence of disciplinary problems in childhood and adolescence, as well as mixed indicators of cerebral dominance or laterality and difficulty with left-right identification);[116] and (6) general physical health (*e.g.*, high

---

who are more lateralized tend to show greater hemispheric specialization in processing information relative to less lateralized individuals. For most (right-handed) individuals, the left cerebral hemisphere specializes in processing verbal stimuli—notably language functions—in a sequential, analytic, and propositional mode, whereas the right hemisphere specializes in processing nonverbal stimuli—particularly spatial functions—in a nonlinguistic, holistic, and synthetic manner. WISC Verbal IQ and other verbal measures are widely used indicators of left-hemispheric abilities; WISC Performance IQ and other spatial measures are indicators of right-hemispheric abilities. Additional factors have also been found to be associated with cerebral lateralization, most notably hand preference and, to a lesser extent, eye and foot preference.

Generally, handedness, gender, and intellectual abilities show three basic interrelationships reported in the literature: (1) a disproportionately higher incidence of males and left-or-mixed-handers among children with language, reading, or learning disorders; (2) evidence that the different patterns of hemispheric specialization in males and females may be related to handedness; and (3) a higher incidence of left-handedness in males relative to females.

Evidence that some left-handers tend to rely on the "less analytic, more emotional, more impulsive response modes" associated with the right hemisphere has been used to explain their greater involvement in delinquency and violence. This tendency may also explain why left-handers and delinquents experience greater deficits in left hemisphere tasks such as reading and language. Some investigators suggest a greater left hemisphere deficit among both delinquents and poor readers irrespective of their lateral preference. Other research points to a right hemisphere deficit among delinquents or evidence of other symptoms of cerebral disorder, such as attention deficit disorder or what the earlier literature labeled as minimal brain dysfunction. *See* DENNO, BIOLOGY AND VIOLENCE, *supra* note 10, at 13-15.

115 Physical growth, even at an early age, is one of several indicators of subsequent health and development and physical maturation during adolescence. Relationships among indicators of physical development and central nervous system and behavioral disorders, however, are inconsistent. *See* DENNO, BIOLOGY AND VIOLENCE, *supra* note 10, at 16.

116 The terminology for such conditions has changed over time. Today, the condition is known as "attention deficit hyperactivity disorder." This Article will refer to the terms attention deficit disorder and hyperactivity separately, however, (as is still done) because this Article is based on older data that have been collected and analyzed with these particular conditions in mind. Attention deficit disorder (ADD), or what much of the earlier literature termed minimal brain dysfunction, and hyperactivity are noted correlates of school failure and delinquency. The term hyperactivity, in particular, describes the heterogenous behaviors of children who show one or more of the following: overactivity, perceptual-motor impairments, impulsivity, emotional lability, attention deficits, minor disturbances of speech, intellectual defects (*e.g.*, learning disabilities), clumsiness, and antisocial responses. By definition, children with below normal intelligence or very severe neurological problems are excluded. Explanations for the causes of ADD include prenatal or birth trauma, neurodevelopmental lag, psychogenic factors, minor physical anomalies, genetic transmission, and poor living environment.

Generally, children with ADD indicate certain learning or behavioral deficiencies associated with central nervous system dysfunctioning. Problem behaviors among ADD children appear to correspond with age. For example, young children (ages 2 to 6 years) may

blood pressure, pica, lead poisoning, and anemia).[117]

This research suggests that both biological and environmental influences, as well as gender, interact and cumulate as risk factors predictive of later mental and behavioral disorders. For example, males "appear to be more vulnerable to all manner of environmental insult and developmental difficulty."[118] Overall, they experience a higher incidence of prenatal and perinatal mortality and complications, childhood diseases, reading and learning disorders, mental retardation,[119] as well as left-handedness and left hemisphere deficits.[120] The incidence for most of these disorders is highest in socioeconomically deprived or "stressed" circumstances.[121] Likewise, researchers found a disproportionate number of delinquents and criminals among individuals with cognitive and developmental difficulties.[122]

B.   CRIMINAL BEHAVIOR AT DIFFERENT AGES

Few studies have examined criminal behavior over a person's life span.[123] Uniform Crime Report data show, however, considerable differences in the types and frequencies of arrests reported according to age. In general, juveniles (ages ten to eighteen) are more likely than young adults to have a police contact for property offenses and relatively less serious crimes, whereas young adults (ages nineteen to twenty-five) are more likely than juveniles to have a police contact for

---

exhibit lack of discipline and hyperactivity; older children (during elementary school and adolescence) may demonstrate reading and learning disorders, academic underachievement, and delinquent or aggressive behaviors. Whereas central nervous system dysfunction may underlie some childhood disorders, evidence suggests that behavioral deviations can result from developmental or maturational lags many children eventually do not outgrow. Longitudinal follow-up studies indicate that children who do not outgrow behavioral disorders may retain antisocial conduct into adulthood. *See id.* at 15-16.

[117] *See id.* at 37-39.

[118] June Machover Reinisch et al., *Prenatal Influences on Cognitive Abilities: Data From Experimental Animals and Human Genetic and Endocrine Syndromes, in* SEX-RELATED DIFFERENCES IN COGNITIVE FUNCTIONING: DEVELOPMENTAL ISSUES 215, 220 (Michele Andrisin Wittig & Anne C. Petersen eds., 1979).

[119] *See id.*

[120] *See* Louise Carter-Salzman, *Patterns of Cognitive Functioning in Relation to Handedness and Sex-Related Differences, in* SEX-RELATED DIFFERENCES IN COGNITIVE FUNCTIONING: DEVELOPMENTAL ISSUES 189, 204-09 (Michele Andrisin Wittig & Anne C. Petersen eds., 1979).

[121] KATHERINE BLICK HOYENGA & KERMIT T. HOYENGA, THE QUESTION OF SEX DIFFERENCES: PSYCHOLOGICAL, CULTURAL, AND BIOLOGICAL ISSUES 236-37 (1979); DENNIS HERBERT STOTT, STUDIES OF TROUBLESOME CHILDREN 9-61 (1966).

[122] For a review of the literature, see DENNO, BIOLOGY AND VIOLENCE, *supra* note 10; Terrie E. Moffitt, *The Neuropsychology of Juvenile Delinquency: A Critical Review, in* CRIMINAL JUSTICE: AN ANNUAL REVIEW OF RESEARCH 99 (Norval Morris & Michael Tonry eds., 1990); Terrie E. Moffitt & Bill Henry, *Neuropsychological Studies of Juvenile Delinquency and Juvenile Violence, in* NEUROPSYCHOLOGY OF AGGRESSION 67 (J. S. Milner ed., 1991).

[123] *See* Marvin E. Wolfgang et al., *Preface, in* FROM BOY TO MAN, FROM DELINQUENCY TO CRIME xiii (Marvin E. Wolfgang et al. eds., 1987).

violent and serious crimes.[124] Moreover, juveniles who evidence relatively more aggressive childhood behavior or delinquent offenses are more likely to be adult offenders than their less delinquent or nondelinquent counterparts.[125]

Among both juveniles and adults, however, research shows that a small percentage of individuals is responsible for the majority of police contacts.[126] For example, a longitudinal study of nearly 10,000 boys born in 1945, and living in Philadelphia from ages ten to eighteen,[127] determined that chronic offenders (those who have five or more offenses) constituted only 6% of the entire cohort of boys and 18% of the offenders. However, chronic offenders were responsible for over half (52%) of all police contacts in the cohort.[128] A subsequent study, of a cohort of Philadelphia boys born in 1958,[129] showed an increase in the number of offenses committed by chronic delinquents. Chronic delinquents comprised 7.5% of the cohort and 23% of the offenders, yet they were responsible for 61% of all police contacts in the cohort.[130] Research has also shown that a small group of adult offenders is responsible for most adult offenses.[131]

The behaviors and characteristics of chronic offenders are important with respect to both social policy and criminal responsibility. For example, "there is excellent evidence that some biological factors are especially useful in distinguishing chronic offenders."[132] Yet, only a limited amount of research has examined gender distinctions among

---

[124] *See* Frank E. Zimring, *American Youth Violence: Issues and Trends, in* CRIME AND JUSTICE: AN ANNUAL REVIEW OF RESEARCH 67, 72-86 (Norval Morris ed., 1979); *see also* Marvin E. Wolfgang et al., *Juvenile and Adult Criminal Careers, in* FROM BOY TO MAN, FROM DELINQUENCY TO CRIME 20, 32 (Marvin E. Wolfgang et al. eds., 1987) (noting that when criminal careers are analyzed up to age 30, "the data clearly indicate that, regardless of offense type, the offenses committed later in an individual's career were, on the average, much more serious than those he committed earlier").

[125] *See* DONALD J. WEST & DAVID P. FARRINGTON, WHO BECOMES DELINQUENT? 11-14 (1973); David. Magnusson, et al., *Aggression and Criminality in a Longitudinal Perspective, in* PROSPECTIVE STUDIES OF CRIME AND DELINQUENCY 277, 277-301 (Sarnoff A. Mednick & Katherine Van Dusen eds., 1983).

[126] *See* HAMPARIAN ET AL., *supra* note 2; PAUL E. TRACY ET AL., DELINQUENCY CAREERS IN TWO BIRTH COHORTS 81-83 (1990); David Farrington, *Offending From 10 to 25 Years of Age, in* PROSPECTIVE STUDIES OF CRIME AND DELINQUENCY 17, 17-37 (Sarnoff A. Mednick & Katherine Van Dusen eds., 1983); Lyle Shannon, *A Longitudinal Study of Delinquency and Crime, in* QUANTITATIVE STUDIES IN CRIMINOLOGY 121, 121-46 (Charles Wellford ed., 1978).

[127] *See* WOLFGANG ET AL., *supra* note 96.

[128] *Id.* at 247-48.

[129] TRACY ET AL., *supra* note 126.

[130] *Id.* at 83.

[131] *See* James J. Collins, *The Disposition of Adult Arrests: Legal and Extralegal Determinants of Outcomes, in* FROM BOY TO MAN, FROM DELINQUENCY TO CRIME 68 (Marvin E. Wolfgang et al. eds., 1987); Farrington, *supra* note 126, at 25.

[132] Mednick et al., *supra* note 15, at 3.

these individuals, or what may be the basis for these distinctions.

The following sections examine data on crime and violence in the Biosocial Study sample to determine the nature and extent of gender differences. Distributions of delinquency are outlined first, followed by distributions of crime during young adulthood. The discussion and illustrations for Figures 1-4 (Appendix C) pertain to the distributions of data provided in Table 1 (Appendix C).

1. Juvenile Delinquency

Nearly 22% of the 987 youths had at least one police contact prior to age eighteen. Thirty-three percent of the males had a police contact, while only 14% of the females had one.[133]

As Figure 1 shows for both genders, the less serious nonindex offenders predominate. More than 40% of the males, and nearly one half of the females, were nonindex offenders. However, more females (39%) were property offenders than males (34%).[134] As expected, gender disparities were greater for crimes of violence. Of the 151 males who became offenders by age eighteen, 36 (nearly ¼) had a police contact for at least one offense that involved violence or injury to one or more persons. In contrast, only 8 (12%) of the 69 female offenders had been involved in a violent or injury-related offense.[135] Overall, most of the delinquent behavior of both males and females was nonviolent, although the amount of violent behavior was sizable— especially among males.

a. Repeat and Chronic Delinquent Offenders

The number of offenses committed by these juveniles reflects their repeat or chronic patterns of delinquency. The number ranged

---

[133] *See* DENNO, BIOLOGY AND VIOLENCE, *supra* note 10, at 40. The proportion of police contacts, particularly for males, was somewhat lower in comparison to the proportion found for other nonwhites raised in Philadelphia at a similar time. In a study of a cohort of males and females who were born in 1958 and lived in Philadelphia, *see* TRACY ET AL., *supra* note 126, 41% of the nonwhite males and 18% of the nonwhite females experienced a police contact prior to age 18. The generally lower prevalence of offense behavior among the Perinatal Project youths may be due to several factors: (1) Perinatal Project youths participated in a medical study for the first seven years of their lives and therefore may have received certain physical and psychological benefits; (2) mothers of the Perinatal Project youths, who were interested enough to participate in a study for seven years, may have had a greater concern about the welfare of their offspring; (3) participation in the Perinatal Project itself may have had a positive effect on youths; and (4) the sample of nonwhites in the study in TRACY ET AL. may have comprised ethnic groups with higher crime rates than blacks and thus rates for the group as a whole were inflated. *See* DENNO, BIOLOGY AND VIOLENCE, *supra* note 10, at 40-41.

[134] *See* DENNO, BIOLOGY AND VIOLENCE, *supra* note 10, at 41-42.

[135] *See id.* at 41.

from 1 to a maximum of 27 offenses across ages seven to seventeen. Consistent with past research, Figure 2 (Appendix C) shows that considerably more females than males were one-time offenders: nearly two-thirds of the female offenders, but less than one-half (45%) of the male offenders, had only one police contact. Further, 38% of the males and 25% of the females were nonchronic repeat offenders.[136]

As mentioned, one of the most important results reported in delinquency research is the finding that chronic offenders are responsible for a highly disproportionate share of the total number of offenses.[137] The domination of chronic offenders in the amount of crime, particularly serious crime, was striking in the present study.[138]

The 25 male chronic offenders represented 5% of the total male sample, and 17% of all male delinquents. These chronic offenders, however, accounted for 51% of the offenses committed by males. Chronic female offenders represented only 1% of the female sample, and 10% of the female delinquents. However, they accounted for 41% of the offenses committed by females.[139]

Chronic offenders also committed a highly disproportionate share of violent crimes. Among males the results were striking: chronic offenders were responsible for 61% of the violent offenses committed by males, 55% of the property offenses, and 46% of the nonindex offenses. Chronic female offenders accounted for 40% of the violent offenses committed by females, 30% of the property offenses, and 48% of the nonindex offenses. Thus, although both male and female chronic offenders dominated the amount of offense behavior, female chronics committed fewer and less severe crimes than their male counterparts.

b.   Incidence and Seriousness of Delinquency

Gender differences in the incidence and seriousness of delinquency are also important considerations. Altogether, the sample of 987 youths committed 588 offenses between the ages of seven and seventeen. Males were responsible for 443, or three quarters of those offenses; females were responsible for 145, or one quarter.[140]

Males committed relatively more violent offenses: 64 (14%) involved violence or injury; 155 (35%) involved property theft or damage; and 224 (51%) were nonindex offenses. In contrast, among females, 10 (7%) of the offenses involved violence; 51 (35%) involved

---

[136] *See id.* at 42-43.
[137] *See* TRACY ET AL., *supra* note 126; WOLFGANG ET AL., *supra* note 127.
[138] *See* DENNO, BIOLOGY AND VIOLENCE, *supra* note 10, at 43.
[139] *See id.* at 43-44.
[140] *See id.* at 43.

property theft or damage; and 84 (58%) were nonindex offenses.[141]

Gender differences were even more significant for offense seriousness. For male offenders, seriousness scores ranged from .3 to 158, with a mean score of 17. For females, they ranged from .3 to 58, with a mean score of 7. Thus, the mean level for males was nearly 2.5 times greater than the mean level for females.[142]

Seriousness levels also differed according to groups of offenders. Among males, the mean seriousness score for one-time offenders was 3, for nonchronic repeat offenders it was 15, and for chronic offenders, 58. Among females, one-time offenders had a mean score of 2, nonchronic repeat offenders a score of 11, and chronic offenders a score of 30. Clearly, chronic offenders deviated from the other groups in terms of the severity of their offenses.[143]

c. Age

The age at which a juvenile begins a delinquent career is strongly related to future offense behavior. In general, juveniles who commit offenses at a young age tend to commit more offenses overall.[144]

Percentages of the age at which juveniles commit their first offense are shown in Figure 3 (Appendix C) and Table 1. The highest percentage of juveniles had a police contact by age thirteen (17%) or fourteen (19%). The lowest percentages occurred at both ends of the distribution, ages eleven (6%) and seventeen (7%).[145]

Gender differences exist with these percentages. For instance, the highest percentage of females became offenders at age thirteen (23%); the highest percentage of males became offenders at age fourteen (20%). Cumulatively, nearly half of the juveniles (46%) became offenders before age fourteen. More than three quarters of both the males (79%) and the females (81%) became offenders before age sixteen. Although the peak age of offending occurred one year earlier for females than it did for males, cumulative percentages are similar

---

[141] *See id.*

[142] *See id.*

[143] *See id.*

[144] *See* WOLFGANG ET AL., *supra* note 127. Moreover, age of onset of violent crime among females may determine a female offender's pattern of criminal activity. One study of violent female offenders, for example, found that

[e]arly initiation into violent crime was accompanied by participation in a wide variety of other offending behaviors and deviant lifestyles. In contrast, those women who began their violent offending later in life did so in the context of a criminal career which, until the beginning of substance abuse, was more specialized and focused on typically nonviolent, gender-congruent activities such as prostitution and shoplifting.

See Baskin & Sommers, *supra* note 2, at 577.

[145] *See* DENNO, BIOLOGY AND VIOLENCE, *supra* note 10, at 44.

for both genders at ages fourteen and sixteen.[146] This result also confirms prior research indicating minor gender differences in the peak ages of criminal activity.[147]

An examination of the mean ages of the onset of delinquency for different offender groups confirms that both nonchronic offenders and chronic repeat offenders start younger. The Biosocial Study examined offender group differences using analysis of variance, a statistical test which determines whether differences are statistically significant at the .05 level.[148]

Mean ages for nonchronic and chronic male offenders (13.5 and 12.9 years, respectively) were significantly lower than the mean age for male one-time offenders (14.6 years) ($F[2,148] = 7.51; p < .001$). Similarly, mean ages for property and violent male offenders (13.6 and 13.3 years, respectively) were significantly lower than the mean age for male nonindex offenders (14.6 years) ($F [2,148] = 5.72; p < .005$). Also, female offenders with two or more offenses were significantly younger (12.8 years) than female one-time offenders (14.9 years) ($F [1,67] = 24.31; p < .001$). No significant differences appeared among the mean ages for types of female offenders.[149]

2. *Young Adult Crime*

Four categories of individuals are used to compare offense behavior between the juvenile and young adult years: (1) those who never experience either a juvenile or an adult police contact; (2) those who experience at least one juvenile contact but no adult contact; (3) those who experience at least one adult contact but no juvenile contact; and (4) those who experience at least one adult and one juvenile contact. The Biosocial Study focused mainly on the last two groups, which were combined in analyses of young adult crime.[150]

Distributions for males and females according to the four groups of possible juvenile or adult offense combinations are presented in Figure 4 (Appendix C) and Table 1. Altogether, 109 (22%) male offenders experienced an adult arrest. Of these, 53 had experienced a juvenile arrest. Of the total sample of 500 female offenders, 24 (5%) experienced an adult arrest. Of these, 8 had previously experienced a

---

[146] *See id.* at 44.

[147] *See* Kruttschnitt, *supra* note 2, at 300.

[148] "Statistical significance" refers to the probability that a particular result occurred by chance. The standard significance level for social science research is .05. Therefore, 5 times out of 100, a factor that appeared to be significant would really not be; the apparent significance would only occur by chance. *See* MONAHAN & WALKER, *supra* note 9, at 80-81.

[149] *See* DENNO, BIOLOGY AND VIOLENCE, *supra* note 10, at 45.

[150] *See id.* at 46.

juvenile arrest.[151]

Of the 109 males who had an adult arrest, 55 had one offense, and 15 were chronic offenders. Of the 24 adult females in this group, 15 had only one offense and 2 were chronic offenders. Altogether, then, the data show that males are considerably more likely than females to: engage in crimes during adulthood, continue crimes into adulthood if they had been delinquents, and commit more than one crime as an adult.[152]

This section is consistent with prior research showing gender differences in the prevalence of crime. Males commit more violent crime, and more offenses, during both the juvenile and the adult years. Contrary to a suggestion in past research,[153] the greater number of offenses for males is a reflection of both their greater participation in crime, and their more frequent offending once they do participate.

The next section considers whether or not comparable differences exist in the prediction of crime by examining three main theories: (1) the biological, psychological, and sociological factors predicting crime among males and females are similar and they interrelate; (2) biological factors are relatively stronger predictors of crime among females, given the greater social and familial constraints on female behavior; and (3) environmental factors are relatively stronger predictors of crime among males, as research indicates that males are somewhat more vulnerable to environmental stressors throughout their lives.

C. GENDER DIFFERENCES IN THE PREDICTION OF CRIME

Most researchers have limited their studies of gender differences to the examination of only one or a few factors. The Biosocial Study, however, determined interrelated associations among many factors at different stages of an individual's development.

This required several steps. The first step involved a statistical screening of several hundred variables to obtain the select predictors of violent and chronic delinquent behavior listed in Appendix A. Variable screening was conducted with three types of regression equations,[154] using two dependent variables: number of offenses and

---

[151] *See id.*

[152] *See id.*

[153] *See* 1 CRIMINAL CAREERS AND "CAREER CRIMINALS," *supra* note 80. *See also, supra* notes 87 to 88 and accompanying text.

[154] The three types of regression equations were: the forward selection technique, the backward elimination technique, and the stepwise regression—forward and backward.

seriousness of offenses.[155]

Those variables found to be significant predictors at the $p \leq .05$ level for either gender with either of the two dependent variables are listed in Appendix B. Appendix B also contains six variables that were not significant predictors in the regression screening but were included in analyses for theoretical reasons, and because they were significant predictors in past delinquency research.[156] Altogether, then, the Biosocial Study examined a total of eight "dependent" variables, designated by the letter "Y," and twenty-two "independent" variables, designated by the letter "X," that predicted the dependent variables.[157]

The Study analyzed these variables in two ways. First, it constructed structural equation models to assess the direct and indirect effects of the twenty-two independent variables across different time periods to determine their simultaneous impact on the eight dependent variables. Second, it examined these structural equation models in their "reduced form," which combines the total impact of direct and indirect effects.

1. Direct and Indirect Effects on Number of Adult Offenses

Structural equation models, which combine features of factor analysis and regression analysis, are useful in many areas of the social and behavioral sciences.[158] Unlike other techniques, such as ordinary least squares regression, where each equation represents an empirical association, the models are appropriate for analyzing longitudinal panel data because each equation represents a "causal link."[159] Thus,

---

[155] *See* DENNO, BIOLOGY AND VIOLENCE, *supra* note 10, at 70.

[156] These variables were: Stanford-Binet, WISC Verbal and Performance IQ, pregnancy and delivery complications, and family income at birth and at age 7. One variable, "otoscopic (hearing) exam," was eventually not included in analyses. Although it demonstrated a highly significant effect on delinquency, the statistical association was unreliably inflated because only two serious delinquents had an abnormal hearing exam. *See id.*

[157] *See id.* at 71. A dependent variable "is that quantity or aspect of nature whose *change or different states* the researcher wants to understand or explain or predict. In cause-and-effect investigations, the effect variable is the dependent variable." MONAHAN & WALKER, *supra* note 9, at 38. The Biosocial Study was unusual because it had more than one dependent variable. An independent variable "is a variable *whose effect upon the dependent variable you are trying to understand.*" *Id.*

[158] *See generally* Karl G. Jöreskog, *A General Method for Estimating A Linear Structural Equation System, in* STRUCTURAL EQUATION MODELS IN THE SOCIAL SCIENCES 85 (Arthur S. Goldberger & Otis Dudley Duncan eds., 1973); ADVANCES IN FACTOR ANALYSIS AND STRUCTURAL EQUATION MODELS (Karl G. Jöreskog & Dåg Sorbom eds., 1979).

[159] *See* Arthur S. Goldberger, *Structural Equation Models in the Social Sciences,* 40 ECONOMETRICA 979, 979-1001 (1972); Arthur S. Goldberger, *Structural Equation Models: An Overview, in* STRUCTURAL EQUATION MODELS IN THE SOCIAL SCIENCES 2 (Arthur S. Goldberg & Otis Dudley Duncan eds., 1973).

"causal terminology" such as "effect on" is appropriate in an analysis of structural equation models, even though it is not intended to suggest that direct or perfect causation exists.

In general, models tested direct and indirect relationships among variables across five different points in time: birth, age four, age seven, ages thirteen through fourteen, and ages seven through twenty-two. Results of model testing for both males and females for number of adult offenses, the final dependent variable, are shown in Tables 2 and 3 (Appendix C), and illustrated in Figures 5 and 6 (Appendix C).[160] Table 4 (Appendix C) isolates those predictors that were statistically significant for the four primary behavioral problem variables: number of adult offenses, number of juvenile offenses, disciplinary problem in school, and language achievement.

In the tables, coefficients can be interpreted in the same way as ordinary least squares regression. The letter "X" represents the effects of independent variables upon dependent variables. The letter "Y" represents the effects of dependent variables upon other dependent variables.

2. *Effects on Male Offenders*

Five factors showed significant effects on the number of adult offenses for males. The strongest factors were the number of juvenile offenses, mother's low educational level, and seriousness of juvenile offenses. The other two factors were father's high educational level and subject's low language achievement. The relationship between the number and seriousness of juvenile offenses and crime at adulthood was predictable, because past criminality is a strong predictor of future behavior. The finding of an expected negative effect of mother's educational level, but an unexpected positive effect of father's educational level, may simply be an artifact because father's educational level was highly related to mother's educational level. These results indicate that parental characteristics have an important effect on adult male crime, perhaps suggesting that lesser educated parents may not provide the kind of social control that is needed in early years to prevent crime in later years. The effect of low language achievement was also predictable in light of past research demonstrating associations between low verbal ability and crime.[161] Indeed, there is

---

[160] Although in the initial model, number of offenses and seriousness of offenses were used as separate, dependent measures for delinquency, only those findings for number of offenses are reported for the final models in Figures 5 and 6 because the results were similar for both measures. Likewise, only number of offenses was used as the dependent measure for young adult crime.

[161] *See* DENNO, BIOLOGY AND VIOLENCE, *supra* note 10, at 10-12.

substantial research indicating evidence of reading or learning disabilities among delinquents and violent offenders.[162]

The effects on juvenile crime are important because of their indirect effects on adult crime, and because they may have a large influence on initiating and perpetuating a youth's involvement in crime. Altogether, in decreasing order of significance, six factors showed significant effects on the number of juvenile offenses for males: number of disciplinary problems in school; amount of time the father was unemployed; evidence of lead intoxication; low language achievement; number of household moves; and abnormal speech.

Evidence of disciplinary problems in school shows the most highly significant association with juvenile offenses for males. This association demonstrates that, not unexpectedly, school-related aggression and behavioral disturbance are strong predictors of future behavioral disorders. Moreover, it appears that delinquents evidence fewer attachments and commitments to conforming and normative behavior, at least in the school setting.

The amount of time the father was unemployed, in addition to number of household moves, are indicators of familial and environmental instability. When combined with lead intoxication, a precursor of physiological and neurological instability,[163] these factors can create the kind of internal and external vulnerability that increases the likelihood of criminal behavior. Evidence of abnormal speech and low language achievement are additional factors that can lead to further instability in school. They also support research suggesting that delinquents have poor communication skills and rely on physical aggression to compensate for what they lack verbally.

Five factors significantly predicted whether males evidenced a disciplinary problem in school: evidence of lead intoxication; anemia; number of household moves; left hand preference; and lack of foster parents. These findings suggest that behavioral problems reflect disorders of the central nervous system and an unstable environment,

---

162 *See id.* at 12.

163 The key source of lead intoxication is lead-based paint, which children ingest by eating paint chips or by swallowing dust derived from the lead paint which settles on walls, windows, and floors. Other sources of lead toxicity are drinking water, soil, food, gasoline, and industry. *See* Deborah W. Denno, *Considering Lead Poisoning As A Criminal Defense*, 22 FORDHAM U.L. J. 377, 392 (1993). Lead exposure can produce devasting physiological and neurobehavioral disorders among young children, including: learning disabilities, delayed nervous system development, deficits in visual motor function, hyperactivity, hypoactivity, and abnormal social and aggressive behavior. *See id.* at 392-93. Although children of all socioeconomic classes are vulnerable to the effects of lead, urban-dwelling black children appear to be most vulnerable. Furthermore, race appears to be a stronger risk factor for lead intoxication than poverty. *See id.* at 390-91.

both of which are precursors of attention deficit disorder and hyper-activity. For example, number of household moves, and lack of foster parents are two of a number of indicators of family instability.[164] Presumably, foster parents provided a relatively more intact, problem-free home than a number of the biological parents with whom children lived.

Placement in a disciplinary program is strongly linked to three variables which, even though they are environmentally created, are typically associated with biological effects: lead intoxication; anemia (which allows for greater lead absorption); and left hand preference. Previous research has shown that left hand preference is one indicator of dominance of the right cerebral hemisphere. It has been associated with a number of behavioral and intellectual disorders, including impulsivity and lack of control.[165] Also, researchers have found considerable evidence of high lead levels among hyperactive and behaviorally disordered children.[166]

Although lead intoxication is generally ignored in crime research, the Biosocial Study showed a significant association between lead intoxication and the number of delinquent offenses committed by males. Similarly, researchers have ignored the effect of iron deficiency anemia on behavioral problems, although the Biosocial Study found that anemia was related to disciplinary problems. Moreover, iron deficiency anemia is one of several factors that increases susceptibility to lead intoxication.[167]

Surprisingly, disciplinary problems in school were not highly correlated with school achievement in language, which showed a significant, direct effect on delinquency. Thus, it appears that behavioral disturbance has a direct effect on delinquency, rather than an indirect or impeding effect through school achievement.

Not surprisingly, prior intelligence test scores were associated with language achievement. Both WISC Verbal IQ and WISC Performance IQ have highly significant direct effects. However, contrary to some past research, early intelligence scores showed no direct effect on delinquency. Thus, the link between intelligence and delinquency is indirect, and mediated through language achievement. In addition, the more dominant effect of Verbal IQ on achievement among males confirms past evidence that poor verbal ability (one indicator of a left hemisphere deficit) is an important factor in aca-

---

[164] *See supra* note 110 and accompanying text.

[165] *See supra* note 114 and accompanying text; DENNO, BIOLOGY AND VIOLENCE, *supra* note 10, at 12-14.

[166] *See* Denno, *supra* note 163.

[167] *See id.* at 392.

demic underachievement.[168]

Early predictors of Verbal and Performance IQ point to other indirect links to delinquency. Not surprisingly, Stanford-Binet at age four had a strong impact on Verbal IQ, Performance IQ, and placement in a program for the mentally retarded during adolescence. The status of having foster parents directly impacted on Performance IQ, indicating that some familial factors contribute to early test scores. Physicians' clinical impressions of the intellectual status of the Biosocial Study children at age seven also predicted Verbal IQ and Performance IQ at age seven, as well as evidence of mental retardation during adolescence. These associations validate physicians' capabilities to determine intellectual performance independent of intelligence tests and to predict intellectual capacity later in life. However, evidence of an abnormal intellectual status at age seven, or of mental retardation during adolescence, does not have a significant direct effect on delinquency.[169]

Importantly, a physician's clinical assessment that a child had abnormal speech at age seven had a significant effect on delinquency. The impact of speech is particularly telling in light of the finding that, of all the tests of adolescent achievement examined as predictors of delinquency at ages thirteen and fourteen, only language ability was significantly associated. In turn, evidence of abnormal speech early in life, in addition to abnormal intellectual status and low Stanford-Binet, predicted placement in a program for the mentally retarded during adolescence.[170]

Contrary to past research, the Biosocial Study did not find a direct link between delinquency and total family income either at the time of the child's birth, or at age seven. It appears, however, that the associations between socioeconomic status and delinquency found in prior research reflected an underlying relationship between factors that were tied to low income, but which have not been examined intensively in delinquency research (*e.g.*, lead intoxication, or detailed familial and parental characteristics). In the Biosocial Study, the number of times the family household moved between the child's birth and seventh birthday demonstrated a significant direct effect on delinquency. The length of time the father was unemployed showed the most highly significant impact, second only to disciplinary problems in school. Thus, patterns of familial instability and disorganization appear to be more important than the amount of income a

---

168 *See* DENNO, BIOLOGY AND VIOLENCE, *supra* note 10, at 85.

169 *See id.*

170 *See id.* at 85-86.

family earns.

Overall, both biological and environmental factors predict crime and violence among males, although environmental factors, such as lead poisoning, appeared to have more impact. The next section discusses the relatively stronger biological effects on crime and violence among females.

3. Effects on Female Offenders

Four factors showed direct effects on the number of adult offenses among females: seriousness of juvenile offenses; number of disciplinary problems in school; low number of juvenile offenses; and father's low educational level. As with males, the seriousness of delinquent offenses was significant; however, unlike males, those most apt to continue to commit crime during adulthood were not always those who committed the most crime during their youth. This result is not surprising, however, since females commit a relatively larger number of petty or status offenses, like shoplifting. Therefore, unlike males, chronic female offenders were not always the most serious offenders—an association that has important distinguishing consequences in terms of social policy. Yet, disciplinary problems in school did show an effect, demonstrating that early problem behavior is predictive of problems in adulthood.[171]

Altogether, nine factors showed direct effects on the number of juvenile offenses among females: disciplinary problems in school; lack of foster parents; abnormal movement; neurological abnormalities; left foot preference; father absence; low language achievement; normal intellectual status; and right eye preference. The strong effect of a disciplinary status is not surprising, given its importance in predicting number of adult offenses. Moreover, the link between delinquency and low language achievement could be expected in light of a comparable link among males. However, the status of not being placed in foster care was a more surprising finding, because it suggested that foster care had a more positive effect on behavior than keeping a child with her own family.[172]

Many of the children who were placed in foster care in the Biosocial Study came from disruptive and abusive homes where at least one parent was absent. Although the children were placed in foster care at any time between infancy and age seven, it appears that their early family experiences had a significant effect on their later delinquency. This conclusion is confirmed by the significant association

---

[171] *See id.* at 86-87.
[172] *See id.* at 87.

found between father absence and delinquency.

Other indicators of number of juvenile offenses—abnormal movements, number of neurological abnormalities, right eye preference, and left foot preference—confirmed prior research indicating that female delinquents have a greater degree of neurological dysfunction than male delinquents.[173] The Biosocial Study assessed abnormal movements during standard tests of coordination, or while observing the child's spontaneous activity. For example, the researchers would ask a test child to hold out both arms horizontally for thirty seconds to ease the detection of abnormal posture, chorea (rapid involuntary jerks), and athetosis (slow, spasmodic repetitions). They recorded many different types of abnormal movements, including fasciculation, tremors, tics, and mirror movements.[174] Also, they asked medical examiners to report, as neurological abnormalities, "conditions, which may not in themselves be neurological but are often related to [central nervous system] disorders, such as abnormalities of skull size and shape, spinal anomalies, and primary muscle disease."[175]

Two factors predicted number of disciplinary problems in school: abnormal movements, which was highly significant, and abnormal vision. Physicians assessed whether a child's vision was abnormal by conducting a visual screening examination. Visual acuity was determined to be abnormal if any one of the following three conditions existed: (1) visual acuity was less than 20:30 (with or without glasses); (2) there was hyperopia test failure; or (3) there was muscle balance test failure.

Eight factors predicted language achievement. Similar to males, WISC Verbal IQ and Performance IQ were the strongest positive predictors. However, in contrast to males, whose language achievement was predicted only by these two factors, six other factors also showed significant effects: lesser number of persons supported; left foot preference; Stanford-Binet; father presence; family income; and mother's education. Thus, socioeconomic factors, such as income, a smaller number of persons in the household to support, father's presence, and mother's education, appeared to have a strong effect on achievement, in addition to indicators of past intellectual ability as measured by the standardized WISC and Stanford-Binet tests. Notably, however, left foot preference was the second strongest predictor.

Other factors showed highly significant effects on both Verbal

---

[173] *See supra* note 94 and accompanying text.

[174] DENNO, BIOLOGY AND VIOLENCE, *supra* note 10, at 87.

[175] *Id.* at 88.

IQ and Performance IQ, most particularly the Stanford-Binet, a lack of neurological abnormalities, and mother's education. Although mother's education had no effect on ability and behavior among juvenile delinquent males, it showed significant effects on Verbal IQ and Performance IQ among females.

The number of times a child entered a program for the mentally retarded showed three effects. Similar to males, a clinician's assessment of abnormal intellectual status had the strongest effect, followed by the amount of time the father was unemployed and number of pregnancy and delivery complications, which are considered to be early predictors of central nervous system dysfunction.

It appears, then, that for both males and females, delinquency and violence are associated with learning difficulties and low achievement, but not with the more debilitating types of mental impairment characteristic of mental retardation or abnormal intellectual status. This finding is consistent with other analyses of these offenders' classifications, which indicated generally that the more violent and chronic delinquents had lower achievement test scores, but that they were not significantly represented in programs for the mentally retarded.[176]

Predictors of female delinquency and violence comprised both biological and environmental effects. Biological factors, however, played a considerably greater role in the delinquency of females than they did in males. Although disciplinary problems and the lack of foster care showed the most highly significant effects on delinquency, neurological abnormalities and factors associated with attention deficit disorder were also important. Those factors—number of neurological abnormalities, mixed cerebral dominance as indicated by left-footedness and right-eyedness, and abnormal movements—influenced language achievement, which had a direct negative impact on delinquency.

Overall, there were two significant effects on delinquency for both genders: disciplinary problems in school—the strongest predictor for males and among the strongest predictors for females—and low language achievement. This finding accords with research[177] which found problems with conduct and academic achievement to be among the principal predictors of delinquency. Apart from academic achievement, however, other factors showed a highly significant impact on delinquency for both genders.

---

[176] *See id.*

[177] *See* R. Loeber & T. Dishion, *Early Predictors of Male Delinquency: A Review*, 94 PSYCH. BULLETIN 68, 68-99 (1983). *See also* DENNO, BIOLOGY AND VIOLENCE, *supra* note 10, for a review of the research.

4. *Total Impact of Effects on Number of Adult Offenses*

An examination of the total impact of independent and dependent variables through the summation of direct and indirect effects provides another way of predicting juvenile and adult offenses, as seen in Tables 5 and 6 (Appendix C). This approach can answer questions relating to the combination of independent effects on intervening variables as they influence crime. For example, this method can determine the total effect of lead intoxication on adult male crime, given that lead has a direct effect on delinquency as well as an indirect effect through disciplinary problems. It can also determine the total effect of left hand preference, given that it has only an indirect effect on delinquency through its impact on disciplinary problems.

In both equations, the strength of the coefficients for reduced form equations is determined by comparisons with other coefficients in the equations. For males in Table 5, the number of adult offenses is most strongly influenced by four factors: mother's high and father's low educational levels; lead intoxication; the amount of time the father was unemployed; and the number of household moves. Number of juvenile offenses was most strongly associated with three factors: the amount of time the father was unemployed; lead intoxication; and number of household moves.

For females in Table 6, the number of adult offenses is most strongly influenced by five factors: father's low educational level; lower number of neurological abnormalities; lack of foster parents; number of abnormal movements; and abnormal vision. Number of Juvenile offenses was most strongly associated with lack of foster parents, abnormal movements, left foot preference, father absence, number of neurological abnormalities, and right eye preference.

In general, then, factors found to be important in the direct and indirect effects were also important in the reduced form models, although the relative strength of their impact shifted somewhat. Yet, the results of the reduced form equations still support the proposition that biological factors (such as abnormal movements, left-foot and right-eye preference, and neurological abnormalities) are more significant predictors of crime among females; whereas environmental factors (such as lead intoxication, father's employment status, and number of household moves) are more significant predictors of crime among males. Indicators of family stability were important for both males and females—the lack of foster parents and father absence were important for females, and father's employment and household moves were important for males.

181

5. Summary of Results

Overall, the results of the Biosocial Study showed that direct, indirect, and total biological, psychological, and sociological influences on juvenile and adult crime were significant for both genders. Similar to past research, regression models demonstrated that some of the same factors that influenced crime among males also influenced crime among females. For example, seriousness of delinquent offenses was a key predictor of adult crime for both males and females, whereas the number of a child's disciplinary problems and low language achievement in school were key shared predictors of juvenile crime. Not surprisingly, WISC Verbal IQ and WISC Performance IQ were the primary predictors of language achievement for both genders. These results confirm prior research that highlighted the importance of past behavior and verbal ability in predicting future crime.

Most significant, however, were the numbers and kinds of predictors that the genders did not share. In general, the Biosocial Study confirmed past proposals suggesting that biological factors have relatively more impact among females, and environmental factors have relatively more impact among males. For example, a comparison among disciplinary problems, juvenile crime, and adult crime shows an interesting gender difference. Among females, the only two factors predicting disciplinary problems—abnormal movements and neurological abnormalities—were also strong predictors of their crime as juveniles, and, in the reduced form equations, their crime as adults. Among males, lead intoxication, the strongest predictor of disciplinary problems, was also a strong predictor of their crime as juveniles, and, in the reduced form equation, their crime as adults. Although lead intoxication results in neurological and physiological impairment,[178] its origins are environmental. The fact that females appeared to be unaffected by lead, even though they were raised in the same or similar environment as males, suggests that males may be relatively more vulnerable to certain kinds of environmental stressors. Similarly, abnormal movements or neurological abnormalities had no effect on ability or behavior among males.

This conclusion warrants some qualification. First, as Figures 5 and 6 illustrate, more factors appeared to influence crime and behavior among females than among males. Moreover, the interrelationships among these factors were more complex. Second, certain biological factors, such as left-handedness, contributed indirectly to crime among males by contributing to disciplinary problems. More-

---

[178] *See supra* note 163 and accompanying text.

over, some environmental factors, such as lack of foster parents, or father absence, contributed directly to juvenile crime among females. Noticeably, however, the few biological predictors of disciplinary problems or crime for males (*e.g.*, left-handedness and perhaps abnormal speech) were not predictors for females, and only one family factor—lack of foster parents—that was significant in predicting juvenile crime for females was also significant in predicting disciplinary problems for males. Thus, more often than not, the genders do not share the same predictors of crime and behavior. This result suggests that researchers must assess different kinds of factors to determine the correlates of gender differences in crime.

Results of the Biosocial Study did not confirm past findings of direct relationships between delinquency and early intelligence, mental retardation, socioeconomic status, or early central nervous system dysfunction as measured by the number of pregnancy complications. The lack of strong, significant associations among these variables may be due to the cultural and demographic characteristics and homogeneity of the sample; the infrequent occurrence of some of the independent variables (for example, particular types of pregnancy and delivery complications), which could mask true associations; or the simultaneous analyses of both biological and environmental variables, which could negate more "traditional" findings. Because much of the research analyzing biological factors and crime has not controlled adequately for social, demographic, and environmental influences, some past findings of biological links to intelligence or to crime may be artifacts of environmental effects. Further, longstanding associations between environmental factors and crime may disguise the significance of biological effects, because researchers rarely incorporate them into delinquency research. Other variables, such as disciplinary problems, may be an outcome of both biological and environmental precursors, although most delinquency research offers only sociological explanations.

Overall, however, the Biosocial Study suggests that delinquency is related to family instability and, most importantly, to a lack of behavioral control associated with neurological and later central nervous system disorders. It appears that attention deficit disorder and hyperactivity, which are part of disciplinary problems, are associated with the learning and behavioral disorders evidenced in some members of the Biosocial Study sample. These disorders would considerably inhibit the ability of young children to create social bonds even before the school experience. Academic failure would perpetuate misconduct and impede attempts at future social bonding. Indeed, a sizable amount of research shows that children who evidence attention deficit disorder and hyperactivity are significantly more likely to retain antisocial tendencies during adulthood, a time when most individuals start to show commitments to socially desirable behavior.[179]

In determining whether gender differences in crime justify a gender-based standard for punishment, the next section first discusses briefly the different theories of punishment. It then examines how the criminal law has applied gender-based defenses. Although such defenses are generally viewed unfavorably by the courts, their popularity is growing. Moreover, defenses for women are somewhat more acceptable than those for men. Next, the section considers whether this gender distinction is based on factors other than gender. It concludes by discussing whether attempts to use gender-based defenses are legitimate, or whether those defenses that are more culturally constructed merely reinforce the gender-related stereotypes of crime that were espoused historically.

IV. GENDER DIFFERENCES AND PREDICTION

A. THEORIES OF PUNISHMENT AND DEFENSES

Commentators have discussed the different theories of punishment and criminal law defenses in great detail,[180] and they are presented only briefly here. Apart from some exceptions, the general presumption in the criminal law is that individuals are responsible actors and that their behavior results from free will.[181] The principles of retributivism and utilitarianism, which differ considerably from one another, provide the theoretical basis for the punishment of criminal behavior. According to retribution theory, offenders deserve to be punished in proportion to the crimes they commit, because they made the choice to engage in social harm.[182] In contrast, utilitarian theory does not view punishment as an end in itself, but instead considers whether it would provide any future social benefit, most particularly in terms of crime prevention. The theory presumes that human actors behave rationally; they will avoid engaging in crime if they be-

---

[179] *See* DENNO, BIOLOGY AND VIOLENCE, *supra* note 10, at 94.

[180] *See* JOSHUA DRESSLER, UNDERSTANDING CRIMINAL LAW (1987); GEORGE P. FLETCHER, RETHINKING CRIMINAL LAW (1978); H.L.A. HART, PUNISHMENT AND RESPONSIBILITY (1968); C.L. TEN, CRIME, GUILT, AND PUNISHMENT: A PHILOSOPHICAL INTRODUCTION (1987); Paul Robinson, *Criminal Law Defenses: A Systematic Analysis*, 82 COLUM. L. REV. 199 (1982); LLoyd L. Weinreb, *Desert, Punishment, and Criminal Responsibility*, 49 LAW & CONTEMP. PROBS. 47 (1986).

[181] *See* HERBERT L. PACKER, THE LIMITS OF THE CRIMINAL SANCTION 74-75 (1968); Richard C. Boldt, *The Construction of Responsibility in the Criminal Law*, 140 U. PA. L. REV. 2245, 2246 (1992); Sanford H. Kadish, *Excusing Crime*, 75 CAL. L. REV. 257, 282 (1987); Stephen J. Morse, *Culpability and Control*, 142 U. PA. L. REV. 1587, 1592-1605 (1994).

[182] *See* Weinreb, *supra* note 180, at 47.

lieve that the potential pain of punishment is greater than the potential pleasure reaped from the crime.[183]

Major types of utilitarian theory include general deterrence, specific deterrence, and rehabilitation. General deterrence presumes that the punishment of a particular defendant will prevent others from engaging in similar conduct because they will be aware of, and fear, the consequences.[184] Specific deterrence purports to deter the future misconduct of the particular defendant being punished, irrespective of the effect such punishment may have on the misconduct engaged in by others.[185] Lastly, rehabilitation attempts to diminish crime by reforming the defendant's behavior.[186]

Despite the conflict between the principles of retributivism and utilitarianism, criminal law scholars generally agree that not all individuals should be subject to criminal punishment.[187] Thus, the available defenses[188] serve two functions: (1) they allow defendants who lack the capacity for rational self control to avoid punishment; and (2) they help clarify the dimensions of the responsible actor by reinforcing the assumption that culpability is based on an actor's ability to control current mental states and physical conduct.[189] Although Robinson has pinpointed five categories of available defenses,[190] for the purposes of evaluating possible gender differences in punishment, this section focuses on two—justifications and excuses.

Typically, justifications and excuses apply to any offense, even though every element of the offense at issue has been satisfied.[191] A justification defense, such as self defense, claims that conduct that would otherwise be criminal is, under the circumstances, socially acceptable or, at least, not wrong. The defense emphasizes the ac-

---

183 DRESSLER, *supra* note 180, § 2.03 at 4.

184 *See id.* § 2.05 at 5.

185 *See id.*

186 *See id.*

187 *See, e.g.,* Weinreb, *supra* note 180, at 50 (noting that the result is about the same irrespective of the theory because criminal law focuses on intentional conduct: "[s]ince desert attaches most easily to such conduct, which also can be deterred by the threat of punishment, desert and utility coincide"); Stephen Morse, *Failed Explanations and Criminal Responsibility: Experts and the Unconscious,* 68 VA. L. REV. 971, 974 (1982) (arguing that the law must accept some notion of subjective mental states when considering appropriate punishment despite the overall presumption of free will in the criminal justice system).

188 *See* Robinson, *supra* note 180, at 203. The term "defense" has been defined as "any set of identifiable conditions or circumstances which may prevent a conviction for an offense." *Id.*

189 *See* Coughlin, *supra* note 19, at 12-13.

190 *See* Robinson, *supra* note 180, at 203. Robinson terms these defenses: failure of proof defenses, offense modification defenses, justifications, excuses, and nonexculpatory public policy defenses. *Id.*

191 *Id.* at 221.

cused's act or conduct. For example, even though killing a human being constitutes criminal conduct, that conduct is justified if the accused killed in self defense (*i.e.*, because the victim was about to use deadly force against the accused for no lawful reason). Thus, even though the accused satisfied all the elements of the crime of homicide, the act was permissible under the circumstances.[192]

An excuse defense, such as insanity or duress, admits that the conduct may be wrong, but claims that the accused should not be responsible because of certain "excusing conditions."[193] The defense emphasizes the accused's personal characteristics to determine the evidence for responsibility.[194] For example, if a woman strikes another person with a deadly weapon, thinking that person wants to control her body by surgically implanting a radio receiver into it, she will have satisfied all of the elements of aggravated assault. She may be excused for this unjustified act, however, if she has a condition (*e.g.*, paranoid delusion) which suggests that she is morally blameless because she had not acted as a result of free will.[195]

---

[192] *See* DRESSLER, *supra* note 180, § 16.03 at 176-77; FLETCHER, *supra* note 180, at § 10.1; HART, *supra* note 180, at 13-14; George Fletcher, *The Right Deed for the Wrong Reason: A Reply to Mr. Robinson*, 23 U.C.L.A. L. REV. 293 (1975); Kent Greenawalt, *The Perplexing Borders of Justification and Excuse*, 84 COLUM. L. REV. 1897 (1984); Paul Robinson, *A Theory of Justification: Social Harm as a Prerequisite for Criminal Liability*, 23 U.C.L.A. L. REV. 266 (1975).

[193] LLOYD L. WEINREB, OEDIPUS AT FENWAY PARK: WHAT RIGHTS ARE AND WHY THERE ARE ANY 50 (1994) ("For the most part, we regard as excuses conditions that have a recognized, identifiable etiology and place a person outside the endless variety of the normal."). *See also* DRESSLER, *supra* note 180, § 16.03 at 177; FLETCHER, *supra* note 180, at § 10.03; HART, *supra* note 180, at 28-53; Kadish, *supra* note 181; Robinson, *supra* note 180, at 221. There are five major tests for determining whether a defendant is insane so as to excuse the conduct. The first is the M'Naghten test, announced by the British House of Lords in M'Naghten's Case, 8 Eng. Rep. 718 (1843). Under this test, defendants are insane if, at the time of their criminal act, they suffered from a disease of the mind that caused them not to know either the nature and quality of their act or that their act was wrong. The second test is the "irresistible impulse test," under which defendants are insane if, as a result of a mental disease or defect, they acted unlawfully due to an irresistible and uncontrollable impulse. The third test is the "product" or Durham test brought to national attention by Durham v. United States, 214 F.2d 862 (D.C. Cir. 1954). This test, which is no longer valid, states that defendants are not guilty if their unlawful act was the result or product of a mental disease or defect. The fourth test is § 4.01 of the Model Penal Code. It states that defendants are not responsible for their conduct if, at the time of the criminal act, as the result of a mental disease or defect, they lacked the substantial capacity either to appreciate the criminality (or wrongfulness) of their actions or to conform their conduct to the law. The fifth and most recent test is the Federal insanity test, 18 U.S.C. § 20(a). Adopted by Congress in 1984, this test excuses defendants only if they prove that, at the time of the crime, as the result of a "severe mental disease or defect," they were unable to appreciate the nature and quality or the wrongfulness of their conduct.

[194] *See generally* DRESSLER, *supra* note 180, § 16.03 at 177; FLETCHER, *supra* note 180, at § 10.03; HART, *supra* note 180, at 28-30; Kadish, *supra* note 181; Robinson, *supra* note 180, at 221.

[195] Robinson, *supra* note 180, at 221.

The law allows excuses for actors who demonstrate a "disability" that causes an excusing condition. The disability (an abnormal condition when the offense occurred) may be: (1) permanent, such as brain damage, or temporary, such as intoxication or automatism; (2) internally-caused, such as insanity, or externally-caused, such as duress; (3) a defect in cognition, because the actor does not realize she is violating the law, or a defect in volition, because the actor cannot stop herself from violating the law.[196]

Similar sorts of conditions may contribute to "failure of proof" defenses, which differ from excuses because the State cannot prove all the elements of an offense, most particularly the element of intent. For example, mental illness can negate the element of intent in a particular crime without constituting the defense of insanity. The "failure of proof" defense for a mentally ill defendant may be called "diminished capacity" or "partial responsibility" in those cases where the defendant was still guilty of a lesser included offense. In turn, the mental illness may prevent conviction altogether if there is no lesser included offense, or if the mental illness also negates the elements of the lesser included offenses.[197]

The next section considers whether these defenses could or should vary according to a gender-based standard. The next section also notes how such differences are explicable in terms of the different theories of punishment.

B. GENDER DIFFERENCES IN PREDICTION AND GENDER-BASED DEFENSES

A gender-based standard for punishment or defenses would most likely incorporate gender differences in the prevalence or prediction of crime. The results of the Biosocial Study presented in this Article help illustrate this point.

First, even though some of the same factors in the Biosocial Study predicted crime among both males and females, most predictors were

---

196 *Id.* at 221-24, 229-30.

197 *See id.*, at 204-06. The defense of "diminished capacity" is an alternative to the insanity defense. With it, defendants claim that even though they suffer from a mental disability that does not constitute insanity, that disability still prevents them from forming the requisite *mens rea* for the offense. Logically, defendants should be excused for any crime for which they lack the requisite *mens rea* (this is the approach taken by Model Penal Code § 4.02(1)), but commonly judges only allow evidence of diminished capacity, if at all, to negate the specific intent of a specific-intent offense. A modified version of this defense is "partial responsibility," a defense based on the premise that mental health is a matter of gradations and thus defendants should be held culpable only to the extent that they are mentally healthy. The Model Penal Code § 210.3(1)(b) provides, for example, that a homicide that would be murder only constitutes manslaughter if the defendant can prove that the actions were the result of "extreme mental or emotional disturbance for which there is a reasonable explanation or excuse." MODEL PENAL CODE § 210.3(1)(b).

different. Yet, similar components to the differences did exist. For example, even though the sources of disciplinary problems varied between the genders, the results were comparable. Both neurological deviations (such as abnormal movements and neurological abnormalities), which were important predictors for females, and lead intoxication, an important predictor for males, resulted in difficulties with impulse control, hyperactivity, and attention deficit disorder—all of which were strong predictors of crime for both genders. Whether some of these predictors are more amenable to an individual's control appears impossible to determine scientifically.[198]

Notably, the Biosocial Study examined only factors that, theoretically, could influence the behaviors of both genders. For example, although lead intoxication did not appear to affect females, it could have. Furthermore, there is no evidence to suggest that females were raised in relatively more lead-free environments, because all subjects were raised in the same types of neighborhoods. Either female children are not as attracted to ingesting lead particles, or such ingestion does not have as strong of an effect on their behavior. In turn, neurological abnormalities among males appeared to have no effect on their behavior. Either the delinquent or criminal behavior of males is predominately influenced by environmental factors, or they are not as affected by certain biological disorders. Thus, the question is whether such "gender-variant" differences in choice or physiology should make a difference in punishment or the use of defenses.[199]

One way of attempting to answer this question is to examine it in the context of how the law has dealt with (albeit inadvertently) a related, but perhaps more problematic, issue—the weighing of potential influences that are gender-based either due to biological or culturally-created conditions. This section discusses four overlapping types of gender-based defenses that represent a continuum ranging from those that are more biologically-based and those that are more culturally-created: (1) gender-specific; (2) gender-dominant; (3) gender-variant; and (4) gender-cultural.

"Gender-specific" defenses rely on conditions that are biologically

---

[198] *See* Denno, *supra* note 10, at 669.

[199] *See generally* Rochelle Cooper Dreyfuss & Dorothy Nelkin, *The Jurisprudence of Genetics*, 45 VAND. L. REV. 313 (1992) (analyzing the impact of genetic research on traditional legal doctrine and our culture's perception of personhood); Lisabeth Fisher DiLalla & Irving I. Gottesman, *Biological and Genetic Contributors to Violence—Widom's Untold Tale*, 109 PSYCH. BULLETIN 125 (1991) (emphasizing the need to examine the relevant biological and genetic literature on the intergenerational transmission of violent behavior); Sandra Scarr, *Three Cheers for Behavior Genetics: Winning the War and Losing Our Indentity*, 17 BEHAV. GENETICS 219 (1987) (discussing psychology's current acceptance and former rejection of theories of genetic diversity in behavior).

or genetically applicable to only one gender. These defenses recognize that gender is one of the few distinguishing characteristics in the criminal law that allows some individuals to have defenses that others could never have.[200] No female could attempt the XYY chromosome defense and no male could claim a defense based on premenstrual syndrome (PMS) or postpartum depression.[201]

"Gender-dominant" defenses predominantly apply to one gender for biological reasons, but theoretically could also apply to the other. For example, only males have relied on high testosterone level defenses, such as the use of anabolic steroids, yet in theory, females could also use these defenses since they too have varying levels of testosterone that appear to be related to aggression.[202] For females, however, defense attorneys typically apply a gender-specific defense for hormonal disorders, such as PMS.

"Gender-variant" defenses are similar to gender-dominant defenses except that, for reasons of biology or culture, the conditions at issue are more applicable to either gender. The results of the Biosocial Study illustrate how a defendant may use a gender-variant defense. For instance, an attorney could defend a male client using a lead intoxication defense by arguing that males are particularly susceptible to lead and its effects on behavior. Similarly, the attorney could defend a female client by relying on her history of neurological disorders.[203]

Lastly, "gender-cultural" defenses primarily pertain to one gender rather than another for psychological, sociological, or cultural reasons. For example, although males have used the battered spouse syndrome,[204] it is typically used by females under the better-known rubric, "battered woman syndrome."[205]

Although courts have begun to accept gender-based defenses for females, they have been largely unsuccessful for both males[206] and females,[207] in the United States.[208] The reasons for the greater flexibility for females are unclear, particularly since the criminal law has

---

[200] Although because of their youth, juveniles are also allowed differential treatment or defenses relative to adults, every one at some point is entitled to rely on a juvenile defense.

[201] *See infra* notes 211 to 310 and accompanying text.

[202] *See infra* note 269 and accompanying text.

[203] *See infra* note 354 and accompanying notes.

[204] *See* Suzanne K. Steinmetz, *The Battered Husband Syndrome*, 2 Victimology 499, 499-509 (1977-78).

[205] *See infra* notes 355 to 377 and accompanying text.

[206] *See infra* notes 211 to 268 and accompanying text.

[207] *See infra* notes 279 to 328 and accompanying text.

[208] Defenses based on PMS, postpartum depression, and battered woman syndrome, are examples. *See infra* notes 279 to 328 and accompanying text.

dabbled with a broad range of new defenses.[209] Some scholars fear that a different standard for females may reinforce the historical, biologically-driven stereotypes of women and their criminal counterparts[210] without providing comparable excuses for men.

The following sections examine a selected number of these defenses to determine how attorneys have used them, why some have had greater success than others, and whether the application of any of these defenses is justified. Because these defenses are still seldomly used, the discussion is primarily theoretical due to the narrow pool of cases available for analysis.

1. *Gender-Specific Defenses for Males: XYY Chromosome Syndrome*

The XYY chromosome syndrome is perhaps the most widely known attempt at a gender-specific defense for males. Genetically normal individuals have one pair of sex chromosomes, typed XX for the normal female, and XY for the normal male.[211] Although a number of different chromosomal deviations can occur,[212] researchers have examined the XYY chromosomal abnormality most extensively in relation to crime because the extra Y chromosome "suggested the possibility of exaggerated maleness, aggressiveness, and violence."[213] Initially, there was some evidence for this conclusion. Although the first discovered XYY male was not a criminal nor abnormally aggressive,[214] subsequent research reported a disproportionate number of XYY males in maximum security institutions in the United States and other countries.[215]

Regardless of these early results, the XYY defense was not successful in the four major XYY cases in the United States in the 1970s.[216]

---

[209] *See* DERSHOWITZ, *supra* note 19; Denno, *supra* note 10; Goldberg, *supra* note 20, at 40; Margot Slade, *At the Bar*, N.Y. TIMES, May 20, 1994, at B20.

[210] With respect to views on the battered woman syndrome, see Coughlin, *supra* note 19; Stephen J. Schulhofer, *supra* note 7, at 116.

[211] HOYENGA & HOYENGA, *supra* note 5, at 53.

[212] *See* Michael Craft, *The Current Status of XYY and XXY Syndromes: A Review of Treatment Implications*, in BIOLOGY, CRIME, AND ETHICS: A STUDY OF BIOLOGICAL EXPLANATIONS FOR CRIMINAL BEHAVIOR 113, 113-15 (Frank H. Marsh & Janet Katz eds., 1985) (discussing the frequency and characteristics of a variety of chromosomal abnormalities, including XXY, YXX, XO, XXX, and XYY).

[213] Sarnoff Mednick, *Biological Factors in Crime Causation: The Reactions of Social Scientists, Introduction* to THE CAUSES OF CRIME: NEW BIOLOGICAL APPROACHES 1, 2 (Sarnoff Mednick et al. eds., 1987).

[214] *See* A.A. Sandberg et al., *An XYY Human Male*, [1961] 2 LANCET 488, 488-89.

[215] *See* Susan Horan, Comment, *The XYY Supermale and the Criminal Justice System: A Square Peg in a Round Hole*, 25 LOY. L.A. L. REV. 1343, 1347-53 (1992); Herman A. Witkin et al., *Criminality in XYY and XXY Men*, 193 SCIENCE 547, 547-55 (1976); Note, *The XYY Chromosome Defense*, 57 GEO. L.J. 892, 892-93 (1969).

[216] *See* People v. Tanner, 91 Cal. Rptr. 656, 657-59 (Cal. Ct. App. 1970) (discussing the

Primarily, the courts rejected the defense because there was insufficient evidence to show a causal link between the XYY chromosome disorder and criminal conduct.[217] In *People v. Yukl*,[218] for example, the trial court denied Yukl's request that a chromosome test be conducted and offered at trial, noting that previous cases had held that XYY evidence failed to meet reasonable standards of a "medical certainty."[219] The trial court set forth a new standard, clarifying that an insanity defense relying on chromosome abnormality "should be possible only if one establishes with a high degree of medical certainty an etiological relationship between the defendant's mental capacity and the genetic syndrome."[220] Moreover, the syndrome's effect on the defendant's thought processes must be so significant that it interferes "substantially with the defendant's cognitive capacity or with his ability to understand or appreciate the basic moral code of his society."[221]

A number of factors complicate arguments suggesting a direct link between the XYY chromosome abnormality and crime.[222] First, evidence that some XYY individuals have impaired intellectual and physiological functioning,[223] or developmental difficulties, such as

---

court's rejection of a causal link between the XYY chromosome disorder and aggressive behavior, or any argument that the extra Y chromosome contributes to legal insanity, despite the testimony of two expert witness geneticists stating that their research and that of others demonstrated a causal link); Millard v. State, 261 A.2d 227, 231-32 (Md. Ct. Spec. App. 1970) (upholding the trial court's refusal to submit the issue of the XYY defendant's insanity to the jury because the expert witness's failed to relate the chromosomal deficiency to a lack of substantial capacity to appreciate the criminality of his conduct); People v. Yukl, 372 N.Y.S.2d 313, 315-20 (N.Y. Sup. Ct. 1975) (denying defendant's request that a chromosome test be conducted and offered as evidence at trial noting that XYY evidence failed to meet reasonable standards of a "medical certainty"); State v. Roberts, 544 P.2d 754, 758 (Wash. Ct. App. 1976) (discussing the appellate court's affirmance of a lower court's denial of the defendant's request for a chromosome test by concluding that the "available medical evidence is unable to establish a reasonably certain causal connection between the XYY defect and criminal conduct"); *see also* Note, *The XYY Syndrome: A Challenge to Our System of Criminal Responsibility*, 16 N.Y.L.F. 232, 246 (1970) (discussing the trial of John Farley, who unsuccessfully attempted to defend himself in New York on charges of committing a brutal murder and rape based upon an XYY genetic defense).

217 *See supra* note 216.

218 372 N.Y.S.2d 313 (N.Y. Sup. Ct. 1975).

219 *See id.* at 318-20 (citing People v. Tanner, 91 Cal. Rptr. 656 (Cal. Ct. App. 1970) and Millard v. State, 261 A.2d 227 (Md. Ct. Spec. App. 1970)).

220 *Yukl*, 372 N.Y.S.2d at 319.

221 *Id.*

222 *See, e.g.*, LAWRENCE TAYLOR, BORN TO CRIME: THE GENETIC CAUSES OF CRIMINAL BEHAVIOR 79 (1984) (arguing that "the evidence seems to point very clearly to the simple fact that the criminal behavior of the super males was genetically caused, with relatively little effect from social or familial influences").

223 *See* WILSON & HERRNSTEIN, *supra* note 1, at 100-02; Witkin et al., *supra* note 215, at 547-55; Horan, *supra* note 215, at 1351-53; Note, *Chromosome Defense, supra* note 215, at 899-901.

speech, learning, or attention disorders,[224] suggests that these intervening factors, and not "supermaleness" alone, may be associated with
crime.[225] Second, severe sample size and methodological limitations
may lead to inconsistent results in many XYY studies.[226] Third, a large
and methodologically sophisticated study conducted on the relationship between the XYY disorder and crime reported that XYY males did
exhibit a higher rate of criminality that was not explained by their
subnormal intelligence; however, these males showed no disproportionate tendency toward violence.[227] In light of the extremely low incidence of the XYY syndrome[228] and other kinds of genetic
abnormalities[229] in the general population, as well as the inconsistent
links between these conditions and crime, it is questionable whether
there is a true association between the XYY chromosome abnormality
and crime. Moreover, the legal community has dismissed consideration of the XYY syndrome as a criminal law defense, including the
insanity defense.[230]

2.   *Gender-Dominant Defenses for Males: High Testosterone Level*

The gender-dominant defenses relying on high testosterone
levels, while not entirely successful, have been influential in some
cases. Moreover, unlike the XYY syndrome, the courts have not totally
dismissed them.

---

[224] *See* Arthur Robinson et al., *Summary of Clinical Findings in Children and Young Adults
with Sex Chromosome Abnormalities*, 26 BIRTH DEFECTS: ORIGINAL ARTICLE SERIES 225, 227
(1991).

[225] *See* WILSON & HERRNSTEIN, *supra* note 1, at 100-02; Witkin et al., *supra* note 215, at
547-55; Horan, *supra* note 215, at 1351-53; Note, *Chromosome Defense, supra* note 215, at 899-
901.

[226] *See* Seymour Kessler & Rudolf H. Moos, *The XYY Karotype and Criminality: A Review*, 7
J. PSYCHIATRIC RES. 153, 160-67 (1970) (identifying several methodological problems associated with XYY studies, including the limited number of XYY males tested so far); Theodore
R. Sarbin & Jeffrey E. Miller, *Demonism Revisited: The XYY Chromosomal Anomaly*, 5 ISSUES IN
CRIMINOLOGY 195, 198-200 (1970) (noting, for example, the heavy reliance on single case
reports, which could create a sampling bias in most of the studies of the relationship between XYY karyotype and criminal behavior).

[227] *See* Witkin et al., *supra* note 215, at 553-54.

[228] *See id.* at 550; Note, *Chromosome Defense, supra* note 215, at 898-99.

[229] *See* Craft, *supra* note 212, at 115-18.

[230] *See* WAYNE R. LAFAVE & AUSTIN W. SCOTT JR., 1 CRIMINAL LAW 379-82 (2d student ed.
1986) (reviewing cases and literature on the XYY as a criminal law defense). Some scholars
nonetheless maintain that the XYY disorder should be considered relevant as a defense to
criminal conduct. *See* Peter T. Farrell, *The XYY Syndrome in Criminal Law: An Introduction*,
44 ST. JOHN'S L. REV. 217, 218 (1969) (arguing that the relevance of the XYY "as part of an
insanity defense should not be opened to serious dispute"); David Skeen, *The Genetically
Defective Offender*, 9 WM. MITCHELL L. REV. 217, 263-65 (1983) (concluding that the courts
should be more open to genetic defenses in the future if trial attorneys are more knowledgeable and prepared).

High testosterone level defenses focus on the association between circulating hormones and aggression. Evidence of an association between androgen levels and aggression in human males is complex and inconclusive.[231] Some research suggests that hormone levels influence behavior indirectly, through their effect on cognitive structure during prenatal and early adolescent development, such as the degree of lateralization of the cerebral cortex.[232] Other research points to a more direct effect on behavior. For example, researchers have associated the behavioral traits of dominance and aggression in the human male with levels or rates of testosterone production.[233]

Research on more direct associations between androgen levels, primarily testosterone, and criminality shows somewhat conflicting results, possibly because of the different types of hormone measures used, the effect of the prison environment on those subjects who are tested, or the differences among the types of offenders examined.[234] In one study of aggression in a sample of young males, researchers found no differences in plasma testosterone levels between groups of nonoffenders and prisoners.[235] However, they found that prisoners with histories of more violent crimes in adolescence had significantly higher levels of testosterone than prisoners without violent histories.[236] Another study showed that imprisoned rapists and child molesters did not have significantly different testosterone levels than normal men. However, the most violent rapists had significantly higher levels than the other subjects.[237] Moreover, recent research on a sample of fifteen- to seventeen-year-old boys showed a "substantial correlation" between testosterone level and self-reports of both verbal

---

231 *See* Kingsley R. Browne, *Biology, Equality, and the Law: The Legal Significance of Biological Sex Differences*, 38 Sw. L.J. 617, 645 (1984).

232 *See* June Machover Reinisch, *Prenatal Exposure to Synthetic Progestins Increases Potential for Aggression in Humans*, 211 SCIENCE 1171, 1171-73 (1981).

233 *See* Moyer, *supra* note 1, at 335; Alan Booth & D. Wayne Osgood, *The Influence of Testosterone on Deviance in Adulthood: Assessing and Explaining the Relationship*, 31 CRIMINOLOGY 93 (1993); Dan Olweus et al., *Testosterone, Aggression, Physical, and Personality Dimensions in Normal Adolescent Males*, 42 PSYCHOSOM. MED. 253 (1980). Evidence also suggests that these rates are linked to age. For example, in one study, the average testosterone production rate of older men (31-66 years old) was half that of younger men (17-28 years old). *See* Harold Persky et al., *Relation of Psychologic Measures of Aggression and Hostility to Testosterone Production in Man*, 33 PSYCHOSOM. MED. 265, 267 (1971).

234 *See* DENNO, BIOLOGY AND VIOLENCE, *supra* note 10, at 627.

235 *See* Leo E. Kreus & Robert M. Rose, *Assessment of Aggressive Behavior and Plasma Testosterone in a Young Criminal Population*, 34 PSYCHOSOM. MED. 321, 327-28 (1972).

236 *See id.* at 327.

237 *See* Richard T. Rada et al., *Plasma Testosterone Levels in the Rapist*, 38 PSYCHOSOM. MED. 257, 263, 265 (1976); *see also* Jerald Bain et al., *Sex Hormones in Murderers and Assaulters*, 5 BEHAVIORAL SCI. & L. 95, 98-100 (1987) (failing to find any demonstrable differences in hormone levels among murderers, assaulters, and a control group, but noting that the study was not definitive).

and physical aggression.[238] Additional research reporting a significant relationship between testosterone level and adult deviance emphasizes that this link is mediated by the effect of testosterone on social integration and history of juvenile delinquency.[239]

Attempts to use testosterone level as a defense or mitigating factor have either been limited, or discouraged. In *People v. Moore*,[240] for example, a prisoner unsuccessfully claimed ineffective assistance of counsel after his attorney pursued a "testosterone defense" rather than the traditional insanity defense.[241] The attorney claimed that the psychiatrists he approached to use as expert witnesses were not willing to testify about a testosterone defense, and employees of the circuit court's Psychiatric Institute also "did not favor" the defense.[242]

Although some courts have acknowledged a link between testosterone and criminal behavior,[243] there is a range in opinion concerning the association's strength. In *People v. Rennert*,[244] for example, the court noted, with respect to the defendant's pursuit of an insanity defense, that other characteristics of the defendant may have contributed to his sexual attack, irrespective of the evidence of defendant's "slightly higher than normal" testosterone levels.[245] Doctors testified that the defendant still suffered from a mental disease or defect even after his treatment with progesterone lowered his level of testosterone to that of a female.[246] According to the court, "[t]he function of testosterone is to immediate sexual and aggressive drives in the body, but there is no clear evidence that the level of testosterone affects individual personalities."[247]

Other courts have not found testosterone evidence to be persuasive,[248] suggesting, as one court concluded, that the "testosterone the-

---

[238] *See* Dan Olweus, *Testosterone and Adrenaline: Aggressive Antisocial Behavior in Normal Adolescent Males, in* THE CAUSES OF CRIME: NEW BIOLOGICAL APPROACHES 263, 264-65 (Sarnoff Mednick et al. eds., 1987).

[239] *See* Booth & Osgood, *supra* note 233, at 93.

[240] 498 N.E.2d 701 (Ill. App. Ct. 1986).

[241] *See id.* at 706.

[242] *See id.*

[243] *See, e.g.,* Parr v. Secretary of the Dep't of Health and Human Serv., No. 90-1324V, 1993 U.S. Claims LEXIS 37, at *8 (Cl. Ct. Apr. 26, 1993) (noting that "[m]ales with organic personality disorder are more likely to become violent than females because of the production of testosterone").

[244] 364 N.E.2d 506 (Ill. App. Ct. 1977).

[245] *See id.* at 508-09.

[246] *See id.* at 508.

[247] *Id.*

[248] *See e.g., In re Maricopa County Juvenile Action,* 838 P.2d 1365, 1369 (Ariz. Ct. App. 1992). In this case, a 13-year-old boy was found to have sexually molested a 3-year-old girl. *Id.* at 1366. Testimony during his trial noted that "pubescent males undergo a biological change, including a surge in the production of testosterone, and become very interested in

ory" has failed to gain "general acceptance in the relevant scientific community."[249] Yet, courts have recognized the beneficial effects of Depo-Provera on the behavior of those using it to lower their testosterone level.[250] Thus, although courts do not accept testosterone level as a defense to criminal culpability, they may recognize its rehabilitative qualities.

A somewhat different issue concerns courts' perspectives on the culpability of those individuals who inject or ingest anabolic steroids.[251] Anabolic steroids are the synthetic analogues of testosterone that mimic the effects of testosterone on the body.[252] Initially, steroids were expected to treat a variety of medical conditions. However, their primary use today is to enhance athletic performance.[253] Steroids have a number of well known side effects, including increased aggression. When used in large doses, however, they can create severe toxic psychosis, a condition that some attorneys have attempted to use to negate criminal responsibility.[254]

---

sexual matters." *Id.* at 1369. The court stated that it did "not believe such expert testimony is necessary to the adjudication of delinquency in this case." *Id.*

[249] State v. Brand, 842 P.2d 470, 472 (Wash. 1992) (denying a convicted murderer's request for a new trial based upon his discovery of evidence concerning the psychiatric effect of the testosterone treatment he had been receiving prior to the murder); *cf.* State v. Krieger, 471 N.W.2d 599 (Wis. Ct. App. 1991). In *Krieger*, the defendant had entered a plea of no contest to eleven counts of sexual exploitation of children. *Id.* at 600. After conviction he sought to withdraw this plea based on the testimony of Fred S. Berlin, Co-Director of the Sexual Disorders Clinic at the John Hopkins Hospital. Berlin testified that Krieger suffered "from pedophilia, which made it impossible for Krieger to be responsible for his criminal conduct . . . . Krieger satisfied both the cognitive component (he did not appreciate the wrongful nature of his acts) and the volitional component (his pedophilia significantly impaired his capacity to conform his behavior to statutory requirements)." *Id.* at 601. Krieger was seeking Depo-Provera treatment to lower his testosterone level and claimed that failure of the trial court to allow him to modify his plea constituted manifest injustice. *Id.* The court rejected these arguments, saying that prior to the plea there had been voluminous evidence of Krieger's mental state available to his counsel, and thus the testimony of Berlin did not constitute new evidence so as to warrant the plea modification. *Id.* at 604.

[250] *See, e.g.*, Paoli v. Lally, 812 F.2d 1489, 1491 (4th Cir. 1987) (commenting on the "beneficial effect" of Depo-Provera treatment and how the prisoner's appearance and behavior have improved dramatically as a result of using it); Commonwealth v. DiVincenzo, 523 A.2d 758, 765 (Pa. Super. 1987) (noting that Depo-Provera "resulted in reductions in erotic fantasies, sexual urges, and related sexual behaviors in all cases. In addition to the sexual inhibitory effects, the drug also had an unmistakable general tranquilizing action.").

[251] *See* Martin T. Bidwill & David L. Katz, *Injecting New Life into an Old Defense: Anabolic Steroid-Induced Psychosis as a Paradigm of Involuntary Intoxication,* 7 ENT. & SPORTS L. REV. 1 (1989).

[252] *See* Herbert A. Haupt & George G. Rovere, *Anabolic Steroids: A Review of the Literature,* 12 AM. J. SPORTS MED. 469, 469 (1984).

[253] *See* Bidwill & Katz, *supra* note 251, at 6-7.

[254] *Id.* at 5; Harrison G. Pope & David L. Katz, *Homicide and Near-Homicide by Anabolic Steroid Users,* 51 J. CLIN. PSYCHIATRY 28, 28 (1990).

In general, courts have not accepted the use of steroids as a defense, either to sexual molestation,[255] violent attacks,[256] or in the context of an insanity defense to first-degree murder.[257] However, steroid use appears to have had some mitigating effect at sentencing in some cases, including cases for attempted murder,[258] and aggravated assault.[259] Moreover, a medical doctor testifying in a major first-degree murder trial stated that the defendant presenting a steroid defense may have been spared the death penalty because of the testimony on the effects of steroids, even though the jury rejected this evidence as a basis for acquittal.[260] A steroid defense may also have more influence in cases where no physical injury occurred. For example, an accused, charged with three counts of arson not involving personal injury, successfully used a defense of steroid-induced insanity.[261]

Others have attempted to use, with mixed results, a variation on the "testosterone theory" in what has been termed the "boys will be boys" defense.[262] The general thesis of this defense is that because of

---

[255] *See, e.g.,* United States v. Seymour, ACM No. 28331, 1991 CMR LEXIS 741 (A.F.C.M.R. Apr. 19, 1991). In this case, an airman claimed that his molestation of his 12-year-old foster daughter was a result of his treatment with methyl testosterone, an anabolic steroid he was taking to increase his fertility. *Id.* The United States Air Force Court of Military Review noted that a psychiatrist had "testified that the appellant's methyl testosterone therapy may have resulted in a toxic psychosis which would limit his ability to conform his conduct to the requirements of the law." *Id.* Two sanity boards disagreed, and the trial judge denied any further pursuit of that defense.

[256] *See* Bidwill & Katz, *supra* note 251, at 4 n.10; Pope & Katz, *supra* note 254, at 28.

[257] *See* Judgment, State v. Horace Williams, No. 86-9257 CF (Fla. 15th Cir. Ct. June 7, 1988), *aff'd,* 573 So.2d 875 (1990). The defendant Williams was convicted of first-degree murder despite his contention that he was insane on the night he brutally killed the victim because of his excessive use of anabolic steroids. *See* Bidwell & Katz, *supra* note 251, at 3-4 & nn.7-8 and accompanying text; *Defense in Slaying Case Cites Steroid Addiction,* N.Y. TIMES, May 30, 1988, at 20. At trial, the defense attempted to introduce a jury instruction maintaining that Williams was insane on the night of the killing due to his use of steroids. The trial judge rejected such an instruction. However, even though the judge did not mention anabolic steroids or the potential influence of any drugs, he did provide an instruction to the jury regarding the defense of voluntary intoxication. *See* Bidwell & Katz, *supra* note 251, at 4-5 & n.11.

[258] *See* Debra Cassens Moss, *And Now the Steroid Defense?,* 74 A.B.A. J. 22, 22 (Oct. 1988).

[259] *See* Slade, *supra* note 209, at B20.

[260] *See* Bidwill & Katz, *supra* note 251, at 5 n.12

[261] *See* State v. Williams, No. C-5630/5631/5634 (Circuit Court for St. Mary's County, Md. filed April 3, 1986). In this case, the defendant Williams had been engaging in the excessive use of steroids as part of his regimen for bodybuilding. The court found Williams guilty, but not criminally responsible, concluding that he "was indeed suffering from an organic personality syndrome caused by the toxic levels of anabolic steroids . . . and that this disorder substantially impaired his ability to appreciate the criminality of his acts and to conform his conduct to the requirements of the law." *See* Opinion and Order, State v. Williams.

[262] *See* MYRIAM MIEDZIAN, BOYS WILL BE BOYS: BREAKING THE LINK BETWEEN MASCULINITY AND VIOLENCE 39 (1991); ELIZABETH A. STANKO, INTIMATE INTRUSIONS 9-11 (1985).

the effects of testosterone, males have "developed highly aggressive and territorial drives that are unalterable."[263] This defense was perhaps most vividly illustrated in the Glen Ridge, New Jersey, rape case, which involved the sexual assault of a mentally defective seventeen-year-old girl by four neighborhood acquaintances.[264] In that case, defense attorneys contended that the victim, who had engaged in sexual intercourse at an early age, was an aggressive temptress who "craved" sex and "had and still has emotional and physical needs."[265] As a result, the defendants would respond in the way that "any boy would." As one attorney contended, "Boys . . . have the same emotional and physical needs . . . Boys will be boys. Pranksters. Fool-arounds. Do crazy things. Experiment with life, and disregard their parents."[266] The "boys will be boys" tactic in the Glen Ridge rape case, which was ridiculed and eventually backfired,[267] relied solely on the "hormonal

---

263 *See* MIEDZIAN, *supra* note 262, at 39.

264 *See In re* B.G., 589 A.2d 637, 640 (N.J. Super. Ct. Law Div. 1991); *see also* PETER LAUFER, A QUESTION OF CONSENT: INNOCENCE AND COMPLICITY IN THE GLEN RIDGE RAPE CASE (1994). In the Glen Ridge case, the victim, considered to be mentally defective, (she had an IQ of 64 and the social capacity of an eight-year-old), was lead by one of the defendants to a basement with the promise that she could have a date with one of the other defendants, who would be there. *In re* B.G., 589 A.2d at 640-41. He was there, along with approximately twelve other boys. *Id.* at 646. The girl was asked to lay down on a couch and disrobe. *Id.* at 641. At this point several of the boys started to leave. *Id.* The girl was then asked to masturbate one boy. Thereafter, others proceeded to insert into her vagina a fungo bat, broomstick, and stick, all of which were wrapped in plastic bags and coated with vaseline (except for the stick). *Id.* There was also mention of a drumstick being inserted into her rectum, but it appears that this evidence was hearsay and thus inadmissible. *Id.* at 640. The victim testified that she was told that, if she failed to cooperate or if she told anyone what was happening, her mother would be told and she would have to leave school. *Id.* at 644. She later discussed the incident with her swimming teacher. *Id.* at 640-41. At this time she sought advice on how to say 'no' in the event of a reoccurrence. *See* Robert Hanley, *Woman in Sex-Abuse Trial Sought Advice On How to Say 'No',* N.Y. TIMES, January 7, 1993, at A11. After talking to her teacher but before a criminal investigation began, the victim refused a subsequent request to go back to the basement for a similar performance, which would be videotaped. *See In re* B.G., 589 A.2d at 645. At the trial, defense attorneys (especially Michael Querques) placed reliance on the "boys will be boys" and "Lolita" defenses. *See* LAUFER, *supra*, at 51-72.

265 LAUFER, *supra* note 264, at 67.

266 *Id.* at 69. As the attorney emphasized,

You think people are going to forget about the girls they knew in high school who were loose and the boys who took? Are men going to forget, Hey, I got a girl who is loose, do you want to join me? Go ahead, forget about it if you want, and then, when you go to bed at night, ask your conscience, Am I being fair to this kid?

Id. at 70.

267 *See id.* at 183-85; Tracy Schroth, *"Lolita" Defense Risky in Glen Ridge Sex Trial,* N.J.L.J., Nov. 2, 1992, at 1. Four defendants (Bryant Grober, Christopher Archer, and Kevin and Kyle Scherzer) were found guilty by a jury, which also found that the victim was legally mentally defective. LAUFER, supra note 264, at 149-50. Bryant Grober was convicted only of conspiracy (in the third-degree) to commit aggravated sexual assault and aggravated sexual contact. *Id.* at 150. Christopher Archer and Kevin and Kyle Scherzer were each convicted of first-degree aggravated sexual assault due to the use of force or coercion, and

stereotypes" of men. Yet, it has been used in other cases, such as the "Spur Posse" incident, with varying degrees of success.[268]

In general, then, the viability of the gender-dominant "testosterone theory" defense for males appears to depend on how, and in what context, it is used. Notably, the outcome of such a defense seems most risky when it relies on extreme gender stereotyping, rather than a depiction of a biological transformation gone astray. As the next section shows, such defenses have been slightly more successful for females in the gender-specific context, although this disparity may be the result of circumstances other than gender.

---

of conspiracy (in the second-degree) to commit aggravated sexual assault and aggravated sexual contact. *Id.* Christopher Archer and Kevin Scherzer were also convicted of first-degree aggravated sexual assault due to penetration of a mentally defective person with foreign objects, while Kyle Scherzer's guilt on this charge was gauged by the jury to be a second-degree offense. *Id.* All four defendants were acquitted on the charges of forced fellatio, fellatio performed by a mentally defective person, improper touching of the victim's breasts, and forced masturbation, by the victim, of the defendants. *Id.* All four defendants were also allowed to remain free on no more than $2,500 bail pending their appeal. *Id.* at 151.

[268] For example, in Lakewood, California, a group of nine high-schoolers calling themselves the "Spur Posse," were charged with molesting and raping neighborhood girls as young as ten years old. *See* LAUFER, *supra* note 264, at 186. The leader of the group claimed 66 conquests, and was called a "virile specimen" by his father. *Id.* Only one of the boys was prosecuted, and he was sent to a juvenile facility for less than a year for molesting a 10-year-old. *Id.* at 187. Charges against the rest of the boys were dropped because the prosecutors believed that the evidence was insufficient to establish lack of consent or forcible rape. *See* Veronica T. Jennings & Stephen Buckley, *Montgomery Teens Accused of Rape: School Superintendent's Son Is Among Five Facing Charges*, WASH. POST, Oct. 30, 1993, at A1; Judy Mann, *Lessons From the Montgomery Seven*, WASH. POST, Dec. 1, 1993, at E19. A similar incident occured in Maryland, where two 14-year-old girls were allegedly gang-raped by a group of youths calling themselves the "Chronics." The group's objective was to have sex with as many girls as possible. Jennings and Buckley, *supra.* Five boys were charged, as adults, with first-degree rape in two separate attacks. *Id.* The charges were dropped, however, when the defense produced sworn affidavits from 14 people who provided details that suggested the sex was consensual. Mann, *supra.* Also in Maryland, 16- and 17-year-old brothers were prosecuted for raping an unconscious party-goer. Their father expressed shock at the prosecution and explained that he thought it was "a mutual thing." LAUFER, *supra* note 264, at 187. Yet again in Maryland, a judge handed out a sentence of probation to a middle-aged man who raped his unconscious former employee, a teenage girl. *Id.* at 188. The judge explained that the girl was "contributorily negligent" in the incident, and noted that intercourse with an unconscious partner was "the dream of quite a lot of males, quite honestly." *Id.* at 188-89. In Montclair, New Jersey, which is immediately adjacent to Glen Ridge, members of a gang calling itself the "Hardhedz Posse" were arrested for molesting a seventh-grade girl on three separate occasions, the incidents spanning a period of several weeks. *Id.* at 190-91. In North Carolina, five teenagers were charged with rape and violation with a foreign object of a mentally handicapped woman whom one of the five had previously dated. *Id.* at 191. The woman was raped and penetrated with a broomstick on New Year's Eve, and raped on videotape at a construction site the following day. *Id.* The defendants in all of these cases appeared to rely heavily on a "boys will be boys" theory for explaining their behavior.

3. Gender-Specific or Gender-Dominant Defenses for Females

A considerable amount of research has been conducted on fluctuating hormonal levels and their relationship to crime among females. Research on the association between testosterone level and human female behavior, however, is scarce. In one study, significantly higher testosterone levels were found among violent female outpatients than among the nonviolent ones, whose levels were similar to those reported for normal females.[269] This study also reported increased irritability among violent patients during menstruation,[270] a finding consistent with other research showing associations between criminality and symptoms of both premenstrual and menstrual periods.[271]

According to Katharina Dalton, who has conducted much of the initial research in this area,[272] the symptoms of PMS[273] vary considerably, although they can include increased aggression, irritability, headaches, edema, psychiatric symptoms, and suicide attempts.[274] These symptoms may be due to a decrease in the level of progesterone, and a relatively greater increase of estrogen in the estrogen-progesterone ratio,[275] although recent research suggests that these fluctuations are

---

[269] *See* C. L. Ehlers et al., *A Possible Relationship Between Plasma Testosterone and Aggressive Behavior in a Female Outpatient Population, in* LIMBIC EPILEPSY AND THE DYSCONTROL SYNDROME 183, 190-93 (M. Girgis & L. Kiloh eds., 1980); *see also* James Dabbs et al., *Saliva Testosterone and Criminal Violence Among Women,* 9 PERSONALITY AND INDIVIDUAL DIFFERENCES 269, 269-75 (1988) (reporting a link between testosterone and violent criminal acts).

[270] *See* Ehlers et. al., *supra* note 269, at 190-91.

[271] *See* Browne, *supra* note 231, at 646-49 (reviewing studies showing that a disproportionate number of violent crimes are committed by women who were menstruating or during the premenstrual week).

[272] Some of Dalton's key publications include: KATHARINA DALTON, THE PREMENSTRUAL SYNDROME (1964); Katharina Dalton, *Menstruation and Crime,* 2 BRIT. MED. J. 1752 (1961); Katharina Dalton, *Menstruation and Examinations,* [1968] 2 LANCET 1386; Katharina Dalton, *Cyclical Criminal Acts in Premenstrual Syndrome,* [1980] 2 LANCET 1070.

[273] PMS has been defined as "the recurrence of symptoms in the premenstruum [premenstruation period] with absence of symptoms in the postmenstruum." KATHARINA DALTON, THE PREMENSTRUAL SYNDROME AND PROGESTERONE THERAPY 3 (2d ed. 1984). The premenstrual syndrome should be distinguished from incidences of "menstrual distress," which Dalton defines as "the presence of intermittent or continuous symptoms present *throughout* the menstrual cycle which increase in severity during the premenstruum or menstruation." *Id.* at 6.

[274] *See* Katharina Dalton, *Premenstrual Syndrome,* 9 HAMLINE L. REV. 143, 148-51 (1986). Dalton examines nine risk factors to diagnose PMS: time of onset, time of increased severity, painless menstruation, increased libido in the premenstruum, intolerance of the pill, adult weight swings beyond twenty-eight pounds, inability to go for long periods without food, impact of pregnancy, and varying inability to tolerate alcohol. *See id.; see also* HOYENGA & HOYENGA, *supra* note 5, at 193-95; KENNETH MOYER, VIOLENCE AND AGGRESSION 49-50 (1987); William R. Keye, Jr. & Eric Trunnell, *Premenstrual Syndrome: A Medical Perspective,* 9 HAMLINE L. REV. 165, 165-67 & n.6 (1986).

[275] *See* MOYER, *supra* note 274, at 49-53.

more complex.[276] Reviews of PMS-crime research indicate, however, that "there is an extremely limited and somewhat inconsistent understanding of the relationship between menstrual symptoms, behavior, and endocrine fluctuations."[277] Moreover, PMS-crime research is fraught with serious methodological difficulties. These include variations in measures of cycle duration, post-hoc correlations that incorrectly imply causation, use of retrospective self-report data, anecdotal methods, small samples, and lack of appropriate control samples or controls for external influences, such as stress.[278]

Whether or not hormonal disorders should provide a criminal defense is a different issue. Although PMS distress has been used successfully as a defense in England,[279] with one recent exception,[280] it has not been accepted as a defense in the United States. In 1982, *People v. Santos*[281] marked the first criminal case in the United States to attempt the defense.[282] Shirley Santos, who faced a charge of first-degree assault against her four-year-old daughter, admitted that she beat her child.[283] At a pre-trial hearing on the defense's motion to dismiss, Santos' lawyer raised the claim that, because of her premenstrual syndrome, Santos was not responsible for her actions.[284] Yet, the defense provided no evidence that Santos had PMS at the time of

---

[276] *See* Hoyenga & Hoyenga, *supra* note 5 at 193-95.

[277] Bruce Harry & Charlotte M. Balcer, *Menstruation and Crime: A Critical Review of the Literature from the Clinical Criminology Perspective*, 5 Behavioral Sci. & L. 307, 317 (1987) (arguing that there is insufficient evidence to know whether there is a link between any phase of the menstrual cycle and crime); *see also* Moyer, *supra* note 274, at 49-53 (reviewing evidence of the link between crime and premenstrual syndrome, but noting that the underlying physiology is obscure); Siann, *supra* note 5, at 38 (noting that "[w]hether or not this syndrome is directly associated with hormonal changes has not been established"); Julie Horney, *Menstrual Cycles and Criminal Responsibility*, 2 L. & Hum. Behav. 25, 29-33 (1978) (raising several critical questions regarding interpretations of research on menstruation and crime).

[278] *See* Harry & Balcer, *supra* note 277.

[279] *See* Candy Pahl-Smith, Comment, *Premenstrual Syndrome as a Criminal Defense: The Need for a Medico-Legal Understanding*, 15 N.C. Cent. L.J. 246, 246 (1985).

[280] *See infra* note 295 and accompanying text.

[281] No. 1KO46299 (Kings County, N.Y. Crim. Ct. Nov. 3, 1982).

[282] Prior to *Santos*, the symptoms of PMS had been discussed in a few civil cases. *See, e.g.*, Hoffman-LaRoche v. Kleindiest, 478 F.2d 1, 9 (3d Cir. 1973); Crockett v. Cohen, 299 F. Supp. 739, 741 (W.D. Va. 1969); Tingen v. Tingen, 446 P.2d 185, 186 (Or. 1968); Reid v. Florida Real Estate Comm'n, 188 So.2d 846, 849 (Fla. Dist. Ct. App. 1966).

[283] *See* Christina L. Hosp, Note, *Has the PMS Defense Gained a Legitimate Toehold in Virginia Criminal Law?*, 14 Geo. Mason U.L. Rev. 427 (1991); Pahl-Smith, *supra* note 279, at 256.

[284] *See* Robert Mark Carney & Brian D. Williams, Note, *Criminal Law—Premenstrual Syndrome: A Criminal Defense*, 59 Notre Dame L. Rev. 253, 262 (1983); Joann D'Emilio, Note, *Battered Woman's Syndrome and Premenstrual Syndrome: A Comparison of Their Possible Use as Defenses to Criminal Liability*, 59 St. John's L. Rev. 558, 570 (1985) (citing defense press release); Elizabeth Holtzman, Letter to the Editor, *Premenstrual Symptoms: No Legal Defense*, 60 St. John's L. Rev. 712, 713-14 (1986); Nora Mulligan, Note, *Premenstrual Syndrome*, 6 Harv. Women's L.J. 219, 222-23 (1983); Pahl-Smith, *supra*, note 279, at 256.

the act or that she had previously experienced PMS.[285] Because a plea bargain allowed Santos to plead guilty to the lesser included charge of harassment, a misdemeanor, the court never officially ruled on the admissibility of PMS testimony.[286] The court did, however, rhetorically question why such evidence should not be admissible when courts regularly admitted similar kinds of psychological evidence.[287]

Santos lost custody of her child, and was required to participate in a counselling program.[288] The claim made by Santos' attorney and others that the PMS defense was valid because the felony charges were dropped,[289] was countered in a strong rebuttal by the prosecutor who claimed that PMS had no influence in prompting a plea bargain.[290] Indeed, Santos herself later stated in a television interview that premenstrual syndrome was never the reason why she hit her child.[291]

The PMS defense was rejected in a subsequent case where the court concluded that the defense lacked scientific support.[292] Thereafter, courts accepted PMS evidence, but not as a defense. Courts continued to deny its legitimacy as a defense either because they considered that the defendant knew right from wrong irrespective of her PMS experiences,[293] or because the defendant lacked a sufficient medical diagnosis.[294] Yet in *Commonwealth v. Richter*,[295] the first case to accept the PMS defense, the court's conclusion that the defendant was not guilty of driving while intoxicated, was based in part on her

---

[285] *See* Pahl-Smith, *supra* at 279.

[286] *See* Carney & Williams, *supra* note 284, at 262; D'Emilio, *supra* note 284, at 570; Holtzman, *supra* note 284, at 714 (citing the minutes of the pre-trial hearing); Mulligan, *supra* note 284, at 222; Pahl-Smith, *supra* note 279, at 257.

[287] *See* Carney & Williams, *supra* note 284, at 262; D'Emilio, *supra* note 284, at 570; Holtzman, *supra* note 284, at 714 (citing the minutes of the pre-trial hearing); Mulligan, *supra* note 284, at 222; Pahl-Smith, *supra* note 279, at 257.

[288] *See* Hosp, *supra* note 283, at 430.

[289] *Id.* at 430-31; D'Emilio, *supra* note 284; Mulligan, *supra* note 284.

[290] *See* Holtzman, *supra* note 284.

[291] *See id.* at 713 (citing television broadcast); Pahl-Smith, *supra* note 279, at 257.

[292] *See In re* Irvin, 31 B.R. 251, 260 (Bankr. D. Colo. 1983) (victim of aggravated assault seeking civil suit against defendant for personal injuries in which the court denied defendant's claim that her conduct was uncontrollable because of PMS).

[293] *See* State v. Lashwood, 384 N.W.2d 319, 321 (S.D. 1986) (affirming defendant's conviction for three counts of forgery and concluding that although the defendant suffered from premenstrual syndrome and "significant memory loss," she "knew right from wrong and had the ability to help in her own defense").

[294] *See* Commonwealth v. Grass, 141 Pa. Cmwlth. 455 (Pa. Commw. Ct. 1991). In *Grass*, the court considered insufficient the defendant's medical evidence supporting her claim that PMS rendered her incapable of making a knowing and conscious decision to take a breathalyzer test following her arrest for driving while intoxicated. *See id.* at 457. Because the defendant offered PMS evidence based only on her own statements and those of her gynecologist and husband, *see id.* at 459, she failed to show a "necessary causal nexus" between her PMS and her conduct. *Id.* at 460.

[295] No. T90-215256 (Fairfax County Gen. Dist. Ct. June 4, 1991) (unreported case).

use of PMS to explain her assaultive and abusive behavior toward police.[296] Police had pulled the defendant off the road for weaving across both lanes of a two-lane highway while driving her three young children.[297] At trial, the defendant stated that the results of her breathalyzer test, which indicated she was intoxicated, were skewed, and that her PMS, which was moderate, made her abusive when she learned that her children would be put in protective services for the night after her arrest.[298] Considering the "totality of the evidence,"[299] the court concluded that either intoxication or PMS could have caused the defendant's behavior—raising a "reasonable doubt" concerning her guilt.[300]

It is unclear whether *Richter* is an isolated case, or important as precedent. No other court has cited it. Moreover, the court applied the PMS defense in an odd way. Because Virginia has rejected the diminished capacity defense,[301] the most common vehicle for introducing PMS, the court used PMS in an effort to explain why the defendant's behavior occurred, rather than to demonstrate the absence of specific intent.[302] Also, the court applied the defense to a well educated, middle class defendant, accused of committing a nonviolent offense, who, as the judge noted, was able to garner "sufficient resources" unavailable to "[y]our average man in the street."[303] Because *Richter* may be an anomaly, this section also examines the postpartum depression defense. Cases relying on that defense provide a broader range of circumstances from which to draw conclusions about the importance of gender-related defenses.

Postpartum psychosis is a temporary condition that occurs to women in about one out of 1000 births.[304] The most severe of the three

---

296 Hosp, *supra* note 283, at 427.

297 *See id.* at 430-33. State troopers reported that the defendant smelled strongly of alcohol, that she freely used profanity toward them, that she refused various field sobriety tests, and that she tried to kick one of the troopers in the groin when he asked her to put her hand on top of her head. She was eventually placed in leg restraints so that she could take the breathalyzer test. *See id.* at 433-34. The defendant showed 0.13% blood alcohol level, more than the legal limit, and admitted to drinking four glasses of wine over a six hour period. *See id.* at 434-36.

298 *Id.* at 435. The expert gynecologist's testimony suggested that the defendant was not being treated for PMS at the time of her arrest, nor that the defendant even knew that she had PMS prior to her examination by the expert. *See id.*

299 *Id.* at 427.

300 *Id.* at 436-37.

301 *See* Stamper v. Commonwealth, 324 S.E.2d 682 (Va. 1985).

302 Hosp, *supra* note 283, at 439.

303 *Id.* at 436-37.

304 *See* Terra Ziporyn, *"Rip van Winkle Period" Ends for Puerperal Psychiatric Problems*, 251 J.A.M.A 2061, 2061-62 (1984); Amy L. Nelson, Comment, *Postpartum Psychosis: A New Defense?*, 95 DICK. L. REV. 625, 625 (1991).

types of postpartum disorders,[305] it can involve loss of sense of reality, delusions, extreme agitation, feelings of persecution, or hallucinations.[306] Typically, it affects women who have no prior criminal record or history of serious mental illness.[307]

Some researchers consider postpartum disorders to be caused by a number of different factors, both internal and external to the individual, which result from the hormonal, psychological, and social changes linked to childbirth.[308] Other researchers believe that nonpsychotic postpartum depression results from social factors, whereas postpartum psychosis is more closely linked to a genetic predisposition.[309]

Women who have attempted to use postpartum psychosis as a criminal defense to infanticide have had varying degrees of success.[310] This section examines thirteen major cases that have relied on postpartum psychosis evidence; seven resulted in an acquittal,[311] and six in

---

[305] In general, experts posit three types of postpartum disorders: postpartum blues, postpartum depression, and postpartum psychosis. The postpartum blues is a temporary period of depression, usually evidenced by crying, which lasts 24 to 48 hours; it occurs in 50% to 60% of new mothers. Postpartum depression, which shares symptoms similar to other kinds of depression, lasts 6-to-8 weeks and occurs in 20% of postpartum women. It is most strongly associated with a previous psychiatric history, as well as self-reported stressful life events and degree of social support. Postpartum psychosis is clinically comparable to nonpospartum depressive psychosis and occurs in only one or two mothers per thousand. *See* Dyanne D. Affonso & George Domino, *Postpartum Depression: A Review,* 11 BIRTH 231, 232-35 (1984); Barry S. Zuckerman & William R. Beardslee, *Maternal Depression: A Concern for Pediatricians,* 79 PEDIATRICS 110 (1987); *see also* CAROL DIX, THE NEW MOTHER SYNDROME: COPING WITH POSTPARTUM STRESS AND DEPRESSION 9-11 (1985) (offering advice with symptoms).

[306] *See* Affonso & Domino, *supra* note 305; Ziporyn, *supra* note 304, at 2061; Jennifer L. Grossman, Note, *Postpartum Psychosis—A Defense to Criminal Responsibility or Just Another Gimmick?,* 67 U. DET. L. REV. 311, 325 (1990).

[307] *See* Nelson, *supra* note 304, at 625.

[308] For example, there are vast hormonal changes that a woman experiences following birth. Although directly prior to delivery, a woman's estrogen and progesterone levels are 50 times higher than they are before pregnancy, hours after birth these levels drop to what they were prior to pregnancy. Other internal changes, such as those required to prepare for milk production, in addition to the external pressures resulting from child birth, such as loss of sleep, can create severe depression or psychosis. *See id.* at 628 n.36; *see also* Ziporyn, *supra* note 304; Grossman, *supra* note 306, at 325-26.

[309] Nelson, *supra* note 304, at 628-29.

[310] *See id.* at 629-33.

[311] *See* People v. Massip, 271 Cal. Rptr. 868 (Cal. Ct. App. 1992) (trial judge substituted his own finding of insanity for the jury's finding of sanity, entered a reduced verdict of voluntary manslaughter, and ordered the defendant, who had placed her infant son under the tire of her car and driven over him, to participate in outpatient treatment program); State v. White, 456 P.2d 797 (Idaho 1969) (a woman who threw her three-month-old daughter on the floor and then placed her in the crib, where she died of blood clotting caused by a skull fracture, was found not guilty of voluntary manslaughter by reason of insanity); People v. Skeoch, 96 N.E.2d 473 (Ill. 1951) (conviction for murder of a woman who asphyxiated her infant son was reversed due to the prosecution's failure to rebut the

a conviction.[312]

The defense was first used in 1951 in *People v. Skeoch*,[313] where the Illinois Supreme Court reversed the defendant's conviction for the murder of her six-day-old child.[314] The court held that a psychiatrist's expert testimony that the defendant was suffering from postpartum psychosis, in addition to the defendant's husband's testimony concerning stressful external circumstances that the defendant was experiencing (such as a theft and his job loss), were sufficient to raise a reasonable doubt of the defendant's insanity at the time she asphyxiated her baby.[315] Although the Idaho Supreme Court allowed a comparable use of the defense nearly twenty years later,[316] another decade passed before the Nevada Supreme Court rejected the defense in affirming the attempted murder conviction of the defendant's daughter.[317]

---

presumption of insanity that the defense established at trial); People v. Thompson (a woman who drowned her nine-month-old son in a bathtub and was charged with manslaughter and felony child abuse was found not guilty by reason of insanity) (*described in* Ann Japenga, *Ordeal of Postpartum Psychosis, Illness Can Have Tragic Consequences for New Mothers*, L.A. TIMES, Feb. 1, 1987, Part VI, at 1); State v. Bartek (a woman who drowned her eight-day-old daughter in the kitchen sink was acquitted of first-degree murder, spending four days in jail and one month in a mental hospital) (*described in* Anastasia Toufexis, *Why Mothers Kill Their Babies*, TIME, June 20, 1988, at 81); People v. Green (N.Y. Sup. Ct. 1988) (a woman who killed her first two children and attempted to kill her third was acquitted of murder because the prosecution could not convince the jury that she was sane) (*described in* Nancy Zeldis, *Post-Partum Psychosis—A Rare Insanity Defense*, N.Y.L.J., Sept. 19, 1988, at 1, *and in* Laura Masnerus, *Postpartum Puzzle; When Do New Mom's 'Blues' Become Serious Illness?*, CHI. TRIB., February 19, 1989, Section 6, at 9).

[312] *See* Clark v. State, 588 P.2d 1027 (Nevada 1979) (a woman who wrapped her two-week-old baby in a blanket and left it on the side of a desert road for three days was convicted of attempted murder); State v. Householder (a woman who pleaded guilty to involuntary manslaughter after she killed her infant daughter by throwing a rock at her, was sentenced to 22 months in jail) (*described in* Dan Trigoboff, *Postpartum Blues: Cases Test Use as Murder Defense*, L.A. DAILY J., Dec. 16, 1987, at 1); Commonwealth v. Dacri (a woman who left her infant son in a bathtub that was filling was convicted of first-degree murder and sentenced to life imprisonment) (*described in* Susan Caba, *Dacri is Sentenced to Life Term*, PHILA. INQUIRER, July 14, 1989, at 1A); Commonwealth v. Weisensale (a woman who drowned her two-month-old daughter was found guilty but mentally ill of third-degree murder, given a suspended five year sentence, and ordered to undergo psychiatric treatment) (described in Judy Pehrson, *The Darkest Side of Postpartum Depression*, YORK (PA) SUNDAY NEWS, May 31, 1987, at E3); Commonwealth v. Comitz, 530 A.2d 473 (Pa. Super. Ct. 1987) (a woman who pleaded guilty but mentally ill to third-degree murder after dropping her one-month-old son into a stream was sentenced to eight to 20 years in prison); Commonwealth v. Smith, No. 1775 Crim. Action 1984 (C.P. York County Ct. May 17, 1985) (a woman who drowned her three-week-old daughter was convicted of third-degree murder and sentenced to probation).

[313] 96 N.E.2d 473 (Ill. 1951).

[314] *See id.* at 475-76.

[315] *See id.* at 474-76.

[316] State v. White, 456 P.2d 797 (Idaho 1969).

[317] *See* Clark v. State, 588 P.2d 1027 (Nevada 1979).

The defense has been used more frequently in the last fifteen years, and with varying results, perhaps attributable in part to the kind of insanity defense that is applied,[318] or evidence of the extent of the psychosis. For example, in one insanity acquittal, the defendant claimed that she thought her nine-month-old son, whom she drowned, was the devil, adding that her postpartum psychosis in an earlier pregnancy ended with a suicide attempt.[319] In another acquittal, the court declared that the defendant, who experienced serious disorders after her child's birth, was insane when she drove her car over her son after unsuccessfully attempting to throw him in front of a moving car.[320] Ann Green's case was perhaps the most controversial. A former pediatric nurse, she was found not guilty by reason of insanity for the murder of her first two children, whom she suffocated soon after their birth, and the attempted murder of a third.[321] One year later she was an outpatient receiving psychiatric treatment.[322]

For convictions, however, there was a wide span of charges, ranging from involuntary manslaughter[323] to first-degree murder,[324] and a

---

[318] *See* Nelson, *supra* note 304.

[319] *See* Japenga, *supra* note 311.

[320] People v. Massip, 271 Cal. Rptr. 868 (Cal. Ct. App. 1992). The People's appeal of the court's overturning of the jury decision in *Massip* was unsuccessful. Even though the trial court abused its discretion and authority in substituting its own finding of insanity for the jury's finding of sanity, the Court of Appeals, Fourth District, Division 3, found that a new trial on the sanity issue would subject the defendant to the danger of a finding of sanity and, therefore, a jail sentence. *Id.* at 872. This result would impermissibly conflict with the rule of People v. Superior Court of Marin County, 446 P.2d 138 (Cal. 1968), which "prohibits review by mandate at the request of the People where . . . there is a danger of further trial or retrial." *Id.* at 147. Furthermore, the court held that the trial court could properly enter a reduced verdict of voluntary manslaughter, rather than the jury's verdict of second-degree murder, based on its finding that "malice actually did not exist." *Massip,* 271 Cal. Rptr. at 874.

This decision, however, was ordered vacated and reconsidered in light of People v. Saille, 820 P.2d 588 (Cal. 1991) (setting forth new guidelines in light of legislative abolition of diminished capacity defense). *See* People v. Massip, 824 P.2d 568 (Cal. 1992) (*en banc*). Even when it is reconsidered in light of *Saille,* the People's appeal will most likely be only partially successful. *Saille* makes clear that the change in California law abolishes the defense of diminished capacity, and thus evidence concerning a defendant's capacity to form a requisite mental state is no longer admissible. *Saille,* 820 P.2d at 593. However, *Saille* also states that a defendant remains "free to show that because of his mental illness or voluntary intoxication, he did not in fact form the intent unlawfully to kill . . . if this evidence is believed, the only supportable verdict would be involuntary manslaughter or an acquittal." *Id.* On reconsideration of *Massip* in light of *Saille,* the Court of Appeals most likely will still find it probative that the trial court found that "malice actually did not exist." *Massip,* 271 Cal. Rptr. at 873.

[321] People v. Green, N.Y.L.J., Sept. 19, 1988, at 1 (N.Y. Sup. Ct. 1988); *Mother Wins Acquittal in 2 Postpartum Killings,* MIAMI HERALD, Oct. 2, 1988, at 18A.

[322] Grossman, *supra* note 306 at 328.

[323] *See* Trigoboff, *supra* note 312, at 24.

[324] *See* Caba, *supra* note 312, at 1A.

gap in sentences, spanning from a suspended sentence[325] to life imprisonment.[326] Yet, apart from the reasons mentioned, such as the reliance on different tests of insanity, there is no clear indication of how these cases differ from acquittals, or how harsher charges and sentences differ from lighter ones. The court in *Commonwealth v. Dacri*[327] conceded that the young defendant, with no prior criminal record, was psychotic when she drowned her son, yet charged her with first-degree murder and sentenced her to life imprisonment.[328]

In general, then, although gender-specific defenses for women have been slightly more successful than those for men, their use and effect are variable. Of all the defenses, courts have viewed postpartum psychosis as the most acceptable. Yet, it is unclear whether the influential factor is gender, particularly with the limited number of defenses available to analyze. The following sections attempt to identify factors that may be most significant.

C. IS GENDER THE CRITICAL FACTOR IN GENDER-BASED DEFENSES?

1. *Gender-specific and Gender-dominant Defenses*

A number of factors other than gender may be driving the apparent differences in courts' willingness to accept certain defenses over others. Three factors seem particularly critical: (1) the permanence of the disorder evidenced, (2) the degree of dangerousness associated with it, and (3) the causal link between the disorder and the crime. A comparison between attempts to argue insanity by applying the XYY chromosome syndrome defense for men, and the postpartum psychosis defense for women, is illustrative:

(1) The XYY syndrome is a life-long genetic condition. In contrast, postpartum psychosis occurs only after childbirth, and even then it is unusual. Most cases last less than a few months, although the more serious cases can last longer.

(2) If XYY is indeed a criminogenic condition, presumably it can be influential at any time. This circumstance raises an awkward predicament for the defendant. He has to contend that the condition caused the crime while, at the same time, concede that he is perpetually dangerous to others. In contrast, women who have evidenced postpartum psychosis are not considered to be dangerous people when they do not have the condition. It is only pregnancy-related.[329]

---

[325] *See* Pehrson, *supra* note 312, at E3.
[326] *See* Caba, *supra* note 312, at 1A.
[327] *See id.*
[328] *See id.*
[329] *See e.g.,* Ziporyn, *supra* note 304.

Moreover, even when they do have it, they are potentially dangerous only to themselves or their children. Most likely, the court considered that Ann Green, who killed two of her children and attempted to kill a third,[330] was not a danger to anyone after her decision to undergo voluntary sterilization, because she was a psychiatric outpatient one year later.[331]

(3) Because a condition like XYY is permanent, it is more difficult to prove that it is causally linked to criminal conduct. Once again, a defendant would need to argue that he is either continually dangerous, that he commits a crime only when he has an opportunity, or he engages in crime when other circumstances in addition to XYY are present. In contrast, women who experience postpartum psychosis typically evidence symptoms that can be more directly linked to their criminal conduct. Furthermore, witnesses routinely report behavioral changes in postpartum psychosis defendants soon or immediately after the birth of their child.[332]

The postpartum psychosis defense is unique. The only defendants are women; the only victims are infants. The defendant's period of dangerousness is temporary, and the disorder is initiated by only one condition—pregnancy, which is often exacerbated by other personal or situational factors. Even though the exact cause of the psychosis remains unclear,[333] the condition initiating it is not.

In light of this comparison, it is more understandable why PMS and testosterone defenses have achieved relatively little success in the United States. It is beyond the scope of this Article to discuss the evidentiary problems associated with these disorders,[334] but it appears that their sources and symptoms are relatively more amorphous than those detected for a disorder such as postpartum psychosis. Yet, even if these conditions were clearly detectable and scientifically reliable, there would also be other differences to consider. Defendants with PMS and high testosterone evidence potentially recurring disorders and their victims can, and have, included anyone. Likewise, defendants can be a recurring danger to society. Thus, it is not surprising that these defenses have been primarily successful for conduct where

---

[330] *See supra* notes 321 to 322 and accompanying text.

[331] *See* Zeldis, *supra* note 311, at 1.

[332] *See supra* notes 304 to 312.

[333] *See supra* notes 308 to 309 and accompanying text.

[334] Presumably, the Federal Rules of Evidence standard affirmed in Daubert v. Merrill Dow Pharmaceuticals, 113 S. Ct. 2786 (1993), would make the admissibility of such evidence more likely compared to the relatively stricter standard espoused in Frye v. United States, 293 F. 1013 (D.C. Cir. 1923). *See, e.g., In re* Irvin, 31 B.R. 251 (Bankr. D. Colo. 1983) (rejecting the admissibility of PMS evidence under the Frye test).

no individual was harmed.[335]

An alternative approach is to compare postpartum psychosis with steroid-induced disorder. First, steroid-induced disorder, like postpartum psychosis, is a temporary condition that ceases when the individual stops using steroids. Second, many of the individuals who have introduced a steroid defense are not considered to be dangerous people either before or after their use of steroids. For example, Pope and Katz, in their case study of three men who committed violent crimes with steroids, reported that the men had no prior history of psychiatric disorder, antisocial personality, or violence, yet their behavior changed dramatically when they started using steroids.[336] Unlike women with postpartum psychosis, however, those with steroid-induced disorder show indiscriminant violence that can last as long as the "rage." Third, similar to postpartum psychosis, a causal link between steroid use and crime can often be substantiated, yet perhaps not as clearly. Homicides induced by postpartum psychosis show characteristics not shared by those induced by steroids.

Foreseeability and sympathy may also be factors. Most individuals who use steroids know that one of the potential consequences will be increased aggression. In contrast, it can be presumed that more sympathy will be invoked for a woman who chooses to have a child, without knowing or even realizing that one of the consequences may be the child's death related to her psychosis. Repeat postpartum psychosis offenders contend that the condition and its consequences may not be clearly foreseeable. Ann Green stated that she did not realize that she had a disorder until a month after the death of her first child and, even then, she "shielded herself from the reality" of this death after a medical examiner attributed it to a narrowing of the aorta.[337]

Yet a disparity in success between these two defenses may simply be a matter of time and sophistication. For example, the first defense of steroid-induced insanity was used in 1988, several decades later than the first case involving postpartum psychosis.[338] In a 1985 trial in which the use of steroids was simply submitted as evidence, it appeared to have little effect on judgment or sentencing, because at that time "virtually no scientific reports on the psychiatric effects of steroids were available."[339] In contrast, in *Commonwealth v. Richter*[340] the court seemed particularly swayed by the extent of the evidence the

---

[335] *See supra* note 329 and accompanying text.

[336] Pope & Katz, *supra* note 254.

[337] *See* Zeldis, *supra* note 311, at 2.

[338] *See* Moss, *supra* note 258, at 22.

[339] Pope & Katz, *supra* note 254, at 29.

[340] No. T90-215256 (Fairfax County Gen. Dist. Ct. June 4, 1991) (unreported case).

defendant submitted on PMS, a defense that had not yet been successful.[341]

Overall, then, an apparent asymmetry in the acceptance of gender-specific or gender-dominant defenses by the courts may be attributable to factors associated with the gender-related condition, or degree of evidence available, rather than a "societal glossing" or favoring of the genetic or biological conditions of one gender over the other. With some exceptions, courts and attorneys also did not appear to emphasize gender per se, or cultural constructs of gender stereotypes, in their introduction or analyses of these defenses. Indeed, the Glen Ridge rape case exemplifies how a defense strategy can backfire when attorneys rely too heavily on extreme gender-stereotyping to give a defense "jury appeal." In light of this conclusion, the next section considers whether there are comparably justified asymmetries for gender-variant or gender-cultural defenses.

2. *Gender-variant and Gender-cultural Defenses*

A question of asymmetry prompts arguments that may apply to any of the four gender-based defenses. This Article uses these arguments to support its conclusion that asymmetries should be avoided if they rely on culturally-created, gender-based, stereotypes. Two tendencies fuel this perspective: (1) a tendency to impose culturally-created stereotypes on gender-specific, gender-dominant, and at times, gender-variant defenses, which rely on genetic or biological differences between the genders; and (2) a tendency to amplify supposed biological or psychological gender differences in gender-cultural, and at times, gender-variant defenses, which focus on sociological and cultural disparities between males and females. Defense attorneys use these tactics to make these defenses more appealing to the jury. Because the criminal law presumes that behavior is a consequence of free will,[342] attorneys attempt to emphasize biological conditions so that their clients' behavior seems less controllable. They also provide cultural explanations for biological conditions, either to elicit sympathy or to convince a jury that their client's environment triggered their internal disorder.

These tactics have a cost. Typically, they rely on a scientifically unfounded social construction, which can perpetuate past or existing gender stereotypes. Also, they may be ineffectual in a particular case or create a backlash for future cases. If these circumstances exist, courts should render them irrelevant and inadmissable.

---

[341] *See supra* notes 279 to 280 and accompanying text.
[342] *See supra* notes 180 to 197 and accompanying text.

a. Arguments Against Using Gender-Specific Defenses

Such drawbacks can be more fully understood in light of the arguments raised against using selected defenses. The first argument concerns the stereotyping of gender-specific defenses. According to some commentators, the PMS or postpartum defenses are degrading or prejudicial to women.[343] These commentators contend that recognizing a link between PMS and violence, for example, would also prevent women from making further progress in their work because employers would expect monthly cycles of irritability or misconduct.[344] But to consider a defense "degrading" because its underlying condition occurs only to women, and therefore puts them in a weak or "flawed" light, misses the point. If a condition truly negates responsibility, either totally or impartially as PMS may, the fact that it applies only to women is irrelevant. Discounting gender-specific conditions in the name of "equality" operates on the pretense that there are no gender differences whatsoever in biology or behavior.[345] This argument unnecessarily imputes cultural or social stereotypes on a biological condition that would otherwise be compared, favorably or not, with the numerous other biological conditions (including hormonal deficiencies, such as hypoglycemia or diabetes) that courts consider with respect to any defendant's responsibility. The focus should not be on the gender to which this condition pertains, but whether it truly negates responsibility.

Curiously, critics of gender-specific defenses for men emphasize their concerns with causality and dangerousness, and not the fear that men will be "degraded" or stereotyped. Even the "boys-will-be-boys" defense used in the Glen Ridge rape case pertained more to the so-called "Lolita-like" behavior of the victim, rather than the gender-stereotyped behavior of the defendants.[346] Attorneys may find ways to avoid potential stereotyping with gender-specific conditions by includ-

---

[343] *See,* Dershowitz, *supra* note 19, at 53-55; Marcia Chambers, *Menstrual Stresses as a Legal Defense,* N.Y. TIMES, May 29, 1982, at 46 (reporting Prof. H. Richard Uviller's criticism of the defense as "degrading"); *see also* Nelson, *supra* note 304, at 649 (noting a district attorney's comment that the postpartum psychosis defense was "demeaning to women, since it implied that they, as a class, were not 'responsible, accountable, equal human beings because of hormonal differences from men'").

[344] *See* DERSHOWITZ, *supra* note 19, at 54; Grossman, *supra* note 306, at 343.

[345] As one commentator explained with respect to the legal system's displeasure with the postpartum psychosis defense:

We are dealing with a type of mental illness that men can't get, and you come into a legal system that's sort of dominated by men and they don't quite see that this could be a sort of mental illness. They don't empathize with it. They can't imagine themselves in this situation.

Nelson, *supra* note 304, at 635 (citation omitted).

[346] *See* LAUFER, *supra* note 264.

ing them within existing defenses, rather than creating specialized, gender-based defenses. For example, one attorney recommends treating postpartum psychosis as simply a "controversial diagnosis" rather than a "new defense."[347]

Others contend that attorneys can use these defenses to inculpate, rather than exculpate.[348] In *Tingen v. Tingen*,[349] for example, the claimant unsuccessfully argued that the court should consider his ex-wife's PMS as a factor for allowing him to receive custody of their children.[350] Likewise, some commentators have suggested that courts will ultimately view PMS as an aggravating condition, rather than a mitigating one. They even believe it will justify a husband's murder of his PMS-afflicted wife, or a court's conclusion that a PMS-afflicted woman should be able to foresee, and thus prevent, the consequences of her monthly condition.[351]

But these risks are inherent in any defense based upon a biological condition. If society viewed PMS as an aggravating condition, it could also view a brain tumor or high testosterone level as one. If society expects an epileptic to foresee the consequences associated with driving a car,[352] it could also expect an individual who theoretically may have a dangerous gender-related disorder to foresee them. Although Ann Green was successful with her insanity defense, a court could have applied a high standard of foreseeability given that, shortly after the murder of her first child, she had some realization that she had done something wrong.[353] The criminal law cannot be expected to provide a one-sided perspective on any particular condition, even if it is gender-related, and even if it can also be used as a defense.

b. Gender-variant Defenses

A more difficult issue concerns defenses that do not rely on gender-specific or gender-dominant conditions, but rather on the way that gender interacts with other biological or environmental factors. For example, a gender-variant defense based on the results of the Biosocial Project discussed in this Article would raise the finding that: (1) lead poisoning is a strong and consistent predictor of crime and behavioral disorders; but that (2) lead poisoning is a significant predictor only among males. Theoretically, a defense attorney could ar-

---

[347] *See, e.g.,* Nelson, *supra* note 304, at 635-36.
[348] *See, e.g.,* Hosp, *supra* note 283, at 445.
[349] 446 P.2d 185 (Or. 1968).
[350] *Id.*
[351] Hosp, *supra* note 283, at 445.
[352] People v. Decina, 138 N.E.2d 799, 803-04 (N.Y. 1956).
[353] *See* Zeldis, *supra* note 311.

gue that males are relatively more vulnerable to environmental influences, such as lead poisoning, which render them more impulsive. Therefore, they are less responsible for their actions. Likewise, females are less responsible if they evidence certain types of neurological disorders that render them more impulsive and biologically less capable of deciding between right and wrong.

These arguments, however, share the same difficulties evidenced by the less successful gender-specific defenses:[354] (1) lead poisoning and neurological disorders are steady, not temporary conditions; (2) for this reason, it is likely that other factors in conjunction with these conditions trigger criminal conduct; and (3) therefore, the causal connection to crime is uncertain. Moreover, a gender-based standard for gender-variant conditions would be misleading. Females are also affected by lead poisoning, but to a lesser degree; males are also affected by neurological disorders. The gender differences described in the Biosocial Study, for example, indicate average, not absolute, variations. A gender-variant defense, therefore, would be both over and under inclusive. The defense could also be open to gender-stereotyping. Recall that historically, female offenders were characterized as biologically deficient and therefore not capable of controlling their behavior.

c.   Gender-cultural Defenses

Gender-cultural defenses are somewhat different. A classic example is the battered woman syndrome defense.[355] According to Lenore Walker, a battered woman is one "in an intimate relationship with a man who repeatedly subjects . . . her to forceful physical and/or psychological abuse."[356] Walker defines "repeatedly" as more than once, and "abuse" as any one of six behaviors, ranging from life-threatening violence to "extreme verbal harassment and expressing comments of a derogatory nature with negative value judgments" and "restriction of her activity through physical or psychological means."[357]

The primary purpose of the defense is not to explain why the

---

[354] *See supra* notes 198 to 210 and accompanying text.

[355] *See generally* Holly Maguigan, *Battered Women and Self-Defense: Myths and Misconceptions in Current Reform Proposals*, 140 U. PA. L. REV. 379 (1991). For a discussion of the constitutional issues pertaining to cases of domestic violence, see Maria L. Marcus, *Conjugal Violence: The Law of Force and the Force of Law*, 69 CAL. L. REV. 1657 (1981).

[356] LENORE E. WALKER, THE BATTERED WOMAN SYNDROME 203 (1984).

[357] *Id.* As Schulhofer notes, however,

[t]his approach includes as battered women the wife whose husband subjects her to derogatory comments twice in two years, the spouse who is slapped across the face six times in six months, and the woman who suffers severe bruises, internal injuries, or broken bones from severe beatings inflicted every week throughout her marriage.

Schulhofer, *supra* note 7, at 117.

woman killed her batterer, but why she did not leave him.[358] Although the defense includes situational factors to explain why a woman did not leave, such as inadequate finances or the failure of police intervention, it focuses on a psychological diagnosis of "learned helplessness."[359] This condition is created when abused women experience a cycle of violence and "loving contrition" which, when combined with low self-esteem, passivity, and fear, makes escape seem impossible.[360] Thus, Walker views the battered woman syndrome as a "mental health disorder"[361] whose sufferers evidence a variety of "cognitive disturbances"[362] that prevent them from seeking avenues of escape, and "motivational" impairments that impede their ability to use such an avenue when they do find one.[363] Even though the empirical basis for Walker's depictions has been severely critiqued,[364] they are widely used in battered women cases.

This Article considers the battered woman syndrome defense to be gender-cultural because individuals concerned with providing a feminist approach to domestic violence created it.[365] Certain commentators believe the defense was constructed from the "patriarchal assumptions" stemming from law and psychology.[366] They contend that the defense does more than simply reinforce negative stereotypes of women; it presumes that women are incapable of choosing a lawful way to avoid the unlawful conduct of their partners. Therefore, the defense reaffirms historical stereotypes that women are incapable of the same kind of rational self-control and self-governance that is expected from men.[367]

Anne Coughlin appropriately recognizes that the provocation defense similarly rests on a gender-cultural stereotype of the uncontrollable male who kills his wife in sight-of-adultery cases. Yet, she notes that the provocation defense also reinforces the hierarchical nature of male-female relationships because the wife is still construed to be an

---

[358] Coughlin, *supra* note 19, at 51.

[359] *See* Lenore E. Walker, *Battered Woman Syndrome and Self-Defense*, 6 Notre Dame L.J. Ethics & Pub. Pol'y 321, 330-32 (1992).

[360] Walker, *supra* note 356, at 86.

[361] *See* Walker, *supra* note 359, at 331.

[362] *See id.* at 327-28.

[363] *See* Lenore E. Walker, Terrifying Love 10-11 (1989).

[364] *See* Dershowitz, *supra* note 19, at 33-37; Schulhofer, *supra* note 7, at 118-22.

[365] *See* Coughlin, *supra* note 19, at 82; Schulhofer, *supra* note 7, at 116.

[366] Coughlin, *supra* note 19, at 7; *see also* Elizabeth M. Schneider, *Describing and Changing: Women's Self-Defense Work and the Problem of Expert Testimony on Battering*, 9 Women's Rts. L. Rep. 200 (1983) (emphasizing the fear that the defense will promote negative and inaccurate stereotypes about women).

[367] *See* Coughlin, *supra* note 19, at 4-8.

object under her husband's control.[368] Furthermore, the defense often succeeds in domestic abuse situations because of the gender-stereotyping applied to the wife's provoking behavior, rather than her husband's reaction to it.[369]

Commentators have critiqued the battered woman syndrome on various grounds that reinforce this Article's concern with the hazards of treating as biological, defenses that are culturally-constructed. "By proving that women suffer from special psychological deficits that make them incapable of resisting illegal pressures exerted by men, [the defense] explicitly locates the source of women's subjugation, not within legal or cultural convention, but within women themselves."[370] Given that the defense views women as passive and irrational, Stephen Schulhofer explains that it is not surprising that the defense has been relatively quickly adopted.[371]

The defense is further scorned by those who claim that it masks "the other side" of statistics on domestic violence that oftentimes get lost in highly publicized spouse killings, such as the O.J. Simpson incident.[372] For example, large scale statistical studies show considerable symmetry in the gender of perpetrators in spouse killings in the United States.[373] For every one hundred men accused of killing their wives, about seventy-five women are accused of killing their husbands. This is an equivalency peculiar to the United States, and does not appear to be related to the availability of guns or increasing "women's liberation."[374] Yet, critics do not recognize a crucial factor—the gender differences in the motives for killing. A large proportion of women kill in self-defense, but men almost never do. Also, women rarely kill in response to the motives that appear to provoke men, such as a failed relationship, infidelity, or long periods of abuse and assaults.[375]

In considering the theoretical acceptability of gender-based de-

---

[368] *See id.* at 5 n.12.

[369] *See* Laurie Taylor, *Provoked Reason: Heat of Passion Manslaughter and Imperfect Self Defense,* 33 U.C.L.A. L. REV. 1679, 1696-97 (1986).

[370] Coughlin, *supra* note 19, at 57.

[371] Schulhofer, *supra* note 7, at 122.

[372] *See, e.g.,* DERSHSOWITZ, *supra* note 19, at 311-12 (noting that "women kill almost as often as men do in the context of *all* family murders"); Katherine Dunn, *Truth Abuse,* 211 NEW REPUBLIC, 16 (Aug. 1, 1994) (claiming that the events surrounding the O.J. Simpson case "are the latest pretext for spreading the anti-male propaganda that passes as socially responsible concern over domestic violence").

[373] *See generally* MURRAY A. STRAUS & RICHARD J. GELLES, PHYSICAL VIOLENCE IN AMERICAN FAMILIES (1990); Margo I. Wilson & Martin Daly, *Who Kills Whom in Spouse Killings? On the Exceptional Sex Ratio of Spousal Homicides in the United States,* 30 CRIMINOLOGY 189 (1992).

[374] *See* Wilson & Daly, *supra* note 373.

[375] *See id.* at 206-07 (noting that this conclusion is countered by other research based on self report evidence, which has been criticized).

fenses, then, the four that this Article discusses provide a continuum based on the degree of their reliance on differences in biology or culture. Even though gender-specific conditions, such as postpartum psychosis, are also influenced by psychological, sociological, and cultural factors, such as familial or economic instability,[376] they are primarily defined by biology. Further, even though gender-cultural conditions, such as the battered woman syndrome, also allege certain "cognitive," motivational, or psychological disorders,[377] they are primarily defined by cultural constructs. The concern here is that the criminal law support scientifically-based efforts to excuse or mitigate conduct, not socially-constructed conditions that may merely pander to a jury's stereotypes.

D. DEFENSES AND THE PROBLEM OF PREDICTION

Irrespective of issues of gender or stereotyping, however, it is not clear whether any of the conditions underlying these defenses actually "cause" crime or mitigate responsibility. It is beyond the scope of this Article to examine the precise causal bases for defenses. Instead, this Article relies on the Biosocial Study's results to question whether there are grounds for assuming that any one condition is considerably more causal or mitigating than another. A "perfect" causal model would be achieved by predicting 100% of an individual's future behavior. Such a high level of prediction has never been accomplished, however, and it is unlikely that it will ever be accomplished. In the Biosocial Study, fairly comprehensive models of biological and environmental variables predicted twenty-five percent of future adult criminality among males, and nineteen percent of future adult criminality among females.[378] These percentages, which were statistically significant, provide acceptable levels of prediction, particularly for social science research. However, seventy-five to eighty percent of behavior is left unexplained, suggesting that most of what predicts crime has not been detected. Furthermore, a higher percentage of female criminal behavior is left unexplained relative to male criminal behavior.[379]

These results give some perspective on evaluating the gender-specific, gender-dominant, or gender-cultural defenses. First, none of the conditions underlying these defenses has any greater predictive link to criminal behavior than the factors examined in the Biosocial

---

[376] *See supra* notes 269 to 328 and accompanying text.

[377] *See* Coughlin, *supra* note 19, at 55-58.

[378] *See* Tables 2 and 3.

[379] Clinicians are also less able to predict violence in women relative to men. *See* Charles W. Lidz et al., *The Accuracy of Predictions of Violence to Others*, 269 JAMA 1007, 1007-11 (1993).

Study. A prior section of this Article[380] discussed how courts could hypothetically view one condition to be more "causal" than another (*e.g.*, postpartum depression relative to XYY chromosome syndrome), but there is no empirical evidence to support their assumptions. Temporal proximity (a condition that is close in time to the criminal act) and impermanence (a condition that is periodic, but not inherent), could be either necessary but insufficient requirements for causality, or, they could simply be unnecessary. Currently, researchers cannot draw firm conclusions.

Second, the Biosocial Study indicated strong biological, sociological, and environmental interactions among predictors of crime for both genders, despite the additional finding of gender differences. This result comports with research or individual reports indicating that the conditions underlying the other gender-based defenses also showed multifactorial effects. For example, postpartum depression was most apt to have a link to an infant's death when other stressful conditions, such as marital or financial conflicts, were present.[381] Therefore, it is unclear whether any defendant could accurately claim that postpartum depression "caused" her behavior, or made her less culpable. Most likely, a constellation of events, biological and sociological or environmental, contributed to her infant's death. Thus, it may not be proper for courts to accept postpartum depression as a defense when it may not have a causal effect without the presence of particular environmental stressors. Similarly, it may not be proper for courts to accept postpartum depression as a defense, and then reject a defense based on the use of anabolic steroids.

If a roomful of experts in the area of biology and violence examined these issues, they would agree that these are philosophical, not legal or factual, inquiries.[382] This view reflects their recognition that science has yet to show anything more than mere propensities toward criminality. In turn, a philosophical determination of what should or should not be causal or mitigating depends upon whatever sentencing philosophy is controlling.

An overriding, oftentimes less visible, influence on courts' amenability to certain defenses could be their recognition of individual differences in the prevalence of crime. In determining future dangerousness, for example, courts will most likely consider whether or not defendants will commit another crime, irrespective of the reasons given for why they may have committed the last crime. The next sec-

---

[380] See *supra* part IV.C.1.

[381] *See supra* notes 304 to 309.

[382] Denno, *supra* note 10, at 669.

tion considers whether there should be a gender-based standard reflecting the vast gender difference in number of offenses, particularly in light of the recent "three-strikes-and-you're-out" legislation concerned with repeat offenders.

V. GENDER DIFFERENCES AND PREVALENCE

The Biosocial Study demonstrated large gender differences in the nature and frequency of offenses. Consistent with prior research, males commit more violent crime.[383] Even though the Biosocial Study relied only on official statistics, which tend to exaggerate gender differences relative to self report studies, the gender differences were substantial. Because official statistics indicate that agents of social control, such as families and the courts, intervene more often in the behavior of girls than boys,[384] the Biosocial Study may exaggerate the level of girls' criminality for less serious crimes.[385]

A. POLICY IMPLICATIONS

In light of the gender differences in prevalence, an argument could be made that the recent "three-strikes-and-you're-out" legislation should not apply to females. Females are far less apt than males to be chronic offenders, and their crimes are less serious. Such deterrence policies are unnecessary for a group which, on the average, is not dangerous. Indeed, Myrna Raeder contends that the United States Sentencing Commission's Sentencing Guidelines, which are gender-neutral,[386] inappropriately ignore evidence demonstrating that females have less serious patterns of offending and more family responsibilities.[387] As a result, gender-neutral sentencing, which is geared toward violent male offenders and drug dealers, dispropor-

---

[383] *See supra* notes 133 to 153 and accompanying text.

[384] *See* Susan K. Datesman & Mikel Aickin, *Offense Specialization and Escalation Among Status Offenders,* 75 J. CRIM. L. & CRIMINOLOGY 1246, 1246-75 (1984).

[385] In general, research indicates that sentencing for girls in juvenile court is more severe than is sentencing for boys. Girls referred to court for having committed status offenses are detained and institutionalized more frequently, and for longer time periods, than males who have committed delinquencies. *See id.* Although, over time, smaller percentages of status offenders than delinquent offenders have been incarcerated, data in 1987 indicated still that substantially more females (10.95%) than males (1.1%) were incarcerated for status offenses. *See* Ira M. Schwartz et al., *Federal Juvenile Justice Policy and the Incarceration of Girls,* 36 CRIME AND DELINQ. 503, 503-20 (1990). However, evidence that patterns of offending for status offenses and minor delinquencies are similar for boys and girls indicates that prosecutions for such crimes vary by gender. *See* Datesman & Aickin, *supra* note 384.

[386] 28 U.S.C. § 994(d) (1992). The Guidelines state that sex is not a relevant factor in how a sentence is to be determined. UNITED STATES SENTENCING GUIDELINES MANUAL § 5H1.10 (1992).

[387] *See* Raeder, *supra* note 18.

tionately harms nonviolent females who have primary parenting responsibilities, or who are involved in drugs because of family relationships.[388]

However, certain factors support gender-neutrality. First, a policy of specific deterrence based on generalizations about immutable individual characteristics, such as gender, offends society's notions of justice. It offends in this proposed context because it would continue to be overinclusive for males (include those nonviolent males who may never repeat again), but would be underinclusive for females (exclude those females who would repeat again and who do not have family responsibilities). Second, because most female offenders are not dangerous or repeat offenders, the "three-strikes-and-you're-out," or similar kinds of "get tough" legislation, will apply less often. Third, there is conflicting evidence on the nature and extent of gender differences in the treatment of violent offenders in the criminal justice system. Some research suggests that the system treats violent female offenders less severely than their male counterparts for pretrial detention and final conviction decisions; other research shows no gender differences or suggests that the system treats females more severely.[389] These disparities reflect conflicts between how judges view their task. Some judges are chivalrous and paternalistic toward females, while others are harsh, punishing females for defying their traditional gender role.[390] Studies of sentencing severity, however, "repeatedly find" that females are less likely than males to receive prison sentences, and more likely to receive shorter terms when they are sentenced.[391] If females are treated more leniently, they are less vulnerable to the "get tough" sanctions.

Some evidence also suggests that such sanctions are less war-

---

[388] *See id.* at 923.

[389] *See* Kruttschnitt, *supra* note 2, at 55-57.

[390] *See id.*; Raeder, *supra* note 18, at 917-18.

[391] *See* Kruttschnitt, *supra* note 2, at 58; *see also* Ilene H. Nagel & John Hagan, *Gender and Crime: Offense Patterns and Criminal Court Sanctions, in* 4 CRIME AND JUSTICE 91, 91-144 (Michael Tonry & Norval Morris eds., 1983). Other research qualifies these results. For example, one recent study concluded that gender shows "a small-to-moderate effect" on incarceration decisions, and that females are jailed less frequently because of legally relevant factors (such as a prior record that is nonviolent). Judges' reasons for enforcing less jail time for females in other cases were based on criteria that, although not strictly "legal," could be justified for other reasons (*e.g.*, childcare responsibilities or signs of remorse). In light of its preview of prior research, this study also concluded that studies with the fewest controls were more likely to show large gender effects, whereas studies with the most controls were most likely to show slight, or nonexistent, gender effects. *See* Darrell Steffensmeier et al., *Gender and Imprisonment Decisions*, 31 CRIMINOLOGY 411, 435-36 (1993). Another study on juvenile offenders reported that although female offenders evidenced greater leniency than their male counterparts overall, they experienced greater punishment when they were repeat offenders committing more serious offenses.

ranted for females given their lower likelihood of repeat offending. For example, research has found that males on probation are more likely than females to be charged with committing new crimes, and that the new crimes for which females are charged are primarily for technical violations of probation.[392] Moreover, the nature and extent of involvement in prison violence is considerably lower for females than for males,[393] perhaps providing one explanation for why females have a relatively greater probability of success when released on parole.[394] Thus, although research suggests that both violent and nonviolent females are treated more leniently than males at the sentencing phase, there is no evidence to suggest that this differential treatment enhances subsequent violence among females.[395] "Both during and after periods of incarceration, women exhibit less violence and subsequent criminality than men."[396]

B. CONCERNS WITH GENDER NEUTRALITY

According to Raeder, the gender-neutral stance of the Sentencing Guidelines has eliminated the prior leniency toward females that existed before the implementation of the Guidelines. Although the trend toward sentencing females more harshly began before the Guidelines, primarily because of mandatory minimums in drug cases, the sentences of females have increased more than those for males.[397] Thus, the Guidelines have increased both the rates and the length of incarceration for female offenders.[398]

Raeder's own analysis, however, points out counterarguments to her ultimate recommendation for a "rational sentencing policy concerning women" that would be integrated into the Guidelines.[399] First, as she notes, all defendants receive relatively longer sentences under the Sentencing Guidelines. The difference is that, prior to the Guidelines, females received more lenient sentences than males, and now they receive sentences that are more comparable.[400] Raeder's argument that the Guidelines treat females more harshly could also

---

392 *See* S. Norland & Pricilla J. Mann, *Being Troublesome—Women on Probation*, 11 CRIM. JUSTICE & BEHAV. 115, 115-35 (1984).

393 *See* Kruttschnitt, *supra* note 2, at 344-45; *see also* Candace Kruttschnitt & Sharon Krompotich, *Aggressive Behavior Among Female Inmates: An Exploratory Study*, 7 CRIMINOLOGY 371, 371-85 (1990) (finding that female aggression in prison is most strongly associated with race and childhood family structure).

394 *See* Kruttschnitt, *supra* note 2, at 346.

395 *See id.*

396 *See id.* at 345-46.

397 *See* Raeder, *supra* note 18, at 925-26.

398 *See id.* at 929.

399 *See id.* at 909.

400 *See id.* at 926.

mean that equity has eliminated the favorable treatment they received.

Second, irrespective of its gender-neutral stance, the Sentencing Commission has reported that females still receive more lenient sentences than males overall, and within the Guideline's intervals. It appears that the relationship between gender and sentencing no longer exists when certain offense characteristics are controlled, such as the presence of a weapon, the amount of drugs used, or the offender's role in a conspiracy.[401] Ignoring Raeder's other concerns, including the effect of sole or primary parenting,[402] this finding supports the argument that females will receive more lenient sentences under the Sentencing Guidelines because they commit less frequent and less serious offenses than males.

Indeed, Raeder's recommendation for a "sentencing policy concerning women" evokes the same themes of paternalism and passivity used to support a battered woman syndrome defense. According to Raeder, female offenders who are themselves the victims of sexual or physical abuse, and who "tend to have low self-esteem and view the world pessimistically," may be "*propelled*" into criminal behavior by "poverty, racism, and sexual discrimination."[403] Wives or girlfriends of male defendants who have fathered their children, "may *find themselves involved* in criminal activity because of social and cultural pressures."[404]

Such characterizations depict women as passive objects under the dominion and control of men, rather than as free thinking agents. Indeed, it appears that Raeder believes this. In arguing for downward departures in the Sentencing Guidelines based on circumstances related to dominance and psychological abuse, Raeder notes that "[w]hile it may be stereotypical to assume that men lead women astray, and therefore women are not fully responsible for their criminal offenses, one federal prison warden has observed, 'Females who make their way to prison have been socialized more toward dependent relationships, as opposed to life activities that promote independence.'"[405] Consequently, Raeder advocates judicial recognition of the "gendered nature of some female crime" in which a woman who is dominated by a male, but who does not meet the criteria required for physical coercion, may be entitled to a departure in culpability for her

---

[401] *See id.* at 931.

[402] *See id.* at 930-31.

[403] *See id.* at 914 (emphasis added).

[404] *See id.* at 906 (emphasis added).

[405] *See id.* at 972-73.

criminal acts.[406]

Raeder's recommendations, however, would perpetuate what appears to be an unfortunate gender hierarchy in the criminal justice system. Moreover, such characterizations ignore the fact that male defendants are also the victims of physical and sexual abuse, poverty, racism, and dominance. It is difficult to contend that a sentencing structure should incorporate the socialization and victimization of women, while ignoring comparable burdens on the lives and behavior of men.

However, this Article recognizes situations where females may be unfairly punished because of their unstereotypical roles in particular crimes. For example, there is considerable evidence that women oftentimes receive more severe penalties than their male counterparts for like crimes, such as the murdering of a mate.[407] As noted, research also indicates that judges may treat females more severely for pretrial detention and final conviction decisions, perhaps because they view women criminals as defying their traditional gender role.[408] A gender neutral sentencing structure should eliminate these kinds of inequities.

A recommendation for gender neutrality is also not intended to ignore the seriously neglected issues pertaining to pregnant women, and sole or primary parents. Although this issue is beyond the scope of this Article, Raeder correctly critiques the disturbing consequences of particular Guideline's decisions on the children of the incarcerated. She also provides sound critiques of other aspects of the Sentencing Guidelines that are too punitive for any actor, irrespective of gender. Yet, not only would a focus on what Raeder calls the "gendered nature of some female crime" reinforce negative stereotypes, it would create an unwarranted gender asymmetry.

---

[406] *See id.*

[407] *See* Coughlin, *supra* note 19, at 3 & n.4; Kit Kinports, *Defending Battered Women's Self-Defense Claims*, 67 OR. L. REV. 393, 454-55 (1988); Victoria M. Mather, *The Skeleton in the Closet: The Battered Woman Syndrome, Self-Defense, and Expert Testimony*, 39 MERCER L. REV. 545, 561 (1988). *See also*, ANN JONES, WOMEN WHO KILL 8-9 (1980) (noting that "for offenses traditionally considered to be 'masculine'—such as armed robbery and felony murder—women tend to receive *heavier* sentences than men"). This disparity was recently illustrated by Baltimore Judge Robert E. Cayhill's sentencing of Kenneth Peacock to 18 months in prison for pleading guilty to killing his wife four hours after finding her in bed, naked, with another man. *See* State's Attorney for Baltimore County, Press Release, Oct. 20, 1994; Tamar Lewin, *What Penalty for a Killing in Passion?*, N.Y. TIMES, Oct. 21, 1994, at A18. A day later, another Baltimore judge gave a three-year sentence to a woman who had pleaded guilty to voluntary manslaughter for killing her husband following 11 years of his abuse. Lewin, *supra.*

[408] *See supra* notes 389 to 390 and accompanying text.

C. WOMEN IN PRISON

Women's lesser involvement in crime does not reap rewards for women prisoners. In 1990, women constituted 5.5% of state prisoners and 7.6% of federal prisoners.[409] Relative to male prisoners, however, they have less adequate physical facilities, health and medical care, psychological counseling, drug and alcohol counseling, and recreational services.[410] They also have fewer work assignments or vocational and educational programs, lower pay for the same job, and more frequent administration of tranquilizers and other medications for purposes of social control.[411] Men are separated into different facilities according to the seriousness of their crimes (*e.g.*, minimum, medium, and maximum security); women are typically housed together regardless of their classification.[412] Ironically, the reasons cited for such disparities return, once again, to the differences between male and female criminals: (1) because the number of female inmates is small, expenditures for them are relatively large; (2) because female inmates are less dangerous than their male counterparts, there is less need to spend money on rehabilitation; and (3) because female inmates are not as demanding, they are less likely to riot over inadequate conditions.[413]

Therefore, gender differences have a further penalizing effect in prison; the women prisoners are neither "bad enough" nor "woman enough." As one study concluded, "the primary goal for female prisoners is often teaching 'femininity'—how to walk, talk, and carry themselves. This is related both to the view that female offenders have 'failed' as women and must be retrained for the role."[414] Yet, females who attempt to fulfill their "feminine" role are also penalized—particularly when that role is one of primary parenthood.[415]

In general, then, the criminal justice system appears to recognize gender differences in the prevalence of crime. According to most research, it provides more lenient sentencing for females than for males. This disparity comports with data indicating that females are relatively less serious and less frequent offenders. Therefore, gender-neutral sentencing schemes reward females by virtue of their behav-

---

[409] ROBYN L. COHEN, BUREAU OF JUSTICE STATISTICS BULLETIN, PRISONERS IN 1990 Table 6 at 4 (1991).

[410] Fletcher & Moon, *supra* note 25; Roslyn Muraskin, *Disparate Treatment in Correctional Facilities, in* IT'S A CRIME: WOMEN AND JUSTICE 211, 218 (Roslyn Muraskin & Ted Alleman eds., 1993).

[411] Fletcher & Moon, *supra* note 25, at 12; Muraskin, *supra* note 410, at 218.

[412] Muraskin, *supra* note 410, at 220.

[413] *See* Fletcher & Moon, *supra* note 25, at 12.

[414] *See id.* (citation omitted).

[415] *See* Raeder, *supra* note 18, at 906.

ior, rather than their gender. A departure from this structure can result in sentencing inequities for men, as well as dangerous stereotyping for both genders.

A recommendation for equity between the genders, however, should not result in penalties for those females who are incarcerated, or their offspring. For this reason, the criminal justice system may need to implement some exceptions to gender neutral sentencing structures, such as considerations for the status of sole or primary parent, until gender neutral family norms are more fully achieved.

VI. CONCLUSION

This Article's examination of gender differences and crime reaches three general conclusions. First, relying on the results of the Biosocial Study, this Article confirmed past research showing gender differences in the prevalence and prediction of crime and violence. With respect to prevalence, males commit more crime and violence than females during both their juvenile and adult years, and they are more frequent and chronic offenders once they do participate in crime. With respect to prediction, results confirmed some past research suggesting that biological factors are generally more predictive of crime among females, whereas environmental factors are generally more predictive of crime among males. At the same time, biological and environmental factors interact in predicting the crime and behaviors of both genders. This finding further reinforces the need for the simultaneous examination of many different indicators in multidisciplinary research.

Second, this Article used these results to propose a new "gender-variant" defense that recognizes the different biological and environmental predictors of male and female crime. It further incorporated these results into a discussion of whether gender differences in the prevalence and prediction of crime should affect the application of four gender-based criminal law defenses which represent a continuum ranging from the most biologically-oriented to the most culturally-constructed: gender-specific, gender-dominant, gender-variant, and gender-cultural. It then critiqued efforts to impose gender-stereotyped social constructions of the more biologically-oriented defenses, as well as tendencies to amplify supposed stereotyped biological and psychological differences in culturally-constructed defenses.

According to Catharine MacKinnon, "arousing the sexism of the judge and jury may appear [to be an accused woman's] only chance of acquittal. A prison term is a big price to pay for principle."[416] Yet, the

---

[416] Catherine A. MacKinnon, *Toward a Feminist Jurisprudence*, 34 STAN. L. REV. 703, 721

consequences of such sexism may be more complex and damaging than she recognizes. First, there is no evidence to suggest that the gender-stereotyped defenses that enhance such sexism have any scientific foundation. For this reason, courts should consider them irrelevant and inadmissible. As this Article discusses, a successful gender-based defense may rest on evidentiary issues or aspects of the particular crime or defendant that may have little or nothing to do with gender or the stereotypical way in which a defense is applied. Therefore, it is unclear whether gender-stereotyped defenses actually enhance an accused's chances of acquittal. Second, as the Glen Ridge rape case illustrated, a gender-stereotyped defense, if poorly applied, can actually enhance a defendant's likelihood of conviction. Third, a gender-stereotyped defense can jeopardize the outcomes of future cases which legitimately rely on a particular defense, because juries will consider the defense controversial and react negatively towards it.[417] Lastly, gender stereotyping can stigmatize individuals or groups, and thereby perpetuate or revive historical depictions of females as socially and biologically incapable of legal responsibility.

Erickson and Murray's recent study of gender differences in cocaine use illustrates the potential for this cyclical effect.[418] They found that, regardless of contradictory scientific evidence, media accounts have portrayed women as particularly susceptible to cocaine addiction and cocaine-related problems. They concluded that this perception reflected an earlier view that cocaine-using women were vulnerable to "sexual corruption." Currently, news media perpetuate this view in their accounts of the "modern woman's" promiscuity with sexual partners who provide cocaine. The media's account of the cocaine-using career woman created an alternative sex role theory that depicted these women as more highly stressed because they attempted to engage in "men's work." Because the successful career woman threatens the traditional female role, the media's message is that cocaine addiction is the penalty she pays for her deviant occupational choices. They conclude, then, that in the 1980s a "double standard has been revived"—cocaine-using women are subject to more negative stereotyping and social ramifications than men.[419] Gender-stereotyped defenses may unwittingly further such sex-based depictions.

Third, this Article recommended a gender-neutral criminal jus-

---

(1982) (reviewing ANN JONES, WOMEN WHO KILL (1980)).

[417] *See* Goldberg, *supra* note 20, at 42 (discussing the backlash created by the more controversially successful cases which rely on defenses such as the battered woman's syndrome).

[418] *See* Erickson & Murray, *supra* note 24, at 135.

[419] *See id.*

tice system. This recommendation, however, is not intended to ignore the potentially devastating consequences that such a stance may have on third parties, most particularly the children of sole or primary caretakers who are incarcerated. Some exceptions may have to be made for social or cultural conditions that are not yet amenable to gender neutrality. Also troubling are the more severe penalties females encounter for either "being bad" by defying an expected gender role, or by not being "bad enough," as is illustrated in the disadvantages they face in prison.

At the same time, there are drawbacks to focusing too much on the differences between males and females. This Article discussed the dangers of oversimplifying, overclaiming, masking, or confusing the relationships and outcomes that researchers try to understand, and of applying rigid, divisive, categories that have no clear scientific base.[420] Gender neutrality should allow society to get beyond such concerns with difference.[421]

---

[420] *See* Rhode, *supra* note 17, at 3-7.
[421] *Id.*

APPENDIX A[422]

SELECTED BIOLOGICAL AND ENVIRONMENTAL MEASURES

MEASURES AT BIRTH

1. Prenatal maternal conditions

Number of prenatal examinations

Number of prenatal conditions (a count of 8 items: mother's heavy cigarette smoking, use of sedatives, single marital status, presence of diabetes, hypertension, number of venereal conditions, number of neurological or psychiatric conditions, number of infectious diseases)

Poor obstetrical history (number of prior abortions, still births, premature siblings, or neonatal death of siblings)

Mother's age

Number of prior pregnancies

2. Pregnancy and delivery conditions

Number of pregnancy and birth complications (a count of 17 items: placenta previa, abruptio placentae, marginal sinus rupture, uterine bleeding during the first, second, or third trimester, anesthetic shock, other anesthetic accident, cesarean or breech delivery, prolapsed cord, irregular fetal heart rate, meconium during labor, use of oxytocic during labor, loose cord around the neck, tight cord around the neck, forceps marks at delivery, multiple birth)

Duration of labor

Apgar at one and five minutes

Gestational age, birth weight

3. Family and social structure

Absence of the father

Amount of time the father is unemployed

Mother's employment status

Mother's marital status

Child's birth order

4. Socioeconomic status

Mother's education

Father's education

Total family income (adjusted to 1970 dollars)

Total family per capita income (adjusted to 1970 dollars)

---

[422] DENNO, BIOLOGY AND VIOLENCE, *supra* note 10, at 34-36.

MEASURES AT AGE 1

   5. Neurological factors
      Hand preference (right, left, or variable)
      Abnormal behavioral control

MEASURES AT AGE 4

   6. Intelligence
      Stanford-Binet Intelligence Scale
   7. Cerebral Dominance
      Hand, eye, foot preference (right, left, or variable)
      Composite index of hand, eye, and foot preference

MEASURES AT AGE 7

   8. Physical growth and development
      Height and weight
      Ponderal index (height/weight^3)
   9. General physical health
      Pica
      Lead intoxication
      Iron deficiency anemia, 5 to 8 gms.
      Systolic and diastolic blood pressure
   10. Neurological factors
      Head shape, head circumference
      Ear size, shape, and position
      Otoscopic exam
      Eye structure
      Referral needed for glasses
      Abnormal visual acuity
      Mental status (clinical impression)
      Speech (clinical impression)
      Number of neurological abnormalities
   11. Soft neurological signs
      Nystagmus
      Abnormal movements
      Gait abnormality
      Coordination, awkwardness
      Right and left identification
      Reflexes
      Abnormal EEG
      Mixed cerebral dominance
      Position sense
      Stereognosis

12. Cerebral dominance

> Hand, eye, and foot preference (right, left, or variable)
> Composite index of hand, eye, and foot preference

13. Intelligence

> WISC Verbal IQ
> WISC Verbal subscales (information, comprehension, vocabulary, digit span)
> WISC Performance IQ
> WISC Performance subscales (picture arrangement, block design, coding)
> WISC Performance IQ-Verbal IQ difference
> Bender Gestalt Test, Koppitz scoring
> Bender Gestalt, time in seconds
> Goodenough-Harris drawing test

14. Achievement

> Wide Range Achievement Test (WRAT) Spelling, Reading, Arithmetic

15. Family and social structure

> Absence of the father
> Absence of the father at birth and at age 7
> Amount of time the father is unemployed
> Mother's religion
> Number of changes in mother's marital status (from birth to age 7)
> Mother's marital stability
> Number of adults, relatives in household
> Total family size
> Presence of grandparents in the household
> Use of childcare
> Foster or adoptive parents, guardian
> Number of household moves (from birth to age 7)

16. Socioeconomic status

> Education, occupation of household head (Census Bureau Index)
> Additional schooling of the mother since child's birth
> Number of persons supported
> Total family income (adjusted to 1970 dollars)
> Total per capita income (adjusted to 1970 dollars)

MEASURES AT AGES 13-14

17. Achievement

> California Achievement Tests (CAT):
> total reading (vocabulary, comprehension)

total math (computation, concepts and problems)
total language (mechanics, usage, and structure)
spelling

18. Disciplinary status

Enrollment in a school program for youths with disciplinary problems at any time during adolescence

19. Mental retardation

Enrollment in a school program for youths with tested evidence of retardation at any time during adolescence

MEASURES AT AGES 7-17

20. Delinquency and violence

Total number of officially recorded offenses (police contacts and arrests)

Seriousness of offenses (based on weights derived from a national survey of crime severity)

Classification of delinquency offenders (nonindex, property, or violent)

MEASURES AT AGES 18-22

21. Young adult crime and violence

Total number of officially recorded offenses (police contacts and arrests)

Classification of criminal offenders (nonindex, property,or violent)

APPENDIX B
STATISTICALLY SCREENED INDEPENDENT AND DEPENDENT
MEASURES

AGES	VARIABLES AND SCALES OF MEASUREMENT	
7	Y_1	WISC Verbal IQ (45-155)
7	Y_2	WISC Performance IQ (44-156)
13-14	Y_3	Disciplinary problem (0 = absent; > 1 = present)
13-14	Y_4	Language achievement (1-99)
13-14	Y_5	Mental retardation (0 = absent; > 1 = present)
7-17	Y_6	Number of juvenile offenses
7-17	Y_7	Seriousness of juvenile offenses
Birth	X_1	Pregnancy and delivery conditions (1-17 items)
Birth	X_2	Mother's education (number of years)
Birth	X_3	Father's education (number of years)
Birth	X_4	Family income (1970 dollars)
Birth	X_5	Time father unemployed (number of months)
1	X_6	Hand preference (0 = right; 1 = left or variable)
4	X_7	Stanford-Binet (25-175)
4	X_8	Hand preference (0 = right; 1 = left)
4	X_9	Eye preference (0 = right; 1 = left)
4	X_{10}	Foot preference (0 = right; 1 = left or variable)
7	X_{11}	Neurological abnormalities (total number)
7	X_{12}	Abnormal movements (0 = absent; 1 = present)
7	X_{13}	Abnormal vision (0 = absent; 1 = present)
7	X_{14}	Lead intoxication (0 = absent; 1 = present)
7	X_{15}	Anemia (0 = absent; 1 = present)
7	X_{16}	Intellectual status (0 = normal; 1 = abnormal)
7	X_{17}	Speech (0 = normal; 1 = abnormal)
7	X_{18}	Foster parents (0 = absent; 1 = present)
Birth-7	X_{19}	Father in household (0 = present; 1 = absent)
Birth-7	X_{20}	Household moves (total number)
7	X_{21}	Persons supported (total number)
7	X_{22}	Family income (1970 dollars)

APPENDIX C

TABLES AND FIGURES

TABLE 1: NUMBERS AND PERCENTAGES FOR FIGURES 1 - 4

FIGURE 1: TYPE OF OFFENDER BY GENDER				
	NUMBER OF PERSONS		PERCENTAGE OF CATEGORY	
	Males	Females	Males	Females
Nonoffender	336	431	69.00	86.20
Nonindex offender	64	34	13.14	6.80
Property offender	51	27	10.47	5.40
Violent offender	36	8	7.39	1.60
Total	487	500	100.00	100.00

FIGURE 2: NUMBER OF OFFENSES BY GENDER				
	NUMBER OF PERSONS		PERCENTAGE OF CATEGORY	
Number of offenses	Males	Females	Males	Females
1	69	45	45.69	65.22
2	35	12	23.19	17.38
3	10	4	6.62	5.79
4	12	1	7.95	1.45
5	5	0	3.31	0.00
6	7	1	4.64	1.45
7	4	0	2.65	0.00
8	1	3	0.66	4.35
9	2	2	1.32	2.91
10+	6	1	3.97	1.45
Total	151	69	100.00	100.00

FIGURE 3: AGE AT FIRST OFFENSE BY GENDER				
	NUMBER OF PERSONS		PERCENTAGE OF CATEGORY	
Age	Males	Females	Males	Females
10 or less	18	5	11.93	7.25
11	11	3	7.28	4.35
12	19	8	12.58	11.59
13	21	16	13.91	23.19
14	30	12	19.87	17.39
15	20	12	13.24	17.39
16	20	9	13.24	13.04
17	12	4	7.95	5.80
Total	151	69	100.00	100.00

FIGURE 4: JUVENILE AND ADULT ARREST CATEGORIES BY GENDER				
	NUMBER OF PERSONS		PERCENTAGE OF CATEGORY	
	Males	Females	Males	Females
No juvenile or adult arrest	280	415	57.50	83.00
Juvenile arrest only	98	61	20.12	12.20
Adult arrest only	56	16	11.50	3.20
Juvenile and adult arrest	53	8	10.88	1.60
Total	487	500	100.00	100.00

Figure 1: Type of Offender by Gender

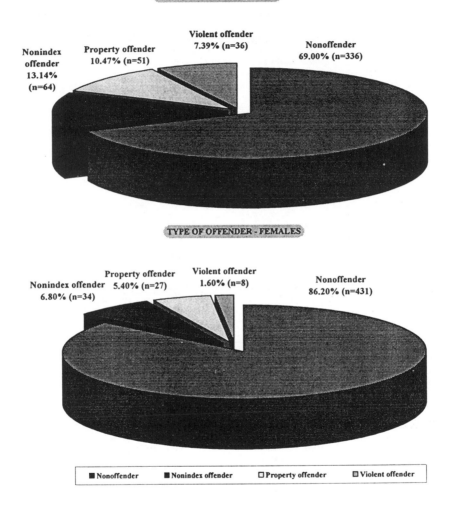

TYPE OF OFFENDER - MALES

Violent offender
7.39% (n=36)

Property offender
10.47% (n=51)

Nonindex
offender
13.14%
(n=64)

Nonoffender
69.00% (n=336)

TYPE OF OFFENDER - FEMALES

Property offender
5.40% (n=27)

Violent offender
1.60% (n=8)

Nonindex offender
6.80% (n=34)

Nonoffender
86.20% (n=431)

■ Nonoffender   ■ Nonindex offender   ☐ Property offender   ▨ Violent offender

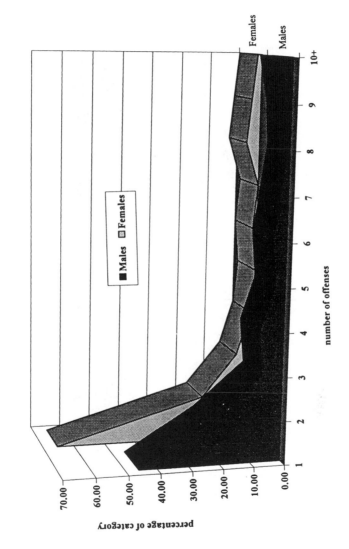

Figure 2: Number of Offenses by Gender

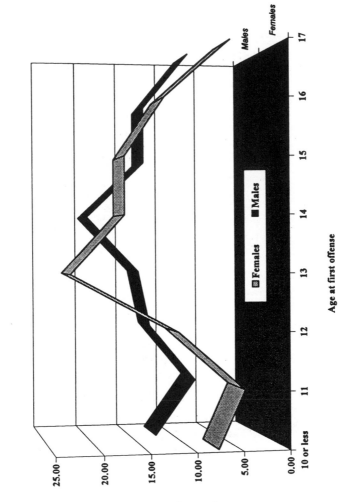

Figure 3: Age at First Offense by Gender

Figure 4: Juvenile and Adult Arrest Categories by Gender

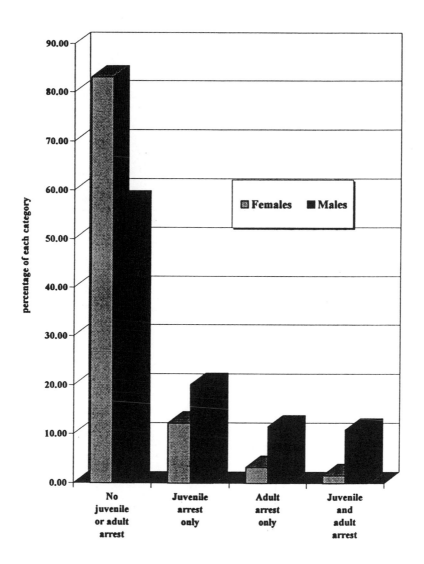

TABLE 2: STRUCTURAL EQUATION MODEL OF BIOLOGICAL AND ENVIRONMENTAL EFFECTS ON JUVENILE AND ADULT CRIME, MALES ONLY

Independent Variables	Ages	Dependent Variables							
		WISC Verbal IQ, age 7 (Y_1)	WISC Performance IQ, age 7 (Y_2)	Disciplinary problem, ages 13-14 (Y_3)	Language achievement, ages 13-14 (Y_4)	Mental retardation, ages 13-14 (Y_5)	Number of Juvenile offenses, ages 7-17 (Y_6)	Seriousness of juvenile offenses, ages 7-17 (Y_7)	Number of adult offenses, ages 18-22 (Y_8)
Y_1 WISC Verbal IQ	7	-	-	-	.306*** (6.95)	-	-	-	-
Y_2 WISC Performance IQ	7	-	-	-	.253*** (5.72)	-	-	-	-
Y_3 Disciplinary problem	13-14	-	-	-	-	-	.220*** (5.04)	.170*** (3.82)	-
Y_4 Language achievement	13-14	-	-	-	-	-	-.096* (-2.32)	-.115** (-2.63)	-.081* (-1.99)
Y_5 Mental retardation	13-14	-	-	-	-	-	-	-	-
Y_6 Number of juvenile offenses	7-17	-	-	-	-	-	-	-	.244*** (3.96)
Y_7 Seriousness of juvenile offenses	7-17	-	-	-	-	-	-	-	.226*** (2.73)
X_1 Pregnancy and delivery conditions	Birth	-	-	-	-	-	-	-	-
X_2 Mother's education	Birth	-	-	-	-	-	-	-	-.120** (-2.92)
X_3 Father's education	Birth	-	-	-	-	-	-	-	.083* (2.02)
X_4 Family income	Birth	-	-	-	-	-	-	-	-
X_5 Time father unemployed	Birth	-	-	-	-	-	.179*** (4.15)	.115** (2.62)	-
X_6 Hand preference	1	-	-	-	-	-	-	-	-

		1	2	3	4	5	6	7	8
X_7 Stanford-Binet	4	.543*** (14.18)	.523*** (7.50)	-	-	-.153*** (-3.45)	-	-	-
X_8 Hand preference	4	-	-	.094* (2.09)	-	-	-	-	-
X_9 Eye preference	4	-	-	-	-	-	-	.059** (2.67)	-
X_{10} Foot preference	4	-	-	-	-	-	-	-	-
X_{11} Neurological abnormalities	7	-	-	-	-	-	-	-	-
X_{12} Abnormal movements	7	-	-	-	-	-	-	-	-
X_{13} Abnormal vision	7	-	-	-	-	-	-	-	-
X_{14} Lead intoxication	7	-	-	.125** (2.77)	-	-	.149*** (3.46)	.143*** (3.26)	-
X_{15} Anemia	7	-	-	.121** (2.67)	-	-	-	.044* (1.95)	-
X_{16} Intellectual status	7	-.136*** (-3.55)	-.158*** (-3.66)	-	-	.263*** (5.97)	-	-	-
X_{17} Speech	7	-	.087* (2.11)	-	-	.092* (2.08)	.045* (2.05)	-	-
X_{18} Foster parents	7	-	-	-.87 (-1.95)	-	-	-	-	-
X_{19} Father absence	Birth-7	-	-	-	-	-	-	-	-
X_{20} Household moves	Birth-7	-	-	.111* (2.48)	-	-	.092* (2.12)	.112 (2.55)	-
X_{21} Persons supported	7	-	-	-	-	-	-	.09** (2.06)	-
X_{22} Family income	7	-	-	-	-	-	-	-	-
R^2		.332	.153	.080	.222	.119	.157	.128	.247

Sample size = 487

Notes: The t-statistic is reported in parentheses (2-tailed test).
*p<.05; **p<.01; ***p<.001.
Male model $\chi^2(166)$ = 150.28; p = .804.

TABLE 3: STRUCTURAL EQUATION MODEL OF BIOLOGICAL AND ENVIRONMENTAL EFFECTS ON JUVENILE AND ADULT CRIME, FEMALES ONLY

Independent Variables	Ages	WISC Verbal IQ, age 7 (Y_1)	WISC Performance IQ, age 7 (Y_2)	Disciplinary problem, ages 13-14 (Y_3)	Language achievement, ages 13-14 (Y_4)	Mental retardation, ages 13-14 (Y_5)	Number of juvenile offenses, ages 7-17 (Y_6)	Seriousness of juvenile offenses, ages 7-17 (Y_7)	Number of adult offenses, ages 18-22 (Y_8)
Y_1 WISC Verbal IQ	7	·	·	·	.225*** (4.56)	·	·	·	·
Y_2 WISC Performance IQ	7	·	·	·	.206*** (4.83)	·	·	·	·
Y_3 Disciplinary problem	13-14	·	·	·	·	·	.232*** (5.40)	.110*** (2.57)	.225*** (5.95)
Y_4 Language achievement	13-14	·	·	·	·	·	-.101* (-2.39)	-.089* (-2.03)	·
Y_5 Mental retardation	13-14	·	·	·	·	·	·	.111** (2.60)	·
Y_6 Number of juvenile offenses	7-17	·	·	·	·	·	·	·	-.267** (-3.10)
Y_7 Seriousness of juvenile offenses	7-17	·	·	·	·	·	·	·	.534*** (6.36)
X_1 Pregnancy and delivery conditions	Birth	·	·	·	·	.090* (2.06)	·	·	·
X_2 Mother's education	Birth	.151*** (3.73)	.062* (1.96)	·	.093* (2.39)	·	·	·	·
X_3 Father's education	Birth	·	·	·	·	·	·	·	-.112** (-2.70)
X_4 Family income	Birth	·	·	·	.096* (2.44)	·	·	·	·
X_5 Time father unemployed	Birth	·	-.062* (-2.10)	·	·	.112* (2.51)	·	·	·
X_6 Hand preference	1	·	·	·	·	·	·	·	·

	df								
X_7 Stanford-Binet	4	.566*** (15.82)	.367*** (8.80)	-	.136*** (2.87)	-	-	-	-
X_8 Hand preference	4	-	-	-	-	-	-	-	-
X_9 Eye preference	4	-	-	-	-	-	-.080* (-1.95)	-.096* (-2.02)	-
X_{10} Foot preference	4	-	-	-	.113*** (3.07)	-	.153*** (3.74)	.101* (2.35)	-
X_{11} Neurological abnormalities	7	-.122*** (-3.39)	-.164*** (-4.00)	-	-	-	.095*** (3.86)	-	-
X_{12} Abnormal movements	7	-	-	.503*** (12.89)	-	-	.062*** (3.94)	-	-
X_{13} Abnormal vision	7	.096** (2.90)	-	.105** (2.68)	-	-	-	-	-
X_{14} Lead intoxication	7	.077* (2.33)	-	-	-	-	-	-	-
X_{15} Anemia	7	-	-	-	-	-	-	-	-
X_{16} Intellectual status	7	-	-	-	-	.146** (3.26)	-.052* (-2.11)	-	-
X_{17} Speech	7	-.104** (-3.05)	-	-	-	-	-	-	-
X_{18} Foster parents	7	-	.113** (2.92)	-	-	-	-.207*** (-5.08)	-.257*** (-6.02)	-
X_{19} Father absence	Birth-7	-	-	-	-.109** (-2.80)	-	.106** (2.60)	.095* (2.20)	-
X_{20} Household moves	Birth-7	-	-	-	-	-	-	-	-
X_{21} Persons supported	7	-	-	-	-.136*** (-3.61)	-	-	-	-
X_{22} Family income	7	-	-	-	-	-	-	-	-
R^2		.437	.232	.262	.348	.045	.206	.134	.166
Sample size = 457									

Notes: The t-statistic is reported in parentheses (2-tailed test).
*p < .05; **p < .01; ***p < .001.
Female model $\chi^2(154) = 116.90$; p = .989.

Figure 5: Structural Equation Model of Biological and Environmental Effects on Juvenile and Adult Crime, Males Only

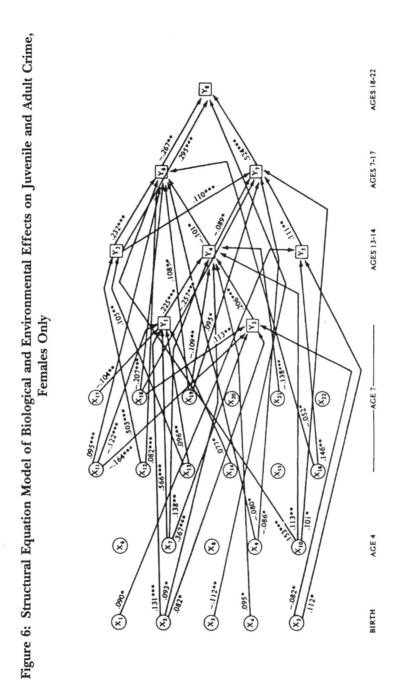

Figure 6: Structural Equation Model of Biological and Environmental Effects on Juvenile and Adult Crime, Females Only

Table 4
GENDER DIFFERENCES IN PREDICTORS OF JUVENILE AND ADULT CRIME
(STATISTICALLY SIGNIFICANT PREDICTORS ONLY FROM TABLES 2 AND 3, IN DECREASING ORDER OF SIGNIFICANCE)

FACTORS PREDICTING NUMBER OF ADULT OFFENSES - MALES
Y_6	Number of juvenile offenses**
X_2	Mother's low education**
Y_7	Seriousness of juvenile offenses**
X_3	Father's high education*
Y_4	Low language achievement*

FACTORS PREDICTING NUMBER OF ADULT OFFENSES - FEMALES
Y_7	Seriousness of juvenile offenses***
Y_3	Disciplinary problem***
Y_6	Low number of juvenile offenses**
X_3	Father's low education**

FACTORS PREDICTING NUMBER OF JUVENILE OFFENSES - MALES
Y_3	Disciplinary problem***
X_5	Time father unemployed***
X_{14}	Lead intoxication***
Y_4	Low language achievement*
X_{20}	Household moves*
X_{17}	Abnormal speech*

FACTORS PREDICTING NUMBER OF JUVENILE OFFENSES - FEMALES
Y_3	Disciplinary problem***
X_{18}	Lack of foster parents***
X_{12}	Abnormal movements***
X_{11}	Neurological abnormalities***
X_{10}	Left foot preference***
X_{19}	Father absence**
Y_4	Low language achievement*
X_{16}	Normal intellectual status*
X_9	Right eye preference*

FACTORS PREDICTING DISCIPLINARY PROBLEM - MALES
X_{14}	Lead intoxication**
X_{15}	Anemia**
X_{20}	Household moves*
X_8	Left hand preference*
X_{18}	Lack of foster parents*

FACTORS PREDICTING DISCIPLINARY PROBLEM - FEMALES
X_{12}	Abnormal movements***
X_{13}	Abnormal vision**

FACTORS PREDICTING LANGUAGE ACHIEVEMENT - MALES
Y_1	WISC Verbal IQ***
Y_2	WISC Performance IQ***

FACTORS PREDICTING LANGUAGE ACHIEVEMENT - FEMALES
Y_2	WISC Performance IQ***
Y_1	WISC Verbal IQ***
X_{21}	Lesser number of persons supported***
X_{10}	Left foot preference**
X_7	Stanford-Binet**
X_{19}	Father presence**
X_4	Family income*
X_2	Mother's education*

TABLE 5: REDUCED FORM EQUATIONS FOR ACHIEVEMENT AND JUVENILE AND ADULT CRIME, MALES ONLY

		Dependent Variables			
Independent Variables	Ages	Language achievement, ages 13-14 (Y_2)	Number of juvenile offenses, ages 7-17 (Y_3)	Seriousness of juvenile offenses, ages 7-17 (Y_7)	Number of adult offenses, ages 18-22 (Y_8)
X_1 Pregnancy and delivery conditions	Birth	—	—	—	-.120
X_2 Mother's education	Birth	—	—	—	.083
X_3 Father's education	Birth	—	—	—	—
X_4 Family income	Birth	—	—	—	—
X_5 Time father unemployed	Birth	—	.179	.115	.070
X_6 Hand preference	1	—	—	—	—
X_7 Stanford-Binet	4	.249	-.024	-.029	-.033
X_8 Hand preference	4	—	.021	.016	.009
X_9 Eye preference	4	—	—	.060	.013
X_{10} Foot preference	4	—	—	—	—
X_{11} Neurological abnormalities	7	—	—	—	—
X_{12} Abnormal movements	7	—	—	—	—
X_{13} Abnormal vision	7	—	.177	.165	.080
X_{14} Lead intoxication	7	—	.027	.065	.021
X_{15} Anemia	7	—	.008	.009	.011
X_{16} Intellectual status	7	-.082	.045	—	.011
X_{17} Speech	7	.022	-.021	-.017	-.011
X_{18} Foster parents	Birth-7	—	—	—	—
X_{19} Father absence	Birth-7	—	—	—	—
X_{20} Household moves	7	—	.116	.131	.058
X_{21} Persons supported	7	—	.078	.091	.039
X_{22} Family income	7	—	—	—	—

Sample size = 487

TABLE 6: REDUCED FORM EQUATIONS FOR ACHIEVEMENT AND JUVENILE AND ADULT CRIME, FEMALES ONLY

Independent Variables	Ages	Dependent Variables			
		Language achievement, ages 13-14 (Y_5)	Number of juvenile offenses, ages 7-17 (Y_6)	Seriousness of juvenile offenses, ages 7-17 (Y_7)	Number of adult offenses, ages 18-22 (Y_8)
X_1 Pregnancy and delivery conditions	Birth	-	-	.010	.004
X_2 Mother's education	Birth	.140	-.014	-.012	-.003
X_3 Father's education	Birth	-	-	-	-.112
X_4 Family income	Birth	.095	-.010	-.008	-.002
X_5 Time father unemployed	Birth	-.017	.009	.014	.005
X_6 Hand preference	1	-	-	-	-
X_7 Stanford-Binet	4	.340	-.034	-.030	-.007
X_8 Hand preference	4	-	-	-	-
X_9 Eye preference	4	-	-.080	-.086	-.024
X_{10} Foot preference	4	.113	.142	.091	.010
X_{11} Neurological abnormalities	7	-.061	.101	.005	-.069
X_{12} Abnormal movements	7	-	.199	.056	.039
X_{13} Abnormal vision	7	.022	.022	.010	.030
X_{14} Lead intoxication	7	.017	-.002	-.002	-
X_{15} Anemia	7	-	-	-	-
X_{16} Intellectual status	7	-.023	-.042	-.016	.020
X_{17} Speech	7	.023	.002	.002	-
X_{18} Foster parents	Birth-7	-.110	-.210	-.259	-.080
X_{19} Father absence	Birth-7	-	.119	.105	.023
X_{20} Household moves	7	-.138	.014	.012	.003
X_{21} Persons supported	7	-	-	-	-
X_{23} Family income		-	-	-	-

Sample size = 500

Juvenile (In)Justice and the Criminal Court Alternative

Barry C. Feld

The juvenile court has been transformed from an informal, welfare agency into a scaled-down, second-class criminal court as a result of a series of reforms that divert status offenders, waive serious offenders to adult criminal courts, punish delinquent offenders, and provide more formal procedures. There are three plausible policy responses to juvenile courts that punish in the name of treatment and deny elementary procedural justice: (a) restructure juvenile courts to fit their original therapeutic purpose; (b) accept punishment as the purpose of delinquency proceedings, but coupled with criminal procedural safeguards; or (c) abolish juvenile courts and try young offenders in criminal courts with certain substantive and procedural modifications.

The Supreme Court's decision in *In re Gault* (1967) began transforming the juvenile court into a very different institution than the Progressives contemplated. Progressive reformers envisioned an informal court whose dispositions reflected the "best interests" of the child. The Supreme Court engrafted formal procedures at trial onto juvenile courts' individualized treatment sentencing schema. Although the Court's decisions were not intended to alter the juvenile courts' therapeutic mission, legislative, judicial, and administrative responses to *Gault* have modified the courts' jurisdiction, purpose, and procedures (Feld 1984, 1988b). The substantive and procedural convergence between juvenile and criminal courts eliminates most of the conceptual and operational differences between social control strategies for youths and adults. With its transformation from an informal, rehabilitative agency into a scaled-down, second-class criminal court, is there any reason to maintain a separate punitive juvenile court whose only distinction is its persisting procedural deficiencies?

Three types of reforms—jurisdictional, jurisprudential, and procedural—reveal the transformation of the contemporary juvenile court (Feld 1991b). Recognizing that juvenile courts often failed to realize their benevolent purposes has led to two jurisdictional changes. Status offenses are misconduct by juveniles, such as truancy or incorrigibility, that would not be a crime

BARRY C. FELD: Centennial Professor of Law, University of Minnesota Law School.

CRIME & DELINQUENCY, Vol. 39 No. 4, October 1993 403-424

if committed by an adult. Recent reforms limit the dispositions that noncriminal offenders may receive or even remove status offenses from juvenile court jurisdiction. A second jurisdictional change is the criminalizing of serious juvenile offenders. Increasingly, courts and legislatures transfer some youths from juvenile courts to criminal courts for prosecution as adults (Feld 1987). As jurisdiction contracts with the removal of serious offenders and noncriminal status offenders, the sentences received by delinquents charged with crimes are based on the idea of just deserts rather than their "real needs." Proportional and determinate sentences based on the present offense and prior record, rather than the best interests of the child, dictate the length, location, and intensity of intervention (Feld 1988b). Increased emphasis on formal procedures at trial has accompanied the enhanced role of punishment in sentencing juveniles (Feld 1984). Although, theoretically, juvenile courts' procedures closely resemble those of criminal courts, in reality, the justice routinely afforded juveniles is lower than the minimum insisted upon for adults.

The Progressive juvenile court. Prior to the creation of the juvenile court, the only special protections received by youths charged with crimes were those afforded by the common law's infancy *mens rea* defense, which conclusively presumed that children less than 7 years old lacked criminal capacity, those 14 years old or older were responsible, and those between 7 years old and 14 years old were rebuttably irresponsible (Fox 1970b). Changes in the cultural conception of children and in strategies of social control during the 19th century led to the creation of the juvenile court (Fox 1970a; Feld 1991b). By the end of the century, children increasingly were seen as vulnerable, innocent, passive, and dependent beings who needed extended preparation for life (Ainsworth 1991; Sutton 1988). The ideology of crime causation changed, as positivistic criminology, which regarded crime as determined rather than chosen, superseded classical explanations that attributed crime to free-willed actors (Allen 1981). Attributing criminal behavior to antecedent causes reduced offenders' moral responsibility, focused efforts on reforming rather than punishing them, and fostered the "rehabilitative ideal." At the dawn of the 20th century, Progressive reformers used the new theories of social control and the new ideas about childhood to create a social welfare alternative to criminal courts to treat criminal and noncriminal misconduct by youths.

By redefining social control, Progressive reformers removed children from the adult criminal system and achieved greater flexibility and supervision of children (Platt 1977; Sutton 1988). Progressives envisioned the juvenile court as a welfare agency in which an expert judge, assisted by social

246

workers and probation officers, made individualized dispositions in a child's best interests (Rothman 1980). The inquiry into the "whole" child accorded minor significance to crime because the specific offense indicated little about a child's real needs. They maximized discretion to provide flexibility in diagnosis and treatment and focused on the child's character and lifestyle. Because juvenile courts separated children from adults and provided an alternative to punishment, they rejected procedural safeguards of criminal law such as juries and lawyers. Informal procedures, euphemistic vocabularies, confidential and private hearings, limited access to court records, and findings of "delinquency" eliminated any stigma or implication of a criminal proceeding. Indeterminate, nonproportional dispositions continued for the duration of the minority, because each child's "treatment" needs differed and no limits could be defined in advance.

THE CONSTITUTIONAL
DOMESTICATION OF THE JUVENILE COURT

The Supreme Court's *Gault* (1967) decision mandated procedural safeguards in delinquency proceedings and focused judicial attention initially on whether the child committed an offense as prerequisite to sentencing (Feld 1984, 1988b). In shifting the focus of juvenile courts from real needs to legal guilt, *Gault* emphasized two crucial gaps between juvenile justice rhetoric and reality: the theory versus practice of rehabilitation, and the differences between the procedural safeguards afforded adults and those available to juveniles (Feld 1990b). The *Gault* Court emphasized that juveniles charged with crimes who faced institutional confinement required elementary procedural safeguards, including notice of charges, a hearing, assistance of counsel, an opportunity to confront and cross-examine witnesses, and a privilege against self-incrimination.

In *In re Winship* (1970), the Court concluded that the risks of erroneous convictions required delinquency to be proven by the criminal standard "beyond a reasonable doubt" rather than by a lower civil standard of proof. In *Breed v. Jones* (1975), the Court posited a functional equivalence between criminal trials and delinquency proceedings and applied the ban on double jeopardy to delinquency convictions.

In *McKeiver v. Pennsylvania* (1970), however, the Court denied juveniles the constitutional right to jury trials and halted the extension of full procedural parity with adult criminal prosecutions. Although *Gault* and *Winship* recognized the need for procedural safeguards against governmental oppression, *McKeiver* denied the need for such protections, invoked the mythology of benevolent juvenile court judges, and justified the procedural differences of juvenile courts by their treatment rationale (*McKeiver* 1970, pp. 550-51; Feld 1988b).

TRANSFORMATION OF THE JUVENILE COURT: REFORMED BUT NOT REHABILITATED

Gault (1967), *Winship* (1970), and *McKeiver* (1970) precipitated a procedural and substantive revolution in juvenile justice that unintentionally but inevitably transformed its Progressive conception. By emphasizing criminal procedural regularity in determining delinquency and formalizing the connection between crime and sentence, the Court made explicit a relationship previously implicit and unacknowledged. Legislative and judicial responses to those decisions—decriminalizing status offenders, waiving serious offenders, punitively sentencing delinquents, and formalizing procedures—further the convergence between criminal and juvenile courts.

Noncriminal status offenders. The definition and administration of status jurisdiction has been criticized extensively in the post-*Gault* decades. The President's Crime Commission (President's Commission on Law Enforcement and Administration of Justice 1967) recommended narrowing the grounds for juvenile court intervention, and many professional organizations subsequently have advocated reform or elimination of status jurisdiction (American Bar Association [ABA] 1982). Some critics focused on its adverse impact on children because, traditionally, status offenses were a form of delinquency and status offenders were detained and incarcerated in the same institutions as criminal delinquents (Handler and Zatz 1982). Others noted its disabling effects on families and other sources of referral, as parents overloaded juvenile courts with intractable family disputes and schools and social agencies used the court as a "dumping ground" to coercively impose solutions (Andrews and Cohn 1974). Legal critics contended that it was "void for vagueness," denied equal protection and procedural justice, and had a disproportionate impact on poor, minority, and female juveniles (Rubin 1985).

Diversion. Disillusionment with juvenile courts' coercive treatment of noncriminal youths led to efforts to divert, deinstitutionalize, and decriminalize them. The Federal Juvenile Justice and Delinquency Prevention Act (1974) required states to begin a process of removing noncriminal offenders from secure detention and correctional facilities and provided an impetus to divert status offenders from juvenile court and decarcerate those remaining in the system (Handler and Zatz 1982).

Progressives created the juvenile court to divert youths from criminal courts and deliver services; now diversion exists to shift otherwise eligible youths away from juvenile court to provide services on an informal basis. Many question whether diversion programs have been implemented coherently or effectively (Klein 1979). Rather than reducing the court's client population, diversion may have had a "net widening" effect, as juveniles who previously would have been released now are subject to informal intervention (Klein 1979).

Deinstitutionalization. Although the numbers of status offenders in secure facilities declined by the mid-1980s, those efforts were frustrated by amendments to the Federal Juvenile Justice Act (1974) in 1980, which weakened the restrictions on secure confinement and allowed youths who ran away from nonsecure placements or violated court orders to be charged with contempt of court and incarcerated (Schwartz 1989). Although subsequent probation violations may result in confinement, juveniles adjudicated for status offenses often receive fewer procedural rights than do youths charged with delinquency (Smith 1992).

Decriminalization. Almost every state "decriminalized" conduct that is illegal only for children by creating nondelinquency classifications such as Persons or Children in Need of Supervision (PINS or CHINS) (Rubin 1985). Such label changes simply shift youths from one jurisdictional category to another without significantly limiting courts' dispositional authority. Using labels of convenience, officials may relabel former status offenders downward as dependent or neglected youths, upward as delinquent offenders, or laterally into a "hidden system" of control in chemical dependency facilities and mental hospitals (Weithorn 1988).

Sentencing juveniles. Historically, juvenile courts imposed indeterminate and nonproportional sentences to achieve the delinquent offender's best interests. In the post-*Gault* era, a fundamental change in the jurisprudence of sentencing occurred as the offense rather than the offender began to dominate the decision (Von Hirsch 1976). A shift in sentencing philosophy from rehabilitation to retribution is evident in the response to serious juvenile offenders and in routine sentencing of delinquent offenders.

Waiver of juvenile offenders to criminal court. Whether to sentence persistent or violent young offenders as juveniles or adults poses difficult theoretical and practical problems and implicates the relationship between juvenile and adult court sentencing practices. Virtually every state has a mechanism for prosecuting some juveniles as adults (Feld 1987). Two types of statutes—judicial waiver and legislative offense exclusion—illustrate the alternative mechanisms and changes in juvenile sentencing philosophies. With judicial waiver, a judge may transfer jurisdiction on a discretionary basis after a hearing to determine whether a youth is "amenable to treatment" or a "threat to public safety" (Feld 1987). With legislative offense exclusion, by statutory definition, youths charged with certain offenses simply are not within juvenile court jurisdiction.

Judicial waiver. Judicial waiver embodies the juvenile court's approach to individual sentencing. In *Kent v. United States* (1966), the Court mandated procedural due process at a waiver hearing where a judge assesses a youth's amenability to treatment or dangerousness. But, if there are no effective treatment programs for serious juvenile offenders, no valid or reliable clinical tests with which to diagnose youths' treatment potential, and no scientific bases by which accurately to predict future dangerousness, then judicial waiver statutes are simply broad grants of standardless discretion (Feld 1978, 1987; Zimring 1991). The inherent subjectivity of discretionary waiver results in racial disparities (Fagan, Forst, and Vivona 1987), and "justice by geography" as different courts within a single state interpret and apply the law inconsistently (Feld 1990a).

Treatment as a juvenile or punishment as an adult is based on an arbitrary line that has no criminological significance other than its legal consequences. There is a relationship between age and crime, and crime rates for many offenses peak in mid- to late adolescence. Rational sentencing requires a coordinated response to active young offenders on both sides of the juvenile/adult line. Because offenders are not irresponsible children one day and responsible adults the next, except as a matter of law, juvenile and criminal courts may work at cross-purposes when juveniles make the transition to criminal courts. Most juveniles judicially waived are charged with property crimes like burglary, rather than with serious offenses against the person; when they appear in criminal courts as adult first offenders, typically they are not imprisoned (Feld 1987; Hamparian et al. 1982).

Legislative exclusion of offenses. Legislative waiver simply excludes from juvenile court jurisdiction youths charged with certain offenses (Feld 1987). Because legislatures create juvenile courts, they may modify their jurisdiction as they please. Increasingly, legislatures use offense criteria either as dispositional guidelines to limit judicial discretion or to automatically exclude certain youths (Feld 1987). Some states amended their judicial waiver statutes to use offense criteria to structure discretion, to reduce inconsistency, and to improve the fit between juvenile waiver and adult sentencing practices. More states reject the juvenile court's individualized sentencing philosophy, at least in part, emphasize retributive policies, and exclude some youths from juvenile court. Exclusion statutes remove judicial sentencing discretion entirely and base the decision to try a youth as an adult on the offense. These statutes emphasizing offenses provide one indicator of the "get-tough" mentality and the shift from a treatment philosophy to a more retributive one. Punishing serious young offenders as adults exposes some youths to the death penalty for the crimes they commit as juveniles (*Stanford v. Kentucky* 1989).

Punishment in juvenile courts. McKeiver denied jury trials and justified a juvenile system separate from the adult one by invoking distinctions between punishment and treatment (Feld 1988b). Whether juvenile courts punish or treat may be determined by examining (a) legislative-purpose clauses and court opinions, (b) juvenile court sentencing statutes and practices, and (c) conditions of confinement and evaluations of treatment effectiveness (Feld 1990b). Despite rehabilitative rhetoric, treating juveniles closely resembles punishing adult criminals.

Purpose of juvenile court. Although 42 states' juvenile codes contain statements of legislative purpose, within the past decade, about one quarter of them have redefined their juvenile codes to de-emphasize rehabilitation and the child's best interest and to assert the importance of public safety and punishing youths for their offenses (Feld 1988b, 1990b). Courts considering these changes in purpose clauses recognize that they signal a basic philosophical reorientation in juvenile justice, even as they endorse punishment as an appropriate juvenile disposition (Feld 1990b).

Juvenile court sentencing statutes. Sentencing statutes provide another indicator of whether juvenile courts punish or treat. Whereas most states' sentencing statutes are indeterminate and nonproportional to achieve a child's best interests, about one third of the states use present offense and/or prior record to regulate some sentencing decisions through determinate or mandatory minimum-sentencing statutes (Feld 1988b, 1990b). Washington state created a juvenile sentencing guidelines commission and based presumptive "just deserts" sentences on a youth's age, present offense, and prior record (Feld 1988b; Walkover 1984). In other states, juvenile court judges

251

consider offense, criminal history, and statutory "aggravating and mitigating" factors when imposing determinate sentences on juveniles (Feld 1988b, 1990b). Some states' mandatory minimum sentences for serious offenses impose terms of confinement ranging from 12 to 18 months up to the age of 21 or to the adult limit for the same offense (Feld 1990b).

Juvenile court sentencing practices. Juvenile court judges enjoy great discretion because of paternalistic assumptions about children and the need to look beyond the offense to their best interests. The exercise of judicial discretion raises concerns about its discriminatory impact, however, because poor and minority youths are disproportionately overrepresented in juvenile correctional institutions (Pope and Feyerherm 1990a, 1990b; Krisberg et al. 1987).

Although evaluations of juvenile court sentencing practices are contradictory, two general findings emerge. First, present offense and prior record account for most of the variance in sentencing that can be explained (McCarthy and Smith 1986; Fagan, Slaughter, and Hartstone 1987; Feld 1989). Second, after controlling for present offense and prior record, individualized discretion is often synonymous with racial disparities in sentencing juveniles (Pope and Feyerherm 1990a, 1990b; Krisberg et al. 1987; Fagan, Slaughter, and Hartstone 1987). A comprehensive review of the influence of race on juvenile sentencing concluded that "race effects may occur at various decision points, they may be direct or indirect, and they may accumulate as youths are processed through the system" (Pope and Feyerherm 1990a, p. 331). Although offense variables exhibit a stronger relationship with dispositions than do social variables, most of the variance in sentencing juveniles remains unexplained. The recent changes in juvenile court sentencing statutes may reflect disquiet with individualized justice, idiosyncratic exercises of discretion, and the inequalities that result (Feld 1988b).

Conditions of juvenile confinement. Gault (1967) belatedly recognized the longstanding contradictions between rehabilitative rhetoric and punitive reality; conditions of confinement motivated the Court to insist upon minimal procedural safeguards for juveniles. Contemporary evaluations of juvenile institutions reveal a continuing gap between rehabilitative rhetoric and punitive reality (Feld 1977, 1981). Simultaneously, lawsuits challenged conditions of confinement, alleged that they violated inmates' "right to treatment," inflicted "cruel and unusual punishment," and provided another outside view of juvenile corrections. A number of courts found inmates beaten by staff, injected with drugs for social control purposes, deprived of minimally adequate care and individualized treatment, routinely locked in solitary confinement, forced to do repetitive and degrading make-work, and provided minimal clinical services (Feld 1990b). The reality for juveniles confined in many treatment facilities is one of violence and punishment.

Effectiveness of treatment. Evaluations of juvenile treatment programs provide scant support for their effectiveness (Whitehead and Lab 1989; Lab and Whitehead 1988). Empirical evaluations question both the efficacy of treatment programs and the scientific underpinnings of those who administer the enterprise. Although the general conclusion that "nothing works" in juvenile corrections has not been persuasively refuted (Melton 1989), it has been strenuously resisted by those who contend that some types of programs may have positive effects on selected clients under certain conditions (Palmer 1991).

The critique of the juvenile court does not rest on the premise that nothing works or ever can work. Even if some demonstration model programs produce positive changes for some youths under some conditions, after a century of unfulfilled promises, a continuing societal unwillingness to commit scare resources to rehabilitative endeavors, and treatment strategies of dubious efficacy, the possibility of effective treatment is inadequate to justify an entire separate justice system.

PROCEDURAL CONVERGENCE
BETWEEN JUVENILE AND CRIMINAL COURTS

A strong nationwide movement, both in theory and in practice, away from therapeutic, individualized dispositions and toward punitive, offense-based sentences eliminates many of the differences between juvenile and adult sentencing practices (Feld 1988b, 1990b). These changes repudiate juvenile courts' original assumptions that youths should be treated differently than adults, that they operate in a youth's best interest, and that rehabilitation is indeterminate and cannot be limited by fixed-time punishment.

The emphasis on punishment contradicts *McKeiver*'s (1970) premise that juveniles require fewer safeguards than do adult defendants and raises questions about the quality of procedural justice (Feld 1990b). Under *Gault*'s (1967) impetus, the formal procedures of juvenile and criminal courts increasingly converge (Feld 1984). There remains, however, a substantial gulf between theory and reality, between the law on the books and the law in action. Theoretically, delinquents are entitled to formal trials and the assistance of counsel. In actuality, juvenile justice is far different. Nearly 3 decades ago, the Supreme Court observed that "the child receives the worst of both worlds: he gets neither the protections accorded to adults nor the solicitous care and regenerative treatment postulated for children" (*Kent v. United States* 1966, p. 556). Despite criminalizing juvenile courts, most states provide neither special procedures to protect juveniles from their own immaturity nor the full panoply of adult procedural safeguards. Instead, states treat juveniles like adult defendants when equality redounds to their disadvantage and use less adequate juvenile court safeguards when those deficient procedures provide an advantage to the state (Feld 1984).

Jury trials in juvenile court. Procedural safeguards are critical when sentences are punitive rather than therapeutic. In denying juries to juveniles, *McKeiver* (1970) posited virtual parity between the accuracy of judges and juries when finding facts. But juries provide special protections to assure factual accuracy, use a higher evidentiary threshold when they apply *Winship*'s (1970) "proof beyond a reasonable doubt" standard, and acquit more readily than do judges (Feld 1984; Ainsworth 1991).

Moreover, *McKeiver* (1970) simply ignored that juries prevent governmental oppression by protecting against weak or biased judges, injecting the community's values into law, and increasing the visibility and accountability of justice administration (Feld 1984; *Duncan v. Louisiana* 1968). Such protections are even more crucial in juvenile courts, which labor behind closed doors immune from public scrutiny.

The right to counsel in juvenile court. Gault (1967) established a constitutional right to an attorney in delinquency proceedings. Despite formal legal changes, the actual delivery of legal services in juvenile courts lags behind; it appears that in many states, half or less of all juveniles receive the assistance of counsel (Feld 1988a, 1989). One study (Feld 1988a) reported that in three of the six states surveyed, only 37.5%, 47.7%, and 52.7% of juveniles charged with delinquency and status offenses were represented. Research in Minnesota (Feld 1989, 1991a) indicates that most juveniles are unrepresented and that many youths removed from their homes or confined in correctional institutions lacked counsel.

The most common explanation for why so many juveniles are unrepresented is that they waive their right to counsel. Courts use the adult standard—"knowing, intelligent, and voluntary" under the "totality of the circumstances"—to assess the validity of juveniles' waivers of constitutional rights (*Fare v. Michael C.* 1979). The crucial issue for juveniles, as for adults, is whether waiver of counsel can be knowing, intelligent, and voluntary when it is made by a child alone without consulting with an attorney. Because juveniles are not as competent as adults, commentators criticize the "totality" approach to waivers as an instance of treating juveniles like adults when equality puts them at a disadvantage (Grisso 1980, 1981).

THE FUTURE OF THE JUVENILE COURT: THREE SCENARIOS

For several decades, juvenile courts have deflected, co-opted, ignored, or accommodated constitutional and legislative reforms with minimal institutional change. The juvenile court remains essentially unreformed despite its transformation from a welfare agency into a scaled-down, second-class criminal court. Public and political concerns about drugs and youth crime encourage repressing rather than rehabilitating young offenders. Fiscal constraints, budget deficits, and competition from other interest groups reduce the likelihood that treatment services for delinquents will expand. Coupling these punitive policies with societal unwillingness to provide for the welfare of children in general, much less those who commit crimes, is there any reason to believe the juvenile court can be rehabilitated?

What is the justification for maintaining a separate court system whose only distinction is that it uses procedures under which no adult would consent to be tried (Feld 1988b; Ainsworth 1991)? Whereas most commentators acknowledge the emergence of a punitive juvenile court, they recoil at the prospect of its outright abolition, emphasize that children are different, and strive to maintain separation between delinquents and criminals (Melton 1989; Rosenberg 1993). Most conclude, however, that juvenile courts need a new rationale that melds punishment with reduced culpability and procedural justice.

There are three plausible responses to a juvenile court that punishes in the name of treatment and simultaneously denies young offenders elementary procedural justice: (a) juvenile courts could be "restructured to fit their original [therapeutic] purpose" (*McKeiver* 1970, p. 557); (b) punishment could be accepted as appropriate in delinquency proceedings but coupled with all criminal procedural safeguards (Melton 1989; ABA 1980c); or (c) juvenile courts could be abolished and young offenders tried in criminal courts with certain substantive and procedural modifications (Feld 1984, 1988b; Ainsworth 1991).

RETURN TO INFORMAL, REHABILITATIVE JUVENILE JUSTICE

Proponents of informal, therapeutic juvenile courts contend that the experiment should not be declared a failure because it has never been

255

implemented effectively (Ferdinand 1989, 1991). From its inception, juvenile courts and correctional facilities have had more in common with penal facilities than welfare agencies (Rothman 1980). Despite its long-standing and readily apparent failures of implementation, proposals persist to reinvigorate the juvenile court as an informal, welfare agency (Edwards 1992).

Even if a flood of resources and a coterie of clinicians suddenly inundated a juvenile court, it would be a dubious policy to recreate it as originally conceived. Despite formal statutes and procedural rules, the "individualized justice" of juvenile courts is substantively and procedurally lawless. To the extent that judges individualize decisions in offenders' best interests, judicial discretion is formally unrestricted. But without practical scientific or clinical bases by which to classify or treat, the exercise of sound discretion is simply a euphemism for judicial subjectivity. Individualization treats similarly situated offenders differently on the basis of personal characteristics and imposes unequal sanctions on invidious bases.

Procedural informality is the concomitant of substantive discretion. If clinical decision making is unconstrained substantively, then it cannot be limited procedurally either, because every case is unique. Although lawyers manipulate legal rules for their clients' advantage, a court without objective laws or formal procedures is unfavorable terrain. But without lawyers to invoke laws, no mechanisms exist to make juvenile courts conform to legal mandates. Closed, informal, confidential proceedings reduce visibility and accountability and preclude external checks on coercive intervention.

Subordinating social welfare to social control. Focusing simply on failures of implementation, inadequate social services or welfare resources, abuses of discretion, and persisting procedural deficiencies, however, systematically misleads both proponents and critics of the juvenile court and prevents either from envisioning alternatives. The fundamental shortcoming of the juvenile court is not just its failures of implementation, but a deeper flaw in its basic concept. The original juvenile court was conceived of as a social service agency operating in a judicial setting, a fusion of welfare and coercion. But providing for the social welfare of young people is ultimately a societal responsibility rather than a judicial one. It is simply unrealistic to expect juvenile courts, or any other legal institution, either to alleviate the social ills afflicting young people or to have a significant impact on youth crime.

Despite claims of being a child-centered nation, we care less about other people's children than we do our own, especially when they are children of other colors or cultures (National Commission on Children 1991). Without a societal commitment to adequately meet the minimum family, medical, housing, nutritional, and educational needs of all young people on a voluntary basis, the juvenile court provides a mechanism for imposing involuntary controls on some youths, regardless of how ineffective it may be in delivering services or rehabilitating offenders.

Juvenile courts' penal emphasis. When social services and social control are combined in one setting, as in juvenile court, custodial considerations quickly subordinate social welfare concerns. Historically, juvenile courts purported to resolve the tension between social welfare and social control by asserting that dispositions in a child's best interests achieved individual and public welfare simultaneously. In reality, some youths who commit crimes do not need social services, whereas others cannot be meaningfully rehabilitated. And, many more children with social service needs do not commit crimes.

Juvenile courts' subordination of individual welfare to custody and control stems from its fundamentally penal focus. Delinquency jurisdiction is not based on characteristics of children for which they are not responsible and for whom intervention could mean an improvement in their lives—their lack of decent education, their lack of adequate housing, their unmet medical needs, or their family or social circumstances (National Commission on Children 1991). Rather, delinquency jurisdiction is based on criminal law violations that are the youths' fault and for which the youths are responsible (Fox 1970b). As long as juvenile courts emphasize criminal characteristics of children least likely to elicit sympathy and ignore social conditions most likely to engender a desire to nurture and help, they reinforce punitive rather than rehabilitative impulses. Operating in a societal context that does not provide adequately for children in general, intervention in the lives of those who commit crimes inevitably serves purposes of penal social control, regardless of the court's ability to deliver social welfare.

Due process and punishment in juvenile court. Acknowledging that juvenile courts punish imposes an obligation to provide all criminal procedural safeguards because "the condition of being a boy does not justify a kangaroo court" (*Gault* 1967, p. 28). Although procedural parity with adults may end the juvenile court experiment, to fail to do so perpetuates injustice. Punishing juveniles in the name of treatment and denying them basic safeguards fosters injustice that thwarts any reform efforts.

Developing rationales to respond to young offenders requires reconciling contradictory impulses engendered when the child is a criminal and the criminal is a child. If juvenile courts provide neither therapy nor justice, then the alternatives are either (a) to make juvenile courts more like criminal courts, or (b) to make criminal courts more like juvenile courts. Whether young offenders ultimately are tried in a separate juvenile court or in a criminal court raises basic issues of substance and procedure. Issues of substantive justice include developing and implementing a doctrinal rationale to sentence young offenders differently, and more leniently, than older defendants (Feld 1988b). Issues of procedural justice include providing youths with *all* of the procedural safeguards adults receive *and* additional protections that recognize their immaturity (Rosenberg 1980; Feld 1984).

Most commentators who recoil from abolishing juvenile court instead propose to transform it into an explicitly penal one, albeit one that limits punishment based on reduced culpability and provides enhanced procedural justice (Melton 1989; ABA 1980a). The paradigm of the "new juvenile court" is the American Bar Association's Juvenile Justice Standards. The Juvenile Justice Standards recommend repeal of jurisdiction over status offenders, use of proportional and determinate sentences to sanction delinquent offenders, use of offense criteria to regularize pretrial detention and judicial transfer decisions, and provision of all criminal procedural safeguards, including nonwaivable counsel and jury trials (Flicker 1983; Wizner and Keller 1977). Although the ABA's "criminal juvenile court" combines reduced culpability sentencing and greater procedural justice, it fails to explain why these principles should be implemented in a separate juvenile court rather than in a criminal court (Melton 1989; Gardner 1989). The ABA's Juvenile Justice Standards assert that "removal of the treatment rationale does not destroy the rationale for a separate system or for utilization of an ameliorative approach; it does, however, require a different rationale" (ABA 1980b, p. 19, note 5). Unfortunately, although the ABA standards virtually replicate the adult criminal process, they provide no rationale for a separate juvenile system.

Some commentators contend that maintaining a separate punishment system for juveniles may avoid some stigmatic effects of a "criminal" label (Gardner 1989). Others speculate that because some specialized juvenile procedures and dispositional facilities will remain, it is more practical and less risky to retain than to abolish juvenile courts (Rubin 1979). Some emphasize criminal courts' deficiencies—overcrowding, ineffective counsel, insufficient sentencing alternatives—as a justification for retaining juvenile courts, even while acknowledging that these are characteristics of juvenile courts as well (Dawson 1990). Given institutional and bureaucratic inertia, however, it might be that only a clean break with the personnel and practices of the past would permit the implementation of procedural justice and sentencing reforms.

The only real difference between the ABA's criminal juvenile court and adult criminal courts is that the former would impose shorter sentences (ABA

1980c; Wizner and Keller 1977). Particularly for serious young offenders, the sanctions imposed in juvenile court are less than those of criminal courts, and a separate court might be the only way to achieve those shorter sentences and insulate youths from criminal courts.

But, recent research suggests that there might be a relationship between increased procedural formality and sentencing severity in juvenile courts. Despite statutes and rules of statewide applicability, juvenile courts are highly variable. Urban courts, which typically are the most formal, also detain and sentence more severely than do their more traditional, rural counterparts (Feld 1991a). If procedural formality increases substantive severity, could a separate criminal juvenile court continue to afford leniency? Will juvenile courts' procedural convergence with criminal courts increase repressiveness and erode present sentencing differences? Can juvenile courts only be lenient because discretion is hidden behind closed doors? Would imposing the rule of law prevent them from affording leniency to most youths? The ABA Standards do not even recognize, much less answer, these questions.

Young offenders in criminal court. If the primary reason a child is in court is because he or she committed a crime, then the child could be tried in criminal courts alongside adult counterparts. Before returning young offenders to criminal courts, however, a legislature must address issues of substance and procedure in order to create a juvenile criminal court. Substantively, a legislature must develop a rationale to sentence young offenders differently and more leniently than older defendants. Procedurally, it must afford youths full parity with adults and additional safeguards.

Substantive justice—juveniles' criminal responsibility. The primary virtue of the contemporary juvenile court is that young serious offenders typically receive shorter sentences than do adults convicted of comparable crimes. One premise of juvenile justice is that youths should survive the mistakes of adolescence with their life chances intact, and this goal would be threatened by the draconian sentences frequently inflicted on 18-year-old "adults." However, even juvenile courts' seeming virtue of shorter sentences for serious offenders is offset by the far more numerous minor offenders who receive longer sentences as juveniles than they would as adults.

Shorter sentences for young people do not require that they be tried in separate juvenile courts. Criminal law doctrines and policies provide rationales to sentence youths less severely than adults in criminal courts (Feld 1988b; Melton 1989). Juvenile courts simply extended upward by a few years the common law's infancy presumptions that immature young people lack

259

criminal capacity (Fox 1970b). "Diminished responsibility" doctrines provide additional rationale for shorter sentences for youths, because within a framework of "deserved" punishments, it would be unjust to sentence youths and adults alike (ABA 1980c). Although an offender's age is of little relevance when assessing harm, youthfulness is highly pertinent when assessing culpability.

Developmental psychological research confirms that young people move through developmental stages with respect to legal reasoning and ethical decision making akin to the common law's infancy defense. Even youths 14 years of age or older, who abstractly may know "right from wrong," might still not be as blameworthy and deserving of comparable punishment as adult offenders. Families, schools, and communities socialize young people and share some responsibility for their offenses (Twentieth Century Fund 1978). To the extent that the ability to make responsible choices is learned behavior, the dependent status of youths systematically deprives them of opportunities to learn to be responsible (Zimring 1982).

The Supreme Court in *Thompson v. Oklahoma* (1988) provided additional support for lesser sentences for reduced culpability even for youths above the common-law infancy threshold of 14 years of age. In vacating Thompson's capital sentence, the Court noted that even though he was criminally responsible, he should not be punished as severely. Despite a later decision upholding the death penalty for 16-year-old or 17-year-old youths (*Stanford* 1989), the Court has repeatedly emphasized that youthfulness is an important mitigating factor at sentencing. The argument for shorter sentences for reduced culpability is not a constitutional claim because the Supreme Court consistently has resisted developing a criminal law mens rea jurisprudence (Rosenberg 1993). Rather, like the juvenile court itself, it is a matter of state legislative sentencing policy.

"Youth discount." Shorter sentences for reduced culpability is a more modest rationale to treat young people differently from adults than the juvenile court's rehabilitative claims. Criminal courts can provide shorter sentences for reduced culpability with fractional reductions of adult sentences in the form of an explicit "youth discount." For example, a 14-year-old might receive 33% of the adult penalty, a 16-year-old 66%, and an 18-year-old the adult penalty, as is presently the case (Feld 1988b). Of course, explicit fractional youth discount sentence reductions can only be calculated against a backdrop of realistic, humane, and determinate adult sentencing practices. For youths younger than 14 years old, the common-law mens rea infancy defense acquires a new vitality for shorter sentences or even noncriminal alternative dispositions (Fox 1970b).

A graduated age-culpability sentencing scheme avoids the inconsistency and injustice played out in binary either/or juvenile versus adult judicial waiver determinations (Feld 1987). Sentences that young people receive might differ by orders of magnitude, depending upon whether or not transfer is ordered. Because of the profound consequences, waiver hearings consume a disproportionate amount of juvenile court time and resources. Abolishing juvenile court eliminates waiver hearings, saves resources that are ultimately expended to no purpose, reduces the "punishment gap" when youths cross from one system to the other, and assures similar consequences for similar offenders.

Trying young people in criminal courts with full procedural safeguards would not appreciably diminish judges' sentencing expertise. Although Progressives envisioned a specialist juvenile court judge possessing the wisdom of a "kadi" (Matza 1964), judges increasingly handle juvenile matters as part of the general docket or rotate through juvenile court on short-term assignments without acquiring any particular dispositional expertise. In most juvenile courts, social services personnel advise judges and possess the information necessary for appropriate dispositions.

Punishing youths does not require incarcerating them with adults in jails and prisons. Departments of corrections already classify inmates, and existing juvenile detention facilities and institutions provide options for age-segregated dispositional facilities. Insisting explicitly on humane conditions of confinement could do as much to improve the lives of incarcerated youths as has the "right to treatment" or the "rehabilitative ideal" (Feld 1977, 1981). Recognizing that most young offenders return to society imposes an obligation to provide resources for self-improvement on a voluntary basis.

Procedural justice for youth. Since *Gault,* most of the procedures of criminal courts are supposed to be routine aspects of juvenile courts as well. Generally, both courts apply the same laws of arrest, search, identification, and interrogation to adults and juveniles, and increasingly subject juveniles charged with felony offenses to similar fingerprinting and booking processes as adults (Feld 1984; Dawson 1990). The more formal and adversarial nature of juvenile court procedures reflects the attenuation between the court's therapeutic mission and its social control functions. The many instances in which states treat juvenile offenders procedurally like adult criminal defendants is one aspect of this process (Feld 1984). Despite the procedural convergence, it remains nearly as true today as 2 decades ago that "the child receives the worst of both worlds" (*Kent* 1966, p. 556). Most states provide neither special safeguards to protect juveniles from the consequences of their immaturity nor the full panoply of adult procedural safeguards to protect them from punitive state intervention.

Youths' differences in age and competence require them to receive more protections than adults, rather than less. The rationales to sentence youths differently and more leniently than adults also justify providing them with *all* of the procedural safeguards adults receive *and* additional protections that recognize their immaturity. This dual-maximal strategy explicitly provides enhanced protection for children because of their vulnerability and immaturity (Feld 1984; Rosenberg 1980; Melton 1989). As contrasted with current practices, for example, a dual-maximal procedural strategy produces different results with respect to waivers of constitutional rights. Although counsel is the prerequisite to procedural justice for juveniles, many youths do not receive the assistance of counsel because courts use the adult standard and find they waived the right in a "knowing, intelligent, and voluntary" manner under the "totality of the circumstances." The Juvenile Justice Standards recognize youths' limitations in dealing with the law and provide that the right to counsel attaches when a youth is taken into custody, that it is self-invoking and does not require an affirmative request as is the case for adults, and that youths must consult with counsel prior to waiving counsel or at interrogation (ABA 1980a).

Providing youths with full procedural parity in criminal courts and additional substantive and procedural safeguards could afford more protection than does the juvenile court. A youth concerned about adverse publicity could waive the right to public trial. If a youth successfully completes a sentence without recidivating, then expunging criminal records and eliminating collateral disabilities could avoid criminal labels and afford as much relief from an isolated act of folly as does the juvenile court's confidentiality.

The conceptual problems of creating a juvenile criminal court are soluble. The difficulty is political. Even though juvenile courts currently provide uneven leniency, could legislators who want to get tough on crime vote for a youth-discount sentencing provision that explicitly recognizes youthfulness as a mitigating factor in sentencing? Even though young people presently possess some constitutional rights, would politicians be willing to provide a justice system that assures those rights would be realistically and routinely exercised? Or, would they rather maintain a juvenile system that provides neither therapy nor justice, that elevates social control over social welfare, and that abuses children while claiming to protect them?

Abolishing juvenile court forces a long overdue and critical reassessment of the meaning of "childhood" (Ainsworth 1991). A society that regards young people as fundamentally different from adults easily justifies an inferior justice system and conveniently rationalizes it on the grounds that children are entitled only to custody, not liberty (*Schall v. Martin* 1984). The ideology of therapeutic justice and its discretionary apparatus persist because the social control is directed at children. Despite humanitarian claims of being a child-centered nation, cultural and legal conceptions of children support institutional arrangements that deny the personhood of young people. Rethinking the juvenile court requires critically reassessing the meaning of childhood and creating social institutions to assure the welfare of the next generation.

REFERENCES

Ainsworth, Janet. 1991. "Re-imagining Childhood and Reconstructing the Legal Order: The Case for Abolishing the Juvenile Court." *North Carolina Law Review* 69:1083-1133.

Allen, Francis A. 1981. *The Decline of the Rehabilitative Ideal: Penal Policy and Social Purpose.* New Haven, CT: Yale University Press.

American Bar Association—Institute of Judicial Administration. 1980a. *Juvenile Justice Standards Relating to Counsel for Private Parties.* Cambridge, MA: Ballinger.

———. 1980b. *Juvenile Justice Standards Relating to Dispositions.* Cambridge, MA: Ballinger.

———. 1980c. *Juvenile Justice Standards Relating to Juvenile Delinquency and Sanctions.* Cambridge, MA: Ballinger.

———. 1982. *Juvenile Justice Standards Relating to Noncriminal Misbehavior.* Cambridge, MA: Ballinger.

Andrews, R. Hale and Andrew H. Cohn. 1974. "Ungovernability: The Unjustifiable Jurisdiction." *Yale Law Journal* 83:1383-1409.

Dawson, Robert. 1990. "The Future of Juvenile Justice: Is It Time to Abolish the System?" *Journal of Criminal Law & Criminology* 81:136-55.

Edwards, Leonard P. 1992. "The Juvenile Court and the Role of the Juvenile Court Judge." *Juvenile and Family Court Journal* 43:1-45.

Fagan, Jeffrey, Martin Forst, and Scott Vivona. 1987. "Racial Determinants of the Judicial Transfer Decision: Prosecuting Violent Youth in Criminal Court." *Crime & Delinquency* 33:259-86.

Fagan, Jeffrey, Ellen Slaughter, and Eliot Hartstone. 1987. "Blind Justice? The Impact of Race on the Juvenile Justice Process. " *Crime & Delinquency* 33: 224-58.

Feld, Barry C. 1977. *Neutralizing Inmate Violence: Juvenile Offenders in Institutions.* Cambridge, MA: Ballinger.

———. 1978. "Reference of Juvenile Offenders for Adult Prosecution: The Legislative Alternative to Asking Unanswerable Questions." *Minnesota Law Review* 62:515-618.

———. 1981. "A Comparative Analysis of Organizational Structure and Inmate Subcultures in Institutions for Juvenile Offenders." *Crime & Delinquency* 27:336-63.

———. 1984. "Criminalizing Juvenile Justice: Rules of Procedure for Juvenile Court." *Minnesota Law Review* 69:141-276.

———. 1987. "Juvenile Court Meets the Principle of Offense: Legislative Changes in Juvenile Waiver Statutes." *Journal of Criminal Law and Criminology* 78:471-533.

———. 1988a. *"In re Gault* Revisited: A Cross-State Comparison of the Right to Counsel in Juvenile Court." *Crime & Delinquency* 34:393-424.

————. 1988b. "Juvenile Court Meets the Principle of Offense: Punishment, Treatment, and the Difference it Makes." *Boston University Law Review* 68:821-915.

————. 1989. "The Right to Counsel in Juvenile Court: An Empirical Study of When Lawyers Appear and the Difference They Make." *Journal of Criminal Law and Criminology* 79:1185-1346.

————. 1990a. "Bad Law Makes Hard Cases: Reflections on Teen-Aged Axe-Murderers, Judicial Activism, and Legislative Default." *Journal of Law and Inequality* 8:1-101.

————. 1990b. "The Punitive Juvenile Court and the Quality of Procedural Justice: Disjunctions Between Rhetoric and Reality." *Crime & Delinquency* 36:443-66.

————. 1991a. "Justice by Geography: Urban, Suburban, and Rural Variations in Juvenile Justice Administration." *Journal of Criminal Law and Criminology* 82:156-210.

————. 1991b. "The Transformation of the Juvenile Court." *Minnesota Law Review* 75:691-725.

Ferdinand, Theodore N. 1989. "Juvenile Delinquency or Juvenile Justice: Which Came First?" *Criminology* 27:79-106.

————. 1991. "History Overtakes the Juvenile Justice System." *Crime & Delinquency* 37:204-24.

Flicker, Barbara. 1983. *Standards for Juvenile Justice: A Summary and Analysis.* 2nd ed. Cambridge, MA: Ballinger.

Fox, Sanford J. 1970a. "Juvenile Justice Reform: An Historical Perspective." *Stanford Law Review* 22:1187-1239.

————. 1970b. "Responsibility in the Juvenile Court." *William & Mary Law Review* 11:659-84.

Gardner, Martin. 1989. "The Right of Juvenile Offenders to be Punished: Some Implications of Treating Kids as Persons." *Nebraska Law Review* 68:182-215.

Grisso, Thomas. 1980. "Juveniles' Capacities to Waive Miranda Rights: An Empirical Analysis." *California Law Review* 68:1134-66.

————. 1981. *Juveniles' Waiver of Rights.* New York: Plenum.

Hamparian, Donna, Linda Estep, Susan Muntean, Ramon Priestino, Robert Swisher, Paul Wallace, and Joseph White. 1982. *Youth in Adult Courts: Between Two Worlds.* Washington, DC: Office of Juvenile Justice and Delinquency Prevention.

Handler, Joel F. and Julie Zatz, eds. 1982. *Neither Angels Nor Thieves: Studies in Deinstitutionalization of Status Offenders.* Washington, DC: National Academy Press.

Klein, Malcolm W. 1979. "Deinstitutionalization and Diversion of Juvenile Offenders: A Litany of Impediments." Pp. 145-201 in *Crime and Justice: An Annual Review,* edited by M. Tonry and N. Morris. Chicago: University of Chicago Press.

Krisberg, Barry, Ira Schwartz, Gideon Fishman, Zvi Eisikovits, Edna Guttman, and Karen Joe. 1987. "The Incarceration of Minority Youth." *Crime & Delinquency* 33:173-205.

Lab, Steven P. and John T. Whitehead. 1988. "An Analysis of Juvenile Correctional Treatment." *Crime & Delinquency* 34:60-83.

Matza, David. 1964. *Delinquency and Drift.* New York: Wiley.

McCarthy, Belinda and Brent L. Smith. 1986. "The Conceptualization of Discrimination in the Juvenile Justice Process: The Impact of Administrative Factors and Screening Decisions on Juvenile Court Dispositions." *Criminology* 24:41-64.

Melton, Gary B. 1989. "Taking *Gault* Seriously: Toward a New Juvenile Court." *Nebraska Law Review* 68:146-81.

National Commission on Children. 1991. *Beyond Rhetoric: A New American Agenda for Children and Families.* Washington, DC: U.S. Government Printing Office.

Palmer, Ted. 1991. "The Effectiveness of Intervention: Recent Trends and Current Issues." *Crime & Delinquency* 37:330-46.

Platt, Anthony. 1977. *The Child Savers.* 2nd ed. Chicago: University of Chicago Press.

Pope, Carl E. and William H. Feyerherm. 1990a. "Minority Status and Juvenile Justice Processing: An Assessment of the Research Literature (Part I)." *Criminal Justice Abstracts* 22:327-35.
———. 1990b. "Minority Status and Juvenile Justice Processing: An Assessment of the
Research Literature (Part II)." *Criminal Justice Abstracts* 22:527-42.
President's Commission on Law Enforcement and Administration of Justice. 1967. *The Challenge of Crime in a Free Society.* Washington, DC: U.S. Government Printing Office.
Rosenberg, Irene M. 1980. "The Constitutional Rights of Children Charged with Crime: Proposal
for a Return to the Not So Distant Past." *University of California Los Angeles Law Review*
27:656-721.
———. 1993. "Leaving Bad Enough Alone: A Response to the Juvenile Court Abolitionists."
Wisconsin Law Review 1993:163-85.
Rothman, David J. 1980. *Conscience and Convenience: The Asylum and Its Alternative in
Progressive America.* Boston: Little, Brown.
Rubin, H. Ted. 1979. "Retain the Juvenile Court? Legislative Developments, Reform Directions
and the Call for Abolition." *Crime & Delinquency* 25:281-98.
———. 1985. *Juvenile Justice: Policy, Practice, and Law.* 2nd ed. New York: Random House.
Schwartz, Ira M. 1989. *(In)Justice for Juveniles: Rethinking the Best Interests of the Child.*
Lexington, MA: Lexington Books.
Smith, Erin. 1992. "In a Child's Best Interest: Juvenile Status Offenders Deserve Procedural
Due Process." *Journal of Law & Inequality* 10:253-303.
Sutton, John R. 1988. *Stubborn Children: Controlling Deliquency in the United States.* Berkeley:
University of California Press.
Twentieth Century Fund Task Force on Sentencing Policy Toward Young Offenders. 1978.
Confronting Youth Crime. New York: Holmes & Meier.
Von Hirsch, Andrew. 1976. *Doing Justice.* New York: Hill and Wang.
Walkover, Andrew. 1984. "The Infancy Defense in the New Juvenile Court." *University of
California Los Angeles Law Review* 31:503-62.
Weithorn, Lois A. 1988. "Mental Hospitalization of Troublesome Youth: An Analysis of
Skyrocketing Admission Rates." *Stanford Law Review* 40:773-838.
Whitehead, John T. and Steven P. Lab. 1989. "A Meta-Analysis of Juvenile Correctional
Treatment." *Journal of Research in Crime and Delinquency* 26:267-95.
Wizner, Steven and Mary F. Keller. 1977. "The Penal Model of Juvenile Justice: Is Juvenile
Court Delinquency Jurisdiction Obsolete?" *New York University Law Review* 52:1120-35.
Zimring, Franklin. 1982. *The Changing Legal World of Adolescence.* New York: Free Press.
———. 1991. "The Treatment of Hard Cases in American Juvenile Justice: In Defense of
Discretionary Waiver." *Notre Dame Journal of Law, Ethics and Public Policy* 5:267-80.

CASES

Breed v. Jones, 421 U.S. 519 (1975).
Duncan v. Louisiana, 391 U.S. 145 (1968).
Fare v. Michael C., 442 U.S. 707 (1979).
In re Gault, 387 U.S. 1 (1967).
Kent v. United States, 383 U.S. 541 (1966).
McKeiver v. Pennyslvania, 403 U.S. 528 (1970).
Schall v. Martin, 467 U.S. 260 (1984).

Stanford v. Kentucky, 109 S.Ct. 2974 (1989).
Thompson v. Oklahoma, 487 U.S. 815 (1988).
In re Winship, 397 U.S. 358 (1970).

STATUTES

Federal Juvenile Justice and Delinquency Prevention Act of 1974. 42 U.S.C. §§ 5601 et seq.

Themes of Injustice: Wrongful Convictions, Racial Prejudice, and Lawyer Incompetence

By Bennett L. Gershman*

The U.S. criminal justice system has undergone radical changes in the past generation. Crime is more complex; prosecutors are more powerful; and courts, corrections agencies, and defense services are burdened with larger case loads and tighter budgets. It is not the best of times to talk about justice. Yet, it is a subject that needs to be constantly addressed, particularly in times of crisis. The following essay focuses on some of the problems that present themselves in the criminal justice system today, including the conviction of innocent defendants, especially in capital cases; racial prejudice; and lawyer incompetence.

There has always existed a tension between justice and law.[1] Contrary to popular belief, justice and law are not coextensive. They may coincide, for example, when law is used to end racial or other invidious discriminatory practices. On the other hand, justice and law may be strikingly at odds, as in the Los Angeles jury's verdict last year acquitting four police officers in the brutal beating of Rodney King. There are just laws. And there are unjust laws. There are judges who believe they should dispense justice. And there are judges who believe they should mechanically apply the law, regardless of the equities.

Notwithstanding the election of a new president, and a potentially new make-up of the Supreme Court, there is much cause for concern over justice in the United States. To borrow from Shakespeare, "the times are out of joint."[2] The Bill of Rights, whose two-hundredth anniversary we celebrated recently, has been sapped of much of its vitality over the past twenty years by a determined Supreme Court, two conservative presidents, and

---

* Professor of Law, Pace University School of Law, White Plains, New York. This essay is based on remarks delivered on Law Day 1992 before the Rockland County Bar Association, New City, N. Y.

[1] For an excellent coursebook addressing this fascinating subject, see A. D'Amato & A. Jacobson, *Justice and the Legal System* (1992).

[2] W. Shakespeare, *Hamlet*, Act I, scene v.

502

a law-and-order Congress. Virtually every key protection of the Bill of Rights has been diluted, eviscerated, or interpreted out of existence.[3] A recent polls shows that few 1990s Americans can identify the Bill of Rights or are aware of its guarantees.[4] Two of its greatest defenders—Justices William J. Brennan and Thurgood Marshall—are gone. And the highest court mirrors the public's insensitivity and apathy by continuing a steady retreat from its long-recognized function "to be watchful for the constitutional rights of the citizen, and against any steady encroachments thereon."[5]

This erosion of judicial protection for individual rights is also reflected in the agonizing death of Habeas Corpus, the Great Writ of liberty second only to the Magna Carta. We have witnessed over the past decade a frantic legal foot-race between a majority of the Supreme Court and some members of Congress to abolish habeas corpus, thereby preventing state inmates from seeking federal judicial redress for constitutional violations. To be sure, as with any legal remedy, habeas corpus can be abused. But statistics show that writs from state prisoners on death row have been found meritorious in one third to one half of all cases.[6] Not long ago, we watched anxiously as a few federal judges in California stayed an execution so that they could decide whether using cyanide gas for executions—the kind used in the concentration camps of World War II—violated evolving constitutional standards of decency.[7] In a tense, early morning battle of judicial power, a majority of the Supreme Court firmly directed the execution to proceed, reminding us of Chief Justice Rehnquist's view about delays in executions: "Let's get on with it."[8]

---

[3] W. Kunstler, "*The Bill of Rights—Can It Survive?*," 26 Gonz. L. Rev. 1 (1991).

[4] "*Poll Finds Only 33% Can Identify Bill of Rights*," N.Y. Times, Dec. 15, 1991, at 33.

[5] Boyd v. United States, 116 U.S. 616, 636 (1886).

[6] J. Liebman, *Federal Habeas Corpus Practice and Procedure* § 2.2, 23–24 n. 97 (1988) (49 percent success rate); Godbold, "Pro Bono Representation of Death Sentenced Inmates," 42 Rec. N.Y. City B. Ass'n 859, 873 (1987) (one third success rate). See also Barefoot v. Estelle, 463 U.S. 880, 915 (1983) (Marshall, J., dissenting) (over 70 percent of cases decided in favor of death sentenced petitioners).

[7] Vasquez v. Harris, 112 S. Ct. 1713, 1714 (1992) ("No further stays of Robert Alton Harris' execution shall be entered by the federal courts except upon order of this Court."). See also Bishop, "After Night of Court Battles, a California Execution," N.Y. Times, Apr. 22, 1992, at 1.

[8] *Id.*

503

Diminished protection for individual liberties parallels diminished protection for civil rights. Blatant prejudice and racial discrimination continue to infect the criminal justice system. There was a time when northerners in this country would deride the southern judicial system for operating a racist justice. Between 1930 and 1974, of the 455 men executed in the south for rape, 405, or 89 percent were black. Virtually all of the complainants were white.[9] But we delude ourselves if we think that racial prejudice is confined to the South. A recent report by the New York State Judicial Commission on Minorities states that minority users of the New York State court system "face many of the same travesties as did their southern counterparts— unequal access, disparate treatment, and frustrated opportunity."[10]

Further, our nation's appetite for executing people, even arguably innocent people, seems to be increasing. There are presently 2,729 inmates on death row.[11] We will execute more men and women this year than in any year since the Supreme Court allowed executions to resume in 1976. At a time in our history when the highest court in the land makes life and death decisions based on technical procedural grounds, rather than justice, and begins an opinion that will decide whether a condemned man will live or die with the words, "This is a case about federalism,"[12] it is important to talk about justice.

However, defining the idea of justice, and the quintessential "just result," often proves a frustrating and elusive task. The term itself is so indefinite and subjective. Is justice done when a condemned prisoner is put to death for murder without an opportunity to present new evidence of his innocence?[13] Is it justice when a court's interpretation of the Civil Rights Act prevents judges from hearing claims against persons charged with obstructing access to an abortion clinic?[14] These examples

---

[9] United States v. Wiley, 492 F.2d 547, 555 (D.C. Cir. 1974) (Bazelon, J., concurring).

[10] *New York State Judicial Commission on Minorities* vii (1990) (letter dated May 16, 1990, from Franklin H. Williams, Esq., Chairman of the Commission, to Chief Justice Sol Wachtler).

[11] Death Row U.S.A. 1 (Spring 1993).

[12] Coleman v. Thompson, 111 S. Ct. 2546, 2552 (1991).

[13] Herrera v. Collins, 113 S. Ct. 853 (1993).

[14] Bray v. Alexandria Women's Health Clinic, 113 S. Ct. 753 (1993).

504

may appear to some to be the antithesis of justice. Others, however, may see them as perfectly neutral applications of law.

Rather than talk about the concept of justice in the abstract, it might be more realistic to talk about the other side of justice, the concept of injustice. For if the meaning of justice eludes us, the meaning of injustice might be easier to grasp. Perhaps participants in the criminal justice system can arrive at greater understanding and sensitivity about their professional obligations, and confront justice issues more effectively and even compassionately, by focusing on the subject of injustice: what broad categories provide the grist for miscarriages of justice; who is responsible for perpetrating those injustices; how they can be corrected, if it is not too late.[15] Three overriding themes of injustice come to mind: convicting the innocent, racial prejudice, and lawyer incompetence.

Convicting the Innocent

Our society, as expressed by the Supreme Court in the landmark case of *In re Winship*,[16] has made a fundamental value judgment that it is far worse to convict an innocent person than to let a guilty person go free. Indeed, we probably could reach a consensus that the greatest injustice any society can perpetrate is to convict, and possibly even put to death, an innocent person. We read recently of two men released from a California state penitentiary after spending seventeen years in jail for what the judge described as a "concocted murder conviction."[17] Of the 2,729 men and women on death row in the United States, there are several persons who, based on reports of newly discovered evidence, probably are innocent. We prefer not to think about such matters. We prefer to trust prosecutors, judges, and juries to do the right thing.

Prosecutors, however, often do not do the right thing, as several recently highly publicized murder cases have docu-

---

[15] The catalyst for the discussion of the subject of justice in terms of injustice came from the late Edmund Cahn's outstanding work, *Confronting Injustice* (1967).

[16] 397 U.S. 358 (1970).

[17] Mydans, "After 17 Years, Sunshine and Freedom," N.Y. Times, Mar. 27, 1992, at A14.

505

mented.[18] Judges also shirk their responsibility to prevent miscarriages of justice, as demonstated by the Supreme Court's anti-habeas crusade.[19] Juries also make mistakes, terrible mistakes, particularly when the prosecution's proof is mistaken or fabricated.[20] Persons who carefully examined the evidence have made a persuasive case that Roger Coleman in Virginia, and Leonel Herrera in Texas, had strong claims to innocence.[21] Indeed, virtually every law-enforcement official in the state of Texas was convinced that Randall Dale Adams was guilty of murdering a police officer, until a courageous film-maker—not a lawyer, prosecutor, or judge—produced a documentary entitled "The Thin Blue Line," which exposed the Texas judicial system at its most vicious and corrupt, and which led to Adam's exoneration.[22]

According to a well-known study published in 1987, more than 350 people in this century have been erroneously convicted in the United States of crimes punishable by death; 116 of those were sentenced to death and 23 actually were executed.[23] This same study found that there have been twenty-nine mistaken convictions in capital cases in New York State, sixteen of which resulted in death verdicts.[24] New York State leads all states in executing the innocent; eight New Yorkers have been executed in error.[25] And a recent study prepared by the New York State Defenders Association concludes that fifty-nine wrongful homi-

---

[18] The cases are those of Randall Dale Adams in Texas, James Richardson and Joseph Brown in Florida, and Eric Jackson in New York. See B. Gershman, *Abuse of Power in the Prosecutor's Office, The World & I* 477, 480 (June 1991).

[19] Greenhouse, "A Window on the Court—Limits on Inmates' Habeas Corpus Petitions Illuminate Mood and Agenda of the Justices," N.Y. Times, May 6, 1992, at A1.

[20] The recent scandal in upstate New York involving fake evidence may be merely an indication of a much more pervasive phenomenon. See "Former State Trooper Explains Ways He Fabricated Evidence," N.Y. Times, Apr. 16, 1993, at B5; "Trooper's Fall Shakes Both Police and Public," N.Y. Times, Nov. 15, 1992, at 41; Suro, "Ripples of a Pathologist's Misconduct in Graves and Courts of West Texas," N.Y. Times, Nov. 22, 1992, at 22; Holloway, "False Changes by Woman Culminate in Her Arrest," N.Y. Times, Oct. 18, 1992, at 47.

[21] *Killing Justice—Government Misconduct and the Death Penalty*, Death Penalty Information Center (1992).

[22] Gershman, "The Thin Blue Line: Art or Trial in the Fact-Finding Process?" 9 Pace L. Rev. 275 (1989).

[23] Bedau & Radelet, "Miscarriages of Justice in Potentially Capital Cases," 40 Stan. L. Rev. 21, 36 (1987).

[24] *Id.* at 37.

[25] Rosenbaum, "Inevitable Error: Wrongful New York State Convictions, 1965–1988," 18 N.Y.U. Rev. L. & Soc. Change 807, 809 (1990–1991).

cide convictions have occurred in New York between 1965 and 1988.[26]

Judges, lawyers, and the general public trust the legal system to make reliable determinations of guilt. The right to counsel, confrontation, compulsory process, trial by jury, and heightened standards of proof manifest our society's commitment to truth. We also trust that claims of innocence will be heard before it is too late. Consider in this context the case of Roger Coleman. He was found guilty of raping and murdering Wanda McCoy in 1981, and sentenced to death. A lengthy article in the *New Republic* makes a powerful case for Coleman's innocence.[27] He was represented at trial by court-appointed lawyers who had never before defended a murder case. Proof of his innocence was presented and rejected by a Virginia trial court. Coleman sought to appeal to the state court of appeals, but Coleman's lawyers filed their notice of appeal two days late. Because of this procedural error, the Virginia court rejected his appeal. Coleman then unsuccessfully sought federal habeas corpus review, seeking to have his claim of innocence examined on the merits. The Supreme Court, in upholding the refusal of the federal courts to entertain Coleman's petition on the merits, never discussed whether Coleman might have been innocent.[28] The majority opinion discussed whether a decision of a state court finding procedural default because a lawyer's filing delay is entitled to respect under principles of federalism. The Court said that it was. Coleman was executed on May 22, 1992.

Consider also the case of Leonel Herrera. Herrera was sentenced to death for the murder of a police officer in Texas in 1981.[29] Herrera maintained from the beginning that he was innocent. His conviction was based largely on his own statements, which he claimed were fabricated by the police. Herrera offered several affidavits and eyewitness accounts to prove his innocence, including an eyewitness affidavit from the real murderer's own son. Last February, a federal district judge stayed the execution to allow Herrera to prove his innocence at an evidentiary hearing. The Texas director of criminal justice appealed, and the Court

---

[26] *Id.* at 808.

[27] Tucker, "Dead End," New Republic 21 (May 4, 1992).

[28] Coleman v. Thompson, 111 S. Ct. 2546 (1991).

[29] Herrera v. Collins, 954 F.2d 1029 (5th Cir. 1992).

507

of Appeals for the Fifth Circuit reversed, ordering Herrera's execution for the following day.[30] In dispensing its swift justice, the court wrote the following chilling words: "Herrera's claim of 'actual innocence' presents no substantial claim for relief. The rule is well established that claims of newly discovered evidence, casting doubt on petitioner's guilt, are not cognizable in federal habeas corpus."[31] The court of appeals held, in essence, that the Constitution does not forbid the execution of an innocent man.

Herrera filed a petition in the Supreme Court hours before his scheduled execution. He sought an appeal and a stay of his execution. The Supreme Court responded in a manner that reflects the nightmarish, Kafkaesque quality that so much of current death penalty jurisprudence was acquired. The Court allowed Herrera the opportunity to bring his appeal. Four justices—Justices Blackmun, Stevens, O'Connor, and Souter—granted certiorari, because that number is required under Supreme Court rules for a case to be heard.[32] The question on which these justices granted certiorari was whether it violates the Eighth and Fourteenth Amendments to execute a person who has been convicted of murder, but who is innocent. However, the Supreme Court rules require a majority of five justices to stay an execution. And a majority of the justices—Chief Justice Rehnquist, and Justices White, Kennedy, Scalia, and Thomas—believed that the execution should proceed on schedule, notwithstanding that the Court had decided to hear the condemned man's case.[33] Herrera's execution was set for April 15. Two days before the execution, the Texas court of criminal appeals, by a five to three vote, stayed Herrera's execution to allow the Supreme Court to consider the merits of the claim.[34]

The Court heard arguments last October, and decided the case in January.[35] Speaking for a five-judge majority, Chief Justice Rehnquist wrote that, although Herrera's proof of innocence had some probative value, it came too late. Moreover, he

---

[30] Id.

[31] Id. at 1033.

[32] Herrera v. Collins, 112 S. Ct. 1074 (1992).

[33] Id.

[34] Suro, "Inmate Given Stay to Argue That Execution Would Violate Rights," N.Y. Times, Apr. 14, 1992, at A21.

[35] Herrera v. Collins, 113 S. Ct. at 853.

508

did not present a sufficient showing to entitle him to a hearing to prove his innocence. His only recourse would be to seek executive clemency. Herrera was executed on May 12, 1993.

Under the U.S. criminal justice system, any death case—indeed, virtually every sort of criminal case—from beginning to end is exclusively an exercise of the prosecutor's use, and abuse, of power.[36] Ethically the prosecutor is obligated "to seek justice, not merely to convict."[37] In pursuit of "justice," the prosecutor alone decides what criminal charges to bring, and whether to charge a murder case as a capital case. The prosecutor alone decides whether to allow a defendant to plead guilty, to grant immunity to accomplices, to rely on the testimony of jailhouse informants, or to disclose to the defense exculpatory evidence. All of these decisions are largely unreviewable, and, therefore, subject to abuse. The prosecutor literally decides who goes to jail, and who goes free; who lives, and who dies. The recent prosecutions of John Gotti and Manual Noriega demonstrated astonishingly broad grants of immunity to murderers and drug traffickers so that they would become government witnesses; these people had criminal records far more extensive and serious than the defendants on trial.[38] Public exposés increasingly describe how purchased, and frequently perjurious, testimony by government informants is used to convict defendants, often with a wink and a nod from the prosecutor.[39] Many prosecutors, if they are candid, would admit that testimony of jailhouse stoolpigeons is often utterly unreliable, but unbelievably effective before a jury. Some prosecutors have even been heard to boast that "Any prosecutor can convict a guilty man; it takes a great prosecutor to convict an innocent man."[40]

Concealment by prosecutors of favorable evidence that would assist a defendant in proving his innocence is pervasive and probably accounts for as many miscarriages of justice as any

---

[36] B. Gershman, *Prosecutorial Misconduct* (1985).

[37] ABA *Standards for Ciminal Justice* § 3-1.2(c) (3d ed. 1992).

[38] Johnston, "*No Victory for Panama*," N.Y. Times, Apr. 11, 1992, at 1 (prosecution called forty witnesses who were convicted drug traffickers, fifteen of whom were granted immunity for crimes more serious than those for which Noriega stood trial).

[39] "Use of Jailhouse Informers Reviewed in Los Angeles," N.Y. Times, Jan. 3, 1989, at A14.

[40] Note 22, *supra* at 275.

509

other single factor.[41] Prosecutors, because of their superior resources and early involvement with police in criminal investigations, invariably accumulate evidence that may cast doubt on a defendant's guilt. A prosecutor is legally and ethically obligated to turn over this evidence to the defense.[42] Many prosecutors obey these rules. Many other prosecutors, however, violate these rules, sometimes inadvertently, sometimes willfully. The published decisions describing such misconduct are merely the tip of the iceberg; most of this misconduct occurs beyond public or judicial scrutiny, in the twilight zone of criminal justice of which only prosecutors and police are aware. Moreover, the absence of meaningful professional discipline of prosecutors for such misconduct makes these tactics almost routine, and a cause for deep concern.[43]

Courts, bar associations, and legislatures should be much more alert to this quagmire in criminal justice. Reversals of convictions should be required automatically for the deliberate suppression of evidence. Disciplinary sanctions against prosecutors should be the norm rather than the exception. Legislation should be enacted making it a crime for prosecutors to willfully suppress evidence resulting in a defendant's wrongful conviction, the degree of the prosecutor's culpability related to the gravity of the conviction.

It should come as no surprise that the Supreme Court and the federal courts have abdicated much of their responsibility to ensure high standards for prosecutors.[44] However, state courts occasionally have filled this breach. Some state courts, notably the New York State Court of Appeals, have affirmatively used

---

[41] The cases of prosecutorial suppression of evidence are legion. See B. Gershman, *Prosecutorial Misconduct*, Ch. 5. Very recently, in People v. Alfred Davis, 81 N.Y.2d 281 (1993), the New York Court of Appeals unanimously reversed a conviction obtained by the Manhattan district attorney for suppressing exculpatory evidence. See also "The 'Brady' Rule: Is It Working?" Nat'l L.J. 1 (May 17, 1993).

[42] Brady v. Maryland, 373 U.S. 83 (1963). See also *ABA Standards for Criminal Justice* § 3-3.11(a) (3d ed. 1992).

[43] Rosen, "Disciplinary Sanctions Against Prosecutors for 'Brady' Violations: A Paper Tiger," 65 N.C.L. Rev. 693 (1987).

[44] See United States v. Williams, 112 S. Ct. 1735 (1992) (federal courts have no supervisory authority over prosecutorial suppression of exculpatory evidence before grand juries); United States v. Hasting, 461 U.S. 499 (1983) (federal courts may not use supervisory power to deter prosecutorial misconduct without first determining whether misconduct was harmless error).

510

their own state constitutions to protect individual rights when the federal Constitution, as interpreted by the Supreme Court, fails to provide adequate protection.[45] This "new federalism" is a healthy and welcome legal development, particularly at a time when fair play for persons charged with crime is not a popular view.

Racial Prejudice

Racial prejudice continues to haunt U.S. criminal justice. In its recent report, the New York State Judicial Commission on Minorities decried what it saw as the many similarities between apartheid and the travesties of justice found to exist in the U.S. South. The commission's findings include the frequency of all-white juries in counties of substantial minority populations; minorities clustered in the worst courthouses in the state; blacks receiving sentences of incarceration where whites do not, and longer sentences than similarly situated whites; underrepresentation of minorities as administgrators, despite their availability in the labor pool; and judges taking twice as long to explain to whites certain of their rights as they do to blacks. In short, the commission concluded, "there is in New York State in the 1990's the reality of a biased court system."[46]

Racial discrimination in the application of the death penalty is a window to racial discrimination generally. One half of the persons on death row in the United States are black or hispanic. But that is not the real story. Perhaps the most shocking statistic reveals that defendants charged with killing white victims are at least four times, and as much as eight times, more likely to receive a death sentence as those charged with killing black victims in otherwise similar cases. The most carefully documented study, the Baldus study, examined over 2,000 murder cases in Georgia, and isolated 230 nonracial variables.[47] The study concluded that a defendant's odds of receiving a death

---

[45] See, e.g., People v. Vilardi, 76 N.Y.2d 67, 556 N.Y.S.2d 518, 555 N.E.2d 915 (1990) (refusing to apply Supreme Court decision limiting prosecutor's disclosure obligations). See also Kaye, "Dual Constitutionalism in Practice and Principle," 61 St. John's L. Rev. 399 (1987); Brennan, "State Constitutions and the Protection of Individual Rights," 90 Harv. L. Rev. 489 (1977).

[46] See note 10, *supra*.

[47] D. Baldus, G. Woodworth & C. Pulaski, Jr., *Equal Justice and the Death Penalty: An Empirical Analysis* (1990).

511

sentence were 4.3 times greater if the victim was white than if the victim was black. In some states, disparities are even higher.[48] In Maryland, killers of whites are eight times more likely to be sentenced to death than killers of blacks; in Arkansas, they are six times more likely; and in Texas, they are five times more likely.[49] The race of the victim also operates as a "silent aggravating circumstance" in the jury's decision to impose the death penalty.[50]

In *McCleskey v. Kemp*,[51] the Supreme Court, although accepting the validity of the Baldus study, declined to find the practice unconstitutionally discriminatory. *McCleskey* has been called the "Dred Scott" decision of this century.[52] Justice Brennan, in one of his greatest dissents, recalled that 130 years ago the Supreme Court denied U.S. citizenship to blacks, and a mere 3 generations ago sanctioned racial segregation. Warren McCleskey's evidence, Justice Brennan wrote, confronts us with "disturbing proof" that "we remain imprisoned by the past as long as we deny its influence in the present."[53] "It is tempting to pretend," he said, "that minorities on death row share a fate in no way connected to our own." This is "an illusion . . . for the reverberations of injustice are not so easily confined. . . . [T]he way in which we choose those who will die reveals the depth of moral commitment among the living." Justice Brennan concluded:

> The court's decision today will not change what attorneys in Georgia tell other Warren McCleskeys about their chances of execution. Nothing will soften the harsh message they must convey, nor alter the prospect that race undoubtedly will continue to be a topic of discussion. McCleskey's evidence will not have obtained judicial acceptance, but that will not affect what is said on death row. However many criticisms of today's decision may be rendered, these painful conversations will serve as the most eloquent dissents of all.[54]

---

[48] "*Killers of Blacks Escape the Death Penalty*," Dallas Times Herald, Nov. 17, 1985, at 1.

[49] *Id.*

[50] Tabak & Lane, "The Execution of Injustice: A Cost and Lack-of-Benefit Analysis of the Death Penalty," 23 Loy. L.A. L. Rev. 59, 90 (1989).

[51] 481 U.S. 279 (1987).

[52] Kennedy, "McCleskey v. Kemp: Race, Capital Punishment, and the Supreme Court," 101 Harv. L. Rev. 1388, 1389 (1988).

[53] 481 U.S. at 344.

[54] *Id.* at 344–345.

512

Warren McCleskey was executed on September 25, 1991.

Racial injustice in jury selection also continues unabated. *Batson v. Kentucky*[55] sought to eliminate such discrimination. But blacks and other minorities continue to be excluded from juries, and both prosecutors and defense lawyers continue to provide spurious reasons for the strikes.[56] The California jury that acquitted the four police officers of beating Rodney King did not include any blacks. The blatant circumvention of *Batson* in New York State recently prompted Judge Bellacosa, in an opinion joined by Chief Judge Wachtler and Judge Titone, to urge the total elimination of peremptory challenges.[57] Judge Bellacosa wrote that ''peremptories have outlived their usefulness and, ironically, appear to be disguising discrimination—not minimizing it, and clearly not eliminating it.''[58]

Incompetence of Counsel

Finally, the inadequacy of representation, which all members of the legal profession should take very seriously, needs to be addressed. The ability of public defenders and appointed counsel to deliver quality defense services is being threatened by lack of funds, huge volume, and often inept training and supervision.[59] The vast majority of criminal defendants in New York State and nationwide are too poor to afford private counsel and therefore must rely for their constitutionally guaranteed defense on legal aid and counsel assigned by the court. There are many talented, although grossly underpaid, attorneys representing indigent defendants. The quality of representation in New York State is probably much higher than the quality of representation nationwide. The dismal level of indigent representation nationwide is particularly noticeable in those jurisdictions that allow capital punishment. An American Bar Association task force recently concluded that ''the inadequacy and inadequate compensation of counsel at trial'' was one of the ''principal failings'' of the capital

---

[55] 476 U.S. 79 (1986).

[56] See, e.g., Hernandez v. New York, 111 S. Ct. 1859 (1991); People v. Kern, 75 N.Y.2d 638, 554 N.E.2d 1235, 555 N.Y.S.2d 647 (1990).

[57] People v. Bolling, 79 N.Y.2d 317, 591 N.E.2d 1136, 582 N.Y.S.2d 950 (1992) (concurring opinion).

[58] 79 N.Y.2d at 326.

[59] Gershman, ''Defending the Poor,'' 29 Trial 47 (March 1993).

513

punishment system.[60] All too often defense lawyers are ill-trained and unprepared. Consider the following examples.[61]

1. Larry Heath was executed last year. His court-appointed lawyer's appellate brief contained only a single page of argument, raised only a single issue, and cited only a single legal precedent.

2. Herbert Richardson was executed in 1989. His appellate brief failed to mention that at his sentencing hearing the prosecutor argued, without any basis in the record, but with no objection by defense counsel, that Richardson should be sentenced to death because he belonged to a black muslim organization in New York, had killed a woman in New Jersey, and had been dishonorably discharged from the military. Richardson's lawyer was later disbarred for other reasons.

3. Arthur Jones was executed in 1986. He was represented at trial by a court-appointed lawyer who made no opening or closing statement and offered no evidence at the penalty phase. During the postconviction phase he was represented by a sole practitioner just two years out of law school who had never handled a capital case.

4. Horace Dunkins, a mentally retarded black man who was executed in 1989, was represented by a lawyer so incompetent that the jury was never told that Dunkins was mentally retarded. Dunkins had an IQ of sixty-five and the mental age of a ten-year-old.

5. The capital trial of a battered woman was interrupted for a day when her defense lawyer appeared in court so intoxicated that he was held in contempt and sent to jail for the day and night.

6. A defense lawyer requested an adjournment between the guilt phase and penalty phase of a murder trial so that he could read the state's death penalty statute.

7. A lawyer's brief was sent back to him by the appellate court because it did not cite a single case.

---

[60] ABA Task Force Report, *Toward a More Just and Effective System of Review in State Death Penalty Cases* 7 (Aug. 1990).

[61] The following examples were provided by Stephen B. Bright, Esq., Director, Southern Center for Human Rights, in a Statement to the Committee on the Judiciary, U.S. Senate, regarding the nomination of Ed Carnes to the U.S. Court of Appeals for the Eleventh Circuit (Apr. 1, 1992).

514

8. A capital defendant was visited only once by his lawyer in eight years. In another case, the lawyer never visited his client in eight years.

One confronts these examples with shock and dismay. Are they merely aberrations? Or do they reflect a much more prevalent condition? Clearly, incompetent lawyering and injustice go hand in hand.

While persons of means are able to obtain "the best counsel money can buy,"[62] these lawyers are also finding their role increasingly more difficult to perform effectively. More and more privately retained lawyers are being subpoenaed to testify against their clients, particularly in connection with their receipt of legal fees, and have been jailed for refusing to testify before grand juries.[63] Prosecutors are increasingly using the statutory summonsing power of the Internal Revenue Service to force criminal defense lawyers to disclose the identities of clients who pay cash.[64] There has been rising incidence of law office searches, disqualification of attorneys, forfeiture of attorney fees, and prosecution of attorneys under obstruction of justice statutes for giving legal advise to clients.[65] The future of our adversary system is at risk by these tactics.

Conclusion

The law can be a vital force for justice, as well as for injustice. We look to it to find rational solutions to problems and disputes, and we hope that these solutions achieve justice. When that happens, the law has a meaning beyond its often arid and sterile language. When that does not happen, when innocent persons are convicted, when racism continues to infect our courts, and when lawyers fail in their obligations, we confront injustice. It is at that time that those who participate in the criminal justice system can more fully appreciate their own responsibility to dispense justice, and to eliminate injustice.

---

[62] Morris v. Slappy, 461 U.S. 1, 23 (1983) (Brennan, J., concurring).

[63] Stern & Hoffman, "Privileged Informers: The Attorney-Subpoena Problem and a Proposal for Reform," 136 U. Pa. L. Rev. 1783 (1988).

[64] United States v. Goldberger & Dubin, 935 F.2d 501 (2d Cir. 1991).

[65] Gershman, "The New Prosecutors," 53 U. Pitt. L. Rev. 393 (1992).

515

Crime, Law and Social Change **21**: 127–154, 1994.

Review essay

The triumph of vengeance over retribution: the United States Supreme Court and the death penalty

KENNETH C. HAAS

University of Delaware, Criminal Justice Program, Newark, DE 19716, USA

Abstract. In this article the author uses a review of Welsh S. White's *The Death Penalty in the Nineties* as a framework for analyzing recent trends in the United States Supreme Court's death penalty jurisprudence. Since 1976 the Supreme Court has upheld the constitutionality of capital punishment at least in part on the notion that the death penalty serves the useful social purpose of retribution. This article, however, contends that it is imperative to distinguish between retribution and vengeance as rationales for criminal punishment. Modern retributive theory calls for punishments to be guided by considerations of proportionality, fairness, and equality. Vengeance-based punishments, on the other hand, are aimed at satisfying the victim's and society's desire for retaliation and are not limited by the retributive principle that punishment must be proportionate to the severity of the crime and the moral blameworthiness of the offender. The article analyzes recent Supreme Court decisions that are not examined in *The Death Penalty in the Nineties* – decisions that allow the introduction of victim-impact evidence into capital sentencing proceedings and permit the death penalty to be imposed on 16-year-old offenders, mentally retarded defendants, and those who neither kill nor intend to kill. These decisions, it is argued, demonstrate that the contemporary Court has bestowed judicial approval on vengeance as an acceptable justification for capital punishment.

Introduction

American opponents of capital punishment were jubilant in 1972 when the United States Supreme Court struck down as unconstitutional the death sentences of all 558 people then on death row.[1] The High Court's ruling in *Furman v. Georgia*[2] invalidated all then-existing state and federal death penalty laws on the ground that these laws were unconstitutional because of the arbitrary and discriminatory way in which they were applied. The major constitutional problem with these laws, according to the five justices who made up the *Furman* majority, was that they granted judges and juries unguided and virtually unregulated discretion to decide whether capital defendants live or die. Although the Court did not declare that capital punishment in and of itself was unconstitu-

---

* Welsh S. White, *The Death Penalty in the Nineties: An Examination of the Modern System of Capital Punishment* (AnnArbor: University of Michigan Press, 1991), 223 pp., hardback S36.50, paperback $18.95.

tional, many abolitionists were convinced that this would surely be the next step.

In 1976, however, the Court upheld new death penalty laws in *Gregg v. Georgia,*[3] *Proffitt v. Florida,*[4] and *Jurek v. Texas.*[5] Although no two states have identical death penalty laws, all of the statutes approved in the 1976 cases require the jury (or, in a few states, the judge) to consider certain "aggravating" and "mitigating" factors concerning the defendant's crime and character, and then sentence him to either death or life imprisonment. A seven-to-two majority soundly rejected both the argument that executions are inherently unconstitutional and the assertion that it is humanly impossible to devise any death penalty system that is not arbitrary and does not discriminate on the basis of race, wealth, age, gender, or other nonlegal factors that have nothing to do with the nature of the offense and the offender's blameworthiness.

In the years since the *Gregg-Proffitt-Jurek* holdings, the Court, increasingly dominated by the appointees of Presidents Nixon, Reagan, and Bush, has become an activist, pro-execution tribunal that has succeeded in pushing the Eighth Amendment's prohibition of cruel and unusual punishment well out of the way of the legislative power. As a result, the United States – the only western industrial nation that still executes criminals – has a death-row population that will soon reach 3,000 men and women.[6]

Since the Supreme Court has played an obvious and prominent role in breathing life back into the death penalty, one would think that there would be more than a few contemporary books that provide a comprehensive and reasonably up-to-date analysis of the Court's death penalty jurisprudence. However, the only book that even comes close to filling the need for such a book is Welsh S. White's *The Death Penalty in the Nineties: An Examination of the Modern System of Capital Punishment.* White, currently Professor of Law at the University of Pittsburgh, is an exceptionally sophisticated legal analyst. He has published extensively on the law of capital punishment, and this book is an updated version of his earlier book, *The Death Penalty in the Eighties.*

It is important to note, however, that *The Death Penalty in the Nineties* is limited both in purpose and in scope. As Professor White makes clear in the introductory chapter, "the purpose of this book is to examine the modern system of capital punishment" (p. 2). Consequently, prospective readers should not be misled by the advertising on the back cover of the paperback edition, which incorrectly states that the book "provides an exposition of the Supreme Court's major capital punishment decisions and examines the effect of these decisions from a number of perspectives." In fact, the book virtually ignores some of the Court's most significant death penalty rulings – rulings that the Court handed down in advance of arguably less momentous decisions that *are* covered in the book. Professor White focuses almost exclusively on procedural aspects of capital trials and the capital-appeals process. Consequently, there is little or no discussion of death penalty cases in which the Court addressed important substantive issues concerning the constitutionality of executing certain kinds of defendants – the young, the mentally retarded, the insane, those who have not actually taken another human life, and other special groups of defendants.

Surprisingly, for example, there is no discussion of *Stanford v. Kentucky*,[7] the 1989 decision upholding state laws that permit the execution of those who commit capital crimes at the age of 16. Not only is this one of the Court's most significant post-*Gregg* holdings, but Justice Antonin Scalia's *Stanford* opinion arguably is the most telling – and troubling – statement the justices have yet issued on the future of capital punishment in the United States.[8] Justice Scalia articulated a theory of extraordinary judicial deference to state legislatures in cases in which death penalty laws are challenged on Eighth Amendment grounds. Such cases, he argued, require the death-sentenced inmate either (1) to prove that his punishment would have been considered cruel and unusual by eighteenth century Americans at the time the Bill of Rights was adopted[9] or (2) to meet the heavy burden of proving that there is a contemporary national consensus that his punishment is cruel and unusual.[10]

Moreover, Justice Scalia asserted that the Court will no longer consider what he calls "ethioscientific" evidence in support of the contention that such a consensus exists.[11] Public opinion studies and the positions adopted by professional associations, therefore, are irrelevant;[12] only "objective indicia", the most important of which are the laws passed by state legislatures, are to be taken into account.[13] The Eighth Amendment, according to *Stanford*, must be taken literally. A challenged punishment must be *both* cruel and unusual to fail the Court's Eighth Amendment tests.[14] In other words, a punishment that is acknowledged to be cruel will nevertheless withstand constitutional challenge if a majority of the justices are satisfied that enough states still authorize it. Just how many are enough will be determined on a case-by-case basis.

This will strike many as a curious way to build a stable, predictable, and principled body of death penalty law, and that is why *Stanford v. Kentucky* deserves careful analysis in a book that supposedly "provides an exposition of the Supreme Court's major capital punishment decisions." *Stanford*, however, is one of several significant death penalty decisions that are not examined in any detail in *The Death Penalty in the Nineties*. Two very important decisions, for example, that are relegated to one-sentence footnotes are *Ford v. Wainwright*[15] and *Penry v. Lynaugh*,[16] In *Ford*, the Court held that a prisoner who has been sentenced to die but who becomes insane by the time of his scheduled execution cannot be executed unless and until his sanity is restored. Yet, in *Penry*, the Court gave the states constitutional permission to execute mentally retarded offenders. Surely, these seemingly contradictory holdings are important enough to deserve a thorough analysis in a book devoted to explaining legal aspects of the American system of capital punishment.

An equally perplexing omission is the *Coker-Enmund-Tison* line of cases, dealing with the question of whether a defendant who does not kill, attempt to kill, or intend to kill can be sentenced to death. Only one paragraph is devoted to *Coker v. Georgia*,[17] the controversial 1977 case in which the Court held that death is an impermissible punishment for rape. Similarly, there is no discussion of the 1982 *Enmund v. Florida*[18] decision, in which the Court declared that those who participate in a felony that leads to murder but who do not actually kill or intend to kill cannot be executed. And to complete this trilogy of neglected but important rulings, Professor White offers no analysis of *Tison v. Arizona*,[19] a major 1987 decision that tore the heart out of *Enmund* by holding that those who neither kill nor intend to kill but who participate in a felony in which someone else commits murder can be executed if their role in the underlying felony was "major" and if their conduct demonstrated a "reckless disregard for human life."[20]

Retribution vs. vengeance

Tison is one of several recent decisions that bestow judicial approval on vengeance – as opposed to retribution – as an acceptable justification for the punishment of death. Unfortunately, these are the very decisions that are either missing or neglected in *The Death Penalty in the Nineties*. As a result, readers will not grasp the extent to which the contemporary Supreme Court has pursued an activist pro-death penalty agenda that has increasingly legitimized vengeance as a primary rationale for criminal punishment generally and for capital punishment in particular.

In recent years, a number of legal scholars, most notably Paul Boudreaux,[21] have challenged the conventional assumption that retribution and vengeance are synonoymous, or as a leading criminal justice textbook puts it, that "[r]etribution is societal vengeance."[22] Boudreaux contends that it is imperative to distinguish between *social retribution*, which means that "as a society we must punish the criminal because he deserves punishment,"[23] and *individual vengeance,* which Boudreaux defines as "an individual's desire to punish a criminal because the individual gains satisfaction from seeing or knowing that the person receives punishment."[24] Aggregated individual vengeance, Boudreaux argues, is superior to social retribution as a rationale for punishment primarily because it can be easily incorporated into a utilitarian model of punishment along with such other traditional justifications for punishment as deterrence, incapacitation, and rehabilitation.[25] Social retribution, on the other hand, fails miserably as a utilitarian rationale because "[b]y punishing a person solely for social retribution, government is making one person worse off – the offender suffers in prison – while no one is made better off."[26]

Who benefits when we frankly acknowledge aggregated individual vengeance rather than social retribution as a leading rationale for inflicting punishment on criminal offenders? According to Boudreaux, the major beneficiaries of this approach are crime victims and all other "[m]embers of society [who] gain satisfaction, or gain 'pleasure,' from seeing or knowing that a criminal offender receives punishment."[27]

> Far from being a vulgar or undesirable human emotion, this satisfaction is an understandable and inescapable facet of human behavior. Every child who has either experienced harassment or witnessed the abuse of a friend by a bully manifests this satisfaction when the bully gets his or her comeuppance. This same emotion, at different levels, exists in nearly every individual.... Today there is no reason why a civilized government may not rationally justify criminal punishment partly on the aggregated desire of individuals in the society to see that a person who has broken its laws receives punishment.[28]

Boudreaux' arguments can be challenged on several fronts, but the major problem is his narrow definition of retribution, or what he calls social retribution. By defining social retribution simply as punishing the offender because he deserves punishment, Boudreaux all but ignores an essential element of retributive theory – the principle of proportionality. Boudreaux simply asserts that social retribution "is related to but separate from the notion of proportionality...."[29] Moreover, he defines proportionality as nothing more than "the moral sense that extreme penalties for many crimes punish the offender too much for our sense of justice."[30]

Most retributive theorists, however, consider proportionality to be an indispensable part of any fair-minded definition of retribution, and they typically define proportionality in terms of actual societal efforts to achieve a proportionate or commensurate relationship between the gravity of the offense and the severity of the punishment (i.e. penal codes, sentencing laws, and court decisions striking down punishments that are found to be excessively harsh).[31] As H.L.A. Hart stressed in *Punishment and Responsibility*, modern retributive theory includes the idea of proportionality to the extent that "the relative gravity of punishments is to reflect [the] moral gravity of offenses; murder is to be punished more severely than theft; intentional killing more severely than unintentionally causing death through carelessness."[32] Indeed, although Hart's theory of punishment emphasized utilitarian considerations, it incorporated this aspect of retributivism by ruling out disproportionately severe punishments, even if they could be shown to be effective in deterring crime, rehabilitating the offender, or achieving other utilitarian objectives.[33]

Proportionality is also an essential element in Igor Primoratz' recent elaboration of a retributive theory of punishment that makes no concession to utilitarianism. In *Justifyinq Legal Punishment*, Primoratz argues that a purely retributive theory of punishment can be best advanced by viewing retribution as a positive principle, one that demands punishment of the guilty, but also recognizes that the specific offense committed is the only legitimate basis of the state's right to punish.[34] It thus is unjust to allow the guilty to go unpunished, to punish the innocent, or to punish the guilty by disproportionately severe sentences.[35] Although overly harsh or otherwise unjust punishments may sometimes serve the purposes of deterrence or other legitimate governmental interests and thus be justifiable on strictly utilitarian grounds, they are not acceptable under Primoratz' variety of retributivism, which holds that the state achieves justice only when it "treat[s] offenders according to their deserts, [giving] them what they deserve, not more and not less."[36]

This is not to say that modern retributivists insist on a literal application of the strict, "eye for an eye" equivalence between crime and punishment established by the *lex talionis*. No retributivist of any repute advocates that we break into the homes of convicted burglars or burn down the homes of convicted arsonists. Modern retributive theory calls for a system of objectively fair punishments that are proportional, not identical, to the offenses committed.[37] It is recognized that the effort to tailor punishments to correspond with the gravity of offenses is central to a fair and workable system of criminal law, but that it is not necessary, desirable, or humanly possible to devise a precise mathematical formula that would give each offender precisely the amount of suffering that his or her offense calls for.[38]

Equally important, one can be a retributivist and still renounce the death penalty.[39] The logic of this position has been succinctly explained by Hugo Adam Bedau:

> [R]etributive justice need not be thought of as consisting in *lex talionis* . One may reject that principle as too crude and still embrace the retributive principle that the severity of punishments should be graded according to the gravity of the offense. Even though one need not claim that life imprisonment (or any kind of punishment other than death) "fits" the crime of murder, one can claim that this punishment is the proper one for murder. To do this, the schedule of punishments accepted by society must be arranged so that this mode of imprisonment is the most severe punishment used. Opponents of the death penalty need not reject this principle of retributive justice, even though they must reject a literal *lex talionis*.[40]

Thus, while advocates of Boudreaux' theory of vengenace seemingly are duty bound to support the death penalty as the appropriate punishment for murder if that is what it takes to give "pleasure"and "satisfaction" to the victim's family and other aggrieved members of society,[41] the retributivist is free (although not obligated) to argue that the death penalty succeeds only in teaching all of us that life is not so sacred after all and that life in prison is the most fitting way to punish convicted murderers.

Modern retributivists take great pains to distinguish their views from those who advocate revenge theories of punishment.[42] By insisting that penalties be scaled commensurately with the seriousness of offenses and the blameworthiness of offenders, they seek to make sure that retribution will not be, as Oliver Wendell Holmes once called it, "only vengeance in disguise."[43] This, however, is no easy task. It is often difficult to distinguish between vengeance and retribution because, as Emile Durkheim stressed, the public's passion for vengeance is an extraordinarily powerful force and it will probably always play a major role in the punishment of criminals.[44] Contemporary penologists may extol the virtues of rationality and sentencing systems based on the unemotional pursuit of utilitarian objectives, but vengeance is "the soul of punishment" and remains the primary motivation underlying the penal practices of modern societies.[45]

But the *motivation for punishment* must not be confused with the question of the *amount of punishment* to be meted out for particular crimes, and this is what ultimately separates vengeance from retribution. Vengeance – whether carried out by the vigilante or by the government – is an unmeasured infliction of punishment on the offender. It is aimed at satisfying the victim's and society's desire for retaliation, and it is not limited by considerations of desert, proportionality, fairness, or equality. Retribution, on the other hand, is a measured infliction of punishment that is imposed by courts and based on careful consideration of the severity of the offense and the offender's blameworthiness and deservedness. It is rooted in the principle of proportionality and the belief that a civilized society must set moral limits on the amount of punishment to be inflicted on wrongdoers. Moreover, retribution, unlike vengeance, reflects "the evolving standards of decency that mark the progress of a maturing society."[46]

The rise of just-deserts retributivism

The view that retribution can – and must – be distinguished from vengeance has achieved increasing acceptance among legal scholars. The distinction between the two is grounded in the understanding that the desire for vengeance often conflicts with the retributive goal of equal and proportionate sentencing. The Report of the Royal Commission on Capital Punishment, for example, took the position that retribution "must always be an essential element in any form of punishment," but only in the sense that "the measure of the punishment must not be greater than the offense deserves."[47] However, vengeance – "the satisfaction by the State of a wronged individual's desire to be avenged"[48] – was dismissed as a primitive concept with little support in modern penological thought.[49]

The flight from vengeance and the call for a principled brand of retribution – one steeped in considerations of fairness and proportionality – gradually gained momentum in the years following the Report of the Royal Commission. In the 1970s and 1980s, the work of Andrew von Hirsch,[50] Richard G. Singer,[51] and Norval Morris[52] was especially influential in asserting that a system of fair and graduated punishments – "just deserts" or "commensurate deserts" – was not only superior to the mindless infliction of vengeance, but offered a way to avoid the injustices, excesses, and failures of punishments that were based overwhelmingly or solely on the utilitarian grounds of rehabilitation, deterrence, and incapacitation. These "new retributivists" never agreed on a single theory of retribution,[53] but they shared a sense of revulsion for the excesses of the indeterminate sentencing laws that dominated American criminal sentencing practices for much of the twentieth century.[54] These laws were premised on the belief that the criminal was morally "sick" and could be rehabilitated by participating in modern correctional treatment programs.[55] But, of course, since there was no way to know how long the "cure" would take in every case, the indeterminate sentence left the release decision to the prison treatment staff and ultimately to the parole board. All too often, correctional discretion led to excessively long sentences – prison terms extending well beyond any reasonable conception of proportionality – for prisoners who refused or never learned how to play the "treatment game."[56] Typically, the losers of this game were young, black offenders, while the beneficiaries were white, middle- or upper-class business and government offenders.[57]

The new retributivists also were concerned about the potential unfairness and exploitability of punishments imposed primarily for purposes of general deterrence.[58] Judges, for example, "will sometimes impose sentences which are markedly more severe than the norm for the express purpose of increasing their deterrent effect."[59] This kind of exemplary sentence is nothing less than the intentional infliction of unequal justice. To the retributivists, such examples convincingly demonstrate that the deterrence rationale can lead to punishments that are just as arbitrary and excessively harsh as those imposed under indeterminate-sentencing schemes.[60]

Similarly, the incapacitation rationale was targeted for considerable criticism by the new retributivists.[61] As Andrew von Hirsch put it, an offender simply "does not *deserve* to be punished more severely on account of a crime he is predicted to commit, however likely its occurrence."[62] Incapacitation has been used as an excuse for imposing lengthy prison sentences on relatively minor offenders who espouse politically unpopular views[63] or who refuse to conform to the prison regimen,[64] and it has been used to justify the death penalty for those who strike jurors as dangerous or threatening not so much because of what *they have done,* but because of *how they are different* in terms of race-,ethnicity, or social background.[65] Incapacitative arguments crumble when confronted with the overwhelming evidence that no one – certainly not psychiatrists, judges, or parole boards – can accurately predict future dangerousness.[66] Incapacitation thus allows harsh and disproportionately severe punishments to be meted out not on the basis of the offender's actual conduct, but on the basis of highly unreliable predictions of recidivism. Having demonstrated that sentencing schemes dominated by the utilitarian goals of rehabilitation, deterrence, and incapacitation so readily lead to excessive and unequal punishments, the new retributivists extolled the virtues of desert and equality as the defining principles of any truly fair system of punishment.

The resurgence of vengeance

Today the just-deserts version of retributivism remains influential both in academia and in American sentencing practices.[67] In recent years, however, the just-deserts model has been challenged by the representatives of two very different schools of thought. First, in their thought-provoking book *Not Just Deserts*, John Braithwaite and Philip Pettit have criticized just-deserts retributivism as an "inherently inadequate theory" that is too narrowly construed to provide satisfactory answers to such important questions as 'Why punish?' and 'How to punish?'[68] It is particularly ironic, contend Braithwaite and Pettit, that although just-deserts theory can be used to rank crimes according to such factors as the harm done and the offender's culpability, it cannot tell us in a theoretically consistent or non-arbitrary manner what the *deserved* level or method of punishments for any given offense should be.[69]

Equally important, Braithwaite and Pettit predict that the just-deserts variety of retributivism inevitably will fall victim to "law and order" politicians who will quickly discard the more humanitarian and egalitarian aspects of just-deserts theory because they know that "their press releases are most likely to get a run by appealing to simple-minded vengeance."[70]

> When you play the game of criminal justice on the field of retribution, you play it on the home ground of conservative law-and-order politicians. You give full rein to those who play to the sense of normality of the majority, urging them to tyrannize the minority. Once all the players agree that retribution, or giving people what they deserve, is the rationale for punishment, the genteel visions of liberal retributivists count for nought.[71]

In the long run, therefore, the new retributivism will "make the community feel more comfortable with punishment," encouraging such policies as doing away with parole, building more prisons, and expanding the reach of the death penalty.[72]

Braithwaite and Pettit proffer an alternative theory – republican theory – advertised as comprehensive, consequentialist, and capable of practical application.[73] Republican theory, if implemented, would foster a host of policies that would promote individual liberty, government accountability, greater access to rehabilitative services, and ultimately, a substantial decline in prison populations.[74] Braithwaite and Pettit also believe that their theory is "capable of incremental application" and thus could result in "politically realistic policy change."[75]

Not Just Deserts is tightly argued and theoretically sophisticated. But by no stretch of the imagination can it be portrayed as politically realistic, at least not as applied to the United States in the 1990s. It may in fact be too late for republican theory in the United States because, as Braithwaite and Pettit feared, just-deserts theories of punishment may have already been co-opted by public officials who understand that the greatest political rewards accrue to those who master the rhetoric of vengeance.

And, indeed, vengeance *is* the second major challenge to the just-deserts brand of retributivism. Paul Boudreaux' argument that aggregated individual vengeance is superior to social retribution as a rationale for criminal punishment is one of several noteworthy efforts to rehabilitate vengeance by stripping it of its usual pejorative connotations. In particular, philosophical defenders of the death penalty have increasingly advanced vengeance as a morally sound rationale for executing criminals. For example, in *For Capital Punishment*, Walter Berns laments our loss of a sense of "moral community"[76] and decries the efforts of "the intellectual community" to make us ashamed of our justifiable anger toward criminals.[77] He urges us, instead, to satisfy that anger by seeing to it that the courts impose punishments that "fit the sentiments of the law-abiding population rather than the crime."[78] "[This] rewards the law-abiding by satisfying the anger he feels at the sight of crime... and by rewarding teaches law-abidingness."[79]

Similarly, Ernest van den Haag condemns our "loss of nerve" when we hesitate to assert our need for lethal revenge.[80] He frankly acknowledges that vengeance is the motive for (though not necessarily the purpose of) the death penalty,[81] and he calls for the government to fulfill the public's desire for revenge:

> The Lord is often quoted as saying "Vengeance is mine." He did not condemn vengeance. He merely reserved it to Himself – and to the government. For in the same epistle He is also quoted as saying that the ruler is "the minister of God, a revenger, to execute wrath upon him that doeth evil." The religious notion of hell indicates that the biblical God favored harsh and everlasting punishment for some. However, particularly in a secular society, we cannot wait for the day of judgment to see murderers

consigned to hell. Our courts must "execute wrath upon him that doeth evil" here and now.[82]

What must be acknowledged – and what is not acknowledged in *The Death Penalty in the Nineties* – is that the vengeance-oriented philosophy advocated by Boudreaux, van den Haag, and Berns is now firmly in control of the United States Supreme Court's death penalty jurisprudence. The just-deserts version of retributivism is rarely evident these days, and republican theory has not yet made an appearance. Instead, the Court's death penalty decision making increasingly reflects the ascendancy of a brand of vengeance that is victim-oriented, arbitrary, discriminatory, and not limited by considerations of proportionality.

Tison v. Arizona: An eye for an eye and then some

The triumph of vengeance is exemplified by the *Tison* decision,[83] which, as noted earlier, scarcely makes an appearance in *The Death Penalty in the Nineties*. Raymond, Ricky, and Donald Tison planned and participated in the prison escape of their father Gary Tison and their father's friend Randy Greenawalt, both of whom were convicted murderers. Although the breakout went smoothly and was accomplished with no injuries or loss of life, the Tisons' Lincoln automobile soon lost a tire on a desert road and the group decided to flag down a passing motorist and steal his car. Raymond Tison stood out in the highway ostensibly seeking help, and a Mazda occupied by John Lyons, his wife, his 2-year-old son, and his 15-year-old niece, pulled over to render aid. The rest of the Tisons and Randy Greenawalt promptly emerged from the side of the road, ordered the Lyons family out of their car, and led them from the Mazda to the Lincoln, which had been driven farther into the desert. Gary Tison then told his three sons to go back to the Mazda to get some water. Shortly thereafter, Gary Tison and Randy Greenawalt lined up their four captives and brutally shotgunned them to death.[84]

Ricky and Raymond subsequently testified that they were surprised by the shooting.[85] Nevertheless, as Justice Sandra Day O'Connor noted in her *Tison* majority opinion, neither brother made an effort to help the victims.[86] Moreover, rather than leave their father at this point, they stayed with the group until they were captured several days later, after a shootout with the police in which Randy Greenawalt was also captured and both their father and their brother Donald were killed.[87] Not surprisingly, Randy Greenawalt was convicted of murder and sentenced to death by an Arizona trial judge who found that the aggravating circumstances surrounding the murder of the Lyons family far outweighed any mitigating circumstances.[88] Randy Greenawalt, after all, had intentionally taken human life, and in 1976 the *Gregg* Court had made it quite clear that no constitutional barriers prevented the execution of "triggermen" who commit first-degree murder.[89]

Ricky and Raymond were also convicted of murder and sentenced to death,[90] but at first glance, their death sentences appeared unlikely to survive constitutional scrutiny. In the 1982 case of *Enmund v. Florida*,[91] the U.S. Supreme Court had reversed the death sentence of a defendant convicted under Florida's felony-murder statute. Earl Enmund had agreed to be the "getaway" driver for a planned robbery of an elderly farm couple. But the victims resisted and in the ensuing shootout, Enmund's accomplices killed the elderly couple.[92] Even though Earl Enmund did not kill or intend to kill anyone, the Florida Supreme Court upheld his death sentence,[93] leading the U.S. Supreme Court to address the question of "whether death is a valid penalty under the Eighth and Fourteenth Amendments for one who neither took life, attempted to take life, nor intended to take life."[94] By a single vote, the Court answered this question in the negative. Citing "overwhelming evidence" of "[s]ociety's rejection of the death penalty for accomplice liability in felony murders,"[95] Justice Byron White's majority opinion concluded:

> For purposes of imposing the death penalty, Enmund's criminal culpability must be limited to his participation in the robbery, and his punishment must be tailored to his personal responsibility and moral guilt. Putting Enmund to death to avenge two killings that he did not commit and had no intention of committing or causing does not measurably contribute to the retributive end of ensuring that the criminal gets his just deserts.[96]

The *Enmund* Court clearly embraced a just-deserts variety of retributivism and just as clearly rejected vengeance as an acceptable goal of capital sentencing. Both the holding and the language of the majority's decision obviously cast considerable doubt on the constitutionality of the death sentences imposed on Ricky and Raymond Tison. Nevertheless, the Arizona Supreme Court affirmed both death sentences in 1984. Although the state tribunal acknowledged that the Tison brothers had not killed anyone, a three-to-two majority adopted an extraordinarily broad definition of "intent to kill" – one that equated "intent to kill" with the forseeability of murder:

> Intend [sic] to kill includes the situation in which the defendant intended, contemplated, or anticipated that lethal force would or might be used or that life would or might be taken in accomplishing the underlying felony.[97]

The court then found that the Tisons should have anticipated that the prison breakout and its aftermath could have led to the use of lethal force. This finding, concluded the majority, was enough to establish that the Tisons "intended" (within the meaning of *Enmund v. Florida*) to kill the Lyons family. Therefore, both death sentences were upheld.[98]

The Tisons next took their case to the United States Supreme Court, no doubt hoping that the justices would repudiate the Arizona Supreme Court's transparent effort to evade the mandate of *Enmund*. But in a five-to-four decision,[99] the Supreme Court went one step further than the state high court, holding that the death penalty is constitutionally permissible even when imposed on a non-triggerman who never formed a specific intent to kill. In her majority opinion Justice O'Connor argued that the longstanding Anglo-American practice of examining whether a defendant intended to kill was not necessarily the best way to determine who deserved to be executed:

> Many who intend to, and do, kill are not criminally liable at all – those who act in self defense or with other justification or excuse. Other intentional homicides, though criminal, are often felt undeserving of the death penalty – those that are the result of provocation. On the other hand, some nonintentional murders may be among the most dangerous and inhumane of all – the person who tortures another not caring whether the victim lives or dies, or the robber who shoots someone in the course of the robbery, utterly indifferent to the fact that the desire to rob may have the unintended consequence of killing the victim as well as taking the victim's property. This reckless indifference to the value of human life may be every bit as shocking to the moral sense as an 'intent to kill'.[100]

To support her argument that the time had come to expand the category of death-eligible defendants, Justice O'Connor pointed out that even after *Enmund*, only ll state death penalty laws specifically forbade the execution of non-triggermen who had demonstrated a reckless disregard for human life while participating in a major way in a felony that led to murder.[101] In cases such as this one, therefore, "the majority of American jurisdictions clearly authorize capital punishment."[102] Reasoning that the Court was not constitutionally obligated to ratify a minority position,[103] Justice O'Connor announced that the Eighth Amendment would no longer bar the death penalty in the case of a defendant who neither killed nor intended to kill: "[W]e simply hold that major participation in [a felony murder], combined with reckless indifference to human life, is sufficient to satisfy the *Enmund* culpability requirement."[104]

Writing on behalf of the four dissenters, Justice Brennan challenged Justice O'Connor's survey of post-*Enmund* state statutes appearing to permit the death penalty for non-triggermen who exhibit a reckless disregard for human life while participating in a felony that leads to murder. It is simply not true, he asserted, that the majority of American jurisdictions authorize capital punishment in such cases.[105] He showed that Justice O'Connor had engaged in results-oriented mathematics by excluding from her survey the states that have abolished capital punishment as well as those that authorize it only in circumstances different from those found in the Tisons' case.[106]

> When these jurisdictions are included, and are considered with those jurisdictions that require a finding of intent to kill in order to impose the death sentence for felony murder, one discovers that approximately three-fifths of American jurisdictions do not authorize the death penalty for a nontriggerman absent a finding that he intended to kill. Thus, contrary to the Court's implication that its view is consonant with that of "the majority of American jurisdictions," the Court's view is itself distinctly the minority position.[107]

Justice Brennan also attacked Justice O'Connor's assertion that limiting the death penalty to those who intend to kill is an inefficious means of identifying the most culpable and dangerous of murderers[108] – an assertion she supported by offering as examples "the person who tortures another not caring whether the victim lives or dies, or the robber who shoots someone in the course of the robbery, utterly indifferent to the fact that the desire to rob may have the unintended consequence of killing the victim as well as taking the victim's property."[109] These examples, Justice Brennan pointed out, are totally inapplicable to the facts of the Tisons' case and in no way support the majority's novel contention that death is a proportionate and constitutional punishment for nontriggermen who neither kill nor intend to kill.[110] The first example, after all, is "the person *who tortures* another not caring whether the victim lives or dies..." and the second is "the robber *who shoots* someone in the course of the robbery...."[111] In both instances the defendant *is* acting as a triggerman – a triggerman who in the traditional legal sense, does intend to kill and, in fact, is quite likely to kill his victim.[112]

Justice O'Connor's two hypothetical cases, according to Justice Brennan, illustrate wanton killings, not unintentional killings.[113] "The element that these wanton killings lack is not intent, but rather premeditation and deliberation."[114] Justice O'Connor's examples would certainly be relevant to the question of whether death is a disproportionate punishment for those *who kill* in a manner that demonstrates a reckless or callous disregard for the value of human life,"[115] "[b]ut the constitutionality of the death penalty for [such] individuals is no more relevant to this case than it was to Enmund, because this case, like *Enmund*, involves accomplices... who not only did not intend to kill, but also have not killed."[116]

Justice Brennan accused the majority of bestowing judicial approval on vengeance as a rationale for the death penalty,[117] and this is precisely what the *Tison* Court did. In *Enmund*, the Court declared that a death sentence must measurably contribute to at least one of the two rationales – retribution and deterrence – that the Court has accepted as justifications for capital punishment.[118] With respect to deterrence, the *Enmund* Court stated that it was "quite unconvinced... that the threat that the death penalty will be imposed for murder will measurably deter one who does not kill and has no intention or purpose that life will be taken."[119] And as noted previously, the *Enmund* majority expressed skepticism that executing Enmund to avenge murders that he did not commit or intend to commit could "measurably contribute to the retributive end of ensuring that the criminal gets his just deserts."[120] The *Tison* Court's decision to approve the death penalty for those who do not kill, attempt to kill, or intend to kill goes beyond even a literal interpretation of the *lex talionis*[121] and can only be viewed as having legitimized vengeance as a third acceptable rationale for imposing the death penalty.[122] Indeed, as Justice Brennan pointed out, *Tison* provides a classic example of Old Testament-style vengeance: "visiting the iniquity of the fathers upon the children...."[123] Unable to punish Gary Tison, the man most responsible for the horrific execution of the Lyons family, the state now has the Supreme Court's blessing to exact vengeance from his sons.[124]

The Booth-Gathers-Payne cases

The triumph of "individual vengeance" over "social retribution," to use Boudreaux' terms, is also epitomized in the *Booth-Gathers-Payne* line of cases. In *Booth v. Maryland*,[125] decided in 1987, the Court held that the Eighth Amendment prohibits capital sentencing juries from considering "victim-impact" evidence – evidence describing the personal characteristics of the victim and the emotional impact of the crime on the victim's family. Writing for the majority, Justice Powell reasoned that this kind of evidence is irrelevant in determining the defendant's moral guilt and poses an impermissible risk of unfair prejudice against the defendant.[126] He pointed out that the Court's precedents require capital juries to make individualized death penalty decisions based on the character of the defendant and the nature of the crime.[127] However, permitting the jury's decision to turn on such idiosyncratic factors as perception that the victim was "a sterling member of the community rather than someone of questionable character" and the extent to which family members happened to be persuasive and articulate in describing their loss would in many cases direct the jury's attention away from the defendant's personal responsibility and moral blameworthiness.[128] This, in turn, "creates a constitutionally unacceptable risk that the jury may impose the death penalty in an arbitrary and capricious manner."[129]

Two years later, in *South Carolina v. Gathers*,[130] the High Court reconsidered the *Booth* ruling, but once again rejected the use of victim-impact evidence. *Gathers* made it clear that *Booth* should be understood to prohibit improper opening and closing statements by the prosecutor regarding the personal qualities and religious convictions of a murder victim.[131] This time Justice Brennan wrote for the Court, emphasizing that prosecutorial arguments focusing on the victim's personal and religious beliefs would introduce factors that in many cases would be irrelevant to the blameworthiness of the defendant.[132] Such arguments thus violate the Court's repeated pronouncements that "[t]he heart of the retribution rationale is that a criminal sentence must be directly related to the personal culpability of the criminal offender."[133]

Both *Booth* and *Gathers* engendered vigorous dissents from the conservative wing of the Court, especially from Justice Scalia.[134] In *Booth*, Justice Scalia made it clear that he saw no constitutional barriers to imposing punishments that violate retributive notions of fairness:

> [T]he principle upon which this Court's opinion rests – that the imposition of capital punishment is to be determined solely on the basis of moral guilt – does not exist, neither in the text of the Constitution, nor in the historic practices of our society, nor even in the opinions of this Court.[135]

Victim-impact evidence enables the sentencing jury to see the full extent of the human suffering inflicted by the defendant, he argued.[136] This may not sufficiently "temper justice with mercy" in all cases, but this was a question "to be decided through the democratic processes of a free people."[137] In his *Gathers* dissent, Justice Scalia urged his colleagues to overrule the *Booth* decision as soon as the opportunity arose, pointedly noting that "[o]verrulings of precedent rarely occur without a change in the Court's personnel."[138]

Surprisingly, the issues raised in *Booth* and *Gathers* are not addressed in *The Death Penalty in the Nineties*. Professor White's failure to analyze the majority and dissenting opinions in *Booth* and *Gathers* is one of the major reasons why readers of the book will not appreciate the extent to which the contemporary Court has become an activist, results-oriented, pro-death penalty tribunal. Justice Scalia's dissenting opinions in *Booth* and *Gathers*, in particular, exemplify the current Court's casual disregard of the cherished doctrine of *stare decisis* – the principle that courts should rarely, and only with the greatest care and circumspection, reverse their settled precedents.[139] Indeed, the conservative justices, most notably Justice Scalia and Chief Justice Rehnquist, have made no effort to camouflage their determination to push the constitutional prohibition against cruel and unusual punishment as far into the woodwork as possible. These justices exercise their power zestfully and with little regard for *stare decisis* and other long-established principles of judicial decision making.

It should come as no surprise, therefore, that shortly after the publication of *The Death Penalty in the Nineties*, Chief Justice Rehnquist triumphantly ended the 1990-91 term by accepting Justice Scalia's invitation to overrule *Booth* and *Gathers*. In *Payne v. Tennesee*[140], the chief justice, joined by Justices Scalia,

O'Connor, White, Kennedy, and Souter, declared that the *Booth* and *Gathers* Courts were simply "wrong in stating that [victim-impact] evidence leads to the arbitrary imposition of the death penalty."[141] *Booth* and *Gathers*, he added, had failed to appreciate the state's legitimate interest in counteracting any mitigating evidence offered on behalf of the defendant by reminding the jury that "just as the murderer should be considered as an individual, so too the victim is an individual whose death represents a unique loss to society and in particular to his family."[142] Accordingly, the Eighth Amendment would no longer prohibit a capital sentencing jury from considering victim-impact evidence concerning the victim's personal characteristics or the emotional impact of the murder on the victim's family.[143]

The *Payne* decision will inevitably lead to the disparate treatment of similarly blameworthy defendants, and in many cases the punishment will be disproportionate to the personal culpability of the offender. The introduction of victim-impact statements can only shift the jury's focus *away* from the actual crime committed by the defendant and encourage sentencing decisions based on passion, prejudice, or caprice. Some defendants will escape the executioner because the victim was not well liked and left no family. Some will receive a life sentence because the victim's family lacked the eloquence to sway the jury toward a death sentence. On the other hand, some defendants will be condemned to death because the victim's family had the will – and the ability – to articulate their craving for revenge in a persuasive manner.[144]

Payne simply cannot be justified as advancing the goal of retribution. The use of emotionally charged victim-impact statements can only distract juries from considering the evidence that truly comports with the retributive rationale – the nature of the crime and the moral blameworthiness of the offender. Chief Justice Rehnquist defended victim-impact evidence as a useful way "to portray for the sentencing authority the actual harm caused by a particular crime,"[145] but he never explained what role evidence of a victim's positive attributes or the family's reaction to the crime is to play in the sentencing decision. The only clear role for this evidence is to appeal to the emotional sympathies of the jurors in an effort to convince them to satisfy the vengeful instincts of the family members.[146]

The chief justice, however, was not simply content to dismantle an evidentiary rule that made it difficult for prosecutors to inspire a spirit of vengeance among the jurors. He announced a radical new exception to the doctrine of *stare decisis*, explaining that although *stare decisis* would remain strong in cases involving property and contract rights, the Court would no longer feel compelled to follow precedent "in cases such as the present one involving procedural and evidentiary rules," especially when such cases "were decided by the narrowest of margins, over spirited dissents challenging the basic underpinnings of those decisions."[147]

This was apparently the last straw for Justice Marshall. Declaring that "[p]ower, not reason, is the new currency of this Court's decision making,"[148] he ended his 24-year career as a justice of the Supreme Court with the following warning:

> Today's decision charts an unmistakable course. If the majority's radical reconstruction of the rules for overturning this Court's decisions is to be taken at face value – and the majority offers us no reason why it should not – then the overruling of *Booth* and *Gathers* is but a preview of an even broader and more far-reaching assault upon this Court's precedents. Cast aside today are those condemned to face society's ultimate penalty. Tomorrow's victims may be minorities, women, or the indigent. Inevitably, this campaign to resurrect yesterday's "spirited dissents" will squander the authority and the legitimacy of this Court as a protector of the powerless.[149]

Conclusion

Is Justice Marshall's final dissent unduly alarmist? My concern is that readers of *The Death Penalty in the Nineties* might think that it is. To be sure, Professor White concludes his book by acknowledging that the Court "holds that maintaining the smooth functioning of our system of capital punishment is a higher priority than protecting the rights of capital defendants."(p. 207). But this conclusion – like the book itself – does not go far enough in capturing the extent to which the present Court has pursued an activist agenda that has legitimized vengeance as an acceptable justification for the death penalty. The cases that are most neglected in *The Death Penalty in the Nineties* are the very cases that best demonstrate the triumph of vengeance over retribution. The omission of any analysis of the victim-impact cases and the *Coker-Enmund-Tison* line of cases is especially perplexing. Moreover, other decisions that are barely mentioned in the book would have provided good examples of the Court's eagerness to approve death penalty laws that simply cannot be justified under the banner of retributivism.

As noted earlier, Professor White provides no discussion or analysis of two very important 1989 decisions – *Stanford v. Kentucky*[150] and *Penry v. Lynaugh*.[151] Both holdings provide good examples of the Court's abandonment of the retributive rationale as a precondition for imposing capital punishment.[152] *Stanford* upheld the constitutionality of executing those who commit capital crimes at 16 or 17 years of age, and *Penry* upheld the death sentence of a mentally retarded defendant convicted of murder. But as Justice Brennan pointed out in his *Stanford* dissent, executing those who lack full responsibility for their actions does make a measurable contribution to the goal of retribution.[153] Juveniles as a class do not have the level of maturity and responsibility that we presume in adults and thus are less blameworthy and culpable than are adults.[154]

Indeed it is because children under 18 are less self-disciplined and more impulsive than adults that all 50 states recognize the age of majority as 18 or older and forbid those below 18 to vote or to serve on a jury.[155] These kinds of age-based classifications "indicate that 18 is the dividing line that society has generally drawn, the point at which it is thought reasonable to assume that persons have an ability to make, and a duty to bear responsibility for their judgments."[156]

Similarly, mentally retarded individuals – those with IQs between 35 and 70 – are limited in their "general ability to meet the standards of maturation, learning, personal independence, and social responsibility expected for an individual's age level and cultural group."[157] The intellectual and behavioral disabilities associated with mental retardation clearly are severe enough to preclude the level of culpability that justifies capital punishment as a retributive goal. In his *Penry* dissenting opinion, Justice Brennan observed that it is often improper and inappropriate to treat the mentally retarded as a single homogeneous group and that such stereotyping can lead to unfair treatment.[158] Nevertheless, "[t]he impairment of a mentally retarded offender's reasoning abilities, control over impulsive behavior, and moral development limits his or her culpability so that, whatever other punishment might be appropriate, the ultimate penalty of death is always... disproportionate to his or her blameworthiness and hence is unconstitutional."[159] This argument, however, will not save the life of Johnny Paul Penry, who was diagnosed as having the mental age of a 6 1/2 year old.[160]

By downplaying the cases in which the Supreme Court approved death penalty laws that arguably serve no valid retributive goals, Professor White missed an opportunity to explore one of the most important philosophical debates surrounding the use of capital punishment in the United States. Instead of addressing Eighth Amendment questions as to who can be executed for what offenses and under what circumstances – questions that lie at the heart of the retributive rationale – *The Death Penalty in the Nineties* concentrates on the technical evidentiary and procedural rules that govern capital trials and appeals. This, however, is something that Professor White does exceptionally well. He provides first-rate insights into court rulings on the capital defendant's right to present mitigating evidence, the limits imposed on prosecutors' closing statements, and the impact of plea-bargaining practices in capital cases. Professor White also does a masterly job of explaining the significance of recent holdings that erect strict procedural roadblocks to federal appellate review of death-row inmates' state criminal convictions. Another highlight is an excellent analysis of *Lockhart v. McCree*,[161] the 1986 Supreme Court decision that rejected the argument that "death qualification" – the practice of removing from capital juries people who admit they could never vote in the penalty phase of a capital trial to impose death – violates the defendant's Sixth Amendment right to a fair trial in the guilt phase of the trial.[162]

301

Chapter seven examines the extent to which racial discrimination affects the outcomes of capital cases, and Professor White's marshaling of the evidence establishing that racism continues to saturate the capital sentencing process will convince many fair-minded readers that *McCleskey v. Kemp*[163] was wrongly decided. In *McCleskey*, the Court conceded that recent studies had shown "that black defendants, such as McCleskey, have the greatest likelihood of receiving the death penalty."[164] Nevertheless, a sharply divided Court held that to establish a violation of the Fourteenth Amendment's equal protection clause, the defendant would have to meet the difficult burden of proving "that the decisionmakers in *his* case acted with discriminatory purpose."[165] Unfortunately, Professor White's analysis of the *McCleskey* decision itself spans less than two pages.[166] His concluding words on *McCleskey*, however, will gladden the hearts of abolitionists: "By essentially accepting that race plays an important part in deciding who is executed, the Court clearly called attention to the most pernicious aspect of our system of capital punishment. In the long run, this can only strengthen the case for abolition" (p. 159).

In short, *The Death Penalty in the Nineties* makes a valuable contribution to our understanding of the legal rules that are applied in capital cases. However, it focuses almost entirely on the procedural aspects of these cases while virtually ignoring significant holdings that demonstrate the growing activism of a Court that has embraced vengeance – not retribution – as the primary social justification for imposing the punishment of death. *The Death Penalty in the Nineties* does not fill the need for a book that takes a critical and comprehensive look at the modern Supreme Court's role in nurturing and maintaining a constitutionally dubious system of a capital punishment. Nevertheless, it remains the best book available for readers who want to understand the disorderly and convoluted process by which the United States metes out the punishment of death.

Notes

1. See James W. Marquart and Jonathan R. Sorensen, "A National Study of the *Furman* – Committed Inmates: Assessing the Threat to Society from Capital Offenders," 23 *Loyola of Los Angeles Law Review* 5 (1989).
2. 408 U.S. 238 (1972).
3. 428 U.S. 153 (1976).
4. 428 U.S. 242 (1976).
5. 428 U.S. 262 (1976).
6. There were 2,632 inmates under sentence of death on October 31, 1992. The death row population has been increasing steadily over the past decade. See *Death Row U.S.A.* (NAACP Legal Defense and Educational Fund, Inc., New York, N.Y.), Fall 1992 at 1.
7. 492 U.S. 361 (1989).
8. Chief Justice Rehnquist and Justices White and Kennedy joined in all aspects of Justice Scalia's opinion. Justice O'Connor concurred in the judgment that the Eighth Amendment per-

mits the execution of 16-year-old offenders and in most other parts of the opinion. However, she refused to join in the portions of the opinion that "[reject] as irrelevant to Eighth Amendment considerations state statutes that distinguish juveniles from adults for a variety of other purposes" and "[suggest] that the use of [proportionality analysis] is improper as a matter of Eighth Amendment jurisprudence." *Id.* at 381-382 (O'Connor, J., concurring in part and concurring in the judgment).

9. *Stanford*, 492 U. S . at 368.

10. *Id.* at 369-377.

11. *Id.* at 379-380.

12. *Id.* at 377-378. Justice Scalia also contended that the laws and sentencing practices of other nations are irrelevant to Eighth Amendment analysis. *Id.* at 369, n.1. In dissent, Justice Brennan pointed out that the Court had often examined international standards of decency in Eighth Amendment cases and that "[w]ithin the world community, the imposition of the death penalty for juvenile crimes appears to be overwhelmingly disapproved." *Id.* at 389-390 (Brennan, J., dissenting).

13. *Id.* at 370-373; 377-380. Having thus limited the criteria to be examined in deciding the constitutionality of the juvenile death penalty, Justice Scalia could summarize his analysis in two sentences:

> Of the 37 states whose laws permit capital punishment, 15 decline to impose it upon 16-year-old offenders and 12 decline to impose it on 17-year-old offenders. This does not establish the degree of national consensus this Court has previously thought sufficient to label a particular punishment cruel and unusual. *Id.* at 370-371.

Justice Brennan's dissent took Justice Scalia to task for excluding from his analysis the District of Columbia and 14 states that do not authorize capital punishment. *Id.* at 384 (Brennan, J., dissenting). He also stressed that 19 of the states that have a death penalty set no minimum age for capital sentences and that these states therefore have not truly "made a conscious moral choice to permit the execution of juveniles." *Id.* at 385.

14. *Id.* at 369. Justice O'Connor joined in this portion of Justice Scalia's opinion. Thus a majority of the Court appears to agree for the first time that there is a significant distinction between the word "cruel" and the word "unusual" and that the Eighth Amendment bars only punishments that are *both* cruel and unusual.

15. 477 U.S. 399 (1986).

16. 492 U.S. 302 (1989).

17. 433 U.S. 584 (1977).

18. 458 U.S. 782 (1982).

19. 481 U.S. 137 (1987).

20. *Id.* at 158.

21. Paul Boudreaux, "*Booth v. Maryland* and the Individual Vengeance Rationale for Criminal Punishment," 80 *Journal of Criminal Law and Criminology* 177 (1989).

22. James A. Inciardi, *Criminal Justice, 3rd ed.* (New York: Harcourt Brace Jovanovich, 1990), 467.

23. P. Boudreaux, *supra* note 21, at 184.

24. *Id.*

25. *Id.* at 189-190.

26. *Id.* at 187.

27. Id. at 188.

28. Id. at 188-189.

29. Id. at 185.

30. See, e.g., A.C. Ewing, *The Morality of Punishment* (London: Kegan Paul, 1929), 13-45 (criticizing retributive theory but conceding that the retributive principle of proportionality

serves to protect the guilty against excessively severe punishments and thus is of great importance and value); Edmund L. Pincoffs, *The Rationale of Legal Punishment* (New York: Humanities Press, 1966) 1-27 (stressing that the principle that a punishment must be proportionate to the crime is central to the retributive theories of Kant, Hegel, and F. W. Bradley); Joel
Feinberg, *Doing and Deserving: Essays in the Theory of Responsibility* (Princeton: Princeton
University Press, 1970), 117-118 (contending that most retributive theories require an effort to
make punishment proportionate to the moral gravity of the offense and call for an assessment
of both the objective severity of the offense and the moral culpability of the offender); Wolf
Middendorff, "Legal Punishment," in Harold H. Hart (ed.), *Punishment: For and Against*
(New York: Hart Publishing Co., 1971), 12-14 (defining retribution as consistent with Cesare
Beccaria's emphasis on the importance of achieving a proportionate relationship between the
crime and the punishment... retribution is "an effort to make the punishment as analogous as
possible to the nature of the crime"); Richard G. Singer, *Just Deserts: Sentencinq Based on
Equality and Desert* (Cambridge, MA: Ballinger Publishing Co., 1979) 1-27 (arguing that proportionality of punishment is an essential element of retributivist sentencing schemes); Marvin Henberg, *Retribution: Evil for Evil in Ethics, Law, and Literature* (Philadelphia, PA: Temple University Press, 1990), 18-19 (emphasizing that "[p]roperly conceiving of retribution requires seeing it in all its parts" and that retribution should be understood to include the idea
that the suffering inflicted on evildoers must be limited by notions of desert); and *infra* notes
32-40 and accompanying text.

31. ?????????

32. H.L.A. Hart, *Punishment and Responsibility: Essays in the Philosophy of Law* (Oxford: Oxford University Press, 1968), 233-234.

33. See *id*. at 210-237.

34. Igor Primoratz, *Justifyinq Legal Punishment* (London: Humanities Press International, Inc.,
1989), 145-154.

35. *Id*. at 145-149.

36. *Id*. at 148.

37. See, e.g., Andrew von Hirsh, *Doing Justice: The Choice of Punishments* (New York: Hill and
Wang, 1976), 66-76, 89-94, 160 n. 4 (explaining the concept of "commensurate deserts" as
holding that the severity of punishment should be proportional to the gravity of the crime but
permitting the proportion to be less than "an eye for an eye"; contending that one can accept
Kantian arguments in favor of proportional punishments while rejecting Kant's espousal of
the *lex talionis);* Norval Morris, *Madness and the Criminal Law* (Chicago, IL: University of
Chicago Press, 1982), 129-176, 179 (arguing that " 'a deserved punishment' when carefully
analyzed does not mean the infliction on the criminal offender of a pain precisely equivalent
to that which he has inflicted on his victim; it means rather a 'not undeserved punishment'
which bears a proportional relationship in a hierarchy of punishments to the harm for which
the criminal has been convicted"); and Jeffrie G. Murphy and Jean Hampton, *Forgiveness and
Mercy* (Cambridge: Cambridge University Press, 1988), 124-138 (arguing that the sophisticated retributivist rejects the lex talionis as the appropriate punishment formula and embrac-
es in its place a formula calling for comparability of punishments with crimes within limits that
reflect the worth of both the victim and the offender).

38. See, e.g., R. Singer, *supra* note 31, at 27-30 (demonstrating that retributivists have long taken
the position that there is no universal moral or scientific standard for determining the precise
punishments that fit particular crimes and that since precise proportionality cannot be at-
tained, good-faith, well-reasoned, and logically consistent efforts to achieve proportionality
will suffice); and Nigel Walker, *Why Punish?* (Oxford;: Oxford University Press, 1991), 105
(acknowledging that "the proportionalist can claim that by striving for consistency he is at
least maximizing proportionality within the limits of the information available to him").

39. Igor Primoratz acknowledges that a retributivist can support the abolition of the death penalty without thereby being inconsistent. See I. Primoratz, *supra* note 34, at 167-169. This is not his position, however. He agrees that the retributive demand for proportionality between crime and punishment can be satisfied by sentencing those who commit crimes other than murder to pay fines and/or serve prison terms. *Id.* at 158. But like Kant, Hegel, and other classical representatives of retributivism, he argues that capital punishment is the *only* proportionate and thus appropriate punishment for "criminal homicide perpetrated voluntarily and intentionally or in wanton disregard for human life." *Id.* at 158-159. He apparently regards murder as the only crime that calls for a literal interpretation of the *lex talionis,* making it clear, for example, that he could not sanction the practice of sentencing a torturer to be tortured. *Id.* at 168-169.

40. Hugo Adam Bedau, "Capital Punishment," in Tom Regan (ed.), *Matters of Life and Death: New Introductory Essays in Moral* Philosophy 2nd ed. (New York: Random House, 1986), 206. See also Mary Ellen Gale, "Retribution, Punishment, and Death," 18 *U. C. Davis Law Review* 973 (1985) (arguing, *inter alia,* that retribution requires that the offender experience and eventually come to accept punishment as his or her just deserts and that the death penalty, because of its unique finality, cannot be experienced in that way and thus is not truly compatible with retributive theory).

41. See *supra* notes 21-28 and accompanying text.

42. See, e.g., Robert Nozick, *Philosophical Explanations* (Cambridge, MA: Harvard University Press, 1981), 363-402 (advancing a nonteleological theory of retributive punishment and stressing that retribution differs from and must not be confused with revenge); Robert C. Solomon, *A Passion for Justice: Emotions and the Origins of the Social Contract* (New York: Addison-Wesley, 1990), 219 (pointing out that "[v]irtually all 'retributivists'... insist on separating retribution from vengeance"); Mark Tunick, *Punishment: Theory and Practice* (Berkeley, CA: University of California Press, 1992), 84-90 (distinguishing between revenge theories and retributive theories of punishment and concluding that "[f]ew retributivists of repute take revenge to be the principle we use to guide us in practice, and most reject the view that the purpose of punishment in a modern state is to satisfy the desire to avenge").

43. Oliver Wendell Holmes, *The Common Law* (Boston, MA: Little, Brown and Co., 1923), 45.

44. Emile Durkheim, *The Division of Labor in Society,* trans. George Simpson (1893; reprinted Glencoe, Ill.: The Free Press, 1933), 73-108. More recently, the long history of vengeance and its importance in guiding and shaping the punishments used by ancient and modern societies have been explored in Susan Jacoby, *Wild Justice: The Evolution of Revenge* (New York: Harper and Row, 1983); Pietro Marongin and Graeme Newman, *Vengeance: The Fight Against Injustice* (Totowa, NJ: Rowman and Littlefield, 1987); and R. Solomon, *supra* note 42.

45. *Id.* at 86-90 For an excellent analysis of Durkheim's theory of punishment, see David Garland, *Punishment and Modern Society: A Study in Social Theory* (Chicago, IL: University of Chicago Press, 1990), 23-81.

46. *Trop v. Dulles,* 356 U.S. 86, 101 (1958).

47. *Report of the Royal Commission on Capital Punishment 1949-1953* (London: H.M.S.O., 1953), 18.

48. *Id.*

49. *Id.* at 17.

50. See A. von Hirsch, *supra* note 37; and von Hirsch, *Past or Future Crimes: Deservedness and Dangerousness in the Sentencing of Criminals* (New Brunswick, NJ: Rutgers University Press, 1985).

51. See R. Singer, *supra* note 31.

52. See Norval Morris, *The Future of Imprisonment* (Chicago, IL: University of Chicago Press, 1974; Morris, *Madness and the Criminal Law* (Chicago, IL: University of Chicago Press, 1982);

and Morris, "Punishment, Desert and Rehabilitation," in Hyman Gross and Andrew von Hirsch (eds.), *Sentencing* (New York: Oxford University Press, 1981), 257-271.

53. Compare, for example, N. Morris, *Madness and the Criminal Law, supra* note 52, at 129-209 (advocating "limiting retributivism" – a system of punishments in which desert sets the upper and lower bounds within which a punishment can be imposed but does not prevent the sentencing authority within those bounds from considering utilitarian objectives in determinating the appropriate punishment) with Andrew von Hirsch, "Ordinal and Cardinal Desert" in Andrew von Hirsch and Andrew Ashworth (eds.), *Principled Sentencing* (Boston, MA.: Northeastern University Press, 1992), 207-219 (criticizing Morris' approach as overly ambiguous and arguing in favor of a model calling for more specificity and a greater emphasis on desert).

54. See, e.g., A. von Hirsch, *supra* note 37, at 11-36; and R. Singer, *supra* note 31, at 1-10. For discussions of the erosion of support for the indeterminate sentence, see Marvin Zalman, "The Rise and Fall of the Indeterminate Sentence," 24 *Wayne Law Review* 45 (1977-78); and A. von Hirsch, "Recent Trends in American Criminal Sentencing Theory," 42 *Maryland Law Review* 6 (1983).

55. The classic case for rehabilitatively-oriented sentencing is articulated in Karl Menninger, *The Crime of Punishment* (New York: The Viking Press, 1968).

56. See, e.g., John Irwin, *Prisons in Turmoil* (Boston, MA: Little, Brown and Co., 1980), 37-65.

57. See, e.g., Jessica Mitford, *Kind and Usual Punishment* (New York: Alfred A. Knopf, 1973), 87-128.

58. See, e.g., A. von Hirsch, *supra* note 31, at 37-55.

59. Nigel Walker, *Sentencing in a Rational Society* (London: Penguin Press, 1969), 69.

60. See Alan H. Goldman, "Beyond the Deterrence Theory," 33 *Rutgers Law Review* 721 (1981).

61. See, e.g., N. Morris, *The Future of Imprisonment, supra* note 53, at 58-84; R. Singer, *supra* note 31, at 12-14; and A. von Hirsch, *Past or Future Crimes, supra* note 51, at 103-146.

62. A. von Hirsch, *supra* note 37, at 125.

63. See, e.g., Vincent Copeland, *The Crime of Martin Sostre* (New York: McGraw-Hill, 1970).

64. See, e.g., Karen Wald, "The San Quentin Six Case: Perspective and Analysis," in Tony Platt and Paul Takagi (eds.), *Punishment and Penal Discipline: Essays on the Prison and the Prisoners' Movement* (San Francisco, CA: Crime and Social Justice Associates, 1980), 165-175.

65. See especially Ron Rosenbaum, *Travels with Dr. Death* (New York: Penguin Books, 1991), 206-237 (chronicling the activities of Dr. Louis Grigson, the controversial Texas psychiatrist who has been extraordinarily successful as a prosecution witness in convincing capital juries that defendants are likely to commit future violent crimes and thus should be sentenced to death; showing that Dr. Grigson's clinical judgments may reflect his – and the jurors' – hostility to the "cultural alienness" of many capital defendants). See also Charles P. Ewing, " 'Dr. Death' and the Case for an Ethical Ban on Psychiatric and Psychological Predictions of Dangerousness in Capital Sentencing Proceedings," 8 *American Journal of Law and Medicine* 407 (1983).

66. Among the large number of studies that raise doubts about the accuracy of predictions of dangerousness are John Monahan, *The Clinical Prediction of Violent Behavior* (Washington, D.C.: Government Printing Office, 1981); John Cocozza and Henry Steadman, "The Failure of Psychiatric Predictions of Dangerousness: Clear and Convincing Evidence," 29 *Rutgers Law Review* 1084 (1976); Harry L. Kozol, "Dangerousness in Society and Law," 13 *University of Toledo Law Review* 241 (1982); James W. Marquart, Sheldon Ekland-Olson, and Jonathan P. Sorensen, "Gazing into the Crystal Ball: Can Jurors Accurately Predict Dangerousness in Capital Cases?" 23 *Law and Society Review* 449 (1989); J. Marquart and J. Sorensen, *supra* note 1; and Charles P. Ewing "Preventive Detention and Execution: The Constitutionality of Punishing Future Crimes," 15 *Law and Human Behavior* 139 (1991). Despite the overwhelm-

ing evidence that psychiatrists cannot reliably predict future violent behavior, the Supreme Court has upheld the use of psychiatric testimony to help the jury determine whether the defendant should be executed because of his future dangerousness. See *Barefoot v. Estelle*, 463 U.S. 880 (1983).

67. See, e.g., Richard N. Ostling, "Let Punishment Fit the Crime: A Controversial Sentencing Scheme Gets a Go-ahead," TIME, Jan. 30, 1989, at 63; Tamar Jacoby, "An End to Judicial Roulette: Similar Crimes, Similar Crooks, Similar Sentences," NEWSWEEK, Jan. 30, 1989, at 76; and Andrew Malcolm, "Sentencing Criminals: Formulas and Fairness," *N.Y. Times*, Feb. 17, 1990, at 10, col. 5.

68. John Braithwaite and Philip Pettit, *Not Just Deserts: A Republican Theory of Criminal Justice* (Oxford: Oxford University Press, 1990), 156-181.

69. *Id.* at 148-152, 178-181.

70. *Id* at 6-7.

71. *Id.*

72. *Id.* at 7.

73. *Id.* at 7-11, 202-204.

74. *Id.* at 86-136.

75. *Id.* at 10, 137-155.

76. Walter Berns, *For Capital Punishment: Crime and the Morality of the Death Penalty* (New York: Basic Books, 1979), 154-155.

77. *Id.* at 149.

78. *Id.* at 136.

79. *Id.* at 147.

80. Ernest van den Haag, *Punishing Criminals: Concerning a Very Old and Painful Question* (New York: Basic Books, 1975), 213.

81. Ernest van den Haag, "The Death Penalty Once More," 18 *U.C. Davis Law Review* 957, 968 (1985).

82. *Id.*

83. *Tison v. Arizona*, 481 U.S. 137 (1987).

84. *Id.* at 139-141.

85. *Id.* at 141.

86. *Id.* at 151-152.

87. *Id.* at 141.

88. *Id.* at 141-142.

89. *Gregg v. Georgia*, 428 U.S. 153 (1976).

90. *Tison*, 481 U.S. at 141-142.

91. 458 U.S. 782 (1982).

92. *Id.* at 783-784.

93. *Id.* at 785-786.

94. *Id.* at 787.

95. *Id.* at 794.

96. *Id.* at 801.

97. *Tison*, 481 U.S. at 143-144.

98. *Id.* at 144-145.

99. The *Tison* majority was composed of Chief Justice Rehnquist and Justices O'Connor, Scalia, Powell, and White. Justice Brennan was joined in dissent by Justices Marshall, Blackmun, and Stevens. *Id.* at 138.

100. *Tison*, 481 U.S. at 157.

101. *Id.* at 154.

102. *Id.* at 155.

103. *Id.* at 158.
104. *Id.*
105. *Id.* at 174-175 (Brennan, J., dissenting).
106. *Id.* at 175.
107. *Id.*
108. *Id.* at 168-169.
109. *Id.* at 169 (quoting *id.* at 157).
110. *Id.* at 169.
111. *Id.* (quoting *id.* at 157).
112. *Id.* at 169-170.
113. *Id.* at 170 n. 9.
114. *Id.*
115. *Id.* at 169.
116. Id. at 169-170.
117. See *id.* at 181 n. 19. Justice Brennan argued that the majority's failure to insist that punishment must always be tailored to the defendant's personal responsibility and moral guilt would permit the government to "replicate the punishment that private vengeance would exact." *Id.* He also quoted Justice Marshall: "[T]he Eighth Amendment is our insulation from our baser selves. The 'cruel and unusual' language limits the avenues through which vengeance can be channeled. Were this not so, the language would be empty and a return to the rack and other tortures would be possible in a given case." *Id.* (quoting *Furman v. Georgia*, 408 U.S. 238, 345 (1972) (Marshall, J., concurring)).
118. *Enmund*, 458 U.S. at 798 (citing *Gregg v. Georgia*, 428 U.S. 153, 183 (1976)).
119. *Id.* at 798-799.
120. *Id.* at 801.
121. In recent years, the Supreme Court also has upheld a number of non-capital sentences that arguably were excessively harsh and sharply disproportionate to the crimes committed. See *Rummel v. Estelle*, 445 U.S. 263 (1980) (holding that the Eighth Amendment permits a sentence of life imprisonment to be imposed on a defendant convicted under a Texas recidivist statute of three non-violent crimes involving the use of fraud to obtain a total of $229.11); *Hutto v. Davis*, 454 U.S. 370 (1982) (citing *Rummel* as controlling precedent and thus upholding a 40-year prison sentence and a fine of $20,000 imposed on a defendant convicted of possession and distribution of approximately nine ounces of marijuana); and *Harmelin v. Michigan*, 111 S. Ct. 2680 (1991) (rejecting an Eighth Amendment challenge to a Michigan statute mandating a sentence of life imprisonment without possibility of parole for anyone – even a first offender – convicted of possession of 650 grams or more of cocaine). But see *Solem v. Helm*, 463 U.S. 277 (1983) (invalidating on Eighth Amendment grounds a sentence of life imprisonment without possibility of parole that had been imposed under a South Dakota recidivist statute on a defendant convicted of seven non-violent felony offenses).
122. Other legal commentators have been highly critical of the *Tison* decision. See, e.g., "The Supreme Court, 1986 Term – Leading Cases," 101 *Harvard Law Review* 138 (1987); and William K. Bass, "*Tison v. Arizona*: A General Intent for Imposing Capital Punishment upon an Accomplice Felony Murderer," 20 *University of Toledo Law Review* 255 (1988). But see James J. Holman, "Redefining a Culpable Mental State for Non-Triggermen Facing the Death Penalty," 33 *Villanova Law Review* 367 (1988).
123. *Tison*, 481 U.S. at 184 n. 20 (citing Exodus 20:5 (King James)).
124. See *id.* at 184 and n. 20 ("[A]n intuition that sons and daughters must sometimes be punished for the sins of the father may be deeply rooted in our consciousness.").
125. 482 U.S. 496 (1987).
126. See *id.* at 502-509.

127. *Id.* at 502 (citing Zant v. Stephens, 462 U.S. 862, 879 (1983); and *Eddings v. Oklahoma,* 455 U.S. 104, 112 (1982)).

128. *Id.* at 505-506.

129. *Id.* at 503.

130. 490 U.S. 805 (1989).

131. See *id.* at 810-812.

132. *Id.* at 810-811.

133. *Id.* at 810 (quoting *Tison v. Arizona,* 481 U.S. 137, 149 (1987))

134. Justice Scalia's dissenting opinion in *Booth* was joined by Chief Justice Rehnquist and Justices White and O'Connor. Justice White also wrote a dissenting opinion that was joined by Chief Justice Rehnquist and Justices Scalia and O'Connor. See *Booth,* 482 U.S. at 515-521. No one joined Justice Scalia's dissenting opinion in *Gathers,* but Justice O'Connor issued a dissenting opinion that was joined by Chief Justice Rehnquist and Justice Kennedy. See *Gathers,* 490 U.S. at 812-825. The four *Gathers* dissenters made it clear that they thought that *Booth* had been wrongly decided and that they were anxious to overrule it. See *Id.* at 813-814, 825. However, they were thwarted by Justice White, who dissented in *Booth* but provided the swing vote in *Gathers,* explaining only that "[u]nless *Booth v. Maryland* (citation omitted) is to be overruled, the judgment below must be affirmed." *Id.* at 812 (White, J., concurring). Perhaps Justice White didn't think that *Booth* was a bad enough precedent to erase in a mere two years. He may have been concerned that overruling so recent a precedent would make the Court's pronouncements appear to be nothing more than the musings of a small group of fickle people who temporarily occupy a position of power. In any event, his reluctance to overrule *Booth* dissolved in another two years when he joined a six-justice majority in *Payne v. Tennessee,* 111 S. Ct. 2597 (1991). See *infra* notes 140-149 and accompanying text.

135. *Booth,* 482 U.S. at 520 (Scalia, J., dissenting).

136. *Id.*

137. *Id.*

138. *Gathers,* 490 U.S. at 824 (Scalia, J., dissenting).

139. See, e.g., *Moragne v. States Marine Lines,* 398 U.S. 375, 403 (1970) (stressing that *stare decisis* is fundamental to the conception of the judiciary as a source of impersonal and reasoned judgments); *Arizona v. Rumsey,* 467 U.S. 203, 212 (1984) (stating that *stare decisis* is the preferred course and that the Court should not depart from it without "special justification"); and *Vasquez v. Hillary,* 474 U.S. 254, 265, 266 (1986) (arguing that *stare decisis* insures the evenhanded, predictable, and consistent development of law and promotes public understanding that the Court implements "principles... founded in the law rather than in the proclivities of individuals").

140. 111 S. Ct. 2597 (1991).

141. *Id.* at 2608.

142. *Id.* (quoting *Booth v. Maryland,* 482 U.S. 496, 517 (White, J. dissenting)).

143. *Id.* at 2609.

144. Ironically, it is not at all clear that victims benefit from making victim-impact statements that call for harsh penalties. Many observers believe that an emphasis on revenge can often undermine recovery from a violent crime and that forgiveness, though difficult to muster, will promote better healing for victims than will revenge. See, e.g., Hannah Arendt, *The Human Condition* (Chicago, IL: University of Chicago Press (1958), 240-241; Lynne N. Henderson, "The Wrongs of Victims' Rights," 37 *Stanford Law Review* 937, 994-999 (1985); and Margaret Vandiver, "Coping with Death: Families of the Terminally Ill, Homicide Victims, and Condemned Prisoners," in Michael L. Radelet (ed.), *Facing the Death Penalty: Essays on a Cruel and Unusual Punishment* (Philadelphia, PA: Temple University Press, 1989), 131-132.

145. *Payne,* 111 S. Ct. at 2606.

146. For commentaries critical of *Payne*, see Michael Ira Oberlander, "The *Payne* of Allowing Victim Impact Statements at Capital Sentencing Hearings," 45 *Vanderbilt Law Review* 1621 (1992); Catherine Bendor, "Defendants' Wrongs and Victims' Rights," 27 *Harvard Civil Rights-Civil Liberties Law Review* 219 (1992); and Angela P. Harris, "The Jurisprudence of Victimhood," 32 *Supreme Court Review* 77 (1992). For an analysis that praises the *Payne* majority's "activist stance in overruling recent precedent," see Keith L. Belknap, Jr., "The Death Penalty and Victim Impact Evidence," 15 *Harvard Journal of Law and Public Policy* 275 (1992).

147. *Payne*, 111 S. Ct. at 2610-2611.

148. *Id.* at 2619 (Marshall, J., dissenting).

149. *Id.* at 2625.

150. 492 U.S. 361 (1989).

151. 492 U.S. 302 (1989).

152. See generally Edward Miller, "Executing Minors and the Mentally Retarded: The Retribution and Deterrence Rationales," 43 *Rutgers Law Review* 15 (1990).

153. *Stanford*, 492 U.S. at 402-403 (Brennan, J., dissenting).

154. *Id.* at 395.

155. *Id.* at 394.

156. *Id.* at 396.

157. *Cleburne v. Cleburne Living Center,* 473 U.S. 432, 442 n.9 (1985).

158. *Penry,* 492 U.S. at 344 (Brennan, J., dissenting).

159. *Id.* at 346.

160. *Penry*, 492 U.S. at 308.

161. 476 U.S. 162 (1986).

162. For a detailed critique of Chief Justice Rehnquist's majority opinion in *Lockhart v. McCree,* see Phoebe C. Ellsworth, "Unpleasant Facts: The Supreme Court's Response to Empirical Research on Capital Punishment," in Kenneth C. Haas and James A. Inciardi (eds.), *Challenging Capital Punishment: Legal and Social Science Approaches* (Newbury Park, CA: Sage Publications, 1988), 177-211.

163. 481 U.S. 279 (1987).

164. Id. at 287.

165. Id. at 292.

166. For a comprehensive analysis of *McCleskey* and the empirical studies that demonstrate the persistence of racial bias in American capital sentencing, see David C. Baldus, George G. Woodworth, and Charles A. Pulaski, Jr., *Equal Justice and the Death Penalty: A Legal and Empirical Analysis* (Boston, MA: Northeastern University Press, 1990).

RACE AND IMPRISONMENT DECISIONS

John Kramer
The Pennsylvania State University;
Darrell Steffensmeir
The Pennsylvania State University

The possible race differences in judicial sentencing have been of long-standing interest to social scientists. We argue, however, that prior research on the issue either uses crude measures of offense severity and prior record, or, if more precise measures are employed, is limited to one or a few offenses. The Pennsylvania guidelines sentencing data used in this report allow a more rigorous test of the racial hypothesis since they include detailed information on these two most important legal variables, on other variables for statistical controls, and on a fairly comprehensive list of common law offenses, with an adequate sample size. The data—analyzed with both additive and interaction models—reveal that race (net of other factors) has a small effect on judicial decision-making as it pertains to the likelihood of incarceration but has negligible effect on the length of imprisonment decision. The small race effect at the in/out decision is accounted for by dispositional departures in sentencing that favor white defendants. Offense severity is overwhelmingly the major factor influencing judicial sentencing, followed at some distance by prior record. At the end of the report, we discuss the implications of our findings for research on sentencing and for policies aimed at reducing the high incarceration rate of black males.

The number of blacks in prison has become an increasingly important issue in American society. Blacks constitute a relatively small share of the general population, but they make up a very large share of federal and state prison populations. Today, blacks comprise 13 percent of the U.S. population and 50 percent of the prison population.

Sociological theories of crime and law disagree about the sources of such a disparity or overrepresentation—whether it is due to disproportionate involvement in criminal offenses or to criminal justice system selection biases (see Bridges and Crutchfield [1988] for a review of the theories). Normative theories reason that punishments are imposed largely (or only) in reaction to criminal acts and that the high black imprisonment rates are due to differences in criminal involvement between blacks and whites, particularly in serious and violent crime. Conflict or stratification theories attribute disparity in imprisonment to the biased treatment of minorities by the legal system, so that while blacks may commit a large percentage of serious crimes, the criminal justice system compounds the

Direct all correspondence to: John Kramer, The Pennsylvania State University, Pennsylvania Commission on Sentencing, P.O. Box 1200, State College, PA 16804.

The Sociological Quarterly, Volume 34, Number 2, pages 357-376.

problem by imposing more severe sanctions on blacks than on whites committing similar types of offenses.

The results from numerous studies of race differences in sentencing outcomes have been mixed, in part because the analyses in many studies have failed to control adequately for legally relevant variables—most importantly, seriousness of the offense and prior criminal record. The need to control for such factors is illustrated in Kleck's review (1981; see also 1985) of 57 studies that examined racial discrimination in sentencing. He reports that 26 studies contradicted the racial bias hypothesis, 15 showed evidence of bias, and 16 had mixed results.

Kleck concluded that some studies failed to include even rudimentary controls for offense severity or defendant's prior record, while most studies used crude and imprecise measures or failed to control simultaneously for both variables. Prior record was operationalized typically as "no prior conviction" vs. "conviction," while offense severity was proxied into broad categories such as "felony" vs. "misdemeanor" or "violent" vs. "property" crimes. These are inexact measures, however, since they include a heterogeneous mix of offenders and offenses that vary considerably in their seriousness.

Recent studies both reflect and reinforce the brunt of Kleck's criticisms. For example, in Myers and Talarico's (1987) well-received study of sentencing practices in Georgia, a control for prior record was included in only two of the counties in their probation sample, whereas the prior record control for their imprisoned sample was restricted to whether the offender had been previously incarcerated in Georgia. Also, although they expand on offense classifications used by many researchers (e.g., Holmes and Daudistel 1984; Unnever and Hembroff 1988), Myers and Talarico simply grouped offenses into common-law violent, robbery, burglary, property theft and damage, and drug offenses. These offense groupings are too imprecise to provide a meaningful control for offense severity.

In light of the controversy that exists, we conducted an analysis that included stringent controls for prior record and offense severity, using data on Pennsylvania sentencing outcomes. The study focused only on sentencing—prison versus non-imprisonment and length of term—of offenders convicted of a range of noncapital offenses. Thus, the study did not address whether racial bias exists in earlier processing or prosecution stages (e.g., in charging), or whether bias exists in capital sentencing. Prior research, nonetheless, does tend to find that the strongest race effects (when they occur) are manifest at the sentencing stage and that the inclusion of process variables in sentencing models contributes little, if anything, to explained variation in sentencing outcomes (see reviews in Eisenstein, Flemming, and Nardulli 1988; Albonetti 1991).

For several reasons, Pennsylvania's data are exceptionally *well-suited* for a study of imprisonment decisions. First, in 1982 the state enacted a *sentencing guidelines* system that takes into account the legal variables of offense severity and prior record such that Pennsylvania's data more accurately reflects the impact of these two variables on sentencing than sentencing statistics from most other jurisdictions. The enactment of a sentencing guidelines system ensures that information about the defendant's prior record will be provided to the court in a standardized format and that its consideration from court to court will be similar. Also, the guidelines system has boosted the likelihood that information about prior record will be accurately collected, recorded, and made available to relevant parties.

Such a situation did not characterize sentencing practices in Pennsylvania prior to passage of the guidelines structure. Nor does it characterize what exists in many states today where criminal history information is irregularly provided to the court at sentencing. Often, because criminal history information requires responses from the state police or the FBI; the courts may rely strictly on local criminal-history information and sentence the offender promptly rather than wait for the more complete criminal history report. Additionally, state criminal history reports often fail to provide the final disposition of the case, so that the court does not know if in fact the defendant was convicted. In Pennsylvania, this recordkeeping process has improved dramatically as the courts have been required to systematically consider the prior record information in applying the sentencing guidelines.[1]

One option used by researchers facing this problem has been to survey **ex post facto** probation or prison records for information on the defendant's prior record and then to merge this information with sentencing outcomes (Petersilia 1983; Myers and Talarico 1987; Spohn, Gruhl and Welch 1987; Unnever and Hembroff 1988). This does not solve the problem, however, since we still do not know whether the sentencing judge in fact was aware of the information compiled in the defendant's dossier. Frequently, the criminal history information in a probationer's or a prisoner's dossier is self-reported by the sentenced felon himself during an intake interview. In many respects, due to the recent enactment of sentencing guidelines systems, researchers (e.g., Miethe and Moore 1986) can better assess the effects of prior record on sentence outcomes because they have more detailed and structured criminal history information.

A second advantage of the Pennsylvania data (again owing partly to changes instituted with the implementation of the guidelines system) is that the state's recordkeeping includes refined classifications not only of prior record but of offense severity as well. The set of offenses is well defined and seriousness is measured with some precision, so that extraneous variation within offense type is limited. In fact, in Pennsylvania some offenses with the same statutory grade are subdivided and given different severity scores. Previous research has had to rely on broadly defined statutes as the basis for classifying offenses.

Third, while Pennsylvania now operates with a guidelines sentencing structure, it is a comparatively "loose" one that still permits significant judicial discretion (Tonry 1987). In addition, the criminal code endorses several sanction philosophies (for deterrence, incapacitation, rehabilitation and retribution), so that opportunities for case, court, and community contexts to affect sentencing are enhanced. Also, there is in fact considerable variation in the sentences imposed, both within and across crime categories (see: Pennsylvania Commission on Sentencing Annual Report, 1990).

Fourth, there are 67 counties and 59 judicial districts in the state. As viable political and social entities, counties vary markedly in demographic, political, economic, and social composition. Previous research has generally been unable to control for the political and social context of sentencing.

Fifth, the large number of cases (about 60,000) allows for the consideration of offenses that range from minor to very serious. Small sample size has plagued prior research conclusions on the issue of race bias in sentencing.

We are not aware of any previous studies on the race/sentencing issue that encompass all the attributes described above, making the present study a significant advance over prior research. That recent research has not overcome many of the shortcomings described above is reflected in a close reading of several major studies of sentencing conducted since Kleck's review. As noted earlier, the ambitious and well-received project by Myers and Talarico (1987) of sentencing practices in Georgia employed broad offense groupings and utilized ambiguous information on prior record. The latter was not included at all for the majority of their sample and, if included, was based on prior arrest and incarceration information collected ex post facto from inmates' files. The problem, as noted, is whether the court in fact used, or even had at its disposal, the prior record information contained in the inmate's dossier. Similarly, the Rand study of *Racial Equity in Sentencing* (Klein, Turner, and Petersilia 1988) considered only a few offenses, was limited to a prison sample, and relied ex post facto on prior record information collected from inmates' files. Also, Miethe and Moore (1986) used data generated by the Minnesota Sentencing Guidelines to show the consequences of model selection for conclusions about race differences in criminal processing. Unfortunately, while their analysis included a 10-point ranking of offense severity, their prior record measure was a dichotomy, restricted to whether the defendant had a prior felony conviction. Finally, a recent study by Bridges and Crutchfield (1988) failed to use any measures of prior record and offense seriousness.

PROCEDURES

This study analyzes Pennsylvania guidelines sentencing data for the years 1985–87, totalling 61,294 cases. The purpose of the guidelines, which apply to any offender convicted of a felony or misdemeanor after July 21 1982, was to reduce unwarranted disparity by establishing that the severity of the convicted offense and the offender's criminal history are the major determinants of sentencing decisions (Kramer and Scirica 1986). A guideline sentence is established for each combination of offense severity and criminal history score. Furthermore, under the guidelines, dispositional or durational departures from the presumptive sentences are permissible but the judge must justify any departure from the guidelines with written statements supporting the departure. Taken together, the Pennsylvania guidelines represent a fairly rigorous and systematically crafted sentencing system, yet it affords ample opportunity for the intrusion of sentencing disparity and racial disparity in particular (Tonry 1987).

The data for this study derive from the monitoring system developed by the Commission. Each sentence given for a separate criminal transaction must be reported to the Commission. The data provide sentencing information on a large number of cases, detailed information on prior record and offense severity, and information on a number of other variables that might affect sentencing outcomes. To our knowledge the resulting statewide data base includes the richest information in the country for analyzing judge's sentencing decisions. Besides race, the independent variables we use in the analysis include a combination of legally-prescribed variables, offender characteristics such as gender and age, and contextual factors. Coding of these variables is straightforward and is presented in Table 1.

The legally-prescribed variables include the severity of the convicted offense (Severity), and criminal history score (History). Severity of the current conviction was measured by a 10-point scale developed by the Commission and by a dummy variable procedure across 20 offense categories. The 10-point severity scale ranks each statutory offense and subdivides certain statutory offenses such as burglary into multiple ranks depending on the specific circumstances of the crime (Kramer and Scirica 1986).[2] The offense dummy variable procedure offered an even more rigorous control of seriousness of offense.

A weighted seven category scale developed by the Commission was used to measure criminal history. The criminal history score measures the number and severity of the

Table 1
Description of Variables

Independent Variables	Description
Legally-Prescribed	
Severity	Severity of the Convicted Offense: 10 category ordinal scale with a range of 1 to 10
History	Criminal History Score: 7 category ordinal scale with a range of 0 to 6
Offense	Twenty dummy coded offenses*
Offender Characteristics	
Race	Binary: Coded 1 if Black, 0 if White
Sex	Binary: Code 1 if male, 0 if female
Age	In years
Type of disposition	Binary: Coded 1 if trial, 0 if plea
Contextual Factors	
Workload	# of cases received/# of judges in county
% Urban	% of county population living in urban areas
% Black	% of county population which is Black
% 15-19	% of county population aged 15-19
% Republican	% of county registered voters registered Republican
Dependent Variables	
Prison/Probation vs. Jail	Binary: Coded 1 if incarcerated, 0 otherwise
Prison vs. Jail/ Probation	Binary: Coded 1 if state incarceration, 0 otherwise
Prison vs. Jail	Binary: Coded 1 if state incarceration, 0 if county incarceration
Sentence length	Midpoint between minimum and maximum in months

Note: *The dummy offense variables are: involuntary manslaughter, robbery felony 1, robbery felony 2, robbery felony 3. Aggravated assault, simple assault, arson, weapons offenses, burglary (7), burglary (6), burglary (5), theft-felony, theft-misdemeanor, retail theft felony, retail theft other, forgery felony 2, forgery felony 3, drug felony. Drug misdemeanor was excluded as the contrast level.

defendant's past convictions. All felonies, as well as misdemeanors (punishable up to five years in Pennsylvania) are included.[3]

Regarding the contextual variables, investigators have identified urbanization and proportion of the population that belongs to minority groups (racial mix) as important contextual factors of the social environment that may affect criminal sentencing (Benson and Walker 1988). Contextual factors also may include differences in organization and caseload processing among courts, such as caseload and type of disposition (Hagan and Bumiller 1983). As a contextual factor to measure conservatism of the social environment, we used "percent republican" (Friedman 1975; Steffensmeier 1976). We also included in the initial regression runs the crime rate of the county, the unemployment rate, and median income levels. Because these variables were highly collinear and redundant with "percent black," we do not report them here.

Sentencing can be thought of as a two-stage process, involving first a decision as to whether to imprison, and second, if incarceration is selected, a decision about the length of sentence. Thus, we employ two dependent variables: incarcerated versus not incarcerated (in/out decision) and length of sentence. For the dependent variable involving the in/out decision, we conducted the analysis using three alternative measures where:

a.   IN refers to confinement in either county jail or state prison, and OUT refers to any combination of non-confinement options (probation, fines, restitution, or suspended sentence—hereafter lumped together as probation). This traditional measure of the In/Out decision is designated as JAIL/PRISON vs. PROBATION.

b.   IN refers to confinement in state prison vs. all other, including jail, probation, etc. This measure is designated as PRISON vs. JAIL/PROBATION.

c.   IN refers to confinement in state prison and OUT refers to confinement in county jail, and is designated as PRISON vs. JAIL. This analysis excludes all defendants who received a sentence of probation, fines, restitution, or suspended sentence.

Since a sentence of "county jail" time is viewed typically as less stigmatizing and as less punitive than "state prison" time (Kramer and Scirica 1986), it is important that confinement in state prison be distinguished from other sentencing options. Based on the legalistic model of sentencing, we expect that the effects of prior record and offense severity on sentencing will be particularly strong when measures (b) and (c) above are employed.

We used both ordinary least squares regression (OLS) and logistic regression to analyze the in/out decision. Each of these procedures has been employed in recent studies of sentencing, and the results from each procedure are displayed for comparison purposes. The two methods revealed similar patterns but we relied mainly on OLS for discussing the study's findings because of its familiarity to most readers and its more straightforward interpretation.[4] We used OLS for the analysis of the length-of-prison term decision because this outcome was a continuous variable.[5]

FINDINGS

Table 2A presents descriptive statistics and bivariate correlations of the variables included in this analysis, including each of the three measures of the In/Out decision as well as sentence length (see methods section). The results indicate that black defendants are more likely to be incarcerated ($r = .08$, for JAIL/PRISON vs. PROBATION) and to receive lengthier jail/prison sentences than white defendants ($r = .11$). But the bivariate correlations in Table 2B also show that black defendants have higher offense severity scores on the average ($r = .15$) than their white counterparts as well as somewhat lengthier prior records of offending (.10). Thus, the bivariate correlations between race and these two legal variables are as strong or stronger than the correlations between race and sentence outcomes. In turn, the two legal variables (Severity, History) are correlated strongly with sentence outcomes (r's of about .40), whereas race and the other variables in the model are correlated only weakly with sentence outcomes.

The bivariate analysis strongly suggests, therefore, that offense severity and prior record have large effects on sentencing outcomes and represent important statistical controls for estimating race effects. As for the other independent variables, their effects turned out to be very small and relatively unimportant, so that, for economy of space, the results observed for these variables are displayed in the tables but are not discussed in the text.

In/Out Decision

We first estimated the effects of race on sentencing, controlling for the other variables in the model. Two separate models were estimated for each dependent variable—one employing the dummy variable procedure as a control for offense seriousness, the other

Table 2
Correlations and Descriptive Statistics

(A) Descriptive Statistics

Variable	Mean	Standard Deviation	Minimum	Maximum
Severity	4.62	2.01	1.00	10.00
History	1.93	2.26	0.00	6.00
Type of Disposition	0.06	.28	0.00	1.00
Race	.38	.39	0.00	1.00
Sex	.91	.29	0.00	1.00
Age	28.69	8.61	14.00	87.00
Workload	308.01	121.96	100.00	571.00
% Urban	70.42	26.55	0.00	100.00
% Black	10.07	13.08	0.03	37.84
% 15-19	7.82	1.01	6.20	12.93
% Republican	42.06	16.48	19.66	71.76
Jail/Prison vs. Probation	0.59	0.49	0.00	1.00
Prison vs. Jail/Probation	0.22	0.41	0.00	1.00
Prison vs. Jail	0.40	0.49	0.00	1.00
Sentence Length	29.19	21.48	1.00	180.00

(continued)

Table 2
(Continued)

(B) Correlations Among Independent Variable

	Severity	History	Race	Sex	Age	Workload	% Urban	% Black	% 15-19	% Republican
Severity	1.00	—	—	—	—	—	—	—	—	—
History	.12	1.00	—	—	—	—	—	—	—	—
Race	.15	.10	1.00	—	—	—	—	—	—	—
Sex	.11	.14	−.01	1.00	—	—	—	—	—	—
Age	−.05	.14	.00	−.08	1.00	—	—	—	—	—
Workload	−.15	−.02	−.26	−.06	.00	1.00	—	—	—	—
% Urban	.15	.04	.44	.02	.02	−.24	1.00	—	—	—
% Black	.23	.04	.48	.07	−.01	−.63	.63	1.00	—	—
% 15–19	−.04	−.04	−.17	.00	−.03	.16	−.39	−.15	1.00	—
% Republican	−.19	−.07	−.32	−.04	−.01	.51	−.48	−.64	.25	1.00

(C) Correlations Between Dependent and Independent Variables

	Jail/Prison vs. Probation	Prison vs. Jail/Probation	Prison v. Jail	Sentence Length
Severity	.38	.39	.34	.50
History	.33	.44	.37	.33
Race	.08	.09	.11	.11
Sex	.17	.11	.07	.09
Age	-.03	.05	.09	.09
Workload	-.04	-.07	-.10	-.11
% Urban	-.06	.02	.10	.13
% Black	.02	.06	.12	.18
% 15–19	.03	-.02	-.05	-.03
% Republican	-.01	-.12	-.19	-.13

Table 3

Results from OLS and Logistic Regression Analysis for Each
of the Four Dependent Variables

Independent Variable	Prison /Jail v. Probation				Prison v. Jail/Probation			
	OLS		*LOGISTIC*		*OLS*		*LOGISTIC*	
	b	*Contribution to R²*	*Beta*	*Odds Ratio*	*b*	*Contribution to R²*	*Beta*	*Odds Ratio*
History	.069	.075	.458	1.58	.080	.143	.527	1.69
Offense Type	—ᵃ	.102	—	—	—	.107	—	—
Race	.084	.008	.429	1.54	.035	.001	.372	1.45
Gender	.119	.006	.572	1.77	.003*	.000	.153	1.17
Age	−.002	.002	−.013	1.01	.000*	.000	.002*	1.00
Type of Disposition	.066	.002	−.497	1.64	.113	.007	.872	2.29
Workload	−.001	.000	−.000*	1.00	−.000*	.000	−.000*	1.00
% Urban	−.003	.009	−.015	1.02	−.001	.002	−.010	1.01
% Black	−.001	.000	−.010	1.01	−.004	.004	−.033	1.03
% 15–19	.006	.001	.045	1.05	.001*	.000	.021*	1.02
% Republican	.001	.001	.004	1.00	−.002	.006	−.026	1.03
Year	.014	.000*	.039*	1.03	.006	.000	.004*	1.00
[Severity]	[.092	.100	.496	1.64]	[.086	.073	.696	2.01]

$R^2 = .2563$ $X^2 = 12511.2$ $R^2 = .3392$ $X^2 = 20300.6$

Note: N   61,294   61,294

* Regression coefficient not statistically significant

ᵃ Results for dummy variable are presented in Appendix A

ᵇ Effect of 10 category offense severity score on the dependent variable when this variable is in the model instead of the offense dummy variable.

employing the severity scale. We rely mainly on the dummy variable procedure in describing our results; it offers a more stringent control of offense seriousness since each of the 10 categories in the offense severity measure includes several specific types of offenses. However, we also display the results from Severity when it is employed in the regression models because it offers a summary or overall indicator of the effects of offense seriousness (as compared to surveying 20 dummy variable coefficients). We also included a control variable for YEAR to partial the effects of trending.

The results are displayed in Table 3. Because the sample size is so large, tests of statistical significance are not very meaningful. Therefore, to identify "predictive" or substantive significance, we calculated for each variable its net contribution to total explained variance or R^2. We ask, after controlling for the effects of all the other variables, how much does race contribute (in terms of explained variance) to the judge's incarceration decision?

Table 3 reveals that judges' sentencing decisions are determined, first and foremost, by the seriousness of the crime committed by the offender and by the length of the offender's prior record. Both are factors of explicit legal relevance to the sentence. Offenders convicted of a more serious offense or having a prior record are punished more harshly.

Table 3
(Continued)

| | Prison vs. Jail | | | | Sentence Length | |
| | OLS | | Logistic | | OLS | |
b	Contribution to R^2	Beta	Odds Ratio	b	Contribution to R^2	
.081	.125	.434	1.54	4.48	.108	
—	.097	—	—	—	.251	
.044	.002	.286	1.33	.695	.000	
−.020	.000	−.093*	1.10	−1.64	.000	
.002	.001	.010	1.01	.146	.002	
.118	.006	.701	2.02	8.36	.008	
−.000*	.000	−.000*	1.00	−.002*	.000	
−.001	.001	−.004	1.00	−.009*	.000	
−.005	.005	−.031	1.03	.013*	.000	
.003*	.000	.028*	1.03	−.033*	.000	
−.005	.004	−.028	1.03	.021	.000	
.004*	.000	.003	1.00	1.21	.001	
[.086	.074	.550	1.73]	[7.54	.159]	

| R^2 = .2905 | | X^2 = 9566.6 | | R^2 = .4354 | |
| 33,527 | | 33,527 | | | 34,487 |

For the traditional in/out measure (JAIL/PRISON vs. PROBATION), type of offense has a net contribution to R^2 of 11 percent while prior record has a net contribution of 7 percent. Together, these two variables account for about three-fourths of the total R^2 (about .26). When the two alternative measures of in/out are considered, type of offense and prior record also account for a large share of the explained variation. The major difference is that prior record now becomes the more powerful predictor of variation in the in/out decision when the principal distinction in sentence outcome is state imprisonment as compared to other sentencing options. Also, it is for the PRISON vs. JAIL/PROBA-TION definition of the In/Out decision that the model as a whole explains the most variation (R^2 of about .36).

Next, we re-estimated the models replacing the offense dummy variables with the offense severity scale (Severity). Across all three in/out decisions, moving from one level of severity to the next results (on the average) in a nine percent greater likelihood of being incarcerated. Again, offense severity and criminal history account for most of the explained variation.

On the other hand, regardless of which control for offense seriousness is employed, race contributes less than one-half of one percent to explained variation in each of the three in/out classifications. The effect of race is somewhat greater when the traditional way of defining in/out is the dependent variable than when "in" refers only to incarceration in a state prison. When the dependent variable is defined as JAIL/PRISON vs.PRO-

BATION, black defendants on the average are 8 percent more likely to be jailed or imprisoned than white defendants, net of all other variables, whereas blacks are only 2 percent more likely than whites to be incarcerated when the definition of in is restricted to state imprisonment (as in PRISON vs. JAIL /PROBATION or PRISON vs. JAIL).[6]

The logistic regression procedure produces similar results.[7] The odds ratio indicates that the odds of blacks being incarcerated (versus not being incarcerated) is 1.54 times higher than the odds of whites being incarcerated. Also, we find that the race effect diminishes considerably when the definition of "in" is restricted to state imprisonment. The odds ratios, on the average, for criminal history and offense severity are 1.58 and 1.64 respectively. This indicates that *each additional increase* in the defendant's criminal history score, or in the offense severity scale, results (on the average) in roughly a 60 percent greater likelihood of being incarcerated when the traditional measure of in/out (PRISON/JAIL vs. PROBATION) is employed.

Lastly, we conducted separate regression analyses (both OLS and logistic) on each of the twenty offenses, for the traditional in/out measure.[8] The results, shown in Table 4, reveal that offender's race has a small effect on the in/out decision that is consistent across all offenses. That is, the effect is not greater for specific offenses—burglary as compared to forgery, for example.

In sum, both OLS and logistic methods indicate that black defendants are slightly more likely than white defendants to be sentenced to jail or prison, with this effect being somewhat stronger for the traditional in/out measure. Also, both methods show that the effect of race on imprisonment decisions is weak compared to the effects of criminal history and offense severity. Ascertaining whether the race effect is substantively significant is not straightforward, however. On the one hand, the race variable adds less than one-half of one percent to explained variation across most offenses. On the other hand, black offenders on the average have about an 8 percent greater likelihood of being incarcerated than white offenders, and the odds ratio favoring whites is about 1.5. We return to this issue later.

Length of Sentence

For defendants who were incarcerated, we employed multiple linear-regression procedures to analyze the relationship between the regressors (independent variables) and the length of sentence. We used regression diagnostics (Belsley, Kuh and Welsch 1980) to detect influential observations (outliers), and we inspected the data for multicollinearity.

Table 2 (shown earlier, right hand column) presents multiple regression results which estimate the effects of race on sentence length while controlling simultaneously for type of offense (using offense gravity score) and prior record as well as for the other variables in the model. As in the analysis above, because of the large sample we consider each variable's net contribution to explained variation or R^2. Not surprisingly, both type of offense and offender's prior record weigh overwhelmingly in judicial decision-making about sentence length. Offense type alone contributes 25 percent to explained variation or 57 percent of the total R^2, while prior record contributes 11 percent to explained variation or 27 percent of the total R^2. The two variables together account for 82 percent of the explained variation in sentence length. On the other hand, the defendant's race accounts for less than one-tenth of one percent of the variation after the other variables are controlled, so that it plays a very small role in decisions about sentence length. The unstandardized regression coefficient for race indicates that black defendants, on the average,

Table 4
Effects of Race on Sentence Outcome by Offense Type

| | | Jail/Prison vs. Probation | | | | Sentence Length | |
| | | OLS | | LOGIT | | OLS | |
	N	b	Contribution to R^2	Beta	Odds Ratio	b	Contribution to R^2
Involuntary Manslaughter	171	.108*	.007	.516	1.68	.781*	.000
Robbery, Felony 1	2428	.005*	.001	.051	1.05	2.44	.000
Robbery, Felony 2	1611	.095	.007	.695	2.00	-1.40*	.000
Robbery, Felony 3	1311	.085	.004	.570	1.80	-1.10*	.002
Aggravated Assault	3411	.107	.010	.565	1.76	4.35	.005
Simple Assault	5047	.107	.008	.561	1.75	-.226*	.000
Arson	449	.155	.017	1.20	3.32	-5.06*	.002
Weapons	2291	.100	.007	.446	1.56	-.349*	.000
Burglary 7	1008	.064	.006	.608	1.84	6.53	.005
Burglary 6	4796	.032	.001	.213	1.24	1.90*	.001
Burglary 5	4792	.117	.009	.680	1.97	1.24*	.000
Criminal Trespass, Felony 2	1110	.117	.008	.568	1.80	.863*	.001
Criminal Trespass, Felony 3	772	.104	.007	.596	1.81	.189*	.000
Theft, Felony 3	6013	.056	.002	.264	1.30	-1.48	.002
Theft, Misdemeanor	5609	.068	.003	.319	1.38	-.335*	.000
Retail Theft, Felony	2675	.134	.015	.751	2.12	.332*	.000
Retail Theft, Other	3309	.111	.010	.556	1.74	.109*	.000
Forgery, Felony 2	990	.105	.007	.543	1.72	4.51	.010
Forgery, Felony 3	2052	.105	.008	.534	1.71	1.86*	.003
Drug Felony	6585	.066	.004	.347	1.41	2.21	.003
Drug Misdemeanor	4314	.058	.003	.352	1.42	2.70	.006

receive .695 months, or about 21 days, longer sentences than white defendants.

Next, we re-estimated the model using the offense severity scale as a control for offense seriousness. Again, prior record and offense severity overwhelmingly account for the explained variation. While the effect of race is statistically significant, its contribution to explained variation in sentence length is less than one-tenth of one percent.

Lastly, we ran the regressions separately for each offense. The results, shown in Table 4, confirm the patterns described above. Across all offenses, race contributes very little to total explained variation. Also, in spite of the large sample size, the race effect does not reach statistical significance for 14 of the 21 offense categories. The variable having by far the largest impact on length of term, as expected, is offender's prior record.

Interaction Analysis

The analysis to this point involved additive models only. To check for the possibility that the effect of race may be conditioned by other variables, we also estimated interaction models. We first repeated the above analysis, with separate models estimated for black and white defendants. For both black and white defendants, seriousness of offense and prior record account for a very large share of explained variation in both the in/out decision and the length-of-term sentence (from about 70 percent to 95 percent of R^2 across all comparisons). We next estimated models which included all possible race interaction terms. Across all dependent variables, none of the interaction terms contribute as much as one-half of one percent to the total R^2. Thus, our results indicate that an interaction model did not produce an improvement of fit over the additive model. Overall, for both the in/out and the sentence length decisions, the effects of the independent variables are virtually identical for black and white defendants.

DISCUSSION

Our major findings are that, net of other factors, race does not have a direct effect on length of sentence, but that black defendants are somewhat more likely than white defendants to be incarcerated. Although race contributes very little to explained variation (less than one percent) in the in/out decision, blacks are about 8 percent more likely than whites to be incarcerated—a pattern that holds fairly consistently across a broad range of offenses.

Whether or not this 8 percent difference (roughly one in twelve) in the black-to-white rate of incarceration is substantively important, there is a need to know more precisely how the offender's race has a bearing on the decision to incarcerate. Some additional data on sentencing practices in Pennsylvania are available that provide at least a partial answer. As noted earlier, the state's sentencing system allows judges to depart from the guidelines schema when they strongly deem it appropriate (see Methods section). When they do depart, judges are asked to justify in writing their reasons for departing; unfortunately, many judges fail to provide reasons or do so only perfunctorily. For our purposes, we are interested in dispositional departures—those having to do with the in/out decision—in which the judge sentences an offender to probation rather than to jail or prison. We ask: To what extent does the race effect described above stem from differences in the propensity of judges to grant "departure" sentences to white more so than black defendants?

To ascertain this, we distinguished the departures by race and found that a higher percentage of white defendants (30 percent) received departure sentences than black defendants (26 percent). We next partitioned the sample to exclude all departure sentences, and found that the results confirmed our suspicions. Once the effects of the departure sentences are removed, the race coefficients are reduced sharply across all offenses; the race effect in the in/out decision becomes essentially negligible. The 8 percent greater likelihood of incarceration is reduced to a virtual zero.

Given the significance of the departure mechanism in "accounting for" the race disparity in "in/out" sentencing, we examined the reasons judges offered for their departure sentences—in order to gauge whether their decision-making was based on legally relevant factors or extra-legal ones. Unfortunately, the analysis here must remain suggestive since some judges gave multiple reasons, some judges gave perfunctory ones (e.g., plea agreement), and many judges did not give any reasons at all for their departure sentences. In addition, we interviewed a number of judges in the state regarding the departures and the consequent racial disparity in their in/out decision-making, with inclusive results.

The responses from the interviews and the departure reasons overlap, so we have combined them here. The major justifications for departure sentences that favor white defendants are as follows: offender has a non-violent prior record or prior conviction occurred a long time ago (e.g., 10–15 years); use of a weapon in the commission of the offense but which is not included in the official charges; no current employment and/or poor employment history; offender is a good candidate for rehabilitation; plea agreement; reluctance to sentence white defendants to jails or prisons that are both overcrowded and disproportionately black.

One judge in explaining why there is still some racial disparity despite the sentencing guidelines, stated:

> I can only speak for myself but there are any number of reasons why, in my court, I'd be more likely to depart if I'm sentencing a white defendant [than a black defendant]. It may not show up in the official charges, but it's more likely a black defendant used a weapon in the crime or was involved in drugs. I'd say, too, black defendants are less likely to be holding a job or supporting a family. These are things you want to take into account.

Another judge responded:

> It's more likely the black defendant is more naive—isn't as knowledgeable about the law and the system . . . so white defendants do better in working out plea agreements. Sometimes the prosecutor makes an aggressive pitch to stay within the guidelines and other times they take no position at all. Generally, this depends on whether the defendant has a high-price attorney [which white defendants are more likely to have].

Another judge responded:

> This [consideration] is becoming more important all the time—especially with the prisons so overcrowded—you are reluctant to send white offenders especially younger ones, to a prison that is largely black. It seems the prisons are becoming more and more black [and hispanic], so judges are leery because they have heard horror stories about what has happened.

Relatedly, another judge answered:

> The overcrowding and the increased violence in state prisons makes it difficult for me to send young, middle-class males to prison. That is extreme punishment.

Finally, one judge responded:

> Especially in drug cases, there is racial disparity. And it is often the police who are
> offering [white] defendants promises in exchange for their cooperation.

It can be debated whether these are legitimate considerations, or are simply convenient justifications. For our purposes, the interviews suggest fruitful lines of empirical inquiry for flushing out the determinants of judicial decision-making and for improving the explained variation achieved by sentencing models. For example, in the present research, we found that offense seriousness and prior record are robust predictors of sentence outcomes and that race has only small or negligible effects. But a large residual variation still remains, suggesting that the model we used only partly fits the actual decision-making process of judges. Consistent with several recent studies (Klein et al. 1988; Myers and Talarico 1987), our model explained 30 percent of the variation in the in/out decision (depending on which measure we used) and about 50 percent of the variation in the sentence-length decisions. It is possible, but unlikely, that this unexplained variation is the result of race (Wilbanks 1987).

We view our findings as an advance over previous work on race and sentencing. The controls for offense seriousness and prior record, the large number of cases and offenses, the division of the sentencing decision, and so forth, have contributed to somewhat more rigorous conclusions about the influence of race on sentencing. But our study also has its limitations.

1. Our data contained only convicted offenders. Individuals who had all charges dropped or were acquitted on all counts were excluded. If there is differential attrition by race through earlier stages of processing, sample selection bias will limit substantive inferences about our population of cases. Racial differences in legal processing may be relatively small at any particular stage of the legal process but may have cumulative effects on overall patterns of imprisonment. While we recognize this limitation in our population of cases, it is questionable whether our results would be modified had such data been available. To begin with, the few empirical studies that exist on the issue report mixed findings but overall offer little evidence of racial bias (or differential treatment) being transmitted indirectly through various presentence and processing outcomes (for reviews, Eisenstein, Flemming, and Nardulli 1988; Albonetti 1991). Also, the existing research typically suffers from the same shortcomings that characterizes the research on sentence outcomes—failure to control adequately for prior record and offense severity. Finally, as Weisburd et al (1990) point out, the practical limitations of research make it virtually impossible to account for all the selection processes that operate in the criminal justice system, such as the decision to prosecute or to the decisions that occur in bargaining over conviction. In this sense, some degree of uncorrected sampling bias is common to every study.

2. Some researchers (e.g., Hagan 1989) have proposed that the race of the defendant may be less important in incarceration and sentencing decisions than the racial composition of the offender-victim dyad. Our data do not allow us to address this question, and the existing research is plagued by inadequate controls. LaFree's (1980; 1989) is the most systematic research on the issue. He reports that black men who sexually assaulted white women received harsher sentences than either

black men who sexually assaulted black women or white men who assaulted white women. (There were too few cases to analyze the white offender-black victim dyad). However, LaFree's findings must be treated skeptically because of the small size of his sample, the use of arrests in his measure of prior record, and the omission of relational aspects (e.g., stranger/acquaintance) of the victim-offender dyad. The latter is important because stranger rapes, which largely comprise the black offender-white victim dyad, tend to be sanctioned more harshly. Related research suffers from similar shortcomings (e.g., Thomson and Zingraff 1981), so that, while intriguing, the effects, if any, of racial composition of offender-victim dyad on sentencing decisions remain largely unknown. (An exception is capital cases, where the effects of race on sentencing appear to be strong, at least in some Southern states—see Baldus, Pulaski, and Woodworth 1986.) Note, moreover, that the above studies only consider crimes involving victims of interpersonal violence (assault, rape), or the threat of it (robbery). These offenses are important, but nonetheless, are only a small part of "the crime problem" in the United States.[9]

3. It is risky to generalize from the findings of one state. Pennsylvania's guidelines sentencing system is somewhat unique and was implemented to reduce judicial discretion. Because of data shortfalls on prior record, it is impossible to ascertain with confidence the extent of racial differences in sentencing prior to enactment of the guidelines. Nonetheless, the strength of the data and the consistency of our findings with Kleck's review suggest that anomalous findings of race effects on sentencing reflect a failure to distinguish good from bad studies as much or more than real race differences.

CONCLUSIONS

Because of its high visibility and symbolic importance to the legal system, the issue of equality of sentencing has led to considerable research aimed at assessing the role of extra-legal influences on sentencing decisions in terms the system itself defines as illegitimate, such as the defendant's race. Many researchers and commentators have concluded that defendant's race strongly influences sentence outcomes and, in so doing, contributes to disproportionate minority populations in state and federal prisons. This view, in fact, has served as an impetus for sentencing reform leading to (more) determinate sentencing systems, including the guidelines format developed in Pennsylvania and some other states (e.g., Minnesota).

At least in Pennsylvania, it appears that racial and other biases in sentencing outcomes may have diminished with the introduction of the guidelines system. Today, if defendants' race affects judges' decisions in sentencing, or if contextual /organization forces result in more severe penalties for black defendants, controlling for legal factors, it does so very weakly or intermittently, if at all. In this regard, the guidelines can be viewed as a policy success.

Simultaneously, however, the passage of the guidelines system has tended to increase rather than decrease the percentage of a state's prison population composed of blacks; in Pennsylvania black admissions to state prison rose from about 45 percent in 1980 to 55 percent in 1990. Petersilia and Turner (1985: v) have noted that when "legitimate standards are applied [they may] have different results for different racial groups." For reasons that are complex, sentencing systems that systematically link severe sentences to offenses most committed by blacks (e.g., robbery) and/or to prior record which may reflect past police and court processing decisions for which blacks may be particularly vulnerable will exacerbate the level of blacks in United States prisons because "serious criminality is disproportionately high in the black population" (Petersilia and Turner).

The results of this study are consistent with other research which finds that high black incarceration rates represent actual behavior and not selection bias. Thus, if the policy goal is to reduce the high black incarceration rate, it will require: (a) either dampening the role of racially linked legal variables, such as offense seriousness and prior record, in the processing of criminal cases; or (b), more realistically, instituting the kinds of structural changes that reduce the high level of serious crime among blacks (especially of young black males in the urban ghetto) which lead to higher rates of incarceration in the first place.

NOTES

1. An analysis by the Sentencing Commission of information available to, or used by, sentencing judges in Pennsylvania prior to enactment of the guidelines found that prior record information was available at time of sentencing in only about 50 percent of the cases. This situation was due largely to the absence of an institutionalized state repository that accurately compiled prior record information on convicted felons and provided this information in a timely fashion. A number of other states have recently instituted, or are considering instituting, a guidelines-type structure with its emphasis on prior record. Personal communication with officials in some of these states (e.g., Delaware, Minnesota, North Carolina, Washington, and Wisconsin) indicates that they had/have similar problems regarding the availability and accuracy of prior record information.

2. The scale of offense severity used by the Pennsylvania Commission ranges from 1 (minor theft) to 10 (murder in the third degree) (Kramer and Scirica 1986). Also, by way of special classification or subdivision of specific offenses (e.g., robbery-1 vs. robbery-2), offense severity includes whether there was victim injury or not and the degree of injury.

3. We also developed several additional measures of criminal history: (a) the number of current convictions at the time of sentencing; (b) a dummy variable representing whether or not the defendant had a violent criminal history; (c) dummy variables representing whether the defendant had a juvenile prior record only, an adult prior record only, or both a juvenile and an adult prior record; and (d) variables representing a combination of the above (e.g., whether the defendant had a violent vs. nonviolent juvenile record; a violent vs. nonviolent record, etc.). We found that these prior record measures did not enhance our understanding of sentence outcomes beyond the seven category prior record score.

4. The OLS regression coefficients indicate the change in the probability of scoring 1 on the dependent variable associated with a unit change in the independent variable—a relatively straightforward interpretation. In the logit model, the coefficients represent the change in the log of the odds of scoring 1 on a dichotomous dependent variable associated with a change in its dependent variable—an interpretation that is relatively difficult to articulate in meaningful terms (see Hanushek and Jackson 1977). Also, the OLS procedure allows for the assessment of the relative contribution of each independent variable to total explained variation—a procedure not possible with logistic regression.

5. In other analyses (available from the authors on request), we included a correction term for selection effects in the regression equation for length of sentence. Sample selection bias is a concern in the modeling of length of sentence, since that decision follows the initial decision about whether or not to incarcerate. In order to correct for this potential bias, a two-stage estimation procedure recommended by Berk (1983) was employed. The results indicated that the predicted probability of exclusion from one stage to the next (the "hazard rate") was highly correlated with offense seriousness. Because of its collinearity with offense seriousness and because the inclusion of the correction term did not significantly affect the magnitudes, signs, or p-values of the variables in the "parti-

tioned" models, we do not include it in this article. The high collinearity we found appears to be a commonplace problem in the research on sentencing (see, e.g., Benson and Walker 1988).

6.   We also analyzed the data using Fisher's discriminant function procedure which allowed us to assess how much the addition of race, net of other independent variables, improves the predictive accuracy of the model. We found that predictive accuracy does not substantially improve when race is added to the model. For the sample as a whole, the addition of race improved predictive accuracy by less than one-half percent (.004 percent). When the offenses were considered separately, the addition of race to the model improved predictive accuracy by at least one percent for only four offenses; for most offenses, the improved accuracy was less than one-half percent. Overall, the results were similar to those described for the OLS and logistic regression models.

7.   Compared to logistic regression, however, the OLS procedure slightly underestimates the race effect in our data. Some analysts (e.g., Hanushek and Jackson 1977) have noted that the OLS regression coefficient multiplied by four should roughly equal the coefficient obtained with logistic regression. In our data, the OLS coefficient for race multiplied by four equals .336, whereas the logistic coefficient is .429. However, when we compared the coefficients obtained from the two procedures across all the independent variables, we found identical patterns—the variables with higher OLS coefficients also have higher logistic coefficients.

8.   For economy of space, only the effects that pertain to race are presented here. Results are available on request.

9.   It is worth noting, moreover, that since in our data the zero-order race effect is null after controlling for prior record and offense severity, a significant effect of racial composition of offender-victim dyad is plausible only if there are offsetting effects from one or more of the other combinations of the victim-offender dyad; for example, if black offenders are treated more harshly in the black offender-white victim combination but they are treated more leniently in the black offender-black victim combination, or that white offenders are treated more harshly in other victim offender combinations.

REFERENCES

Albonetti, Celesta. 1991. "An Integration of Theories to Explain Judicial Discretion." *Social Problems* 38: 247–266.

Baldus, David., C. Pulaski and G. Woodworth. 1986. "Arbitrariness and Discrimination in the Administration of the Death Penalty: A Challenge to State Supreme Courts." *Stetson Law Review* 15: 133–261.

Belsley, David A., Edwin Kuh and Roy E. Welch. 1980. *Regression Diagnostics, Identifying Influential Data and Sources of Collinearity*. New York: Wiley.

Benson, Michael L. and Esteban Walker. 1988. "Sentencing the White Collar Offender." *American Sociological Review* 53: 294–302.

Berk, Richard. 1983. "An Introduction to Sample Selection Bias in Sociological Data." *American Sociological Review* 48: 386–398.

Bridges, George S. and Robert D. Crutchfield. 1988. "Law, Social Standing and Racial Disparities in Imprisonment." *Social Forces* 66: 699–724.

Eisenstein, James, Roy Flemming and Peter Nardulli. 1988. *The Contours of Justice: Communities and Their Courts*. Boston: Little, Brown.

Friedman, Lawrence. 1975. *The Legal System: A Social Science Perspective*. New York: Russell Sage.

Hagan, John. 1977. "Criminal Justice in Rural and Urban Communities: A Study of the Bureaucatization of Justice." *Social Forces* 55: 597–612.

Hagan, John and Kristen Bumiller. 1983. "Making Sense of Sentencing: A Review and Critique of Sentencing Research." Pp 1–54 In *Research in Sentencing: The Search for Reform*, Vol. 2, edited by Alfred Blumstein, Jacqueline Cohen, Susan Martin and Michael Tonry. Washington, D.C.: National Academy Press.

Hagan, John. 1989. *Structural Criminology*. New Brunswick, NJ: Rutgers University Press.

Hanushek, Eric and John Jackson. 1977. *Statistical Methods for Social Scientists*. NY: Academic Press.

Holmes, Malcolm and Howard Daudistel. 1984. "Ethnicity and Justice in the Southwest: The Sentencing of Anglo, Black, and Mexican Origin Defendants." *Social Science Quarterly* 65: 265–277.

Kleck, Gary. 1981. "Racial Discrimination in Criminal Sentencing: A Critical Evaluation of the Evidence with Additional Evidence on the Death Penalty." *American Sociological Review* 46: 783–805.

———. 1985 . "Life Support for Ailing Hypothesis: Modes of Summarizing the Evidence for Racial Discrimination in Sentencing." *Law and Human Behavior* 9: 271–85.

Klein, Stephen P., Susan Turner and Joan Petersilia. 1988. *Racial Equity in Sentencing*. Santa Monica, CA: Rand Corp.

Kramer, John H. and Anthony J. Scirica. 1986. "Complex Policy Choices - The Pennsylvania Commission on Sentencing." *Federal Probation* 50: 15–23.

LaFree, Gary. 1980. "The effect of sexual stratification by race on official reactions to rape." *American Sociological Review* 45: 842–854.

———. 1989. "Rape and Criminal Justice: The Social Construction of Sexual Assault." Belmont, CA: Wadsworth.

Maynard, Douglas. 1984. *Inside Plea Bargaining*. Englewood Cliffs, NJ: Plenum Press.

Miethe, Terance D. and Charles A. Moore. 1989. "Sentencing Guidelines, Their Effect in Minnesota." Office of Justice Programs, National Institute of Justice.

———. 1985. "Socio-economic Disparities under Determinate Sentencing Systems: A Comparison of Pre-and Post-Guideline Practices in Minnesota." *Criminology* 23: 337–346

Myers, Martha A. and Susette M. Talarico. 1987. *The Social Contexts of Criminal Sentencing*. New York: Springer- Verlag.

Pennsylvania Commission on Sentencing. 1990. *Sentencing in Pennsylvania: Annual Report*. University Park, PA: Pennsylvania Commission on Sentencing.

Petersilia, Joan. 1983. *Racial Disparities in the Criminal Justice System*. Santa Monica, CA: Rand Corp.

Petersilia, Joan and Susan Turner. 1985. "Guideline-Based Justice: The Implications for Racial Minorities." Santa Monica, CA: Rand Corp.

Spohn, Cassia, John Gruhl and Susan Welch. 1987. "The Impact of Ethnicity and Gender of Defendants on the Decision to Reject or Dismiss Felony Charges." *Criminology* 25: 175–192.

Steffensmeier, Darrell. 1976. "Advocates of Law and Order." *Criminal Justice and Behavior* 3: 273–285.

Thomson, R. and M. Zingraff. 1981. "Detecting Sentencing Disparity: Some Problems and Evidence." *American Journal of Sociology* 86: 869–80.

Tonry, Michael. 1987. "Sentencing Guidelines and Their Effects." Pp. 16–46 in *The Sentencing Commission and Its Guidelines*, edited by Andrew von Hirsch, Kay A. Knapp and Michael Tonry. Boston, MA: Northeastern University Press.

Unnever, James and Larry Hembroff. 1988. "The Prediction of Racial/Ethnic Sentencing Disparities: An Expectation States Approach." *Journal of Research in Crime and Delinquency* 25: 53–82.

Weisburd, David, Elin Waring and Stanton Wheeler. 1990. "Class, Status, and the Punishment of White-Collar Criminals." *Law and Social Inquiry* 15: 223–246.

Wilbanks, William. 1987. *The Myth of a Racist Criminal Justice System*. Monterey, CA: Brooks/Cole Publishing Company.

William S. Laufer*

Culpability and the Sentencing of Corporations

TABLE OF CONTENTS

I. INTRODUCTION

In the fifty years since Edwin Sutherland coined the term "white collar crime" there has been periodic interest in the subject of corporate criminality.[1] The most recent period of interest emerged in 1980

* Assistant Professor, Legal Studies, The Wharton School, University of Pennsylvania; B.A., Johns Hopkins University; J.D., Northeastern University; Ph.D., Rutgers University.

My appreciation to Kip Schlegel for his important contribution to sections IV and V of this manuscript. Thomas W. Dunfee, Andrew von Hirsch, and D. Bruce Johnsen made helpful comments on earlier drafts of this article.

1. MARSHALL B. CLINARD & PETER C. YEAGER, CORPORATE CRIME (1980); MARSHALL B. CLINARD ET AL., ILLEGAL CORPORATE BEHAVIOR (1979); DONALD R. CRESSEY, CRIMINAL ORGANIZATION: ITS ELEMENTARY FORMS (1972); M. DAVID ERMANN & RICHARD L. LUNDMAN, CORPORATE AND GOVERNMENTAL DEVIANCE: PROBLEMS OF ORGANIZATIONAL BEHAVIOR IN CONTEMPORARY SOCIETY (1982);

with ground-breaking scholarship examining the law violations of the largest corporations in the United States.[2] Within the last five years, research has focused on sentencing. Even though there have been relatively few empirical studies of the sentencing of corporations, as compared with the sentencing of individuals, there is no shortage of serious discussion regarding corporate sanctions.[3] Legal scholars, economists, and sociologists have engaged in a lengthy debate over proposals for organizational sanctions issued by the United States Sentencing Commission ("Sentencing Commission").[4]

Gilbert Geis, *White Collar Crime: The Heavy Electrical Equipment Antitrust Cases of 1961*, in CRIMINAL BEHAVIOR SYSTEMS, A TYPOLOGY 139 (Marshall B. Clinard & Richard Quinney eds., 1967); SUSAN P. SHAPIRO, WAYWARD CAPITALISTS: TARGET OF THE SECURITIES AND EXCHANGE COMMISSION (1984); Edwin H. Sutherland, *Crime of Corporations*, in THE SUTHERLAND PAPERS 78 (Albert K. Cohen et al. eds., 1956); EDWIN H. SUTHERLAND, WHITE COLLAR CRIME (1949); Marshall B. Clinard, *Criminological Theories of Violations of Wartime Regulations*, 11 AM. SOC. REV. 258 (1946); Robert E. Lane, *Why Businessmen Violate the Law*, 44 J. CRIM. L., CRIMINOLOGY, & POLICE SCI. 151 (1953); Edwin H. Sutherland, *Is 'White Collar Crime' Crime?* 10 AM. SOC. REV. 132 (1945); Edwin H. Sutherland, *White Collar Criminality*, 5 AM. SOC. REV. 1 (1940).

2. See CLINARD & YEAGER, *supra* note 1; *see also* MARSHALL B. CLINARD ET AL., *supra* note 1. For a general discussion of the nature corporate crime research, see Donald R. Cressey, *The Poverty of Theory in Corporate Crime Research*, in 1 ADVANCES IN CRIMINOLOGICAL THEORY 31 (William S. Laufer & Freda Adler eds., 1988); and John Braithwaite & Brent Fisse, *The Plausibility of Corporate Crime Research*, in 2 ADVANCES IN CRIMINOLOGICAL THEORY 21 (William S. Laufer & Freda Adler eds., 1990).

3. Three reasons may be offered for the dearth of empirical work: (1) there is a conspicuous absence of theories of corporate crime causation—theories that might promote both a qualitative and quantitative body of literature, (2) until the United States Sentencing Commission initiated its surveys on organizational sanctions, data on corporate prosecutions and convictions were difficult, if not impossible, to obtain, and (3) convictions of corporations under state or federal law are infrequent events, as compared with convictions of individuals. Clinard and Yeager comment on the lack of scholarship in writing: "Only recently has corporate crime begun seriously to concern the public, government agencies, and scholars. . . . Public concern of course influences both legislatures and law enforcement agencies and affects research trends in law, sociology, and particularly, criminology. Accordingly, textbooks purporting to analyze social problems have, with few exceptions, focused on more conventional crimes." CLINARD & YEAGER, *supra* note 1, at 12-13 (citation omitted); *cf.* Mark A. Cohen, *Corporate Crime and Punishment: A Study of Social Harm and Sentencing Practice in the Federal Courts 1984-1987*, 26 AM. CRIM. L. REV. 605 (1989); Mark A. Cohen et al., *Organizations as Defendants in Federal Court: A Preliminary Analysis of Prosecutions, Convictions, and Sanctions, 1984-1987*, 10 WHITTIER L. REV. 103 (1988).

4. An extensive literature has developed tracking the progress of the United States Sentencing Commission and its draft proposals. The most recent collection of articles appeared in a symposium issue of the Boston University Law Review entitled Sentencing the Corporation. *See, e.g.*, Michael K. Block, *Optimal Penalties, Criminal Law and the Control of Corporate Behavior*, 71 B.U. L. REV. 395 (1991); John C. Coffee, Jr., *Does "Unlawful" Mean "Criminal"?: Reflections on the Disappearing Tort/Crime Distinction in American Law*, 71 B.U. L. REV. 193 (1991);

The early Sentencing Commission proposals rested on a weak foundation, it is argued, because they treated sentencing as a single, largely isolated phenomenon independent of the basic premises of the substantive criminal law.[5] Such treatment neglected the existence of a direct relation between the assessment of culpability and the deservedness of punishment.[6] This neglect may be attributed in part to the confusion and controversy that surrounds criminal liability of corporate offenders appearing in the form of "non-human" persons.[7] More likely, it resulted from a steadfast commitment to an intellectual para-

---

Mark A. Cohen, *Corporate Crime and Punishment: An Update on Sentencing Practice in the Federal Courts, 1988-1990*, 71 B.U. L. REV. 247 (1991); Jonathan R. Macey, *Agency Theory and the Criminal Liability of Organizations*, 71 B.U. L. REV. 315 (1991); Stephen A. Saltzburg, *The Control of Criminal Conduct in Organizations*, 71 B.U. L. REV. 421 (1991). For references to earlier work, see KIP SCHLEGEL, JUST DESERTS FOR CORPORATE CRIMINALS (1990).

5. *See infra* notes 54-102 and accompanying text.

6. Throughout this paper I will use the term culpability to reflect the notion of blameworthiness. As discussed in Parts I to III, culpability or blameworthiness is raised as an issue both prior to and after conviction. Prior to conviction, culpability is raised in relation to liability. After conviction, culpability is raised in relation to severity of sentence. *See, e.g.*, HYMAN GROSS, A THEORY OF CRIMINAL JUSTICE 76, 436-38 (1979)("The criminal law adheres in general to the principle of proportionality in prescribing liability according to the culpability of each kind of criminal conduct . . . . Punishment that fits the crime is punishment in proportion to the culpability of the criminal conduct and it is what the perpetrator deserves for his crime."); JEROME HALL, GENERAL PRINCIPLES OF CRIMINAL LAW 317 (1960)("[P]unishment implies the criminal's moral culpability and is apt (fitting, correct) in light of that."); ANDREW VON HIRSCH, DOING JUSTICE: THE CHOICE OF PUNISHMENTS 80 (1976)("Here there is one well-established principle: that prohibited behavior causing (or risking) the same harm varies in seriousness depending on whether it is intentional, reckless, negligent, or punishable regardless of the actor's intent . . . .").

7. Following New York Central and Hudson River Railroad v. United States, 212 U.S. 481 (1909), there has been considerable debate over the logic and wisdom of imputing mens rea to corporate entities. *See* R.A. DUFF, INTENTION, AGENCY & CRIMINAL LIABILITY: PHILOSOPHY OF ACTION AND THE CRIMINAL LAW (1990); PETER A. FRENCH, COLLECTIVE AND CORPORATE RESPONSIBILITY (1984); Virginia Held, *Corporations, Persons and Responsibility, in* SHAME, RESPONSIBILITY AND THE CORPORATION 159 (Hugh Curtler ed., 1986); Henry W. Edgerton, *Corporate Criminal Responsibility*, 36 YALE L.J. 827 (1927); James R. Elkins, *Corporations and the Criminal Law: An Uneasy Alliance*, 65 KY. L.J. 73 (1976); Peter A. French, *The Corporation as a Moral Person*, 16 AM. PHIL. Q. 207 (1979); Michael Keeley, *Organizations as Non-persons*, 15 J. VALUE INQUIRY 149 (1981); Frederic P. Lee, *Corporate Criminal Liability*, 28 COLUM. L. REV. 1 (1928); Larry May, *Vicarious Agency and Corporate Responsibility*, 43 PHIL. STUD. 69 (1983); Michael McDonald, *The Personless Paradigm*, 37 U. TORONTO L.J. 212 (1987); Gerhard O.W. Mueller, *Mens Rea and the Corporation—A Study of the Model Penal Code Position on Corporate Criminal Liability*, 19 U. PITT. L. REV. 21 (1957); Comment, *Developments in the Law—Corporate Crime: Regulating Corporate Behavior Through Criminal Sanctions*, 92 HARV. L. REV. 1227 (1979); Note, *Corporate Criminal Liability*, 68 NW. U. L. REV. 870 (1973); Note, *Criminal Liability of Corporations*, 14 COLUM. L. REV. 241 (1914).

digm that does not require an assessment of culpability in relation to harm at the time of sentencing. Notably, the debate that accompanied the deliberations of the Sentencing Commission over organizational sanctions was grounded in differences over ideology. Economists, who proposed economic models derived from theories of deterrence, searched for efficiency in optimal penalties. Others, including interest groups in the business community, fought hard for a more eclectic consideration of harm, culpability, and mitigation in fashioning organizational sanctions.[8]

The last effort by the Sentencing Commission, codified in law on November 1, 1991,[9] did a masterful job in addressing culpability in relation to corporate sanctions.[10] What is left, however, is a less than adequate corporate criminal law. The assessment of culpability in relation to liability remains couched in a poorly drafted and presented federal criminal law. The federal criminal law relies upon obscure and antiquated culpability provisions. Differing interpretations of culpability provisions in both individual and corporate prosecutions are nearly impossible to reconcile. These problems, as well as others, contribute to the commonly-held view that the federal criminal law is no more than a "hodgepodge of conflicting, contradictory, and imprecise laws with little relevance to each other or to the state of the criminal law as a whole."[11]

---

8. This debate resulted in three draft proposals from the Sentencing Commission, and numerous conferences and public forums. For a detailed description of the Sentencing Commission's work, see UNITED STATES SENTENCING COMMISSION, SUPPLEMENTARY REPORT ON SENTENCING GUIDELINES FOR ORGANIZATIONS (1991). For additional commentary, see Block, *supra* note 4; Macey, *supra* note 4, at 316-17 ("Notably, the Sentencing Commission's proposal for organizational sanctions was wholly devoid of empirical or theoretical foundation. Its proposals were politically oriented, rather than policy oriented. Indeed, if nothing else, the process of establishing sentencing guidelines has made it clear that the work of the Sentencing Commission has entered the realm of special-interest politics."); Jeffrey S. Parker, *Criminal Sentencing Policy for Organizations: The Unifying Approach of Optimal Penalties*, 26 AM. CRIM. L. REV. 513 (1989); Jeffrey S. Parker, *The Current Corporate Sentencing Proposals: History and Critique*, 3 FED. SENTENCING REP. 133 (1990); and Cohen, The New Corporate Sentencing Guidelines: The Beginning or the End of the Controversy? 1 (1991)(unpublished manuscript, on file with the NEBRASKA LAW REVIEW)("A large part of the disagreement over corporate sentencing appears to be grounded in ideological differences").

9. 18 U.S.C. app. §§ 8A1.1-8E1.3 (1992).

10. *See infra* notes 129-34 and accompanying text.

11. S. REP. No. 605, 95th Cong., 1st Sess. 3 (1977)(Senate Report for S. 1437, the Criminal Justice Code Reform Act of 1977). If this assessment appears overly critical, consider the remarks of former Attorney General Richard Thornburgh who only recently called for a recodification of the federal criminal code:

> Our federal criminal laws are presently scattered among 50 titles of the United States Code, containing over 23,000 pages of text. They cannot be understood without review of case decisions encompassed in 2300

It would be unfair to place the burden of federal criminal law reform upon the Sentencing Commission. But it is equally true that any genuine effort to consider culpability in relation to sentence severity, no matter how successful, would be frustrated by the obfuscation of existing federal statutory law.[12] The current fascination with organizational sentencing has completely overlooked the fact that the substantive law upon which the new sentencing guidelines are based is wholly inadequate. This article argues that Congress' failure to make meaningful statutory reforms to the United States Code over the last twenty years has compromised the value of the recently enacted sentencing guidelines for organizations. In passing the Sentencing Reform Act of 1984 ("SRA"), which gave rise to these new guidelines, Congress proceeded as if there were no logical connection between the substantive law and the law of sentencing.[13] So the question remains: If the SRA was enacted in order to achieve honesty, uniformity, and proportionality in sentencing, can this be achieved given the current state of federal law?

Part I of this Article reviews general principles of corporate liability. Part II examines pre-conviction assessment of culpability. Part III considers post-conviction assessment of culpability. Part IV discusses sentencing in relation to culpability. Part V briefly contrasts proposals for determining genuine corporate intent with culpability provisions found in extant law.

II. CORPORATE CRIMINAL LIABILITY

Corporate criminal law requires both a basis of liability and an at-

---

volumes, containing over 3,000,000 pages. They are contaminated, if you will, by the inclusion of over 1700 essentially regulatory violations . . . . The traditionally recognized forms of wrongdoing are lost among multiple and confused citations.

Richard Thornburgh, Address to the Conference of the Society for the Reform of the Criminal Law, in FED. NEWS SERVICE, January 22, 1990.

12. See infra notes 90-102 and accompanying text.
13. The Sentencing Reform Act of 1984 (SRA) found in Title II of the Comprehensive Crime Control Act of 1984, 18 U.S.C. § 3553, was passed by Congress to structure the discretion of federal judges and, thus, diminish unwarranted sentencing disparity. The SRA led to: (1) the dismantling of the United States Parole Commission, (2) the development of determinate rather than indeterminate sentencing in federal courts, (3) sentence review by U.S. Courts of Appeal, and (4) the establishment of the United States Sentencing Commission. For a recent criticism of the effects of the SRA, see Daniel J. Freed, Federal Sentencing in the Wake of Guidelines: Unacceptable Limits on the Discretion of Sentencers, 101 YALE L.J. 1681 (1992).

The SRA was designed by Congress to promote fairness in sentencing. Fairness was to be achieved by moving toward some very admirable goals: (1) honesty in sentencing, (2) uniformity in sentencing, and (3) proportionality in sentencing. UNITED STATES SENTENCING COMMISSION, GUIDELINES MANUAL 2-4 (1990).

tribution of culpability. Liability becomes a threshold issue—"should the act in question be subjected to criminal punishment?"[14] In federal courts, liability rules for corporations are derived from agency principles, and have evolved in case law.[15] This may be contrasted with liability rules for state law violations which generally follow the provisions in the Model Penal Code ("MPC").[16] Of course, both state

14. VON HIRSCH, *supra* note 6, at 80 ("Culpability, it should be noted, affects both questions of liability ('Should the person be punished at all?') and questions of allocation ('How severely should he be punished?'). Liability is a threshold question: Whether the behavior involved sufficient culpability to be punishable at all."); *see also* Stanislaw Frankowski, *Mens Rea and Punishment in England: In Search of Interdependence of the Two Basic Components of Criminal Liability (A Historical Perspective)*, 63 U. DET. L. REV. 393 (1986).

15. *See, e.g.*, New York Cent. and Hudson River R.R. v. United States, 212 U.S. 481 (1909); United States v. Illinois Cent. R.R., 303 U.S. 239 (1938); United States v. Gold, 743 F.2d 800 (11th Cir. 1984)(upholding corporation's conviction for employee's filing of false Medicare claims); Apex Oil Co. v. United States, 530 F.2d 1291 (8th Cir. 1976), *cert. denied*, 429 U.S. 827 (1976)(knowledge of supervisory employee is knowledge of the corporation); Steere Tank Lines, Inc. v. United States, 330 F.2d 719 (5th Cir. 1963)(conviction of corporate motor carrier upheld for employee's falsification of logs); Standard Oil Co. v. United States, 307 F.2d 120, 127 (5th Cir. 1962)("The corporations can be found guilty, therefore, only if the evidence shows that each, acting through its human agents, deliberately did these acts, that is, with the corporation "knowing" that they were being done."); Magnolia Motor & Logging Co. v. United States, 264 F.2d 950 (9th Cir. 1959)(conviction of corporation for employees' conversion and stealing of property); Riss & Co. v. United States, 262 F.2d 245 (8th Cir. 1958)(corporations can be found guilty for "knowing and willful" violations of federal statutes through the doctrine of respondeat superior); *cf.* United States v. Sherpix, Inc., 512 F.2d 1361, 1368 (D.C. Cir. 1975)("Individuals or corporations used without their knowledge or consent by others in the commission of offenses may not possess the requisite criminal intent to be guilty of an offense." (citation omitted)); United States v. Gibson Products Co., 426 F. Supp 768 (S.D. Texas 1976)(corporation's conviction for employee's false entries upheld under theory of respondeat superior); United States v. T.I.M.E.-D.C., Inc., 381 F. Supp. 730, 738 (W.D. Vir. 1974)("A corporation can only act through its employees and, consequently, the acts of its employees, within the scope of their employment, constitute the acts of the corporation."); United States v. Griffin, 401 F. Supp. 1222 (S.D. Ind. 1975)(conviction of corporation for acts of bribery by its president); United States v. Thompson-Powell Drilling Co., 196 F. Supp. 571 (N.D. Texas 1961)(corporation found liable for employees' violation of the Hot Oil Act, 15 U.S.C. § 715).

16. MODEL PENAL CODE § 2.07(1)(Proposed Official Draft 1962) sets forth the liability rules:

(1) A corporation may be convicted of the commission of an offense if:
(a) the offense is a violation or the offense is defined by a statute other than the Code in which a legislative purpose to impose liability on corporations plainly appears and the conduct is performed by an agent of the corporation acting in behalf of the corporation within the scope of his office or employment, except that if the law defining the offense designates the agents for whose conduct the corporation is accountable or the circumstances under which it is accountable, such provisions shall apply; or
(b) the offense consists of an omission to discharge a specific duty of af-

and federal law provide for the imputation or attribution of liability of agents and employees to corporate entities.[17]

A. Federal Corporate Criminal Liability

Courts interpreting federal statutory law find corporations criminally liable for the conduct of employees acting within the scope of employment or with apparent authority, and with an intent to benefit the corporation.[18] Under the doctrine of respondeat superior corporations are viewed as principals. Officers, directors, and all employees—whether managers or subordinates—are considered agents of the corporation.[19] Thus, criminal liability extends to the corporation for criminal acts committed by: (1) officers and directors,[20] (2) managers and supervisors,[21] (3) subordinate employees,[22] and (4) independent

---

firmative performance imposed on corporations by law; or (c) the commission of the offense was authorized, requested, commanded, performed or recklessly tolerated by the board of directors or by a high managerial agent acting in behalf of the corporation within the scope of his office or employment.

Id.

For an interpretation of these rules, see Mueller, *supra* note 7; and Herbert L. Packer, *The Model Penal Code and Beyond*, 63 COLUM. L. REV. 594 (1963), and see also Kathleen F. Brickey, *Rethinking Corporate Liability Under the Model Penal Code*, 19 Rutgers L.J. 593 (1988), in a special issue of the Rutgers Law Journal devoted to the 25th Anniversary of the Model Penal Code.

17. For a thorough review of both state and federal imputation cases, see KATHLEEN F. BRICKEY, CORPORATE CRIMINAL LIABILITY (1984).

18. The term "scope of employment" includes "acts on the corporation's behalf in performance of the agent's general line of work." United States v. Automated Medical Laboratories, Inc., 770 F.2d 399, 407 (4th Cir. 1985); *cf.* United States v. Gold, 743 F.2d 800, 823 (upholding the following jury instruction: "Whether the agents' acts or omissions were committed within the scope of their employment is a question of fact. To be acting within his employment, the agent first must have intended that his act would have produced some benefit to the corporation or some benefit to himself and the corporation second."). The requirement of "intent to benefit the corporation" has been considered a critical factor in "equating the agent's action with that of the corporation." Standard Oil Co. v. United States, 307 F.2d 120, 128 (5th Cir. 1962); *see also* BRICKEY, *supra* note 16, at §§ 3:01-3:08.

19. The unqualified application of the doctrine of respondeat superior ("let the master answer") to corporations has spurred some debate. Critics argue that it is unfair to hold officers, directors, and high managerial agents liable for the acts of low level employees. *See, e.g.*, Mueller, *supra* note 7; Comment, *supra* note 7.

20. *See, e.g.*, United States v. Empire Packing Co., 174 F.2d 16 (7th Cir. 1949), *cert. denied*, 337 U.S. 959 (1949); United States v. Carter, 311 F.2d 934 (6th Cir. 1963). For a discussion of the these different levels of liability, see Elkins, *supra* note 7.

21. *See* C.I.T. Corp. v. United States, 150 F.2d 85 (9th Cir. 1945); United States v. American Radiation & Sanitary Corp., 433 F.2d 174 (3d Cir. 1970).

22. *See* United States v. Uniroyal, Inc., 300 F. Supp. 84 (S.D.N.Y. 1969). The rationale for holding subordinates liable as stated in United States v. E. Brooke Matlack, Inc., 149 F. Supp. 814 (D. Md. 1957) is that:

While the primary responsibility for conducting the operations of the

contractors.[23]

A recent statement of the general rule of corporate criminal liability under federal law is found in *United States v. Basic Construction Co.*,[24] in which the Fourth Circuit Court of Appeals affirmed a conviction under section 1 of the Sherman Act[25] for bid rigging in state road-paving contracts. At trial, Basic Construction Company argued that the bid rigging activities were performed by low-level employees without the knowledge of high-level officials, and that the Company had a strict policy against such practices. In a per curiam opinion, the Court ruled that "a corporation may be held criminally responsible for antitrust violations committed by its employees if they were acting within the scope of their authority, or apparent authority, and for the benefit of the corporation even if . . . such acts were against corporate policy or express instructions."[26]

More elaborate rules for the federal courts, however, have been proposed. Liability rules were first discussed at length by the National Commission on Reform of Federal Criminal Laws ("Brown Commission") over twenty years ago.[27] The Brown Commission re-

---

corporation lay with its principal officers, it was their duty in delegating authority to lesser agents to take effective measures to supervise and assure performance of the affirmative duty imposed upon the corporation. Thus the corporation cannot avoid responsibility by merely saying that a subordinate agent neglected his duty.

Id. at 820.

23. *See* United States v. Parfait Powder Puff Co., 163 F.2d 1008 (7th Cir. 1947).
24. United States v. Basic Const. Co., 711 F.2d 570 (4th Cir. 1983), *cert. denied*, 464 U.S. 956 (1983); *see also* United States v. Hilton Hotels Corp., 467 F.2d 1000 (9th Cir. 1972), *cert. denied*, 409 U.S. 1125 (1973); Continental Baking Co. v. United States, 281 F.2d 137 (6th Cir. 1960). In *Continental Baking*, the Sixth Circuit Court of Appeals stated that:

There is an officer or agent of a corporation with broad express authority, generally holding a position of some responsibility, who performs a criminal act related to the corporate principal's business. Under such circumstances, the courts have held that so long as the criminal act is directly related to the performance of the duties which the officer or agent has the broad authority to perform, the corporate principal is liable for the criminal act also, and must be deemed to have "authorized" the criminal act.

Continental Baking Co. v. United States, 281 F.2d 137, 149 (6th Cir. 1960).
25. 15 U.S.C. § 1 (1992).
26. United States v. Basic Const. Co., 711 F.2d 570, 573 (4th Cir. 1983). This statement of law has been interpreted broadly to include all federal criminal law violations. For example, in United States v. Automated Medical Laboratories, Inc., 770 F.2d 399 (4th Cir. 1985), the Court held: "We believe that Basic Construction states a generally applicable rule on corporate criminal liability despite the fact that it addresses violations of the antitrust laws." *Id.* at 407, n.5. *See also* Old Monastery Co. v. United States, 147 F.2d 905 (4th Cir. 1945); United States v. Hilton Hotels Corp., 467 F.2d 1000 (9th Cir. 1972); United States v. Am. Radiator & Standard Sanitary Corp., 433 F.2d 174 (3d Cir. 1970).
27. The Honorable Edmund G. Brown, Chairman of the National Commission on Re-

commended corporate liability for any offense committed by an agent who was authorized, commanded, or requested to act by: (1) the board of directors, (2) an executive officer, (3) a person who controls the organization or is responsible for policy formation, or (4) a person otherwise considered responsible under a statute.[28] According to the Brown Commission, a successful effort to codify liability rules would have the effect of addressing two critical problems: (1) the existing uncertainty regarding the extent of liability for acts committed by agents of the corporation, and (2) the "inappropriateness" of extant rules of accountability.[29]

A number of versions of these liability rules appeared in draft proposals for the revision of the Federal Criminal Code during the late 1970s and early 1980s. In the last proposal, found in the Criminal Code Reform Act of 1981, organizations would be liable for the acts of any agent that: (a) occur in the performance of their duties, (b) are intended to benefit the organization, and (c) are ratified or adopted by the organization. Alternatively, liability may be found where there is a failure on the part of the organization to discharge a specific duty imposed by law.[30]

B. State Corporate Criminal Liability

It is worthwhile, for purposes of comparison, to examine analogous state liability rules. The codification of the MPC by the American Law Institute in 1962 ushered in a new era in uniform liability for state corporate criminal law violations.[31] The MPC identifies three

---

form of Federal Criminal Laws, submitted a final report to the President and Congress on January 7, 1971. In this report, the Brown Commission described the many features of the proposed criminal code, including the fact that:

> Unlike existing Title 18, the [proposed] Code is comprehensive. It brings together all federal felonies, many of which are presently found outside Title 18; it codifies common defenses, which presently are left to conflicting common law decisions by the courts; it establishes standard principles of criminal liability and standard meanings for terms employed in the definitions of offenses and defenses.

NATIONAL COMMISSION ON REFORM OF FEDERAL CRIMINAL LAWS, at xii (Final Report 1971).

28. NATIONAL COMMISSION ON REFORM OF THE FEDERAL CRIMINAL LAWS, 1 WORKING PAPERS 214 (1970).
29. *Id.* at 163.
30. S. 1630, 97th Cong., 2d Sess. § 402 (1982). This section superseded the liability rules found in S. 1722, 96th Cong., 1st Sess. (1979). Congress never passed S. 1722 due, in part, to insufficient time. Subsequently, according to Norman Abrams, "The steam went out of the effort to adopt a comprehensive criminal code revision and Congress began again to consider crime bills that treat substantive criminal law issues piecemeal." NORMAN ABRAMS, FEDERAL CRIMINAL LAW AND ITS ENFORCEMENT 67 (1986).
31. *See* MODEL PENAL CODE, § 2.07(1)(Proposed Official Draft 1962). For a discussion of the efforts to change state penal codes, see Robert G. Lawson, *Kentucky Penal*

distinct forms of liability, *i.e.*, regulatory offenses, failures to discharge duties imposed by law, and penal law violations. First, corporations are liable for minor, regulatory offenses where a clear legislative purpose to impose liability is present, and the agent's actions were on behalf of the corporation and within the scope of his authority.[32] The basis of liability here is vicarious, found in the doctrine of respondeat superior. Notably, the use of a due diligence defense limits the reach of this liability rule by allowing a corporation to escape conviction if it can establish that a responsible supervisory officer used due diligence to prevent the offense. Second, a corporation is liable where the offense is based on a failure to discharge a specific duty of performance imposed by law.[33] Finally, corporations are liable for all penal law violations, with few exceptions, where the "offense was authorized, requested, commanded, performed or recklessly tolerated by the board of directors or by a high managerial agent acting in behalf of the corporation within the scope of his office or employment".[34] This final category, which has been the subject of much deliberation and debate, does not adopt the broad respondeat superior approach of section 207(1)(a) and confines liability to a narrow class of criminal acts— those concerning high managerial agents whose acts reflect the policy of the corporate body.[35] Some states' legislatures have found section 207(1)(c) too restrictive and, thus, have proceeded cautiously in adopting this section. Most states, however, have used section 207(1)(c) as a rough guide for drafting less restrictive provisions.[36]

Code: The Culpable Mental States and Related Matters, 61 KY. L.J. 657 (1973); Note, *The Mens Rea Provisions of the Proposed Ohio Criminal Code—The Continuing Uncertainty*, 33 OHIO ST. L.J. 354 (1972); Note, *The Proposed Tennessee Criminal Code—General Interpretive Provisions and Culpability*, 41 TENN. L. REV. 131 (1973).

32. MODEL PENAL CODE § 2.07(1)(a)(Proposed Official Draft 1962).
33. MODEL PENAL CODE § 207(1)(b)(Proposed Official Draft 1962).
34. MODEL PENAL CODE § 2.07(1)(c)(Proposed Official Draft 1962).
35. This is in sharp contrast to federal liability rules. *Cf.* United States v. Basic Constr. Co., 711 F.2d 570 (4th Cir. 1983); Holland Furnace Co. v. United States, 158 F.2d 2 (6th Cir. 1946).
36. For example, according to Brickey,
    [T]o the extent that section 2.07 has served as a model rule of corporate liability for crime, its role has been closer to that of rough theoretical model than that of model law. In its first twenty-five years, section 2.07 has succeeded in providing an organizing principle around which many state laws have been modeled, but is has yet to achieve the goal of bringing order and rationality to this unruly branch of the law.
    Brickey, *supra* note 16, at 632. A host of state cases discuss corporate liability issues. Consider, for example, Commonwealth v. Penn Valley Resorts, Inc., 494 A.2d 1139 (Pa. Super. 1985)(involuntary manslaughter); State v. Christy Pontiac-GMC, Inc., 354 N.W.2d 17 (Minn. 1984)(theft and forgery); State v. Chapman Dodge Center, Inc., 428 So. 2d 413 (La. 1983)(theft); Granite Constr. Co. v. Superior Court, 197 Cal. Rptr. 3 (Ct. App. 1983)(manslaughter); Vaughan & Sons, Inc. v. State, 649 S.W.2d 677 (Tex. Crim. App. 1983)(manslaughter); State v. Shepherd

III. PRE-CONVICTION CULPABILITY

An assessment of an agent's or corporation's culpability serves two distinct functions. First, it satisfies one of a number of elements necessary to establish liability, *i.e.*, the mental element, and, thus, provides a basis for criminal punishment. After all, it is axiomatic that theories of criminal punishment require the finding of mens rea.[37] Thus, the prosecution must establish a requisite mental state in order to satisfy its burden of proving each and every material element of an offense.[38] As Professor H. L. A. Hart noted, the central question of culpability prior to conviction is: "Can this man be convicted of this crime?"[39] Thus, the pre-conviction use of culpability is typically more restricted, limited to finding willfulness or knowledge on the part of an actor in the federal courts, or purpose, knowledge, recklessness, or negligence in state courts.[40] A second brand of culpability is considered after conviction at which point the concern is with the allocation of punishment.[41] Here the question is: "How severely is the accused to be punished?"[42] The post-conviction assessment of culpability reflects an interest in assessing the interaction between blameworthiness and harm, in addition to the actor's intent. As will become evident, a host of other factors may be considered in assessing blameworthiness at sentencing.

Constr. Co., 281 S.E.2d 151 (Ga. 1981)(restraint of trade); People v. Warner Lambert Co., 51 N.Y.2d 295 (1980)(manslaughter); Commonwealth v. McIlwain Sch. Bus Lines, Inc., 423 A.2d 413 (Pa. 1980)(homicide by vehicle); Commonwealth v. J.P. Mascaro and Sons, Inc., 402 A.2d 1050 (Pa. 1979)(theft by deception, deceptive business practices, and unsworn falsification to authorities); People v. Ebasco Services, Inc., 354 N.Y.S.2d 807 (1974)(negligent homicide); State v. Adjustment Dept. Credit Bureau, Inc., 483 P.2d 687 (Idaho 1971)(extortion); and State v. Pacific Powder Co., 360 P.2d 530 (Oregon 1961)(involuntary manslaughter).

37. *See, e.g.*, H.L.A. HART, PUNISHMENT AND RESPONSIBILITY: ESSAYS IN THE PHILOSOPHY OF LAW 114 (1988)("All civilized penal systems make liability to punishment for at any rate serious crime dependent not merely on the fact that the person to be punished has done the outward act of a crime, but on his having done it in a certain state of mind or will."). For a recent review of different conceptualizations of mens rea, see Stephen J. Morse, *The "Guilty Mind:" Mens Rea*, *in* THE HANDBOOK OF PSYCHOLOGY AND LAW 207 (D.K. Kagehiro & W.S. Laufer eds. 1992).

38. *In re* Winship, 397 U.S. 358 (1970); Mullaney v. Wilbur, 421 U.S. 684 (1975); Patterson v. New York, 432 U.S. 197 (1977); *see* Herbert L. Packer, *Making the Punishment Fit the Crime*, 77 HARV. L. REV. 1071 (1964); Herbert L. Packer, *Mens Rea and the Supreme Court*, 1962 SUP. CT. REV. 107. For an interesting revisionist perspective on mens rea in relation to due process, see Gary V. Dubin, *Mens Rea Reconsidered: A Plea for a Due Process Concept of Criminal Responsibility*, 18 STAN. L. REV. 322 (1966).

39. HART, *supra* note 37, at 114.

40. *See infra* notes 43-102 and accompanying text.

41. *See infra* notes 103-109 and accompanying text.

42. HART, *supra* note 37, at 115.

State law culpability provisions are elaborate and generally well-conceived—much more so than federal provisions. Thus, after briefly considering the many advances made in state culpability provisions with the passage of the MPC, the discussion will focus on the pre- and post-conviction usages of culpability in federal law.

A. Culpability under State Law

It is the presence or absence of mens rea, an evil intent or guilty state of mind, that provides a natural division between blameworthy and non-blameworthy acts, between crimes and accidental acts.[43] In assessing culpability prior to conviction, the focus is squarely on establishing a material mental state, required under a particular statute, which reflects a criminal intent.

Prior to the codification of the MPC, state legislatures had little guidance in crafting uniform criminal statutes that consistently defined mental states. In fact, a host of mental states with varied meanings were found in state codes, including fault provisions that are quite difficult to interpret, e.g., "unlawfully," "maliciously," "fraudulently," and "designedly."[44] Courts, for example, were forced to decipher the meaning of "heedlessly," "wickedly," "wantonly," and "wrongfully."[45]

---

43. See, e.g., JOEL P. BISHOP, 1 BISHOP ON CRIMINAL LAW 192-93 (9th ed. 1923)("There can be no crime, large or small, without an evil mind. In other words, punishment is the sequence of wickedness . . . . It is therefore a principle of our legal system . . . that the essence of an offence is the wrongful intent, without which it cannot exist." (citations omitted)); HALL, supra note 6, at 243 ("Even apart from the enormous extent of tort law devoted to negligence and strict liability, it follows that moral culpability is not essential in tort law—immoral conduct is simply one of various ways by which individuals suffer economic damage."); Gerhard O.W. Mueller, On Common Law Mens Rea, 42 MINN. L. REV. 1043 (1958); Francis B. Sayre, Mens Rea, 45 HARV. L. REV. 974 (1932); see also Morse, supra note 37.

For a fascinating discussion of the crime/tort distinction, see Coffee, supra note 4.

44. For a review of the development of culpability in state law, consider Ronald L. Gainer, The Culpability Provisions of the Model Penal Code, 19 RUTGERS L.J. 575, 578-79 (1988)("The disorder of the American criminal law concerning culpable mental states assured the drafters of the Model Penal Code of a daunting task. It also assured the drafters of at least some degree of success; there was virtually no chance that their product would be worse than that produced over the centuries by a succession of judges and legislators."); and Paul H. Robinson & Jane A. Grall, Element Analysis in Defining Criminal Liability: The Model Penal Code and Beyond, 35 STAN. L. REV. 681 (1983).

45. These mens rea requirements come from Alabama's pre-MPC criminal laws. See English v. Jacobs, 82 So. 2d 542 (Ala. 1955); Padgett v. State, 56 So. 2d 116 (Ala. App. 1952); Martin v. State, 25 So. 255 (Ala. 1898); Burton v. State, 107 Ala. 108 (1894). Lawson observed that: "Without question the most significant single accomplishment of the entire code is the clarification that has been provided by doctrine of mens rea. The confusion which previously existed in this area of the law is not totally describable." Lawson, supra note 31, at 658 (citation omitted).

With the MPC, four culpable mental states were selected that represent a continuum or hierarchy of culpability—ranging from conduct that is purposeful, or consciously designed to bring about a certain result, to negligent conduct where the actor should have known of a substantial risk of injury. Thus, liability under the MPC requires that one act purposely ("with a conscious object to engage in conduct"), knowingly ("aware that it is practically certain that his conduct will cause a result"), recklessly ("consciously disregards a substantial and unjustifiable risk"), or negligently ("should be aware of a substantial and unjustifiable risk") with respect to a material element of an offense.[46]

The MPC also brought with it a critical advance in the interpretation of offense descriptions. Prior to the MPC, in some states, proof of one culpable mental state was required for each offense or class of offenses. For example, there were statutes for which knowledge alone was required for a particular offense description, and there were classes of offenses characterized simply as requiring a "general intent." This "offense analysis" was replaced in the MPC with the recognition that offense descriptions may necessitate separate proof of a culpable state of mind for the conduct, result, or circumstance elements of an offense.[47] The analysis of the elements of offense descrip-

---

Lawson noted 10 pre-MPC mens rea terms for crimes against property in Kentucky (willful; wanton; reckless; negligence; unlawfully; forcibly; willfully and maliciously, intent; willfully, knowingly and maliciously; and knowingly) and six for crimes against property (willfully and maliciously; willfully, intentionally, or maliciously; unlawfully; feloniously; willfully and knowingly; willfully and fraudulently). *Id.* at 658-59.

46. *See* Paul H. Robinson, *A Brief History of Distinctions in Criminal Culpability*, 31 HASTINGS L.J. 815 (1980).

47. The MPC defines these four states of mind as follows:

(2)(a) A person acts *purposely* with respect to a material element of an offense when: (i) if the element involves the nature of his conduct or a result thereof, it is his conscious object to engage in conduct of that nature or to cause such a result; and (ii) if the element involves the attendant circumstances, he is aware of the existence of such circumstances or he believes or hopes that they exist.

(b) A person acts *knowingly* with respect to a material element of an offense when: (i) if the element involves the nature of his conduct or the attendant circumstances, he is aware that his conduct is of that nature or that such circumstances exist; and (ii) if the element involves a result of his conduct, he is aware that it is practically certain that his conduct will cause such a result.

(c) A person acts *recklessly* with respect to a material element of an offense when he consciously disregards a substantial and unjustifiable risk that the material element exists or will result from his conduct. The risk must be of such a nature and degree that, considering the nature and purpose of the actor's conduct and the circumstances known to him, its disregard involves a gross deviation from the standard of conduct that a law-abiding person would observe in the actor's situation.

(d) A person acts *negligently* . . . when he should be aware of a sub-

tions ensures clarity and consistency. Most important, element analysis recognizes complex factual situations requiring more than one mental state. Grouping the act, circumstance, and results elements runs the risk of obscuring critically important state of mind distinctions. As Professor Sayre noted over fifty years ago, "A mens rea does not mean a single precise state of mind which must be proved as a prerequisite for all criminality. Mens rea, chameleon-like, takes on different colors in different surroundings."[48]

The codification of four culpable mental states added significant rationality and fairness to state penal law. It has been observed that the MPC gives "fair warning of what will constitute a crime, limits governmental discretion in determining whether a particular individual has violated the criminal law, and provides the distinctions among degrees of harm and degrees of culpability that create the foundation of a fair sentencing system."[49]

Indeed, even though the focus here is on establishing liability through proof of a mental state, culpable mental states also provide an initial basis for the determination of a sentence. This may be seen in one of two ways. First, sentencing judges under most state statutes use the grade or degree of an offense in order to calculate a propor-

---

stantial and unjustifiable risk that a material elements exists or will result from his conduct. The risk must be of such a nature and degree that the actor's failure to perceive it, considering the nature and purpose of his conduct and the circumstances known to him, involves a gross deviation from the standard of care that a reasonable person would observe in the actor's situation.

MODEL PENAL CODE § 2.02(2)(a)-(d)(Proposed Official Draft 1962).

For a discussion of the importance of element analysis, see Robinson & Grall, *supra* note 44, at 683 ("The majority of American jurisdictions have adopted criminal codes that incorporate this Model Penal Code innovation by requiring courts to apply an element analysis to each offense and theory of liability." (citation omitted)); and Gainer, *supra* note 44, at 588 ("Perhaps the greatest potential value of the overall analytical approach employed by the Code lies in its restrained application to the drafting of the penal offenses themselves. The possibility of a superior structure is suggested. If a building block technique can so simplify the law with regard to mental elements through recasting them better to accord with distinctions among acts, circumstances, and results, and through re-examining the continued utility of traditional offense categories."). *See also* Sayre, *supra* note 43; Francis B. Sayre, *The Present Signification of Mens Rea in the Criminal Law, in* HARVARD LEGAL ESSAYS 399 (Roscoe Pound ed., 1934).

48. Francis B. Sayre, *The Present Signification of Mens Rea in the Criminal Law, in* HARVARD LEGAL ESSAYS 399, 402 (Roscoe Pound ed., 1934); *see also* Robinson & Grall, *supra* note 44, at 687 ("The Model Penal Code's move towards 'element analysis' continued this refinement process by adding to the specific mental state concept detailed definitions of the required culpable states of mind. In addition, the concept of a different mens rea for each offense acquired a larger, more precise meaning. Under the Code, a culpable state of mind requirement may exist for '*each* material *element*' of an offense. Further, the culpability requirement may be different for different elements of the same offense." (citation omitted)).

49. Robinson & Grall, *supra* note 44, at 689 (citations omitted).

tional sentence.[50] As Professor Ashworth has noted, "Much of the doctrine of the criminal law concerns—implicitly and even expressly in places—the different levels of seriousness of crimes. Different maximum penalties may be assigned to offences which turn on the distinction between intention and recklessness . . . ."[51] Thus, in states that have adopted the MPC in whole or in part, offenses may be hierarchically graded by culpable mental states. For example, in many jurisdictions the types and degrees of criminal homicide are organized by hierarchical mental states.[52] Second, judges often use culpable mental states as a threshold showing of blameworthiness. It is simply the most logical starting point for a more detailed pre-sentence assessment of culpability.[53]

B. Culpability under Federal Law

The contrast between state and federal law in regard to culpability provisions is dramatic. The failure of Congress to incorporate uniform and hierarchical culpable mental states in the Federal Criminal Code, as well as a host of federal criminal laws is more than remarkable.[54]

---

50. *See, e.g.*, ME. REV. STAT. ANN. tit. 17-A, § 1252 (West 1991); N.J. STAT. ANN. § 2C:44-1 (West 1992). See Robinson & Grall, *supra* note 44, who make the connection between degrees of harm, degrees of culpability, and sentencing guidelines.

51. ANDREW ASHWORTH, PRINCIPLES OF CRIMINAL LAW 14 (1991).

52. *See, e.g.*, N.J. STAT. ANN. § 2c:11-2 to -6 (West 1992); 18 PA. CONST. STAT. ANN. § 2501-06 (1992).

53. *See* DAVID WEISBURD ET AL., CRIMES OF THE MIDDLE CLASSES: WHITE COLLAR OFFENDERS IN THE FEDERAL COURTS (1991).

54. Every year, approximately 50% of all convictions of corporations in federal district courts are for violations of non-Title 18 federal statutes. During the period January 1, 1989 to June 30, 1990, for example, the distribution of convictions by U.S. Code Title was as follows:

Title	Number	Percent
7	2	0.4%
8	2	0.4%
12	1	0.2%
15	85	19.1%
16	5	1.1%
18	227	51.0%
19	6	1.3%
20	1	0.2%
21	33	7.4%
22	1	0.2%
26	23	5.2%
29	4	0.9%
30	1	0.2%
31	6	1.3%
33	15	3.4%
42	23	5.2%
43	1	0.2%
47	1	0.2%

Federal criminal law relating to culpability has been described as "hopelessly confused," "bewildering," and "elusive."[55] Clearly, the effort to reform the Federal Criminal Code has held out the greatest hope.[56] The Brown Commission criticized the "confused and inconsis-

49	2	0.4%
50	6	1.3%
Total	445*	99.0%

*One missing case

UNITED STATES SENTENCING COMMISSION, ORGANIZATIONS SENTENCED IN FEDERAL CRIMINAL COURTS 1989-90, (1991).

55. *See* SENATE COMM. ON THE JUDICIARY, 96th CONG., 2d SESS., REPORT ON CRIMINAL CODE REFORM ACT OF 1979, 59 (1980)("Present Federal criminal law is composed of a bewildering array of terms used to describe the mental elements of an offense. . . . Not surprisingly, the proliferation of these terms has left the criminal justice system with confusing and even conflicting laws. Justice Jackson characterized the mental element concepts in Federal law as being 'elusive' because of the 'variety, disparity and confusion' of judicial definitions." (footnotes omitted)).

56. The debate over the possible reform of the Federal Criminal Code has persisted for over twenty years. *See, e.g., Reform of the Federal Criminal Laws, Hearings Before the Subcomm. on Criminal Laws and Procedure of the Senate Comm. on the Judiciary,* 91st-94th Cong., (1971-1975); Edward M. Kennedy, *Federal Criminal Code: An Overview,* 47 GEO. WASH. L. REV. 451 (1979); John L. McClellan, *Codification, Reform, and Revision: The Challenge of a Modern Federal Criminal Code,* 1971 DUKE L.J. 663; Paul F. Rothstein, *Federal Criminal Code Revision: Some Problems With Culpability Provisions,* 15 CRIM. L. BULL. 157 (1979).

This debate continues with a recent report of the Federal Courts Study Committee unanimously recommending that: "Congress should enact a comprehensive recodification of the federal criminal laws and should create a code revision commission to expedite the process." FEDERAL COURTS STUDY COMM., 100TH CONG., 2D SESS., REPORT OF THE FEDERAL COURTS STUDY COMM. 106 (1990).

Recently, Senator Howell Heflin proposed the creation of the National Commission on Federal Criminal Law Reform as part of the Federal Courts Study Committee Implementation Act of 1991 (S. 1569). The Commission would consider, along with a series of proposed reforms, mens rea requirements in criminal statutes. *See* 137 CONG. REC. S11,062 (1991)(daily ed. July 26, 1991)(Statement of Sen. Heflin). The proposal met with mixed reviews. In testimony given before the Senate Committee on the Judiciary, Subcommittee on Courts and Administrative Practice, by Paul Maloney, Deputy Assistant Attorney General, Criminal Division, Department of Justice, on October 17, 1991, the proposal was called "ill-advised." According to Maloney:

Although the Department of Justice has long supported the concept of comprehensive federal criminal code reform, we do not favor the enactment of the proposal in Title II. . . . The nearly decade-long period since the abandonment of the criminal code reform effort has been a time of unprecedented legislative activity in the area of federal criminal law, and one that has resulted in the attainment of some of the goals of the reform bills. Comprehensive laws affecting the federal criminal justice system have been enacted by Congress in 1984, 1986, 1988, and 1990, and this year Congress is again considering, at the President's request, another important bill addressed primarily to violent crime. The 1984 Act was especially important, since it embodied the sentencing and bail reforms that had been included in prior Senate criminal code reform bills, as well as other substantial changes, such as a limitation of the insanity

tent ad hoc approach" to culpability in the federal courts and called for a "new departure."[57] The need for this new departure was made clear by the Brown Commission's identification of seventy-eight different mens rea terms and combinations of terms in the Federal Criminal Code. As the Appendix suggests, there was no new departure. There are currently one hundred and one culpable mental state terms and combinations of terms in Title 18.[58] This is a significant increase over the already unmanageable number of terms and combinations of terms found by the Brown Commission in 1970. Moreover, the inventory of Title 18 terms in Appendix A fails to consider the culpability provisions in criminal statutes found outside of the Federal Criminal Code.[59]

Mens rea terms found in the Federal Criminal Code are left undefined, and no federal statute existed at the time of the Brown Commission, or exists now, providing rules of construction for requisite states of mind and their many combinations. This results in two significant problems with the construction of mens rea requirements: interpreta-

---

defense. Other reforms in recent years have included new offenses aimed at drug trafficking and money laundering, and the enactment of statutes permitting both civil and criminal forfeiture for a wide panoply of federal crimes.

Given the extent to which federal criminal laws have undergone revision over the last ten years—a degree of legal revolution, as it were, far greater than has been experienced in the entire previous history of the nation—we believe this is not the time for another comprehensive overhaul.

(Statement of Paul Maloney, Department of Justice, concerning the Implementation of Federal Courts Study Committee Recommendations, S.1569, at 6).

On the other hand, support was voice by J. Vincent April II, who testified: "It is an inevitable reality that any body of statutory criminal law which is regularly revisited for purposes of modification, deletion, and addition, will eventually require a comprehensive revamping to guarantee a consistent and uniform relationship between various criminal offenses which make up the body of that law." (Statement of J. Vincent April II, concerning the Implementation of Federal Courts Study Committee Recommendations, S.1569, at 3).

57. See SENATE COMM. ON THE JUDICIARY, *supra* note 55, at 60. For an excellent discussion of culpable mental states in federal statutory law, see United States v. Bailey, 444 U.S. 394 (1980). This opinion is remarkable for its consideration of mens rea in federal law, and for its cautions against an overly critical approach to the limitations of federal statutory law. In analyzing the culpability requirements for 18 U.S.C. § 751(a), Justice Rehnquist cautioned that "[t]his system could easily fall of its own weight if courts or scholars become obsessed with hairsplitting distinctions, either traditional or novel, that Congress neither stated nor implied when it made the conduct criminal." *Id.* at 406-07.

58. 18 U.S.C. §§ 1-2711 (1992).

59. See UNITED STATES SENTENCING COMMISSION, *supra* note 54. With a significant number of corporate convictions obtained for non-Title 18 offenses, it is necessary to consider whether or not similar state of mind problems exist in these regulatory and non-regulatory statutes. *See, e.g.,* George E. Garvey, *The Sherman Act and the Vicious Will: Developing Standards for Criminal Intent in Sherman Act Prosecutions,* 29 CATH. U.L. REV. 389 (1980).

tive variations and redundant combinations. The former may be seen in differing interpretations by courts of identical mens rea requirements within a particular statute, as well as across statutes. The latter is evident in statutes that combine mens rea terms that possibly have the same meaning, e.g., willfully and knowingly.[60]

Federal courts are left to interpret one hundred and one mental state combinations using prior case law, legislative history, and intuition as a guide.[61] Meaningful interpretation is further limited by problems of generality, vagueness, and ambiguity in federal statutory law.[62] Moreover, as shall be seen below, "willfulness"—perhaps the most obscure of all mens rea requirements—is less than ideal for such an ad hoc approach to determining culpability.[63] Willfulness is currently used in twenty-three different combinations in the Federal Criminal Code, e.g., "willfully and corruptly," "falsely and willfully," and "willfully and unlawfully." A more detailed consideration of the use of this term in the United States Code will reveal its limitations.

---

60. See *infra* notes 80-89 and accompanying text.

61. The process of choosing a mens rea requirement for a particular statute is equally obscure. Consider the history of the bank bribery provisions found in 18 U.S.C. § 215. These provisions originated in the 1984 Comprehensive Crime Control Act, 18 U.S.C. § 1107, and, for a period of two years, failed to have a mens rea requirement, e.g., a corrupt intention. The result was that normal banking and business activities often were prohibited under the statute. For example, in its strict liability form, the statute prohibited a bank official from seeking anything of value for another in connection with bank business. It also prohibited anyone from giving anything of value to a bank official in connection with bank business. In order to cure this defect, considerable debate took place over the selection of an appropriate mental state. This debate ended with the choice of the term "corruptly," which allegedly conveys the meaning of corrupt intention. This choice was made with the knowledge that the term was both unclear and offered little guidance to those governed by the Act in the financial industry. For debate over the Bank Bribery Amendments, see 132 CONG. REC. 943 (1986); 131 CONG. REC. 9274 (1985); 131 CONG. REC. 2591 (1985); and 131 CONG. REC. 7081 (1985).

62. For a discussion of these problems in relation to 18 U.S.C. § 207, see Matthew T. Fricker & Kelly Gilchrist, Comment, *United States v. Nofziger and the Revision of 18 U.S.C. § 207: The Need for a New Approach to the Mens Rea Requirements of Federal Criminal Law*, 65 NOTRE DAME L. REV. 803, 809-812 (1990). These problems are not typical of all statutes. See, e.g., P.S. ATIYAH & ROBERT S. SUMMERS, FORM AND SUBSTANCE IN ANGLO-AMERICAN LAW 98 (1991)("Because statute law is a better source of rules than case-law, and because many rules are susceptible of highly formal treatment, this also tends to make statute law a more formal kind of law. Case law can be extremely *ad hoc*—simply a method of deciding disputes without providing much, if any guidance for the future. Indeed, in some cases the courts appear exclusively concerned with the past, with clearing up a mess after the fact. The usual statute is not like this at all: it is prospective, and operates through rules, many of which are hard and fast rules.").

63. For an excellent treatment of willfulness in federal law, see Kenneth R. Feinberg, *Toward a New Approach to Proving Culpability: Mens Rea and the Proposed Federal Criminal Code*, 18 AM. CRIM. L. REV. 123, 125-128 (1980).

1. Willfulness

The first statutory codification of a willful state of mind has been traced to England and the Uniformity of Service Act of 1548.[64] Since the creation of that act, the term "willful" has served in English statutory law, and subsequently in American law, as an elastic proxy for a host of mental states ranging from "malicious" to "not accidental." In fact, the term is so elastic that its meaning in any particular statute is said to depend, at least in part, on a judge's view of mens rea generally.[65] More likely, its meaning is tied to the subject matter of the statute.[66] After *United States v. Murdock*,[67] there has been an evolving consensus that the meaning of a willful state of mind can be determined only through an examination of the context in which it is used. In *Murdock*, Justice Roberts acknowledged that the term willful should reflect an intentional, knowing, and voluntary state of mind. He noted as well that, depending on the statute, courts have used the term to reflect acts done with a bad purpose, without excuse, stubbornly, obstinately, perversely, and with a careless disregard.[68] A resolution of this inconsistency is achieved by courts accepting a contextual approach to the interpretation of mens rea requirements in federal statutory law. Such an approach allows courts to develop statute-specific interpretations of mens rea terms. This may be contrasted with Justice Marshall's recent call for a plain language approach that would require uniform interpretations of identical mens rea terms across statutes.[69] The architects of the MPC choose a variation of the

---

64. J. LL. J. EDWARDS, MENS REA IN STATUTORY OFFENCES 30 (1955).
65. *Id.* at 31.
66. *See, e.g.*, United States v. Murdock, 290 U.S. 389, 395 (1933)("Aid in arriving at the meaning of the word 'willfully' may be afforded by the context in which it is used . . . ."); Spies v. United States, 317 U.S. 492, 497 (1943)("[W]illful, as we have said, is a word of many meanings, its construction often being influenced by its context.").
67. United States v. Murdock, 290 U.S. 389 (1933).
68. This characterization comes directly from *Murdock*, where the Court defined "willful":

   The word often denotes an act which is intentional, or knowing, or voluntary, as distinguished from accidental. But, when used in a criminal statute, it generally means an act done with a bad purpose . . . without justifiable excuse . . . stubbornly, obstinately, perversely. . . . The word is also employed to characterize a thing done without ground for believing it is lawful . . . or conduct marked by careless disregard whether or not one has the right so to act.

   United States v. Murdock, 290 U.S. 389, 394-95 (1933).
69. This distinction was made clear in McLaughlin v. Richland Shoe Co., 486 U.S. 128 (1988), where the Court defined a willful violation of the Fair Labor Standards Act to include an employer's knowledge or "reckless disregard for the matter of whether its conduct was prohibited by the statute . . . ." *Id.* at 133. This definition was borrowed from an earlier decision, Trans World Airlines, Inc. v. Thurston, 469 U.S. 111, 125-130 (1985), where Justice Powell interpreted the willfulness pro-

plain language approach, but could not do so with the term willful. Quite simply, the term willful was "unusually ambiguous standing alone."[70]   Instead, a provision was added to the MPC that substituted the mental state of knowledge for all statutory references to willful states.[71]

The contextual approach to the determination of a willful mental state has resulted in a significant number of differing judicial interpretations under Title 18 and other federal statutory laws.[72] With regard

---

vision of the Age Discrimination in Employment Act of 1967. Justice Marshall's dissent in *McLaughlin* illustrates the contrasting approaches:

> The Court today imports into a limitations provision of the Fair Labor Standards Act (FLSA) the "knowing or reckless" definition of "willful" that we previously adopted in construing a liquidated damages provision of the Age Discrimination in Employment Act of 1967. . . . In doing so, the Court departs from our traditional contextual approach to the definition of the term "willful" . . . . The Court's apparent abandonment of this approach in favor of a nonexistent "plain language" definition of "willful" . . . is unprecedented and unwise.

McLaughlin v. Richland Shoe Co., 486 U.S. 128, 135-37 (1988)(Marshall, J., dissenting)(citations omitted).

70. MODEL PENAL CODE § 2.02(8) note on term willful (Proposed Official Draft 1962). Along the same lines, in the American Law Institute Proceedings, an exchange between the Reporter and Judge Learned Hand was recorded:

> JUDGE HAND: Do you use . . . [willfully] throughout? How often do you use it? It's a very dreadful word.
> MR. WECHSLER: We will never use it in the Code, but we are superimposing this on offenses outside the Code. It was for that purpose that I thought that this was useful. I would never use it.
> JUDGE HAND: Maybe it is useful. It's an awful word! It is one of the most troublesome words in a statute that I know. If I were to have the index purged, "wilful" would lead all the rest in spite of its being at the end of the alphabet.
> MR. WECHSLER: I agree with you Judge Hand, and I promise you unequivocally that the word will never be used in the definition of any offense in the Code. But because it is such a dreadful word and so common in the regulatory statutes, it seemed to me useful to superimpose some norm of meaning on it. . . .

A.L.I. PROC. 160 (1955).

71. MODEL PENAL CODE § 2.02(8)(Proposed Official Draft 1962). The provision reads: "*Requirement of Wilfulness Satisfied by Acting Knowingly*. A requirement that an offense be committed wilfully is satisfied if a person acts knowingly with respect to the material elements of the offense, unless a purpose to impose further requirements appears."

72. *See, e.g.*, Feinberg, *supra* note 63, at 127. Feinberg's review of federal decisions reveals seven definitional variations of the term willful: (1) knowledge of illegality, or an intent to further an objective known to be illegal; (2) recklessness as to legality; (3) negligence as to legality; (4) immoral objective, or knowledge immorality—such as bad purpose, evil intent, and conscious wrongdoing; (5) intent to defraud or injure; (6) intent or knowledge with respect to ordinary elements of the offense; and (7) recklessness with respect to ordinary elements of the offense. *Id.* Even a cursory analysis of these mental states reveals a full range of culpability (excluding negligence)—from intention or purpose, to recklessness. Commentators have overlooked the fact that the obscure nature of wilfulness

to the latter, willfulness under the Fair Labor Standards Act is knowing or reckless conduct, or conduct that is "not merely negligent."[73] The requirement of proving willfulness under the Age Discrimination in Employment Act is satisfied by establishing knowledge of the statute or a reckless disregard of it.[74] Under the Securities and Exchange Act of 1934, courts have found willful action to be deliberate and intentional.[75] Willful infringement of Federal copyright laws requires purposive action.[76] The Currency and Foreign Transactions Reporting Act has a willfulness requirement that is satisfied by both a knowing failure to obey the law, and a specific intent to disobey the law.[77] Most recently, the United States Supreme Court has ruled that willfulness under criminal tax law requires an intentional and voluntary violation of a known duty.[78]

The existence of differing interpretations of willfulness across different regulatory statutes is problematic, and is made more so by differences between judicial decisions regarding definitions and interpretations of a single mental state within a particular statute. This is true for those statutes providing a basis for the prosecution of corporations found inside and outside the Federal Criminal Code.[79]

---

is only furthered by the nature of the corporate form. Courts appear unsure as to whether wilfulness is established by direct reference to employee acts (or omissions) or proof of willful corporate behavior which is essentially independent of employee behavior, *e.g.*, an entity's reaction or lack of reaction to the discovery of illegal behavior. *See, e.g.,* United States Bank of New England, 821 F.2d 844 (1st Cir. 1987)(direct evidence of bank employees state of mind used to establish wilfulness); United States v. Sawyer, 337 F. Supp. 29 (D. Minn. 1971)(wilfulness established by proof of a corporation's plain indifference to the requirements of the statute); United States v. T.I.M.E.-D.C., Inc., 381 F. Supp. 730 (W.D. Vir. 1974)(evidence of a "hands off" attitude by the corporation toward compliance with the regulation constitutes wilfulness).

73. McLaughlin v. Richland Shoe Co., 486 U.S. 128, 133 (1988).
74. Trans World Airlines, Inc. v. Thurston, 469 U.S. 111, 127-28 (1985).
75. United States v. Dixon, 536 F.2d 1388, 1396-98 (2d Cir. 1976).
76. *See, e.g.,* United States v. Heilman, 614 F.2d 1133, 1137 (7th Cir. 1980)(the court followed a two-part test for willfulness which includes acting with the purpose of depriving the victim of an interest protected by a copyright); *see also* United States v. Wise, 550 F.2d 1180 (9th Cir. 1977); United States v. Cross, 816 F.2d 297 (7th Cir. 1987).
77. United States v. Sans, 731 F.2d 1521, 1530 (1984).
78. Cheek v. United States, 111 S. Ct. 604 (1991). Justice White announced that: "Willfulness, as construed by our prior decisions in criminal tax cases, requires the Government to prove that the law imposed a duty on the defendant, that the defendant knew of this duty, and that he voluntarily and intentionally violated that duty." *Id.* at 610. Justice Scalia concurred in the judgment of the court but disagreed with the definition of willfulness. "I find it impossible to understand how one can derive from the lonesome word 'willfully' the proposition that belief in the nonexistence of a textual prohibition excuses liability, but belief in the invalidity (*i.e.*, the legal nonexistence) of a textual prohibition does not." *Id.* at 614. (Scalia, J., concurring).
79. Within the Federal Criminal Code, consider the differing interpretations of the

To make matters even more obscure, judges who face questions relating to the distinctions between "willful" and "knowing" states of mind often refer back to Justice Butler's attempt to distinguish these two seemingly different culpable mental states: "'Wilfully' means something not expressed by 'knowingly,' else both would not be used conjunctively . . . ."[80] However, the effort to distinguish the requirement of willfulness from other mens rea requirements may be no more than a semantic one. As one commentator has observed, supporting a "decision as an interpretation of statutory 'willfulness' rather than of intention . . . [is] a distinction without a difference."[81] In fact, the most reasonable view is that willfulness is no more than a term of art which may encompass all culpable mental states that exceed negligence.[82] In this sense, it resembles the common law conceptualization of general intent.[83]

In part because of its broad reach, the unsparing use of willfulness by Congress has had a truncating effect on the presence of different

---

mens rea requirement for the mail fraud statute, 18 U.S.C. § 1341, found in United States v. Gordon, 780 F.2d 1165 (5th Cir. 1986)(specific intent must be established); United States v. Dick, 744 F.2d 546 (7th Cir. 1984)(reckless disregard is sufficient); United States v. Glick, 710 F.2d 639 (10th Cir. 1983)(deliberate ignorance is sufficient); and United States v. Massa, 740 F.2d 629 (8th Cir. 1984)(willful blindness is sufficient). Outside the Federal Criminal Code, consider the differing mens rea interpretations under the anti-fraud provisions of § 17 of the Securities Act of 1933, 15 U.S.C. §§ 77q, 77x, found in Elbel v. United States, 364 F.2d 127 (10th Cir. 1966), *cert. denied*, 385 U.S. 939 (1966)(willful intent judged according to a reckless indifference test); United States v. Amik, 439 F.2d 351 (7th Cir. 1971), *cert. denied*, 403 U.S. 918 (1971)(reckless misinterpretation is sufficient); United States v. Brown, 578 F.2d 1280 (9th Cir. 1978)(specific intent is required); and United States v. Vandersee, 279 F.2d 176 (3rd Cir. 1960)(fraudulent intent is required). For a discussion of scienter under the Securities Exchange Act of 1934, see Craig L. Griffin, *Corporate Scienter Under the Securities Exchange Act of 1934*, 34 B.Y.U. L. REV. 1227 (1989).

80. St. Louis & S.F.R. Co. v. United States, 169 F. 69, 71 (8th Cir. 1909).
81. GLANVILLE L. WILLIAMS, THE MENTAL ELEMENT IN CRIME 39 (1965).
82. As was noted by the National Commission on the Reform of the Federal Criminal Law,

There may be no word in the Federal criminal lexicon which has caused as much confusion as the word "willfully" (or "willful"). In ordinary speech, the word probably connotes something between purpose and malice, and also something of obstinacy. Despite the confusion that the word has engendered, it has an accepted place in Federal criminal law and can be eliminated only with difficulty. The next best thing to eliminating it entirely is to attempt to give it a clear, fixed meaning. This has been done by providing that a person engages in conduct "willfully" if he engages in it "intentionally," "knowingly," or "recklessly." So confined, the word offers a useful means of referring to the more serious degrees of culpability. None of its connotations have significance for the criminal law.

NATIONAL COMMISSION ON REFORM OF THE FEDERAL CRIMINAL LAWS, *supra* note 27, at 128 (citation omitted).
83. *See* HALL, *supra* note 6, at 143.

mens rea terms in federal statutes. The full range of culpable mental states in the MPC hierarchy is absent, for example, from the Federal Criminal Code. Consider the use of recklessness, or the conscious disregard of a substantial and unjustifiable risk. It is identified in only seven provisions of the Code.[84] Over time, however, courts have ruled that the mens rea requirements of an additional twelve statutes, which most often require willful and knowing acts, may be satisfied by a reckless state of mind.[85]

---

84. The term reckless appears in the following provisions of the Federal Criminal Code: 18 U.S.C. § 33 (1991)("Destruction of motor vehicles or motor vehicle facilities. Whoever willfully, with intent to endanger the safety of any person on board or anyone who he believes will board the same, or with a reckless disregard for the safety of human life . . . ."); 18 U.S.C. § 35(b)(1991)("Imparting or conveying false information. . . . (b) Whoever willfully and maliciously, or with reckless disregard for the safety of human life . . . ."); 18 U.S.C. § 831(b)(1)(B)(i)(II)(1991)("Prohibited transactions involving nuclear materials. . . . [The punishment for an offense is imprisonment if] the offender, under circumstances manifesting extreme indifference to the life of an individual, knowingly engages in any conduct and thereby recklessly causes the death of or serious bodily injury to any person . . . ."); 18 U.S.C. § 922 (1991)("Unlawful acts. . . . (2)(A) Except as provided in subparagraph (B), it shall be unlawful for any person, knowingly or with reckless disregard for the safety of another, to discharge or attempt to discharge a firearm at a place that the person knows is a school zone."); 18 U.S.C. § 1365(a)(1991) "Tampering with consumer products. (a) Whoever, with reckless disregard for the risk that another person will be placed in danger of death or bodily injury and under circumstances manifesting extreme indifference to such risk, tampers with any consumer product that affects interstate or foreign commerce . . . ."); 18 U.S.C. § 1861 (1991)("Deception of prospective purchasers. Whoever . . . in reckless disregard of the truth, falsely represents to any such person that any tract of land shown to him is public land of the United States subject to sale, settlement, or entry, or that it is of a particular surveyed description, thereby deceiving the person to whom such representation is made . . . ."); 18 U.S.C. § 1864(a)(1991)("Hazardous or injurious devices on Federal lands. (a) Whoever— . . . (3) with reckless disregard to the risk that another person will be placed in danger of death or bodily injury and under circumstances manifesting extreme indifference to such risk, uses a hazardous or injurious device on Federal land, . . . shall be punished . . . .").

85. The following judicial decisions have held that recklessness is sufficient to satisfy a mens rea requirement other than recklessness in particular provisions of the Federal Criminal Code: United States v. Thomas, 610 F.2d 1166 (3rd Cir. 1979)(holding that reckless disregard sufficient to satisfy intent element under 18 U.S.C. § 656 (1991)("Theft, embezzlement or misapplication by bank officer or employee")); United States v. Felice, 481 F. Supp. 79 (N.D. Ohio 1978)(holding that reckless disregard is sufficient to find intent to defraud under 18 U.S.C. § 664("Theft or embezzlement from employee benefit plan")); Zimmerman v. United States, 1 F.2d 712, (6th Cir. 1924)(holding that recklessness may justify inference of intent under 18 U.S.C. § 755 (1991)("Permitting an officer to escape")); United States v. Evans, 559 F.2d 244 (5th Cir. 1977), cert. denied, 434 U.S. 1015 (1978)(holding that proof of specific intent may be made by showing of reckless disregard under 18 U.S.C. § 1001 (1991)("Statements or entries generally")); United States v. Bernstein, 533 F.2d 775 (2nd Cir. 1976)(holding that recklessness satisfies knowledge element of 18 U.S.C. § 1010 (1991)("Department of Housing

The problem of truncation by a broad interpretation of willfulness may help explain the absence of references to reckless states of mind in Title 18. It cannot, however, assist in explaining the conspicuous absence of references to negligent mental states. There are four explicit statutory provisions requiring proof of a negligent mental state in the entire Federal Criminal Code.[86] Only two statutes allow for a

---

and Urban Development and Federal Housing Administration Transactions")); United States v. Tolkow, 532 F.2d 853 (2nd Cir. 1976)(holding that reckless disregard may satisfy the knowledge requirement of 18 U.S.C. § 1027 (1991)("False statements and concealment of facts in relation to documents required by the Employee Retirement Income Security Act of 1974")); United States v. Pardee, 368 F.2d 368 (4th Cir. 1966)(holding that gross negligence may be established by proof of reckless disregard for human life under 18 U.S.C. § 1112 (1991)("Manslaughter")); United States v. Farris, 614 F.2d 634 (9th Cir. 1979)(holding that reckless disregard satisfies requirements of 18 U.S.C. § 1341 (1991)("Frauds and Swindles")); United States v. Hathaway, 798 F.2d 902 (6th Cir. 1986)(holding that reckless indifference to truth or falsity is sufficient under 18 U.S.C. § 1341 (1991)("Frauds and Swindles")); United States v. Armstrong, 654 F.2d 1328, (9th Cir. 1981)(holding that reckless disregard of truth about fraudulent nature of activities satisfies 18 U.S.C. § 1343 (1991)("Fraud by wire, radio, or television")); United States v. Gullett, 713 F.2d 1203 (6th cir. 1983)(holding that reckless disregard for truth is sufficient under 18 U.S.C. § 2314 (1991)("Transportation of stolen goods, securities, moneys, fraudulent State tax stamps, or articles used in counterfeiting")); United States v. Jacobs, 475 F.2d 270 (2nd Cir. 1973)(holding that reckless disregard of whether bills were stolen may satisfy 18 U.S.C. § 2315 (1991)("Sale or receipt of stolen goods, securities, moneys, or fraudulent State tax stamps")); Farroni v. Farroni, 862 F.2d 109 (6th Cir. 1988)(holding that willful action may be proved by evidence of reckless disregard of known legal duty under 18 U.S.C. § 2511 (1991)("Interception and disclosure of wire, oral, or electronic communications prohibited")).

86. The following statutes contain explicit reference to negligent states of mind: 18 U.S.C. § 492 (1991) ("Forfeiture of counterfeit paraphernalia. Whenever . . . any person interested in any article, device, or other thing, or material or apparatus seized under this section files with the Secretary of the Treasury, before the disposition thereof, a petition for the remission or mitigation of such forfeiture, the Secretary of the Treasury, if he finds that such forfeiture was incurred without willful negligence or without any intention on the part of the petitioner to violate the law, or finds the existence of such mitigating circumstances as to justify the remission or the mitigation of such forfeiture, may remit or mitigate the same upon such terms and conditions as he deems reasonable and just."); 18 U.S.C. § 755 (1991)("Officer permitting escape. Whoever . . . negligently suffers [a prisoner in his custody] to escape, . . . shall be fined not more than $ 500 or imprisoned not more than one year, or both."); 18 U.S.C. § 793(f)(1991)("Gathering, transmitting, or losing defense information. . . . Whoever . . . having . . . control of any document, writing, code book, signal book, sketch, photograph, photographic negative, blueprint, plan, map, model, instrument, appliance, note, or information, relating to the national defense, (1) through gross negligence permits the same to be removed from its proper place of custody or delivered to anyone in violation of his trust, or to be lost, stolen, abstracted, or destroyed, . . . [s]hall be fined not more than $ 10,000 or imprisoned not more than ten years, or both."); 18 U.S.C. § 1115 (1991)("Misconduct or neglect of ship officers. Every captain, engineer, pilot, or other person employed on any steamboat or vessel, by whose misconduct, negligence, or inattention to his duties on such vessel the life of any person is

substitution of negligence with other mens rea requirements.[87]

It is certainly true that the inclusion of negligence in penal statutes has been hotly debated for many years.[88] However, the relative absence of recklessness in combination with the near complete absence of negligence results in a body of federal criminal law that is insufficiently inclusive. The full range of culpability provisions found in state law, for example, is missing. And the problem of inclusivity and truncated mens rea requirements is made even more serious by the haphazard collection of mens rea terms.[89]

2. Inadequate Statutory Law

The most promising solution to this ad hoc, intuitive approach to culpability, according to the Brown Commission is to adopt the MPC's

---

destroyed, and every owner, charterer, inspector, or other public officer, through whose fraud, neglect, connivance, misconduct, or violation of law the life of any person is destroyed, shall be fined . . . or imprisoned . . . .").

87. The following decisions allow negligence to satisfy other mens rea requirements found in particular provisions of the Federal Criminal Code: Shaw v. United States, 357 F.2d 949 (Ct. Cl. 1966)(holding that proof of negligence is sufficient to satisfy 18 U.S.C. § 650 (1991)("Depositaries failing to safeguard deposits")); United States v. Pardee, 368 F.2d 368 (4th Cir. 1966)(holding that gross negligence supports a conviction for involuntary manslaughter under 18 U.S.C. § 1112 (1991)("Manslaughter")).

88. See James B. Brady, *Punishment for Negligence: A Reply to Professor Hall*, 22 BUFF. L. REV. 107 (1972); Robert P. Fine & Gary M. Cohen, *Is Criminal Negligence a Defensible Basis for Penal Liability?*, 16 BUFF. L. REV. 749 (1967); Jerome Hall, *Negligent Behavior Should be Excluded from Penal Liability*, 63 COLUM. L. REV. 632 (1963).

89. The Brown Commission was extremely critical of the culpability requirements in the Federal Criminal Code.

Unsurprisingly, the courts have been unable to find substantive correlates for all these varied descriptions of mental states, and, in fact, the opinions display far fewer mental states than the statutory language. Not only does the statutory language not reflect accurately or consistently what are the mental elements of the various crimes; there is no discernible pattern or consistent rationale which explains why one crime is defined or understood to require one mental state and another crime another mental state or indeed no mental state at all.

NATIONAL COMMISSION ON REFORM OF THE FEDERAL CRIMINAL LAWS, *supra* note 28, at 120.

Professor Rothstein has written that:

There is no question that the federal criminal law badly needs codification. It is currently scattered in conflicting measures spread through most of the fifty titles and a dozen or so of the volumes of the U.S. Code, and an estimated 50,000 viable decisions. Often quite a few of the provisions relate to the same conduct. The statutes were enacted piecemeal over two hundred years, with little regard for one another or consistency between them, and with little modernization to meet changing conditions. They were separate and unrelated responses to the particular problems and moral notions of the day and its Congress.

Rothstein, *supra* note 56, at 157.

hierarchical state of mind organization, along with provisions that would require element analysis of culpable mental states and corresponding offense elements. Thus, four mental states would be analyzed in relation to the elements of conduct, existing circumstances, and result.[90] This solution would yield significant rewards for courts interpreting the intent of Congress in passing certain legislation. There is no doubt that explicit liability rules and clearly defined culpable mental states would go a long way in providing certainty, predictability, and structure to such reasoning.

The absence of rules guiding liability and culpability is both unfortunate and conspicuous. Drafters of the proposed Code worked for well over a decade to provide liability rules and culpability reformulations.[91] Certainly, the analogous MPC reformulation produced clarity and promoted fairness. Thus, it is fair to ask: What is it that makes Congress willing to settle for less in the federal criminal law? Or, more specifically, why is the focus in the area of federal law reform on the creation of new offenses and the standardization of sanctions? Why is there more concern with culpability in relation to sentence severity, than culpability in relation to liability?

Answers to the first two questions seem straightforward. Congress passed comprehensive legislation affecting the federal criminal law in 1984, 1986, 1988, and 1990. Therefore, it appears as if there has been a significant evolution in the substance of federal criminal law. Proponents of this view argue that now is simply not the time to engage in comprehensive criminal law reform. Such an effort, it is argued, would entail significant costs in terms of a major "retooling of the system." Jury instructions and indictment forms would have to be changed. Practitioners would have to learn the new law. A new body of law

---

90. The Brown Commission alleged that:

> The Federal Criminal Code, as reported, discards the confused and inconsistent *ad hoc* approach to culpability that now characterizes Federal criminal law. Instead it reduces the number of terms used to describe the requisite mental state to four: *intentional, knowing, reckless, or negligent.* All other statutory formulations within title 18, United States Code, are eliminated. The four degrees of culpability that are retained express the significant distinctions in defining offenses. . . . By classifying the offense elements into three types, *viz.,* the nature of conduct, the circumstances surrounding the conduct and the results of the conduct, and by considering the state of mind required in relation to each component offense element, the Code avoids confusing proof required with respect to each element. Although many offenses prescribe the same state of mind for each type of element, some do not. Clear analysis therefore requires that the question of the kind of culpability required to establish the commission of an offense be considered separately with respect to each of the elements of the offense.

SENATE COMM. ON THE JUDICIARY, *supra* note 55, at 60-61.

91. *See* Rothstein, *supra* note 56.

would have to evolve in order to interpret the statutory changes.[92] Perhaps a more satisfactory answer is that the legislative revision that has taken place, in such areas as bail reform, violent crime, drug offenses, and sentencing reform, reflects a particular political agenda—one that would not be served by a focus on the notion of culpability.[93]

The answer to the last question appears a bit less transparent. A glimpse of the truth, though, may be gleaned from two caveats noted in Justice Rehnquist's opinion in *United States v. Bailey*.[94] After extolling the virtues of the MPC's approach to culpability and the move toward element analysis, he cautioned:

> First . . . courts obviously must follow Congress' intent as to the required level of mental culpability for any particular offense. Principles derived from common law as well as precepts suggested by the American Law Institute must bow to legislative mandates. . . . Second, while the suggested element-by-element analysis is a useful tool for making sense of an otherwise opaque con-

---

92. *See supra* note 56.

93. *See, e.g.*, Robert Drinan et al., *The Federal Criminal Code: The Houses are Divided*, 18 AM. CRIM. L. REV. 509, 531 (1981)(arguing that the hurdles inhibiting the passage of comprehensive reform of federal criminal laws are neither technical nor philosophical—they are political in nature); Barbara A. Stolz, *Interest Groups and Criminal Law: The Case of Federal Criminal Code Revision*, 30 CRIME & DELINQ. 91 (1984); *see also* Feinberg, *supra* note 63, at 124. ("In particular, there has been surprisingly little discussion of the proposed definitions of states of mind and the rules governing proof of culpability. This is probably due to the technical complexities of the subject and the relatively non-controversial nature of the particular provisions. There is an obvious reluctance to debate culpability concepts in the new code when more visible and exciting issues, such as sentencing reform, new rules governing corporate liability, and the appropriate scope of federal inchoate offenses, continue to occupy public attention." (citation omitted)). It is somewhat ironic that the Sentencing Reform Act of 1984, Comprehensive Crime Control Act of 1984, Pub. L. No. 98-473, 98 Stat. 1837, 1976, 1987-2040 (codified as amended in scattered sections of 26 U.S.C.), which gave rise to the Sentencing Commission, has its roots in the effort to reform *and* recodify the federal criminal law.

It is also revealing to examine the evolution of proposed federal criminal laws following the Criminal Code Reform Acts of 1979 and 1981. Such an examination uncovers the dual focus on crime control and sentencing to the exclusion of any effort at recodification. *See, e.g.*, Sentencing Reform Act of 1983, Pub. L. No. 99-646, §§ 4, 5, 6, 27, 29(a), 100 Stat. 3592, 3597, 3600 (codified in scattered sections of 28 U.S.C.); Sentencing Reform Act of 1984, Pub. L. No. 98-473, 98 Stat. 1987; Comprehensive Crime Control Act of 1984, Pub. L. Nos. 98-473, -596, 98 Stat. 1976, 3140; Criminal Law and Procedure Technical Amendments Act of 1986, Pub. L. No. 99-646, 100 Stat. 3592, Pub. L. No. 100-185, 101 Stat. 1279, Pub. L. No. 100-690, 102 Stat. 4395; Criminal Justice Act Revision of 1986, Pub. L. No. 99-651, 100 Stat. 3642; Criminal Fine Improvements Act of 1987, Pub. L. No. 100-185, 101 Stat. 1279; The Minor and Technical Criminal Law Amendments Act of 1988, Pub. L. No. 100-690, 102 Stat. 4395; Pollution Prosecution Act of 1990, Pub. L. No. 101-593, 104 Stat. 2962; Comprehensive Thrift and Bank Fraud Prosecution and Taxpayer Recovery Act of 1990, Pub. L. No. 101-647, 104 Stat. 4859; Crime Control Act of 1990, Pub. L. No. 101-647, 104 Stat. 4789, Pub. L. No. 102-190, 105 Stat. 1488.

94. United States v. Bailey, 444 U.S. 394 (1980).

cept, it is not the only principle to be considered. The administration of the federal system of criminal justice is confided to ordinary mortals, whether they be lawyers, judges, or jurors. This system could easily fall of its own weight if courts or scholars become obsessed with hair-splitting distinctions, either traditional or novel, that Congress neither stated nor implied when it made the conduct criminal.[95]

Thus, the simple answer is that distinctions in culpable mental states must give way to revelations of legislative intent. Such a view trivializes the problem with interpreting Congressional intent.[96] Moreover, because there is so little evidence of legislative intent, it suggests that the idea of culpability in relation to liability is not too important. Of course, the weakness of this view is made clear by the connectedness of culpability assessments. As has been noted, culpability assessments at both the pre- and post-conviction stage are often inextricably intertwined.[97] A clear and concise set of liability rules and culpability standards would be of little value without a sentencing scheme that considers the blameworthiness of the defendant. Likewise, a well-crafted set of sentencing guidelines that considers blameworthiness is far less valuable where the assessment of culpability in relation to liability is obscure.[98]

The absence of needed reforms is also conspicuous because the Sentencing Commission's last-minute effort to consider an assessment of culpability produced greater clarity for federal judges assessing blameworthiness after conviction, than the Federal Criminal Code does prior to conviction.[99] As shall be discussed later, the Sentencing Commission was more explicit than Congress has been in identifying and defining culpable mental states for the purpose of assessing blameworthiness, even in the absence of statutory law that requires the same for the purpose of conviction.

The risks associated with a poorly articulated federal statutory law

---

95. *Id.* at 406-07.
96. *See, e.g.,* ATIYAH & SUMMERS, *supra* note 62, at 110. ("As is well known, a wide range of sources may be consulted by American courts in their search for legislative intent. These include Congressional (or state legislative) debates; reports of committees; statements of those sponsoring the legislation; comments and view of legislators, officials, and other parties at legislative hearings; and other similar material. Much of this material is not only unhelpful in ascertaining 'legislative intention' but deliberately distorting—such as speeches inserted in the *Congressional Record,* but never actually delivered, or statements made with the deliberate aim of influencing judicial interpretation, even though they did not represent the general view in the Congress." (citations omitted)).
97. *See supra* notes 50-53 and accompanying text.
98. Herbert L. Packer states the argument in terms of fairness: "And whatever fairness may be thought to mean on the procedural side, its simplest (if most neglected) meaning is that no one should be subjected to punishment without having an opportunity to litigate the issue of his culpability." HERBERT L. PACKER, THE LIMITS OF THE CRIMINAL SANCTION 69 (1968).
99. *See infra* note 137.

are twofold. First, the confusion that surrounds culpability assessment—within and across statutes—may make liability judgments suspect. Lack of definitions and guidance concerning construction of seemingly redundant terms remains an ongoing and significant problem.[100] This problem is compounded by the absence of a hierarchy of culpable mental states and distinct material elements in offense descriptions which allow for something more than a mere offense analysis. It is further complicated by the complex nature of the corporate form. The well-accepted legal fiction of imputing the culpability of an agent to an entity is stretched to its logical limit where there is no overriding consensus as to what that culpability consists of. Commentators have argued that state criminal law, before the MPC, was often confused and arbitrary.[101] Current federal law is certainly no better.

A second concern relates to the connection between pre- and post-conviction assessments of culpability. As discussed above, ascribing culpability is a central feature of finding liability. Even though it is narrowly focused, the ascription does provide a threshold measure of blameworthiness that reflects on the deservedness of a sanction. Indeed, it is this connection between pre-conviction ascription of culpability and post-conviction decisionmaking with regard to proportional sanctions that makes a remedy for inadequate statutory law all the more important. Obscure culpability requirements compromise the more general assessment of blameworthiness that takes place after conviction in accordance with sentencing guidelines.[102]

IV.   POST-CONVICTION CULPABILITY

Principles of commensurate dessert acknowledge the critical role of culpability and harm in sentencing. Punishment, it is alleged, ascribes or imparts blame. Thus, the extent of a sanction carries with it a message concerning the degree of blameworthiness and seriousness of an offense.[103] Judgments of seriousness may be based upon the na-

---

100. It may be argued that this is more of a theoretical than practical problem. In other words, federal prosecutors and judges concern themselves, more generally, with finding "scienter" or a "general intent" even when an element of a statute specifies a particular culpable mental state. Accordingly, an actor's intention may be inferred from the very act of fraud, for example, without the necessity of providing any separate proof of a mental state. Such a view is unsatisfactory for a number of reasons. First, transforming specific mens rea requirements into a general requirement for finding scienter alters the meaning of the statute. Second, such a practice may result in a lack of notice concerning the ingredients of an offense.
101. *See* Robinson & Grall, *supra* note 44.
102. *See infra* notes 135-37 and accompanying text.
103. Cardinal proportionality requires that "the overall level of the penalty scale, both maximum punishment and actual sentence ranges, should not be disproportionate to the magnitude of the offending behaviour . . . [T]his concept of proportion-

ture of the injury (harm), the intensity of the harm, the proximity of the harm, and the degree of culpability.[104]

Culpability, harm, and seriousness form the basis of what has been called a "normative lens" through which judges view criminal cases.[105] Interestingly, such a lens permits judgments that transcend the strictures of the written law. Thus, judges often look beyond statutes and codes in order to conceptualize harm and culpability. In an examination of the sentencing practices of federal district court judges, it was observed that "the conventional elements of criminal intent that are essential to establishing grounds for conviction in a criminal case are often the starting point for a judge's consideration of blameworthiness. But this consideration usually reaches beyond the starting point to include a broader moral sphere."[106] What is encompassed by the broad moral sphere of culpability? In federal practice, generally, the early history of a defendant, details regarding a defendant's role in an offense, a defendant's motive, and, of course, the defendant's mental state are all important considerations bearing on a post-conviction assessment of culpability.[107]

This broad moral sphere is grounded not only in judicial practice but is also explicitly found in law. In capital sentencing, for example, the United States Supreme Court recently held that a jury may hear victim impact evidence.[108] Victim impact statements reflect an offender's culpability. To deprive a jury of such evidence would unreasonably restrict relevant information bearing on culpability. In the past, the Supreme Court has given judges close to free reign in conducting broad and nearly unlimited inquiries on blameworthiness. The constitutional limit is with evidence that may unduly prejudice a defendant.[109] Given these boundaries, it seems only logical that the Sentencing Commission would place significant weight on an organization's culpability in crafting appropriate guidelines. The wisdom of this intuition is considered below.

V. GUIDELINES AND CULPABILITY

A. Proposed Guidelines

The United States Sentencing Commission was established by the

---

ality involves preserving a correspondence between the relative seriousness of the crime and relative severity of the sentence." ASHWORTH, *supra* note 51, at 15.

104. *Id.* at 37.
105. WEISBURD ET AL., *supra* note 53.
106. STANTON WHEELER ET AL., SITTING IN JUDGMENT: THE SENTENCING OF WHITE COLLAR CRIMINALS 20 (1988).
107. *Id.* at 93-123.
108. Payne v. Tennessee, 111 S. Ct. 2597 (1991).
109. *See, e.g.*, Williams v. New York, 337 U.S. 241 (1949); United States v. Tucker, 404 U.S. 443 (1972).

Sentencing Reform Act of 1984 in order to create sentencing policies and practices for the federal courts.[110] The Sentencing Commission took its mandate from Congress in 1985 to create guidelines for organizational sanctions. Three proposals[111] predated the issuance of final guidelines.[112] In the first two proposals, little concern was expressed for either pre- or post-conviction assessments of culpability.

Though the Sentencing Commission's mandate called for an untenable integration of "just punishment, deterrence, public protection and rehabilitation," the underlying theoretical position taken in the first two proposals reflected an economic model of deterrence best represented by the writings of Gary Becker.[113] The central tenet of this model is that punishment represents disincentives to engage in crime, or, viewed differently, incentives to engage in compliance, by altering the means by which offenders calculate the gains of crime and the costs of punishment. Simply put, because corporations are affected largely by monetary concerns, sanctions such as fines, restitution and forfeitures are most appropriate, and the policy undergirding their distribution is determined by reference to the monetary loss caused by the offense, the likelihood of apprehension, and the enforcement costs that result in investigation, prosecution and punishment.[114]

This model has been subject to numerous criticisms that shall not be explored here, e.g., difficulty in determining harm, questions regarding the calculations performed by the multiplier, and the role of offender characteristics.[115] What is open to discussion here is the tenuous relationship of this early approach of the Sentencing Commission to the substantive criminal law, principally as it concerns both pre- and post-conviction assessments of culpability.

---

110. 18 U.S.C. §§ 3551-80 (1991); 28 U.S.C. §§ 991-98 (1991).
111. UNITED STATES SENTENCING COMMISSION, SENTENCING OF ORGANIZATIONS (Discussion Draft 1988); UNITED STATES SENTENCING COMMISSION, SENTENCING OF ORGANIZATIONS (Preliminary Draft 1989); UNITED STATES SENTENCING COMMISSION, SENTENCING OF ORGANIZATIONS (Proposed Guidelines 1990).
112. For a recent discussion of the sequence and spirit of these proposals, see Jonathan R. Macey, *Agency Theory and the Criminal Liability of Organizations*, 71 B.U. L. REV. 315 (1991).
113. Gary S. Becker, *Crime and Punishment: An Economic Approach*, 76 J. POL. ECON. 169 (1968); M.K. Block & J.M. Heineke, *A Labor Theoretic Analysis of the Criminal Choice*, 65 AM. ECON. REV. 314 (1975); Richard A. Posner, *An Economic Theory of the Criminal Law*, 85 COLUM. L. REV. 1193 (1985); *see also* Parker, *supra* note 8. For a summary of the philosophical bases for imposing sanctions, as specified by Congress, see 28 U.S.C. § 991(b)(1)(A)(1991).
114. Block, *supra* note 4; *see also* Parker, *supra* note 8, at 517 ("My analysis concludes that monetary sanctions are by far the most desirable form of sentence for organizational offenders in general, because a monetary penalty both minimizes the societal losses resulting from the sanctioning process and affects most directly the monetary incentives that drive organizational behavior.").
115. *See* UNITED STATES SENTENCING COMMISSION, *supra* note 8, at 9-15.

Essentially, the early work of the Sentencing Commission ignored the relationship between sentencing aims and the larger aims of the substantive criminal law. To the extent that such aims were considered, they were reduced to the single, general claim that the fundamental aim of the criminal law is to prevent harm. Such a view is correct, of course, from a minimalist perspective, yet the pursuit of that general aim is clearly imbedded in important collateral notions as well, which are represented most clearly by culpability requirements. The criminal sanction is a stigmatizing instrument, functioning as a condemnatory response to an actor's culpability and the harm done. The convention that society has chosen to reflect that condemnation takes the form of adverse economic consequences or deprivations of liberty. Out of fairness, the criminal law affords a host of procedural safeguards to those not responsible for, and thus not worthy of, blame. Of course, this view of the criminal law is a moral interpretation, and those taking this position point out that it is the moral connotation given to blameworthiness that distinguishes criminal liability and punishment from liability under administrative regulations and corresponding civil sanctions.[116]

The Sentencing Commission initially failed to address the fact that culpability is essential for purposes of crime control.[117] It is unreasonable to expect to control crime when criminal sanctions are not commensurate with culpability. Punishment will lose much of its deterrent value if the entity receiving or threatened with punishment is incapable of controlling present or future conduct.[118]

In considering organizational sanctions, little attention was paid by the Sentencing Commission to the moral connotations represented in the intent requirements found in the criminal law. That blame, in general, can be imposed only when the actor is "responsible" for its actions, and that the extent of culpability must affect the degree to which an actor may be held blameworthy went largely unaddressed in the first two proposals. It is worthwhile examining each one of these concerns in more detail.

The stated objective of punishment under the economic approach is to provide corporations with realistic and compelling disincentives to engage in crime.[119] By confronting the corporation with an effec-

---

116. *See supra* note 43.
117. ASHWORTH, *supra* note 51, at 12-16.
118. *See* HART, *supra* note 37, at 133-34 ("[M]any writers, including Professor Glanville Williams, have shared an assumption that to be a deterrent the threat of punishment must be capable of entering into the deliberations of the criminal as a guide at the moment when he contemplates his crime.").
119. *See* RICHARD A. POSNER, ECONOMIC ANALYSIS OF LAW 397 (3d ed. 1986)("An important question about the social responsibility of corporations is whether the corporation should always obey the law or just do so when the expected punishment costs outweigh the expected benefits of violation. If the expected punish-

tive response to non-compliance, the entity will take the desired steps to ensure that its employees comply with the law. At least three alternative paths are available to achieve this aim. The state may impose monetary sanctions directly on the corporation, it may adopt a series of incapacitative sanctions that allow for intervention in the management and operations of the corporation, or it may encourage self-enforcement through the creation and maintenance of compliance programs, ethics training programs, and other more informal means of self-policing.[120] The Sentencing Commission's early work followed the first path. The rationale for monetary sanctions may be derived from the economic model of deterrence. First, since corporations operate largely to produce profit, sanctions that are not directly relevant to that goal are incidental. For costs to be weighed against benefits, the unit of analysis for both must be equal. Such a position devalues any alternative goal that may be operating; *e.g.*, power, prestige, corporate social responsibility; or maintains that such alternative goals are means to the larger goal of profit. The converse of this latter point is that any non-monetary sanctions, such as community service and probation, found in subsequent Sentencing Commission proposals, work only by their impact in economic terms.[121] Adverse publicity sanctions, for example, contain meaning only by virtue of the reduced profitability rising from the abandonment by customers and suppliers.[122]

Second, the economic model of deterrence generally employs some determination of illegal gain in order to produce either incentives or disincentives. Yet, the gains derived through corporate crime are not necessarily equivalent to the harms typically produced. Corporate crimes may result in little distinguishable gain and significant social costs. Reliance on gain alone, therefore, cannot be reconciled with the criminal law doctrine that the punishment imposed be proportionate to the harm caused or risked by the offense.[123] To the extent that the Sentencing Commission considered this point, the model undergirding

---

ment costs are set at the efficient level, the question answers itself; the corporation will violate the law only when it is efficient to do so.").

120. *See* John Braithwaite, *Enforced Self-Regulation: A New Strategy for Corporate Crime Control*, 80 MICH. L. REV. 1466 (1982).

121. *See, e.g.*, Richard Gruner, *To Let the Punishment Fit the Organization: Sanctioning Corporate Offenders Through Corporate Probation*, 16 AM. CRIM. L. REV. 1 (1988); Christopher Kennedy, Comment, *Criminal Sentences for Corporations: Alternative Fining Mechanisms*, 73 CAL. L. REV. 443 (1985); Fred L. Rush, *Corporate Probation: Invasive Techniques for Restructuring Institutional Behavior*, 21 SUFFOLK U. L. REV. 33 (1986).

122. *See, e.g.*, JOHN BRAITHWAITE, CRIME, SHAME, AND REINTEGRATION (1989); BRENT FISSE & JOHN BRAITHWAITE, THE IMPACT OF PUBLICITY ON CORPORATE OFFENDERS (1983); Brent Fisse, *The Use of Publicity as a Criminal Sanction Against Business Corporations*, 8 MELB. U. L. REV. 107 (1971).

123. *Cf.* Block, *supra* note 4.

the first set of guidelines substitutes social loss for corporate gain. Given this proposition, it may be argued that monetary sanctions are the only penalties that may reflect offense harm.

The ultimate impact of non-monetary sanctions cannot be controlled in a fashion that does not risk over-deterrence. Because it is difficult to assess how much intervention is necessary to force the corporation to discontinue its illegal activity, the likely result, so the logic goes, is that the intervention may exceed what is actually required within the organizational structure. Finally, since punishment entails costs to the government, monetary sanctions appear to present fewer burdens in administration than do non-monetary sanctions, which the courts are ill-equipped to provide.

What is striking about this early approach is the lack of any meaningful connection to the concept of corporate culpability. That the Sentencing Commission initially adopted a "black box" approach to corporate control through sanctions is not overstated. The first proposal noted the relevance of this concern by commenting that the goals of the corporation may not necessarily be the same as the goals of individuals acting at various levels within the corporate bureaucracy. Yet, the response offered suggested an unwillingness to delve into the mire of corporate accountability.

The Sentencing Commission's early failure to give credence to the moral connotations implied by the culpability requirements of substantive criminal law is best demonstrated by their unwillingness to adequately address the role that culpability plays in determining the seriousness of corporate offenses. Clearly, as has been noted,[124] the severity of punishment is a function of the seriousness of the offense. Yet, the Sentencing Commission was single-minded in its definition of offense seriousness, initially limiting discussion to social loss as it is defined through property loss, *e.g.*, placing the focus on the estimated monetary value of human life as determined in safety regulations. Subsequently, the Commission appeared to enlarge its conception of loss to include: (a) losses to direct victims, (b) enforcement costs, and (c) social losses, *e.g.*, loss of market efficiency.[125]   Still, the idea of culpability was secondary and almost incidental. Loss was said to include the notion of culpability.[126]

B. Final Proposals

Fortunately, the third set of proposed guidelines attempted to capture the moral sphere of culpability. In these guidelines, the Sentencing Commission required judges to consider four mitigating factors

---

124. *See supra* notes 103-09 and accompanying text.
125. Parker, *supra* note 8, at 577.
126. *Id.* at 565.

that reflected culpability. Evidence of such factors, in the form of a mitigation score, would have reduced the multiplier.[127]   Courts would consider the following questions: (a) Did the offense occur without the knowledge of any person who exercised control over the organization? (b) Did the offense occur despite a meaningful compliance program? (c) Did the organization voluntarily and promptly report the offense? and (d) After discovering the offense, did the organization take reasonable steps to remedy the harm, discipline those responsible, and prevent a reoccurrence?   In addition to these mitigating circumstances, courts would be required to consider, among other things, the "nature and circumstances of the offense and history and characteristics of the defendants."[128]

This "carrot and stick" proposal was widely criticized. Part of the criticism was based on concerns over the mitigation score. Would large publicly-held corporations fare better than small privately-held firms?   Would reduced penalties for compliance programs or monitoring lead to cosmetic programs and lax regulatory oversight? Significant criticism resulted in a new and final proposal.[129]

The final proposal took some additional steps. The Sentencing Commission agreed that fines should reflect the seriousness of an offense, as well as the culpability of the offending corporation. The former would be determined by the pre-tax gain to the corporation, amount of loss caused by the corporation, and a pre-defined ranking of offense seriousness. The latter would be approximated by a culpability score calculated on the basis of an organization's: (a) involvement in or tolerance of criminal activity (scaled according to the size of the organization and highest level of corporate knowledge), (b) prior history, (c) record of violations of orders, (d) attempts to obstruct justice, (e) maintenance of an effective compliance program, and (f) willingness to self-report, cooperate, and accept responsibility.[130]

The Sentencing Commission decided that organizations are more culpable when a "high-level" employee "participated in, condoned, or was wilfully ignorant of the offense."[131]   Here "condone" means knowledge of *and* a failure to prevent or terminate an offense. Willful ignorance approximates the mental state of recklessness insofar as it concerns a conscious disregard of a substantial and unjustifiable risk.

---

127. UNITED STATES SENTENCING COMMISSION, SENTENCING OF ORGANIZATIONS § 8C2.1(d)(Tent. Draft 1990).

128. *Id.* § 8C2.2.

129. *See* UNITED STATES SENTENCING COMMISSION, GUIDELINES MANUAL 3 (1991). For a critical review of the 1990 Draft, see John C. Coffee, *"Carrot and Stick" Sentencing: Structuring Incentives for Organizational Defendants*, 3 FED. SENTENCING REP. 126 (1990).

130. 18 U.S.C. app. § 8C2.5 (b)-(g)(1992).

131. 18 U.S.C. app. § 8C2.5(b)(1)(A)(i)(1992).

Alternatively, organizations are more culpable where "tolerance of the offense by substantial authority personnel was pervasive throughout the organization."[132] In this provision, tolerance appears as a reasonable proxy for negligence, *i.e.*, a high managerial agent should have known of a substantial and unjustifiable risk.

Thus, in these two provisions, the Commission has astutely and creatively provided judges with a culpability assessment that hierarchically grades blameworthiness by proxies for knowledge, recklessness, and negligence.[133] The Commission also provided five appropriate post-conviction culpability measures, ranging from an assessment of prior history, which considers the number of previous adjudications, to the maintenance of an effective compliance program. Thus, the guidelines cover an organization's action prior to the offense, during the offense, and after the offense. This is notable as it is a rare but certainly welcomed acknowledgement of differences in individual versus organizational culpability.[134]

C. Guidelines and Federal Statutory Law

In evaluating the success of the sentencing guidelines it is critical to consider their relation to federal statutory law. Once again, it is worthwhile considering the assessment of culpability, both before and after conviction: To what extent are these new guidelines limited by extant law? To what extent could the guidelines address or remedy the weakness in federal statutory law?

The significant assessment of culpability in the new guidelines provided a remedy for the post-conviction culpability assessment. As of their codification in 1991, federal district court judges are able to assess culpability in relation to the deservedness of sanctions by a threshold measure of hierarchical mental states *and* by five more broad indices of blameworthiness, all of which acknowledge the complexity of organizational life and serve as proxies for corporate culpability. This is a significant advance over the state of the law prior to the passage of the guidelines. Notably, the sentencing guidelines for individuals, passed in 1987, provided similar benefit. For a series of offenses where no grade of culpability existed, a template of culpability was imposed.[135] For example, involuntary manslaughter, which under 18 U.S.C. § 1112 requires a mental state of "without due cau-

---

132. 18 U.S.C. app. § 8C2.5 (b)(1)(A)(ii)(1992).

133. UNITED STATES SENTENCING COMMISSION, *supra* note 129, at 71.

134. *Cf.* Leonard Orland, *Corporate Punishment by the U.S. Sentencing Commission*, 4 FED. SENTENCING REP. 50 (1991)(Orland criticizes the Sentencing Commission's conception of corporate culpability, finding it to be based upon assumptions that run counter to organizational theory).

135. *See, e.g.*, UNITED STATES SENTENCING COMMISSION, *supra* note 13, at §§ 2A1, 2A6.1, 2F.1(4), 2H3.1, 2K1.4(b)(1), 251.1(b)(1).

tion," has been transformed in the sentencing guidelines to ten points if the conduct was criminally "negligent," or fourteen points if the conduct was "reckless."[136] The Sentencing Commission has provided needed clarification for judges.

The culpability assessment that the guidelines did not address, and could not address, was culpability in relation to liability. Providing clarification concerning mens rea requirements at the time of sentencing does nothing to address the limitations of federal statutory law described in section II. As has been argued, the reliance on willfulness and obscure combinations of mens rea terms, the absence of hierarchical mental states, and the failure to consider material elements of offenses, make the finding of corporate criminal liability vulnerable to significant discretion and disparity in federal statutory law.

Additionally, such vulnerability calls into question the seriousness of proposals that search for genuine corporate intent. Commentators who suggest the importance of determining corporate culpability, rather than individual mens rea which is imputed to an entity, may have underestimated how far the federal statutory law has strayed into obscurity. In Section V, several proposals for genuine corporate culpability are contrasted with culpability provisions found in federal statutory law.

VI.   GENUINE CORPORATE CULPABILITY

The evolution of corporate criminal law scholarship demonstrates a trend toward thinking about the behavior of organizations in the context of organizational theory.[137] Commentators have argued that it is possible to identify culpability from specific corporate action, as opposed to individual action.[138] The MPC and federal statutory law rely significantly upon a model of "managerial mens rea," *i.e.*, where

---

136. *Id.* at § 2A1.4.

137. *See, e.g.*, Barry B. Baysinger, *Organizational Theory and the Criminal Liability of Organizations*, 71 B.U. L. REV. 341 (1991); Michael B. Metzger, *Organizations and the Law*, 25 AM. BUS. L. REV. 407 (1987); Laura S. Schrager & James F. Short, *Toward a Sociology of Organizational Crime*, 25 SOC. PROBS. 407 (1978); Diane Vaughan, *Toward Understanding Unlawful Organizational Behavior*, 80 MICH. L. REV. 1377 (1982).

138. For a discussion of the different forms of corporate culpability, see Brent Fisse, *Reconstruction Corporate Criminal Law: Deterrence, Retribution, Fault, and Sanctions*, 56 S. CAL. L. REV. 1141, 1186-1192 (1983). In this article, Fisse finds the managerial (mental state of manager is imputed to entity), composite (mens rea of employees grouped and then imputed), and strategic (mens rea found in organizational policy) forms of mens rea to be inadequate. Instead, he proposes reactive corporate fault, where the court would assess culpability on the basis of a corporation's attempt to employ preventive or corrective measures upon commission of an offense. *Id.* at 1195-97.

the mental state of an agent is simply imputed to the entity.[139]

In a recent article, Professor Foerschler argues that the imputation of intent from the employees within the corporation to the corporate entity fails to properly consider the organizational basis for corporate action.[140] Drawing from the work of Dan-Cohen,[141] she notes that corporate criminal liability can be effective only when based on an understanding of the decisionmaking process within corporations. Organizational theory informs us that corporate actions are not simply the product of individual choice, but the melding of individual decisions set within an organizational structure and embedded in an organizational culture. The author reviews two models of organizational decisionmaking:[142] the Organizational Process Model, represented by the writings of Simon,[143] and Bureaucratic Politics Model, found in the work of Cyert and March.[144]

Drawing on scattered principles from these models, as well as from a model of analysis based on segregational intent,[145] Foerschler offers a framework for imputing corporate intent based on three criteria: (1) did a corporate practice or policy violate the law,[146] or (2) was it reasonably foreseeable that a corporate practice or policy would result in

---

139. *See supra* notes 42-99 and accompanying text.
140. Ann Foerschler, *Corporate Criminal Intent: Toward a Better Understanding of Corporate Misconduct*, 78 CAL. L. REV. 1287, 1288 (1990).
141. *See* MEIR DAN-COHEN, RIGHTS, PERSONS AND ORGANIZATIONS: A LEGAL THEORY FOR BUREAUCRATIC SOCIETY (1986); *see also* Richard B. Stewart, *Organizational Jurisprudence*, 101 HARV. L. REV. 371 (1987).
142. Foerschler, *supra* note 140, at 1298-1302.
143. *See* JAMES G. MARCH & HERBERT A. SIMON, ORGANIZATIONS (1958).
144. *See* RICHARD M. CYERT & JAMES G. MARCH, A BEHAVIORAL THEORY OF THE FIRM (1963); *see also* GRAHAM T. ALLISON, ESSENCE OF DECISION: EXPLAINING THE CUBAN MISSILE CRISIS (1971).
145. Foerschler, *supra* note 140, at 1303. This analysis is based on the notion of "segregational intent" as discussed by the Supreme Court and set forth in Keyes v. Sch. Dist. No. 1, 413 U.S. 189 (1973). The concept of institutional intent was applied by the Sixth Circuit Court of Appeals in its finding that the school board's policies served no legitimate educational objectives. Oliver v. Michigan State Bd. of Educ., 508 F.2d 178, 184-86 (6th Cir. 1974), *cert. denied*, 421 U.S. 963 (1975).
146. Foerschler, *supra* note 140, at 1307. This first criterion addresses whether the policy itself violates the law. She notes,

> To determine what qualifies as a corporate practice or policy, the law should turn to the organization theory models of decisionmaking explained above in Section II(B). Both the BP [Bureaucratic Politics] and OP [Organizational Process] models should be incorporated into the concept of a corporate practice or procedure because, depending on the facts of the case, one theory may be more appropriate than the other. This choice will be left to the prosecutor's discretion.

Id. The court should examine either or both the bargaining process (through memoranda and minutes of meetings in which policies were set) that ultimately produce the corporate practices and policies, (as suggested by the BP model) and/or the standard operating procedures used by the organization or organizational units (as suggested by the OP model) to determine this point. In addition, the

a corporate agent's violation of the law,[147] or (3) did the corporation adopt a corporate agent's violation of the law?[148] Such a framework shifts the focus away from individuals within the corporation and toward the corporate structure as a means of locating corporate intent.

A system of liability that reflects genuine corporate fault is one that places less emphasis on the particular hierarchical position of the actors involved and more attention on the corporation's practices, procedures, and policies. Professor French has crafted perhaps the most articulate argument in support of corporate intentionality and it is this approach that serves as a philosophical basis for Professor Fisse's conceptualization of strategic mens rea, i.e., where culpability is assessed with reference to corporate policy.[149] According to French, the components of the corporation's internal decision structure (CID structure), consisting of the corporation's flowchart and procedural and recognition rules, make up the elements that define corporate intention. Whether or not the action is legal or illegal, the corporation establishes certain goals and objectives for the purpose of carrying forth the action or intention. Following this reasoning, a corporation may be held responsible when the act reflects a corporate decision and not simply the decisions of particular individuals within the corporation.[150]

> court should also examine the level at which the task or action in question took place.

147. This second test "responds to those instances in which the corporate practice or policy does not explicitly violate the law but is designed so as to instigate violation." *Id.* at 1308-09. Criminal liability attaches only when there is clear evidence of an industry awareness of illegal activity and evidence that the corporation's policies and practices, such as an employee incentive system, could reasonably be foreseen as leading to the commission of the crime. *Id.* at 1309-10.

148. This final test "is intended to attribute intent to a corporation not for instigating violation of a law, but for acquiescing in an agent's violation of the law." *Id.* at 1310. When a corporation knowingly allows and acquiesces to criminal behavior by its employees, it can be said to "adopt a policy" in favor of criminal activity.

149. Fisse, *supra* note 138, at 1190-92; *see* PETER A. FRENCH, COLLECTIVE AND CORPORATE RESPONSIBILITY (1984).

150. FRENCH, *supra* note 143, at 44. French writes,

> [w]hen the corporate act is consistent with an instantiation or an implementation of established corporate policy, then it is proper to describe it as having been done for corporate reasons, as having been caused by a corporate desire coupled with a corporate belief and so, in other words, as corporate intentional.

Id. Larry May proposes an impressive variation of the French proposal with the following model rules for corporate vicarious negligence:

> A corporation is vicariously negligent for the harmful acts of one of its members if: a) *causal factor*—the member of the corporation was enabled or facilitated in his or her harmful conduct by the general grant of authority given to him or her by a corporate decision; and b) *fault factor*—appropriate members of the corporation failed to take preventive measures to thwart the potential harm by those who could harm due to the above general part of authority, even though: 1. the appropriate

Most recently, Professor Bucy has proposed an extension of this work by providing a corporate criminal liability standard that requires proof of an ethos or personality that encouraged the commission of the criminal act.[151] Under this ethos standard, courts that grapple with cases that raise issues of corporate liability and culpability would consider the organization's: (a) hierarchy, *e.g.*, the board of director's role, (b) goals and practices, *e.g.*, whether goals are lawful, (c) reaction to current and prior offenses, *e.g.*, whether current or past offenses are recklessly tolerated, (d) existing compliance programs, *e.g.*, whether internal audits are performed, and (e) compensation and indemnification schemes, *e.g.* whether unlawful awards are bestowed.[152] Such a consideration would reveal the corporate personality, and the extent to which it encouraged or facilitated criminal conduct. Criminal liability attaches and corporate intention is found in an organization that perpetuates an ethos favorable to law violation.[153]

The search for genuine corporate culpability by French, Fisse, Braithwaite and other scholars reflects an interest in fairly and accurately capturing the intentionality of an entity. Most of the calls for genuine corporate culpability acknowledge the difference between human and entity intentionality, and allow for the unique characteristics of non-human persons by considering the complexity of organizational life.[154] When set against the confusion created by the ill-defined and obscure culpability provisions described earlier, even a cursory consideration of these proposals reveal the woeful inadequacy of existing federal statutory law.

These proposals also point to the inadequacy of those attempts by some federal courts to use existing culpability provisions in order to approximate genuine corporate intention. Beginning in 1951 with *In-*

---

members could have taken such precautions, and 2. these appropriate members could reasonably have predicted that the harm would occur.

LARRY MAY, THE MORALITY OF GROUPS: COLLECTIVE RESPONSIBILITY, GROUP-BASED HARM, AND CORPORATE RIGHTS 85 (1987)(emphasis added).

151. Pamela H. Bucy, *Corporate Ethos: A Standard for Imposing Corporate Criminal Liability*, 75 MINN. L. REV. 1095 (1991).

152. *Id.* at 1129-46.

153. As Bucy notes: "If this examination shows that a corporation whose employees violated the law perpetuated an ethos that encouraged this violation, the corporation is criminally liable for the acts of its agents." *Id.* at 1183.

154. Proposals for genuine corporate culpability find their source in discussions of the moral responsibility of collectives. *See, e.g.*, THOMAS DONALDSON, CORPORATIONS AND MORALITY (1982); JOEL FEINBERG, DOING AND DESERVING: ESSAYS IN THE THEORY OF RESPONSIBILITY (1970); David Copp, *Collective Actions and Secondary Actions*, 16 AM. PHIL. Q. 177 (1979); Peter A. French, *Types of Collectivities and Blame*, 56 THE PERSONALIST 160 (1975); Kenneth E. Goodpaster, *The Concept of Corporate Responsibility*, 2 J. OF BUS. ETHICS 1 (1983); Keeley, *supra* note 7; May, *supra* note 7; Jerry Surber, *Individual and Corporate Responsibility: Two Alternative Approaches*, 2 BUS. & PROF. ETHICS J. 67 (1983).

land Freight Lines v. United States,[155] a handful of courts have deciphered an aggregate, collective, or composite mens rea from the knowledge of more than one agent or employee.[156] The rationale for a collective intention is straightforward. Corporate knowledge is compartmentalized—found with employees in various divisions, branches, or subsidiaries. A composite of this knowledge, it is argued, reflects true corporate knowledge. After all, corporations are thought to have notice, either actual or constructive, of the collective knowledge of all employees.[157]

As commentators have suggested, however, there is no reason to believe that the imputation of aggregated mental states to an entity achieves genuine corporate culpability.[158] This is so even when the finding of composite mens rea reveals the sum of all employee intentions.[159] Quite simply, courts that use aggregated mental states in or-

---

155. Inland Freight Lines v. United States, 191 F.2d 313 (10th Cir. 1951). In this appeal from a conviction of a common carrier under the Interstate Commerce Act, the court ruled that knowledge of different material facts by different corporate agents could be grouped and then imputed to the corporation. Thus, corporate knowledge and wilfulness may be based upon inferences "drawn from a combination of acts, conduct, and circumstances." *Id.* at 315.

156. Commentators have been less than kind with the idea of a collective or composite mens rea. Fisse, for example, calls it a "mechanical concept of mental state that fails to reflect true corporate fault." Fisse, *supra* note 138, at 1189-90. May concludes that composite mens rea is inadequate to explain purposive group action because it fails to consider group structure. MAY, *supra* note 150, at 66. Finally, Bucy labels the fiction a "desperate, but disingenuous, application of the respondeat superior or MPC standards." Bucy, *supra* note 151, at 1157.

157. United States Bank of New England, 821 F.2d 844, 856 (1st Cir. 1987), *cert. denied*, 484 U.S. 943 (1987)("Corporations compartmentalize knowledge, subdividing the elements of specific duties and operations into smaller components. The aggregate of those components constitutes the corporation's knowledge of a particular operation."); United States v. T.I.M.E.-D.C., Inc., 381 F. Supp. 730, 738 (W.D.Va. 1974)("[T]he corporation is considered to have acquired the collective knowledge of its employees . . . ."); United States v. Sawyer Transport, 337 F. Supp. 29, 31 (D. Minn. 1971), *aff'd*, 463 F.2d 175 (8th Cir. 1972)(knowledge of employees may be joined and imputed to the corporation). For a recent reference to collective knowledge, see United States v. LBS Bank-New York, 757 F. Supp. 496, 501 (E.D. Pa. 1990)(knowledge from different employees can be joined in order to establish corporate knowledge, but specific intent cannot be so aggregated); Camacho v. Bowling, 562 F. Supp. 1012, 1025 (N.D. Ill. 1983)("Other organizations, such as private corporations or partnerships, are held to have constructive notice of the collective knowledge of all the employees and departments within the organization."); and People v. American Medical Centers, 324 N.W.2d 782, 793 (Mich. App. 1982)("The combined knowledge of those employees may be imputed to the corporation to find it liable for fraudulent acts.").

158. *See supra* note 156.

159. Composite mens rea cannot exist unless at least one employee (but more likely two employees) have some material knowledge. Consider Judge Mukasey's decision in First Equity Corp. v. Standard & Poor's Corp., 690 F. Supp. 256 (S.D.N.Y. 1988) which stated:

While it is not disputed that a corporation may be charged with the col-der to establish corporate knowledge most often stop short of discussing corporate knowledge as independent of employee knowledge.[160] The corporation's knowledge is "constructive" or "acquired," rather than actual or real. Indeed, genuine corporate culpability should not be wholly contingent or dependent upon principles of vicarious agency.[161] Finally, it is worth noting the striking resemblance of the new organizational guidelines with models of genuine corporate culpability. Both move away from notions of agency and the imputation of intention, to various measures of entity intentionality, e.g., aspects of reactive corporate fault. Their similarity makes it easy to forget that the former relate culpability to sentence severity, while the latter concern culpability in relation to liability. This fact might suggest that the law of sentencing is only as strong as the substantive law that serves as its foundation.

VII. CONCLUSION

In urging Congress to resume the task of recodifying the federal criminal law, the Federal Courts Study Committee observed that some of the recent criticisms of the sentencing guidelines may reflect the "arbitrary structure of the federal criminal laws, a structure [that] is made transparent by the guidelines."[162] A more reasonable interpretation is that the sentencing guidelines, at least with respect to organizations, highlight the inadequacy of the federal criminal law. The guidelines confirm the feasibility of assessing organizational culpability—but they look strange when compared with current substantive law. On the one hand, the federal law determines culpability in relation to liability by the identification of one or more of over one hundred mental states. On the other hand, the federal law determines culpability in relation to sentence severity through an elaborate examination of an organization's actions prior to the offense, during the offense, and after the offense.

The development of sentencing guidelines for organizations has

---

lective knowledge of its employees, it does not follow that the corporation may be deemed to have a culpable state of mind when that state of mind is possessed by no single employee. A corporation can be held to have a particular state of mind only when that state of mind is possessed by a single individual.

Id. at 260; *cf.* Note, *Corporate Crime: Regulating Corporate Behavior Through Criminal Sanctions*, 92 HARV. L. REV. 1227, 1248-49 (1978).

160. *Cf.* United States v. Bank of New England, 821 F.2d 844 (1st Cir. 1987), *cert. denied*, 484 U.S. 943 (1987). Foerschler has argued to the contrary and that the collective knowledge cases, like *Bank of New England*, "virtually eliminate the distinction between individual and institutional intent." Foerschler, *supra* note 134, at 1306.

161. *Cf.* May, *supra* note 7.

162. FEDERAL COURTS STUDY COMM., *supra* note 56, at 23.

confirmed, as well, that order may not be brought to an otherwise disordered body of law through sentencing reform alone. The SRA, with its lofty goals of honesty, uniformity, and proportionality in sentencing, is compromised if issues relating to culpability and liability remain unresolved. After all, what does proportionality mean? What good is uniformity and honesty at time of sentencing when both may be missing in the determination of liability? These questions mirror the Federal Courts Study Committee conclusion, that the "lack of a rational criminal code has also hampered the development of a rational sentencing system."[163]

---

163. *Id.* at 106.

VIII. APPENDIX

	Title 18 Sections 1970	1992
willful	542	542
willfully	2	2
willfully refuses or neglects		2076
willfully and corruptly	2271	1917
willfully or maliciously	1362	1362
willfully and maliciously	35	35
willfully and maliciously . . . with the intent		1991
willfully and unlawfully	2071	2071
willfully and knowingly		1752
willfully and knowingly . . . [with] knowledge or reason to believe . . .	954	954
willfully . . . with intent to . . .	32	32
corruptly	201	201
corruptly . . . with intent to . . .	201	201
maliciously	549	549
maliciously . . ., with an intent unlawfully to	1659	1659
maliciously . . . knowing		844
willfully, deliberate, malicious, and premeditated	1111	1111
from a premeditated design unlawfully and maliciously to . . .	1111	1111
without malice . . . voluntary [manslaughter]	1112	1112
without malice . . . involuntary . . . without due caution and circumspection [manslaughter]	1112	1112
voluntarily	755	755
unlawfully	1427	1427
unlawfully and willfully	664	664
unlawfully or . . . wantonly		1853
improperly	1703	1703
feloniously	1506	1506
wantonly	1852	1852
wrongfully		654
falsely	185	485
falsely . . . for the purpose of		709
falsely and willfully	911	911
fraudulently	331	331
with the specific intent to destroy	1091	
with intent to defraud	472	471
with intent to defraud . . . or to deceive	1006	1006
fraudulently . . . knowing . . .	331	331

	Title 18 1970	Sections 1992
with intent to defraud, knowingly_____	658	658
with intent to defraud, knowing_____	483	483
with fraudulent intent . . . knowing . . . _____	506	506
with intent to defraud, falsely_____	482	478
fraudulently or knowingly_____	545	545
with intent to deceive or mislead_____	703	703
for the fraudulent purpose of . . . _____	706	706
with intent to defraud . . . for the purpose of__	707	707
falsely or fraudulently . . . for the purpose of__	917	917
through the fault or . . . with a fraudulent intent_____	332	332
fraudulently or wrongfully_____	1017	1017
for any purpose_____	371	371
for any purpose not prescribed by law_____	653	653
with any intent . . . that . . . _____	964	964
with unlawful or fraudulent intent_____	2314	2314
with intent wrongfully_____		1851
for the purpose_____		47
with the purpose of fraudulently . . . _____	500	500
with intent to . . . _____	114	513
with intent that . . . _____	794	373
with the intent that . . . _____	473	473
intentionally or maliciously_____	1367	
with the intention of . . . _____	663	663
with intent unlawfully_____		1426
intending to . . . _____	1343	1343
intentionally_____		247
for the purpose of . . . _____	288	288
with intent or reason to believe that . . . _____	794	794
knows, or reasonable grounds to believe or suspect_____		568
knowingly_____	43	46
knowing or intentional_____		403
knowingly and willfully_____	288	288
knowingly or willfully_____	550	550
knowingly and unlawfully_____	1857	1424
knowingly and fraudulently_____	152	152
knowingly and falsely_____	289	289
knowingly and with intent to defraud_____	479	479
knowingly and willfully, with intent to defraud_____	545	545
knowingly and with fraudulent intent_____	2318	
knowingly, willfully and corruptly_____	1158	1158

	Title 18 1970	Sections 1992
knowingly and, with a design to . . .	1657	1657
knowingly, willfully, or wantonly		2152
knowingly . . ., for the purpose of . . .	877	713
knowingly . . ., with the intent		207
knowing . . .	287	287
knowing or having reason to know or intending		231
with knowledge that . . .	224	224
having knowledge of . . .	4	4
knowing that . . .	3	3
with knowledge or reason to believe that . . .	491	491
without reasonable cause to believe . . .	542	542
neglect	1115	1115
with the knowledge or intent		1588
negligently		755
negligence, or inattention to . . . duties	1115	1115
through gross negligence	793	793
willfully neglects	1421	1421
by willful breach of duty	2196	2196
by will breach of duty or by neglect of duty	2196	2196
recklessly		831
conscious or reckless risk		1031
with reckless disregard for the risk		1365
in reckless disregard of the truth		1861
with reckless disregard for the safety of human life [ ]	35	33
otherwise than in the proper discharge of his official duties	205	205
without willful negligence or without any intention . . . to violate the law [forfeiture provision]	492	492

Twenty years of sentencing reform: steps forward, steps backward

by Michael Tonry, symposium issue editor

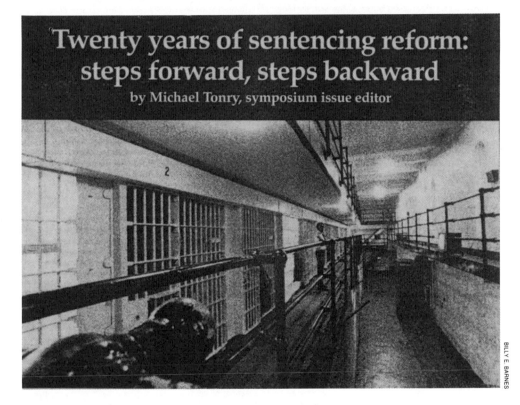

If a time machine were to transport a group of state and federal judges from 1970 to a national conference on sentencing in 1995, most would be astonished by a quarter century's changes. Many, perhaps all, would be disapproving.

This article is drawn from the author's book, SENTENCING MATTERS, to be published by Oxford University Press later this year.
1. Blumstein, Cohen, Martin, and Tonry, eds. RESEARCH ON SENTENCING: THE SEARCH FOR REFORM, 2 vols. (Washington, D.C.: National Academy Press, 1983), chap. 3.

Their astonishment would result from the number and enormity of the changes they would learn about. Sentencing, as they knew it, had not changed significantly for many years.[1] In 1970, every American state and the federal government had indeterminate sentencing systems, in which lawmakers enacted and amended the criminal code and set maximum penalties. A few jurisdictions had minimum penalties, which many judges disliked. These penalties generally required

one- or two-year minimums except for murder, which carried a mandatory life sentence in some jurisdictions.

Subject only to statutory maximums

MICHAEL TONRY is Sonosky Professor of Law and Public Policy at the University of Minnesota Law School.

and the occasional minimums, judges had the authority to sentence convicted defendants either to probation

377

(and under what conditions) or to prison (and for what maximum term). Parole boards decided when prisoners were released. Usually, prisoners became eligible for release after serving a third of the maximum sentence, but they could be held until the maximum term expired. Prison managers typically were allowed to reduce sentences by awarding time off for good behavior.

In 1995, the time-traveling judges would learn that since the mid-1970s, the federal system and many states had rejected indeterminate sentencing and repealed much of its apparatus, often on tough-on-crime political grounds. More than 20 jurisdictions had adopted sentencing guidelines to limit judicial discretion, more than 15 had eliminated parole release, 20 had adopted parole guidelines, most had narrowed time off for good behavior, and all had enacted mandatory minimum sentence legislation, which often included 10-, 20-, or 30-year minimum terms and life without possibility of parole.[2] Most recently, the judges would learn, Congress in 1994 authorized billions of federal dollars to states that abolish parole release, establish guidelines to constrain judicial sentencing discretion, and require abolition or narrowing of time off for good behavior.

There can be little doubt that the time-traveling judges would disapprove much of what they would find. Partly this can be attributed to parochialism. Human beings tend to prefer the familiar over the new and what we know over what we don't. Because the broad outlines of indeterminate sentencing had been the same everywhere since 1930, few judges at work in 1970 would have had experience working in any other system.

Some of their objections would, however, concern matters of principle and conceptions of justice that transcend parochialism. Rigid sentencing laws, including mandatory penalties, they would insist, create unacceptable risks of injustice because they make it impossible to take account of important differences among defendants. Laws that specify penalties for particular cases are unwise, they would argue, because legislators are far likelier than judges to be influenced by short-term

emotions and concern for political advantage. Limits on judicial discretion are unsound, they would urge, because they shift discretion into the hands of prosecutors who will exercise it less judiciously than judges.

We can predict that these arguments would be made because many judges from the early 1970s today have opposed sentencing reforms in these terms, and many judges (and nonjudges) still do. There is, however, one 1970s argument that is seldom heard today—that there is no need for substantial changes in sentencing because there is no convincing evidence that indeterminate sentencing was afflicted by unwarranted sentencing disparities or racial and gender bias. These arguments are seldom heard because the weight of the research evidence has become clear. Unwarranted disparities, explicable more in terms of the judge's personality, beliefs, and background than the offender's crime or criminal history, have repeatedly been demonstrated.[3] So has substantial gender disparity in indeterminate sentencing—in favor of women.[4] The evidence is unclear on the causes of racial disparities, but their existence is well-documented.[5]

State versus federal reforms

The overall impression the time-traveling judges would take back with them would probably be shaped by whether they learn first about federal or state sentencing reforms. If they were to study the changes brought about by the federal Sentencing Reform Act of 1984, they would return to 1970 determined to fight the first signs of the sentencing reform movement. But if they were to study the experiences of states like Delaware, Minnesota, Pennsylvania, Oregon, and Washington, they would be likely to go back apprehen-

sive but with an understanding that meliorable injustices did exist under indeterminate sentencing that can be mitigated without creating larger injustices in their place.

For the time-traveling judges to be able to understand contemporary sentencing issues, they would need a briefing on developments since 1970. Here is what they would learn: Sentencing became a focus of criminal justice reform efforts in the mid-1970s, influenced by several contemporaneous developments. First, civil rights activists, concerned by what they perceived to be racial bias in sentencing and correctional administration, called for controls on the discretion of judges and other officials.[6] Second, research reviews by social scientists reported that little systematic empirical evidence showed that corrections programs successfully reduced recidivism, which undermined the rehabilitative foundation on which indeterminate sentencing stood.[7] Third, proceduralists throughout the legal system—who had been working to make legal processes fairer and decision makers more accountable—argued that sentencing too should be subject to rules and review procedures.[8] And finally, political conservatives, concerned about a specter of "lenient judges," supported sentencing reforms as a way to set and enforce harsher sentencing standards.[9]

Most of these influences shaped an influential book, *Criminal Sentences: Law without Order*, by then-U.S. district judge Marvin Frankel.[10] On fairness grounds, he decried the absence of standards for the sentences federal judges set and the related absence of meaningful opportunities for sentence appeals. As a solution, Judge Frankel proposed creation of a specialized administrative agency, called a sentencing commission, that would

2. Tonry, *Sentencing Commissions and Their Guidelines*, in Tonry, ed., CRIME AND JUSTICE: A REVIEW OF RESEARCH, vol. 17, (Chicago: University of Chicago Press, 1993).

3. *Supra* n. 1, at chap. 2.

4. Knapp, THE IMPACT OF THE MINNESOTA SENTENCING GUIDELINES: THREE YEAR EVALUATION (St. Paul: Minnesota Sentencing Guidelines Commission, 1984).

5. Tonry, MALIGN NEGLECT: RACE, CRIME, AND PUNISHMENT IN AMERICA (New York: Oxford University Press, 1995).

6. American Friends Service Committee, STRUGGLE FOR JUSTICE: A REPORT ON CRIME AND PUNISHMENT

IN AMERICA (New York: Hill & Wang, 1971).

7. Lipton, Martinson, and Wilks. THE EFFECTIVENESS OF CORRECTIONAL TREATMENT: A SURVEY OF TREATMENT EVALUATION STUDIES (New York: Praeger, 1975).

8. Davis, DISCRETIONARY JUSTICE: A PRELIMINARY INQUIRY (Baton Rouge: Louisiana State University Press, 1969).

9. Messinger and Johnson, *California's Determinate Sentencing Laws*, in DETERMINATE SENTENCING: REFORM OR REGRESSION (Washington, D.C.: U.S. Government Printing Office, 1978).

10. Frankel, CRIMINAL SENTENCES: LAW WITHOUT ORDER (New York: Hill & Wang. 1972).

378

develop guidelines for judges to use in making sentencing decisions. The guidelines would be presumptively applicable, and their application would be subject to appeal by aggrieved parties.

Judge Frankel's proposals were based partly on the concerns that influenced sentencing reform generally, but they were also shaped by appreciation of the institutional properties of administrative agencies and legislatures. Over time, agencies such as Judge Frankel's proposed commission develop specialized expertise that legislatures cannot match. Moreover, because commissioners are typically appointed for fixed terms and are ordinarily outside day-to-day political battles, such agencies can be somewhat insulated from emotionalism and short-term political pressures.

Judge Frankel's sentencing commission proposal became the most widely adopted vehicle for sentencing reform. In the 1970s, several states—most notably Minnesota and Pennsylvania—created sentencing commissions. Several others—including California, Illinois, and Indiana—replaced indeterminate sentencing with statutory determinate sentencing schemes, in which criminal codes specified specific prison terms for particular crimes.

The comparative merits of sentencing commissions soon became clear. Evaluations in Minnesota and Pennsyl-

vania (and later in Oregon and Washington) showed that use of sentencing guidelines reduced disparities generally and lessened racial and gender disparities in particular. (Since the effect was to increase sentences for women, some might see this as a mixed blessing.)[11] In addition, many judges in those states came to favor guidelines for two reasons—guidelines provided a starting point for considering sen-

Judge Frankel's sentencing commission proposal became the most widely adopted vehicle for sentencing reform.

tences, and judges recognized that guidelines reduced disparities. By contrast, the statutory determinate sentencing systems were shown to have had no significant effects on sentencing processes or outcomes.[12]

More importantly, experience confirmed Judge Frankel's ideas about administrative agencies. For instance, Minnesota's commission tied sentencing policy to available prison resources and managed to hold the prison population within capacity throughout the 1980s, while most states experienced record increases. Commissions in Oregon and Kansas and, for a time, Washington also helped insulate sentencing policy from political pressure. But in states like California, where fine-grained sentencing policies were left in legislative hands, statutory sentencing provisions were amended upwards nearly every year, and the prison population increased by 400 percent between 1980 and 1994.[13]

Success and disaster

By 1995, the success of Judge Frankel's innovation was clear. Twenty-two states have created commissions, guidelines are in effect in 17 of these states, and new commissions are at work in the other five.[14] No state adopted a statu-

tory determinate sentencing scheme after the mid-1980s, and some that had, like Colorado, diluted its effects by reintroducing parole release.[15]

Because the federal commission had the prior experiences of the states to draw on, ample resources, and the capacity to recruit staff from throughout the country, all of the auguries would have predicted that the U.S. Sentencing Commission would build on the state experiences and produce the most successful guidelines system to date.

The Sentencing Reform Act of 1984 abolished parole release prospectively and directed the newly created sentencing commission to develop guidelines for federal sentencing. Few outside the federal commission would disagree that the federal guidelines have been a disaster. The highly detailed guidelines divide crimes into 43 different categories, and the rules governing their application are highly mechanistic. The commission has forbidden judges to take account in sentencing of many factors—such as the effect of the sentence on the defendant or his family, or the defendant's mental health or drug or alcohol dependence, or a severely deprived background or victimization by sexual abuse—that many judges believe to be ethically relevant to sentencing. The guidelines are based not on the offense of which the defendant was convicted, but his "actual offense behavior" including alleged crimes of which he was acquitted or never charged. The guidelines allow virtually no role for non-imprisonment sentences.[16]

For all these reasons, the federal guidelines are deeply disliked by most federal judges and lawyers who practice in federal courts, and they are widely circumvented.[17] In addition, a majority of federal judges surveyed in 1991 said they believe sentencing disparities were as bad or worse under the guidelines as before their adoption.[18] Even commission-sponsored research demonstrates that prosecutors and judges disingenuously circumvent the

11. *Supra* n. 2.
12. *Supra* n. 1.
13. Zimring and Hawkins, INCAPACITATION: PENAL CONFINEMENT AND THE RESTRAINT OF CRIME (New York: Oxford University Press, 1995).
14. *See* Frase, *Sentencing guidelines in the states: still going strong,* 78 JUDICATURE 173 (1995).
15. Wesson, *Sentencing Reform in Colorado: Many Changes, Little Progress,* 4 OVERCROWDED TIMES 14-17, 20 (1993).
16. U.S. Sentencing Commission, SENTENCING COMMISSION GUIDELINES MANUAL (St. Paul, Minn.: West Publishing, 1994).
17. U.S. SENTENCING COMMISSION, THE FEDERAL SENTENCING GUIDELINES: A REPORT ON THE OPERATION OF THE GUIDELINES SYSTEM AND SHORT-TERM IMPACTS ON DISPARITY IN SENTENCING, USE OF INCARCERATION, AND PROSECUTORIAL DISCRETION AND PLEA BARGAINING (Washington, D.C.: U.S. Sentencing Commission, 1991).
18. *Id.*

guidelines in a third of cases,[19] while the true rate is probably higher.

Staff of newly created state commissions report that negative stereotypes created by the federal guidelines have been a major obstacle to their work. Commissions in Texas, Ohio, and North Carolina recently adopted resolutions repudiating the federal guidelines as a model for any policies they might later develop. Both the North Carolina commission and the American Bar Association's sentencing standards project (which proposed that states create sentencing commissions) avoided use of the word "guidelines" because of the negative connotations associated with the federal guidelines.[20]

No one factor can explain why the federal guidelines have been so much less successful than state guidelines. Some judges use words like arrogant and hostile to describe the commission's attitude to the federal judiciary. Some observers argue that the failure was in management: With all of its resources, a better-managed commission that consulted more widely and made efforts to learn from the state experiences could have done better. Others note that only two of the initial commissioners had ever imposed a sentence (one of them 30 years earlier), and three were full-time academics. Still others point out that a number of the initial commissioners were long known to be aspirants for higher judicial office and suggest that the guidelines were an effort to show that the commission's policies were consonant with the views of influential congressional conservatives.

No doubt there is truth in all these explanations. The primary explanation, however, is a structural one: The federal sentencing commission legislation was formulated and agreed on in one political era, in which Judge Frankel's ideas and goals were widely shared. However, they were implemented in a different political era, in which Judge Frankel's ideas had little weight.

The first commission legislation, introduced in Congress in 1974, was a direct outgrowth of a Yale Law School seminar that attempted to convert Judge Frankel's general proposal into

proposed legislation.[21] After reintroduction in successive Congresses as a stand-alone bill, the proposal was folded into then-pending federal criminal code bills. By 1979, Senators Edward Kennedy and Strom Thurmond, the ranking Democratic and Republican members of the Senate Judiciary Committee (who succeeded one another as chairs), agreed to support the legislation, which the Senate went on to approve overwhelmingly. Although the House of Representatives did not act that year, the Senate agreement held. The bill including the sentencing commission sections repeatedly thereafter passed both the Senate Judiciary Committee and the full Senate by wide margins.

Eventually, the proposed criminal code was abandoned as unpassable, but the less controversial commission sections became part of an omnibus crime bill enacted in 1984. Unfortunately, when this good-government, rationalistic proposal, initially intended to make sentencing fairer and to distance sentencing policy from politics, took effect, the government in power did not hold those goals.[22]

The crime-control policies of the Reagan administration in 1985, when the commissioners were appointed, were oriented more toward toughness than fairness. It should not therefore be a surprise that many of the commissioners who were appointed did not share Judge Frankel's belief that sentencing policy should be, to the extent possible, insulated from partisan politics. Instead, influential commissioners demonstrated that they too were tough on crime and had little sympathy for "lenient" judges.[23] (This stereotype of judges is odd, since a large percentage of federal district judges by 1987, when the guidelines took effect, were Reagan appointees—as today are a large percentage of the guidelines' fiercest critics).

Mixed results

So the picture the time-traveling judges would see is mixed—federal guidelines that at least match their worst preconceptions of what would happen if indeterminate sentencing were abandoned, and state guidelines that turned out much better than they

would have predicted.

This issue of *Judicature* could serve as a briefing document for the judges from 1970. It demonstrates there is merit in most of their concerns and that some good has been achieved in the shift from indeterminate to determinate sentencing. Richard Frase's article summarizes developments in the states and provides information on guidelines activities in more than 20 jurisdictions. Marc Miller's article demonstrates that the eight-year-old federal sentencing guidelines remain deeply disliked and offers suggestions for reform.

An article by Kevin and Curtis Reitz describes the American Bar Association's effort in its sentencing standards project to learn from the combined state and federal experiences and to offer guidance to states that have not yet overhauled their sentencing laws. David Boerner's article traces the evolution of policy and practice concerning prosecutorial powers under guidelines, and concludes, with Frase, that there have been both gains and losses. Saul Pilchen discusses the effects of the "organizational guidelines," a version of the federal guidelines that applies to sentences for corporations and other collective entities. Finally, a transcript of an American Judicature Society panel discussion offers the insights of state and federal judges and academics regarding sentencing guidelines.

The conclusion the time-traveling judges would most likely take back is that the judiciary itself must listen to complaints about sentencing and work to address them. Otherwise, other agencies of government will, with results ranging from tolerable to awful. ⚖⚖

19. Nagel and Schulhofer, *A Tale of Three Cities: An Empirical Study of Charging and Bargaining Practices under the Federal Sentencing Guidelines*, 66 S. CAL. L. REV. 501-566 (1992).
20. Orland and Reitz, *Epilogue: A Gathering of State Sentencing Commissions*, 64 COL. L. REV. 837-845 (1993); Reitz and Reitz, *Building a sentencing reform agenda: the ABA's new sentencing standards*, 78 JUDICATURE 189 (1995).
21. O'Donnell, Curtis and Churgin, TOWARD A JUST AND EFFECTIVE SENTENCING SYSTEM (New York: Praeger, 1977).
22. Stith and Koh, *The Politics of Sentencing Reform: The Legislative History of the Federal Sentencing Guidelines*, 28 WAKE FOREST L.REV. 223-290 (1993).
23. *Id.*

380

COMMENTARY

The *Lex Talionis* Before and After Criminal Law

ERNEST VAN DEN HAAG

I

The *lex talionis* established a right to revenge. It responds to a common feeling: one who wrongfully inflicted harm should not benefit and should compensate the person he harmed. The actual feeling is something like this: Why should he, who deprived me of one eye, continue to enjoy two eyes? More generally, why should he, who harmed me, be unharmed? There may be, as well, a kind of restitution through sympathetic magic, as though, by depriving him of the eye he owes me, mine is somehow restored. This is not possible. However, equality can be restored. Originally we were equal, each possessing two eyes; we became unequal when he deprived me of one. If his eye is taken, we are equal once more, each having one eye. By restoring equality, the original attacker is deprived of any relative gain. This has a deterrent effect too, which, though not part of revenge, may have played a role in the social approval thereof.

Among primitives the *lex talionis* was practiced in a literal manner by the interested parties. It still is in vendettas and blood feuds. These occur whenever injuries are suffered which the law cannot, or is not trusted to, settle in an acceptable manner.[1] However, as social authorities became more involved, the *lex talionis* was refined, to become, in the

Ernest van den Haag's Punishing Criminals *has just been reissued by University Press of America.*

main, a right to compensation.

II

The *lex talionis* also limited the retaliatory injury that rightfully could be done by the injured party to the original offender, or the compensation that could be exacted from him for the harm, or loss, suffered. (In this respect the *lex talionis* was more rational than current American liability practice appears to be.) Apart from equity, the social need for this limitation is quite obvious. Without it, a wrongful injury might give rise to wrongful retaliatory injuries in excess of the original loss or harm, which, in turn, would be retaliated for, and so on *ad infinitum*. Custom tended to enforce the limitations imposed. The injured person, or surviving relatives, were entitled to retaliation or compensation. Absent the claimants, nothing was due. In short, the *lex talionis* treated as torts what today are considered crimes. Indeed, compensation came to include the elements of modern tort law.

Since the *lex talionis* was to make the injured party whole, by restoring, as much as possible, the *status quo ante*, including the degree of equality or inequality that originally prevailed, a number of questions arise: What if either party was one-eyed to begin with? Or was much younger or more beautiful than the other? Or pursued an occupation totally impeded by the harm inflicted? What about different social statuses and incomes? Pain and suffering? Lost earnings? Indirect adverse physical and psychological effects to which

the harm is claimed to have contributed? Obviously problems arise in the application of the *lex talionis*. Therefore many rabbinical commentaries have interpreted the original biblical injunction punctiliously. These commentaries are irrelevant to criminal law, whatever their relevance to tort law. I shall not add to them. Rather, I turn to the relation of the *lex talionis* to criminal law.

III

The *lex talionis* is not relevant to criminal law except by suggesting that the punishment of criminals must be perceived as sufficiently punitive so that crime victims will resist the temptation to resort to private revenge. The punishment inflicted by the criminal law is likely to be the only satisfaction the victim receives since attempts to obtain compensation *via* tort law fail most of the time because the offender cannot pay. Yet it is not the main task of criminal punishment to gratify the desire for revenge.

In moral and philosophical discourse about the criminal law, the *lex talionis* is sometimes used to contend that the pain or harm inflicted by punishment should not exceed the pain or harm inflicted by the offender on his victim.[2] As noted, such a limitation made sense when what today we call crimes were, in effect, conceived as torts. But the *lex talionis* makes no sense whatever when used to limit the punishments of the criminal

continued on page 62

Commentary
continued from page 2

law.

Crimes are offenses against the social and legal order, as distinct from torts, which are wrongful harms suffered by individual victims. The purpose of criminal punishment is neither retaliation nor compensation. Indeed, the notions of revenge, retaliation, restitution, or compensation are irrelevant to the criminal law *sensu strictiori*. Unlike torts, crimes are prosecuted in the name of "the people." The victim is but a witness for the prosecution. The retributive punishments of the law are meant to vindicate the social order and to deter from violating it. The harm done to any specific victim may influence legislators and courts in their judgment of the gravity of the offense against the public order, which judgment, together with the culpability of the offender, and the need to deter others, determines the severity of the punishment needed. However, that punishment is in no way limited by the harm suffered by the individual victim. The punishment depends entirely on the harm, moral and material, suffered by society. There is nothing morally wrong, then, with imposing four years of imprisonment on a kidnapper who imprisoned his victim for just three days; nor with punishing an offender who had no specific victim: a person who evaded military service or taxes, or illegally imported drugs, or seduced a consenting minor, or unsuccessfully attempted to commit any crime.

Finally, even if the *lex talionis* were to influence criminal punishments, it would raise the question: Why limit the punishment to the harm suffered by the victim? Why not double as much? After all, the victim was innocent, but the offender was not. The offender volunteered to do harm; the victim did not volunteer to have harm done. Not least, the offender volunteered for the risk of punishment; the victim did not. Why use tort reasoning for crimes? Since nothing compensatory is involved, retaliation would be unlimited. On the other hand, why should the punishment not impose only half the suffering the offender imposed? Society may be charitable.

The harm done by the offender to the victim does not determine the harm done to society in breaking its laws, or the punishment required by that harm, except that that harm is unlikely to be less than the harm done to the individual victim. Therefore, the punishment, however different in kind, rarely should be less than that which the *lex talionis* exacted although it may be more, since the social harm may well exceed the harm suffered by the individual. Thus the *lex talionis* suggests a minimum, but no maximum, criminal punishment, although before the criminal law was invented and as long as it was conceived mainly as socialized revenge or compensation, the *lex talionis* suggested the maximum harm or compensation the victim could exact.

NOTES

1 The Italian movie *The Seduction of Mimi*, directed by Lina Wertmuller, may serve as an illustration: although not attracted to her, the protagonist goes to great lengths to seduce the wife of a man who had seduced *his* wife, as an act of literal retaliation.

2 *See* Goldman, *Beyond the Deterrence Theory: Comments on van den Haag's "Punishment as a Device for Controlling the Crime Rate,"* 33 RUTGERS L. REV. 721-29 (1981); Reiman, *Justice, Civilization and the Death Penalty: Answering van den Haag,* 14 PHIL. & PUB. AFF. 115-48 (1985); A. CAMUS, in RESISTANCE, REBELLION AND DEATH 131, 151-52 (trans. X. O'Brien 1960).

Should Penal Rehabilitationism be Revived?

ANDREW VON HIRSCH AND LISA MAHER

Penal rehabilitationism has been in eclipse since the early 1970s.[1] Treatment efforts seemed to offer only limited hope for success.[2] Relying on treatment to decide the sentence seemed also to lead to unjust results—for example, to excessive intrusion into offenders' lives in the name of cure.[3]

Recently, however, there have been hints of an attempted revival. Some researchers claim striking new successes in treatment techniques. These successes, Ted Palmer concludes in a recent survey of treatment methods, suggest that rehabilitative intervention has gained "increased moral and philosophical legitimacy," and that it is no longer the case that rehabilitation "should be secondary to punishment . . . whether for short- or long-term goals."[4] Some penologists—for example, Francis Cullen and Karen Gilbert—argue that a revival of the penal treatment ethic could help lead to a gentler and more caring penal system.[5] Interestingly, such arguments sometimes come from penologists of the left[6]—who once had been so critical of treatment-based punishments.[7] There is by no means unanimity, however, even from these sources. Some researchers—for example, John Whitehead and Steven Lab in their recent survey of juvenile treatments[8]—continue to be quite pessimistic about those treatments' effects. Some writers of the left—for example, Thomas Mathiesen[9]—still strongly resist treatment as the basis for sanctioning. Nevertheless, there is enough ferment to prompt the question in our title, "Should penal rehabilitationism be revived?"

Reinstatement of a treatment ethic would raise a number of questions. How much more is known about the treatment of offenders now than was known a few years ago? How often can treatment give us answers about how severely to sentence convicted offenders? Is treatment really as humane as it is made out to be? How fair is it to base the sentence on an offender's supposed rehabilitative needs? Rehabilitationism went into eclipse some years ago partly because it could not answer those questions satisfactorily. Are better answers available today?

We approach these issues from heterogeneous viewpoints. One of us (von Hirsch) is a philosophical liberal, and has long been an advocate of the desert model.[10] The other (Maher) has a more left and feminist orientation,[11] and is skeptical of a retributive penal ethic. In our present discussion of the new rehabilitationism, we will not be assuming another articulated sentencing philosophy. What we agree on are the questions, not the answers.

Questions of Effectiveness

During the late 60s and the 70s, critics of penal treatment sometimes were tempted to assert that "nothing works."

Andrew von Hirsch, author of Past or Future Crimes, *is a Professor in the School of Criminal Justice, Rutgers University, and Research Fellow at Uppsala University, Sweden; Lisa Maher ia a doctoral candidate in the School of Criminal Justice, Rutgers University.*

The phrase now haunts them, and confuses analysis. It implies that the main problem of treatment is that of establishing its effectiveness; and that treatment can be declared a "success" once some programs are shown to work. Both assumptions are erroneous. Even when treatments succeed, their use to decide sentencing questions raises important normative questions (discussed below). And occasional successes are not enough.

The last large-scale survey and analysis of treatments,

undertaken by a panel of the National Academy of Sciences,[12] is over a decade old. It was distinctly pessimistic in its conclusions: when subjected to close scrutiny, few programs seemed to succeed in reducing offender recidivism. Since then there has been continued experimentation, and successes have been reported.[13] Some treatment advocates, such as Paul Gendreau and Robert Ross, have suggested that such findings show that rehabilitation has been "revivified."[14]

Perhaps, however, caution is in order. The extent of recent treatment successes remains very much in dispute—as witness a recent debate among researchers who have surveyed juvenile treatment programs.[15] A source of continuing difficult is that the "whys" of treatment (that is, the processes by which successes are achieved) are seldom understood.[16] Without knowing the processes by which experimental programs produce given outcomes, it is difficult to tell which features "work," and will continue to work, when programs are extended beyond experimental groups and implemented more widely.

Programs appear to have better prospects for success when they focus on selected subgroups of offenders, carefully screened for amenability.[17] Such a screening approach, however, necessarily limits the scope for rehabilitation. Perhaps this or that type of program can be shown to succeed with this or that subgroup of offenders. Treatments do not (and are not likely to) exist, however, that can be relied upon to decide sentences routinely—that can inform the judge, when confronted with the run-of-the-mill robbery, burglary, or drug offense, what the appropriate sanction should be, and can provide even a modicum of assurance that the sanction will contribute to the offender's desistance from crime. Even Palmer concedes that recent treatment surveys do not "indicate that generic types of programs have been found that consistently produce major recidivism reductions"; and that programs that have positive effects for selected offender subgroups "may have limited relevance to the remaining [offender] subtypes—those which might comprise much of the sample."[18] If treatment lacks such routine, predictable applicability, how can it serve as a principal sentencing rationale?

Success depends, also, on the resources available for implementation. The programs that succeed tend to be well-funded, well-staffed, and vigorously implemented.[19] These features are easiest to achieve when the program is tried in an experimental setting. When the same programs are carried out more widely, program quality tends to deteriorate. Even Gendreau and Ross admit that "[we are] still . . . absolutely amateurish at implementing . . . experimentally demonstrated programs within . . . systems provided routinely by government."[20]

Questions of Humaneness

Some new advocates of penal rehabilitationism, such as Cullen and Gilbert, stress its humaneness. Reemphasizing treatment, they assert, is humane because it is more caring: it looks to the needs of the offender rather than seeking merely to punish or prevent.[21] Is it true that rehabilitation is concerned chiefly with meeting the offender's needs? That depends on whether one is speaking of social service or of measures aimed at preventing recidivism.

Social service is benevolent in intent, if not necessarily in actual application: The aim is to help the offender lead a less deprived life. It can sometimes be achieved by fairly modest interventions: the unskilled offender, for example, might be taught certain skills that make him better able to cope. Providing these services is, we agree, desirable,[22] although it is far from clear to what extent they reduce recidivism. The offender who is taught to read will not necessarily desist from crime as a result.

Treatment programs, however, seldom aim merely at social service. Their objective, instead, is recidivism prevention: protecting us against future depredations on the offender's part. To accomplish that crime-preventive aim, the intervention may well have to be more drastic. It will take more to get the drug-abusing robber to stop committing further robberies than to teach him/ her a skill. (A recent review of current research suggests that the best indicator of successful drug treatment outcomes is length of time in treatment.)[23] To describe such strategies as intrinsically humane or caring is misleading: it confuses humanitarian concerns with treatment-as-crime-prevention.

Cullen and Gilbert admit this last point—that rehabilitation is aimed at recidivism prevention. They argue, however, that few people care much about being humane or benevolent to convicted criminals as an end in itself. Rehabilitationism, they argue, offers a more attractive reason — a crime-preventive one — for decent penal policies.[24] There is something circular about this argument. It assumes that rehabilitative punishments are capable of reducing crime significantly, or at least that people will believe they are. And it assumes that treatment-oriented punishments are inherently gentle.

Are rehabilitative responses intrinsically less onerous? Not necessarily. Consider offenders convicted of crimes of intermediate or lesser gravity. A proportionate sanction for such offenses should be of no more than moderate severity.[25] What of a rehabilitative response? That would depend on how much intervention, and how long, is required to alter the offender's criminal propensities—and to succeed, the intervention may have to be quite substantial (as in the just-noted case of drug treatments).[26]

A rehabilitative ethic also tends to shift attention from the offender's actual criminal conduct to his or her lifestyle or social/moral character. For example, the cultural presumption that women are less "rational" often results in their lawbreaking being perceived as symptomatic of social (or biological) pathology. Women found guilty of relatively minor offenses thus may be subjected to substantial treatment interventions.[27] Concerns about offenders' attitudes may elicit intrusive responses aimed at "correcting" individual ways of thinking and feeling.[28]

Cullen and Gilbert, and some other new rehabilitationists, argue for a return to a treatment model, on grounds that other models (for example, desert) have led to harsh results.[29] How supportable are such claims? The severity or leniency with which a given sentencing philosophy is implemented will vary with the manner of its implementation and the criminal-justice politics of the jurisdiction involved. That legislatively mandated "deserved" penalties were harsh in California may be attributable, perhaps, to the character of criminal-justice politics in that state, and to having given the legislature the task of setting the specific penalties.[30] A similar philosophy led to different (and less harsh) results in places such as Minnesota and Oregon, where both the form of guidance and the criminal-justice politics were different.[31] Similar considerations apply also to rehabilitationism. Were California to return to a rehabilitative ethos, it is far from certain (given California's politics) how "humane" or benevolent the results would be.

Some new rehabilitationists' rejection of other models, such as desert, is based on a "socially critical" perspective: how the rationale is likely to be implemented in a society characterized by race, class, and gender inequalities.[32] Such a critique, however, cuts both ways: one also needs to consider how rehabilitationism might be implemented in such an unpropitious social setting. It is fallacious to reject desert, for example, because of how "they" might carry it out, and then urge a treatment ethic on the basis of how "we" might implement it — that is, on the assumption of a much more supportive social system and legal culture than exists today. If rehabilitation is kinder, gentler, or better because that is how good people would implement it, then please tell us when and how, in a society such as our own, the good people take over.

While the new rehabilitationists are taking such a critical stance, they might also apply it to the rehabilitative ethic itself. Historically, the treatment ethos supported (as Michel Foucault has pointed out[33]) the expansion of official and expert power/knowledge. If penal rehabilitationism is revived, what checks are there against a further proliferation of these powers?

Questions of Fairness

Criminal punishment, by its nature, condemns. The sanction not only visits deprivation but also conveys that the conduct is wrong and the offender to blame for having committed it. This holds whatever purpose is adopted for deciding sentences. Whether the sentence is based on the seriousness of the offender's crime or on his/her need(s) for treatment, it will still imply something about the impropriety of the behavior.

The theoretical basis for the principle of proportionality of sentence is that it comports with the criminal sanction's censuring implications. Conduct that is more blameworthy—in the sense of involving greater harm or culpability—is to be punished (and thereby condemned) more severely; conduct that is less reprehensible is to be punished (and hence censured) more mildly.[34]

Treatment, however, can seldom rely on criteria relating to the blameworthiness of the conduct; whether the offender is amenable to a particular treatment depends, instead, on his/her social and personal characteristics. This creates the potential problem of fairness: one is using criminal punishment, a blame-conveying response, and yet deciding the intervention on the basis of those personal and social variables that have little to do with how reprehensible the behavior is.[35]

How serious is this problem? The answer depends, of course, on how much emphasis proportionality receives. A thoroughgoing desert conception would require the severity of the penal response to depend heavily on the degree of reprehensibleness of the conduct—thus leaving limited scope for rehabilitative considerations (except for deciding among responses of comparable severity[36]). Not everyone supports a desert model, and some new rehabilitationists say they reject it.[37] But then, it needs to be explained what role, if any, the degree of blameworthiness of the conduct should have.

One possibility would be to give proportionality a limiting role: the seriousness of the criminal conduct would set upper and lower bounds on the quantum of punishment—within which rehabilitation could be invoked to fix the sentence.[38] That kind of solution requires one to specify how much weight its desert elements should have—that is, how narrow or broad the offense-based limits on the sentence should be.[39] Here, one faces the familiar dilemma; the narrower one sets those limits, the less room there would be for treatment considerations; whereas the wider one sets the limits, the more one would need to worry about seemingly disparate or disproportionate responses.

Another possibility would be to try to dispense with notions of proportionality altogether.[40] Such a strategy, however, would pose its own difficulties. It would, first, have to be explained how it is justifiable to employ punishment—a blaming institution—without regard to the blameworthiness of the conduct.[41] Or, if one proposes to eliminate the censuring element in punishment, it needs to be explained how this may possibly be accomplished. (The juvenile justice system, for example, long purported to convey no blame, but who was fooled?) Second, the absence of significant proportionality constraints could open the way for abuses of the kind that discredited the old rehabilitation—for example, long-term, open-ended intervention against those deemed to be in special need of treatment. (One thinks of the young car thief who was confined for sixteen years at Patuxent Institution because he refused to talk to the therapists.) One might hope that we are more sophisticated now about the therapeutic value of such interventions—but is such hope enough without principled restraints upon rehabilitative responses?

Finally, one could be more ambitious and think of replacing the criminal sanction with a wholly different set of measures. Nils Christie has urged that state punishment be supplanted by communitarian responses aimed at resolution of conflicts.[42] Some feminist writers have been exploring alternative conceptions of justice.[43] These theorists are, however, aware of the scope of this undertaking: it would involve, not a change in sentencing philosophy, but a completely new set of institutions for responding to what is now termed criminal behavior. One would have to consider whether, and how, these new institutions could afford protection against excessive, or seemingly unfair, intrusions. Whatever one thinks of such suggestions (and one of us has been skeptical of Christie's[44]), they constitute a different level of argument, one that concerns basic social and institutional change. These writers are not speaking, as the new rehabilitationists are, about retaining the criminal sanction and merely giving sentencing more of a treatment emphasis.

Concluding Thoughts

In offering the foregoing criticisms of the new rehabilitationists, we are not denying that treatment might have a legitimate role in a fair system of sanctions. How large that role should be depends not only on how much is known about treatment but also on what other assumptions one makes—including those regarding proportionality.[45] Rehabilitation, however, cannot be the primary basis for deciding the sentence, nor can it be the rationale for supporting less harsh sanctions than we have today. If we want sanctions scaled down, as they surely should be, the main and explicitly stated reason for so doing should concern equity and the diminution of suffering.

The most dangerous temptation is to treat the treatment ethos as a kind of edifying fiction:[46] If we only act as though we cared—and minister treatment to offenders as a sign of our caring—a more humane penal system will emerge. No serious inquiry is needed, on this view, about the criteria for deciding what constitutes a humane penal system or about how a renewed treatment emphasis could achieve its intended effects or lead to reasonably just outcomes.

Such thinking is a recipe for failure. It is likely to cause the new treatment ethos to be rejected once its specifics (or lack of them) are subject to critical scrutiny. And it could do no more good than the old, largely hortatory treatment ethic: create a facade of treatment behind which decision makers act as they choose. Those who wish to revive penal rehabilitationism have yet to address the hard questions, including the ones we have tried to raise here.

NOTES

The authors are grateful for the comments of Andrew Ashworth, David Dixon, Jeffrey Fagan, and John Kleinig.

1 *See* F. ALLEN, THE DECLINE OF THE REHABILITATIVE IDEAL (1981), ch. 3.

2 *See, e.g., infra* note 15.

3 AMERICAN FRIENDS SERVICE COMMITTEE, STRUGGLE FOR JUSTICE (1971); A. VON HIRSCH, DOING JUSTICE (1976), ch. 15; N. MORRIS, THE FUTURE OF IMPRISONMENT (1974), ch. 1.

4 Palmer, *The Effectiveness of Intervention: Recent Trends and Current Issues*, 37 CRIME & DELINQ. 330, 342 (1991).

5 F. CULLEN & K. GILBERT, REAFFIRMING REHABILITATION (1982).

6 B. HUDSON, JUSTICE THROUGH PUNISHMENT (1987); Carlen, *Crime, Inequality, and Sentencing*, in PAYING FOR CRIME (P. Carlen & D. Cook eds. 1989); *see also* J. BRAITHWAITE & P. PETTIT, NOT JUST DESERTS (1990), at 124-25.

7 *See, e.g.*, AMERICAN FRIENDS SERVICE COMMITTEE, STRUGGLE FOR JUSTICE (1971).

8 *See infra* note 15.

9 T. MATHIESEN, PRISON ON TRIAL (1989).

10 A. VON HIRSCH, *supra* note 3; A. VON HIRSCH, PAST OR FUTURE CRIMES (1985).

11 Maher, *Criminalizing Pregnancy*, 17 SOCIAL JUSTICE 111 (1990). Maher, *Punishment and Welfare: Crack Cocaine and the Regulation of Mothering*, 3 WOMEN & CRIM. JUSTICE __ (1991) (in press).

12 Panel on Research on Rehabilitative Effects, *Report*, in THE REHABILITATION OF CRIMINAL OFFENDERS (L. Sechrest, S. White & E. Brown eds. 1979).

13 *See, e.g.*, Fagan, *Social and Legal Policy Dimensions of Violent Juvenile Crime*, 17 CRIM. JUST. & BEHAVIOR 93 (1990).

14 Gendreau & Ross, *The Revivification of Rehabilitation: Evidence from the 1980's*, 4 JUST. Q. 349 (1988).

15 *Compare* Lab & Whitehead, *An Analysis of Juvenile Treatment*, 34 CRIME & DELINQ. 60 (1988), and Lab & Whitehead, *From "Nothing Works" to "The Appropriate Works,"* 28 CRIMINOLOGY 405 (1990), *with* Andrews, Zinger, Hoge, Bonta, Gendreau & Cullen, *Does Correctional Treatment Work?* 28 CRIMINOLOGY 369 (1990), and Andrews, Zinger, Hoge, Bonta, Gendreau & Cullen, *A Human Science Approach or More Pessimism*, 28 CRIMINOLOGY 419 (1990).

16 *See* Fagan, *supra* note 13.

17 Palmer, *Treatment and the Role of Classification*, 30 CRIME & DELINQ. 245 (1984); Sechrest, *Classification for Treatment*, in PREDICTION AND CLASSIFICATION (D. Gottfredson & M. Tonry eds. 1987); *see also* Palmer, *supra* note 4.

18 Palmer, *supra* note 4, at 339.

19 *See* Fagan, *supra* note 13.

20 Gendreau & Ross, *supra* note 14, at 345.

21 *See, e.g.*, F. CULLEN & K. GILBERT, *supra* note 5, ch. 7.

22 For discussion of social services for offenders, see A. VON HIRSCH & K. HANRAHAN, THE QUESTION OF PAROLE (1979), ch. 8.

23 Anglin & Hser, *The Treatment of Drug Offenders*, in DRUGS & CRIME (J. Wilson & M. Tonry eds. 1990).

24 F. CULLEN & K. GILBERT, *supra* note 5, ch. 7.

25 von Hirsch, Wasik & Greene, *Punishments in the Community and the Principles of Desert*, 20 RUTGERS L.J. 595, 615-16 (1989).

26 *See supra* note 23 and accompanying text.

27 *See, e.g.*, Pearson, *Women Defendants in Magistrates' Courts*, 3 BRITISH J.L. & SOCIETY 265 (1976); Phillips & De Fleur, *Gender Ascription and the Stereotyping of Deviants*, 20 CRIMINOLOGY 431 (1982); *see also* C. SMART, WOMEN, CRIME AND CRIMINOLOGY (1976).

28 For an exploration of the problem of humiliating and intrusive penalties, see von Hirsch, *The Ethics of Community-*

Based Sanctions, 36 CRIME & DELINQ. 162, 165-73 (1990).

29 *See, e.g.,* F. CULLEN & K. GILBERT, supra note 5; B. HUDSON, supra note 6.

30 von Hirsch, *The Politics of "Just Deserts,"* 32 CANADIAN J. CRIMINOLOGY 397, 400-02 (1990).

31 *Id.;* A. VON HIRSCH, K. KNAPP & M. TONRY, THE SENTENCING COMMISSION AND ITS GUIDELINES (1987), chs. 2 and 5.

32 *See, e.g.,* B. HUDSON, supra note 6, ch. 4.

33 M. FOUCAULT, DISCIPLINE AND PUNISH (1977).

34 A. VON HIRSCH, PAST OR FUTURE CRIMES (1985), chs. 3-5.

35 Some personal or social variables—for example, facts relating to diminished capacity—do have a bearing on blameworthiness. However, treatment programs rely on other variables that concern the offender's amenability to the program, and that seldom have such a bearing.

36 *See* von Hirsch, Wasik & Greene, *supra* note 25, at 604.

37 *See supra* notes 4 and 5.

38 For a sketch of such a model, see N. MORRIS, MADNESS AND THE CRIMINAL LAW (1982), ch. 5. For a critique, see A. VON HIRSCH, *supra* note 34, chs. 4, 12.

39 A. VON HIRSCH, *supra* note 34, ch. 12.

40 An attempt to develop an alternative penal theory that dispenses with desert principles is set forth in J. BRAITHWAITE & P. PETTIT, *supra* note 6. That theory, however, relies primarily on deterrence and incapacitation rather than treatment. In our view, the theory has manifold difficulties, discussed in von Hirsch and Ashworth, *Not Not Just Deserts:*

A Critique of Braithwaite and Pettit, 12 OXFORD J. LEGAL STUDIES No. 1 (1992) (forthcoming).

41 BRAITHWAITE & PETTIT, *supra* note 6, try to detach censure from proportionality requirements, but their arguments are unconvincing in our judgment for reasons set forth in VON HIRSCH & ASHWORTH, *supra* note 40.

42 N. CHRISTIE, LIMITS TO PAIN (1981).

43 *See, e.g.,* Lahey, *Until Women Have Told All They Have To Tell,* 23 OSGOODE HALL L. REV. 519 (1985); Heidensohn, *Models of Justice: Portia or Persephone?,* 14 INT'L J. SOCIOLOGY OF L. 287 (1986); Howe, *Social Injury Revisited: Towards a Feminist Theory of Social Justice,* 15 INT'L J. SOCIOLOGY OF L. 423 (1987); West, *Jurisprudence and Gender,* 55 U. CHICAGO L. REV. 1 (1988); C. SMART, FEMINISM AND THE POWER OF LAW (1989); Daly, *Criminal Justice Ideologies and Practices in Different Voices: Some Feminist Questions About Justice,* 17 INT'L J. SOCIOLOGY OF L. 1 (1989); Smart, *Law's Truth/Women's Experience,* in DISSENTING OPINIONS: FEMINIST EXPLORATIONS IN LAW AND SOCIETY (R. Graycar ed. 1990).

44 von Hirsch, Review of N. Christie, 28 CRIME & DELINQ. 315 (1982). For arguments in favor of a censuring penal response, see von Hirsch, *Proportionality in the Philosophy of Punishment,* 1 CRIM. L. FORUM 259, 270-79 (1990).

45 For a limited suggested role of treatment considerations under a desert model, see von Hirsch, Wasik & Greene, supra note 25, 615-16. For a somewhat expanded role under a "mixed" model, see N. MORRIS & M. TONRY, BETWEEN PRISON AND PROBATION (1990), ch. 7. For a comparison of these models, see von Hirsch, *Scaling Intermediate Punishments,* in SMART SENTENCING: EXPANDING OPTIONS FOR INTERMEDIATE SANCTIONS (J. Byrne, A. Lurigio & J. Petersilia eds. 1991) (forthcoming).

46 *See* Rothman, *Decarcerating Prisoners and Patients,* 1 CIVIL LIBERTIES REV. 8 (1973).

Mandatory Minimums and the Betrayal of Sentencing Reform: A Legislative Dr. Jekyll and Mr. Hyde*

By Henry Scott Wallace

Senior Fellow, Criminal Justice Policy Foundation, Washington, DC

He put the glass to his lips and drank at one gulp. A cry followed; he reeled, staggered, clutched at the table and held on, staring with injected eyes, gasping with open mouth; and as I looked there came, I thought, a change—he seemed to swell—his face became suddenly black and the features seemed to melt and alter—and the next moment, I had sprung to my feet and leaped back against the wall, my arm raised to shield me from that prodigy, my mind submerged in terror.

"O God!" I screamed, and "O God!" again and again.

—Robert Louis Stevenson
Dr. Jekyll and Mr. Hyde

CONGRESS IS of two minds on sentencing reform. One mind is dispassionate and learned, deliberating for decades in search of a rational, comprehensive solution. The other is impulsive, reckless, driven by unquenchable political passions, and impatient with its plodding alter-ego.

The two are polar opposites, hardly aware of each other's existence, yet existing together within the same body, commonly within the same individual legislator. Both are strong, and have accomplished much to shape sentencing reform in their own image. From the dispassionate one came the Sentencing Reform Act of 1984, creating the United States Sentencing Commission and the federal sentencing guidelines under which all federal crimes since 1987 have been punished.[1] From the impulsive one—in random, angry bursts—came mandatory minimums.

They are a legislative Dr. Jekyll and Mr. Hyde, and their simultaneous existence is a mortal danger to themselves and society.

Different Paths to the Same Goal

Both Jekyll and Hyde are trying to accomplish the same thing: determinate sentencing. The goal is to reduce judicial sentencing discretion and the arbitrary and unpredictable sentencing disparities that have accompanied it.[2]

As recognized in 1983 by the one Senator who opposed both the Sentencing Reform Act and mandatory minimums, Senator Mathias (R-Md), "hardly anyone disagrees" (in 1983) that there is too much disparity in criminal sentences and that prison sentences are too indeterminate in duration.[3] The problem, he wrote, is in figuring out "how best to reduce the disparity and indeterminacy."[4]

If longevity were the test of merit, mandatory punishments would excel. They are as old as civilization. The biblical *lex talionis*—an eye for eye, a tooth for

tooth—is mandatory,[5] and envisions "neither mercy nor mitigation of punishment."[6] Mandatory punishments are enshrined in earliest Anglo-Saxon law. King Alfred, who reigned in England around 900 A.D., prescribed mandatory fines for every conceivable injury, including:

> If a wound an inch long is made under the hair, one shilling shall be paid . . .
> If an ear is cut off, 30 shillings shall be paid . . .
> If one knocks out another's eye, he shall pay 66 shillings, 6⅓ pence . . .
> If the eye is still in the head, but the injured man can see nothing with it, one-third of the payment shall be withheld. . . .[7]

In America, mandatory punishments date back to the earliest days of the Republic, starting with various capital offenses in 1790.[8] Throughout the 19th century, mandatory prison terms were added for lesser offenses, such as refusing to testify before Congress, failure to report seaboard saloon purchases, or causing a ship to run aground by use of a false light.[9]

Mandatory minimums of broad applicability did not surface until the Boggs Acts of the 1950's, setting drug distribution penalties of a mandatory five years for a first offense, ten for a second or for any drug distribution to a minor, and a life sentence or the death penalty for a third offense.[10] The Senate report recognized the controversial nature of such severe penalties without possibility of probation, parole or suspension of sentence, particularly for first offenses, but concluded, significantly, that it could think of no alternative way "to define the gravity of the crime and the assured penalty to follow."[11] The federal Boggs Acts were mimicked by "Little Boggs Acts" in the states.[12]

But fourteen years later, Congress confessed error and repealed virtually all mandatory minimums for drug offenses,[13] citing the severity and inflexibility of the sentences.[14] Mandatory minimums were criticized for "treat[ing] casual violators as severely as they treat hardened criminals," raising qualms even with prosecutors, interfering with the judicial role of making individualized sentencing judgments, and perhaps most

*This article was originally published in the March/April 1993 issue of the *Federal Bar News & Journal*, Vol. 40, No. 3. It has been reprinted here with permission of the Federal Bar Association.

importantly, producing no reduction in drug viola- tions.[15] The repeal was even praised by freshman Congressman George Bush for promoting "more equi- table action by the courts . . . and fewer disproportion- ate sentences."[16]

It was about this time that the idea of sentencing guidelines was born. A national crime commission issued a report in 1971 calling attention to the need for more uniform federal sentencing.[17] Shortly there- after, Federal District Judge Marvin Frankel outlined the sentencing system that, thirteen years later, would become law: a national commission writing federal sentencing guidelines which would assume the force of legislation in the absence of a congressional veto.[18]

The federal guidelines system enacted in 1984 seems to have been conceived as a middle ground between mandatory sentences and completely inde- terminate sentencing. The Senate report on the Sen- tencing Reform Act, while emphasizing the need to curtail judicial sentencing discretion, stressed that the guidelines are not intended to be imposed "in a mecha- nistic fashion."[19] The purpose, the report stated, is "to provide a structure for evaluating the fairness and appropriateness of the sentence for an individual of- fender,"[20] but not to "remove all of the judge's sentenc- ing discretion."[21] Sentencing schemes in four states that relied on statutorily mandated sentences were discussed and rejected.[22] As one Senator said in 1975 in introducing one of the precursor bills of the Sentenc- ing Reform Act: "An inflexible scheme is hardly an improvement on a arbitrary one."[23]

The resulting sentencing system, though open to criticism for tilting too far toward inflexibility[24] or for being a gutless abdication of Congress's fundamental responsibility to set criminal punishments,[25] seems at least to have been a compromise rationally arrived at.

But the appearance of a rational evolution of sen- tencing policy is fleeting. In the very same comprehen- sive crime bill that contained the Sentencing Reform Act of 1984—which in every aspect appeared to em- body a complete repudiation of mandatory mini- mums—Congress, incredibly, included significant new mandatory minimums, harbingers of what has become the most sweeping regime of mandatory punishments in the nation's history.

The most significant ones in the 1984 bill were a mandatory five years for possessing a gun during a crime of violence, on top of the sentence for the crime of violence itself,[26] and a mandatory fifteen years for simple possession of a firearm by a person with three previous state or federal convictions for burglary or robbery.[27] Nowhere in the legislative history was any irony or inconsistency with the Sentencing Reform Act noted.

New mandatory minimums came every two years, in election-eve crime bills hundreds of pages long. In the 1986 Anti-Drug Abuse Act came numerous drug- related mandatory minimums, including the most widely used ones currently on the books: the five- and ten-year mandatory sentences for drug distribution or importation, tied to the quantity of any "mixture or substance" containing a "detectable amount" of the prohibited drugs.[28] Incredibly, although these provi- sions had been duly processed in committee, with a written report (a rare occurrence for mandatory mini- mum provisions over the past decade),[29] there was not a word of acknowledgement of the momentousness of the undertaking—not a word explaining why the les- sons of the failure of the Boggs Acts were now being ignored; and not a word of discussion of any potential inconsistency with the guideline system of determi- nate sentencing that Congress had set in motion just two years earlier.

Instead, what appeared to be driving the drug bill was unprecedented media attention on drugs. Univer- sity of Maryland basketball star Len Bias had died of a crack overdose during House consideration of the bill, and thoughts of sentencing uniformity and the integrity of the guidelines system were quickly eclipsed by the day's headlines. An anguished Con- gressman Robert Dornan (R-Cal.) explained: "I think it comes down to one young man not dying in vain."[30]

In 1988 came yet another Anti-Drug Abuse Act,[31] containing numerous mandatory minimums, includ- ing 20 years for "continuing criminal enterprise" drug offenses[32] or using a weapon during a violent or drug- related crime,[33] and mandatory life for use of a ma- chine gun or silencer[34] or for any drug offender with three prior state or federal drug felony convictions.[35] Drug conspiracies and attempts were made subject to the same mandatory minimums as the completed of- fenses.[36]

The 1988 Act also contained the most bizarre and anomalous mandatory minimum in federal law: a five- year mandatory minimum for simple possession of five grams of "crack" cocaine—the weight of about two pennies.[37] Simple possession of any amount of other drugs, including powder cocaine and heroin—or 4.9 grams or less of crack—remained a misdemeanor, with a mandatory sentence required only for a second of- fense, and a mere fifteen days at that.

A few more mandatory minimums were approved in the 1990 crime bill, including 10 years for the Crime du Jour—being a savings-and-loan "kingpin."[38] But in a sign of emerging concern about the compatibility of mandatory minimums with the guideline system, a variety of other stiff mandatory minimums passed by the Senate were deleted in House-Senate conference, while a provision mandating a Sentencing Commission study of the impact and effectiveness of mandatory minimums was retained.[39]

This report, submitted to Congress in August 1991 and entitled *Special Report to the Congress: Mandatory Minimums in the Federal Criminal Justice System*, is the most authoritative and thorough—and thoroughly devastating—review of mandatory minimums to date.[40]

Still another large crime bill was poised for enactment in 1992, containing several new mandatory minimums—though fewer and less severe than those approved in the Senate's version—but died at the end of the Congress due to controversies over gun control and habeas corpus reform.[41]

In federal law today, although there are over 60 statutes containing mandatory minimum penalties, only four are used with any frequency. These four, covering drug and weapons offenses,[42] account for 94 percent of all federal mandatory minimum cases.

For the present, although harsh and radical mandatory minimums continue to be shouted through in floor deliberations on crime legislation, particularly under the less formal Senate rules, the momentum for new mandatory minimums appears to be slowing. Armed with the Sentencing Commission report and increasingly vociferous opposition from every federal judicial circuit in the country,[43] Judiciary Committee leaders are beginning to debate the merits of mandatory minimums openly and are able to hold the line on the most excessive new ones in House-Senate conference negotiations.

Thus, federal sentencing policy today is stalled with one foot in both camps, with Congress wise enough not to complete the "mandatorization" of federal criminal law, but far from bold enough to tamper with existing mandatory minimums and bear the very real risk of being savaged as "soft on crime" in the next election.

Uneven Prosecutorial Application

Perhaps the greatest appeal of mandatory minimums is the promise of universal, impartial application. On their face, they treat all offenders the same; as Senator Phil Gramm (R-Tex.) warned in proposing a ten-year mandatory sentence for first-offense sale of drugs to a minor in 1991, everybody who violates the statute must pay the same price, "no matter who your daddy is, and no matter how society has done you wrong."[44] But as the Sentencing Commission report found, the expectation that mandatory minimums would be applied to all cases that meet the statutory criteria of eligibility has not been fulfilled.

The prosecution's power to unilaterally reward a defendant's cooperation introduces significant disparities. The only available statutory basis for a judge to sentence below a federal mandatory minimum is the

defendant's "substantial assistance" in prosecuting somebody else.[45] Since a judge may do this only "upon motion of the Government," and since U.S. Attorneys around the country are free to define "substantial" as they wish, the prosecutor, in effect, has sole, untrammeled and unreviewable discretion to grant a sentence below a mandatory minimum.[46]

A common problem with this cooperation discount is that higher level drug offenders, who have more "substantial" information to give to prosecutors, end up with lesser sentences than bit players. One press account compared the case of Stanley Marshall, who sold less than one gram of LSD and got a twenty-year mandatory sentence, to that of Jose Cabrera, who the government estimates made more than $40 million importing cocaine and who would have qualified for life plus 200 years in prison, but was able to cut a deal for only eight years because he knew Manuel Noriega and agreed to testify against him.[47]

One judge who imposed a mandatory sentence on a woman convicted of conspiracy in her boyfriend's drug dealing called it a "gross miscarriage of justice . . . to pick the one who may be the least involved of all and sentence her to over six times the time of . . . the real actors in this case [who cooperated]."[48]

U.S. District Judge Terry J. Hatter, Jr. commented: "The people at the very bottom who can't provide substantial assistance end up getting [punished] more severely than those at the top."[49]

The Sentencing Commission's report found that plea bargains were used to circumvent clearly applicable mandatory minimums in more than a third of the cases studied.[50] The report also found that prosecutors file mandatory minimum charges unpredictably. Prosecutorial practices included:

- Filing drug distribution charges specifying no amount of drugs, thus avoiding any mandatory minimums, or specifying a lower quantity than appeared supportable;

- Not charging the mandatory five-year weapon enhancement in almost half the cases where it would have been appropriate; and

- Not seeking mandatory sentence enhancements for prior felony convictions in almost two-thirds of the possible cases.[51]

Overall, the Commission's empirical data indicated, defendants do not receive mandatory minimum sentences in approximately 41 percent of the cases where they appear warranted.[52]

The Commission concluded: "To the extent that prosecutorial discretion is exercised with preference to some and not to others, and to the extent that some are convicted of conduct carrying a mandatory minimum penalty while others who engage in the same or similar conduct are not so convicted, disparity is reintroduced" into the sentencing system.[53]

Arbitrary State/Federal Case Allocation

The Sentencing Commission did not even discuss the most gaping hole in federal mandatory minimums' promise of uniform application: the reality that the vast majority of drug and weapons offenses which are subject to federal mandatory penalties are in fact prosecuted under state statutes covering the same offense conduct and resulting in far less severe punishments.

State and federal prosecutors are under no obligation to develop or publish standards governing the selection of cases to receive the more severe federal penalties. The Federal Courts Study Committee's 1990 final report, observing that the federal courts were being "flooded" with minor drug cases formerly prosecuted in state court, urged the Justice Department to "develop clear national policies governing which drug cases to prosecute in the federal courts," drawing the line, for example, at cases that do not involve "international or interstate elements."[54]

Bizarrely, selective use of federal mandatory minimums in random state cases often appears to be a specific legislative goal of Congress. The sponsor of the lengthiest mandatory minimum of the ground-breaking 1984 crop, the Armed Career Criminal Act (fifteen years for gun possession by a three-time burglar or robber),[55] expressly touted selective prosecution and disparate sentencing as the greatest advantages of his proposal. Prosecuting only "a handful" of possible cases in each jurisdiction would "set an example," he argued, that would have "a tremendous leveraging or rippling effect" on other offenders:

Career criminals with cases pending in the state courts, once made aware of the risks of a federal prosecution and the certainty of 15 years in prison, would suddenly find themselves motivated to enter a guilty plea in the state case, in the hope of obtaining some lesser sentence. The result can be expected to be sentences of 5 to 10 years or 7 to 14 years—less than the expected federal sentence, but substantially more than [routine state] sentences....[56]

A similar intent was expressed by the sponsor of one of the most sweeping and ambitious mandatory minimums ever proposed. In a 1991 crime bill debate, Senator Alfonse D'Amato (R-NY) sponsored an amendment to make virtually every offense in the nation committed with a firearm into a federal offense carrying mandatory federal prison terms of ten, twenty, or thirty years.[57] According to Justice Department figures, there are about 640,000 crimes committed every year with handguns[58]—about fourteen times the entire capacity of the federal prison system, which is already overloaded to 160 percent of its capacity. D'Amato added a proviso that his amendment should

be used "to supplement but not supplant" state prosecutions, but did not suggest standards for how this selectivity should be exercised. He conceded that his proposal, which passed the Senate overwhelmingly,[59] might not solve the problem of gun-related crime, but argued that "it does bring about a sense that we are serious."[60]

These policy rationales—conveying a "sense" of seriousness rather than actually being serious, or randomly selecting a "handful" of possible offenders to "set an example" in the hope that others will plead guilty in order to receive lesser sentences—make a shameless mockery of sentencing uniformity and certainty of punishment. The extreme disparity between the harsh federal mandatory sentences for the same conduct, together with the overwhelming odds against any individual offender becoming one of the few singled out for federal prosecution, not only vitiate the deterrent power of the law, but threaten to do affirmative harm to the credibility and integrity of both state and federal criminal justice systems.

Judges Reduced to Automatons

As the discussion above suggests, prosecutors have enormous power under a mandatory minimum regime to decide what the sentence will be. They can decide what to charge, what quantity of drugs to allege, whether to "swallow the gun," whether to accept a lesser plea, whether to certify "substantial assistance," or which offenders are to be "made examples of" in federal court. Judges are all but superfluous. Echoing one of Congress's key themes in the 1970 repeal of mandatory minimums,[61] federal Circuit Judge Franklin S. Billings recently wrote:

[The existence of mandatory minimums denies] judges of this court, and of all courts, the right to bring their conscience, experience, discretion and sense of what is just into the sentencing procedure, and it, in effect, makes a judge a computer, automatically imposing sentences without regard to what is right and just.[62]

The refrain is increasingly heard from sentencing judges in mandatory minimum cases that they recognize the required sentence to be unjust and disproportionate, but their "hands are tied," in cases such as—

- David Schoolcraft, a successful businessman with a dozen-year-old felony record, sentenced to fifteen years under the Armed Career Criminal Act for a gun-possession offense that would have been a misdemeanor in state court.

- Bobby Joe Ward, a 60-year-old retired coal miner with black lung disease, caught accompanying his son to his son's marijuana patch; the sentencing judge lamented his inability to consider the father's disability and clean record.[63]

- Richard Anderson, a crane operator with no criminal record who accepted $5 to give an acquaintance a lift to a Burger King where the acquaintance was arrested for selling 100 grams of crack to an undercover drug agent; the Republican-appointed judge who imposed the mandatory ten-year sentence was moved to tears and called the sentence "a grave miscarriage of justice."[64]

On the premise of removing discretion from the sentencing process, mandatory minimums have succeeded only in shifting it from one place to another—from the judge, in public proceedings conducted on the record in the courtroom, to the prosecutor's office, off the record and behind closed doors. Since the charging and plea negotiation processes which handcuff the sentencing judge are "neither open to public review nor generally reviewable by the courts," concluded the Sentencing Commission in its report, "the honesty and truth in sentencing intended by the guidelines system is compromised."[65]

Perhaps because mandatory minimums suggest a profound congressional mistrust of judges' ability to do justice, even when guided and constrained by the guideline system, federal judges have risen up with one voice in protest. The judiciary in every federal circuit in the country has passed resolutions condemning mandatory minimums and call for their repeal.[66]

Unwarranted Sentencing Uniformity

When they are charged and applied, mandatory minimums are to sentencing uniformity what a meat axe is to brain surgery. As the Sentencing Commission observed in one of its earliest explorations of the subject, mandatory minimums operate "crudely," failing to "differentiate among dissimilarly situated defendants convicted of the same crime."[67]

The problem is that Congress, in setting these *minimum* sentences, consistently focuses on cases of *maximum* culpability. Drug mandatory minimums are passed amid speeches about "kingpins" and "major" dealers, with no discussion that the statute will apply equally to the lowest level flunky of the dealer—the lookout, the floor sweeper, or the impoverished Colombian peasant who risks his life for $100 by swallowing a cocaine-filled condom for an airplane flight to America.

Special mandatory minimums for any drug offense within 1,000 feet of a school are passed amid speeches about dealers hanging around schoolyards peddling poison to the nation's youth, with no mention that the statute will also punish an addict possessing drugs for personal use whose home happens to be within 1,000 feet of a school,[68] or every "mule" arrested on an Amtrak train passing through New York City because

a business school is located in a skyscraper high above.[69]

Recently, when Senator John Seymour (R-Cal.) proposed an amendment setting a three-year mandatory sentence add-on for any adult who "encourages" a minor to commit any federal offense, he spoke of "young kids . . . being recruited as foot solders [for] organized crime activities, such as gambling, money laundering, and extortion," and of force, coercion and threats against the child's life or safety.[70] He did not dwell on the amendment's equal applicability to less coercive scenarios and less serious offenses, even misdemeanors, such as, conceivably, an eighteen-year-old telling a fifteen-year-old that he might enjoy trying marijuana sometime. There had been no hearings, nobody argued against the amendment, and it passed in minutes by voice vote.[71]

As Justice White pointed out in *Harmelin* v. *Michigan*, to be consistent with the notion of a "minimum" sentence, "the offense should be one which will *always* warrant that punishment."[72]

The distortion caused by this calibration of "minimum" sentences to maximum offense conduct is not limited to drug and firearm cases. It has corrupted the entire federal sentencing system, as the Sentencing Commission skews the ranges for all other offenses in a struggle to maintain system-wide proportionality.[73]

Requiring judges to impose on peripheral players sentences designed for their higher-ups has led to an endless parade of individual cases of excessively harsh, disproportionate and inconsistent punishment. For example:

- A migrant farmworker with no criminal record, single and the sole support of her five young daughters, serving a ten-year mandatory minimum for agreeing to drive a van with hidden drugs across the border from Mexico;[74]

- A Michigan man convicted of first-offense simple possession of a pound and a half of cocaine under state law and sentenced to mandatory life imprisonment;[75] when arrested, he voluntarily surrendered a concealed, registered handgun, perhaps not realizing that the penalty for his drug offense was the same as the penalty for murdering a police officer;[76] and

- A Washington, D.C. secretary sentenced to a five-year mandatory minimum because her drug-dealing son hid 120 grams of crack in her attic.[77]

Some of the most egregious inconsistencies in federal mandatory minimums are in drug cases, where statutory language ties the penalty not just to the amount of the drug involved, but to the amount of any "mixture or substance" containing a "detectable amount" of the drug. Customarily, drugs such as heroin and cocaine are mixed with increasing amounts of non-narcotic mixing substances as they move further down the distribution chain; a street dealer may be handling drugs that are more than ninety percent powdered sugar. But for purposes of federal mandatory minimums, the sugar counts just as much as the drug. The sentence is tied to the weight of the entire mixture; purity is irrelevant. Thus, echoing the irony of the "substance assistance" discount discussed above, the more small-time the dealer, the more severe the relative punishment.

Nowhere is this problem more pronounced than in LSD cases. LSD, a highly concentrated drug, is placed on a carrier for retail sale; one dose, weighing only .05 mg, is commonly placed on a sugar cube weighing some two grams. The result is sentencing disparities that have been described as "crazy," "loony," and "absurd "[78] A person who sells five doses of LSD on sugar cubes will receive a ten-year mandatory minimum, based almost exclusively on the weight of the sugar cubes, while a person who sells 19,999 doses in pure liquid form is not even subject to the five-year mandatory minimum.[79] Depending on the carrier—ranging from sugar cubes to gelatin cubes to blotter paper to pure liquid form—the sentence for selling 1,000 doses can soar from fifteen months to thirty years.[80]

And these intra-drug disparities are compounded by inexplicable discrepancies between the various hard-core drugs subject to mandatory minimums. As Justice Stevens has written, one defendant who received a mandatory twenty-year prison term for selling less than 12,000 doses of LSD would have had to sell about 50,000 doses of crack, between one and two million doses of heroin, or between 325,000 and five million doses of powder cocaine (depending on purity) to get the same sentence.[81]

The anti-mandatory-minimum resolutions of the various federal judicial circuits characterize mandatory minimums often as being "manifestly unjust" or "inordinately harsh."[82] The Federal Courts Study Committee gently suggested that "Congress may not realize the impact" of mandatory minimums.[83]

Proportionality, wrote the Sentencing Commission, is "a fundamental premise for just punishment, and a primary goal of the Sentencing Reform Act," but it is compromised by mandatory minimums.[84] Though sentencing uniformity may be the desired goal of mandatory minimums, the Commission concluded that "an unintended effect of mandatory minimums is *unwarranted* sentencing uniformity."[85] The Commission wrote that:

> Deterrence . . . is dependent on certainty and appropriate severity. While mandatory minimum sentences may increase severity, the data suggest that uneven application may dramatically reduce certainty. The consequence . . . is likely to thwart the deterrent value of mandatory minimums.[86]

The alternative, the Commission modestly notes, is the guidelines' "finely calibrated . . . smooth continuum" of sentences,[87] permitting differentiation on the basis of offender and offense characteristics, role in the offense, criminal history and acceptance of responsibility, resulting in penalties that are not only "certain" and "substantial," but also "proportionate and fair."[88]

Racial Disparities

One of the Sentencing Commission's most disturbing findings was that whites are more likely than non-whites to be sentenced below the applicable mandatory minimum.[89] Whites are less likely than Black or Hispanic defendants to be indicted or convicted at the indicated mandatory minimum level, more likely to plead guilty, and more likely to receive a "substantial assistance" reduction.[90]

Such findings may produce an upsurge in race-based constitutional challenges to mandatory minimums. The Minnesota Supreme Court ruled that it violates federal equal protection guarantees for a statutory scheme to punish offenses involving crack cocaine—the drug of choice among Black cocaine users—more severely than powder cocaine—preferred among White users.[91] Federal law contains an even greater crack/cocaine differential than the Minnesota statue.[92]

Interestingly, the *prevention* of racial and social discrimination was at one point a reason cited in *support* of mandatory minimums. Senator Edward Kennedy (D-Mass.), today the Senate's strongest opponent of mandatory minimums, introduced one of the first post-1970 bills to restore federal mandatory minimums, citing the need to impose sentences "evenhandedly [on] all offenders." Because the poor "often pay a heavier price for crime than others in society," he explained, "[w]e must end that shameful double standard and assure that mandatory sentences will be applied with an equal hand."[93]

Overloaded Courts, Prisons, But No Reduction in Crime

A consistent finding of the various studies is that because of the high stakes involved, mandatory minimums reduce the number of cases settled by plea, and correspondingly increase the number of cases going to trial. The Federal Courts Study Committee reported:

> [L]engthy mandatory minimum sentences seriously frustrate the normal and salutary process of pretrial settlements in criminal cases. Even defendants who have little doubt of the likelihood that they will be found guilty are more likely to take their chances on a trial when faced with the possibility of a lengthy minimum sentence.[94]

And as the Committee noted, "even a 5 percent reduction in guilty pleas means 33 to 50 percent increase in trials."[95]

Mandatory sentences in drug and weapons cases are fueling an unprecedented increase in federal prison populations. The federal prison population roughly tripled during the 1980's, and may double again the next decade.[96] By far the largest component of this increase is in the drug area; drug case fillings increased 280 percent during the 1980's, with the trend continuing upward.[97] About half of the cases sentenced in federal court now are drug cases[98]—the mother lode of mandatory minimums in federal law.

There are several effects of this trend. One is cost: keeping up with rapidly expanding federal prison populations will add billions to the annual federal corrections budget, with the cost of building a single new federal prison space as high as $100,000,[99] and construction costs accounting for only about five percent of a facility's total operating costs over its lifecycle.[100] Another is prison discipline: the head of the federal Bureau of Prisons told Congress in 1991 that mandatory sentences were creating severe discipline problems and asked for legislative authority to grant new "good time" sentence reductions.[101] And a looming risk is that, as the proportion of prisoners serving mandatory minimums increase and budget pressures make it more difficult to build the necessary prison space, the early release of other offenders, perhaps more serious but not serving mandatory minimums, may become necessary. This is precisely what happened when Florida instituted an aggressive new regime of mandatory sentences in drug cases,[102] with one-third of those released early committing new crimes after their release.[103]

One irony is that avoiding prison overcrowding was one of Congress's key goals back when the present regime of mandatory minimums was launched. In 1984, the Sentencing Commission was specifically directed to formulate the sentencing guidelines "to minimize the likelihood that the Federal prison population will exceed the capacity of the Federal prisons."[104]

But the bottom line is clear: in the midst of all this explosive growth of budgets, prisons, and court dockets, aimed primarily at drugs and violent crime, drug offenses and violent crime have continued to grow at an unprecedented rate. The U.S. is now experiencing the highest rate of violent crime in history, a 45 percent increase since 1982.[105] Hard-core drug use is dramatically increasingly.[106] And new young drug offenders are starting up at an alarming rate: juvenile drug arrests have jumped 713 percent in the past decade.[107]

Is There Hope?

The Supreme Court has washed its hands of the debate over mandatory minimums. Even the massive disparities of LSD cases have withstood constitutional attack.[108] Proportionality and individualized sentences are policy issues, says the Court, not constitutional ones.[109]

And as a policy matter, for all the foregoing reasons, mandatory minimums are worse than useless; they are counterproductive. They serve no purpose that is not served equally well or better by sentencing guidelines. Yet advocates of mandatory minimums have spilled precious little ink explaining specifically the need for mandatory minimums vis-a-vis the vast new guideline system painstakingly fashioned to accomplish precisely the same goal.

The Sentencing Commission has endorsed an important first step to restrain new mandatory minimums in the future. The Commission's central recommendation was that all new legislation increasing sentences should be written as directions to the Commission to incorporate increases into the "established process of the sentencing guidelines, permitting the sophistication of the guidelines structure to work." By doing so, the Commission concluded, "Congress can achieve the purposes of mandatory minimums while not compromising other goals to which it is simultaneously committed."[110] Congress started doing this sporadically in 1988,[111] and must finally resolve to make a consistent habit of it.

Congress should also stop letting sentencing legislation be drafted on the floor of the House and Senate and passed without review or debate. A procedure should be instituted requiring objective review by the Sentencing Commission of any legislation affecting criminal punishment, to determine its impact on the courts, prisons, budgets, sentencing uniformity, proportionality and certainty, and importantly, on crime, as well as whether it is procedurally compatible with the existing sentencing guideline system. This can be accomplished either by rules changes in both Houses, by legislation (a requirement for "prison impact assessments" was included in last year's unenacted omnibus crime bill),[112] or at the least, by obtaining commitments from the Judiciary Committee chairmen and the leadership of each chamber that they will put a substance-neutral hold on any amendment that has not been through this process.

But the more challenging task is doing something about the mandatory minimums already on the books. For the first time since 1970, a bill has been introduced in Congress to repeal mandatory minimums—not just some, but every single one, to give the sentencing guidelines a chance to work. The legislation is entitled the Sentencing Uniformity Act, H.R. 6079, and was introduced on October 1, 1992 by Rep. Don Edwards (D-Cal.), Chairman of the House Judiciary Subcommittee on Civil and Constitutional Rights.[113]

Such legislation, hopeless a year ago, now faces a possible favorable reception by the Clinton administration. During the campaign, candidate Clinton spoke about the need to get "smarter" about crime and about use of scarce prison space.[114] As Governor, he refused to allow the extradition of a young woman from Arkansas, an honor student at a Connecticut prep school charged with helping her boyfriend smuggle 300 grams of cocaine through JFK Airport, to stand trial in New York, saying that it would be "unconscionable" to expose her to New York's harsh fifteen-year mandatory minimum. She ended up pleading to lesser charges in Connecticut and being sentenced to probation but no prison.[115] Perhaps most significantly, President Clinton may be mindful that his own brother's fifteen-month federal prison sentence for a 1984 cocaine sale, which his brother credits with turning his life around, would have been a mandatory—and uselessly punitive—five or even ten years had his offense occurred after 1985.[116]

The key concept is balance. Prison has an important function in incapacitation, deterrence and retribution. But because it is the costliest sanction by far, and inimical to rehabilitation, it must be parsed wisely, to produce the biggest crime-control bang for the scarce federal buck. Complete sentencing uniformity is a nice ideal, but in fact an unattainable one, since docket pressures chronically require the vast majority of criminal cases to be resolved by deals and pleas. The best practical goal is rationality, fairness, and reasonable predictability.

These are complex and delicate balancing tasks, which Congress can either attempt itself—in the one minute of floor time routinely allotted to debate new mandatory minimums—or entrust to the expert body it created eight years ago for precisely such purposes.

The key question is whether Congress trusts the Sentencing Commission to produce appropriate sentences according to Congress's directions. If it does—and not even the biggest congressional champions of mandatory minimums have said a word against the Commission in this regard—it should junk all mandatory minimums and let the Commission do its job. To retain mandatory minimums is to call into question the integrity and, ultimately, the viability of the Commission.

A choice must be made. Continued legislative schizophrenia will be destructive of the goals of sentencing reform—just as the depraved Edward Hyde finally overwhelmed the good Dr. Jekyll, and in the end, both were sent to the gallows together.

NOTES

[1]Enacted as Chapter II of Title II of the Comprehensive Crime Control Act of 1984, Pub. L. No. 98-473, 98 Stat. 1837 (1984).

[2]The overriding goal of the Sentencing Reform Act was the elimination of "unwarranted sentencing disparity." S. REP. NO. 225, 98th Cong., 2d Sess., at 52 [hereinafter *Senate Report*]. 28 U.S.C.§ 991(b)(1)(B). Reducing disparity is likewise a goal of manda-

tory minimums. See UNITED STATES SENTENCING COMM'N, SPECIAL REPORT TO THE CONGRESS: MANDATORY MINIMUM PENALTIES IN THE FEDERAL CRIMINAL JUSTICE SYSTEM 14 (Aug. 1991) (reducing judicial discretion and disparity commonly cited by supporters of mandatory minimums) [hereinafter SENTENCING COMM'N REPORT]; statement of Senator Kennedy, Senate Judiciary Committee Chairman, in introducing S.2698, to establish mandatory minimums for certain firearms offenses, violent robberies, and heroin sales (goal is to make "certainty of punishment more of a reality"). 121 CONG. REC. 37561 (NOV. 20, 1975).

[3]*See* studies cited in UNITED STATES SENTENCING COMM'N, THE FEDERAL SENTENCING GUIDELINES: A REPORT ON THE OPERATION OF THE GUIDELINES SYSTEM AND SHORT-TERM IMPACTS ON DISPARITY IN SENTENCING, USE OF INCARCERATION, AND PROSECUTORIAL DISCRETION AND PLEA BARGAINING, Vol. 1, at 14, n.58 (Dec. 1991).

[4]*Senate Report, supra* note 2, at 792 (minority views of Senator Mathias, explaining his vote against the Sentencing Reform Act) *id.* at 422.

[5]Leviticus 24:19-20.

[6]Granucci, *"Nor Cruel and Unusual Punishments Inflicted": The Original Meaning*, 57 CALIF. L. REV. 839,844 (1969).

[7]J. Dawson, *The Development of Law and Legal Institutions* 44 (unpublished, Harvard Law School 1965), cited in Granucci, *supra* note 6, at 845 n.25.

[8]See § 3, 1 Stat. 112, 113.

[9]2 U.S.C. § 192; 19 U.S.C. § 283; 18 U.S.C. § 1658, as cited in a historical section on mandatory minimums in the SENTENCING COMM'N REPORT, *supra* note 2, at 5-10 and Appendix A.

[10]These penalties are from the second "Boggs Act," the Narcotic Control Act of 1956, Pub. L. No. 84-728, 70 Stat. 651 (1956). An earlier version with lesser mandatory penalties was passed in 1951. Pub. L. No. 82-255, 65 Stat. 767 (1951) (two years for a first offense, five for a second, and ten for a third).

[11]S. REP. NO. 1997, 84th Cong., 2d Sess. 6 (1956).

[12]Zeese, *Mandatory Minimum Sentences and Drug Control: A Brief History* (unpublished), at 1, Drug Policy Foundation (1991).

[13]Comprehensive Drug Abuse Prevention and Control Act of 1970, Pub. L. No. 91-513, 84 Stat. 1236 (1970).

[14]S. REP. NO. 613, 91st Cong., 1st Sess. 2 (1969).

[15]*Id*; H.R. REP. NO. 1444, 91st Cong., 2d Sess. 11 (1970). *See* discussion in SENTENCING COMM'N REPORT, *supra* note 2, at 6-7.

[16]116 CONG. REC. 33314 (Sept. 23, 1970).

[17]NATIONAL COMMISSION ON REFORM OF FEDERAL CRIMINAL LAWS, FINAL REPORT (1971) (the Brown Commission). The Commission was established by Congress by Act of November 8, 1966, Pub. L. No. 89-801, 80 Stat. 1516.

[18]Marx Lectures, November 3-5, 1971, published as Frankel, *Lawlessness in Sentencing*, 41 U. CINN. L. REV. 1 (1972), *reprinted in Reform of the Federal Criminal Laws: Hearings Before the Subcommittee on Criminal Laws and Procedures of the Senate Committee on the Judiciary*, 92d Cong., 1st Sess., Part IV, at 3923 (1972).

[19]*Senate Report, supra* note 2, at 52.

[20]*Id.*

[21]*Id.* at 51.

[22]*Id.* at 62. The systems in Pennsylvania, California, Illinois and Indiana were contrasted with "a more flexible sentencing guidelines system," such as the Minnesota system upon which the Sentencing Reform Act was modeled.

[23]121 CONG. REC. 37565 (1975) (statement of Senator Tunney upon introducing S.2699, to establish a United States Commission on Sentencing Guidelines).

[24]Senator Mathias' prescient objection in 1983 was that the mandatory guidelines would strip federal judges of their traditional sentencing discretion and force them "to adhere to preordained guidelines except in the most extraordinary circumstances," consigning judges to the task of "operating a sentencing decision machine designed and built by somebody else." *Senate Report, supra* note 2, at 792. At the same time, the House Judiciary Committee had approved legislation establishing a voluntary system of guidelines, to be developed by the judiciary itself (H.R. 6012, 98th Cong., 2d Sess. (1984); H.R. REP. NO. 1017, 98th Cong., 2d Sess. (1984)), but it was never considered by the full House. Concerns about the inflexibility and mandatory nature of the guidelines have persisted, dominated by the unanimous recommendation of the bipartisan, congressionally-established Federal Courts Study Committee, in its April 2, 1990 Final Report, at 135-40, that "serious consideration" be given to making the guideline system noncompulsory [hereinafter *Final Report*].

[25]This abdication of legislative responsibility, I have written elsewhere, lies in the process by which the guidelines become law—automatic enactment if Congress neither vetoes or modifies them within six months. Wallace, *Congressional Abdication,* 10 NAT'L L. J. 13 (1987). It is a system that results in the maximum possible diffusion of responsibility for any individual prison sentence. Congress is not responsible because it did not write the guidelines. The Sentencing Commission is not responsible because it was Congress which, through inaction, enacted them. And the sentencing judge is responsible only for toting up the points and entering the defendant's score on the predetermined guideline grid.

[26]Pub. L. No. 98-473, § 1005(a), amending 18 U.S.C. § 924(c).

[27]*Id.,* Chapter XVIII, The Armed Career Criminal Act of 1984, currently codified at 18 U.S.C.§ 924(e).

[28]21 U.S.C. § 841(b)(1). Also in 1986, a variety of firearms-related mandatory sentences were included in the Firearms Owners' Protection Act, Pub. L. No. 99-308, 100 Stat. 449 (1986).

[29]H.R. REP. NO. 845, pt. I, 99th Cong., 2d Sess. (1986).

[30]Wallace, *A Bias in the War on Drugs,* X THE CHAMPION 20 (Dec. 1986). In the resulting "can-you-top-this atmosphere," editorialized the Washington Post, "if someone had offered an amendment to execute pushers only after flogging and hacking them, it probably would have passed."

[31]Pub. L. No. 100-690, 102 Stat. 4377 (1988).

[32]*Id.,* § 6481, amending 21 U.S.C. § 848(a).

[33]*Id.,* § 6460, amending 18 U.S.C. § 924(c)(1).

[34]*Id.*

[35]*Id.,* § 6452, amending 21 U.S.C. § 841(b)(1)(A).

[36]*Id.,* § 6470, amending 21 U.S.C. § 846.

[37]*Id.,* § 6371, amending 21 U.S.C. § 844(a). Under the amendment, the five-year mandatory minimum is triggered also by a second offense involving three grams, or a third offense involving one gram.

[38]Comprehensive Crime Control Act of 1990, Pub. L. No. 101-647, 104 Stat. 4846, § 2510 (establishing a new offense of "continuing financial crimes enterprise" as part of Title XXV of the bill, sepa-

rately entitled the Comprehensive Thrift and Bank Fraud Prosecution and Taxpayer Recovery Act of 1990).

[39]*Id.,* § 1703.

[40]*See* note 2 *supra.* A second government study, by the Government Accounting Office, an independent auditing arm of the Congress, has been under way for two years, with a report expected this spring.

[41]Violent Crime and Law Enforcement Act, Conference Report on H.R. 3371, H.R. REP. NO. 102-405; also printed in CONG. REC. H11686 (Nov. 26, 1991).

[42]*See* 21 U.S.C. §§ 841 (drug distribution), 844 (possession), 960 (importation), and 18 U.S.C. § 924(c) (firearm enhancement). The full range of federal mandatory minimum provisions is catalogued in the SENTENCING COMM'N REPORT, *supra* note 2, at 10 *et seq.* and Appendix A.

[43]*See* note 66 *infra.*

[44]CONG. REC. S8888 (June 27, 1991). The amendment was approved by unanimous consent without further debate, but was dropped in House-Senate conference; the conference bill was never passed. *See* note 41, *supra* and accompanying text.

[45]18 U.S.C. § 3553(e).

[46]*See* United States v. Roberts, 726 F. Supp. 1359, 1373-77 (D.D.C. 1989), *rev'd sub nom.* United States v. Doe, 934 F.2d 353, *cert. denied,* 112 S. Ct. 268, *reh'g denied,* 112 S. Ct. 959 (1991) (prosecutor's arbitrary withholding of motion for sentence reduction for the defendant's actual cooperation held by district court to violate due process).

[47]*Long LSD Prison Terms—It's All in the Packaging,* LOS ANGELES TIMES, July 27, 1992, at 8-9.

[48]United States v. Richardson (D. Ala. March 16, 1992) (unpublished transcript of sentencing).

[49]LOS ANGELES TIMES, *supra* note 47, at 9.

[50]SENTENCING COMM'N REPORT, *supra* note 2, at ii, 58.

[51]*Id.* at 57.

[52]*Id.* at 89.

[53]*Id.* at iii.

[54]*Final Report, supra* note 24, at 37,

[55]*See* note 27 and accompanying text, *supra.*

[56]Statement of Senator Arlen Specter (R-Pa.) on passage of Comprehensive Crime Control Act of 1984, 130 CONG. REC. S13080-81 (Oct. 4, 1984); A. Specter, *Juvenile Justice Issues, Justice Assistance, Career Criminal Provisions, and the Insanity Defense,* 32 FED. BAR NEWS & J. 76 (Feb. 1985).

[57]Debate on Biden-Thurmond Violent Crime Control Act of 1991, S.1241, § 1213, CONG. REC. S8666 (June 26, 1991).

[58]U.S. DEPARTMENT OF JUSTICE, BUREAU OF JUSTICE STATISTICS, CRIME IN THE UNITED STATES 1989 (Sept. 1990). This includes roughly 407,000 assaults, 210,000 robberies, 12,100 rapes, and 9,200 murders.

[59]*See* debate on Biden-Thurmond crime bill, *supra* note 57. The vote was 88-11. The provision was subsequently deleted in House-Senate Conference negotiations after federalism and budgetary objections were raised by the U.S. Judicial Conference. *See* letter from Chief Justice William H. Rehnquist to Rep. William J. Hughes, House Judiciary Committee, transmitting a resolution of the Judicial Conference, September 19, 1991.

[60]*Senate's Rule for Its Anti-Crime Bill: The Tougher the Provision, the Better,* New York Times, July 8, 1991, at A6.

[61]See S. REP. NO. 613, 91st Cong., 1st Sess. 2 (1969) (mandatory minimums infringe "on the judicial function by not allowing the judge to use his discretion in individual cases"). See notes 15-17 and accompanying text supra.

[62]United States v. Medkour, 930 F.2d 234 (2d Circ. 1991).

[63]Both these cases, and others, are summarized in FAMILIES AGAINST MANDATORY MINIMUMS, MANDATORY MINIMUM CASES (1992) [hereinafter FAMM SUMMARY].

[64]Stuart Taylor, Jr., Ten Years for Two Ounces: Congress is Packing Prisons With Bit Players in Small-Time Drug Deals, AM. LAW. (Mar. 1990) (reprinted in CONG. REC. S9013 et seq. (June 28, 1990)).

[65]SENTENCING COMM'N REPORT, supra note 2, at ii.

[66]See Resolutions collected in id., Appendix G. These resolutions do not necessarily suggest complete judicial unanimity; the Sentencing Commission surveyed federal judges and found a small percentage (2 of 48) who had nothing but positive comments about mandatory minimums, and a slightly larger minority (6 of 48) who had mixed comments (e.g., finding some deterrent benefit, but injustices at low levels of culpability). Id. at 93-96.

[67]Letter of Commission Chairman William W. Wilkins to Senator Sam Nunn (Aug. 23, 1988).

[68]FAMM SUMMARY, supra note 63, at 3 (case of Huey Johnson, serving ten-year mandatory minimum; already convicted and sentenced on overlapping state charges, but a federal agent told him he felt the state sentence was not severe enough). See United States v. Holland, 810 F.2d 1215 (D.C. Cir.), cert. denied 481 U.S. 1057 (1987) (defendant's residence within school zone).

[69]See United States v. Liranzo, 729 F. Supp. 1012 (S.D.N.Y. 1990); United States v. Coates, 739 F. Supp. 146 (S.D.N.Y. 1990).

[70]CONG. REC. S8886 (June 27, 1991) (text of proposed Criminal Exploitation of Minors Control Act and comments of Senator Seymour).

[71]Id. The provision was subsequently deleted in House-Senate Conference negotiations on the 1991 crime bill, supra note 41 and accompanying text.

[72]Harmelin v. Michigan, 111 S. Ct. 2680, 2716 (White, J., dissenting) (emphasis in the original).

[73]SENTENCING COMM'N REPORT, supra note 2, at 112.

[74]See Taylor, supra note 64.

[75]See Harmelin, 111 S. Ct. 2680.

[76]Stuart Taylor, Jr., Don't Throw Away That Key, LEGAL TIMES, October 22, 1990, at 25.

[77]CONG. REC. S9000 (June 28, 1990) (Statement of Senator Kennedy).

[78]Chapman v. United States, 111 S. Ct. 1919, 1933 (1991) (dissenting opinion of Justice Stevens).

[79]See Chapman, 111 St. Ct. 1919, 1932 (citing Judge Posner's dissent in United States v. Marshall, 908 F.2d 1312, 1333 (7th Cir. 1990)).

[80]Id.

[81]Id. at n.12.

[82]See note 66 and accompanying text supra.

[83]See Final Report, supra note 24, at 134.

[84]SENTENCING COMM'N REPORT, supra note 2, at iii.

[85]Id. at ii.

[86]Id. at ii-iii.

[87]Id.

[88]Id. at 25-26.

[89]Id. at ii.

[90]Id. at 76, 82.

[91]State v. Russell, 477 N.W.2d 886 (Minn. 1991) (en banc).

[92]Under 21 U.S.C. § 841(b)(1), as well as the "kingpin" provisions of § 848, the amount of powder cocaine which triggers the various mandatory minimums is 100 times the amount of crack which triggers the same sentence.

[93]121 CONG. REC. 37560 (Nov. 11, 1975) (statement of Senator Kennedy introducing S.2698, containing two-year mandatory minimums for any gun crime, robbery with serious bodily injury, or heroin sale; exceptions were included of juveniles, mental disease, duress, or "mere accomplices").

[94]Final Report, supra note 24, at 134. See BOSTON BAR ASSOCIATION TASK FORCE ON DRUGS AND THE COURTS FINAL REPORT, DRUGS IN THE COMMUNITY: A SCOURGE BEYOND THE SYSTEM (Mar. 15, 1990) (citing the "tremendous negative impact on the ability to move cases swiftly and surely through an underfunded criminal justice system").

[95]Final Report, supra note 24, at 137.

[96]UNITED STATES SENTENCING COMM'N, 1990 ANN. REP. 96-97.

[97]Final Report, supra note 24, at 36.

[98]UNITED STATES SENTENCING COMM'N, 1990 ANN. REP. 42-43.

[99]CRIMINAL JUSTICE INSTITUTE, CORRECTIONS YEARBOOK (1992) (federal maximum security costs $98,000 per space, $65,000 for medium security; total 1992 federal prison budget: $2.7 billion).

[100]Projections for U.S. Corrections, MONDAY MORNING HIGHLIGHTS (U.S. Department of Justice Federal Prison System) (July 15, 1991).

[101]Testimony of J. Michael Quinlan before the House Judiciary Subcomm. on Crime and Criminal Justice, April 24, 1991. Quinlan never followed up by submitting draft legislation, presumably due to political pressure from above, and the issue has gone nowhere.

[102]Florida's Crackdown on Crime Forces Early Release of Inmates, WASHINGTON POST, Dec. 28, 1990, at A14.

[103]NATIONAL COUNCIL ON CRIME AND DELINQUENCY, THE NCCD PRISON POPULATION FORECAST: THE IMPACT OF THE WAR ON DRUGS 5 (Dec. 1989) (citing Final Report of the Florida Consensus: Criminal Justice Estimating Conference (Feb. 23, 1989)).

[104]28 U.S.C. § 994(g).

[105]FEDERAL BUREAU OF INVESTIGATION, CRIME IN THE UNITED STATES 1991: UNIFORM CRIME REPORTS 11 (Aug. 30, 1992).

[106]According to figures released in December 1992 by the National Institute on Drug Abuse, the number of persons using cocaine about once a week rose from 606,000 to 855,000 in one year. Cocaine- and heroin-related hospital emergency room visits increased 31 and 26 percent respectively. 1991 NIDA Household Survey, CRIMINAL JUSTICE NEWSLETTER 5 (Dec. 16, 1991).

[107]FBI Finds Major Increase in Juvenile Violence in Past Decade, WASHINGTON POST, August 30, 1992, at A13. The juvenile drug arrest rate includes arrests for use or sale of heroin or cocaine.

[108]*Chapman*, 111 S. Ct. 1919 (1991).

[109]Lockett v. Ohio, 438 U.S. 586, 604-05 (1978) (plurality opinion); *Harmelin*, 111 S. Ct. 2680 (Eighth Amendment challenge).

[110]SENTENCING COMM'N REPORT, *supra* note 2, at iv.

[111]*See* Pub. L. No. 100-690 (1988), §§ 6453, 6454 (directing the Sentencing Commission to raise the guideline levels for certain drug importation offenses and drug offenses involving children to "in no event less than level 26"); Pub. L. No. 101-647 (1990), §§ 321 (suggesting the Sentencing Commission might raise the guidelines to provide "more substantial penalties" for sexual crimes against children if it finds current penalties "inadequate"), 401 (ordering the Commission to raise guidelines by three levels for certain aggravated child-kidnapping offenses); and 2701 (ordering a two-level guideline increase for offenses involving methamphetamine in its "smokable crystal" form). Both Acts, however, also contained mandatory minimums. *See* notes 31-38 and accompanying text *supra*.

[112]*See* note 41 and accompanying text *supra*.

[113]*See* CONG. REC. E2901-02 (Oct. 2, 1992) (statement of Rep. Edwards and cosponsor Rep. Ed Jenkins (D-Ga.)).

[114]*See Bush v. Clinton: The Candidates on Legal Issues*, A.B.A.J., 61 (Oct. 1992).

[115]*Clinton Interceded in N.Y. Drug Case*, WASHINGTON POST, Oct. 5, 1992, at A6.

[116]Stuart Taylor, Jr., *Mandatory Sentence, Minimum Sense*, LEGAL TIMES, Nov. 16, 1992, at 25.

Acknowledgments

Acker, James R. and Charles S. Lanier. "The Dimensions of Capital Murder." *Criminal Law Bulletin* 29 (1993): 379–417. Reprinted with the permission of the publisher, *Criminal Law Bulletin*, a division of Research Institute of America, Inc.

Alexander, Rudolph, Jr. "Hands-off, Hands-on, Hands-semi-off: A Discussion of the Current Legal Test Used by the United States Supreme Court to Decide Inmates' Rights." *Journal of Crime and Justice* 17 (1994): 103–28. Reprinted with the permission of the Anderson Publishing Company.

Bachman, Ronet and Raymond Paternoster. "A Contemporary Look at the Effects of Rape Law Reform: How Far Have We Really Come?" *Journal of Criminal Law and Criminology* 84 (1993): 554–74. Reprinted with the special permission of the Northwestern University School of Law, *Journal of Criminal Law and Criminology*.

Benekos, Peter J. and Alida V. Merlo. "Three Strikes and You're Out!: The Political Sentencing Game." *Federal Probation* 59 (1995): 3–9. Reprinted with the permission of the Administrative Office of the U.S. Courts.

Bowers, David A. and Jerold L. Waltman. "Do More Conservative States Impose Harsher Felony Sentences? An Exploratory Analysis of 32 States." *Criminal Justice Review* 18 (1993): 61–70. Reprinted with the permission of the College of Public and Urban Affairs, Georgia State University.

Callahan, Lisa A., Margaret A. McGreevy, Carmen Cirincione, and Henry J. Steadman. "Measuring the Effects of the Guilty but Mentally Ill (GBMI) Verdict: Georgia's 1982 GBMI Reform." *Law and Human Behavior* 16 (1992): 447–62. Reprinted with the permission of Plenum Press.

Davey, Joseph D. "The Death of the Fourth Amendment Under the Rehnquist Court: Where Is Original Intent When We Need It?" *Journal of Crime and Justice* 17 (1994): 129–48. Reprinted with the permission of the Anderson Publishing Company.

Denno, Deborah W. "Gender, Crime, and the Criminal Law Defenses." *Journal of Criminal Law and Criminology* 85 (1994): 80–180. Reprinted with the special permission of the Northwestern University School of Law, *Journal of Criminal Law and Criminology*.

Feld, Barry C. "Juvenile (In)Justice and the Criminal Court Alternative." *Crime and*

Delinquency 39 (1993): 403–24. Reprinted with the permission of Sage Publications, Inc.

Gershman, Bennett L. "Themes of Injustice: Wrongful Convictions, Racial Prejudice, and Lawyer Incompetence." *Criminal Law Bulletin* 29 (1993): 502–15. Reprinted with the permission of the publisher, *Criminal Law Bulletin*, a division of Research Institute of America, Inc.

Haas, Kenneth C. "The Triumph of Vengeance Over Retribution: The United States Supreme Court and the Death Penalty." *Crime, Law and Social Change* 21 (1994): 127–54. Reprinted with the permission of Kluwer Academic Publishers.

Kramer, John and Darrell Steffensmeier. "Race and Imprisonment Decisions." *Sociological Quarterly* 34 (1993): 357–76. Reprinted with the permission of JAI Press, Inc.

Laufer, William S. "Culpability and the Sentencing of Corporations." *Nebraska Law Review* 71 (1992): 1049–94. Reprinted with the permission of the *Nebraska Law Review*.

Tonry, Michael. "Twenty Years of Sentencing Reform: Steps Forward, Steps Backward." *Judicature* 78 (1995): 169–72. Reprinted with the permission of the American Judicature Society.

Van den Haag, Ernest. "The *Lex Talionis* Before and After Criminal Law." *Criminal Justice Ethics* 11 (1992): 2, 62. Reprinted with the permission of the Institute for Criminal Justice Ethics.

Von Hirsch, Andrew and Lisa Maher. "Should Penal Rehabilitation Be Revived?" *Criminal Justice Ethics* 11 (1992): 25–30. Reprinted with the permission of the Institute for Criminal Justice Ethics.

Wallace, Henry Scott. "Mandatory Minimums and the Betrayal of Sentencing Reform: A Legislative Dr. Jekyll and Mr. Hyde." *Federal Probation* 57 (1993): 9–19. Reprinted with the permission of the Administrative Office of the U.S. Courts.